BERLITZ

german-english
english-german
dictionary

wörterbuch
deutsch-englisch
englisch-deutsch

By the Staff of Berlitz Guides

Revised edition 1979
Library of Congress Catalog Card Number: 78-78082

18th printing 1991
Printed in Switzerland

BERLITZ TRAVEL GUIDES

Africa
- ○ Algeria
- Kenya
- Morocco
- South Africa
- Tunisia

Asia, Middle East
- ○ China
- Hong Kong
- ○ India
- ○ Indonesia*
- ○ Japan
- Nepal
- Singapore
- Sri Lanka
- Thailand
- Egypt
- Jerusalem/Holy Land
- Saudi Arabia

Australasia
- ○ Australia
- New Zealand

Austria/Switzerland
- Tyrol
- Vienna
- ○ Switzerland

British Isles
- Channel Islands
- Ireland
- London
- Oxford and Stratford
- Scotland

Belgium/Netherlands
- Brussels
- Amsterdam

France
- Brittany
- ○ France
- French Riviera
- Loire Valley
- Normandy
- Paris

Germany
- Berlin
- Munich
- The Rhine Valley

Greece, Cyprus and Turkey
- Athens
- Corfu
- Crete
- Greek Islands Aegean
- Peloponnese
- Rhodes
- Salonica/N. Greece
- Cyprus
- Istanbul/Aegean Coast
- ○ Turkey

Italy and Malta
- Florence
- Italian Adriatic
- Italian Riviera
- ○ Italy
- Naples/Amalfi Coast*
- Rome
- Sicily
- Venice
- Malta

Scandinavia
- Copenhagen
- Helsinki
- Oslo/Bergen
- Stockholm

Spain
- Barcelona
- Canary Islands
- Costa Blanca
- Costa Brava
- Costa del Sol/Andalusia
- Costa Dorada/Barcelona
- Ibiza and Formentera
- Madrid
- Majorca and Minorca
- Seville

Portugal
- Algarve
- Lisbon
- Madeira

Eastern Europe
- Budapest
- Dubrovnik/S. Dalmatia
- ○ Hungary
- Istria and Croatian Coast
- Moscow and Leningrad

- The Hermitage, Leningrad*
- Prague
- Split and Dalmatia
- ○ Yugoslavia

North America
- ○ U.S.A.
- California
- Florida
- Hawaii
- Miami
- New York
- Washington
- ○ Canada
- Montreal
- Toronto

Caribbean, Lat. Am.
- Bahamas
- Bermuda
- French West Indies
- Jamaica
- Puerto Rico
- Southern Caribbean
- Virgin Islands
- Brazil (Highlights of)
- ○ Mexico*
- Mexico City
- Rio de Janeiro

Address Books
- London/New York
- Paris/Rome

Blueprint Guides
- Europe A-Z/France
- Germany/Britain
- Greece/Hungary
- Italy/Spain/USSR*

More for the $
- France/Italy

Cruise Guides
- Alaska
- Caribbean
- Handbook to Cruising

Ski Guides
- Austria/France
- Italy/Switzerland
- Skiing the Alps

Europe
- Business Travel Guide
- Train Travel
- Pocket Guide-Europe
- Cities of Europe

* in preparation/○ country guides 192 or 256 p.

Berlitz Dictionaries

Dansk	Engelsk, Fransk, Italiensk, Spansk, Tysk
Deutsch	Dänisch, Englisch, Finnisch, Französisch, Italienisch, Niederländisch, Norwegisch, Portugiesisch, Schwedish, Spanisch
English	Danish, Dutch, Finnish, French, German, Italian, Norwegian, Portuguese, Spanish, Swedish, Turkish
Español	Alemán, Danés, Finlandés, Francés, Holandés, Inglés, Noruego, Sueco
Français	Allemand, Anglais, Danois, Espagnol, Finnois, Italien, Néerlandais, Norvégien, Portugais, Suédois
Italiano	Danese, Finlandese, Francese, Inglese, Norvegese, Olandese, Svedese, Tedesco
Nederlands	Duits, Engels, Frans, Italiaans, Portugees, Spaans
Norsk	Engelsk, Fransk, Italiensk, Spansk, Tysk
Português	Alemão, Francês, Holandês, Inglês, Sueco
Suomi	Englanti, Espanja, Italia, Ranska, Ruotsi, Saksa
Svenska	Engelska, Finska, Franska, Italienska, Portugisiska, Spanska, Tyska

Contents

Inhaltsverzeichnis

Preface

In selecting the 12.500 word-concepts in each language for this dictionary, the editors have had the traveller's needs foremost in mind. This book will prove invaluable to all the millions of travellers, tourists and business people who appreciate the reassurance a small and practical dictionary can provide. It offers them—as it does beginners and students—all the basic vocabulary they are going to encounter and to have to use, giving the key words and expressions to allow them to cope in everyday situations.

Like our successful phrase books and travel guides, these dictionaries—created with the help of a computer data bank—are designed to slip into pocket or purse, and thus have a role as handy companions at all times.

Besides just about everything you normally find in dictionaries, there are these Berlitz bonuses:

● imitated pronunciation next to each foreign-word entry, making it easy to read and enunciate words whose spelling may look forbidding

● a unique, practical glossary to simplify reading a foreign restaurant menu and to take the mystery out of complicated dishes and indecipherable names on bills of fare

● useful information on how to tell the time and how to count, on conjugating irregular verbs, commonly seen abbreviations and converting to the metric system, in addition to basic phrases.

While no dictionary of this size can pretend to completeness, we expect the user of this book will feel well armed to tackle foreign travel with confidence. We should, however, be very pleased to receive comments, criticism and suggestions that you think may be of help in preparing future editions.

Vorwort

Bei der Auswahl der 12 500 Begriffe, die in jedem der beiden Teile dieses Wörterbuchs enthalten sind, standen die Bedürfnisse des Reisenden stets im Vordergrund. Dieses handliche und praktische, mit Hilfe einer Datenbank erstellte Wörterbuch wird sich deshalb für alle Reisende – ob Touristen oder Geschäftsleute –, aber auch für Anfänger und Sprachschüler als unschätzbarer Helfer erweisen. Es enthält den Grundwortschatz und alle wichtigen Ausdrücke, die man benötigt, um sich im Alltag in jeder Lage zurechtzufinden.

Wie unsere Sprachführer und Reiseführer paßt auch dieses Wörterbuch in jede Jacken- oder Handtasche und ist so immer griffbereit. Neben all dem, was man von einem Wörterbuch erwartet, bietet es noch diese besonderen Vorteile:

● Die internationale Lautschrift (IPA) nach jedem Stichwort in der Fremdsprache löst alle Ausspracheprobleme.

● Ein einzigartiges kulinarisches Lexikon hilft beim Lesen der Speise- und Getränkekarte und enträtselt all die unbekannten Gerichte und Zutaten.

● Nützliche Hinweise über Zeitangaben, Grund- und Ordnungszahlen, unregelmäßige Verben und übliche Abkürzungen werden ergänzt durch einige Sätze, die in alltäglichen Situationen zustatten kommen.

Selbstverständlich kann kein Wörterbuch dieses Formats Anspruch auf Vollständigkeit erheben. Wir glauben jedoch, daß der Benutzer dieses Buches sich mit Zuversicht auf die Reise machen kann. Es versteht sich, daß wir jede Art von Kommentar, Kritik oder Anregung begrüßen, die uns helfen, zukünftige Auflagen zu verbessern.

german-english

deutsch-englisch

Abbreviations

adj	adjective	*ntpl*	neuter plural
adv	adverb	*num*	numeral
Am	American	*p*	past tense
art	article	*pl*	plural
conj	conjunction	*plAm*	plural (American)
f	feminine	*pp*	past participle
fpl	feminine plural	*pr*	present tense
m	masculine	*pref*	prefix
mpl	masculine plural	*prep*	preposition
n	noun	*pron*	pronoun
nAm	noun (American)	*v*	verb
nt	neuter	*vAm*	verb (American)

Introduction

The dictionary has been designed to take account of your practical needs. Unnecessary linguistic information has been avoided. The entries are listed in alphabetical order, regardless of whether the entry word is printed in a single word or in two or more separate words. As the only exception to this rule, reflexive verbs and a few idiomatic expressions are listed alphabetically as main entries, according to the verb or the most significant word of the expression.

> e.g. *sich befassen mit* is found under **b**
> *auf Wiedersehen* is found under **w**

When an entry is followed by sub-entries such as expressions and locutions, these, too, have been listed in alphabetical order.

Each main-entry word is followed by a phonetic transcription (see Guide to pronunciation). Following the transcription is the part of speech of the entry word whenever applicable. When an entry word may be used as more than one part of speech, the translations are grouped together after the respective part of speech.

Considering the complexity of the rules for constructing the plural of German nouns, we have supplied the plural form whenever in current use.

Each time an entry word is repeated in plural or in sub-entries, a tilde (~) is used to represent the full entry word. Two dots above the tilde (≈) means that, in the plural, the word takes an *Umlaut*.

In plurals of compounds only the part that changes is written out fully, whereas the unchanged part is represented by a hyphen.

Entry: Abenteuer (pl ~)	Plural: Abenteuer
Abend (pl ~e)	Abende
Satz (pl ≈e)	Sätze
Geschäftsmann (pl -leute)	Geschäftsleute

An asterisk (*) in front of a verb indicates that the verb is irregular. For details, refer to the lists of irregular verbs.

Guide to Pronunciation

Each main entry in this part of the dictionary is followed by a phonetic transcription which shows you how to pronounce the words. This transcription should be read as if it were English. It is based on Standard British pronunciation, though we have tried to take account of General American pronunciation also. Below, only those letters and symbols are explained which we consider likely to be ambiguous or not immediately understood.

The syllables are separated by hyphens, and stressed syllables are printed in *italics*.

Of course, the sounds of any two languages are never exactly the same, but if you follow carefully our indications, you should be able to pronounce the foreign words in such a way that you'll be understood. To make your task easier, our transcriptions occasionally simplify slightly the sound system of the language while still reflecting the essential sound differences.

Consonants

g	always hard, as in go
kh	a k-sound where the tongue doesn't quite touch the roof of the mouth, so that the air continues to come out, with a sound of friction between the tongue and the roof of the mouth; after back vowels (e.g. **ah**, **o**, **oo**) like **ch** in Scottish lo**ch**, otherwise more like **h** in **h**uge
r	pronounced in the back of the mouth
s	always hard, as in so
zh	a soft, voiced **sh**, like s in pleasure

Vowels and Diphthongs

aa	long **a**, as in c**a**r
ah	a short version of **aa**; between **a** in c**a**t and **u** in c**u**t
ai	like **air**, without any **r**-sound
eh	like **e** in g**e**t
er	as in oth**er**, without any **r**-sound
ew	a "rounded **ee**-sound"; say the vowel sound **ee** (as in s**ee**), and while saying it, round your lips as for **oo** (as in s**oo**n), without moving your tongue; when your lips are in the **oo** position, but your tongue is in the **ee** position, you should be pronouncing the correct sound
igh	as in s**igh**
o	always as in h**o**t (British pronunciation)
ou	as in l**ou**d
ur	as in f**ur**, but with rounded lips and no **r**-sound

1) A bar over a vowel symbol (e.g. $\overline{ew}$) shows that this sound is long.

2) Raised letters (e.g. ᵃaa) should be pronounced only fleetingly.

3) German vowels (i.e. not diphthongs) are pure. Therefore, you should try to read a transcription like **oa** without moving tongue or lips while pronouncing the sound.

4) Some German words borrowed from French contain nasal vowels, which we transcribe with a vowel symbol plus **ng** (e.g. **ahng**). This **ng** should *not* be pronounced, and serves solely to indicate nasal quality of the preceding vowel. A nasal vowel is pronounced simultaneously through the mouth and the nose.

A

Aal (aal) *m* (pl ~e) eel

ab (ahp) *prep* as from; *adv* off; ~ **und zu** occasionally

abändern (*ahp*-ehn-derrn) *v* change

Abbildung (*ahp*-bil-doong) *f* (pl ~en) picture

abbremsen (*ahp*-brehm-zern) *v* slow down

Abbruch (*ahp*-brookh) *m* demolition

abdrehen (*ahp*-dráy-ern) *v* turn off

Abend (aa-bernt) *m* (pl ~e) night, evening

Abenddämmerung (aa-bernt-deh-mer-roong) *f* dusk

Abendessen (aa-bernt-eh-sern) *nt* supper; dinner

abends (aa-bernts) *adv* at night

Abenteuer (aa-bern-toi-err) *nt* (pl ~) adventure

aber (aa-berr) *conj* but

Aberglaube (aa-berr-glou-ber) *m* superstition

****abfahren** (*ahp*-faa-rern) *v* pull out

Abfahrt (*ahp*-faart) *f* departure

Abfahrtszeit (*ahp*-faarts-tsight) *f* (pl ~en) time of departure

Abfall (*ahp*-fahl) *m* (pl ~e) garbage; litter, rubbish, refuse

Abfalleimer (*ahp*-fahl-igh-merr) *m* (pl ~) rubbish-bin, dustbin; trash can

Am

****abfallen** (*ahp*-fah-lern) *v* slope

abfassen (*ahp*-fah-sern) *v* *draw up

abfertigen (*ahp*-fehr-ti-gern) *v* dispatch

Abfluß (*ahp*-flooss) *m* drain

Abführmittel (*ahp*-fewr-mi-terl) *nt* (pl ~) laxative

abgelegen (*ahp*-ger-láy-gern) *adj* far-off, remote

abgeneigt (*ahp*-ger-nighkt) *adj* averse

abgenutzt (*ahp*-ger-nootst) *adj* worn-out

Abgeordnete (*ahp*-ger-or-dner-ter) *m* (pl ~n) deputy; Member of Parliament

abgerundet (*ahp*-ger-roon-dert) *adj* rounded

Abgesandte (*ahp*-ger-zahn-ter) *m* (pl ~n) delegate, envoy

abgeschieden (*ahp*-ger-shee-dern) *adj* isolated

abgesehen von (*ahp*-ger-záy-ern) apart from

Abgott (*ahp*-got) *m* (pl ~er) idol

Abgrund (*ahp*-groont) *m* (pl ~e) abyss, precipice

Abhandlung (*ahp*-hahn-dloong) *f* (pl ~en) essay

Abhang (*ahp*-hahng) *m* (pl ~e) slope

****abhängen von** (*ahp*-hehng-ern) depend on

abhängig (*ahp*-hehng-ikh) *adj* dependant

*****abheben** (*ahp*-hāy-bern) *v* *draw

abholen (*ahp*-hōa-lern) *v* pick up, collect, fetch

abhorchen (*ahp*-hor-khern) *v* eavesdrop

Abkommen (*ahp*-ko-mern) *nt* (pl ~) agreement

Abkürzung (*ahp*-kewr-tsoong) *f* (pl ~en) abbreviation

*****abladen** (*ahp*-laa-dern) *v* unload

Ablagerung (*ahp*-laa-ger-roong) *f* (pl ~en) deposit

*****ablaufen** (*ahp*-lou-fern) *v* expire

ablehnen (*ahp*-lāy-nern) *v* reject

ableiten (*ahp*-ligh-tern) *v* deduce, infer

Ablenkung (*ahp*-lehng-koong) *f* diversion

abliefern (*ahp*-lee-ferrn) *v* deliver

ablösen (*ahp*-lūr-zern) *v* relieve

abmachen (*ahp*-mah-khern) *v* stipulate

sich abmelden (*ahp*-mehl-dern) check out

sich abmühen (*ahp*-mēw-ern) labour

Abnahme (*ahp*-naa-mer) *f* (pl ~n) decrease

*****abnehmen** (*ahp*-nāy-mern) *v* *take away; decrease; slim

Abneigung (*ahp*-nigh-goong) *f* dislike, antipathy

abnorm (ahp-*norm*) *adj* abnormal

Abonnement (ah-bo-ner-*mahng*) *nt* (pl ~s) subscription

Abonnent (ah-bo-*nehnt*) *m* (pl ~en) subscriber

Abordnung (*ahp*-or-dnoong) *f* (pl ~en) delegation

Abortus (ah-*bor*-tooss) *m* (pl ~) abortion

*****abraten** (*ahp*-raa-tern) *v* dissuade from

Abreise (*ahp*-righ-zer) *f* departure

abreisen (*ahp*-righ-zern) *v* depart, *set out

Absatz (*ahp*-zahts) *m* (pl ~̈e) heel; paragraph

abschaffen (*ahp*-shah-fern) *v* abolish

abschalten (*ahp*-shahl-tern) *v* *cut off

abscheulich (ahp-*shoi*-likh) *adj* hideous, terrible

Abschied (*ahp*-sheet) *m* parting

*****abschießen** (aab-shee-sern) *v* launch

*****abschließen** (*ahp*-shlee-sern) *v* *shut

Abschluß (*ahp*-shlooss) *m* issue

*****abschneiden** (*ahp*-shnigh-dern) *v* *cut off; chip

Abschnitt (*ahp*-shnit) *m* (pl ~e) section; extract

abschrauben (*ahp*-shrou-bern) *v* unscrew

Abschrift (*ahp*-shrift) *f* (pl ~en) copy

abschüssig (*ahp*-shew-sikh) *adj* sloping, slanting

*****absenden** (*ahp*-zehn-dern) *v* *send off

Absicht (*ahp*-zikht) *f* (pl ~en) purpose, intention

absichtlich (*ahp*-zikht-likh) *adj* deliberate, on purpose, intentional

absolut (ahp-zoa-*lōot*) *adj* sheer

absplittern (*ahp*-shpli-terrn) *v* chip

Abstammung (*ahp*-shtah-moong) *f* origin

Abstand (*ahp*-shtahnt) *m* space

Abstieg (*ahp*-shteek) *m* descent

Abstimmung (*ahp*-shti-moong) *f* vote

Abstinenzler (ahps-ti-*nehn*-tslerr) *m* (pl ~) teetotaller

abstoßend (*ahp*-shtōa-sernt) *adj* revolting, repellent

abstrakt (ahps-*trahkt*) *adj* abstract

abstürzen (*ahp*-shtewr-tsern) *v* crash

absurd (ahp-*zoort*) *adj* absurd

Abszeß (ahps-tsehss) *m* (pl -esse) abscess

Abtei (ahp-*tigh*) *f* (pl ~en) abbey

Abteil (ahp-*tighl*) nt (pl ~e) compartment

Abteilung (ahp-*tigh*-loong) f (pl ~en) division, department; section

*****abtragen** (ahp-traa-gern) v wear out

abtrocknen (ahp-tro-knern) v dry

abwärts (ahp-vehrts) adv downwards

*****abwaschen** (ahp-vah-shern) v wash up

Abwasserkanal (ahp-vah-serr-kah-naal) m (pl ~e) sewer

abwechselnd (ahp-veh-kserlnt) adj alternate

Abwechslung (ahp-veh-ksloong) f variation

Abwehr (ahp-vāyr) f defence

*****abweichen** (ahp-vigh-khern) v deviate

Abweichung (ahp-vigh-khoong) f (pl ~en) aberration

abwenden (ahp-vehn-dern) v avert

Abwertung (ahp-vair-toong) f devaluation

abwesend (ahp-vāy-zernt) adj absent

Abwesenheit (ahp-vāy-zern-hight) f absence

abwischen (ahp-vi-shern) v wipe

abzahlen (ahp-tsaa-lern) v *pay on account

abzeichnen (ahp-tsighkh-nern) v initial; endorse

*****abziehen** (ahp-tsee-ern) v deduct

Abzug (ahp-tsōōk) m (pl ~e) print; trigger

Achse (ah-kser) f (pl ~n) axle

Acht (ahkht) f notice; **sich in ~**
*****nehmen** beware

acht (ahkht) num eight

achtbar (ahkht-baar) adj respectable

achte (ahkh-ter) num eighth

achten (ahkh-tern) v respect; ~ **auf** mind; *pay attention to

*****achtgeben** (ahkht-gāy-bern) v look out; ~ **auf** watch; attend to; mind

Achtung (ahkh-toong) f esteem; respect

achtzehn (ahkh-tsāyn) num eighteen

achtzehnte (ahkh-tsāyn-ter) num eighteenth

achtzig (ahkh-tsikh) num eighty

Acker (ah-kerr) m (pl ~) field

addieren (ah-dee-rern) v count; add

Addition (ah-di-tsᵞōān) f (pl ~en) addition

Adel (aa-derl) m nobility

Ader (aa-derr) f (pl ~n) vein

Adler (aa-dlerr) m (pl ~) eagle

adlig (aa-dlikh) adj noble

administrativ (aht-mi-ni-strah-teef) adj administrative

Admiral (aht-mi-raal) m (pl ~e) admiral

adoptieren (ah-dop-tee-rern) v adopt

Adressat (ah-dreh-saat) m (pl ~en) addressee

Adresse (ah-dreh-ser) f (pl ~n) address

adressieren (ah-dreh-see-rern) v address

Adverb (aht-vehrp) nt (pl ~ien) adverb

Affe (ah-fer) m (pl ~n) monkey

Afrika (ah-fri-kaa) Africa

Afrikaner (ah-fri-kaa-nerr) m (pl ~) African

afrikanisch (ah-fri-kaa-nish) adj African

Agent (ah-gehnt) m (pl ~en) agent

Agentur (ah-gehn-tōōr) f (pl ~en) agency

aggressiv (ah-greh-seef) adj aggressive

agrarisch (ah-graa-rish) adj agrarian

Ägypten (eh-gewp-tern) Egypt

Ägypter (eh-gewp-terr) m (pl ~) Egyptian

ägyptisch (eh-gewp-tish) adj Egyptian

ähnlich (ain-likh) adj similar; alike

Ähnlichkeit (*ain*-likh-kight) *f* (pl ~en) similarity; resemblance

Ahnung (*aa*-noong) *f* notion

Ahorn (*aa*-horn) *m* (pl ~e) maple

Akademie (ah-kah-day-*mee*) *f* (pl ~n) academy

Akkord (ah-*kort*) *m* (pl ~e) agreement

Akkreditiv (ah-kray-di-*teef*) *nt* (pl ~e) letter of credit

Akku (*ah*-koo) *m* (pl ~s) battery

Akne (*ah*-kner) *f* acne

Akt (ahkt) *m* (pl ~e) act; nude

Akte (*ahk*-ter) *f* (pl ~n) record; **Akten file**

Aktentasche (*ahk*-tern-tah-sher) *f* (pl ~n) briefcase, attaché case

Aktie (*ahk*-ts^{y}er) *f* (pl ~n) share; **Aktien stocks and shares**

Aktion (ahk-ts^y*ōan*) *f* (pl ~en) action

aktiv (ahk-*teef*) *adj* active

Aktivität (ahk-ti-vi-*tait*) *f* (pl ~en) activity

aktuell (ahk-too-*ehl*) *adj* topical

akut (ah-*kōot*) *adj* acute

Akzent (ahk-*tsehnt*) *m* (pl ~e) accent

akzeptieren (ahk-tsehp-*tee*-rern) *v* accept

Alarm (ah-*lahrm*) *m* alarm

alarmieren (ah-lahr-*mee*-rern) *v* alarm

albern (*ahl*-berrn) *adj* foolish, silly

Album (*ahl*-boom) *nt* (pl Alben) album

Algebra (*ahl*-gay-brah) *f* algebra

Algerien (ahl-*gāy*-r^{y}ern) Algeria

Algerier (ahl-*gāy*-r^{y}err) *m* (pl ~) Algerian

algerisch (ahl-*gāy*-rish) *adj* Algerian

Alimente (ah-li-*mayn*-ter) *ntpl* alimony

Alkohol (*ahl*-koa-hol) *m* alcohol

alkoholisch (ahl-koa-*hōa*-lish) *adj* alcoholic

all (ahl) *num* all; **alle** *num* all; *adv* finished

Allee (ah-*lāy*) *f* (pl ~n) avenue

allein (ah-*lighn*) *adv* alone

allenfalls (*ah*-lern-fahls) *adv* at most

allerdings (*ah*-lerr-dings) *adv* of course

Allergie (ah-lehr-*gee*) *f* (pl ~n) allergy

allerlei (*ah*-lerr-ligh) *adj* various, all sorts of

alles (*ah*-lerss) *pron* everything; ~ **inbegriffen** all in

allgemein (ahl-ger-*mighn*) *adj* general; public; common; universal; **im allgemeinen** in general

Alliierten (ah-li-*eer*-tern) *mpl* Allies pl

allmächtig (ahl-*mehkh*-tikh) *adj* omnipotent

allmählich (ahl-*mai*-likh) *adj* gradual

alltäglich (ahl-*tāyk*-likh) *adj* ordinary, everyday; daily

Almanach (*ahl*-mah-nahkh) *m* (pl ~e) almanac

Alphabet (ahl-fah-*bāyt*) *nt* alphabet

als (ahls) *conj* when; than; ~ **ob** as if

alsbald (ahls-*bahlt*) *adv* soon

also (*ahl*-zōa) *conj* so

Alt (ahlt) *m* (pl ~e) alto

alt (ahlt) *adj* old, ancient; aged

Altar (ahl-*taar*) *m* (pl ~e) altar

altbacken (*ahlt*-bah-kern) *adj* stale

Alteisen (*ahlt*-igh-zern) *nt* scrap-iron

Alter (*ahl*-terr) *nt* age; old age

Alternative (ahl-tehr-nah-*tee*-ver) *f* (pl ~n) alternative

Altertum (*ahl*-terr-tōom) *nt* antiquity

Altertumskunde (*ahl*-terr-tōoms-koonder) *f* archaeology

ältlich (*ehlt*-likh) *adj* elderly

altmodisch (*ahlt*-mōa-dish) *adj* oldfashioned, ancient; quaint

Ambulanz (ahm-boo-*lahnts*) *f* (pl ~en) ambulance

Ameise (*aa*-migh-zer) *f* (pl ~n) ant

Amerika (ah-*māy*-ri-kah) America

Amerikaner (ah-may-ri-*kaa*-nerr) *m* (pl

~) American

amerikanisch (ah-may-ri-*kaa*-nish) *adj* American

Amethyst (ah-may-*tewst*) *m* (pl ~en) amethyst

Amnestie (ahm-nay-*stee*) *f* amnesty

Amsel (*ahm*-zerl) *f* (pl ~n) blackbird

Amt (ahmt) *nt* (pl ~er) office

Amulett (ah-moo-*leht*) *nt* (pl ~e) lucky charm, charm

amüsant (ah-mew-*zahnt*) *adj* entertaining

Amüsement (ah-mew-zer-*mahng*) *nt* entertainment

amüsieren (ah-mew-*zee*-rern) *v* amuse; entertain

an (ahn) *prep* on

Analphabet (ah-nahl-fah-*bāȳt*) *m* (pl ~en) illiterate

Analyse (ah-nah-*lēw*-zer) *f* (pl ~n) analysis

analysieren (ah-nah-lew-*zee*-rern) *v* analyse

Analytiker (ah-nah-*lēw*-ti-kerr) *m* (pl ~) analyst

Ananas (*ah*-nah-nahss) *f* pineapple

Anarchie (ah-nahr-*khee*) *f* anarchy

Anatomie (ah-nah-toa-*mee*) *f* anatomy

anbauen (*ahn*-bou-ern) *v* cultivate, raise

in Anbetracht (in *ahn*-ber-trahkht) considering, regarding

*anbieten (*ahn*-bee-tern) *v* offer; present

Anblick (*ahn*-blik) *m* sight; look

*anbrennen (*ahn*-breh-nern) *v* *burn

Andenken (*ahn*-dehng-kern) *nt* (pl ~) souvenir; remembrance; memory

ander (*ahn*-derr) *adj* other; different

ändern (*ehn*-derrn) *v* change; alter

anders (*ahn*-derrs) *adv* otherwise

andersherum (*ahn*-derrs-heh-room) *adv* the other way round

anderswo (*ahn*-derrs-*vōā*) *adv* else-

where

Änderung (*ehn*-der-roong) *f* (pl ~en) change; alteration

andrehen (*ahn*-drāȳ-ern) *v* turn on

*anempfehlen (*ahn*-aym-pfāȳ-lern) *v* recommend

*anerkennen (*ahn*-ehr-keh-nern) *v* recognize

Anerkennung (*ahn*-ehr-keh-noong) *f* (pl ~en) recognition

Anfall (*ahn*-fahl) *m* (pl ~e) fit

Anfang (*ahn*-fahng) *m* start, beginning; **Anfangs-** initial; primary

*anfangen (*ahn*-fahng-ern) *v* start, commence, *begin

Anfänger (*ahn*-fehng-err) *m* (pl ~) learner, beginner

anfänglich (*ahn*-fehng-likh) *adv* originally

anfangs (*ahn*-fahngs) *adv* at first

Anfangsbuchstabe (*ahn*-fahngs-bōōkh-shtaa-ber) *m* (pl ~n) initial

anfeuchten (*ahn*-foikh-tern) *v* moisten

anflehen (*ahn*-flāȳ-ern) *v* beg

Anführer (*ahn*-fēw-rerr) *m* (pl ~) leader

Anführungszeichen (*ahn*-fēw-roongs-tsigh-khern) *ntpl* quotation marks

Angabe (*ahn*-gaa-ber) *f* (pl ~n) data *pl*

*angeben (*ahn*-gāȳ-bern) *v* indicate; declare

angeboren (*ahn*-ger-bōā-rern) *adj* natural

Angebot (*ahn*-ger-bōat) *nt* (pl ~e) offer; supply

angebracht (*ahn*-ger-brahkht) *adj* proper

angegliedert (*ahn*-ger-glee-derrt) *adj* affiliated

*angehen (*ahn*-gāȳ-ern) *v* concern

Angeklagte (*ahn*-ger-klaak-ter) *m* (pl ~n) accused

Angelegenheit (*ahn*-ger-lāȳ-gern-hight) *f* (pl ~en) affair, business, concern

Angelgeräte (*ahng-erl-ger-rai-ter*) *ntpl* fishing tackle, fishing gear

Angelhaken (*ahng-erl-haa-kern*) *m* (pl ~) fishing hook

angeln (*ahng-erln*) *v* fish, angle

Angelrute (*ahng-erl-rōō-ter*) *f* (pl ~n) fishing rod

Angelschein (*ahng-erl-shighn*) *m* (pl ~e) fishing licence

Angelschnur (*ahng-erl-shnōōr*) *f* (pl ~e) fishing line

angemessen (*ahn-ger-meh-sern*) *adj* appropriate; adequate, convenient, suitable

angenehm (*ahn-ger-naym*) *adj* pleasant; enjoyable, pleasing, agreeable

Angestellte (*ahn-ger-shtehl-ter*) *m* (pl ~n) employee

*****angreifen** (*ahn-grigh-fern*) *v* attack, assault

Angriff (*ahn-grif*) *m* (pl ~e) attack

Angst (ahngst) *f* (pl ~e) fright, fear; dread; ~ **haben** *be afraid

ängstlich (*ehngst-likh*) *adj* afraid

*****anhaben** (*ahn-haa-bern*) *v* *wear

anhaken (*ahn-haa-kern*) *v* tick off

*****anhalten** (*ahn-hahl-tern*) *v* halt; pull up; prevent; **anhaltend** continuous

Anhalter (*ahn-hahl-terr*) *m* (pl ~) hitchhiker; **per** ~ *fahren hitch-hike

Anhang (*ahn-hahng*) *m* (pl ~e) annex

Anhänger (*ahn-hehng-err*) *m* (pl ~) supporter; advocate; pendant; trailer

anhäufen (*ahn-hoi-fern*) *v* pile

anheften (*ahn-hayf-tern*) *v* attach

Anhöhe (*ahn-hūr-er*) *f* (pl ~n) rise

anhören (*ahn-hūr-rern*) *v* listen

Anker (*ahng-kerr*) *m* (pl ~) anchor

Anklage (*ahn-klaa-ger*) *f* (pl ~n) charge

anklagen (*ahn-klaa-gern*) *v* accuse, charge

ankleben (*ahn-klay-bern*) *v* *stick

ankleiden (*ahn-kligh-dern*) *v* dress

Ankleideraum (*ahn-kligh-der-room*) *nt* (pl ~e) dressing-room

*****ankommen** (*ahn-ko-mern*) *v* arrive

ankreuzen (*ahn-kroi-tsern*) *v* mark

ankündigen (*ahn-kewn-di-gern*) *v* announce

Ankündigung (*ahn-kewn-di-goong*) *f* (pl ~en) announcement

Ankunft (*ahn-koonft*) *f* arrival; coming

Ankunftszeit (*ahn-koonfts-tsight*) *f* (pl ~en) time of arrival

Anlage (*ahn-laa-ger*) *f* (pl ~n) investment; public garden

Anlaß (*ahn-lahss*) *m* (pl Anlässe) cause, occasion

Anlasser (*ahn-lah-serr*) *m* starter motor

anlegen (*ahn-lay-gern*) *v* dock; invest

Anleihe (*ahn-ligh-er*) *f* (pl ~n) loan

Anmeldebogen (*ahn-mehl-der-bōa-gern*) *m* (pl ~) registration form

sich anmelden (*ahn-mehl-dern*) check in

anmerken (*ahn-mehr-kern*) *v* note

Anmut (*ahn-mōōt*) *f* grace

anmutig (*ahn-mōō-tikh*) *adj* graceful

annähernd (*ahn-nai-errnt*) *adj* approximate

*****annehmen** (*ahn-nay-mern*) *v* accept; assume, suppose; adopt; **angenommen daß** supposing that

annullieren (*ah-noo-lee-rern*) *v* cancel

Annullierung (*ah-noo-lee-roong*) *f* (pl ~en) cancellation

anonym (ah-noa-*newm*) *adj* anonymous

anpassen (*ahn-pah-sern*) *v* adapt; adjust

Anproberaum (*ahn-prōa-ber-room*) *m*

(pl ~e) fitting room

anprobieren (*ahn*-proa-bee-rern) *v* try on

*****anraten** (*ahn*-raa-tern) *v* recommend

anregen (*ahn*-rāy-gern) *v* incite

Anregung (*ahn*-rāy-goong) *f* impulse

anrichten (*ahn*-rikh-tern) *v* cause

Anruf (*ahn*-rōōf) *m* (pl ~e) telephone call, call

*****anrufen** (*ahn*-rōō-fern) *v* phone, ring up, call; call up *Am*

anrühren (*ahn*-rēw-rern) *v* touch

anschauen (*ahn*-shou-ern) *v* look at

Anschauung (*ahn*-shou-oong) *f* (pl ~en) idea, outlook

Anschein (*ahn*-shighn) *m* semblance

anscheinend (*ahn*-shigh-nernt) *adv* apparently

Anschlagzettel (*ahn*-shlaak-tseh-terl) *m* (pl ~) poster

*****anschließen** (*ahn*-shlee-sern) *v* connect; **sich ~** join

Anschluß (*ahn*-shlooss) *m* (pl Anschlüsse) connection

*****anschreiben** (*ahn*-shrigh-bern) *v* score

Anschrift (*ahn*-shrift) *f* (pl ~en) address

Ansehen (*ahn*-zāy-ern) *nt* reputation

*****ansehen** (*ahn*-zāy-ern) *v* look at; regard

Ansicht (*ahn*-zikht) *f* (pl ~en) view, opinion; **der ~ *sein** consider; **zur ~** on approval

Ansichtskarte (*ahn*-zikhts-kahr-ter) *f* (pl ~n) picture postcard, postcard

Anspannung (*ahn*-shpah-noong) *f* (pl ~en) strain

anspornen (*ahn*-shpor-nern) *v* stimulate

Ansprache (*ahn*-shpraa-kher) *f* (pl ~n) speech

*****ansprechen** (*ahn*-shpreh-khern) *v* address

Anspruch (*ahn*-shprookh) *m* (pl ~e) claim

Anstalt (*ahn*-shtahlt) *f* (pl ~en) institute; asylum

Anstand (*ahn*-shtahnt) *m* decency

anständig (*ahn*-shtehn-dikh) *adj* decent

anstatt (ahn-*shtaht*) *prep* instead of

anstecken (*ahn*-shteh-kern) *v* infect

ansteckend (*ahn*-shteh-kernt) *adj* contagious, infectious

anstellen (*ahn*-shteh-lern) *v* appoint; engage

Anstoß (*ahn*-shtōāss) *m* kick-off

anstößig (*ahn*-shtǖr-sikh) *adj* offensive

*****anstreichen** (*ahn*-shtrigh-khern) *v* paint

Anstrengung (*ahn*-shtrehng-oong) *f* (pl ~en) effort, strain

Antenne (ahn-*teh*-ner) *f* (pl ~n) aerial

Anthologie (ahn-toa-loa-*gee*) *f* (pl ~n) anthology

Antibiotikum (ahn-ti-bi-*ōā*-ti-koom) *nt* (pl -ka) antibiotic

antik (ahn-*teek*) *adj* antique

Antipathie (ahn-ti-pah-*tee*) *f* dislike

Antiquität (ahn-ti-kvi-*tait*) *f* (pl ~en) antique

Antiquitätenhändler (ahn-ti-kvi-*tai*-tern-hehn-dlerr) *m* (pl ~) antique dealer

Antrag (*ahn*-traak) *m* (pl ~e) motion

*****antreiben** (*ahn*-trigh-bern) *v* propel

Antwort (*ahnt*-vort) *f* (pl ~en) answer; reply; **als ~** in reply

antworten (*ahnt*-vor-tern) *v* answer; reply

anvertrauen (*ahn*-fehr-trou-ern) *v* commit

*****anwachsen** (*ahn*-vah-ksern) *v* increase

Anwalt (*ahn*-vahlt) *m* (pl ~e) solicitor, attorney

*****anweisen** (*ahn*-vigh-zern) *v* designate

Anweisung (*ahn*-vigh-zoong) *f* (pl ~en) direction; money order

***anwenden** (*ahn*-vehn-dern) *v* apply

Anwendung (*ahn*-vehn-doong) *f* (pl ~en) application

anwesend (*ahn*-vāy-zernt) *adj* present

Anwesenheit (*ahn*-vāy-zern-hight) *f* presence

Anzahl (*ahn*-tsaal) *f* (pl ~en) number; quantity

Anzahlung (*ahn*-tsaa-loong) *f* (pl ~en) down payment

Anzeichen (*ahn*-tsigh-khern) *nt* (pl ~) indication

Anzeige (*ahn*-tsigh-ger) *f* (pl ~n) notice; advertisement; ticket

***anziehen** (*ahn*-tsee-ern) *v* attract; *put on

anziehend (*ahn*-tsee-ernt) *adj* attractive

Anziehung (*ahn*-tsee-oong) *f* attraction

Anzug (*ahn*-tsōōk) *m* (pl ˜e) suit

anzünden (*ahn*-tsewn-dern) *v* *light

Anzünder (*ahn*-tsewn-derr) *m* (pl ~) lighter

apart (ah-*pahrt*) *adv* separately

Aperitif (ah-peh-ri-*teef*) *m* (pl ~s) aperitif; drink

Apfel (*ah*-pferl) *m* (pl ˜) apple

Apfelsine (ah-pferl-*zee*-ner) *f* (pl ~n) orange

Apotheke (ah-poa-*tāy*-ker) *f* (pl ~n) pharmacy, chemist's; drugstore *nAm*

Apotheker (ah-poa-*tāy*-kerr) *m* (pl ~) chemist

Apparat (ah-pah-*raat*) *m* (pl ~e) machine, apparatus

Appartement (ah-pahr-ter-*mahng*) *nt* (pl ~e) apartment *nAm*

Appell (ah-*pehl*) *m* (pl ~e) appeal

Appetit (ah-pay-*teet*) *m* appetite

Appetithappen (ah-pay-*teet*-hah-pern) *m* (pl ~) appetizer

Aprikose (ah-pri-*kōā*-zer) *f* (pl ~n) apricot

April (ah-*pril*) April

Aquarell (ah-kvah-*rehl*) *nt* (pl ~e) water-colour

Äquator (eh-*kvaa*-tor) *m* equator

Araber (*aa*-rah-berr) *m* (pl ~) Arab

arabisch (ah-*raa*-bish) *adj* Arab

Arbeit (*ahr*-bight) *f* (pl ~en) labour, work; job

arbeiten (*ahr*-bigh-tern) *v* work; operate

Arbeiter (*ahr*-bigh-terr) *m* (pl ~) workman, labourer, worker

Arbeitgeber (*ahr*-bight-gāy-berr) *m* (pl ~) employer

Arbeitnehmer (*ahr*-bight-nāy-merr) *m* (pl ~) employee

Arbeitsamt (*ahr*-bights-ahmt) *nt* (pl ˜er) employment exchange

Arbeitsbewilligung (*ahr*-bights-ber-vi-li-goong) *f* (pl ~en) work permit; labor permit *Am*

arbeitslos (*ahr*-bights-lōāss) *adj* unemployed

Arbeitslosigkeit (*ahr*-bights-lōā-zikh-kight) *f* unemployment

Arbeitszimmer (*ahr*-bights-tsi-merr) *nt* (pl ~) study

Archäologe (ahr-kheh-oa-*lōā*-ger) *m* (pl ~n) archaeologist

Archäologie (ahr-kheh-oa-loa-*gee*) *f* archaeology

Architekt (ahr-khi-*tehkt*) *m* (pl ~en) architect

Architektur (ahr-khi-tehk-*tōōr*) *f* architecture

Archiv (ahr-*kheef*) *nt* (pl ~e) archives *pl*

Argentinien (ahr-gehn-*tee*-nᵞern) Argentina

Argentinier (ahr-gehn-*tee*-nᵞerr) *m* (pl

~) Argentinian

argentinisch (ahr-gehn-*tee*-nish) *adj* Argentinian

Ärger (*ehr*-gerr) *m* anger

ärgerlich (*ehr*-gerr-likh) *adj* annoying

ärgern (*ehr*-gerrn) *v* annoy

Argument (ahr-goo-*mehnt*) *nt* (pl ~e) argument

argumentieren (ahr-goo-mehn-*tee*-rern) *v* argue

Argwohn (*ahrk*-vōan) *m* suspicion

argwöhnisch (*ahrk*-vūr-nish) *adj* suspicious

Arkade (ahr-*kaa*-der) *f* (pl ~n) arcade

Arm (ahrm) *m* (pl ~e) arm; ~ **in Arm** arm-in-arm

arm (ahrm) *adj* poor

Armaturenbrett (ahr-mah-*tōo*-rern-breht) *nt* dashboard

Armband (*ahrm*-bahnt) *nt* (pl ~er) bracelet

Armbanduhr (*ahrm*-bahnt-ōor) *f* (pl ~en) wrist-watch

Armee (ahr-*māy*) *f* (pl ~n) army

Ärmel (*ehr*-merl) *m* (pl ~) sleeve

Ärmelkanal (*ehr*-merl-kah-naal) *m* English Channel

Armlehne (*ahrm*-lāy-ner) *f* (pl ~n) arm

Armleuchter (*ahrm*-loikh-terr) *m* (pl ~) candelabrum

ärmlich (*ehrm*-likh) *adj* poor

Armreif (*ahrm*-righf) *m* (pl ~en) bangle

Armut (*ahr*-mōot) *f* poverty

Aroma (ah-*rōa*-mah) *nt* aroma

Art (ahrt) *f* (pl ~en) species, sort; way, manner

Arterie (ahr-*tāy*-r^yer) *f* (pl ~n) artery

artig (*ahr*-tikh) *adj* good

Artikel (ahr-*tee*-kerl) *m* (pl ~) article

Artischocke (ahr-ti-*sho*-ker) *f* (pl ~n) artichoke

Arznei (ahrts-*nigh*) *f* (pl ~en) drug

Arzneimittellehre (ahrts-*nigh*-mit-terl-lāy-rer) *f* pharmacology

Arzt (ahrtst) *m* (pl ~e) doctor, physician; **praktischer** ~ general practitioner

ärztlich (*ehrtst*-likh) *adj* medical

Asbest (ahss-*behst*) *m* asbestos

Asche (*ah*-sher) *f* ash

Aschenbecher (*ah*-shern-beh-kherr) *m* (pl ~) ashtray

Asiate (ah-z^y*aa*-ter) *m* (pl ~n) Asian

asiatisch (ah-z^y*aa*-tish) *adj* Asian

Asien (*aa*-z^yern) Asia

Aspekt (ahss-*pehkt*) *m* (pl ~e) aspect

Asphalt (ahss-*fahlt*) *m* asphalt

Aspirin (ahss-pi-*reen*) *nt* aspirin

Assistent (ah-siss-*tehnt*) *m* (pl ~en) assistant

assoziieren (ah-soa-tsi-*ee*-rern) *v* associate

Ast (ahst) *m* (pl ~e) branch, bough

Asthma (*ahst*-mah) *nt* asthma

Astronomie (ah-stroa-noa-*mee*) *f* astronomy

Asyl (ah-*zēwl*) *nt* (pl ~e) asylum

Atem (*aa*-term) *m* breath

Atheist (ah-tay-*ist*) *m* (pl ~en) atheist

Äther (*ai*-terr) *m* ether

Äthiopien (eh-ti-*ōa*-p^yern) Ethiopia

Äthiopier (eh-ti-*ōa*-p^yerr) *m* (pl ~) Ethiopian

äthiopisch (eh-ti-*ōa*-pish) *adj* Ethiopian

Athlet (aht-*lāyt*) *m* (pl ~en) athlete

Athletik (aht-*lāy*-tik) *f* athletics *pl*

Atlantik (aht-*lahn*-tik) *m* Atlantic

atmen (*aat*-mern) *v* breathe

Atmosphäre (aht-moa-*sfai*-rer) *f* atmosphere

Atmung (*aat*-moong) *f* respiration, breathing

Atom (ah-*tōam*) *nt* (pl ~e) atom; **Atom-** atomic

atomar (ah-toa-*maar*) *adj* atomic

Attest (ah-*tehst*) *nt* (pl ~e) certificate

Attraktion (ah-trahk-*ts*ʸ*ōān*) *f* (pl ~en) attraction

Aubergine (oa-behr-*zhee*-ner) *f* eggplant

auch (oukh) *adv* too, also; as well

auf (ouf) *prep* on, upon; at

aufbauen (*ouf*-bou-ern) *v* construct; erect

aufblähen (*ouf*-blai-ern) *v* inflate

aufblasbar (*ouf*-blaass-baar) *adj* inflatable

aufdecken (*ouf*-deh-kern) *v* uncover

Aufenthalt (*ouf*-ehnt-hahlt) *m* (pl ~e) stay; delay

Aufenthaltsgenehmigung (*ouf*-ehnt-hahlts-ger-nāy-mi-goong) *f* (pl ~en) residence permit

***auffallen** (*ouf*-fah-lern) *v* *strike

auffallend (*ouf*-fah-lernt) *adj* striking

auffassen (*ouf*-fah-sern) *v* conceive

auffordern (*ouf*-for-derrn) *v* invite

Aufführung (*ouf*-fēw-roong) *f* (pl ~en) show, performance

Aufgabe (*ouf*-gaa-ber) *f* (pl ~n) duty, task; exercise

***aufgeben** (*ouf*-gāy-bern) *v* *give up, quit; post, mail

***aufgehen** (*ouf*-gāy-ern) *v* *rise

aufgliedern (*ouf*-glee-derrn) *v* *break down

aufgrund (ouf-*groont*) *prep* owing to, because of

sich *aufhalten (*ouf*-hahl-tern) stay

aufhängen (*ouf*-hehng-ern) *v* *hang

Aufhänger (*ouf*-hehng-err) *m* (pl ~) hanger

Aufhängung (*ouf*-hehng-oong) *f* suspension

***aufheben** (*ouf*-hāy-bern) *v* lift

aufheitern (*ouf*-high-terrn) *v* cheer up

aufhören (*ouf*-hūr-rern) *v* cease, expire, stop; ~ **mit** discontinue, quit

aufknöpfen (*ouf*-knur-pfern) *v* unbutton

aufknoten (*ouf*-knōa-tern) *v* untie

Auflage (*ouf*-laa-ger) *f* (pl ~n) issue

auflauern (*ouf*-lou-errn) *v* watch for

auflösen (*ouf*-lūr-zern) *v* dissolve; **sich ~** dissolve

aufmachen (*ouf*-mah-khern) *v* *undo; unfasten

aufmerksam (*ouf*-mehrk-zaam) *adj* attentive

Aufmerksamkeit (*ouf*-mehrk-zaam-kight) *f* attention; notice

Aufnahme (*ouf*-naa-mer) *f* (pl ~n) reception; shot; recording

***aufnehmen** (*ouf*-nāy-mern) *v* pick up

aufopfern (*ouf*-o-pfern) *v* sacrifice

aufpassen (ouf-pah-sern) *v* *pay attention; watch out; ~ **auf** look after

aufräumen (*ouf*-roi-mern) *v* tidy up

aufrecht (*ouf*-rehkht) *adj* upright, erect; *adv* upright

***aufrechterhalten** (*ouf*-rehkht-ehr-hahl-tern) *v* maintain

aufregen (*ouf*-rāy-gern) *v* excite; **aufregend** exciting

Aufregung (*ouf*-rāy-goong) *f* excitement

aufreihen (*ouf*-righ-ern) *v* thread

aufrichten (*ouf*-rikh-tern) *v* erect; **aufgerichtet** erect

aufrichtig (*ouf*-rikh-tikh) *adj* sincere, honest; true

Aufruhr (*ouf*-rōōr) *m* revolt, rebellion; riot

Aufsatz (*ouf*-zahts) *m* (pl ~̈e) essay

***aufschieben** (*ouf*-shee-bern) *v* delay; postpone

***aufschließen** (*ouf*-shlee-sern) *v* unlock

Aufschrei (*ouf*-shrigh) *m* (pl ~e) cry

***aufschreiben** (*ouf*-shrigh-bern) *v* *write down

Aufschub (*ouf*-shōōp) *m* delay; respite

aufsehenerregend (*ouf*-zāy-ern-ehr-rāy-gernt) *adj* sensational

Aufseher (*ouf*-zāy-err) *m* (pl ~) supervisor; warden

Aufsicht (*ouf*-zikht) *f* supervision

Aufsichtsbeamte (*ouf*-zikhts-ber-ahm-ter) *m* (pl ~n) inspector

Aufstand (*ouf*-shtahnt) *m* (pl ~e) rebellion; revolt, rising

*****aufstehen** (*ouf*-shtāy-ern) *v* *rise, *get up

*****aufsteigen** (*ouf*-shtigh-gern) *v* ascend

Aufstieg (*ouf*-shteek) *m* climb; ascent; rise

auftauen (*ouf*-tou-ern) *v* thaw

Auftrag (*ouf*-traak) *m* (pl ~e) order

*****auftreten** (*ouf*-trāy-tern) *v* appear

Auftritt (*ouf*-trit) *m* (pl ~e) appearance

aufwachen (*ouf*-vah-khern) *v* wake up

Aufwand (*ouf*-vahnt) *m* expenditure

aufwärts (*ouf*-vehrts) *adv* upwards

aufzeichnen (*ouf*-tsighkh-nern) *v* record

Aufzeichnung (*ouf*-tsighkh-noong) *f* (pl ~en) note

*****aufziehen** (*ouf*-tsee-ern) *v* *wind; raise

Aufzug (*ouf*-tsōōk) *m* (pl ~e) lift; elevator *nAm*

Auge (*ou*-ger) *nt* (pl ~n) eye

Augenarzt (*ou*-gern-ahrtst) *m* (pl ~e) oculist

Augenblick (*ou*-gern-blik) *m* (pl ~e) moment; second, instant

augenblicklich (*ou*-gern-blik-likh) *adv* instantly

Augenbraue (*ou*-gern-brou-er) *f* (pl ~n) eyebrow

Augenbrauenstift (*ou*-gern-brou-ern-shtift) *m* (pl ~e) eye-pencil

Augenlid (*ou*-gern-leet) *nt* (pl ~er) eyelid

Augenschminke (*ou*-gern-shming-ker) *f* eye-shadow

Augenwimper (*ou*-gern-vim-perr) *f* (pl ~n) eyelash

Augenzeuge (*ou*-gern-tsoi-ger) *m* (pl ~n) eye-witness

August (ou-*goost*) August

aus (ouss) *prep* out of; from; for

ausarbeiten (*ouss*-ahr-bigh-tern) *v* elaborate

ausatmen (*ouss*-aat-mern) *v* expire, exhale

ausbessern (*ouss*-beh-serrn) *v* mend

ausbeuten (*ouss*-boi-tern) *v* exploit

ausbilden (*ouss*-bil-dern) *v* educate; train

Ausbildung (*ouss*-bil-doong) *f* training

ausbreiten (*ouss*-brigh-tern) *v* expand; *spread

Ausbruch (*ouss*-brookh) *m* (pl ~e) outbreak

ausdehnen (*ouss*-dāy-nern) *v* expand

Ausdehnung (*ouss*-dāy-noong) *f* extension

*****ausdenken** (*ouss*-dehng-kern) *v* devise

Ausdruck (*ouss*-drook) *m* (pl ~e) term, expression; ~ *geben express

ausdrücken (*ouss*-drew-kern) *v* express

ausdrücklich (*ouss*-drewk-likh) *adj* express, explicit

Auseinandersetzung (ouss-igh-*nahn*-derr-zeh-tsoong) *f* (pl ~en) discussion, argument; dispute

auserlesen (*ouss*-ehr-lāy-zern) *adj* exquisite, select

Ausfahrt (*ouss*-faart) *f* (pl ~en) exit

Ausflug (*ouss*-flōōk) *m* (pl ~e) excursion; trip

Ausfuhr (*ouss*-fōōr) *f* exports *pl*, exportation

ausführbar (*ouss*-fewr-baar) *adj* realizable

ausführen (*ouss*-few-rern) v perform; export; execute, implement

ausführlich (*ouss*-fewr-likh) adj detailed

ausfüllen (*ouss*-few-lern) v fill in; fill out Am

Ausgabe (*ouss*-gaa-ber) f (pl ~n) issue, edition; expense

Ausgang (*ouss*-gahng) m (pl ~e) way out, exit

Ausgangspunkt (*ouss*-gahngs-poongkt) m (pl ~e) starting-point

* **ausgeben** (*ouss*-gay-bern) v *spend; issue

ausgedehnt (*ouss*-ger-daynt) adj extensive; broad

* **ausgehen** (*ouss*-gay-ern) v *go out

ausgenommen (*ouss*-ger-no-mern) prep except

ausgesetzt (*ouss*-ger-zehtst) subject to

ausgezeichnet (*ouss*-ger-tsighkh-nert) adj fine, excellent

Ausgleich (*ouss*-glighkh) m (pl ~e) compensation

* **ausgleichen** (*ouss*-gligh-khern) v equalize; compensate

ausgleiten (*ouss*-gligh-tern) f slip

Ausgrabung (*ouss*-graa-boong) f (pl ~en) excavation

Ausguß (*ouss*-gooss) m (pl -güsse) sink

* **aushalten** (*ouss*-hahl-tern) v sustain

ausharren (*ouss*-hah-rern) v *keep up

Auskunft (*ouss*-koonft) f (pl ~e) information

Auskunftsbüro (*ouss*-koonfts-bew-roa) nt (pl ~s) information bureau, inquiry office

* **ausladen** (*ouss*-laa-dern) v discharge, unload

Auslage (*ouss*-laa-ger) f (pl ~n) display

im Ausland (im *ouss*-lahnt) abroad

Ausländer (*ouss*-lehn-derr) m (pl ~) foreigner, alien

ausländisch (*ouss*-lehn-dish) adj foreign, alien

* **auslassen** (*ouss*-lah-sern) v *leave out, omit

auslegen (*ouss*-lay-gern) v display

Auslegung (*ouss*-lai-goong) f (pl ~en) explanation

* **auslesen** (*ouss*-lay-zayn) v select

ausliefern (*ouss*-lee-ferrn) v deliver; extradite

auslöschen (*ouss*-lur-shern) v extinguish, *put out

Ausmaß (*ouss*-maass) nt (pl ~e) extent; size

Ausnahme (*ouss*-naa-mer) f (pl ~n) exception

* **ausnehmen** (*ouss*-nay-mern) v exempt

ausnutzen (*ouss*-noo-tsern) v exploit

auspacken (*ouss*-pah-kern) v unpack, unwrap

Auspuff (*ouss*-poof) m (pl ~e) exhaust

Auspuffgase (*ouss*-poof-gaa-zer) ntpl exhaust gases

Auspufftopf (*ouss*-poof-topf) m silencer; muffler nAm

ausrangieren (*ouss*-rahng-zhee-rern) v discard

ausrechnen (*ouss*-rehkh-nern) v calculate

* **ausreißen** (*ouss*-righ-sern) v extract

Ausreißer (*ouss*-righ-serr) m (pl ~) runaway

Ausruf (*ouss*-roof) m (pl ~e) exclamation

* **ausrufen** (*ouss*-roo-fern) v exclaim

ausruhen (*ouss*-roo-ern) v rest

ausrüsten (*ouss*-rewss-tern) v equip

Ausrüstung (*ouss*-rewss-toong) f outfit, equipment; gear, kit

ausrutschen (*ouss*-roo-chern) v slip

aussaugen (*ouss*-zou-gern) v *bleed

ausschalten (*ouss*-shahl-tern) v switch

off; disconnect

ausschimpfen (*ouss*-shim-pfern) *v* call names

Ausschlag (*ouss*-shlaak) *m* rash

*****ausschließen** (*ouss*-shlee-sern) *v* exclude

ausschließlich (*ouss*-shleess-likh) *adv* exclusively; solely

Ausschreitung (*ouss*-shrigh-toong) *f* (pl ~en) excess

Ausschuß (*ouss*-shooss) *m* (pl -schüsse) committee

Aussehen (*ouss*-zāy-ern) *nt* look

*****aussehen** (*ouss*-zāy-ern) *v* look

Außenbezirke (*ou*-sern-ber-tseer-ker) *mpl* outskirts *pl*

Außenseite (*ou*-sern-zigh-ter) *f* exterior, outside

außer (*ou*-serr) *prep* beyond, besides; but, except; out of; ~ wenn unless

äußer (*oi*-serr) *adj* outward; **äußerst** *adj* extreme, utmost; very

außerdem (*ou*-serr-dāym) *adv* moreover

Äußere (*oi*-ser-rer) *nt* outside

außergewöhnlich (*ou*-serr-ger-vūrn-likh) *adj* exceptional

außerhalb (*ou*-serr-hahlp) *prep* outside

äußerlich (*oi*-serr-likh) *adj* external, exterior

äußern (*oi*-serrn) *v* express; utter

außerordentlich (ou-serr-*or*-dernt-likh) *adj* extraordinary

Äußerung (*oi*-ser-roong) *f* (pl ~en) expression

Aussetzung (*ouss*-zay-tsoong) *f* exposure

Aussicht[1] (*ouss*-zikht) *f* view; sight

Aussicht[2] (*ouss*-zikht) *f* (pl ~en) prospect, outlook

Aussprache (*ouss*-shpraa-kher) *f* pronunciation

*****aussprechen** (*ouss*-shpreh-khern) *v* pronounce

ausstatten (*ouss*-shtah-tern) *v* equip

*****aussteigen** (*ouss*-shtigh-gern) *v* *get off

ausstellen (*ouss*-shteh-lern) *v* exhibit; *show

Ausstellung (*ouss*-shteh-loong) *f* (pl ~en) exhibition; display, show, exposition

Ausstellungsraum (*ouss*-shteh-loongs-roum) *m* (pl ~e) showroom

Ausstoß (*ouss*-shtōass) *m* output

austauschen (*ouss*-tou-shern) *v* exchange

austeilen (*ouss*-tigh-lern) *v* *deal

Auster (*ouss*-terr) *f* (pl ~n) oyster

Australien (ouss-*traa*-lᵞern) Australia

Australier (ouss-*traa*-lᵞerr) *m* (pl ~) Australian

australisch (ouss-*traa*-lish) *adj* Australian

ausüben (*ouss*-ēw-bern) *v* exercise; practise

Ausverkauf (*ouss*-fehr-kouf) *m* clearance sale

ausverkauft (*ouss*-fehr-kouft) *adj* sold out

Auswahl (*ouss*-vaal) *f* choice; selection; assortment; variety

auswählen (*ouss*-vai-lern) *v* select

Auswanderer (*ouss*-vahn-der-rerr) *m* (pl ~) emigrant

auswandern (*ouss*-vahn-derrn) *v* emigrate

Auswanderung (*ouss*-vahn-der-roong) *f* emigration

auswechseln (*ouss*-veh-kserln) *v* exchange

Ausweg (*ouss*-vāyk) *m* (pl ~e) issue

Ausweis (*ouss*-vighss) *m* (pl ~e) identity card

*****ausweisen** (*ouss*-vigh-zern) *v* expel

auswendig (*ouss*-vehn-dikh) *adv* by heart

auswischen (*ouss*-vi-shern) v wipe

sich auszeichnen (*ouss*-tsighkh-nern) excel

*ausziehen (*ouss*-tsee-ern) v extract

Auszug (*ouss*-tsōōk) m (pl ⁓e) excerpt

authentisch (ou-*tehn*-tish) adj authentic

Auto (*ou*-toa) nt (pl ⁓s) automobile; **im ⁓ *fahren** motor

Autobahn (*ou*-toa-baan) f (pl ⁓en) motorway; highway nAm

Autofahrer (*ou*-toa-faa-rerr) m (pl ⁓) motorist

Autokarte (*ou*-toa-kahr-ter) f (pl ⁓n) road map

Automat (ou-toa-*maat*) m (pl ⁓en) slot-machine

automatisch (ou-toa-*maa*-tish) adj automatic

Automatisierung (ou-toa-mah-ti-*zee*-roong) f automation

Automobilismus (ou-toa-moa-bi-*liss*-mooss) m motoring

Automobilklub (ou-toa-moa-*beel*-kloop) m (pl ⁓s) automobile club

autonom (ou-toa-*nōam*) adj autonomous

Autopsie (ou-toa-*psee*) f autopsy

Autor (*ou*-tor) m (pl ⁓en) author

autoritär (ou-toa-ri-*tair*) adj authoritarian

Autovermietung (*ou*-toa-fehr-mee-toong) f car hire; car rental Am

B

Baby (*bāy*-bi) nt (pl ⁓s) baby

Babysitter (*bāy*-bi-si-terr) m (pl ⁓) babysitter

Baby-Tragetasche (*bāy*-bi-traa-ger-tah-sher) f (pl ⁓n) carry-cot

Bach (bahkh) m (pl ⁓e) brook, stream

Backbord (*bahk*-bord) nt port

backen (*bah*-kern) v bake

Backenbart (*bah*-kern-bahrt) m whiskers pl

Backenknochen (*bah*-kern-kno-khern) m (pl ⁓) cheek-bone

Backenzahn (*bah*-kern-tsaan) m (pl ⁓e) molar

Bäcker (*beh*-kerr) m (pl ⁓) baker

Bäckerei (beh-ker-*righ*) f (pl ⁓en) bakery

Backofen (*bahk*-ōa-fern) m (pl ⁓) oven

Backpflaume (*bahk*-pflou-mer) f (pl ⁓n) prune

Bad (baat) nt (pl ⁓er) bath

Badeanzug (*baa*-der-ahn-tsōōk) m (pl ⁓e) swim-suit, bathing-suit

Badehose (*baa*-der-hōa-zer) f (pl ⁓n) swimming-trunks, bathing-trunks, bathing-suit

Bademantel (*baa*-der-mahn-terl) m (pl ⁓) bathrobe

Bademütze (*baa*-der-mew-tser) f (pl ⁓n) bathing-cap

baden (*baa*-dern) v bathe

Badesalz (*baa*-der-zahlts) nt (pl ⁓e) bath salts

Badetuch (*baa*-der-tōōkh) nt (pl ⁓er) bath towel

Badezimmer (*baa*-der-tsi-merr) nt (pl ⁓) bathroom

Bahn (baan) f (pl ⁓en) railway; track

Bahnhof (*baan*-hōaf) m (pl ⁓e) station; depot nAm

Bahnsteig (*baan*-shtighk) m (pl ⁓e) platform

Bahnsteigkarte (*baan*-shtighk-kahr-ter) f (pl ⁓n) platform ticket

Bahnübergang (*baan*-ēw-berr-gahng) m (pl ⁓e) crossing, level crossing

Bakterie (bahk-*tāy*-rʸer) f (pl ⁓n) bacterium

bald (bahlt) adv soon; shortly

Balken (*bahl*-kern) *m* (pl ~) beam

Balkon (bahl-*kawng*) *m* (pl ~s) balcony; circle

Ball (bahl) *m* (pl ˷e) ball

Ballett (bah-*leht*) *nt* (pl ~s) ballet

Ballon (bah-*lawng*) *m* (pl ~e) balloon

Ballsaal (*bahl*-zaal) *m* (pl -säle) ballroom

Bambus (*bahm*-booss) *m* bamboo

Banane (bah-*naa*-ner) *f* (pl ~n) banana

Band[1] (bahnt) *nt* (pl ˷er) band; ribbon; tape

Band[2] (bahnt) *m* (pl ˷e) volume

Bande (*bahn*-der) *f* (pl ~n) gang

Bandit (bahn-*deet*) *m* (pl ~en) bandit

Bandmaß (*bahnt*-maass) *nt* (pl ~e) tape-measure

bange (*bahng*-er) *adj* afraid

Bank[1] (bahngk) *f* (pl ~en) bank

Bank[2] (bahngk) *f* (pl ˷e) bench

Bank-Einlage (*bahngk*-ighn-laa-ger) *f* (pl ~n) deposit

Bankettsaal (bahng-*keht*-zaal) *m* (pl -säle) banqueting-hall

Bankkonto (*bahngk*-kon-toa) *nt* (pl -konten) bank account

Banknote (*bahngk*-nōā-ter) *f* (pl ~n) banknote

bankrott (bahng-*krot*) *adj* bankrupt

Banner (*bah*-nerr) *nt* (pl ~) banner

Bar (baar) *f* (pl ~s) bar; saloon

Bär (bair) *m* (pl ~en) bear

Bardame (*baar*-daa-mer) *f* (pl ~n) barmaid

Bargeld (*baar*-gehlt) *nt* cash

Bariton (*baa*-ri-ton) *m* (pl ~e) baritone

barmherzig (bahrm-*hehr*-tsikh) *adj* merciful

Barmherzigkeit (bahrm-*hehr*-tsikh-kight) *f* mercy

barock (bah-*rok*) *adj* baroque

Barometer (bah-roa-*māy*-terr) *nt* (pl ~) barometer

Barsch (bahrsh) *m* (pl ~e) perch, bass

Bart (bahrt) *m* (pl ˷e) beard

Base (*baa*-zer) *f* (pl ~n) cousin

Baseball (*bāyss*-bōal) *m* baseball

Basilika (bah-*zee*-li-kah) *f* (pl -ken) basilica

Basis (*baa*-ziss) *f* (pl Basen) basis; base

Baskenmütze (*bahss*-kern-mew-tser) *f* (pl ~n) beret

Baß (bahss) *m* (pl Bässe) bass

Bastard (*bahss*-tahrt) *m* (pl ~e) bastard

Batterie (bah-ter-*ree*) *f* (pl ~n) battery

Bau (bou) *m* construction

Bauch (boukh) *m* (pl ˷e) belly

Bauchschmerzen (*boukh*-shmehr-tsern) *mpl* stomach-ache

bauen (*bou*-ern) *v* construct, *build

Bauer (*bou*-err) *m* (pl ~n) farmer; peasant; pawn

Bäuerin (*boi*-er-rin) *f* (pl ~nen) farmer's wife

Bauernhaus (*bou*-errn-houss) *nt* (pl ˷er) farmhouse

Bauernhof (*bou*-errn-hōāf) *m* (pl ˷e) farm

baufällig (*bou*-feh-likh) *adj* dilapidated

Bauholz (*bou*-holts) *nt* timber

Baukunst (*bou*-koonst) *f* architecture

Baum (boum) *m* (pl ˷e) tree

Baumschule (*boum*-shōō-ler) *f* (pl ~n) nursery

Baumwolle (*boum*-vo-ler) *f* cotton; **Baumwoll-** cotton

Baumwollsamt (*boum*-vol-zahmt) *m* velveteen

Bazille (bah-*tsi*-ler) *f* (pl ~n) germ

beabsichtigen (ber-*ahp*-zikh-ti-gern) *v* intend; aim at

beachten (ber-*ahkh*-tern) *v* attend to; observe

beachtlich (ber-*ahkht*-likh) *adj* considerable

Beachtung (ber-*ahkh*-toong) *f* consideration

Beamte (ber-*ahm*-ter) *m* (pl ~n) clerk

beanspruchen (ber-*ahn*-shproo-khern) *v* claim

beantworten (ber-*ahnt*-vor-tern) *v* answer

beaufsichtigen (ber-*ouf*-zikh-ti-gern) *v* supervise

bebauen (ber-*bou*-ern) *v* cultivate

beben (*bay*-bern) *v* tremble

Becher (*beh*-kherr) *m* (pl ~) mug, tumbler

Becken (*beh*-kern) *nt* (pl ~) basin; pelvis

bedächtig (ber-*dehkh*-tikh) *adj* wary

Bedarf (ber-*dahrf*) *m* want

Bedauern (ber-*dou*-errn) *nt* regret

bedauern (ber-*dou*-errn) *v* regret

bedecken (ber-*deh*-kern) *v* cover

bedenklich (ber-*dehngk*-likh) *adj* critical

bedeuten (ber-*doi*-tern) *v* *mean

bedeutend (ber-*doi*-ternt) *adj* considerable, big; important; capital, substantial

Bedeutung (ber-*doi*-toong) *f* (pl ~en) meaning, sense; importance; **von ~** *sein matter

bedeutungsvoll (ber-*doi*-toongs-fol) *adj* significant

bedienen (ber-*dee*-nern) *v* serve; wait on, attend on

Bedienung (ber-*dee*-noong) *f* service

bedingt (ber-*dingkt*) *adj* conditional

Bedingung (ber-*ding*-oong) *f* (pl ~en) condition; term

bedingungslos (ber-*ding*-oongs-lôáss) *adj* unconditional

bedrohen (ber-*drōā*-ern) *v* threaten

bedrohlich (ber-*drōā*-likh) *adj* threatening

Bedrohung (ber-*drōā*-oong) *f* (pl ~en) threat

bedrücken (ber-*drew*-kern) *v* oppress

Bedürfnis (ber-*dewrf*-niss) *nt* (pl ~se) need

sich beeilen (ber-*igh*-lern) hurry

beeindrucken (ber-*ighn*-droo-kern) *v* impress

beeinflussen (ber-*ighn*-floo-sern) *v* influence; affect

beenden (ber-*ehn*-dern) *v* end, finish

beerdigen (ber-*air*-di-gern) *v* bury

Beere (*bay*-rer) *f* (pl ~n) berry; currant

befähigen (ber-*fai*-i-gern) *v* enable

Befähigung (ber-*fai*-i-goong) *f* (pl ~en) qualification

befahrbar (ber-*faar*-baar) *adj* navigable

***befahren** (ber-*faa*-rern) *v* sail

sich befassen mit (ber-*fah*-sern) *deal with

Befehl (ber-*fáȳl*) *m* (pl ~e) order; command

***befehlen** (ber-*fáȳ*-lern) *v* order; command

Befehlshaber (ber-*fáȳls*-haa-berr) *m* (pl ~) commander

befestigen (ber-*fehss*-ti-gern) *v* fasten; attach

befeuchten (ber-*foikh*-tern) *v* damp

beflecken (ber-*fleh*-kern) *v* stain

befördern (ber-*furr*-derrn) *v* promote

Beförderung (ber-*furr*-der-roong) *f* (pl ~en) transport; promotion

befragen (ber-*fraa*-gern) *v* query

befreien (ber-*frigh*-ern) *v* exempt

befreit (ber-*fright*) *adj* exempt

Befreiung (beh-*frigh*-oong) *f* liberation; exemption

befriedigen (ber-*free*-di-gern) *v* satisfy

Befriedigung (ber-*free*-di-goong) *f* satisfaction

Befugnis (ber-*fōōk*-niss) *f* (pl ~se)

authority

befugt (ber-*fōōkt*) adj qualified

befürchten (ber-*fewrkh*-tern) v dread

begabt (ber-*gaapt*) adj gifted, talented

Begabung (ber-*gaa*-boong) f faculty, talent

begegnen (ber-*gāy*-gnern) v *meet; encounter, *come across; **zufällig ~** run into

Begegnung (ber-*gāy*-gnoong) f (pl ~en) encounter

***begehen** (ber-*gāy*-ern) v commit

Begehren (ber-*gāy*-rern) nt wish

begehren (ber-*gāy*-rern) v wish; desire

begehrenswert (ber-*gāy*-rerns-*vāyrt*) adj desirable

begeistern (ber-*gighss*-terrn) v inspire; **begeistert** adj enthusiastic; keen

Begeisterung (ber-*gighss*-ter-roong) f enthusiasm

begierig (ber-*gee*-rikh) adj eager

Beginn (ber-*gin*) m beginning

***beginnen** (ber-*gi*-nern) v *begin; **wieder ~** recommence

begleiten (ber-*gligh*-tern) v accompany; conduct

beglückwünschen (ber-*glewk*-vewnshern) v congratulate, compliment

Beglückwünschung (ber-*glewk*-vewnshoong) f (pl ~en) congratulation

Begnadigung (ber-*gnaa*-di-goong) f (pl ~en) pardon

***begraben** (ber-*graa*-bern) v bury

Begräbnis (ber-*graip*-niss) nt (pl ~se) funeral, burial

***begreifen** (ber-*grigh*-fern) v *understand; *see

Begriff (ber-*grif*) m (pl ~e) notion

begünstigen (ber-*gewns*-ti-gern) v favour

Beha m (pl ~s) brassiere

behaglich (ber-*haak*-likh) adj cosy, easy

Behaglichkeit (ber-*haak*-likh-kight) f (pl ~en) comfort

***behalten** (ber-*hahl*-tern) v remember

Behälter (ber-*hehl*-terr) m (pl ~) container

behandeln (ber-*hahn*-derln) v treat; handle

Behandlung (ber-*hahn*-dloong) f (pl ~en) treatment; **kosmetische ~** beauty treatment

Behandlungsweise (ber-*hahn*-dloongs-vigh-zer) f (pl ~n) approach

beharren (ber-*hah*-rern) v insist

behaupten (ber-*houp*-tern) v claim

sich *behelfen mit (ber-*hehl*-fern) *make do with

behende (ber-*hehn*-der) adj skilful

beherbergen (ber-*hehr*-behr-gern) v lodge

beherrschen (ber-*hehr*-shern) v master

beherzt (ber-*hehrtst*) adj brave

behexen (ber-*heh*-ksern) v bewitch

Behörde (ber-*hürr*-der) f (pl ~n) authorities pl

behutsam (ber-*hōōt*-zaam) adj gentle

bei (bigh) prep at, with; near, by

Beichte (*bighkh*-ter) f (pl ~n) confession

beichten (*bighkh*-tern) v confess

beide (*bigh*-der) adj both, either; **einer von beiden** either

Beifall (*bigh*-fahl) m applause; **~ klatschen** clap

beifügen (*bigh*-few-gern) v attach

beige (bāyzh) adj beige

Beil (bighl) nt (pl ~e) axe

Beilage (*bigh*-laa-ger) f (pl ~n) enclosure; supplement

beiläufig (*bigh*-loi-fikh) adj casual

beilegen (*bigh*-lāy-gern) v enclose

Bein (bighn) nt (pl ~e) leg; bone

beinahe (*bigh*-naa-er) adv nearly, almost

***beischließen** (*bigh*-shlee-sern) v enclose

beiseite (*bigh-zigh*-ter) *adv* aside

Beispiel (*bigh*-shpeel) *nt* (pl ~e) instance, example; **zum ~** for instance, for example

*****beißen** (*bigh*-sern) *v* *bite

Beistand (*bigh*-shtahnt) *m* assistance

Beitrag (*bigh*-traak) *m* (pl ~̈e) contribution

beiwohnen (*bigh*-vōa-nern) *v* attend, assist at

bejahen (ber-*Yaa*-ern) *v* approve; **bejahend** affirmative

bejahrt (ber-*Yaart*) *adj* aged

bekämpfen (ber-*kehm*-pfern) *v* combat

bekannt (ber-*kahnt*) *adj* well-known

Bekannte (ber-*kahn*-ter) *m* (pl ~n) acquaintance

bekanntmachen (ber-*kahnt*-mah-khern) *v* announce

Bekanntmachung (ber-*kahnt*-mah-khoong) *f* (pl ~en) announcement; communiqué

Bekanntschaft (ber-*kahnt*-shahft) *f* (pl ~en) acquaintance

bekehren (ber-*kāy*-rern) *v* convert

*****bekennen** (ber-*keh*-nern) *v* confess

*****bekommen** (ber-*ko*-mern) *v* *get; receive

bekömmlich (ber-*kurm*-likh) *adj* wholesome

bekrönen (ber-*krūr*-nern) *v* crown

bekümmert (ber-*kew*-merrt) *adj* sorry

Belagerung (ber-*laa*-ger-roong) *f* (pl ~en) siege

belanglos (ber-*lahng*-lōāss) *adj* insignificant

belasten (ber-*lahss*-tern) *v* charge

belästigen (ber-*lehss*-ti-gern) *v* bother

Belästigung (ber-*lehss*-ti-goong) *f* (pl ~en) bother

Belastung (ber-*lahss*-toong) *f* (pl ~en) charge

Beleg (ber-*lāyk*) *m* (pl ~e) voucher

beleibt (ber-*lighpt*) *adj* corpulent

beleidigen (ber-*ligh*-di-gern) *v* offend, insult; **beleidigend** *adj* offensive

Beleidigung (ber-*ligh*-di-goong) *f* (pl ~en) offence, insult

Beleuchtung (ber-*loikh*-toong) *f* lighting, illumination

Belgien (*behl*-gYern) Belgium

Belgier (*behl*-gYerr) *m* (pl ~) Belgian

belgisch (*behl*-gish) *adj* Belgian

Belichtung (ber-*likh*-toong) *f* exposure

Belichtungsmesser (ber-*likh*-toongs-meh-serr) *m* (pl ~) exposure meter

beliebig (ber-*lee*-bikh) *adj* optional

beliebt (ber-*leept*) *adj* popular

bellen (*beh*-lern) *v* bark, bay

belohnen (ber-*lōā*-nern) *v* reward

Belohnung (ber-*lōā*-noong) *f* (pl ~en) reward; prize

sich bemächtigen (ber-*mehkh*-ti-gern) secure

bemerken (ber-*mehr*-kern) *v* notice; note; remark

bemerkenswert (ber-*mehr*-kerns-vāyrt) *adj* noticeable

Bemerkung (ber-*mehr*-koong) *f* (pl ~en) remark

bemitleiden (ber-*mit*-ligh-dern) *v* pity

bemühen (ber-*mēw*-ern) *v* trouble; **sich ~** try

Bemühung (ber-*mēw*-oong) *f* (pl ~en) effort

benachbart (ber-*nahkh*-baart) *adj* neighbouring

benachrichtigen (ber-*naakh*-rikh-ti-gern) *v* notify

sich *benehmen (ber-*nāy*-mern) act, behave

beneiden (ber-*nigh*-dern) *v* envy

Benennung (ber-*neh*-noong) *f* (pl ~en) denomination

benutzen (ber-*noo*-tsern) *v* use; utilize

Benutzer (ber-*noo*-tserr) *m* (pl ~) user

Benzin (behn-*tseen*) *nt* petrol; fuel; gasoline *nAm*, gas *nAm*

Benzinpumpe (behn-*tseen*-poom-per) *f* (pl ~n) petrol pump; fuel pump *Am*; gas pump *Am*

Benzintank (behn-*tseen*-tahngk) *m* petrol tank

beobachten (ber-*ōa*-bahkh-tern) *v* watch

Beobachtung (ber-*ōa*-bahkh-toong) *f* (pl ~en) observation

bequem (ber-*kvāym*) *adj* comfortable; convenient, easy

Bequemlichkeit (ber-*kvāym*-likh-kight) *f* (pl ~en) comfort

beratschlagen (ber-*raat*-shlaa-gern) *v* deliberate

Beratung (ber-*raa*-toong) *f* (pl ~en) deliberation

Beratungsstelle (ber-*raa*-toongs-shteh-ler) *f* (pl ~n) health centre

berauscht (ber-*rousht*) *adj* intoxicated

berechnen (ber-*rehkh*-nern) *v* calculate

berechtigt (ber-*rehkh*-tikht) *adj* just

bereden (ber-*rāy*-dern) *v* persuade

Bereich (ber-*righkh*) *m* reach; range

bereit (ber-*right*) *adj* ready; prepared

bereits (ber-*rights*) *adv* already

bereitwillig (ber-*right*-vi-likh) *adj* cooperative

Berg (behrk) *m* (pl ~e) mountain; mount

Bergbau (*behrk*-bou) *m* mining

Bergkette (*behrk*-keh-ter) *f* (pl ~n) mountain range

Bergmann (*behrk*-mahn) *m* (pl -leute) miner

Bergschlucht (*behrk*-shlookht) *f* (pl ~en) glen

Bergsteigen (*behrk*-shtigh-gern) *nt* mountaineering

Bergwerk (*behrk*-vehrk) *nt* (pl ~e) mine

Bericht (ber-*rikht*) *m* (pl ~e) account, report; notice

berichten (ber-*rikh*-tern) *v* inform; report

Berichterstatter (ber-*rikht*-err-shtah-terr) *m* (pl ~) reporter

Berichtigung (ber-*rikh*-ti-goong) *f* (pl ~en) correction

Bernstein (*behrn*-shtighn) *m* amber

*****bersten** (*behrs*-tern) *v* *burst; crack

berüchtigt (ber-*rewkh*-tikht) *adj* notorious

Beruf (ber-*rōof*) *m* (pl ~e) profession; trade

beruflich (ber-*rōof*-likh) *adj* professional

beruhigen (ber-*rōō*-i-gern) *v* calm down; reassure

Beruhigungsmittel (ber-*rōō*-i-goongs-mi-terl) *nt* (pl ~) sedative; tranquillizer

berühmt (ber-*rēwmt*) *adj* famous, noted

berühren (ber-*rēw*-rern) *v* touch

Berührung (ber-*rēw*-roong) *f* (pl ~en) touch, contact

besagen (ber-*zaa*-gern) *v* imply

Besatzung (ber-*zah*-tsoong) *f* (pl ~en) crew

beschädigen (ber-*shai*-di-gern) *v* damage

beschaffen (ber-*shah*-fern) *v* provide

beschäftigen (ber-*shehf*-ti-gern) *v* employ; **beschäftigt** *adj* engaged, busy; **sich ~ mit** attend to

Beschäftigung (ber-*shehf*-ti-goong) *f* (pl ~en) business, occupation; employment; job

beschämt (ber-*shaimt*) *adj* ashamed

Bescheid (ber-*shight*) *m* message

bescheiden (ber-*shigh*-dern) *adj* modest; humble

Bescheidenheit (ber-*shigh*-dern-hight) *f* modesty

Bescheinigung (ber-*shigh*-ni-goong) *f* (pl ~en) certificate

beschlagnahmen (ber-*shlaak*-naa-mern) *v* impound, confiscate

beschleunigen (ber-*shloi*-ni-gern) *v* accelerate

***beschließen** (ber-*shlee*-sern) *v* decide

Beschluß (ber-*shlooss*) *m* (pl Beschlüsse) decision

beschmutzt (ber-*shmootst*) *adj* soiled

beschränken (ber-*shrehng*-kern) *v* limit

***beschreiben** (ber-*shrigh*-bern) *v* describe

Beschreibung (ber-*shrigh*-boong) *f* (pl ~en) description

beschriften (ber-*shrif*-tern) *v* label

beschuldigen (ber-*shool*-di-gern) *v* accuse; blame

Beschwerde (ber-*shvayr*-der) *f* (pl ~n) complaint

Beschwerdebuch (ber-*shvayr*-der-bookh) *nt* (pl ~er) complaints book

sich beschweren (ber-*shvay*-rern) complain

beschwindeln (ber-*shvin*-derln) *v* cheat

beseitigen (ber-*zigh*-ti-gern) *v* eliminate; remove

Beseitigung (ber-*zigh*-ti-goong) *f* removal

Besen (*bay*-zern) *m* (pl ~) broom

besessen (ber-*zeh*-sern) *adj* possessed

Besessenheit (ber-*zeh*-sern-hight) *f* obsession

besetzen (ber-*zeh*-tsern) *v* occupy; **besetzt** *adj* engaged; occupied

Besetzung (ber-*zeh*-tsoong) *f* (pl ~en) occupation

besichtigen (ber-*zikh*-ti-gern) *v* view

besiegen (ber-*zee*-gern) *v* *beat; defeat; conquer

Besitz (ber-*zits*) *m* possession; property

***besitzen** (ber-*zi*-tsern) *v* possess, own

Besitzer (ber-*zi*-tserr) *m* (pl ~) owner

besonder (ber-*zon*-derr) *adj* special, particular; separate

besonders (ber-*zon*-derrs) *adv* most of all, especially

besonnen (ber-*zo*-nern) *adj* sober

besorgen (ber-*zor*-gern) *v* procure; look after, *do; **besorgt** anxious, concerned

Besorgtheit (ber-*zorkt*-hight) *f* worry, anxiety

bespötteln (ber-*shpur*-terln) *v* ridicule

Besprechung (ber-*shpreh*-khoong) *f* (pl ~en) discussion; review

bespritzen (ber-*shpri*-tsern) *v* splash

besser (*beh*-serr) *adj* better; superior

best (behst) *adj* best; **zum besten** ***haben** fool

beständig (ber-*shtehn*-dikh) *adj* permanent; constant, steady

Bestandteil (ber-*shtahnt*-tighl) *m* (pl ~e) element; ingredient

bestätigen (ber-*shtai*-ti-gern) *v* acknowledge, confirm

Bestätigung (ber-*shtai*-ti-goong) *f* (pl ~en) confirmation

Bestattung (ber-*shtah*-toong) *f* (pl ~en) burial

***bestechen** (ber-*shteh*-khern) *v* bribe, corrupt

Bestechung (ber-*shteh*-khoong) *f* (pl ~en) bribery, corruption

Besteck (ber-*shtehk*) *nt* cutlery

***bestehen** (ber-*shtay*-ern) *v* exist; insist; pass; ~ **aus** consist of

***besteigen** (ber-*shtigh*-gern) *v* mount, ascend

bestellen (ber-*shteh*-lern) *v* order

Bestellung (ber-*shteh*-loong) *f* (pl ~en) order; **auf ~ gemacht** made to order

Bestellzettel (ber-*shtehl*-tseh-terl) *m*

(pl ~) order-form

besteuern (ber-*shtoi*-errn) *v* tax

Besteuerung (ber-*shtoi*-er-roong) *f* taxation

bestimmen (ber-*shti*-mern) *v* define, determine; destine

bestimmt (ber-*shtimt*) *adj* certain; definite

Bestimmung (ber-*shti*-moong) *f* (pl ~en) definition

Bestimmungsort (ber-*shti*-moongs-ort) *m* (pl ~e) destination

bestrafen (ber-*shtraa*-fern) *v* punish

bestrebt (ber-*shtraypt*) *adj* anxious

*****bestreiten** (ber-*shtrigh*-tern) *v* dispute

bestürzt (ber-*shtewrtst*) *adj* upset

Besuch (ber-*zookh*) *m* (pl ~e) visit; call

besuchen (ber-*zoo*-khern) *v* visit; call on

Besuchsstunden (ber-*zookhs*-shtoon-dern) *fpl* visiting hours

betasten (ber-*tahss*-tern) *v* *feel

Betäubung (ber-*toi*-boong) *f* (pl ~en) anaesthesia

Betäubungsmittel (ber-*toi*-boongs-mi-terl) *nt* (pl ~) anaesthetic

Bete (*bay*-ter) *f* (pl ~n) beetroot

sich beteiligen an (ber-*tigh*-li-gern) join

beteiligt (ber-*tigh*-likht) *adj* involved, concerned

beten (*bay*-tern) *v* pray

Beton (bay-*tawng*) *m* concrete

betonen (ber-*toa*-nern) *v* emphasize, stress

Betonung (ber-*toa*-noong) *f* accent, stress

betrachten (ber-*trahkh*-tern) *v* consider; regard

beträchtlich (ber-*trehkht*-likh) *adj* considerable; *adv* pretty, quite

Betrag (ber-*traak*) *m* (pl ~e) amount

Betragen (ber-*traa*-gern) *nt* conduct, behaviour

*****betragen** (ber-*traa*-gern) *v* amount to

*****betreffen** (ber-*treh*-fern) *v* concern; touch

betreffs (ber-*trehfs*) *prep* about, regarding, concerning

*****betreten** (ber-*tray*-tern) *v* enter

Betrieb (bertreep) *m* working

Betriebsanlage (ber-*treeps*-ahn-laa-ger) *f* (pl ~n) plant

Betriebsstörung (ber-*treeps*-shtür-roong) *f* (pl ~en) breakdown

Betrübnis (ber-*trewp*-niss) *f* sorrow, grief

betrübt (ber-*trewpt*) *adj* sad

Betrug (ber-*trook*) *m* deceit; fraud, swindle

*****betrügen** (ber-*trew*-gern) *v* cheat; deceive; swindle

Betrüger (ber-*trew*-gerr) *m* (pl ~) swindler

betrunken (ber-*troong*-kern) *adj* drunk

Bett (beht) *nt* (pl ~en) bed

Bettdecke (*beht*-deh-ker) *f* (pl ~n) counterpane

betteln (*beh*-terln) *v* beg

Bettler (*beht*-lerr) *m* (pl ~) beggar

Bettzeug (*beht*-tsoik) *nt* bedding

beugen (*boi*-gern) *v* bow

Beule (*boi*-ler) *f* (pl ~n) dent; lump

sich beunruhigen (ber-*oon*-roo-i-gern) worry

beunruhigt (ber-*oon*-roo-ikht) *adj* worried

beurteilen (ber-*oor*-tigh-lern) *v* judge

Beutel (*boi*-terl) *m* (pl ~) pouch

Bevölkerung (ber-*furl*-ker-roong) *f* population

bevor (ber-*foar*) *conj* before

bevorrechten (ber-*foar*-rehkh-tern) *v* favour

bewachen (ber-*vah*-khern) *v* guard

bewaffnen (ber-*vahf*-nern) *v* arm

bewahren (ber-*vaa*-rern) *v* *keep; preserve

Bewahrung (ber-*vaa*-roong) *f* preservation

bewaldet (ber-*vahl*-dert) *adj* wooded

bewegen (ber-*vāy*-gern) *v* move, stir

beweglich (ber-*vāyk*-likh) *adj* mobile; movable

Bewegung (ber-*vāy*-goong) *f* (pl ~en) movement, motion

Beweis (ber-*vighss*) *m* (pl ~e) proof, evidence; token

***beweisen** (ber-*vigh*-zern) *v* prove; *show, demonstrate

sich *bewerben (ber-*vehr*-bern) apply

Bewerber (ber-*vehr*-berr) *m* (pl ~) candidate

Bewerbung (ber-*vehr*-boong) *f* (pl ~en) application

bewilligen (ber-*vi*-li-gern) *v* allow; grant

Bewilligung (ber-*vi*-li-goong) *f* permission

bewillkommnen (ber-*vil*-kom-nern) *v* welcome

bewirten (ber-*veer*-tern) *v* entertain

bewohnbar (ber-*vōān*-baar) *adj* habitable, inhabitable

bewohnen (ber-*vōā*-nern) *v* inhabit

Bewohner (ber-*vōā*-nerr) *m* (pl ~) inhabitant

bewölkt (ber-*vurlkt*) *adj* cloudy, overcast

Bewölkung (ber-*vurl*-koong) *f* clouds

bewundern (ber-*voon*-derrn) *v* admire

Bewunderung (ber-*voon*-der-roong) *f* admiration

bewußt (ber-*voost*) *adj* conscious; aware

bewußtlos (ber-*voost*-lōāss) *adj* unconscious

Bewußtsein (ber-*voost*-zighn) *nt* consciousness

bezahlen (ber-*tsaa*-lern) *v* *pay

Bezahlung (ber-*tsaa*-loong) *f* (pl ~en) payment

bezaubernd (ber-*tsou*-berrnt) *adj* enchanting; glamorous

bezeichnen (ber-*tsighkh*-nern) *v* mark; **bezeichnend** typical, characteristic

bezeugen (ber-*tsoi*-gern) *v* testify

sich *beziehen auf (ber-*tsee*-ern) affect

Beziehung (ber-*tsee*-oong) *f* (pl ~en) relation, connection; reference

Bezirk (ber-*tseerk*) *m* (pl ~e) district

in Bezug auf (in ber-*tsook* ouf) as regards

Bezugsschein (ber-*tsōōks*-shighn) *m* (pl ~e) coupon

bezwecken (ber-*tsveh*-kern) *v* aim at

bezweifeln (ber-*tsvigh*-ferln) *v* doubt, query

BH (bay-*haa*) *m* bra

Bibel (*bee*-berl) *f* (pl ~n) bible

Biber (*bee*-berr) *m* (pl ~) beaver

Bibliothek (bi-bli-oa-*tāyk*) *f* (pl ~en) library

***biegen** (*bee*-gern) *v* *bend

biegsam (*beek*-zaam) *adj* flexible; supple

Biegung (*bee*-goong) *f* (pl ~en) turn, bend; curve

Biene (*bee*-ner) *f* (pl ~n) bee

Bienenkorb (*bee*-nern-korp) *m* (pl ~e) beehive

Bier (beer) *nt* (pl ~e) beer; ale

***bieten** (*bee*-tern) *v* offer

Bilanz (bi-*lahnts*) *f* (pl ~en) balance

Bild (bilt) *nt* (pl ~er) picture; image

bilden (*bil*-dern) *v* shape

Bildhauer (*bilt*-hou-err) *m* (pl ~) sculptor

Bildschirm (*bilt*-sheerm) *m* (pl ~e) screen

Billard (*bi*-l^yahrt) *nt* billiards *pl*

billig (*bi*-likh) *adj* cheap, inexpensive; reasonable

billigen (*bi*-li-gern) *v* approve of

Billigung (*bi*-li-goong) *f* approval

Bimsstein (*bims*-shtighn) *m* pumice stone

***binden** (*bin*-dern) *v* tie; *bind

Bindestrich (*bin*-der-shtrikh) *m* (pl ~e) hyphen

Binse (*bin*-zer) *f* (pl ~n) rush

Biologie (bi-oa-loa-*gee*) *f* biology

Birke (*beer*-ker) *f* (pl ~n) birch

Birne (*beer*-ner) *f* (pl ~n) pear; light bulb

bis (biss) *prep* to, till, until; *conj* till; ~ **zu** till

Bischof (*bi*-shof) *m* (pl ̈-e) bishop

bisher (biss-*hāyr*) *adv* so far

Biß (biss) *m* (pl Bisse) bite; **bißchen** bit

Bissen (*bi*-sern) *m* (pl ~) bite

Bitte (*bi*-ter) *f* (pl ~n) request

bitte (*bi*-ter) please; here you are

***bitten** (*bi*-tern) *v* ask; request; beg

bitter (*bi*-terr) *adj* bitter

Bittschrift (*bit*-shrift) *f* (pl ~en) petition

blank (blahngk) *adj* broke

Blase (*blaa*-zer) *f* (pl ~n) blister; bladder; bubble

***blasen** (*blaa*-zern) *v* *blow

Blasenentzündung (*blaa*-zern-ehnt-tsewn-doong) *f* cystitis

Blaskapelle (*blaass*-kah-peh-ler) *f* (pl ~n) brass band

Blatt (blaht) *nt* (pl ̈-er) leaf; sheet; page

Blattgold (*blaht*-golt) *nt* gold leaf

blau (blou) *adj* blue

Blazer (*blāy*-zerr) *m* (pl ~) blazer

Blei (bligh) *nt* lead

***bleiben** (*bligh*-bern) *v* stay; remain; *keep; **bleibend** lasting

bleich (blighkh) *adj* pale

bleichen (*bligh*-khern) *v* bleach

Bleistift (*bligh*-shtift) *m* (pl ~e) pencil

Bleistiftspitzer (*bligh*-shtift-shpi-tserr) *m* (pl ~) pencil-sharpener

blenden (*blehn*-dern) *v* blind; **blendend** glaring

Blick (blik) *m* (pl ~e) look; glimpse, glance

blind (blint) *adj* blind

Blinddarm (*blint*-dahrm) *m* (pl ̈-e) appendix

Blinddarmentzündung (*blint*-dahrm-ehnt-tsewn-doong) *f* appendicitis

Blindenhund (*blin*-dern-hoont) *m* (pl ~e) guide-dog

Blinker (*bling*-kerr) *m* (pl ~) indicator

Blitz (blits) *m* (pl ~e) lightning; flash

Blitzlicht (*blits*-likht) *nt* (pl ~er) flash-bulb

blockieren (blo-*kee*-rern) *v* block

blöde (*blūr*-der) *adj* dumb

blond (blont) *adj* fair

Blondine (blon-*dee*-ner) *f* (pl ~n) blonde

bloß (blōass) *adj* naked, bare; *adv* only

Bluejeans (*blōo*-jeens) *pl* Levis *pl*, jeans *pl*

blühen (*blēw*-ern) *v* flower

Blume (*blōo*-mer) *f* (pl ~n) flower

Blumenbeet (*blōo*-mern-bāyt) *nt* (pl ~e) flowerbed

Blumenblatt (*blōo*-mern-blaht) *nt* (pl ̈-er) petal

Blumenhändler (*blōo*-mern-hehn-dlerr) *m* (pl ~) florist

Blumenhandlung (*blōo*-mern-hahn-dloong) *f* (pl ~en) flower-shop

Blumenkohl (*blōo*-mern-kōal) *m* cauliflower

Blumenzwiebel (*blōo*-mern-tsvee-berl) *f* (pl ~n) bulb

Bluse (*blōo*-zer) *f* (pl ~n) blouse

Blut (blōot) *nt* blood

Blutarmut (*blōot*-ahr-mōot) *f* anaemia

Blutdruck (*blōot*-drook) *m* blood

pressure

bluten (*blōō*-tern) v *bleed

Blutgefäß (*blōōt*-ger-faiss) nt (pl ~e) blood-vessel

Blutsturz (*blōōt*-shtoorts) m (pl ~e) haemorrhage

Blutvergiftung (*blōōt*-fehr-gif-toong) f blood-poisoning

Boden[1] (*bōā*-dern) m soil, earth

Boden[2] (*bōā*-dern) m (pl ~) bottom, ground; attic

Bogen (*bōā*-gern) m (pl ~) arch; bow

bogenförmig (*bōā*-gern-furr-mikh) adj arched

Bogengang (*bōā*-gern-gahng) m (pl ~e) arcade

Bohne (*bōā*-ner) f (pl ~n) bean

bohren (*bōā*-rern) v bore, drill

Bohrer (*bōā*-rerr) m (pl ~) drill

Boje (*bōā*-Yer) f (pl ~n) buoy

Bolivianer (boa-li-*vYaa*-nerr) m (pl ~) Bolivian

bolivianisch (boa-li-*vYaa*-nish) adj Bolivian

Bolivien (boa-*lee*-vYern) Bolivia

Bolzen (*bol*-tsern) m (pl ~) bolt

bombardieren (bom-bahr-*dee*-rern) v bomb

Bombe (*bom*-ber) f (pl ~n) bomb

Bonbon (bawng-*bawng*) m (pl ~s) sweet; candy nAm

Boot (bōāt) nt (pl ~e) boat

an Bord (ahn bort) aboard

Bordell (bor-*dehl*) nt (pl ~e) brothel

borgen (*bor*-gern) v borrow

Börse (*būr*-zer) f (pl ~n) stock exchange; stock market, exchange; purse

bösartig (*būrss*-ahr-tikh) adj vicious, malignant

Böse (*būr*-zer) nt harm

böse (*būr*-zer) adj cross, angry; ill, wicked, evil

boshaft (*bōāss*-hahft) adj malicious

Botanik (boa-*taa*-nik) f botany

Bote (*bōā*-ter) m (pl ~n) messenger

Botengang (*bōā*-tern-gahng) m (pl ~e) errand

Botschaft (*bōāt*-shahft) f (pl ~en) embassy

Botschafter (*bōāt*-shahf-terr) m (pl ~) ambassador

Boutique (boo-*tik*) f (pl ~n) boutique

Bowling (*bōā*-ling) nt bowling

boxen (bo-ksern) v box

Boxkampf (boks-kahmpf) m (pl ~e) boxing match

brach (braakh) adj waste

Brand (brahnt) m (pl ~e) fire

Brandmarke (*brahnt*-mahr-ker) f (pl ~n) brand

Brandwunde (*brahnt*-voon-der) f (pl ~n) burn

Brasilianer (brah-zi-*lYaa*-nerr) m (pl ~) Brazilian

brasilianisch (brah-zi-*lYaa*-nish) adj Brazilian

Brasilien (brah-*zee*-lYern) Brazil

Brassen (*brah*-sern) m (pl ~) bream

***braten** (*braa*-tern) v fry; roast

Bratensoße (*braa*-tern-zōā-ser) f (pl ~n) gravy

Bratpfanne (*braat*-pfah-ner) f (pl ~n) frying-pan

Bratrost (*braat*-rost) m (pl ~e) grill

Bratspieß (*braat*-shpeess) m (pl ~e) spit

Brauch (broukh) m (pl ~e) usage

brauchbar (*broukh*-baar) adj useful; usable

brauchen (*brou*-khern) v need

brauen (*brou*-ern) v brew

Brauerei (brou-er-*righ*) f (pl ~en) brewery

braun (broun) adj brown; tanned

Brause (*brou*-zer) f fizz

Braut (brout) f (pl ~e) bride

Bräutigam (*broi*-ti-gahm) m (pl ~e)

bridegroom

brav (braaf) *adj* good

Brecheisen (*brehkh*-igh-zern) *nt* (pl ~) crowbar

*****brechen** (*breh*-khern) *v* *break; crack; fracture

breit (bright) *adj* broad, wide

Breite (*brigh*-ter) *f* (pl ~n) breadth, width

Breitengrad (*brigh*-tern-graat) *m* (pl ~e) latitude

Breitling (*bright*-ling) *m* (pl ~e) whitebait

Bremse (*brehm*-zer) *f* (pl ~n) brake

Bremslichter (*brehms*-likh-terr) *ntpl* brake lights

Bremstrommel (*brehms*-tro-merl) *f* (pl ~n) brake drum

*****brennen** (*breh*-nern) *v* *burn

Brennpunkt (*brehn*-poongkt) *m* (pl ~e) focus

Brennschere (*brehn*-shāy-rer) *f* (pl ~n) curling-tongs *pl*

Brennspiritus (*brehn*-shpee-ri-tooss) *m* methylated spirits

Brennstoff (*brehn*-shtof) *m* (pl ~e) fuel

Bresche (*breh*-sher) *f* (pl ~n) breach

Brett (breht) *nt* (pl ~er) plank, board

Bridge (brij) *nt* bridge

Brief (breef) *m* (pl ~e) letter; eingeschriebener ~ registered letter

Briefkasten (*breef*-kahss-tern) *m* (pl ~) letter-box; pillar-box; mailbox *nAm*

Briefmarke (*breef*-mahr-ker) *f* (pl ~n) postage stamp, stamp

Brieföffner (*breef*-urf-nerr) *m* (pl ~) paper-knife

Briefpapier (*breef*-pah-peer) *nt* notepaper

Brieftasche (*breef*-tah-sher) *f* (pl ~n) pocket-book, wallet

Briefumschlag (*breef*-oom-shlaak) *m*

(pl ~e) envelope

Briefwechsel (*breef*-veh-kserl) *m* correspondence

brillant (bri-*lYahnt*) *adj* brilliant

Brille (*bri*-ler) *f* (pl ~n) spectacles, glasses

*****bringen** (*bring*-ern) *v* *bring; *take

Brise (*bree*-zer) *f* (pl ~n) breeze

Brite (*bri*-ter) *m* (pl ~n) Briton

britisch (*bri*-tish) *adj* British

Brocken (*bro*-kern) *m* (pl ~) lump

Brombeere (*brom*-bāy-rer) *f* (pl ~n) blackberry

Bronchitis (bron-*khee*-tiss) *f* bronchitis

Bronze (*brawng*-ser) *f* bronze

bronzen (*brawng*-sern) *adj* bronze

Brosche (*bro*-sher) *f* (pl ~n) brooch

Broschüre (bro-*shew*-rer) *f* (pl ~n) brochure

Brot (brōat) *nt* (pl ~e) bread

Brötchen (*brūrt*-khern) *nt* (pl ~) roll, bun

Bruch (brookh) *m* (pl ~e) fracture, break; hernia

Bruchstück (*brookh*-shtewk) *nt* (pl ~e) fraction; fragment

Brücke (*brew*-ker) *f* (pl ~n) bridge

Bruder (*brōo*-derr) *m* (pl ~) brother

Bruderschaft (*brōo*-derr-shahft) *f* (pl ~en) congregation

Brüderschaft (*brēw*-derr-shahft) *f* fraternity

Brüllen (*brew*-lern) *nt* roar

brüllen (*brew*-lern) *v* roar

brummen (*broo*-mern) *v* growl

Brünette (brew-*neh*-ter) *f* (pl ~n) brunette

Brunnen (*broo*-nern) *m* (pl ~) well

Brunnenkresse (*broo*-nern-kreh-ser) *f* watercress

Brust (broost) *f* (pl ~e) chest; breast, bosom

Brustkasten (*broost*-kahss-tern) *m*

chest

Brustschwimmen (*broost*-shvi-mern) *nt* breaststroke

Brüstung (*brewss*-toong) *f* (pl ~en) rail

brutal (broo-*taal*) *adj* brutal

brutto (*broo*-toa) *adj* gross

Bub (boop) *m* (pl ~en) boy

Bube (*boo*-ber) *m* (pl ~n) knave

Buch (bookh) *nt* (pl ~er) book

Buche (*boo*-kher) *f* (pl ~n) beech

buchen (*boo*-khern) *v* book

Bücherstand (*bew*-kherr-shtahnt) *m* (pl ~e) bookstand

Buchhändler (*bookh*-hehn-dlerr) *m* (pl ~) bookseller

Buchhandlung (*bookh*-hahn-dloong) *f* (pl ~en) bookstore

Buchladen (*bookh*-laa-dern) *m* (pl ~) bookstore

Büchse (*bew*-kser) *f* (pl ~n) tin, can

Büchsenöffner (*bew*-ksern-urf-nerr) *m* (pl ~) can opener

Buchstabe (*bookh*-shtaa-ber) *m* (pl ~n) letter

buchstabieren (bookh-shtah-*bee*-rern) *v* *spell

Bucht (bookht) *f* (pl ~en) creek, bay, inlet

sich bücken (*bew*-kern) *bend down

Bude (*boo*-der) *f* (pl ~n) booth

Budget (bew-*jāy*) *nt* (pl ~s) budget

Büfett (bew-*feht*) *nt* (pl ~e) buffet

Bügeleisen (*bew*-gerl-igh-zern) *nt* (pl ~) iron

bügelfrei (*bew*-gerl-frigh) *adj* drip-dry, wash and wear

bügeln (*bew*-gerln) *v* iron; press

Bühne (*bew*-ner) *f* (pl ~n) stage

Bühnenautor (*bew*-nern-ou-tor) *m* (pl ~en) playwright

Bulgare (bool-*gaa*-rer) *m* (pl ~n) Bulgarian

Bulgarien (bool-*gaa*-rʸern) Bulgaria

bulgarisch (bool-*gaa*-rish) *adj* Bulgarian

Bummel (*boo*-merl) *m* stroll

bummeln (*boo*-merln) *v* stroll

Bummelzug (*boo*-merl-tsook) *m* (pl ~e) stopping train

Bund (boont) *m* (pl ~e) league; **Bundes-** federal

Bündel (*bewn*-derl) *nt* (pl ~) bundle

bündeln (*bewn*-derln) *v* bundle

bündig (*bewn*-dikh) *adj* brief

Bündnis (*bewnt*-niss) *nt* (pl ~se) alliance

bunt (boont) *adj* colourful; gay; **buntes Glas** stained glass

Burg (boork) *f* (pl ~en) castle, stronghold

Bürge (*bewr*-ger) *m* (pl ~n) guarantor

Bürger (*bewr*-gerr) *m* (pl ~) citizen; **Bürger-** civilian, civic

bürgerlich (*bewr*-gerr-likh) *adj* middle-class

Bürgermeister (*bewr*-gerr-mighss-terr) *m* (pl ~) mayor

Bürgersteig (*bewr*-gerr-shtighk) *m* (pl ~e) pavement; sidewalk *nAm*

Bürgschaft (*bewr*-gerr-shahft) *f* (pl ~en) guarantee

Büro (bew-*rōā*) *nt* (pl ~s) office

Büroangestellte (bew-*rōā*-ahn-ger-shtehl-ter) *m* (pl ~n) clerk

Bürokratie (bew-roa-krah-*tee*) *f* bureaucracy

Bürostunden (bew-*rōā*-shtoon-dern) *fpl* office hours

Bursche (*boor*-sher) *m* (pl ~n) boy, guy, lad

Bürste (*bewrs*-ter) *f* (pl ~n) brush

bürsten (*bewrs*-tern) *v* brush

Bus (booss) *m* (pl ~se) bus

Busch (boosh) *m* (pl ~e) bush

Busen (*boo*-zern) *m* (pl ~) bosom

Buße (*boo*-ser) *f* (pl ~n) penalty

Büste (*bewss*-ter) *f* (pl ~n) bust

Büstenhalter (*bewss*-tern-hahl-terr) *m* (pl ~) brassiere, bra

Butter (*boo*-terr) *f* butter

Butterbrot (*boo*-terr-brōat) *nt* (pl ~e) sandwich

C

Café (kah-*fāy*) *nt* (pl ~s) café

Camper (*kehm*-perr) *m* (pl ~) camper

Camping (*kehm*-ping) *nt* (pl ~s) camping

Campingplatz (*kehm*-ping-plahts) *m* (pl ~e) camping site

Celsius (*tsehl*-zi-ooss) centigrade

Cembalo (*chehm*-bah-loa) *nt* (pl ~s) harpsichord

Chalet (shah-*lāy*) *nt* (pl ~s) chalet

Champignon (*shahm*-pi-n^yawng) *m* (pl ~s) mushroom

Chance (*shahng*-ser) *f* (pl ~n) chance

Chaos (*kaa*-oss) *nt* chaos

chaotisch (kah-*ōa*-tish) *adj* chaotic

Charakter (kah-*rahk*-terr) *m* (pl ~e) character

charakterisieren (kah-rahk-ter-ri-*zee*-rern) *v* characterize

charakteristisch (kah-rahk-ter-*riss*-tish) *adj* characteristic

Charakterzug (kah-*rahk*-terr-tsōok) *m* (pl ~e) characteristic

charmant (shahr-*mahnt*) *adj* charming

Charterflug (*chahr*-terr-flōok) *m* (pl ~e) charter flight

Chauffeur (sho-*fūrr*) *m* (pl ~e) chauffeur

Chaussee (shoa-*sāy*) *f* (pl ~n) causeway

Chef (shehf) *m* (pl ~s) boss; manager

Chemie (khay-*mee*) *f* chemistry

chemisch (*khāy*-mish) *adj* chemical

Chile (*chee*-lay) Chile

Chilene (chi-*lāy*-ner) *m* (pl ~n) Chilean

chilenisch (chi-*lāy*-nish) *adj* Chilean

China (*khee*-nah) China

Chinese (khi-*nāy*-zer) *m* (pl ~n) Chinese

chinesisch (khi-*nāy*-zish) *adj* Chinese

Chinin (khi-*neen*) *nt* quinine

Chirurg (khi-*roork*) *m* (pl ~en) surgeon

Chlor (klōar) *nt* chlorine

Choke (chōak) *m* choke

Chor (kōar) *m* (pl ~e) choir

Christ (krist) *m* (pl ~en) Christian

christlich (*krist*-likh) *adj* Christian

Christus (*kriss*-tooss) Christ

Chrom (krōam) *nt* chromium

chronisch (*krōa*-nish) *adj* chronic

chronologisch (kroa-noa-*lōa*-gish) *adj* chronological

Clown (kloun) *m* (pl ~s) clown

Cocktail (*kok*-tāyl) *m* (pl ~s) cocktail

Conférencier (kawng-fay-rahng-s^y*āy*) *m* (pl ~s) entertainer

Container (kon-*tāy*-nerr) *m* (pl ~) container

Curry (*kur*-ri) *m* curry

D

da (daa) *conj* as, since, because

Dach (dahkh) *nt* (pl ~er) roof

Dachziegel (*dahkh*-tsee-gerl) *m* (pl ~) tile

damalig (*daa*-maa-likh) *adj* contemporary

damals (*daa*-maals) *adv* then

Dame (*daa*-mer) *f* (pl ~n) lady

Damebrett (*daa*-mer-breht) *nt* (pl ~er) draught-board

Damenbinde (*daa*-mern-bin-der) *f* (pl ~n) sanitary towel

Damentoilette (*daa*-mern-twah-leh-ter) *f* (pl ~n) powder-room, ladies' room

Damenunterwäsche (*daa*-mern-oon-terr-veh-sher) *f* lingerie

Damespiel (*daa*-mer-shpeel) *nt* draughts; checkers *plAm*

damit (dah-*mit*) *conj* so that

Damm (dahm) *m* (pl ·̈e) dam; dike; embankment

Dampf (dahmpf) *m* (pl ·̈e) steam

Dampfer (*dahm*-pferr) *m* (pl ~) steamer

Däne (*dai*-ner) *m* (pl ~n) Dane

Dänemark (*dai*-ner-mahrk) Denmark

dänisch (*dai*-nish) *adj* Danish

dankbar (*dahngk*-baar) *adj* thankful, grateful

Dankbarkeit (*dahngk*-baar-kight) *f* gratitude

danken (*dahng*-kern) *v* thank; **danke schön** thank you

dann (dahn) *adv* then

darauf (dah-*rouf*) *adv* then

darlegen (*daar*-lāy-gern) *v* state

Darm (dahrm) *m* (pl ·̈e) gut, intestine; **Därme** bowels *pl*

darstellen (*daar*-shteh-lern) *v* interpret

Darstellung (*daar*-shteh-loong) *f* (pl ~en) diagram; version

darum (daa-*room*) *conj* therefore

das (dahss) *pron* that

Dasein (*daa*-zighn) *nt* existence

daß (dahss) *conj* that

Dattel (*dah*-terl) *f* (pl ~n) date

Datum (*daa*-toom) *nt* (pl Daten) date

Dauer (*dou*-err) *f* duration

dauerhaft (*dou*-err-hahft) *adj* lasting, permanent

Dauerkarte (*dou*-err-kahr-ter) *f* (pl ~n) season-ticket

dauern (*dou*-errn) *v* last; **dauernd** permanent

Dauerwelle (*dou*-err-veh-ler) *f* perma-nent wave

Daumen (*dou*-mern) *m* (pl ~) thumb

Daune (*dou*-ner) *f* (pl ~n) down

Daunendecke (*dou*-nern-deh-ker) *f* (pl ~n) eiderdown

Debatte (day-*bah*-ter) *f* (pl ~n) debate

Deck (dehk) *nt* (pl ~s) deck

Decke (*deh*-ker) *f* (pl ~n) blanket; ceiling

Deckel (*deh*-kerl) *m* (pl ~) lid; top, cover

Deckkajüte (*dehk*-kah-Yew-ter) *f* (pl ~n) deck cabin

Defekt (day-*fehkt*) *m* (pl ~e) fault

Definition (day-fi-ni-tsYōan) *f* (pl ~en) definition

definieren (day-fi-*nee*-rern) *v* define

Defizit (*dāy*-fi-tsit) *nt* (pl ~e) deficit

dehnbar (*dāyn*-baar) *adj* elastic

dehnen (*dāy*-nern) *v* stretch

Deich (dighkh) *m* (pl ~e) dike; dam

dein (dighn) *pron* your

Dekoration (day-koa-rah-tsYōan) *f* (pl ~en) decoration

Delegation (day-lay-gah-tsYōan) *f* (pl ~en) delegation

Delinquent (day-ling-*kvehnt*) *m* (pl ~en) criminal

Demokratie (day-moa-krah-*tee*) *f* (pl ~n) democracy

demokratisch (day-moa-*kraa*-tish) *adj* democratic

Demonstration (day-mon-strah-tsYōan) *f* (pl ~en) demonstration

demonstrieren (day-mon-*stree*-rern) *v* demonstrate

*****denken** (*dehng*-kern) *v* *think; guess, reckon; ~ **an** *think of; **sich** ~ imagine

Denker (*dehng*-kerr) *m* (pl ~) thinker

Denkmal (*dehngk*-maal) *nt* (pl ·̈er) monument; memorial

denkwürdig (*dehnk*-vewr-dikh) *adj* memorable

denn (dehn) *conj* for

dennoch (*deh*-nokh) *adv* still, however; *conj* yet

Deodorant (day-oa-doa-*rahnt*) *nt* deodorant

deponieren (day-poa-nee-rern) *v* bank

Depot (day-*pōā*) *nt* (pl ~s) warehouse

deprimieren (day-pri-*mee*-rern) *v* depress

der (dāyr) *art* (f die, nt das) the *art*; *pron* that; which

derartig (*dāyr*-ahr-tikh) *adj* similar

dermaßen (*dāyr*-maa-sern) *adv* so

desertieren (day-zehr-*tee*-rern) *v* desert

deshalb (*dehss*-hahlb) *adv* therefore

Desinfektionsmittel (dehss-in-fehk-tsʸōāns-mi-terl) *nt* (pl ~) disinfectant

desinfizieren (dehss-in-fi-*tsee*-rern) *v* disinfect

deswegen (*dehss*-vāy-gern) *adv* therefore

Detektiv (day-tehk-*teef*) *m* (pl ~e) detective

deutlich (*doit*-likh) *adj* clear; distinct, plain

deutsch (doich) *adj* German

Deutsche (*doi*-cher) *m* (pl ~n) German

Deutschland (*doich*-lahnt) Germany

Devise (day-*vee*-zer) *f* (pl ~n) motto

Dezember (day-*tsehm*-berr) December

Dezimalsystem (day-tsi-*maal*-zewss-tāym) *nt* decimal system

Dia (*dee*-ah) *nt* (pl ~s) slide

Diabetes (di-ah-*bāy*-tehss) *m* diabetes

Diabetiker (di-ah-*bāy*-ti-kerr) *m* (pl ~) diabetic

Diagnose (di-ah-*gnōā*-zer) *f* (pl ~n) diagnosis

diagnostizieren (di-ah-gnoss-ti-*tsee*-rern) *v* diagnose

diagonal (di-ah-goa-*naal*) *adj* diagonal

Diagonale (di-ah-goa-*naa*-ler) *f* (pl ~n) diagonal

Diagramm (di-ah-*grahm*) *nt* (pl ~e) chart

Diamant (di-ah-*mahnt*) *m* (pl ~en) diamond

Diät (di-*ait*) *f* diet

dich (dikh) *pron* yourself

dicht (dikht) *adj* thick; dense; ~ **bevölkert** populous

Dichter (*dikh*-terr) *m* (pl ~) poet

Dichtung (*dikh*-toong) *f* poetry

dick (dik) *adj* thick, fat; corpulent, stout, big; bulky

Dicke (*di*-ker) *f* thickness

Dieb (deep) *m* (pl ~e) thief

Diebstahl (*deep*-shtaal) *m* (pl ˜e) robbery, theft

dienen (*dee*-nern) *v* serve

Diener (*dee*-nerr) *m* (pl ~) servant; domestic, valet; boy

Dienst (deenst) *m* (pl ~e) service

Dienstag (*deens*-taak) *m* Tuesday

Dienstmädchen (*deenst*-mait-khern) *nt* (pl ~) maid

Dienstpflichtige (*deenst*-pflikh-ti-ger) *m* (pl ~n) conscript

Dienstraum (*deenst*-roum) *m* (pl ˜e) office

Dienststelle (*deenst*-steh-ler) *f* (pl ~n) agency

dies (deess) *pron* this

diese (*dee*-zer) *pron* these

Diesel (*dee*-zerl) *m* diesel

dieser (*dee*-zerr) *pron* this

diesig (*dee*-zikh) *adj* hazy

Diktat (dik-*taat*) *nt* (pl ~e) dictation

Diktator (dik-*taa*-tor) *m* (pl ~en) dictator

diktieren (dik-*tee*-rern) *v* dictate

Diktiergerät (dik-*teer*-ger-rait) *nt* (pl ~e) dictaphone

Ding (ding) *nt* (pl ~e) thing

Diphtherie (dif-tay-*ree*) *f* diphtheria

Diplom (di-*plōām*) *nt* (pl ~e) certificate; diploma; **ein ~ erlangen** graduate

Diplomat (di-ploa-*maat*) *m* (pl ~en) diplomat

dir (deer) *pron* you

direkt (di-*rehkt*) *adj* direct

Direktor (di-*rehk*-tor) *m* (pl ~en) manager, director; headmaster; principal

Dirigent (di-ri-*gehnt*) *m* (pl ~en) conductor

dirigieren (di-ri-*gee*-rern) *v* conduct

Diskontsatz (diss-*kont*-zahts) *m* (pl ~e) bank-rate

Diskussion (diss-koo-s^y*ōān*) *f* (pl ~en) discussion

diskutieren (diss-koo-*tee*-rern) *v* discuss; argue

Distel (*diss*-terl) *f* (pl ~n) thistle

Disziplin (diss-tsi-*pleen*) *f* discipline

doch (dokh) *conj* yet

Dock (dok) *nt* (pl ~s) dock

Doktor (*dok*-tor) *m* (pl ~en) doctor

dolmetschen (*dol*-meh-chern) *v* interpret

Dolmetscher (*dol*-meh-cherr) *m* (pl ~) interpreter

Dom (dōam) *m* (pl ~e) cathedral

Donator (doa-*naa*-tor) *m* (pl ~en) donor

Donner (*do*-nerr) *m* thunder

donnern (*do*-nerrn) *v* thunder

Donnerstag (*do*-nerrs-taak) *m* Thursday

Doppelbett (*do*-perl-beht) *nt* (pl ~en) twin beds

doppelsinnig (*do*-perl-zi-nikh) *adj* ambiguous

doppelt (*do*-perlt) *adj* double

Dorf (dorf) *nt* (pl ~er) village

Dorn (dorn) *m* (pl ~en) thorn

dort (dort) *adv* there

dorthin (*dort*-hin) *adv* there

Dose (*dōā*-zer) *f* (pl ~n) canister

Dosenöffner (*dōā*-zern-urf-nerr) *m* (pl ~) tin-opener

Dosis (*dōā*-ziss) *f* (pl Dosen) dose

Dotter (*do*-terr) *nt* (pl ~) yolk

Drache (*drah*-kher) *m* (pl ~n) dragon

Draht (draat) *m* (pl ~e) wire

Drama (*draa*-mah) *nt* (pl Dramen) drama

Dramatiker (drah-*maa*-ti-kerr) *m* (pl ~) dramatist

dramatisch (drah-*maa*-tish) *adj* dramatic

drängen (*drehng*-ern) *v* push; urge

draußen (*drou*-sern) *adv* outside, outdoors; **nach ~** outwards

Dreck (drehk) *m* muck

dreckig (*dreh*-kikh) *adj* dirty, filthy

drehen (*drāy*-ern) *v* twist

Drehtür (*drāy*-tewr) *f* (pl ~en) revolving door

Drehung (*drāy*-oong) *f* (pl ~en) turn, twist

drei (drigh) *num* three

Dreieck (*drigh*-ehk) *nt* (pl ~e) triangle

dreieckig (*drigh*-eh-kikh) *adj* triangular

dreißig (*drigh*-sikh) *num* thirty

dreißigste (*drigh*-sikhs-ter) *num* thirtieth

dreiviertel (drigh-*feer*-terl) *adj* three-quarter

dreizehn (*drigh*-tsāyn) *num* thirteen

dreizehnte (*drigh*-tsāyn-ter) *num* thirteenth

dressieren (dreh-*see*-rern) *v* train

dringend (*dring*-ernt) *adj* pressing, urgent

dringlich (*dring*-likh) *adj* pressing

Dringlichkeit (*dring*-likh-kight) *f* urgency

Drink (dringk) *m* (pl ~s) drink

drinnen (*dri*-nern) *adv* inside

dritte (*dri*-ter) *num* third

Droge (*drōā*-ger) *f* (pl ~n) drug

Drogerie (droa-ger-*ree*) *f* (pl ~n) pharmacy, chemist's; drugstore *nAm*

drohen (*dro͞a*-ern) *v* threaten

Drohung (*dro͞a*-oong) *f* (pl ~en) threat

Drossel (*dro*-serl) *f* (pl ~n) thrush

drüben (*dre͞w*-bern) *adv* across; over there

Druck (drook) *m* pressure

drucken (*droo*-kern) *v* print

drücken (*dre͞w*-kern) *v* press

Druckknopf (*drook*-knopf) *m* (pl ~̈e) push-button

Drucksache (*drook*-zah-kher) *f* (pl ~n) printed matter

Drüse (*dre͞w*-zer) *f* (pl ~n) gland

Dschungel (*joong*-erl) *m* jungle

du (do͞o) *pron* you

dulden (*dool*-dern) *v* *bear

dumm (doom) *adj* dumb, stupid

Düne (*de͞w*-ner) *f* (pl ~n) dune

Dünger (*dewng*-err) *m* dung, manure

dunkel (*doong*-kerl) *adj* dark, dim; obscure

Dunkelheit (*doong*-kerl-hight) *f* dark

dünn (dewn) *adj* thin; sheer; weak

Dunst (doonst) *m* (pl ~̈e) haze; vapour

durch (doorkh) *prep* through; by

durchaus (doorkh-*ouss*) *adv* quite

durchbohren (doorkh-*bo͞a*-rern) *v* pierce

***durchdringen** (doorkh-*dring*-ern) *v* penetrate

Durcheinander (doorkh-igh-*nahn*-derr) *m* (nt) muddle, mess

***durcheinanderbringen** (doorkh-igh-*nahn*-derr-bring-ern) *v* muddle

Durchfahrt (*doorkh*-faart) *f* passage

Durchfall (*doorkh*-fahl) *m* diarrhoea

***durchfallen** (*doorkh*-fah-lern) *v* fail

durchführbar (*doorkh*-fe͞wr-baar) *adj* feasible

durchführen (*doorkh*-fe͞w-rern) *v* carry

out

Durchgang (*doorkh*-gahng) *m* (pl ~̈e) passage

Durchgangsstraße (*doorkh*-gahngs-shtraa-ser) *f* (pl ~n) thoroughfare

durchmachen (*doorkh*-mah-khern) *v* *go through

durchnässen (doorkh-*neh*-sern) *v* soak

durchqueren (doorkh-*kvāy*-rern) *v* pass through

durchscheinend (*doorkh*-shigh-nernt) *adj* sheer

Durchschlag (*doorkh*-shlaak) *m* (pl ~̈e) carbon copy; strainer

Durchschnitt (*doorkh*-shnit) *m* average, mean

durchschnittlich (*doorkh*-shnit-likh) *adj* medium, average; *adv* on the average

durchsichtig (*doorkh*-zikh-tikh) *adj* transparent

durchsuchen (doorkh-*zo͞o*-khern) *v* search

***dürfen** (*dewr*-fern) *v* *be allowed to; *may

dürr (dewr) *adj* arid

Dürre (*dew*-rer) *f* drought

Durst (doorst) *m* thirst

durstig (*doors*-tikh) *adj* thirsty

Dusche (*doo*-sher) *f* (pl ~n) shower

Düsenflugzeug (*de͞w*-zern-flo͞ok-tsoik) *nt* (pl ~e) jet

düster (*de͞wss*-terr) *adj* sombre, gloomy

Düsterkeit (*de͞wss*-terr-kight) *f* gloom

Dutzend (*doo*-tsernt) *nt* (pl ~e) dozen

Dynamo (dew-*naa*-moa) *m* (pl ~s) dynamo

E

Ebbe (*eh*-ber) *f* low tide

eben (*āy*-bern) *adj* level, flat; smooth, even

Ebene (*āy*-ber-ner) *f* (pl ~n) plain

ebenfalls (*āy*-bern-fahls) *adv* as well, likewise, also

Ebenholz (*āy*-bern-holts) *nt* ebony

ebenso (*āy*-bern-zōa) *adv* as, equally; likewise; ~ **wie** as well as

ebensosehr (*āy*-bern-zoa-zāyr) *adv* as much

ebensoviel (*āy*-bern-zoa-feel) *adv* as much

Echo (*eh*-khoa) *nt* (pl ~s) echo

echt (ehkht) *adj* true; genuine, authentic

Ecke (*eh*-ker) *f* (pl ~n) corner

edel (*āy*-derl) *adj* noble

Edelstein (*āy*-derl-shtighn) *m* (pl ~e) gem, stone

Efeu (*āy*-foi) *m* ivy

Effektenbörse (eh-*fehk*-tern-būrr-zer) *f* (pl ~n) stock exchange

egal (ay-*gaal*) *adj* like

egoistisch (ay-goa-*iss*-tish) *adj* egoistic

Ehe (*āy*-er) *f* (pl ~n) marriage; matrimony

ehe (*āy*-er) *conj* before

ehelich (*āy*-er-likh) *adj* matrimonial

ehemalig (*āy*-er-maa-likh) *adj* former

Ehepaar (*āy*-er-paar) *nt* (pl ~e) married couple

eher (*āy*-err) *adv* before; rather

Ehering (*āy*-er-ring) *m* (pl ~e) wedding-ring

ehrbar (*āyr*-baar) *adj* respectable

Ehre (*āy*-rer) *f* (pl ~n) honour; glory

ehren (*āy*-rern) *v* honour

ehrenwert (*āy*-rern-vāyrt) *adj* honourable

ehrerbietig (*āyr*-ehr-bee-tikh) *adj* respectful

Ehrerbietung (*āyr*-ehr-bee-toong) *f* respect

Ehrfurcht (*āyr*-foorkht) *f* respect

Ehrgefühl (*āyr*-ger-fewl) *nt* sense of honour

ehrgeizig (*āyr*-gigh-tsikh) *adj* ambitious

ehrlich (*āyr*-likh) *adj* honest; straight

Ehrlichkeit (*āyr*-likh-kight) *f* honesty

ehrwürdig (*āyr*-vewr-dikh) *adj* venerable

Ei (igh) *nt* (pl ~er) egg

Eiche (*igh*-kher) *f* (pl ~n) oak

Eichel (*igh*-kherl) *f* (pl ~n) acorn

Eichhörnchen (*ighkh*-hurrn-khern) *nt* (pl ~) squirrel

Eid (ight) *m* (pl ~e) vow, oath

Eidotter (*igh*-do-terr) *nt* (pl ~) egg-yolk

Eierbecher (*igh*-err-beh-kherr) *m* (pl ~) egg-cup

Eierkuchen (*igh*-err-kōō-khern) *m* (pl ~) omelette

Eifer (*igh*-ferr) *m* zeal; diligence

Eifersucht (*igh*-ferr-zookht) *f* jealousy

eifersüchtig (*igh*-ferr-zewkh-tikh) *adj* envious, jealous

eifrig (*igh*-frikh) *adj* zealous, diligent

eigen (*igh*-gern) *adj* own

Eigenschaft (*igh*-gern-shahft) *f* (pl ~en) property, quality

Eigenschaftswort (*igh*-gern-shahfts-vort) *nt* (pl ˜er) adjective

eigentlich (*igh*-gernt-likh) *adv* really

Eigentum (*igh*-gern-tōōm) *nt* property

Eigentümer (*igh*-gern-tēw-merr) *m* (pl ~) proprietor, owner

eigentümlich (*igh*-gern-tēwm-likh) *adj* peculiar

Eigentümlichkeit (*igh*-gern-tēwm-likh-kight) *f* (pl ~en) peculiarity

sich eignen (*igh*-gnern) qualify

Eile (*igh*-ler) *f* haste, hurry; speed; **Eil-** express

eilen (*igh*-lern) *v* hurry; hasten, rush

eilig (*igh*-likh) *adv* in a hurry

Eilpost (*ighl*-post) special delivery

Eimer (*igh*-merr) *m* (pl ~) bucket, pail

ein (ighn) *art* (f eine, nt ein) a *art*; ~ **anderer** another

Einakter (*ighn*-ahk-terr) *m* (pl ~) one-act play

einander (igh-*nahn*-derr) *pron* each other

Einäscherung (*ighn*-eh-sher-roong) *f* (pl ~en) cremation

einatmen (*ighn*-aat-mern) *v* inhale

Einbahnverkehr (*ighn*-baan-fehr-kāyr) *m* one-way traffic

Einband (*ighn*-bahnt) *m* (pl ~̈e) binding

sich einbilden (*ighn*-bil-dern) fancy, imagine

Einbildung (*ighn*-bil-doong) *f* fantasy, imagination

***einbrechen** (*ighn*-breh-khern) *v* burgle

Einbrecher (*ighn*-breh-kherr) *m* (pl ~) burglar

einbüßen (*ighn*-bēw-sern) *v* *lose

***eindringen** (*ighn*-dring-ern) *v* invade; trespass

Eindringling (*ighn*-dring-ling) *m* (pl ~e) trespasser

Eindruck (*ighn*-drook) *m* (pl ~̈e) impression; sensation

eindrucksvoll (*ighn*-drooks-fol) *adj* impressive

einfach (*ighn*-fahkh) *adj* simple

Einfahrt (*ighn*-faart) *f* (pl ~en) entry

Einfall (*ighn*-fahl) *m* (pl ~̈e) idea; invasion, raid

Einfluß (*ighn*-flooss) *m* (pl -flüsse) influence

einflußreich (*ighn*-flooss-righkh) *adj* influential

einfügen (*ighn*-fēw-gern) *v* insert

Einfuhr (*ighn*-fōōr) *f* import

einführen (*ighn*-fēw-rern) *v* import; introduce

Einführung (*ighn*-fēw-roong) *f* (pl ~en) introduction

Einfuhrzoll (*ighn*-fōōr-tsol) *m* duty, import duty

Eingang (*ighn*-gahng) *m* (pl ~̈e) entry; entrance, way in; **kein ~** no admittance

eingebildet (*ighn*-ger-bil-dert) *adj* conceited

Eingeborene (*ighn*-ger-bōā-rer-ner) *m* (pl ~n) native

eingehend (*ighn*-gāy-ernt) *adj* detailed

eingeschlossen (*ighn*-ger-shlo-sern) included

Eingeweide (*ighn*-ger-vigh-der) *pl* bowels *pl*, intestines, insides

Eingreifen (*ighn*-grigh-fern) *nt* interference

einheimisch (*ighn*-high-mish) *adj* native

Einheit (*ighn*-hight) *f* (pl ~en) unit; unity

einholen (*ighn*-hōā-lern) *v* gather

einige (*igh*-ni-ger) *pron* some

einkassieren (*ighn*-kah-see-rern) *v* cash

einkaufen (*ighn*-kou-fern) *v* shop

Einkaufstasche (*ighn*-koufs-tah-sher) *f* (pl ~n) shopping bag

Einkaufszentrum (*ighn*-koufs-tsehn-troom) *nt* (pl -zentren) shopping centre

einkerben (*ighn*-kehr-bern) *v* carve

Einkommen (*ighn*-ko-mern) *nt* (pl ~) revenue, income

Einkommenssteuer (*ighn*-ko-merns-shtoi-err) *f* income-tax

einkreisen (*ighn*-krigh-zern) *v* encircle

Einkünfte (*ighn*-kewnf-ter) *fpl* revenue

*einladen (*ighn*-laa-dern) *v* invite; ask

Einladung (*ighn*-laa-doong) *f* (pl ~en) invitation

*einlassen (*ighn*-lah-sern) *v* admit

einleitend (*ighn*-ligh-ternt) *adj* preliminary

einmachen (*ighn*-mah-khern) *v* preserve

einmal (*ighn*-maal) *adv* once; some time

sich einmischen (*ighn*-mi-shern) intervene; interfere with

Einnahme (*ighn*-naa-mer) *f* capture; **Einnahmen** earnings *pl*

*einnehmen (*ighn*-nāy-mern) *v* cash; occupy, *take up; capture

einpacken (*ighn*-pah-kern) *v* pack up

einräumen (*ighn*-roi-mern) *v* admit

einrichten (*ighn*-rikh-tern) *v* furnish; institute

Einrichtung (*ighn*-rikh-toong) *f* (pl ~en) installation; institution

eins (ighns) *num* one

einsam (*ighn*-zaam) *adj* lonely

einsammeln (*ighn*-zah-merln) *v* collect

Einsatz (*ighn*-zahts) *m* (pl ~̈e) bet

einschalten (*ighn*-shahl-tern) *v* turn on, switch on

einschenken (*ighn*-shehng-kern) *v* pour

sich einschiffen (*ighn*-shi-fern) embark

Einschiffung (*ighn*-shi-foong) *f* embarkation

*einschließen (*ighn*-shlee-sern) *v* include, comprise; involve; encircle, *shut in, circle

einschließlich (*ighn*-shleess-likh) *adv* inclusive

Einschnitt (*ighn*-shnit) *m* (pl ~e) cut

Einschränkung (*ighn*-shrehng-koong) *f* (pl ~en) restriction, qualification

*einschreiben (*ighn*-shrigh-bern) *v* book; enter, register

Einschreibung (*ighn*-shrigh-boong) *f* (pl ~en) booking

*einschreiten (*ighn*-shrigh-tern) *v* interfere

*einsehen (*ighn*-zāy-ern) *v* *see

einseitig (*ighn*-zigh-tikh) *adj* one-sided

Einsicht (*ighn*-zikht) *f* vision; insight

einsperren (*ighn*-shpeh-rern) *v* lock up

einspritzen (*ighn*-shpri-tsern) *v* inject

einst (ighnst) *adv* once

*einsteigen (*ighn*-shtigh-gern) *v* *get on; embark

einstellen (*ighn*-shteh-lern) *v* stop, discontinue; tune in; garage

Einstellung (*ighn*-shteh-loong) *f* (pl ~en) attitude

einstimmig (*ighn*-shti-mikh) *adj* unanimous

einstöpseln (*ighn*-shtur-pserln) *v* plug in

einstufen (*ighn*-shtōō-fern) *v* grade

einteilen (*ighn*-tigh-lern) *v* classify

*eintragen (*ighn*-traa-gern) *v* list, book

einträglich (*ighn*-traik-likh) *adj* profitable

Eintragung (*ighn*-traa-goong) *f* (pl ~en) entry; registration

Eintreffen (*ighn*-treh-fern) *nt* arrival

*eintreffen (*ighn*-treh-fern) *v* arrive

*eintreten (*ighn*-trāy-tern) *v* enter

Eintritt (*ighn*-trit) *m* entrance; entry; admission; ~ **verboten** no entry

Eintrittsgeld (*ighn*-trits-gehlt) *nt* entrance-fee

einverleiben (*ighn*-fehr-ligh-bern) *v* annex

einverstanden! (*ighn*-fehr-shtahn-dern) all right!

Einverständnis (*ighn*-fehr-shtehnt-niss) *nt* approval

Einwand (*ighn*-vahnt) *m* (pl ~̈e) objection; ~ *erheben gegen object to

Einwanderer (*ighn*-vahn-der-rerr) *m* (pl ~) immigrant

einwandern (*ighn*-vahn-derrn) *v* immigrate

Einwanderung (*ighn*-vahn-der-roong) *f* immigration

einwandfrei (*ighn*-vahnt-frigh) *adj* faultless

einweichen (*ighn*-vigh-khern) *v* soak

*****einwenden** (*ighn*-vehn-dern) *v* object; **etwas einzuwenden *haben gegen** mind

einwickeln (*ighn*-vi-kerln) *v* wrap

einwilligen (*ighn*-vi-li-gern) *v* consent

Einwilligung (*ighn*-vi-li-goong) *f* consent

Einwohner (*ighn*-vōa-nerr) *m* (pl ~) inhabitant

Einzahl (*ighn*-tsaal) *f* singular

Einzelhandel (*ighn*-tserl-hahn-derl) *m* retail trade

Einzelhändler (*ighn*-tserl-hehn-dlerr) *m* (pl ~) retailer

Einzelheit (*ighn*-tserl-hight) *f* (pl ~en) detail

einzeln (*ighn*-tserln) *adj* individual; **im einzelnen** specially

Einzelne (*ighn*-tserl-ner) *m* (pl ~n) individual

*****einziehen** (*ighn*-tsee-ern) *v* confiscate

einzig (*ighn*-tsikh) *adj* only; sole, single

einzigartig (*ighn*-tsikh-ahr-tikh) *adj* unique

Eis (ighss) *nt* ice; ice-cream

Eisbahn (*ighss*-baan) *f* (pl ~en) skating-rink

Eisbeutel (*ighss*-boi-terl) *m* (pl ~) ice-bag

Eisen (*igh*-zern) *nt* iron

Eisenbahn (*igh*-zern-baan) *f* (pl ~en) railway; railroad *nAm*

Eisenbahnfähre (*igh*-zern-baan-fai-rer) *f* (pl ~n) train ferry

Eisenhütte (*igh*-zern-hew-ter) *f* (pl ~n) ironworks

Eisenwaren (*igh*-zern-vaa-rern) *fpl* hardware

Eisenwarenhandlung (*igh*-zern-vaa-rern-hahn-dloong) *f* (pl ~en) hardware store

eisern (*igh*-zerrn) *adj* iron

eisig (*igh*-zikh) *adj* freezing

*****eislaufen** (*ighss*-lou-fern) *v* skate

Eisschrank (*ighss*-shrahngk) *m* (pl ~e) refrigerator

Eiswasser (*ighss*-vah-serr) *nt* iced water

eitel (*igh*-terl) *adj* vain

Eiter (*igh*-terr) *m* pus

ekelhaft (*āy*-kerl-hahft) *adj* disgusting

Ekuador (ay-kvah-*dōar*) Ecuador

Ekuadorianer (ay-kvah-doa-r*ʸaa*-nerr) *m* (pl ~) Ecuadorian

Ekzem (ehk-tsā*ym*) *nt* eczema

elastisch (ay-*lahss*-tish) *adj* elastic

Elch (ehlkh) *m* (pl ~e) moose

Elefant (ay-lay-*fahnt*) *m* (pl ~en) elephant

elegant (ay-lay-*gahnt*) *adj* smart, elegant

Eleganz (ay-lay-*gahnts*) *f* elegance

Elektriker (ay-*lehk*-tri-kerr) *m* (pl ~) electrician

elektrisch (ay-*lehk*-trish) *adj* electric

Elektrizität (ay-lehk-tri-tsi-*tait*) *f* electricity

elektronisch (ay-lehk-*trōa*-nish) *adj* electronic

Element (ay-lay-*mehnt*) *nt* (pl ~e) element

elementar (ay-lay-mern-*taar*) *adj* primary

Elend (*āy*-lehnt) *nt* misery

elend (*āy*-lehnt) *adj* miserable

Elendsviertel (*āy*-lehnts-feer-terl) *nt*

slum

elf (ehlf) *num* eleven; **Elf** *f* soccer team

Elfe (*ehl*-fer) *f* (pl ~n) elf

Elfenbein (*ehl*-fern-bighn) *nt* ivory

elfte (*ehlf*-ter) *num* eleventh

Ellbogen (*ehl*-bōa-gern) *m* (pl ~) elbow

Elster (*ehls*-terr) *f* (pl ~n) magpie

Eltern (*ehl*-terrn) *pl* parents *pl*

Email (ay-*migh*) *f* enamel

emailliert (ay-mah-ᵞeert) *adj* enamelled

Emanzipation (ay-mahn-tsi-pah-tsᵞōan) *f* emancipation

Embargo (ehm-*bahr*-goa) *nt* embargo

Emblem (ehm-blāym) *nt* (pl ~e) emblem

eminent (ay-mi-*nehnt*) *adj* outstanding

Empfang (ehm-*pfahng*) *m* (pl ⁓e) reception; receipt

*****empfangen** (ehm-*pfahng*-ern) *v* receive

Empfängnis (ehm-*pfehng*-niss) *f* conception

Empfangsdame (ehm-*pfahngs*-daa-mer) *f* (pl ~n) receptionist

Empfangsschein (ehm-*pfahngs*-shighn) *m* (pl ~e) receipt

Empfangszimmer (ehm-*pfahngs*-tsi-merr) *nt* (pl ~) drawing-room

*****empfehlen** (ehm-*pfāy*-lern) *v* recommend; advise

Empfehlung (ehm-*pfāy*-loong) *f* (pl ~en) recommendation; advice

Empfehlungsschreiben (ehm-*pfāy*-loongs-shrigh-bern) *nt* (pl ~) letter of recommendation

empfindlich (ehm-*pfint*-likh) *adj* sensitive

Empfindung (ehm-*pfin*-doong) *f* (pl ~en) perception; sensation

empor (ehm-*pōar*) *adv* up

empörend (ehm-*pūr*-rernt) *adj* revolting, shocking

Ende (*ehn*-der) *nt* end; ending, issue

enden (*ehn*-dern) *v* end; finish

endgültig (*ehnt*-gewl-tikh) *adj* eventual

endlich (*ehnt*-likh) *adv* at last

Endstation (*ehnt*-shtah-tsᵞōan) *f* (pl ~en) terminal

Energie (ay-nehr-*gee*) *f* energy; power

energisch (ay-*nehr*-gish) *adj* energetic

eng (ehng) *adj* narrow; tight; **enger machen** tighten; **enger *werden** tighten

Engel (*ehng*-erl) *m* (pl ~) angel

England (*ehng*-lahnt) England; Britain

Engländer (*ehng*-lehn-derr) *m* (pl ~) Englishman; Briton

englisch (*ehng*-lish) *adj* English; British

Engpaß (*ehng*-pahss) *m* (pl -pässe) bottleneck

engstirnig (*ehng*-shteer-nikh) *adj* narrow-minded

Enkel (*ehng*-kerl) *m* (pl ~) grandson

Enkelin (*ehng*-ker-lin) *f* (pl ~nen) granddaughter

entbehren (ehnt-*bāy*-rern) *v* spare

entbeinen (ehnt-*bigh*-nern) *v* bone

*****entbinden von** (ehnt-*bin*-dern) discharge of

Entbindung (ehnt-*bin*-doong) *f* (pl ~en) delivery, childbirth

entdecken (ehnt-*deh*-kern) *v* discover; detect

Entdeckung (ehnt-*deh*-koong) *f* (pl ~en) discovery

Ente (*ehn*-ter) *f* (pl ~n) duck

entfalten (ehnt-*fahl*-tern) *v* unfold; expand

entfernen (ehnt-*fehr*-nern) *v* *take away

entfernt (ehnt-*fehrnt*) *adj* distant; far-

away, remote; **entferntest** furthest
Entfernung (ehnt-*fehr*-noong) *f* (pl
~en) distance; way
Entfernungsmesser (ehnt-*fehr*-noongs-
meh-serr) *m* (pl ~) range-finder
entgegengesetzt (ehnt-*gāy*-gern-ger-
zehtst) *adj* opposite; contrary
entgegenkommend (ehnt-*gāy*-gern-ko-
mernt) *adj* oncoming
*entgehen** (ehnt-*gāy*-ern) *v* escape
*enthalten** (ehnt-*hahl*-tern) *v* contain,
include; deny; **sich** ~ abstain from
Enthärtungsmittel (ehnt-*hehr*-toongs-
mi-terl) *nt* (pl ~) water-softener
Entheiligung (ehnt-*high*-li-goong) *f*
sacrilege
enthüllen (ehnt-*hew*-lern) *v* reveal
Enthüllung (ehnt-*hew*-loong) *f* (pl
~en) revelation
sich entkleiden (ehnt-*kligh*-dern) undress
*entkommen** (ehnt-*ko*-mern) *v* escape
entkorken (ehnt-*kor*-kern) *v* uncork
*entladen** (ehnt-*laa*-dern) *v* discharge
entlang (ehnt-*lahng*) *prep* along, past
*entlassen** (ehnt-*lah*-sern) *v* dismiss,
fire
entlegen (ehnt-*lāy*-gern) *adj* out of the
way
*entleihen** (ehnt-*ligh*-ern) *v* borrow
Entlohnung (ehnt-*lōā*-noong) *f* (pl
~en) remuneration
*entnehmen** (ehnt-*nāy*-mern) *v* deprive of
Entrüstung (ehnt-*rewss*-toong) *f* indignation
entschädigen (ehnt-*shai*-di-gern) *v* remunerate
Entschädigung (ehnt-*shai*-di-goong) *f*
(pl ~en) indemnity
*entscheiden** (ehnt-*shigh*-dern) *v* decide
Entscheidung (ehnt-*shigh*-doong) *f* (pl
~en) decision

sich *entschließen (ehnt-*shlee*-sern)
decide
entschlossen (ehnt-*shlo*-sern) *adj* resolute, determined
Entschluß (ehnt-*shlooss*) *m* (pl
-schlüsse) decision
entschuldigen (ehnt-*shool*-di-gern) *v*
excuse; *forgive; **sich** ~ apologize
Entschuldigung (ehnt-*shool*-di-goong)
f (pl ~en) apology, excuse; **Entschuldigung!** sorry!
Entsetzen (ehnt-*zeh*-tsern) *nt* horror
entsetzlich (ehnt-*zehts*-likh) *adj* horrible
sich *entsinnen (ehnt-*zi*-nern) *v* recollect
sich entspannen (ehnt-*shpah*-nayn) relax
Entspannung (ehnt-*shpah*-noong) *f* (pl
~en) relaxation
entsprechend (ehnt-*shpreh*-khernt) *adj*
adequate; equivalent
*entstehen** (ehnt-*shtāy*-ern) *v* *arise
entstellt (ehnt-*shtehlt*) *adj* deformed
enttäuschen (ehnt-*toi*-shern) *v* disappoint; *let down; *be disappointing
Enttäuschung (ehnt-*toi*-shoong) *f* (pl
~en) disappointment
entwässern (ehnt-*veh*-serrn) *v* drain
entweder ... oder (*ehnt*-vāy-derr ...
ōā-derr) either ... or
*entwerfen** (ehnt-*vehr*-fern) *v* design
entwerten (ehnt-*vāyr*-tern) *v* devalue
entwickeln (ehnt-*vi*-kerln) *v* develop
Entwicklung (ehnt-*vi*-kloong) *f* (pl
~en) development
entwischen (ehnt-*vi*-shern) *v* slip
Entwurf (ehnt-*voorf*) *m* (pl ~̃e) design
entzücken (ehnt-*tsew*-kern) *v* delight;
entzückend delightful; **entzückt**
delighted
entzündbar (ehnt-*tsewnt*-baar) *adj* inflammable
entzünden (ehnt-*tsewn*-dern) *v* *be-

come septic

Entzündung (ehnt-*tsewn*-doong) *f* (pl ~en) inflammation

entzwei (ehnt-*tsvigh*) *adj* broken

Enzyklopädie (ehn-tsew-kloa-peh-*dee*) *f* (pl ~n) encyclopaedia

Epidemie (ay-pi-day-*mee*) *f* (pl ~n) epidemic

Epilepsie (ay-pi-leh-*psee*) *f* epilepsy

Epilog (ay-pi-*lōag*) *m* (pl ~e) epilogue

episch (*āy*-pish) *adj* epic

Episode (ay-pi-*zōa*-der) *f* (pl ~n) episode

Epos (*āy*-poss) *nt* (pl Epen) epic

er (*āyr*) *pron* he

erbärmlich (ehr-*behrm*-likh) *adj* miserable

erben (*ehr*-bern) *v* inherit

erblich (*ehrp*-likh) *adj* hereditary

erblicken (ehr-*bli*-kern) *v* glance; glimpse

* **erbrechen** (ehr-*breh*-khern) *v* vomit

Erbschaft (*ehrp*-shahft) *f* (pl ~en) inheritance; legacy

Erbse (*ehr*-pser) *f* (pl ~n) pea

Erdball (*āyrt*-bahl) *m* globe

Erdbeben (*āyrt*-bāy-bern) *nt* (pl ~) earthquake

Erdbeere (*āyrt*-bāy-rer) *f* (pl ~n) strawberry

Erdboden (*āyrt*-bōa-dern) *m* soil

Erde (*āyr*-der) *f* earth; soil

Erdgeschoß (*āyrt*-ger-shoss) *nt* ground floor

Erdichtung (ehr-*dikh*-toong) *f* (pl ~en) fiction

Erdkunde (*āyrt*-koon-der) *f* geography

Erdnuß (*āyrt*-nooss) *f* (pl -nüsse) peanut

Erdteil (*āyrt*-tighl) *m* (pl ~e) continent

sich ereignen (ehr-*igh*-gnern) happen; *v* occur

Ereignis (ehr-*igh*-gniss) *nt* (pl ~se) event; happening, occurrence

erfahren (ehr-*faa*-rern) *adj* experienced; skilled

* **erfahren** (ehr-*faa*-rern) *v* experience

Erfahrung (ehr-*faa*-roong) *f* (pl ~en) experience

* **erfinden** (ehr-*fin*-dern) *v* invent

Erfinder (ehr-*fin*-derr) *m* (pl ~) inventor

erfinderisch (ehr-*fin*-der-rish) *adj* inventive

Erfindung (ehr-*fin*-doong) *f* (pl ~en) invention

Erfolg (ehr-*folk*) *m* (pl ~e) success

erfolglos (ehr-*folk*-lōass) *adj* unsuccessful

erfolgreich (ehr-*folk*-righkh) *adj* successful

erforderlich (ehr-*for*-derr-likh) *adj* requisite

erfordern (ehr-*for*-derrn) *v* require

Erfordernis (ehr-*for*-derr-niss) *nt* (pl ~se) requirement

erforschen (ehr-*for*-shern) *v* explore

erfreulich (ehr-*froi*-likh) *adj* enjoyable

erfreut (ehr-*froit*) *adj* pleased, glad

erfrischen (ehr-*fri*-shern) *v* refresh; **erfrischend** fresh

Erfrischung (ehr-*fri*-shoong) *f* refreshment

sich * **ergeben** (ehr-*gāy*-bern) result; surrender

Ergebnis (ehr-*gāyp*-niss) *nt* (pl ~se) result; issue, effect, outcome

* **ergreifen** (ehr-*grigh*-fern) *v* seize; *catch, grasp

* **erhalten** (ehr-*hahl*-tern) *v* obtain

erhältlich (ehr-*hehlt*-likh) *adj* obtainable

* **erheben** (ehr-*hāy*-bern) *v* raise; **sich** ~ *arise

Erhebung (ehr-*hāy*-boong) *f* (pl ~en) mound, hillock

erhöhen (ehr-*hūr*-ern) *v* raise

Erhöhung (ehr-*hūr*-oong) *f* (pl ~en)

increase; rise; raise *nAm*

sich erholen (ehr-*hōā*-lern) *v* recover

Erholung (ehr-*hōā*-loong) *f* recreation; recovery

Erholungsheim (ehr-*hōā*-loongs-highm) *nt* (pl ~e) rest-home

Erholungsort (ehr-*hōā*-loongs-ort) *m* (pl ~e) holiday resort

erinnern (ehr-*i*-nerrn) *v* remind; **sich ~** recall, remember

Erinnerung (ehr-*i*-ner-roong) *f* (pl ~en) memory; remembrance

sich erkälten (ehr-*kehl*-tern) catch a cold

Erkältung (ehr-*kehl*-toong) *f* (pl ~en) cold

ermitteln (ehr-*mi*-terln) *v* ascertain

*erkennen (ehr-*keh*-nern) *v* recognize; acknowledge

erkenntlich (ehr-*kehnt*-likh) *adj* grateful

erklärbar (ehr-*klair*-baar) *adj* accountable

erklären (ehr-*klai*-rern) *v* explain; declare

Erklärung (ehr-*klai*-roong) *f* (pl ~en) explanation; statement; declaration

Erkrankung (ehr-*krahng*-koong) *f* (pl ~en) affection

sich erkundigen (ehr-*koon*-di-gern) enquire, inquire

Erkundigung (ehr-*koon*-di-goong) *f* (pl ~en) enquiry

erlangen (ehr-*lahng*-ern) *v* obtain

erlauben (ehr-*lou*-bern) *v* allow, permit; **erlaubt *sein** *be allowed

Erlaubnis (ehr-*loup*-niss) *f* permission

erläutern (ehr-*loi*-terrn) *v* explain; elucidate

Erläuterung (ehr-*loi*-ter-roong) *f* (pl ~en) explanation

erleben (ehr-*lāy*-bern) *v* experience

erledigen (ehr-*lāy*-di-gern) *v* settle

erleichtern (ehr-*lighkh*-terrn) *v* relieve

Erleichterung (ehr-*lighkh*-ter-roong) *f*

(pl ~en) relief

*erleiden (ehr-*ligh*-dern) *v* suffer

erlesen (ehr-*lāy*-zern) *adj* select

erleuchten (ehr-*loikh*-tern) *v* illuminate

*erliegen (ehr-*lee*-gern) *v* succumb

Erlös (ehr-*lūrss*) *m* (pl ~e) produce

erlösen (ehr-*lūr*-zern) *v* deliver, redeem

Erlösung (ehr-*lūr*-zoong) *f* delivery

Ermächtigung (ehr-*mehkh*-ti-goong) *f* (pl ~en) authorization

Ermäßigung (ehr-*mai*-si-goong) *f* (pl ~en) rebate

ermitteln (ehr-*mi*-terln) *v* ascertain

ermüden (ehr-*mēw*-dern) *v* tire

ermutigen (ehr-*mōō*-ti-gern) *v* encourage

ernähren (ehr-*nai*-rern) *v* *feed

*ernennen (ehr-*neh*-nern) *v* nominate, appoint

Ernennung (ehr-*neh*-noong) *f* (pl ~en) nomination, appointment

erneuern (ehr-*noi*-errn) *v* renew

Ernst (ehrnst) *m* gravity, seriousness

ernst (ehrnst) *adj* serious; grave; severe

ernsthaft (*ehrnst*-hahft) *adj* bad

Ernte (*ehrn*-ter) *f* (pl ~n) crop; harvest

Eroberer (ehr-*ōā*-ber-rerr) *m* (pl ~) conqueror

erobern (ehr-*ōā*-berrn) *v* conquer

Eroberung (ehr-*ōā*-ber-roong) *f* (pl ~en) conquest

erörtern (ehr-*urr*-terrn) *v* discuss; argue

Erörterung (ehr-*urr*-ter-roong) *f* (pl ~en) deliberation

erpressen (ehr-*preh*-sern) *v* blackmail; extort

Erpressung (ehr-*preh*-soong) *f* (pl ~en) blackmail; extortion

erregen (ehr-*rāy*-gern) *v* excite

Erregung (ehr-*ray*-goong) *f* emotion; excitement

erreichbar (ehr-*righkh*-baar) *adj* attainable

erreichen (ehr-*righ*-khern) *v* reach, attain; achieve; *catch

errichten (ehr-*rikh*-tern) *v* construct; erect; found

erröten (ehr-*rur*-tern) *v* blush

Ersatz (ehr-*zahts*) *m* substitute

Ersatzfüllung (ehr-*zahts*-few-loong) *f* (pl ~en) refill

Ersatzreifen (ehr-*zahts*-righ-fern) *m* (pl ~) spare tyre

Ersatzteil (ehr-*zahts*-tighl) *nt* (pl ~e) spare part

erschaffen (ehr-*shah*-fern) *v* create

erschallen (ehr-*shah*-lern) *v* sound

Erscheinen (ehr-*shigh*-nern) *nt* appearance

*erscheinen** (ehr-*shigh*-nern) *v* appear; seem

Erscheinung (ehr-*shigh*-noong) *f* (pl ~en) appearance; apparition

erschöpfen (ehr-*shur*-pfern) *v* exhaust; **erschöpft** tired

*erschrecken** (ehr-*shreh*-kern) *v* *be frightened; frighten, terrify, scare

ersetzen (ehr-*zeh*-tsern) *v* replace, substitute

*ersinnen** (ehr-*zi*-nern) *v* invent

Ersparnisse (ehr-*shpaar*-ni-ser) *fpl* savings pl

erstarrt (ehr-*shtahrt*) *adj* numb

Erstaunen (ehr-*shtou*-nern) *nt* amazement, astonishment

erstaunen (ehr-*shtou*-nern) *v* amaze; surprise

erstaunlich (ehr-*shtoun*-likh) *adj* astonishing, striking

erste (*ayrs*-ter) *num* first; *adj* initial; foremost

ersticken (ehr-*shti*-kern) *v* choke

erstklassig (*ayrst*-klah-sikh) *adj* first-

class

erstrangig (*ayrst*-rahng-ikh) *adj* first-rate

Ertrag (ehr-*traak*) *m* (pl ~e) produce

*ertragen** (ehr-*traa*-gern) *v* endure, *bear

erträglich (ehr-*trayk*-likh) *adj* tolerable

*ertrinken** (ehr-*tring*-kern) *v* drown; *be drowned

erwachsen (ehr-*vah*-ksern) *adj* adult, grown-up

Erwachsene (ehr-*vah*-kser-ner) *m* (pl ~n) adult, grown-up

*erwägen** (ehr-*vai*-gern) *v* consider

Erwägung (ehr-*vai*-goong) *f* (pl ~en) consideration

erwähnen (ehr-*vai*-nern) *v* mention

Erwähnung (ehr-*vai*-noong) *f* (pl ~en) mention

erwarten (ehr-*vahr*-tern) *v* expect; anticipate; await

Erwartung (ehr-*vahr*-toong) *f* (pl ~en) expectation

erweitern (ehr-*vigh*-terrn) *v* extend; enlarge, widen

Erwerb (ehr-*vehrp*) *m* purchase

*erwerben** (ehr-*vehr*-bern) *v* acquire; *buy

erwischen (ehr-*vi*-shern) *v* *catch

erwürgen (ehr-*vewr*-gern) *v* strangle, choke

Erz (*ayrts*) *nt* (pl ~e) ore

erzählen (ehr-*tsai*-lern) *v* *tell; relate

Erzählung (ehr-*tsai*-loong) *f* (pl ~en) tale

Erzbischof (*ehrts*-bi-shof) *m* (pl ~e) archbishop

erzeugen (ehr-*tsoi*-gern) *v* generate

*erziehen** (ehr-*tsee*-ern) *v* *bring up

Erziehung (ehr-*tsee*-oong) *f* education

es (ehss) *pron* it

Esel (*ay*-zerl) *m* (pl ~) donkey; ass

eskortieren (ehss-kor-*tee*-rern) *v* escort

Essay (*eh*-say) *m* (pl ~s) essay
eßbar (*ehss*-baar) *adj* edible
Essen (*eh*-sern) *nt* food
***essen** (*eh*-sern) *v* *eat; **zu Abend ~**
dine
Essenz (eh-*sehnts*) *f* essence
Essig (*eh*-sikh) *m* vinegar
Eßlöffel (*ehss*-lur-ferl) *m* (pl ~) tablespoon
Eßlust (*ehss*-loost) *f* appetite
Eßservice (*ehss*-sehr-veess) *nt* dinner-
service
Etage (ay-*taa*-zher) *f* (pl ~n) storey;
apartment *nAm*
Etappe (ay-*tah*-per) *f* (pl ~n) stage
Etikett (ay-ti-*keht*) *nt* (pl ~e) label,
tag
etliche (*eht*-li-kher) *adj* several
Etui (eht-*vee*) *nt* (pl ~s) case
etwa (*eht*-vah) *adv* about, approximately
etwas (*eht*-vahss) *pron* something; **irgend ~** anything
euch (oikh) *pron* you; yourselves
euer (*oi*-err) *pron* your
Eule (*oi*-ler) *f* (pl ~n) owl
Europa (oi-*rōa*-pah) Europe
Europäer (oi-roa-*pai*-err) *m* (pl ~)
European
europäisch (oi-roa-*pai*-ish) *adj* European
evakuieren (ay-vah-koo-*ee*-rern) *v*
evacuate
Evangelium (ay-vahng-*gāy*-lʸoom) *nt*
(pl -ien) gospel
eventuell (ay-vehn-too-*ehl*) *adj* possible
Evolution (ay-voa-loo-tsʸ*ōan*) *f* (pl
~en) evolution
ewig (*āy*-vikh) *adj* eternal
Ewigkeit (*āy*-vikh-kight) *f* eternity
exakt (eh-*ksahkt*) *adj* precise, very
Examen (eh-*ksaa*-mern) *nt* (pl ~) examination

Exemplar (eh-ksehm-*plaar*) *nt* (pl ~e)
specimen; copy
exklusiv (ehks-kloo-*zeef*) *adj* exclusive
exotisch (eh-*ksoā*-tish) *adj* exotic
Expedition (ehks-pay-di-tsʸ*ōan*) *f* (pl
~en) expedition
Experiment (ehks-pay-ri-*mehnt*) *nt* (pl
~e) experiment
experimentieren (ehks-pay-ri-mehn-
tee-rern) *v* experiment
explodieren (ehks-ploa-*dee*-rern) *v* explode
Explosion (ehks-ploa-zʸ*ōan*) *f* (pl ~en)
blast, explosion
explosiv (ehks-ploa-*zeef*) *adj* explosive
Export (ehks-*port*) *m* export
exportieren (ehks-por-*tee*-rern) *v* export
extravagant (*ehks*-trah-vah-gahnt) *adj*
extravagant
Extrem (ehks-*trāym*) *nt* (pl ~e) extreme
extrem (ehks-*trāym*) *adj* extreme

F

Fabel (*faa*-berl) *f* (pl ~n) fable
Fabrik (fah-*breek*) *f* (pl ~en) factory;
mill, works *pl*
Fabrikant (fah-bri-*kahnt*) *m* (pl ~en)
manufacturer
fabrizieren (fah-bri-*tsee*-rern) *v* manufacture
Fach (fahkh) *nt* (pl ¨er) section;
trade, profession
Fächer (*feh*-kherr) *m* (pl ~) fan
fachkundig (*fahkh*-koon-dikh) *adj* expert
Fachmann (*fahkh*-mahn) *m* (pl -leute)
expert
Fackel (*fah*-kerl) *f* (pl ~n) torch
Faden (*faa*-dern) *m* (pl ¨) thread

fähig (*fai*-ikh) *adj* able; capable

Fähigkeit (*fai*-ikh-kight) *f* (pl ~en) ability; faculty, capacity

Fahne (*faa*-ner) *f* (pl ~n) flag

Fahrbahn (*faar*-baan) *f* (pl ~en) carriageway; lane; roadway *nAm*

Fährboot (*fair*-bōat) *nt* (pl ~e) ferryboat

*****fahren** (*faa*-rern) *v* *drive; *ride; sail

Fahrer (*faa*-rerr) *m* (pl ~) driver

Fahrgeld (*faar*-gehlt) *nt* fare

Fahrgestell (*faar*-ger-shtehl) *nt* (pl ~e) chassis

Fahrkarte (*faar*-kahr-ter) *f* (pl ~n) ticket

Fahrkartenautomat (*faar*-kahr-tern-ou-toa-maat) *m* (pl ~en) ticket machine

Fahrplan (*faar*-plaan) *m* (pl ~e) timetable, schedule

Fahrrad (*faar*-raat) *nt* (pl ~er) cycle, bicycle

Fahrt (faart) *f* (pl ~en) ride, drive

Fährte (*fair*-ter) *f* (pl ~n) trail

Fahrzeug (*faar*-tsoik) *nt* (pl ~e) vehicle

Faktor (*fahk*-tor) *m* (pl ~en) factor

Faktur (fahk-*tōōr*) *f* (pl ~en) invoice

fakturieren (fahk-too-*ree*-rern) *v* bill

Fakultät (fah-kool-*tait*) *f* (pl ~en) faculty

Falke (*fahl*-ker) *m* (pl ~n) hawk

Fall (fahl) *m* (pl ~e) case; instance; **auf jeden ~** at any rate; **im ~** in case of

Falle (*fah*-ler) *f* (pl ~n) trap

*****fallen** (*fah*-lern) *v* *fall; **~ *lassen** drop

fällig (*feh*-likh) *adj* due

Fälligkeitstermin (*feh*-likh-kights-tehr-meen) *m* (pl ~e) expiry

falls (fahls) *conj* in case, if

falsch (fahlsh) *adj* wrong, mistaken; false

fälschen (*fehl*-shern) *v* forge, counterfeit

Fälschung (*fehl*-shoong) *f* (pl ~en) fake

Falte (*fahl*-ter) *f* (pl ~n) fold; crease; wrinkle

falten (*fahl*-tern) *v* fold

Familie (fah-*mee*-l^yer) *f* (pl ~n) family

Familienname (fah-*mee*-l^yern-naa-mer) *m* surname

fanatisch (fah-*naa*-tish) *adj* fanatical

*****fangen** (*fahng*-ern) *v* *catch; capture

Farbe (*fahr*-ber) *f* (pl ~n) colour; paint; dye

farbecht (*fahrb*-ehkht) *adj* fast-dyed

Färbemittel (*fehr*-ber-mi-terl) *nt* (pl ~) colourant

färben (*fehr*-bern) *v* dye

farbenblind (*fahr*-bern-blint) *adj* colour-blind

farbenfroh (*fahr*-bern-frōa) *adj* colourful

Farbfilm (*fahrp*-film) *m* (pl ~e) colour film

farbig (*fahr*-bikh) *adj* coloured

Farbton (*fahrp*-tōan) *m* (pl ~e) shade

Fasan (fah-*zaan*) *m* (pl ~e) pheasant

Faschismus (fah-*shiss*-mooss) *m* fascism

Faschist (fah-*shist*) *m* (pl ~en) fascist

faschistisch (fah-*shiss*-tish) *adj* fascist

Faser (*faa*-zerr) *f* (pl ~n) fibre

Faß (fahss) *nt* (pl Fässer) barrel; cask

Fassade (fah-*saa*-der) *f* (pl ~n) façade

Fäßchen (*fehss*-khern) *nt* (pl ~) keg

fassen (*fah*-sern) *v* grip

Fassung (*fah*-soong) *f* (pl ~en) socket

fast (fahst) *adv* nearly, almost

faul (foul) *adj* lazy, idle

Faust (foust) *f* (pl ~e) fist

Fausthandschuhe (*foust*-hahnt-shōō-er) *mpl* mittens *pl*

Faustschlag (*foust*-shlaak) *m* (pl ~e) punch

Favorit (fah-voa-*reet*) *m* (pl ~en) favourite

Fayence (fah-*Yahngss*) *f* (pl ~n) faience

Fazilität (fah-tsi-li-*tait*) *f* (pl ~en) facility

Februar (*fāy*-broo-aar) February

*fechten (*fehkh*-tern) *v* fence

Feder (*fāy*-derr) *f* (pl ~n) feather; pen; spring

Federung (*fāy*-der-roong) *f* suspension

Fee (fāy) *f* (pl ~n) fairy

fegen (*fāy*-gern) *v* *sweep

Fehlen (*fāy*-lern) *v* want

fehlen (*fāy*-lern) *v* fail; **fehlend** missing

Fehler (*fāy*-lerr) *m* (pl ~) mistake; error, fault

fehlerhaft (*fāy*-lerr-hahft) *adj* faulty

Fehlgeburt (*fāyl*-ger-bōort) *f* (pl ~en) miscarriage

Fehlschlag (*fāyl*-shlaak) *m* (pl ˜e) failure

Fehltritt (*fāyl*-trit) *m* slip

Feier (*figh*-err) *f* (pl ~n) celebration

feierlich (*figh*-err-likh) *adj* solemn

Feierlichkeit (*figh*-err-likh-kight) *f* (pl ~en) ceremony

feiern (*figh*-errn) *v* celebrate

Feiertag (*figh*-err-taak) *m* (pl ~e) holiday

Feige (*figh*-ger) *f* (pl ~n) fig

feige (*figh*-ger) *adj* cowardly

Feigling (*fighk*-ling) *m* (pl ~e) coward

Feile (*figh*-ler) *f* (pl ~n) file

fein (fighn) *adj* fine; delicate

Feind (fighnt) *m* (pl ~e) enemy

feindlich (*fighnt*-likh) *adj* hostile

Feinkost (*fighn*-kost) *f* delicatessen

Feinkostgeschäft (*fighn*-kost-ger-shehft) *nt* (pl ~e) delicatessen

Feinschmecker (*fighn*-shmeh-kerr) *m* (pl ~) gourmet

Feld (fehlt) *nt* (pl ~er) field

Feldbett (*fehlt*-beht) *nt* (pl ~en) camp-bed

Feldstecher (*fehlt*-shteh-kherr) *m* (pl ~) field glasses, binoculars *pl*

Felge (*fehl*-ger) *f* (pl ~n) rim

Fell (fehl) *nt* (pl ~e) skin

Felsblock (*fehls*-blok) *m* (pl ˜e) boulder

Felsen (*fehl*-zern) *m* (pl ~) rock

felsig (*fehl*-zikh) *adj* rocky

Fenster (*fehns*-terr) *nt* (pl ~) window

Fensterbrett (*fehns*-terr-breht) *nt* (pl ~er) window-sill

Fensterladen (*fehns*-terr-laa-dern) *m* (pl ˜) shutter

Ferien (*fāy*-rYern) *pl* vacation

Ferienlager (*fāy*-rYern-laa-gerr) *nt* (pl ~) holiday camp

Ferkel (*fehr*-kerl) *nt* (pl ~) piglet

fern (fehrn) *adj* far; **ferner** *adj* further; *adv* moreover

Ferngespräch (*fehrn*-ger-shpraikh) *nt* (pl ~e) trunk-call

Fernsehen (*fehrn*-zāy-ern) *nt* television

Fernsehgerät (*fehrn*-zāy-ger-rait) *nt* television set

Fernsprecher (*fehrn*-shprai-kherr) *m* phone

Fernsprechverzeichnis (*fehrn*-shprehkh-fehr-tsighkh-niss) *nt* (pl ~se) telephone book *Am*

Fernsprechzelle (*fehrn*-shprehkh-tseh-ler) *f* (pl ~n) telephone booth

Ferse (*fehr*-zer) *f* (pl ~n) heel

fertig (*fehr*-tikh) *adj* ready; finished

Fertigkeit (*fehr*-tikh-kight) *f* art, skill

fertigmachen (*fehr*-tikh-mah-khern) *v* prepare; finish

fesseln (*feh*-serln) *v* fascinate

Fest (fehst) *nt* (pl ~e) feast

fest (fehst) *adj* firm; fixed, permanent; solid; *adv* tight

*festhalten (*fehst*-hahl-tern) *v* *hold;

sich ~ *hold on
Festival (*fehss*-ti-vahl) *nt* (pl ~s) festival
Festkörper (*fehst*-kurr-perr) *m* (pl ~) solid
Festland (*fehst*-lahnt) *nt* mainland; continent
festlich (*fehst*-likh) *adj* festive
festmachen (*fehst*-mah-khern) *v* fasten
Festmahl (*fehst*-maal) *nt* (pl ~er) banquet
Festnahme (*fehst*-naa-mer) *f* (pl ~n) arrest; capture
festsetzen (*fehst*-zeh-tsern) *v* determine; stipulate
feststecken (*fehst*-shteh-kern) *v* pin
feststellen (*fehst*-shteh-lern) *v* notice; ascertain, establish; diagnose
Festung (*fehss*-toong) *f* (pl ~en) fortress
Fett (feht) *nt* (pl ~e) grease, fat
fett (feht) *adj* fat; greasy
Fettheit (*feht*-hight) *f* fatness
fettig (*feh*-tikh) *adj* greasy, fatty
feucht (foikht) *adj* wet; damp, moist, humid
Feuchtigkeit (*foikh*-tikh-kight) *f* damp; moisture, humidity
Feuchtigkeitskrem (*foikh*-tikh-kights-krāym) *f* (pl ~s) moisturizing cream
feudal (foi-*daal*) *adj* feudal
Feuer (*foi*-err) *nt* (pl ~) fire
Feueralarm (*foi*-err-ah-lahrm) *m* fire-alarm
feuerfest (*foi*-err-fehst) *adj* fireproof
Feuerlöscher (*foi*-err-lur-sherr) *m* (pl ~) fire-extinguisher
feuersicher (*foi*-err-zi-kherr) *adj* fireproof
Feuerstein (*foi*-err-shtighn) *m* (pl ~e) flint
Feuerwehr (*foi*-err-vāyr) *f* fire-brigade
Feuerzeug (*foi*-err-tsoik) *nt* (pl ~e) cigarette-lighter

Feuilleton (*furee*-er-tawng) *nt* (pl ~s) serial
Fieber (*fee*-berr) *nt* fever
fiebrig (*fee*-brikh) *adj* feverish
Figur (fi-*goor*) *f* (pl ~en) figure
Fiktion (fik-*tsyōān*) *f* (pl ~en) fiction
Film (film) *m* (pl ~e) film; movie
filmen (*fil*-mern) *v* film
Filmleinwand (*film*-lighn-vahnt) *f* screen
Filter (*fil*-terr) *m* (pl ~) filter
Filz (filts) *m* felt
Fimmel (*fi*-merl) *m* (pl ~) craze
Finanzen (fi-*nahn*-tsern) *pl* finances *pl*
finanziell (fi-nahn-*tsyehl*) *adj* financial
finanzieren (fi-nahn-*tsee*-rern) *v* finance
***finden** (*fin*-dern) *v* *find; *come across; consider
Finger (*fing*-err) *m* (pl ~) finger; **kleine** ~ little finger
Fingerabdruck (*fing*-err-ahp-drook) *m* (pl ~e) fingerprint
Fingergelenk (*fing*-err-ger-lehngk) *nt* (pl ~e) knuckle
Fingerhut (*fing*-err-hōōt) *m* (pl ~e) thimble
Fink (fingk) *m* (pl ~en) finch
Finne (*fi*-ner) *m* (pl ~n) Finn
finnisch (*fi*-nish) *adj* Finnish
Finnland (*fin*-lahnt) Finland
finster (*fins*-terr) *adj* dark
Finsternis (*fins*-terr-niss) *f* (pl ~sen) dark; eclipse
Firma (*feer*-mah) *f* (pl -men) firm, company
Firnis (*feer*-niss) *m* varnish
Fisch (fish) *m* (pl ~e) fish
fischen (*fi*-shern) *v* fish
Fischer (*fi*-sherr) *m* (pl ~) fisherman
Fischerei (fi-sher-*righ*) *f* fishing industry
Fischgräte (*fish*-grai-ter) *f* (pl ~n) fishbone

Fischhandlung (*fish*-hahn-dloong) *f* (pl ~en) fish shop

Fischnetz (*fish*-nehts) *nt* (pl ~e) fishing net

Fjord (f^yort) *m* (pl ~e) fjord

FKK-Strand (ehf-kaa-*kaa*-shtrahnt) *m* (pl ~e) nudist beach

flach (flahkh) *adj* smooth, plane, level, flat

Fläche (*fleh*-kher) *f* (pl ~n) area

Flakon (flah-*kawng*) *nt* (pl ~s) flask

Flamingo (flah-*ming*-goa) *m* (pl ~s) flamingo

Flamme (*flah*-mer) *f* (pl ~n) flame

Flanell (flah-*nehl*) *m* flannel

Flasche (*flah*-sher) *f* (pl ~n) bottle

Flaschenöffner (*flah*-shern-urf-nerr) *m* (pl ~) bottle opener

Fleck (flehk) *m* (pl ~e) stain; spot, speck; **blauer** ~ bruise

fleckenlos (*fleh*-kern-lōass) *adj* spotless, stainless

Fleckenreinigungsmittel (*fleh*-kern-righ-ni-goongs-mi-terl) *nt* stain remover

flegelhaft (*flāy*-gerl-hahft) *adj* impertinent

Fleisch (flighsh) *nt* meat; flesh

Fleischer (*fligh*-sherr) *m* (pl ~) butcher

Fleiß (flighss) *m* diligence

fleißig (*fligh*-sikh) *adj* diligent, industrious

flicken (*fli*-kern) *v* mend, patch

Fliege (*flee*-ger) *f* (pl ~n) fly; bow tie

***fliegen** (*flee*-gern) *v* *fly

***fliehen** (*flee*-ern) *v* escape

***fließen** (*flee*-sern) *v* flow; **fließend** fluent

Flitterwochen (*fli*-terr-vo-khern) *fpl* honeymoon

Floß (flōass) *nt* (pl ~e) raft

Flöte (*flū̄r*-ter) *f* (pl ~n) flute

Flotte (*flo*-ter) *f* (pl ~n) fleet

Fluch (flōōkh) *m* (pl ~e) curse

fluchen (*flōō*-khern) *v* curse, *swear

Flucht (flookht) *f* escape

flüchten (*flewkh*-tern) *v* escape

Flug (flōōk) *m* (pl ~e) flight

Flügel (*flē̄w*-gerl) *m* (pl ~) wing; grand piano

Flughafen (*flōōk*-haa-fern) *m* (pl ~) airport

Flugkapitän (*flōōk*-kah-pi-tain) *m* (pl ~e) captain

Fluglinie (*flōōk*-lee-n^yer) *f* (pl ~n) airline

Flugplatz (*flōōk*-plahts) *m* (pl ~e) airfield

Flugzeug (*flōōk*-tsoik) *nt* (pl ~e) aeroplane; plane, aircraft; airplane *nAm*

Flugzeugabsturz (*flōōk*-tsoik-ahp-shtoorts) *m* (pl ~e) plane crash

Flur (flōōr) *m* (pl ~e) corridor

Fluß (flooss) *m* (pl Flüsse) river

flüssig (*flew*-sikh) *adj* liquid, fluid

Flüssigkeit (*flew*-sikh-kight) *f* (pl ~en) fluid

Flußufer (*flooss*-ōō-ferr) *nt* (pl ~) riverside, river bank

flüstern (*flewss*-terrn) *v* whisper

Flut (flōōt) *f* high tide, flood

Focksegel (*fok*-sāy-gerl) *nt* (pl ~) foresail

Föderation (fur-day-rah-ts^y*ōān*) *f* (pl ~en) federation

Folge (*fol*-ger) *f* (pl ~n) result, issue, consequence; sequel; series, sequence

folgen (*fol*-gern) *v* follow; **folgend** following, subsequent

folglich (*folk*-likh) *adv* consequently

Folklore (folk-*lōā*-rer) *f* folklore

Fön (fūrn) *m* (pl ~e) hair-dryer

Fonds (fawng) *m* (pl ~) fund

foppen (*fo*-pern) *v* kid

forcieren (for-*see*-rern) *v* strain; force

fordern (*for*-derrn) v demand, claim
fördern (*furr*-derrn) v promote
Forderung (*for*-der-roong) f (pl ~en) demand, claim
Forelle (foa-*reh*-ler) f (pl ~n) trout
Form (form) f (pl ~en) form, shape
Formalität (for-mah-li-*tait*) f (pl ~en) formality
Format (for-*maat*) nt (pl ~e) size
Formel (*for*-merl) f (pl ~n) formula
formen (*for*-mern) v form; model
förmlich (*furrm*-likh) adj formal
Formular (for-moo-*laar*) nt (pl ~e) form
Forschung (*for*-shoong) f (pl ~en) research
Forst (forst) m (pl ~e) forest
Förster (*furrs*-terr) m (pl ~) forester
Fort (fōar) nt (pl ~s) fort
fort (fort) adv gone
fortdauern (*fort*-dou-errn) v continue
*fortfahren** (*fort*-faa-rern) v carry on, *go on, *go ahead, proceed; continue; ~ mit *keep on
fortgeschritten (*fort*-ger-shri-tern) adj advanced
fortlaufend (*fort*-lou-fernt) adj continuous
fortschicken (*fort*-shi-kern) v dismiss
*fortschreiten** (*fort*-shrigh-tern) v advance
Fortschritt (*fort*-shrit) m (pl ~e) advance, progress
fortschrittlich (*fort*-shrit-likh) adj progressive
fortsetzen (*fort*-zeh-tsern) v continue
fortwährend (*fort*-vai-rernt) adv continually
Foyer (fwah-*ʸāy*) nt (pl ~s) foyer, lobby
Fracht (frahkht) f (pl ~en) freight, cargo
Frage (*fraa*-ger) f (pl ~n) inquiry, question, query; issue, problem, matter

fragen (*fraa*-gern) v ask; **fragend** interrogative; **sich** ~ wonder
Fragezeichen (*fraa*-ger-tsigh-khern) nt (pl ~) question mark
Fragment (frah-*gmehnt*) nt (pl ~e) fragment
frankieren (frahng-*kee*-rern) v stamp
franko (*frahng*-koa) adj post-paid
Frankreich (*frahng*-righkh) France
Franse (*frahn*-zer) f (pl ~n) fringe
Franzose (frahn-*tsōā*-zer) m (pl ~n) Frenchman
französisch (frahn-*tsūr*-zish) adj French
Frau (frou) f (pl ~en) woman; wife; **gnädige** ~ madam
Frauenarzt (*frou*-ern-ahrtst) m (pl ~e) gynaecologist
Fräulein (*froi*-lighn) nt (pl ~) miss
frech (frehkh) adj bold, impertinent, insolent
frei (frigh) adj free; vacant
freigebig (*frigh*-gāy-bikh) adj generous, liberal
*freihalten** (*frigh*-hahl-tern) v *hold
Freiheit (*frigh*-hight) f (pl ~en) freedom; liberty
Freikarte (*frigh*-kahr-ter) f (pl ~n) free ticket
Freispruch (*frigh*-shprookh) m (pl ~e) acquittal
Freitag (*frigh*-taak) m Friday
freiwillig (*frigh*-vi-likh) adj voluntary
Freiwillige (*frigh*-vi-li-ger) m (pl ~n) volunteer
Freizeit (*frigh*-tsight) f spare time
fremd (frehmt) adj strange; foreign
Fremde (*frehm*-der) m (pl ~n) stranger; foreigner
Fremdenheim (*frehm*-dern-highm) nt (pl ~e) guest-house
Fremdenverkehr (*frehm*-dern-fehr-kāyr) m tourism

Fremdling (*frehmt*-ling) *m* (pl ~e) alien

Frequenz (fray-*kvehnts*) *f* (pl ~en) frequency

Freude (*froi*-der) *f* (pl ~n) joy; pleasure, gladness

freudig (*froi*-dikh) *adj* joyful

sich freuen (*froi*-ern) *be delighted

Freund (froint) *m* (pl ~e) friend

Freundin (*froin*-din) *f* (pl ~nen) friend

freundlich (*froint*-likh) *adj* friendly, kind

Freundschaft (*froint*-shahft) *f* (pl ~en) friendship

freundschaftlich (*froint*-shahft-likh) *adj* friendly

Frieden (*free*-dern) *m* peace

Friedhof (*freet*-hōāf) *m* (pl ~e) cemetery

friedlich (*freet*-likh) *adj* peaceful

***frieren** (*free*-rern) *v* *freeze

frisch (frish) *adj* fresh

Friseur (fri-*zūrr*) *m* (pl ~e) hairdresser, barber

Frisierkommode (fri-*zeer*-ko-mōā-der) *f* (pl ~n) dressing-table

Frist (frist) *f* (pl ~en) term

Frisur (fri-*zōōr*) *f* (pl ~en) hair-do

froh (frōā) *adj* glad, joyful

fröhlich (*frū̄*-likh) *adj* merry, jolly, cheerful

Fröhlichkeit (*frū̄r*-likh-kight) *f* gaiety

fromm (from) *adj* pious

Frosch (frosh) *m* (pl ~e) frog

Frost (frost) *m* frost

Frostbeule (*frost*-boi-ler) *f* (pl ~n) chilblain

Frösteln (*frurss*-terln) *nt* shiver, chill

frösteln (*frurss*-terln) *v* shiver; **fröstelnd** *adj* shivery

Frottierstoff (fro-*teer*-shtof) *m* (pl ~e) towelling

Frucht (frookht) *f* (pl ~e) fruit

fruchtbar (*frookht*-baar) *adj* fertile

Fruchtsaft (*frookht*-zahft) *m* (pl ~e) squash

früh (frew) *adj* early

früher (*frew*-err) *adj* former, prior, previous; *adv* formerly

Frühling (*frew*-ling) *m* spring; springtime

Frühstück (*frew*-shtewk) *nt* breakfast

Fuchs (fooks) *m* (pl ~e) fox

fühlbar (*fewl*-baar) *adj* palpable

fühlen (*few*-lern) *v* *feel

führen (*few*-rern) *v* carry; *lead, guide, direct, conduct; **führend** *adj* leading

Führer (*few*-rerr) *m* (pl ~) guide; guidebook

Führerschein (*few*-rerr-shighn) *m* driving licence

Führung (*few*-roong) *f* leadership; management

Fülle (*few*-ler) *f* plenty

füllen (*few*-lern) *v* fill

Füller (*few*-lerr) *m* (pl ~) fountain-pen

Füllung (*few*-loong) *f* (pl ~en) stuffing, filling

Fundbüro (*foont*-bew-rōā) *nt* (pl ~s) lost property office

Fundsachen (*foont*-zah-khern) *fpl* lost and found

fünf (fewnf) *num* five

fünfte (*fewnf*-ter) *num* fifth

fünfzehn (*fewnf*-tsāyn) *num* fifteen

fünfzehnte (*fewnf*-tsāyn-ter) *num* fifteenth

fünfzig (*fewnf*-tsikh) *num* fifty

funkelnd (*foong*-kerlnt) *adj* sparkling

Funken (*foong*-kern) *m* (pl ~) spark

Funktion (foongk-ts^yōān) *f* (pl ~en) function; operation

funktionieren (foongk-ts^yoa-*nee*-rern) *v* work

funktionsunfähig (foongk-ts^yōāns-oon-fai-ikh) *adj* out of order

für (fewr) *prep* for

Furcht (foorkht) *f* terror, fear

furchtbar (foorkht-baar) *adj* terrible, dreadful, awful

fürchten (fewrkh-tern) *v* fear

fürchterlich (fewrkh-terr-likh) *adj* frightful

furchterregend (foorkht-ehr-rāy-gernt) *adj* terrifying

Furt (foort) *f* (pl ~en) ford

Furunkel (foo-*roong*-kerl) *m* (pl ~) boil

Fürwort (fewr-vort) *nt* (pl ~er) pronoun

Fusion (foo-z^yōān) *f* (pl ~en) merger

Fuß (fōōss) *m* (pl ~e) foot; **zu ~** walking, on foot

Fußball (fōōss-bahl) *m* (pl ~e) football; soccer

Fußballspiel (fōōss-bahl-shpeel) *nt* (pl ~e) football match

Fußboden (fōōss-bōa-dern) *m* (pl ~) floor

Fußbremse (fōōss-brehm-zer) *f* (pl ~n) foot-brake

Fußgänger (fōōss-gehng-err) *m* (pl ~) pedestrian; ~ **verboten** no pedestrians

Fußgängerübergang (fōōss-gehng-err-ēw-berr-gahng) *m* (pl ~e) pedestrian crossing

Fußknöchel (fōōss-knur-kherl) *m* (pl ~) ankle

Fußpfleger (fōōss-pflāy-gerr) *m* (pl ~) pedicure, chiropodist

Fußpuder (fōōss-pōō-derr) *m* foot powder

Fußtritt (fōōss-trit) *m* (pl ~e) kick

Fußweg (fōōss-vāyk) *m* (pl ~e) footpath

Futter (foo-terr) *nt* (pl ~) lining

G

Gabe (gaa-ber) *f* (pl ~n) gift; faculty

Gabel (gaa-berl) *f* (pl ~n) fork

sich gabeln (gaa-berln) fork

Gabelung (gaa-ber-loong) *f* (pl ~en) fork

gähnen (gai-nern) *v* yawn

Galerie (gah-ler-ree) *f* (pl ~n) gallery

Galgen (gahl-gern) *m* (pl ~) gallows pl

Galle (gah-ler) *f* gall; bile

Gallenblase (gah-lern-blaa-zer) *f* (pl ~n) gall bladder

Gallenstein (gah-lern-shtighn) *m* (pl ~e) gallstone

Galopp (gah-*lop*) *m* gallop

Gang¹ (gahng) *m* (pl ~e) aisle; course; gear

Gang² (gahng) *m* gait, walk, pace; **in ~ *bringen** launch

gangbar (gahng-baar) *adj* current

Gangschaltung (gahng-shahl-toong) *f* gear lever

Gans (gahns) *f* (pl ~e) goose

Gänsehaut (gehn-zer-hout) *f* gooseflesh

ganz (gahnts) *adj* whole; total, entire, complete; *adv* entirely; quite

Ganze (gahn-tser) *nt* whole

gänzlich (gehnts-likh) *adj* total, utter; *adv* altogether, wholly, completely

Garage (gah-*raa*-zher) *f* (pl ~n) garage

Garantie (gah-rahn-tee) *f* (pl ~n) guarantee

garantieren (gah-rahn-tee-rern) *v* guarantee

Garderobe (gahr-der-rōā-ber) *f* (pl ~n) cloakroom; wardrobe; checkroom *nAm*

Garderobenschrank (gahr-der-rōā-bern-shrahngk) *m* (pl ~e) closet *nAm*

Garderobenständer (gahr-der-*rōä*-bern-shtehn-derr) *m* (pl ~) hat rack

***gären** (*gai*-rern) *v* ferment

Garn (gahrn) *nt* (pl ~e) yarn

Garnele (gahr-*nāy*-ler) *f* (pl ~n) shrimp

garstig (*gahrs*-tikh) *adj* nasty

Garten (*gahr*-tern) *m* (pl ~̈) garden; **zoologischer** ~ zoological gardens

Gartenbau (*gahr*-tern-bou) *m* horticulture

Gärtner (*gehrt*-nerr) *m* (pl ~) gardener

Gas (gaass) *nt* (pl ~e) gas

Gasherd (*gaass*-hāyrt) *m* (pl ~e) gas cooker

Gasofen (*gaass*-ōä-fern) *m* (pl ~̈) gas stove

Gaspedal (*gaass*-pay-daal) *nt* (pl ~e) accelerator

Gasse (*gahss*-ser) *f* alley, lane

Gast (gahst) *m* (pl ~̈e) visitor, guest

Gästezimmer (*gehss*-ter-tsi-merr) *nt* (pl ~) spare room, guest-room

gastfreundlich (*gahst*-froint-likh) *adj* hospitable

Gastfreundschaft (*gahst*-froint-shahft) *f* hospitality

Gastgeber (*gahst*-gāy-berr) *m* (pl ~) host

Gastgeberin (*gahst*-gāy-ber-rin) *f* (pl ~nen) hostess

Gasthof (*gahst*-hōäf) *m* (pl ~̈e) inn

gastrisch (*gahss*-trish) *adj* gastric

Gaststätte (*gahst*-shteh-ter) *f* (pl ~n) roadhouse; roadside restaurant

Gastwirt (*gahst*-veert) *m* (pl ~e) innkeeper

Gaswerk (*gaass*-vehrk) *nt* (pl ~e) gasworks

Gatte (*gah*-ter) *m* (pl ~n) husband

Gatter (*gah*-terr) *nt* (pl ~) fence

Gattin (*gah*-tin) *f* (pl ~nen) wife

Gattung (*gah*-toong) *f* (pl ~en) breed

Gaze (*gaa*-zer) *f* gauze

Gebäck (ger-*behk*) *nt* cake, pastry

Gebärde (ger-*bair*-der) *f* (pl ~n) sign

Gebärmutter (ger-*bair*-moo-terr) *f* womb

Gebäude (ger-*boi*-der) *nt* (pl ~) building; construction, house, premises *pl*

***geben** (*gāy*-bern) *v* *give

Gebet (ger-*bāyt*) *nt* (pl ~e) prayer

Gebiet (ger-*beet*) *nt* (pl ~e) zone, area, region; territory; field

Gebirge (ger-*beer*-ger) *nt* (pl ~) mountain range

gebirgig (ger-*beer*-gikh) *adj* mountainous

Gebirgspaß (ger-*beerks*-pahss) *m* (pl -pässe) mountain pass

Gebiß (ger-*biss*) *nt* (pl Gebisse) denture; **künstliches** ~ false teeth

geboren (ger-*bōä*-rern) *adj* born

Gebrauch (ger-*broukh*) *m* use

gebrauchen (ger-*brou*-khern) *v* apply, use; **gebraucht** *adj* second-hand

Gebrauchsanweisung (ger-*broukhs*-ahn-vigh-zoong) *f* (pl ~en) directions for use

Gebrauchsgegenstand (ger-*broukhs*-gāy-gern-shtahnt) *m* (pl ~̈e) utensil

Gebühr (ger-*bēwr*) *f* (pl ~en) charge; **Gebühren** dues *pl*; **gebühren-pflichtige Verkehrsstraße** turnpike *nAm*

gebührend (ger-*bēw*-rernt) *adj* proper

Geburt (ger-*bōōrt*) *f* (pl ~en) birth

Geburtsort (ger-*bōōrts*-ort) *m* (pl ~e) place of birth

Geburtstag (ger-*boorts*-taak) *m* (pl ~e) birthday

Gedächtnis (ger-*dehkht*-niss) *nt* memory

Gedanke (ger-*dahng*-ker) *m* (pl ~n) thought; idea

gedankenlos (ger-*dahng*-kern-lōass)
adj careless

Gedankenstrich (ger-*dahng*-kern-
shtrikh) *m* (pl ~e) dash

Gedeckkosten (ger-*dehk*-koss-tern) *pl*
cover charge

Gedenkfeier (ger-*dehngk*-figh-err) *f* (pl
~n) commemoration

Gedicht (ger-*dikht*) *nt* (pl ~e) poem

Geduld (ger-*doolt*) *f* patience

geduldig (ger-*dool*-dikh) *adj* patient

geeignet (ger-*igh*-gnert) *adj* convenient, suitable, proper, appropriate

Gefahr (ger-*faar*) *f* (pl ~en) danger;
risk, peril

gefährlich (ger-*fair*-likh) *adj* dangerous; perilous

Gefährte (ger-*fair*-ter) *m* (pl ~n) companion

Gefälle (ger-*feh*-ler) *nt* gradient

*gefallen** (ger-*fah*-lern) *v* please

gefällig (ger-*feh*-likh) *adj* obliging; enjoyable

Gefälligkeit (ger-*feh*-likh-kight) *f* (pl
~en) favour

Gefangene (ger-*fahng*-er-ner) *m* (pl
~n) prisoner

*gefangennehmen** (ger-*fahng*-ern-
nāy-mern) *v* capture

Gefängnis (ger-*fehng*-niss) *nt* (pl ~se)
gaol, jail, prison

Gefängniswärter (ger-*fehng*-niss-vehr-
terr) *m* (pl ~) jailer

Gefäß (ger-*faiss*) *nt* (pl ~e) vessel

Gefecht (ger-*fehkht*) *nt* (pl ~e) combat

Geflügel (ger-*flēw*-gerl) *nt* fowl, poultry

Geflügelhändler (ger-*flēw*-gerl-hehn-
dlerr) *m* (pl ~) poulterer

Geflüster (ger-*flewss*-terr) *nt* whisper

gefräßig (ger-*frai*-sikh) *adj* greedy

*gefrieren** (ger-*free*-rern) *v* *freeze

Gefrierpunkt (ger-*freer*-poongkt) *m*
freezing-point

Gefrierschutzmittel (ger-*freer*-shoots-
mi-terl) *nt* (pl ~) antifreeze

Gefrierwaren (ger-*freer*-vaa-rern) *fpl*
frozen food

Gefühl (ger-*fēwl*) *nt* (pl ~e) feeling

gefüllt (ger-*fewlt*) *adj* stuffed

gegen (*gāy*-gern) *prep* against; versus

Gegend (*gāy*-gernt) *f* (pl ~en) region,
area; district, country

Gegensatz (*gāy*-gern-zahts) *m* (pl ~e)
contrast

gegensätzlich (*gāy*-gern-zehts-likh) *adj*
opposite

gegenseitig (*gāy*-gern-zigh-tikh) *adj*
mutual

Gegenstand (*gāy*-gern-shtahnt) *m* (pl
~e) article, object

Gegenteil (*gāy*-gern-tighl) *nt* reverse,
contrary; **im** ~ on the contrary

gegenüber (gāy-gern-*ēw*-berr) *prep*
opposite, facing

*gegenüberstehen** (gāy-gern-*ēw*-berr-
shtāy-ern) *v* face

Gegenwart (*gāy*-gern-vahrt) *f* present;
presence

gegenwärtig (*gāy*-gern-vehr-tikh) *adj*
present; current

Gegner (*gāy*-gnerr) *m* (pl ~) opponent

Gehalt (ger-*hahlt*) *nt* (pl ~er) salary,
pay

Gehaltserhöhung (ger-*hahlts*-ehr-hūr-
oong) *f* (pl ~en) rise

gehässig (ger-*heh*-sikh) *adj* spiteful

geheim (ger-*highm*) *adj* secret

Geheimnis (ger-*highm*-niss) *nt* (pl
~se) secret; mystery

geheimnisvoll (ger-*highm*-niss-fol) *adj*
mysterious

*gehen** (*gāy*-ern) *v* *go; walk

Gehirn (ger-*heern*) *nt* (pl ~e) brain

Gehirnerschütterung (ger-*heern*-ehr-
shew-ter-roong) *f* concussion

Gehör (ger-*hūrr*) *nt* hearing

gehorchen (ger-*hor*-khern) *v* obey

gehören (ger-*hūr*-rern) *v* belong

Gehorsam (ger-*hōar*-zaam) *m* obedience

gehorsam (ger-*hōar*-zaam) *adj* obedient

Gehweg (*gāy*-vāyk) *m* (pl ~e) sidewalk *nAm*

Geier (*gigh*-err) *m* (pl ~) vulture

Geige (*gigh*-ger) *f* (pl ~n) violin

Geisel (*gigh*-zerl) *f* (pl ~n) hostage

Geist (gighst) *m* (pl ~er) ghost, soul, spirit, mind; spook

Geistesblitz (*gighss*-terss-blits) *m* (pl ~e) brain-wave

geistig (*gighss*-tikh) *adj* mental; spiritual

Geistliche (*gighst*-li-kher) *m* (pl ~n) minister, clergyman

geistreich (*gighst*-righkh) *adj* witty

geizig (*gigh*-tsikh) *adj* avaricious

gekrümmt (ger-*krewmt*) *adj* curved

Gelächter (ger-*lehkh*-terr) *nt* laughter

gelähmt (ger-*laimt*) *adj* lame

Gelände (ger-*lehn*-der) *nt* terrain; site

Geländer (ger-*lehn*-derr) *nt* (pl ~) rail

gelassen (ger-*lah*-sern) *adj* quiet

gelb (gehlp) *adj* yellow

Gelbsucht (*gehlp*-zookht) *f* jaundice

Geld (gehlt) *nt* money; **zu Gelde machen** cash

Geldanlage (*gehlt*-ahn-laa-ger) *f* (pl ~n) investment

Geldbeutel (*gehlt*-boi-terl) *m* (pl ~) purse

Geldschrank (*gehlt*-shrahngk) *m* (pl ~e) safe

Geldstrafe (*gehlt*-shtraa-fer) *f* (pl ~n) fine

Gelee (zhay-*lāy*) *nt* jelly

gelegen (ger-*lāy*-gern) *adj* situated

Gelegenheit (ger-*lāy*-gern-hight) *f* (pl ~en) chance, opportunity, occasion

Gelegenheitskauf (ger-*lāy*-gern-hights-kouf) *m* (pl ~e) bargain

gelegentlich (ger-*lāy*-gernt-likh) *adv* occasionally

Gelehrte (ger-*lāyr*-ter) *m* (pl ~n) scholar

Geleit (ger-*light*) *nt* escort

Gelenk (ger-*lehngk*) *nt* (pl ~e) joint

gelenkig (ger-*lehng*-kikh) *adj* supple

geliebt (ger-*leept*) *adj* beloved

***gelingen** (ger-*ling*-ern) *v* manage, succeed

***gelten** (*gehl*-tern) *v* apply

Gelübde (ger-*lewp*-der) *nt* (pl ~) vow

Gemälde (ger-*mail*-der) *nt* (pl ~) picture, painting

gemäß (ger-*maiss*) *prep* according to; in accordance with

gemäßigt (ger-*mai*-sikht) *adj* moderate

gemein (ger-*mighn*) *adj* vulgar, coarse

Gemeinde (ger-*mighn*-der) *f* (pl ~n) community; congregation

gemeinsam (ger-*mighn*-zaam) *adj* common; *adv* jointly

Gemeinschaft (ger-*mighn*-shahft) *f* community

gemeinschaftlich (ger-*mighn*-shahft-likh) *adj* joint

gemischt (ger-*misht*) *adj* mixed

Gemüse (ger-*mēw*-zer) *nt* (pl ~) greens *pl*, vegetable

Gemüsegarten (ger-*mēw*-zer-gahr-tern) *m* (pl ~) kitchen garden

Gemüsehändler (ger-*mēw*-zer-hehn-dlerr) *m* (pl ~) greengrocer; vegetable merchant

gemütlich (ger-*mēwt*-likh) *adj* cosy

genau (ger-*nou*) *adj* exact; precise, accurate, careful, punctual; correct; *adv* just, exactly

genehmigen (ger-*nāy*-mi-gern) *v* approve

Genehmigung (ger-*nāy*-mi-goong) *f*

(pl ~en) permission, authorization; permit

geneigt (ger-*nighkt*) *adj* inclined

General (gay-nay-*raal*) *m* (pl ̈e) general

Generalvertreter (gay-nay-*raal*-fehr-trāy-terr) *m* (pl ~) distributor

Generation (gay-nay-rah-ts^y*ōān*) *f* (pl ~en) generation

Generator (gay-nay-*raa*-tor) *m* (pl ~en) generator

*genesen** (ger-*nāy*-zern) *v* recover

Genesung (ger-*nāy*-zoong) *f* cure, recovery

Genie (zhay-*nee*) *nt* (pl ~s) genius

*genießen** (ger-*nee*-sern) *v* enjoy

Genosse (ger-*no*-ser) *m* (pl ~n) comrade

Genossenschaft (ger-*no*-sern-shahft) *f* (pl ~en) co-operative

genug (ger-*nōōk*) *adv* enough

genügend (ger-*nēw*-gernt) *adj* enough, sufficient

Genugtuung (ger-*nōōk*-tōō-oong) *f* satisfaction

Genuß (ger-*nooss*) *m* (pl Genüsse) enjoyment, delight

Geologie (gay-oa-loa-*gee*) *f* geology

Geometrie (gay-oa-may-*tree*) *f* geometry

Gepäck (ger-*pehk*) *nt* luggage, baggage

Gepäckaufbewahrung (ger-*pehk*-ouf-ber-vaa-roong) *f* left luggage office; baggage deposit office *Am*

Gepäcknetz (ger-*pehk*-nehts) *nt* (pl ~e) luggage rack

Gepäckwagen (ger-*pehk*-vaa-gern) *m* (pl ~) luggage van

Geplauder (ger-*plou*-derr) *nt* chat

gerade (ger-*raa*-der) *adj* straight; even; *adv* just

geradeaus (ger-raa-der-*ouss*) *adv* straight on, straight ahead

geradewegs (ger-*raa*-der-vāyks) *adv* straight

Gerät (ger-*rait*) *nt* (pl ~e) appliance; tool, implement, utensil

geräumig (ger-*roi*-mikh) *adj* spacious, roomy, large

Geräusch (ger-*roish*) *nt* (pl ~e) noise

gerecht (ger-*rehkht*) *adj* fair; righteous, right, just

Gerechtigkeit (ger-*rehkh*-tikh-kight) *f* justice

Gericht (ger-*rikht*) *nt* (pl ~e) court; dish

Gerichtshof (ger-*rikhts*-hōaf) *m* (pl ̈e) law court

Gerichtsverfahren (ger-*rikhts*-fehr-faa-rern) *nt* (pl ~) lawsuit, trial

Gerichtsvollzieher (ger-*rikhts*-fol-tsee-err) *m* (pl ~) bailiff

gering (ger-*ring*) *adj* minor, small; **geringer** inferior; **geringst** least

geringfügig (ger-*ring*-fēw-gikh) *adj* petty, slight

Geringschätzung (ger-*ring*-sheh-tsoong) *f* contempt

*gerinnen** (ger-*ri*-nern) *v* coagulate

Gerippe (ger-*ri*-per) *nt* (pl ~) skeleton

gern (gehrn) *adv* willingly; ~ *haben** like, care for, love; ~ *mögen** like, *be fond of

gerne (*gehr*-ner) *adv* gladly

Gerste (*gehrs*-ter) *f* barley

Geruch (ger-*rookh*) *m* (pl ̈e) smell, odour

Gerücht (ger-*rewkht*) *nt* (pl ~e) rumour

Gerüst (ger-*rewst*) *nt* (pl ~e) scaffolding

gesamt (ger-*zahmt*) *adj* overall

Gesamtsumme (ger-*zahmt*-zoo-mer) *f* (pl ~n) total

Gesandtschaft (ger-*zahnt*-shahft) *f* (pl ~en) legation

Gesäß (ger-*zaiss*) *nt* (pl ~e) bottom

Geschädigte (ger-*shai*-dikh-ter) *m* (pl ~n) victim

Geschäft (ger-*shehft*) *nt* (pl ~e) shop; business; deal; **Geschäfte machen mit** *deal with

Geschäftigkeit (ger-*shehf*-tikh-kight) *f* bustle

geschäftlich (ger-*shehft*-likh) *adj* on business

Geschäftsführer (ger-*shehfts*-fēw-rerr) *m* (pl ~) executive

Geschäftsmann (ger-*shehfts*-mahn) *m* (pl -leute) tradesman, businessman

geschäftsmäßig (ger-*shehfts*-mai-sikh) *adj* business-like

Geschäftsreise (ger-*shehfts*-righ-zer) *f* (pl ~n) business trip

Geschäftszeit (ger-*shehfts*-tsight) *f* (pl ~en) business hours

*geschehen** (ger-*shāy*-ern) *v* happen, occur

gescheit (ger-*shight*) *adj* smart, clever

Geschenk (ger-*shehngk*) *nt* (pl ~e) gift, present

Geschichte (ger-*shikh*-ter) *f* (pl ~n) history; story, tale

geschichtlich (ger-*shikht*-likh) *adj* historical

Geschick (ger-*shik*) *nt* fortune

geschickt (ger-*shikt*) *adj* skilful, skilled

Geschirrtuch (ger-*sheer*-tōōkh) *nt* (pl ~er) tea-cloth

Geschlecht (ger-*shlehkht*) *nt* (pl ~er) sex; gender

geschlechtlich (ger-*shlehkht*-likh) *adj* genital

Geschlechtskrankheit (ger-*shlehkhts*-krahngk-hight) *f* (pl ~en) venereal disease

geschlossen (ger-*shlo*-sern) *adj* shut, closed

Geschmack (ger-*shmahk*) *m* taste; flavour

geschmacklos (ger-*shmahk*-lōass) *adj* tasteless

geschmeidig (ger-*shmigh*-dikh) *adj* supple, flexible; smooth

Geschöpf (ger-*shurpf*) *nt* (pl ~e) creature

Geschoß (ger-*shoss*) *nt* (pl Geschosse) floor

Geschwader (ger-*shvaa*-derr) *nt* (pl ~) squadron

Geschwätz (ger-*shvehts*) *nt* chat

geschwind (ger-*shvint*) *adj* swift

Geschwindigkeit (ger-*shvin*-dikh-kight) *f* (pl ~en) speed; rate

Geschwindigkeitsbegrenzung (ger-*shvin*-dikh-kights-ber-grehn-tsoong) *f* (pl ~en) speed limit

Geschwindigkeitsmesser (ger-*shvin*-dikh-kights-meh-serr) *m* (pl ~) speedometer

Geschwindigkeitsübertretung (ger-*shvin*-dikh-kights-ēw-berr-trāy-toong) *f* (pl ~en) speeding

Geschwulst (ger-*shvoolst*) *f* (pl ~̈e) tumour, growth; swelling

Geschwür (ger-*shvēwr*) *nt* (pl ~e) sore, ulcer

Gesellschaft (ger-*zehl*-shahft) *f* (pl ~en) society, company; **Gesellschafts-** social

Gesellschaftsanzug (ger-*zehl*-shahfts-ahn-tsōōk) *m* (pl ~̈e) evening dress

Gesellschaftsraum (ger-*zehl*-shahfts-roum) *m* (pl ~̈e) lounge

Gesetz (ger-*zehts*) *nt* (pl ~e) law

gesetzlich (ger-*zehts*-likh) *adj* lawful; legal

gesetzmäßig (ger-*zehts*-mai-sikh) *adj* legal

gesetzt (ger-*zehtst*) *adj* sedate

Gesicht (ger-*zikht*) *nt* (pl ~er) face

Gesichtskrem (ger-*zikhts*-krāym) *f* (pl ~s) face-cream

Gesichtsmassage (ger-*zikhts*-mah-saazher) *f* (pl ~n) face massage

Gesichtspackung (ger-*zikhts*-pah-koong) *f* (pl ~en) face-pack

Gesichtszug (ger-*zikhts*-tsōōk) *m* (pl ~e) feature

gesondert (ger-*zon*-derrt) *adv* apart

gespannt (ger-*shpahnt*) *adj* curious; tense

Gespenst (ger-*shpehnst*) *nt* (pl ~er) spook, phantom

Gespräch (ger-*shpraikh*) *nt* (pl ~e) conversation, talk; discussion

gesprächig (ger-*shprai*-khikh) *adj* talkative

gesprenkelt (ger-*shprehng*-kerlt) *adj* spotted

Gestalt (ger-*shtahlt*) *f* (pl ~en) figure

Geständnis (ger-*shtehnt*-niss) *nt* (pl ~se) confession

gestatten (ger-*shtah*-tern) *v* allow, permit

*****gestehen** (ger-*shtāy*-ern) *v* confess

Gestell (ger-*shtehl*) *nt* (pl ~e) frame

gestern (*gehss*-terrn) *adv* yesterday

gestikulieren (gehss-ti-koo-*lee*-rern) *v* gesticulate

gestreift (ger-*shtrighft*) *adj* striped

Gestrüpp (ger-*shtrewp*) *nt* (pl ~e) scrub

Gesuch (ger-*zōōkh*) *nt* (pl ~e) request; application

gesund (ger-*zoont*) *adj* healthy, well

Gesundheit (ger-*zoont*-hight) *f* health

Gesundheitsattest (ger-*zoont*-hights-ah-tehst) *nt* (pl~e) health certificate

Getränk (ger-*trehngk*) *nt* (pl ~e) beverage; **alkoholfreies** ~ soft drink; **alkoholische Getränke** spirits

Getreide (ger-*trigh*-der) *nt* corn, grain

getrennt (ger-*trehnt*) *adj* separate; *adv* apart

Getriebe (ger-*tree*-ber) *nt* gear-box

Getue (ger-*tōō*-er) *nt* fuss

geübt (ger-*ēwpt*) *adj* skilled

Gewächshaus (ger-*vehks*-houss) *nt* (pl ~er) greenhouse

gewagt (ger-*vaakt*) *adj* risky

gewähren (ger-*vai*-rern) *v* grant, extend

Gewalt (ger-*vahlt*) *f* violence, force; **vollziehende** ~ executive

Gewaltakt (ger-*vahlt*-ahkt) *m* (pl ~e) outrage

gewaltig (ger-*vahl*-tikh) *adj* huge

gewaltsam (ger-*vahlt*-zaam) *adj* violent

Gewand (ger-*vahnt*) *nt* (pl ~er) robe

gewandt (ger-*vahnt*) *adj* smart, skilful

Gewebe (ger-*vāy*-ber) *nt* (pl ~) tissue

Gewehr (ger-*vāyr*) *nt* (pl ~e) rifle, gun

Geweih (ger-*vigh*) *nt* (pl ~e) antlers *pl*

Gewerbe (ger-*vehr*-ber) *nt* (pl ~) trade, business

Gewerkschaft (ger-*vehrk*-shahft) *f* (pl ~en) trade-union

Gewicht (ger-*vikht*) *nt* (pl ~e) weight

gewillt (ger-*vilt*) *adj* inclined

Gewinn (ger-*vin*) *m* (pl ~e) benefit; gain, profit, winnings *pl*

*****gewinnen** (ger-*vi*-nern) *v* gain, *win

gewiß (ger-*viss*) *adj* certain

Gewissen (ger-*vi*-sern) *nt* conscience

Gewitter (ger-*vi*-terr) *nt* (pl ~) thunderstorm

gewitterschwül (ger-*vi*-terr-shvēwl) *adj* thundery

gewöhnen (ger-*vūr*-nern) *v* accustom

Gewohnheit (ger-*vōān*-hight) *f* (pl ~en) custom, habit

gewöhnlich (ger-*vūrn*-likh) *adj* customary, plain, ordinary, usual; common; *adv* as a rule, usually

gewohnt (ger-*vōānt*) *adj* accustomed; habitual, regular, normal; ~ *****sein** *be used to

gewöhnt (ger-*vūrnt*) *adj* accustomed

Gewölbe (ger-*vurl*-ber) *nt* (pl ~) arch; vault

gewunden (ger-*voon*-dern) *adj* winding

gewürfelt (ger-*vewr*-ferlt) *adj* chequered

Gewürz (ger-*vewrts*) *nt* (pl ~e) spice

gewürzt (ger-*vewrtst*) *adj* spiced

geziert (ger-*tseert*) *adj* affected

Gicht (gikht) *f* gout

Giebel (*gee*-berl) *m* (pl ~) gable

Gier (geer) *f* greed

gierig (*gee*-rikh) *adj* greedy

*gießen** (*gee*-sern) *v* pour

Gift (gift) *nt* (pl ~e) poison

giftig (*gif*-tikh) *adj* poisonous

Gipfel (*gi*-pferl) *m* (pl ~) height, top, summit, peak

Gips (gips) *m* plaster

Gitarre (gi-*tah*-rer) *f* (pl ~n) guitar

Gitter (*gi*-terr) *nt* (pl ~) railing

Glanz (glahnts) *m* glare, gloss

glänzen (*glehn*-tsern) *v* *shine

glänzend (*glehn*-tsernt) *adj* brilliant, magnificent; glossy

Glanzleistung (*glahnts*-lighss-toong) *f* (pl ~en) feat

glanzlos (*glahnts*-lōass) *adj* mat

Glas (glaass) *nt* (pl ~er) glass

gläsern (*glai*-zerrn) *adj* glass

glasieren (glah-*zee*-rern) *v* glaze

glatt (glaht) *adj* even; smooth

Glattbutt (*glaht*-boot) *m* (pl ~e) brill

Glaube (*glou*-ber) *m* belief; faith

glauben (*glou*-bern) *v* believe

Gläubiger (*gloi*-bi-gerr) *m* (pl ~) creditor

glaubwürdig (*gloub*-vewr-dikh) *adj* credible

gleich (glighkh) *adj* equal; alike; level, even; *adv* alike

*gleichen** (*gligh*-khern) *v* resemble

gleichfalls (*glighkh*-fahls) *adv* also

gleichförmig (*glighkh*-furr-mikh) *adj* uniform

gleichgesinnt (*glighkh*-ger-zint) *adj* like-minded

Gleichgewicht (*glighkh*-ger-vikht) *nt* balance

gleichgültig (*glighkh*-gewl-tikh) *adj* indifferent

Gleichheit (*glighkh*-hight) *f* equality

*gleichkommen** (*glighkh*-ko-mern) *v* equal

gleichlaufend (*glighkh*-lou-fernt) *adj* parallel

gleichmachen (*glighkh*-mah-khern) *v* level

Gleichstrom (*glighkh*-shtrōam) *m* direct current

gleichwertig (*glighkh*-vāyr-tikh) *adj* equivalent

gleichzeitig (*glighkh*-tsigh-tikh) *adj* simultaneous

Gleis (glighss) *nt* (pl ~e) track

*gleiten** (*gligh*-tern) *v* glide, *slide

Gletscher (*gleh*-cherr) *m* (pl ~) glacier

Glied (gleet) *nt* (pl ~er) limb; link

glitschig (*gli*-chikh) *adj* slippery

global (gloa-*baal*) *adj* broad

Globus (*glōa*-booss) *m* (pl Globen) globe

Glocke (*glo*-ker) *f* (pl ~n) bell

Glockenspiel (*glo*-kern-shpeel) *nt* (pl ~e) chimes *pl*

Glück (glewk) *nt* luck; happiness; fortune

glücklich (*glewk*-likh) *adj* lucky; happy, fortunate

Glückwunsch (*glewk*-voonsh) *m* (pl ~e) congratulation

Glühbirne (*glēw*-beer-ner) *f* (pl ~n) light bulb

glühen (*glēw*-ern) *v* glow

Glut (glōot) *f* glow

Gnade (*gnaa*-der) *f* grace; mercy

Gobelin (goa-ber-*lang*) *m* (pl ~s) tapestry

Gold (golt) *nt* gold

golden (*gol*-dern) *adj* golden

Goldgrube (*golt*-grōō-ber) *f* (pl ~n) goldmine

Goldschmied (*golt*-shmeet) *m* (pl ~e) goldsmith

Golf (golf) *m* (pl ~e) gulf; *nt* golf

Golfklub (*golf*-kloop) *m* (pl ~s) golf-club

Golfplatz (*golf*-plahts) *m* (pl ~̈e) golf-links, golf-course

Gondel (*gon*-derl) *f* (pl ~n) gondola

Gosse (*go*-ser) *f* (pl ~n) gutter

Gott (got) *m* (pl ~̈er) god

Gottesdienst (*go*-terss-deenst) *m* (pl ~e) worship

Göttin (*gur*-tin) *f* (pl ~nen) goddess

göttlich (*gurt*-likh) *adj* divine

Gouvernante (goo-vehr-*nahn*-ter) *f* (pl ~n) governess

Gouverneur (goo-vehr-*nūr*) *m* (pl ~e) governor

Grab (graap) *nt* (pl ~̈er) grave, tomb

Graben (*graa*-bern) *m* (pl ~̈) ditch

*graben (*graa*-bern) *v* *dig

Grabstein (*graap*-shtighn) *m* (pl ~e) gravestone, tombstone

Grad (graat) *m* (pl ~e) degree

Graf (graaf) *m* (pl ~en) earl, count

Gräfin (*grai*-fin) *f* (pl ~nen) countess

Grafschaft (*graaf*-shahft) *f* (pl ~en) county

sich grämen (*grai*-mern) grieve

Gramm (grahm) *nt* (pl ~e) gram

Grammatik (grah-*mah*-tik) *f* grammar

grammatikalisch (grah-mah-ti-*kaa*-lish) *adj* grammatical

Grammophon (grah-moa-*fōan*) *nt* (pl ~e) record-player, gramophone

Granit (grah-*neet*) *m* granite

Graphik (*graa*-fik) *f* (pl ~en) graph

graphisch (*graa*-fish) *adj* graphic

Gras (graass) *nt* grass

Grashalm (*graass*-hahlm) *m* (pl ~e) blade of grass

Grat (graat) *m* (pl ~e) ridge

Gräte (*grai*-ter) *f* (pl ~n) bone, fishbone

gratis (*graa*-tiss) *adv* free

gratulieren (grah-too-*lee*-rern) *v* congratulate, compliment

grau (grou) *adj* grey

grauenhaft (*grou*-ern-hahft) *adj* horrible

grausam (*grou*-zaam) *adj* cruel, harsh

Graveur (grah-*vūrr*) *m* (pl ~e) engraver

gravieren (grah-*vee*-rern) *v* engrave

greifbar (*grighf*-baar) *adj* tangible

*greifen (*grigh*-fern) *v* *take

Grenze (*grehn*-tser) *f* (pl ~n) frontier, border; boundary, limit, bound

Grieche (*gree*-kher) *m* (pl ~n) Greek

Griechenland (*gree*-khern-lahnt) Greece

griechisch (*gree*-khish) *adj* Greek

Griff (grif) *m* (pl ~e) grip, grasp; clutch

Grille (*gri*-ler) *f* (pl ~n) cricket; whim

grillen (*gri*-lern) *v* grill

Grillroom (*gril*-rōōm) *m* (pl ~s) grillroom

Grinsen (*grin*-zern) *nt* grin

grinsen (*grin*-zern) *v* grin

Grippe (*gri*-per) *f* flu, influenza

grob (grawp) *adj* rude, coarse, gross

Gros (gross) *nt* gross

groß (grōass) *adj* big; great, large, tall; major

großartig (*grōass*-ahr-tikh) *adj* terrific, grand, superb, magnificent

Großbritannien (grōass-bri-*tah*-nʸern) Great Britain

Großbuchstabe (*grōass*-bōōkh-shtaaber) *m* (pl ~n) capital letter

Größe (*grūr*-ser) *f* (pl ~n) size

Großeltern (*grōass*-ehl-terrn) *pl* grandparents *pl*

Großhandel (*groass*-hahn-derl) *m* wholesale

Großhändler (*groass*-hehn-dlerr) *m* (pl ~) wholesale dealer

Großmama (*groass*-mah-maa) *f* (pl ~s) grandmother

Großmut (*groass*-mōot) *m* generosity

Großmutter (*groass*-moo-terr) *f* (pl ~̈) grandmother

Großpapa (*groass*-pah-paa) *m* (pl ~s) grandfather

Großvater (*groass*-faa-terr) *m* (pl ~̈) grandfather

*****großziehen** (*groass*-tsee-ern) *v* *bring up; rear

großzügig (*groass*-tsew-gikh) *adj* generous, liberal

Grotte (*gro*-ter) *f* (pl ~n) grotto

Grube (*grōo*-ber) *f* (pl ~n) hole, pit

grün (*grewn*) *adj* green; **grüne Versicherungskarte** green card

Grund (*groont*) *m* (pl ~̈e) ground; cause, reason; **Grund-** primary

gründen (*grewn*-dern) *v* establish, found; base

Grundgesetz (*groont*-ger-zehts) *nt* (pl ~e) constitution

Grundlage (*groont*-laa-ger) *f* (pl ~n) basis, base

grundlegend (*groont*-lāy-gernt) *adj* fundamental, essential, basic

gründlich (*grewnt*-likh) *adj* thorough

Grundriß (*groont*-riss) *m* (pl -risse) plan

Grundsatz (*groont*-zahts) *m* (pl ~̈e) principle

Grundstück (*groont*-shtewk) *nt* (pl ~e) grounds

Gruppe (*groo*-per) *f* (pl ~n) group; set, party

Grus (*grōoss*) *m* grit

gruselig (*grōo*-zer-likh) *adj* creepy

Gruß (*grōoss*) *m* (pl ~̈e) greeting

grüßen (*grew*-sern) *v* greet; salute

gucken (*goo*-kern) *v* look

gültig (*gewl*-tikh) *adj* valid

Gummi (*goo*-mi) *m* rubber; gum

Gummiband (*goo*-mi-bahnt) *nt* (pl ~̈er) rubber band, elastic

Gummilinse (*goo*-mi-lin-zer) *f* (pl ~n) zoom lens

Gunst (*goonst*) *f* grace

günstig (*gewns*-tikh) *adj* favourable

gurgeln (*goor*-gerln) *v* gargle

Gurke (*goor*-ker) *f* (pl ~n) cucumber

Gürtel (*gewr*-terl) *m* (pl ~) belt

Gußeisen (*gooss*-igh-zern) *nt* cast iron

gut (*gōot*) *adj* good; right; *adv* well; **gut!** all right!; well!

Güter (*gew*-terr) *ntpl* goods *pl*

Güterzug (*gew*-terr-tsōok) *m* (pl ~̈e) goods train; freight-train *nAm*

gutgelaunt (*gōot*-ger-lount) *adj* good-tempered, good-humoured

gutgläubig (*gōot*-gloi-bikh) *adj* credulous

gütig (*gew*-tikh) *adj* kind

gutmütig (*gōot*-mew-tikh) *adj* good-natured

Gutschein (*gōot*-shighn) *m* (pl ~e) voucher

Gynäkologe (gew-neh-koa-*loā*-ger) *m* (pl ~n) gynaecologist

H

Haar (haar) *nt* (pl ~e) hair

Haarbürste (*haar*-bewrs-ter) *f* (pl ~n) hairbrush

Haarfixativ (*haar*-fi-ksah-teef) *nt* setting lotion

haarig (*haa*-rikh) *adj* hairy

Haarklemme (*haar*-kleh-mer) *f* (pl ~n) hair-grip; bobby pin *Am*

Haarkrem (*haar*-krāym) *f* (pl ~s) hair

cream

Haarlack (*haar*-lahk) *m* (pl ~e) hairspray

Haarnadel (*haar*-naa-derl) *f* (pl ~n) hairpin

Haarnetz (*haar*-nehts) *nt* (pl ~e) hairnet

Haaröl (*haar*-ürl) *nt* hair-oil

Haarschnitt (*haar*-shnit) *m* (pl ~e) haircut

Haartonikum (*haar*-tōā-ni-koom) *nt* hair tonic

Haartracht (*haar*-trahkht) *f* (pl ~en) hair-do

Habe (*haa*-ber) *f* possessions, belongings *pl*

* **haben** (*haa*-bern) *v* *have

Habicht (*haa*-bikht) *m* (pl ~e) hawk

hacken (*hah*-kern) *v* chop

Hafen (*haa*-fern) *m* (pl ~̈) harbour, port

Hafenarbeiter (*haa*-fern-ahr-bigh-terr) *m* (pl ~) docker

Hafer (*haa*-ferr) *m* oats *pl*

Haft (hahft) *f* custody, imprisonment

haftbar (*hahft*-baar) *adj* responsible

Haftbarkeit (*hahft*-baar-kight) *f* responsibility

Häftling (*hehft*-ling) *m* (pl ~e) prisoner

Hagel (*haa*-gerl) *m* hail

Hahn (haan) *m* (pl ~̈e) cock; tap

Hai (high) *m* (pl ~e) shark

Hain (highn) *m* (pl ~e) grove

häkeln (*hai*-kerln) *v* crochet

Haken (*haa*-kern) *m* (pl ~) hook

halb (hahlp) *adj* half; **Halb-** semi-

halbieren (hahl-*bee*-rern) *v* halve

Halbinsel (*hahlp*-in-zerl) *f* (pl ~n) peninsula

Halbkreis (*hahlp*-krighss) *m* (pl ~e) semicircle

halbwegs (*hahlp*-vāyks) *adv* halfway

Halbzeit (*hahlp*-tsight) *f* half-time

Hälfte (*hehlf*-ter) *f* (pl ~n) half

Halle (*hah*-ler) *f* (pl ~n) hall

hallo! (hah-*lōā*) hello!

Hals (hahls) *m* (pl ~̈e) neck; throat

Halsband (*hahls*-bahnt) *nt* (pl ~̈er) collar; beads *pl*

Halsentzündung (*hahls*-ehnt-tsewn-doong) *f* (pl ~en) laryngitis

Halskette (*hahls*-keh-ter) *f* (pl ~n) necklace

Halsschmerzen (*hahls*-shmehr-tsern) *mpl* sore throat

Halt (hahlt) *m* grip

* **halten** (*hahl*-tern) *v* *hold, *keep; **halt!** stop!; ~ **für** reckon, count

Haltestelle (*hahl*-ter-shteh-ler) *f* (pl ~n) stop

Haltung (*hahl*-toong) *f* (pl ~en) position

Hammelfleisch (*hah*-merl-flighsh) *nt* mutton

Hammer (*hah*-merr) *m* (pl ~̈) hammer

Hämorrhoiden (heh-moa-roa-*ee*-dern) *fpl* piles *pl*, haemorrhoids *pl*

Hand (hahnt) *f* (pl ~̈e) hand; **Hand-** manual

Handarbeit (*hahnt*-ahr-bight) *f* (pl ~en) handwork, handicraft; needlework

Handbremse (*hahnt*-brehm-zer) *f* (pl ~n) hand-brake

Handbuch (*hahnt*-bōōkh) *nt* (pl ~̈er) handbook

Händedruck (*hehn*-der-drook) *m* handshake

Handel (*hahn*-derl) *m* trade, commerce; business; **Handels-** commercial

handeln (*hahn*-derln) *v* act; trade; bargain

Handelsrecht (*hahn*-derls-rehkht) *m* commercial law

Handelsware (*hahn*-derls-vaa-rer) *f* merchandise

Handfläche (*hahnt*-fleh-kher) *f* (pl ~n) palm

handgearbeitet (*hahnt*-ger-ahr-bigh-tert) *adj* hand-made

Handgelenk (*hahnt*-ger-lehngk) *nt* (pl ~e) wrist

Handgepäck (*hahnt*-ger-pehk) *nt* hand luggage, hand baggage *Am*

Handgriff (*hahnt*-grif) *m* (pl ~e) handle

handhaben (*hahnt*-haa-bern) *v* handle

Handkoffer (*hahnt*-ko-ferr) *m* (pl ~) suitcase

Handkrem (*hahnt*-kraym) *f* (pl ~s) hand cream

Händler (*hehn*-dlerr) *m* (pl ~) merchant; trader, dealer

handlich (*hahnt*-likh) *adj* handy; manageable

Handlung (*hahn*-dloong) *f* (pl ~en) deed, action; plot

Handschellen (*hahnt*-sheh-lern) *fpl* handcuffs *pl*

Handschrift (*hahnt*-shrift) *f* (pl ~en) handwriting

Handschuh (*hahnt*-shoo) *m* (pl ~e) glove

Handtasche (*hahnt*-tah-sher) *f* (pl ~n) handbag, bag

Handtuch (*hahnt*-tookh) *nt* (pl ~er) towel

Handvoll (*hahnt*-fol) *f* handful

Handwerk (*hahnt*-vehrk) *nt* handicraft

Hanf (hahnf) *m* hemp

Hang (hahng) *m* (pl ~e) hillside

Hängebrücke (*hehng*-er-brew-ker) *f* (pl ~n) suspension bridge

Hängematte (*hehng*-er-mah-ter) *f* (pl ~n) hammock

***hängen** (*hehng*-ern) *v* *hang

Harfe (*hahr*-fer) *f* (pl ~n) harp

Harke (*hahr*-ker) *f* (pl ~n) rake

harmlos (*hahrm*-lōass) *adj* harmless

Harmonie (hahr-moa-*nee*) *f* harmony

hart (hahrt) *adj* hard

hartnäckig (*hahrt*-neh-kikh) *adj* dogged, obstinate, stubborn

Harz (hahrts) *m* resin

Hase (*haa*-zer) *m* (pl ~n) hare

Haselnuß (*haa*-zerl-nooss) *f* (pl -nüsse) hazelnut

Haß (hahss) *m* hatred, hate

hassen (*hah*-sern) *v* hate

häßlich (*hehss*-likh) *adj* ugly

Hast (hahst) *f* haste

hastig (*hahss*-tikh) *adj* hasty

Haufen (*hou*-fern) *m* (pl ~) heap, lot; pile; bunch

häufig (*hoi*-fikh) *adj* frequent; *adv* often

Häufigkeit (*hoi*-fikh-kight) *f* frequency

Haupt (houpt) *nt* (pl ~er) head; chief; **Haupt-** capital; leading, main, chief; major

Hauptbahnhof (*houpt*-baan-hōāf) *m* (pl ~e) central station

Hauptleitung (*houpt*-ligh-toong) *f* (pl ~en) mains *pl*

Häuptling (*hoipt*-ling) *m* (pl ~e) chieftain

Hauptmahlzeit (*houpt*-maal-tsight) *f* (pl ~en) dinner

Hauptquartier (*houpt*-kvahr-teer) *nt* (pl ~e) headquarters *pl*

hauptsächlich (*houpt*-zehkh-likh) *adj* cardinal, primary; *adv* especially, mainly

Hauptstadt (*houpt*-shtaht) *f* (pl ~e) capital

Hauptstraße (*houpt*-shtraa-ser) *f* (pl ~n) main road; main street

Hauptstrecke (*houpt*-shtreh-ker) *f* (pl ~n) main line

Hauptverkehrsstraße (*houpt*-fehr-kāyrs-shtraa-ser) *f* (pl ~n) thoroughfare

Hauptverkehrszeit (*houpt*-fehr-kāyrs-tsight) *f* (pl ~en) rush-hour, peak hour

Hauptwort (*houpt*-vort) *nt* (pl ̈er) noun

Haus (houss) *nt* (pl ̈er) house; home; **im** ~ indoors, indoor; **nach Hause** home; **zu Hause** home, at home

Hausangestellte (*houss*-ahn-ger-shtehl-ter) *f* (pl ~n) housemaid

Hausarbeit (*houss*-ahr-bight) *f* (pl ~en) housekeeping

Hausbesitzer (*houss*-ber-zi-tserr) *m* (pl ~) landlord

Häuserblock (*hoi*-zerr-blok) *m* (pl ~s) house block *Am*

Häusermakler (*hoi*-zerr-maak-lerr) *m* (pl ~) house agent

Hausfrau (*houss*-frou) *f* (pl ~en) housewife

Haushalt (*houss*-hahlt) *m* (pl ~e) housekeeping, household

Haushälterin (*houss*-hehl-ter-rin) *f* (pl ~nen) housekeeper

Haushaltsarbeiten (*houss*-hahlts-ahr-bigh-tern) *fpl* housework

Hausherrin (*houss*-heh-rin) *f* (pl ~nen) mistress

Hauslehrer (*houss*-lāy-rerr) *m* (pl ~) tutor

häuslich (*hoiss*-likh) *adj* domestic

Hausmeister (*houss*-mighss-terr) *m* (pl ~) janitor, caretaker, concierge

Hausschlüssel (*houss*-shlew-serl) *m* (pl ~) latchkey

Hausschuh (*houss*-shōō) *m* (pl ~e) slipper

Haustier (*houss*-teer) *nt* (pl ~e) pet

Haut (hout) *f* skin; hide

Hautausschlag (*hout*-ouss-shlaak) *m* rash

Hautkrem (*hout*-krāym) *f* (pl ~s) skin cream

Hebamme (*hāyp*-ah-mer) *f* (pl ~n) midwife

Hebel (*hāy*-berl) *m* (pl ~) lever

*heben (*hāy*-bern) *v* lift; raise

Hebräisch (hay-*brai*-ish) *nt* Hebrew

Hecht (hehkht) *m* (pl ~e) pike

Hecke (*heh*-ker) *f* (pl ~n) hedge

Heckenschütze (*heh*-kern-shew-tser) *m* (pl ~n) sniper

Heer (hāyr) *nt* (pl ~e) army

Hefe (*hāy*-fer) *f* yeast

Heft (hehft) *nt* (pl ~e) note-book; issue

heftig (*hehf*-tikh) *adj* fierce; violent, severe, intense

Heftklammer (*hehft*-klah-merr) *f* (pl ~n) staple

Heftpflaster (*hehft*-pflahss-terr) *nt* (pl ~) adhesive tape, plaster

Heide (*high*-der) *f* (pl ~n) heath, moor; *m* heathen, pagan

Heidekraut (*high*-der-krout) *nt* heather

heidnisch (*hight*-nish) *adj* heathen, pagan

heikel (*high*-kerl) *adj* precarious, critical

Heilbad (*highl*-baat) *nt* (pl ̈er) spa

Heilbutt (*highl*-boot) *m* (pl ~e) halibut

heilen (*high*-lern) *v* cure, heal

heilig (*high*-likh) *adj* holy, sacred

Heilige (*high*-li-ger) *m* (pl ~n) saint

Heiligtum (*high*-likh-tōōm) *nt* (pl ̈er) shrine

Heilmittel (*highl*-mi-terl) *nt* (pl ~) remedy

Heim (highm) *nt* (pl ~e) home; asylum

Heimatland (*high*-maat-lahnt) *nt* (pl ̈er) native country

*heimgehen (*highm*-gāy-ern) *v* *go home

Heimweh (*highm*-vāy) *nt* homesickness

Heirat (*high*-raat) *f* (pl ~en) wedding

heiraten (*high*-raa-tern) *v* marry

heiser (*high*-zerr) *adj* hoarse

heiß (highss) *adj* warm, hot

*****heißen** (*high*-sern) *v* *be called

heiter (*high*-terr) *adj* cheerful

Heiterkeit (*high*-terr-kight) *f* gaiety

heizen (*high*-tsern) *v* heat

Heizkörper (*hights*-kurr-perr) *m* (pl ~) radiator

Heizofen (*hights*-ōa-fern) *m* (pl ~̈) heater

Heizöl (*hights*-ūrl) *nt* fuel oil

Heizung (*high*-tsoong) *f* (pl ~en) heating

Held (hehlt) *m* (pl ~en) hero

*****helfen** (*hehl*-fern) *v* help; assist, aid

Helfer (*hehl*-ferr) *m* (pl ~) helper

hell (hehl) *adj* bright, light; pale

hellhörig (*hehl*-hūr-rikh) *adj* noisy

hellviolett (*hehl*-vi-oa-leht) *adj* mauve

Helm (hehlm) *m* (pl ~e) helmet

Hemd (hehmt) *nt* (pl ~en) shirt; vest

Henne (*heh*-ner) *f* (pl ~n) hen

her (hāyr) *adv* ago

herab (heh-*rahp*) *adv* down

herabsetzen (heh-*rahp*-zeh-tsern) *v* reduce, lower

*****herabsteigen** (heh-*rahp*-shtigh-gern) *v* descend

herannahend (heh-*rahn*-naa-ernt) *adj* oncoming

heraus (heh-*rouss*) *adv* out

herausfordern (heh-*rouss*-for-derrn) *v* challenge, dare

Herausforderung (heh-*rouss*-for-der-roong) *f* (pl ~en) challenge

*****herausgeben** (heh-*rouss*-gāy-bern) *v* publish

*****herausnehmen** (heh-*rouss*-nāy-mern) *v* *take out

sich herausstellen (heh-*rouss*-shteh-lern) *v* prove

Herberge (*hehr*-behr-ger) *f* (pl ~n) hostel

Herbst (hehrpst) *m* autumn; fall *nAm*

Herd (hāyrt) *m* (pl ~e) hearth; stove

Herde (*hāyr*-der) *f* (pl ~n) herd, flock

Hering (*hāy*-ring) *m* (pl ~e) herring

Herkunft (*hāyr*-koonft) *f* origin

hernach (hehr-*naakh*) *adv* afterwards

Hernie (*hehr*-nᵞer) *f* slipped disc

Herr (hehr) *m* (pl ~en) gentleman; mister; **mein ~** sir

Herrentoilette (*heh*-rern-twah-leh-ter) *f* (pl ~n) men's room

Herrin (*heh*-rin) *f* (pl ~nen) mistress

herrlich (*hehr*-likh) *adj* wonderful, lovely; splendid

Herrschaft (*hehr*-shahft) *f* domination; dominion, rule, reign

Herrschaftshaus (*hehr*-shahfts-houss) *nt* (pl ~̈er) mansion, manor-house

herrschen (*hehr*-shern) *v* rule

Herrscher (*hehr*-sherr) *m* (pl ~) ruler; sovereign

herstellen (*hāy*-r-shteh-lern) *v* manufacture; produce

herum (heh-*room*) *adv* about

herunter (heh-*roon*-terr) *adv* down

*****herunterlassen** (heh-*roon*-terr-lah-sern) *v* lower

hervorragend (hehr-*fōar*-raa-gernt) *adj* outstanding, excellent

Herz (hehrts) *nt* (pl ~en) heart

Herzklopfen (*hehrts*-klo-pfern) *nt* palpitation

herzlich (*hehrts*-likh) *adj* hearty, cordial

herzlos (*hehrts*-lōass) *adj* heartless

Herzog (*hehr*-tsōak) *m* (pl ~̈e) duke

Herzogin (*hehr*-tsōa-gin) *f* (pl ~nen) duchess

Herzschlag (*hehrts*-shlaak) *m* (pl ~̈e) heart attack

heterosexuell (*hay*-tay-roa-zeh-ksoo-ehl) *adj* heterosexual

Heu (hoi) *nt* hay

Heuchelei (hoi-kher-*ligh*) *f* hypocrisy

heucheln (*hoi*-kherln) *v* simulate

Heuchler (*hoikh*-lerr) *m* (pl ~) hypocrite

heuchlerisch (*hoikh*-ler-rish) *adj* hypocritical

heulen (*hoi*-lern) *v* roar

Heuschnupfen (*hoi*-shnoo-pfern) *m* hay fever

Heuschrecke (*hoi*-shreh-ker) *f* (pl ~n) grasshopper

heute (*hoi*-ter) *adv* today; ~ **abend** tonight; ~ **morgen** this morning; ~ **nachmittag** this afternoon; ~ **nacht** tonight

heutzutage (*hoit*-tsoo-taa-ger) *adv* nowadays

Hexe (*heh*-kser) *f* (pl ~n) witch

Hexenschuß (*heh*-ksern-shooss) *m* lumbago

hier (heer) *adv* here

Hierarchie (hi-ay-rahr-*khee*) *f* (pl ~n) hierarchy

Hilfe (*hil*-fer) *f* help; assistance, aid; **erste** ~ first-aid

hilfreich (*hilf*-righkh) *adj* helpful

Himbeere (*him*-bāy-rer) *f* (pl ~n) raspberry

Himmel (*hi*-merl) *m* sky; heaven

hinab (hi-*nahp*) *adv* down

hinauf (hi-*nouf*) *adv* up

***hinaufsteigen** (hi-*nouf*-shtigh-gern) *v* ascend

hinaus (hi-*nouss*) *adv* out

hindern (hin-derrn) *v* hinder, embarrass; impede

Hindernis (*hin*-derr-niss) *nt* (pl ~se) obstacle; impediment

hinein (hi-*nighn*) *adv* in

***hineingehen** (hi-*nighn*-gāy-ern) *v* *go in

hinken (*hing*-kern) *v* limp

hinreichend (*hin*-righ-khernt) *adj* sufficient

Hinrichtung (*hin*-rikh-toong) *f* (pl ~en) execution

hinsichtlich (hin-zikht-likh) *prep* as regards, regarding, about, with reference to, concerning

hinten (*hin*-tern) *adv* behind

hinter (*hin*-terr) *prep* behind; after

Hinterbacke (*hin*-terr-bah-ker) *f* (pl ~en) buttock

Hintergrund (*hin*-terr-groont) *m* (pl ~̈e) background

Hinterhalt (*hin*-terr-hahlt) *m* (pl ~e) ambush

hinterlegen (hin-terr-*lāy*-gern) *v* deposit

Hintern (*hin*-terrn) *m* bottom

Hinterseite (*hin*-terr-zigh-ter) *f* (pl ~n) rear

***hinübergehen** (hi-*nēw*-berr-gāy-ern) *v* cross

hinunter (hi-*noon*-terr) *adv* downstairs

hinzufügen (hin-*tsōō*-fēw-gern) *v* add

Hinzufügung (hin-*tsōō*-fēw-goong) *f* (pl ~en) addition

Hirt (heert) *m* (pl ~en) shepherd

Historiker (hiss-*tōa*-ri-kerr) *m* (pl ~) historian

historisch (hiss-*tōa*-rish) *adj* historic

Hitze (*hi*-tser) *f* heat

hoch (hōakh) *adj* high; tall

Hochebene (*hōakh*-āy-ber-ner) *f* (pl ~n) plateau

Hochland (*hōakh*-lahnt) *nt* uplands *pl*

hochmütig (*hōakh*-mēw-tikh) *adj* haughty, proud

hochnäsig (*hōakh*-nai-zikh) *adj* snooty

Hochsaison (*hōakh*-zeh-zawng) *f* high season, peak season

Hochsommer (*hōakh*-zo-merr) *m* midsummer

höchst (hūrkhst) *adj* extreme

höchstens (*hūrkhst*-erns) *adv* at most

Höchstgeschwindigkeit (*hūrkhst*-ger-shvin-dikh-kight) *f* speed limit

Hochzeit (*hokh*-tsight) *f* (pl ~en) wedding

Hochzeitsreise (*hokh*-tsights-righ-zer) *f* (pl ~n) honeymoon

hochziehen (*hōākh*-tsee-ern) *v* hoist

Hof (hoaf) *m* (pl ~e) yard ; court

hoffen (*ho*-fern) *v* hope

Hoffnung (*hof*-noong) *f* (pl ~en) hope

hoffnungslos (*hof*-noongs-lōass) *adj* hopeless

hoffnungsvoll (*hof*-noongs-fol) *adj* hopeful

höflich (*hūrf*-likh) *adj* polite, courteous, civil

Höhe (*hūr*-er) *f* (pl ~n) height ; altitude

Höhepunkt (*hūr*-er-poongkt) *m* (pl ~e) height ; zenith

höher (*hūr*-err) *adj* upper

hohl (hōāl) *adj* hollow

Höhle (*hūr*-ler) *f* (pl ~n) cavern, cave ; den

Höhlung (*hūr*-loong) *f* (pl ~en) cavity

Hohn (hōan) *m* scorn

holen (*hōā*-lern) *v* fetch ; *get, collect

Holland (*ho*-lahnt) Holland

Holländer (*ho*-lehn-derr) *m* (pl ~) Dutchman

holländisch (*ho*-lehn-dish) *adj* Dutch

Hölle (*hur*-ler) *f* hell

holperig (*hol*-per-rikh) *adj* rough, bumpy

Holz (holts) *nt* wood

hölzern (*hurl*-tserrn) *adj* wooden

Holzhammer (*holts*-hah-merr) *m* (pl ~) mallet

Holzkohle (*holts*-kōā-ler) *f* charcoal

Holzschnitzerei (*holts*-shni-tser-righ) *f* (pl ~en) wood-carving

Holzschuh (*holts*-shōō) *m* (pl ~e) wooden shoe

homosexuell (*hoa*-moa-zeh-ksoo-ehl) *adj* homosexual

Honig (*hōā*-nikh) *m* honey

Honorar (hoa-noa-*raar*) *nt* (pl ~e) fee

Hopfen (*ho*-pfern) *m* hop

hörbar (*hūrr*-baar) *adj* audible

hören (*hūr*-rern) *v* *hear

Horizont (hoa-ri-*tsont*) *m* horizon

Horn (horn) *nt* (pl ~er) horn

Horsd'œuvre (or-*dūrvr*) *nt* (pl ~s) hors-d'œuvre

Hose (*hōā*-zer) *f* (pl ~n) trousers *pl*, slacks *pl* ; pants *plAm* ; **kurze ~** shorts *pl*

Hosenanzug (*hōā*-zern-ahn-tsōōk) *m* (pl ~e) pant-suit

Hosenträger (*hōā*-sern-trai-gerr) *mpl* braces *pl* ; suspenders *plAm*

Hotel (hoa-*tehl*) *nt* (pl ~s) hotel

Hotelpage (hoa-*tehl*-paa-zher) *m* (pl ~n) page-boy, bellboy

hübsch (hewpsh) *adj* good-looking, pretty ; nice, fair, lovely

Huf (hōōf) *m* (pl ~e) hoof

Hufeisen (*hōōf*-igh-zern) *nt* (pl ~) horseshoe

Hüfte (*hewf*-ter) *f* (pl ~n) hip

Hüfthalter (*hewft*-hahl-terr) *m* (pl ~) girdle, suspender belt ; garter belt *Am*

Hügel (*hēw*-gerl) *m* (pl ~) hill

hügelig (*hēw*-ger-likh) *adj* hilly

Huhn (hōōn) *nt* (pl ~er) hen ; chicken

Hühnerauge (*hēw*-nerr-ou-ger) *nt* (pl ~n) corn

huldigen (*hool*-di-gern) *v* honour

Huldigung (*hool*-di-goong) *f* (pl ~en) tribute, homage

Hülle (*hew*-ler) *f* (pl ~n) sleeve

Hummer (*hoo*-merr) *m* (pl ~) lobster

Humor (hoo-*mōar*) *m* humour

humorvoll (hoo-*mōar*-fol) *adj* humorous

Hund (hoont) *m* (pl ~e) dog

Hundehütte (*hoon*-der-hew-ter) *f* (pl ~n) kennel

hundert (*hoon*-derrt) *num* hundred

Hundezwinger (*hoon*-der-tsving-err) *m* (pl ~) kennel

Hündin (*hewn*-din) *f* (pl ~nen) bitch

Hunger (*hoong*-err) *m* hunger

hungrig (*hoong*-rikh) *adj* hungry

Hupe (*hōō*-per) *f* (pl ~n) hooter; horn

hupen (*hōō*-pern) *v* hoot; toot *vAm*, honk *vAm*

Hupf (hoopf) *m* (pl ~e) hop

hüpfen (*hew*-pfern) *v* hop, skip

Hure (*hōō*-rer) *f* (pl ~n) whore

Husten (*hōōss*-tern) *m* cough

husten (*hōōss*-tern) *v* cough

Hut (hōōt) *m* (pl ~e) hat

sich hüten (*hew*-tern) beware

Hütte (*hew*-ter) *f* (pl ~n) cabin, hut

Hygiene (hew-gʸ*ay*-ner) *f* hygiene

hygienisch (hew-gʸ*ay*-nish) *adj* hygienic

Hymne (*hewm*-ner) *f* (pl ~n) hymn

hypokritisch (hew-poa-*kree*-tish) *adj* hypocritical

Hypothek (hew-poa-*tāyk*) *f* (pl ~en) mortgage

hysterisch (hewss-*tāy*-rish) *adj* hysterical

I

ich (ikh) *pron* I

ichbezogen (*ikh*-ber-tsōa-gern) *adj* self-centred

Ideal (i-day-*aal*) *nt* (pl ~e) ideal

ideal (i-day-*aal*) *adj* ideal

Idee (i-*dāy*) *f* (pl ~n) idea

identifizieren (i-dehn-ti-fi-*tsee*-rern) *v* identify

Identifizierung (i-dehn-ti-fi-*tsee*-roong) *f* (pl ~en) identification

identisch (i-*dehn*-tish) *adj* identical

Identität (i-dehn-ti-*tait*) *f* identity

Idiom (i-dʸ*ōam*) *nt* (pl ~e) idiom

idiomatisch (i-dʸoa-*maa*-tish) *adj* idiomatic

Idiot (i-dʸ*ōat*) *m* (pl ~en) idiot

Idol (i-*dōal*) *nt* (pl ~e) idol

Igel (*ee*-gerl) *m* (pl ~) hedgehog

ignorieren (i-gnoa-*ree*-rern) *v* ignore

ihm (eem) *pron* him

ihn (een) *pron* him

Ihnen (*ee*-nern) *pron* you

ihnen (*ee*-nern) *pron* them

Ihr (eer) *pron* your

ihr (eer) *pron* you; their; her; her

Ikone (i-*kōa*-ner) *f* (pl ~n) icon

illegal (*i*-lay-gaal) *adj* illegal

Illusion (i-loo-zʸ*ōan*) *f* (pl ~en) illusion

Illustration (i-looss-trah-*tsʸōan*) *f* (pl ~en) illustration

illustrieren (i-looss-*tree*-rern) *v* illustrate

imaginär (i-mah-gi-*nair*) *adj* imaginary

Imbiß (*im*-biss) *m* (pl Imbisse) lunch; snack

Imitation (i-mi-tah-*tsʸōan*) *f* (pl ~en) imitation

immer (*i*-merr) *adv* always; ever; ~ **wieder** again and again

immerzu (i-merr-*tsōō*) *adv* all the time

immunisieren (i-mōō-ni-*zee*-rern) *v* immunize

Immunität (i-mōō-ni-*tait*) *f* immunity

impfen (*im*-pfern) *v* vaccinate, inoculate

Impfung (*im*-pfoong) *f* (pl ~en) vaccination, inoculation

imponieren (im-poa-*nee*-rern) *v* impress

Import (im-*port*) *m* import

Importeur (im-por-*tūrr*) *m* (pl ~e) importer

importieren (im-por-*tee*-rern) *v* import

imposant (im-poa-*zahnt*) *adj* imposing

impotent (*im*-poa-tehnt) *adj* impotent

Impotenz (*im*-poa-tehnts) *f* impotence

improvisieren (im-proa-vi-*zee*-rern) *v*

improvise

Impuls (im-*pools*) *m* (pl ~e) impulse, urge

impulsiv (im-pool-*zeef*) *adj* impulsive

imstande (im-*shtahn*-der) *adv* able; ~ *sein zu* *be able to

in (in) *prep* in; at, into, inside

indem (in-*dáym*) *conj* whilst

Inder (*in*-derr) *m* (pl ~) Indian

Index (*in*-dehks) *m* (pl ~e) index

Indianer (in-*d*ʸ*aa*-nerr) *m* (pl ~) Indian

indianisch (in-*d*ʸ*aa*-nish) *adj* Indian

Indien (*in*-dʸern) India

indirekt (*in*-di-rehkt) *adj* indirect

indisch (*in*-dish) *adj* Indian

individuell (in-di-vi-doo-*ehl*) *adj* individual

Individuum (in-di-*vee*-doo-oom) *nt* (pl -duen) individual

Indonesien (in-doa-*nay*-zʸern) Indonesia

Indonesier (in-doa-*nay*-zʸerr) *m* (pl ~) Indonesian

indonesisch (in-doa-*nay*-zish) *adj* Indonesian

indossieren (in-do-*see*-rern) *v* endorse

Industrie (in-dooss-*tree*) *f* (pl ~n) industry

Industriegebiet (in-dooss-*tree*-ger-beet) *nt* (pl ~e) industrial area

industriell (in-dooss-tri-*ehl*) *adj* industrial

Infanterie (in-fahn-ter-*ree*) *f* infantry

Infektion (in-fehk-tsʸ*oan*) *f* (pl ~en) infection

Infinitiv (*in*-fi-ni-teef) *m* (pl ~e) infinitive

Inflation (in-flah-tsʸ*oan*) *f* inflation

infolge (in-*fol*-ger) *prep* owing to

informell (in-for-*mehl*) *adj* informal

informieren (in-for-*mee*-rern) *v* inform

infrarot (*in*-frah-rōat) *adj* infra-red

Ingenieur (in-zhay-nʸ*ūrr*) *m* (pl ~e) engineer

Ingwer (*ing*-verr) *m* ginger

Inhaber (*in*-haa-berr) *m* (pl ~) occupant; bearer

inhaftieren (in-hahf-*tee*-rern) *v* imprison

Inhalt (*in*-hahlt) *m* contents *pl*

Inhaltsverzeichnis (*in*-hahlts-fehr-tsighkh-niss) *nt* (pl ~se) table of contents

Initiative (i-ni-tsʸah-*tee*-ver) *f* initiative

Injektion (in-ʸehk-tsʸ*oan*) *f* (pl ~en) injection

inländisch (*in*-lehn-dish) *adj* domestic

inmitten (in-*mi*-tern) *prep* among, amid

innen (*i*-nern) *adv* inside

Innenseite (*i*-nern-zigh-ter) *f* (pl ~n) inside

inner (*i*-nerr) *adj* inside; internal

Innere (*i*-ner-rer) *nt* interior; *im Innern* within, inside

innerhalb (*i*-nerr-hahlp) *prep* within, inside

Inschrift (*in*-shrift) *f* (pl ~en) inscription

Insekt (in-*zehkt*) *nt* (pl ~en) insect; bug *nAm*

Insektengift (in-*zehk*-tern-gift) *nt* (pl ~e) insecticide

Insektenschutzmittel (in-*zehk*-tern-shoots-mi-terl) *nt* (pl ~) insect repellent

Insel (*in*-zerl) *f* (pl ~n) island

insgesamt (ins-ger-*zahmt*) *adv* altogether

Inspektion (in-spehk-tsʸ*oan*) *f* (pl ~en) inspection

inspizieren (in-spi-*tsee*-rern) *v* inspect

Installateur (in-stah-lah-*tūrr*) *m* (pl ~e) plumber

installieren (in-stah-*lee*-rern) *v* install

Instandhaltung (in-*shtahnt*-hahl-toong)

f maintenance

Instandsetzung (in-*shtahnt*-zeh-tsoong) *f* repair

Instinkt (in-*stingkt*) *m* (pl ~e) instinct

Institut (in-sti-*tōōt*) *nt* (pl ~e) institute

Institution (in-sti-too-ts^y*ōān*) *f* (pl ~en) institution

Instrument (in-stroo-*mehnt*) *nt* (pl ~e) instrument

Intellekt (in-teh-*lehkt*) *m* intellect

intellektuell (in-teh-lehk-too-*ehl*) *adj* intellectual

intelligent (in-teh-li-*gehnt*) *adj* clever, intelligent

Intelligenz (in-teh-li-*gehnts*) *f* intelligence

intensiv (in-tehn-*zeef*) *adj* intense

interessant (in-tay-reh-*sahnt*) *adj* interesting

Interesse (in-tay-*reh*-ser) *nt* (pl ~n) interest

interessieren (in-tay-reh-*see*-rern) *v* interest

interessiert (in-tay-reh-*seert*) *adj* interested

intern (in-*tehrn*) *adj* internal; resident

Internat (in-tehr-*naat*) *nt* (pl ~e) boarding-school

international (in-tehr-nah-ts^yoa-*naal*) *adj* international

Intervall (in-tehr-*vahl*) *nt* (pl ~e) interval

Interview (in-tehr-*v^yōō*) *nt* (pl ~s) interview

intim (in-*teem*) *adj* intimate

Invalide (in-vah-*lee*-der) *m* (pl ~n) invalid

invalide (in-vah-*lee*-der) *adj* disabled, invalid

Invasion (in-vah-z^y*ōān*) *f* (pl ~en) invasion

Inventar (in-vehn-*taar*) *nt* (pl ~e) inventory

investieren (in-vehss-*tee*-rern) *v* invest

Investition (in-vehss-ti-ts^y*ōān*) *f* (pl ~en) investment

inwendig (*in*-vehn-dikh) *adj* inner

inzwischen (in-*tsvi*-shern) *adv* in the meantime, meanwhile

Irak (i-*raak*) Iraq

irakisch (i-*raa*-kish) *adj* Iraqi

Iran (i-*raan*) Iran

Iranier (i-*raa*-n^yerr) *m* (pl ~) Iranian

iranisch (i-*raa*-nish) *adj* Iranian

Ire (*ee*-rer) *m* (pl ~n) Irishman

irgendein (*eer*-gernt-ighn) *adj* any

irgendwie (*eer*-gernt-vee) *adv* anyhow

irgendwo (*eer*-gernt-vōā) *adv* somewhere

irisch (*ee*-rish) *adj* Irish

Irland (*eer*-lahnt) Ireland

Ironie (i-roa-*nee*) *f* irony

ironisch (i-*rōā*-nish) *adj* ironical

Irre (*i*-rer) *m* (pl ~n) lunatic

irre (*i*-rer) *adj* mad

irreal (*i*-ray-aal) *adj* unreal

irren (*i*-rern) *v* err; **sich ~** *be mistaken

irreparabel (i-reh-pah-*raa*-berl) *adj* irreparable

Irrgarten (*eer*-gahr-tern) *m* (pl ~̈) maze

irritieren (i-ri-*tee*-rern) *v* annoy, irritate

Irrsinn (*eer*-zin) *m* lunacy

irrsinnig (*eer*-zi-nikh) *adj* lunatic

Irrtum (*eer*-tōōm) *m* (pl ~̈er) error, mistake

Island (*eess*-lahnt) Iceland

Isländer (*eess*-lehn-derr) *m* (pl ~) Icelander

isländisch (*eess*-lehn-dish) *adj* Icelandic

Isolation (i-zoa-lah-ts^y*ōān*) *f* (pl ~en) isolation; insulation

Isolator (i-zoa-*laa*-tor) *m* (pl ~en) insulator

isolieren (i-zoa-*lee*-rern) *v* isolate; insulate

Isolierung (i-zoa-*lee*-roong) *f* (pl ~en) isolation

Israel (*iss*-rah-ehl) Israel

Israeli (iss-rah-*ā̄y̆*-li) *m* (pl ~s) Israeli

israelisch (iss-rah-*ā̄y̆*-lish) *adj* Israeli

Italien (i-*taa*-l Yern) Italy

Italiener (i-tah-*l Yā̄y̆*-nerr) *m* (pl ~) Italian

italienisch (i-tah-*l Yā̄y̆*-nish) *adj* Italian

J

ja (Yaa) yes

Jacht (Yahkht) *f* (pl ~en) yacht

Jacke (Yah-ker) *f* (pl ~n) jacket

Jackett (zhah-*kehrt*) *nt* (pl ~s) jacket

Jade (Yaa-der) *m* jade

Jagd (Yaakt) *f* hunt, chase

Jagdhaus (Yaakt-houss) *nt* (pl ~er) lodge

jagen (Yaa-gern) *v* hunt

Jäger (Yai-gerr) *m* (pl ~) hunter

Jahr (Yaar) *nt* (pl ~e) year

Jahrbuch (Yaar-bōōkh) *nt* (pl ~er) annual

Jahrestag (Yaa-rerss-taak) *m* (pl ~e) anniversary

Jahreszeit (Yaa-rerss-tsight) *f* (pl ~en) season

Jahrhundert (Yaar-*hoon*-derrt) *nt* (pl ~e) century

jährlich (Yair-likh) *adj* yearly, annual; *adv* per annum

jähzornig (Yai-tsor-nikh) *adj* hot-tempered, irascible

Jalousie (zhah-loo-*zee*) *f* (pl ~n) blind; shutter

Jammer (Yah-merr) *m* misery

jämmerlich (Yeh-merr-likh) *adj* lamentable

Januar (Yah-noo-aar) January

Japan (Yaa-pahn) Japan

Japaner (Yah-*paa*-nerr) *m* (pl ~) Japanese

japanisch (Yah-*paa*-nish) *adj* Japanese

je ... je (Yā̄y̆) the ... the

jedenfalls (Yā̄y̆-dern-fahls) *adv* at any rate

jeder (Yā̄y̆-derr) *pron* each, every; everyone

jedermann (Yā̄y̆-derr-mahn) *pron* everyone, everybody; anyone

jedoch (Yay-*dokh*) *conj* yet, but, only, however; *adv* though

jemals (Yā̄y̆-maals) *adv* ever

jemand (Yā̄y̆-mahnt) *pron* someone, somebody; **irgend** ~ anybody

jene (Yā̄y̆-ner) *pron* those; those

jener (Yā̄y̆-nerr) *pron* that; that

jenseits (Yā̄y̆n-zights) *prep* across, beyond; *adv* beyond

Jersey (jurr-si) *m* (pl ~s) jersey

jetzt (Yehtst) *adv* now; **bis** ~ so far

jeweilig (Yā̄y̆-vigh-likh) *adj* respective

Joch (Yokh) *nt* (pl ~e) yoke

Jockei (jo-ki) *m* (pl ~s) jockey

Jod (Yōat) *nt* iodine

Johannisbeere (Yoa-hah-niss-bā̄y̆-rer) *f* (pl ~n) black-currant

Jolle (Yo-ler) *f* (pl ~n) dinghy

Jordanien (Yor-*daa*-n Yern) Jordan

Jordanier (Yor-*daa*-n Yerr) *m* (pl ~) Jordanian

jordanisch (Yor-*daa*-nish) *adj* Jordanian

Journalismus (zhoor-nah-*liss*-mooss) *m* journalism

Journalist (zhoor-nah-*list*) *m* (pl ~en) journalist

Jubiläum (Yoo-bi-*lai*-oom) *nt* (pl -läen) jubilee

Jucken (Yoo-kern) *nt* itch

jucken (Yoo-kern) *v* itch

Jude (Yōō-der) *m* (pl ~n) Jew

jüdisch (ᵞeᵂ-dish) adj Jewish

Jugend (ᵞoͦo-gernt) f youth

Jugendherberge (ᵞoͦo-gernt-hehr-behr-ger) f (pl ~n) youth hostel

jugendlich (ᵞoͦo-gernt-likh) adj juvenile

Jugoslawe (ᵞoo-goa-slaa-ver) m (pl ~n) Yugoslav, Jugoslav

Jugoslawien (ᵞoo-goa-slaa-vᵞern) Yugoslavia, Jugoslavia

jugoslawisch (ᵞoo-goa-slaa-vish) adj Jugoslav

Juli (ᵞoͦo-li) July

Jumper (jahm-perr) m (pl ~) jumper

jung (ᵞoong) adj young

Junge (ᵞoong-er) m (pl ~n) boy; lad

Jungfrau (ᵞoongk-frou) f (pl ~en) virgin

Junggeselle (ᵞoong-ger-zeh-ler) m (pl ~n) bachelor

Juni (ᵞoͦo-ni) June

Jurist (ᵞoo-rist) m (pl ~en) lawyer

Juwel (ᵞoo-vaᵞl) nt (pl ~en) jewel; gem

Juwelier (ᵞoo-vay-leer) m (pl ~e) jeweller

K

Kabarett (kah-bah-reht) nt (pl ~e) cabaret; revue, floor show

Kabel (kaa-berl) nt (pl ~) cable; flex; electric cord

Kabeljau (kaa-berl-ᵞou) m (pl ~e) cod

Kabine (kah-bee-ner) f (pl ~n) cabin

Kabinett (kah-bi-neht) nt (pl ~e) cabinet

Kachel (kah-kherl) f (pl ~n) tile

Kader (kaa-derr) m (pl ~) cadre

Käfer (kai-ferr) m (pl ~) beetle; bug

Kaffee (kah-fay) m coffee

Kaffeemaschine (kah-fay-mah-shee-ner) f (pl ~n) percolator

Käfig (kai-fikh) m (pl ~e) cage

kahl (kaal) adj bald; naked, bare

Kai (kigh) m (pl ~s) dock, wharf, quay

Kaiser (kigh-zerr) m (pl ~) emperor

Kaiserin (kigh-zer-rin) f (pl ~nen) empress

kaiserlich (kigh-zerr-likh) adj imperial

Kaiserreich (kigh-zerr-righkh) nt (pl ~e) empire

Kajüte (kah-ᵞeᵂ-ter) f (pl ~n) cabin

Kalamität (kah-lah-mi-tait) f (pl ~en) calamity

Kalb (kahlp) nt (pl ~̈er) calf

Kalbfleisch (kahlp-flighsh) nt veal

Kalbleder (kahlp-lāy-derr) nt calf skin

Kalender (kah-lehn-derr) m (pl ~) calendar

Kalk (kahlk) m lime

Kalkulation (kahl-koo-lah-tsᵞoͦan) f (pl ~en) calculation

Kalorie (kah-loa-ree) f (pl ~n) calorie

kalt (kahlt) adj cold

Kälte (kehl-ter) f cold

Kalvinismus (kahl-vi-niss-mooss) m Calvinism

Kalzium (kahl-tsᵞoom) nt calcium

Kamee (kah-māy) f (pl ~n) cameo

Kamel (kah-māyl) nt (pl ~e) camel

Kamera (kah-may-rah) f (pl ~s) camera

Kamin (kah-meen) m (pl ~e) fireplace

Kamm (kahm) m (pl ~̈e) comb

kämmen (keh-mern) v comb

Kammgarn (kahm-gahrn) nt worsted

Kampagne (kahm-pah-nᵞer) f (pl ~n) campaign

Kampf (kahmpf) m (pl ~̈e) battle; combat, struggle, fight

kämpfen (kehm-pfern) v *fight; combat, struggle, battle

Kanada (kah-nah-dah) Canada

Kanadier (kah-naa-dᵞerr) m (pl ~) Canadian

kanadisch (kah-*naa*-dish) *adj* Canadian

Kanal (kah-*naal*) *m* (pl ~e) canal; channel

Kanarienvogel (kah-*naa*-rʸern-fōa-gerl) *m* (pl ~) canary

Kandidat (kahn-di-*daat*) *m* (pl ~en) candidate

Känguruh (kehng-goo-roo) *nt* (pl ~s) kangaroo

Kaninchen (kah-*neen*-khern) *nt* (pl ~) rabbit

Kanone (kah-*nōa*-ner) *f* (pl ~n) gun

Kante (*kahn*-ter) *f* (pl ~n) edge

Kantine (kahn-*tee*-ner) *f* (pl ~n) canteen

Kanu (kah-*nōō*) *nt* (pl ~s) canoe

Kanzel (*kahn*-tserl) *f* (pl ~n) pulpit

Kap (kahp) *nt* (pl ~s) cape

Kapelle (kah-*peh*-ler) *f* (pl ~n) band; chapel

Kaper (*kaa*-perr) *m* (pl ~) hijacker

kapern (*kaa*-perrn) *v* hijack

Kapital (kah-pi-*taal*) *nt* capital

Kapitalgeber (kah-pi-*taal*-gāy-berr) *m* (pl ~) investor

Kapitalismus (kah-pi-tah-*liss*-mooss) *m* capitalism

Kapitän (kah-pi-*tain*) *m* (pl ~e) captain

Kapitulation (kah-pi-too-lah-tsʸ*ōan*) *f* (pl ~en) capitulation

Kaplan (kah-*plaan*) *m* (pl ~e) chaplain

Kapsel (*kah*-pserl) *f* (pl ~n) capsule

kaputt (kah-*poot*) *adj* broken

Kapuze (kah-*pōō*-tser) *f* (pl ~n) hood

Karaffe (kah-*rah*-fer) *f* (pl ~n) carafe

Karamelle (kah-rah-*meh*-ler) *f* (pl ~n) caramel

Karat (kah-*raat*) *nt* carat

Kardinal (kahr-di-*naal*) *m* (pl ~e) cardinal; **Kardinal-** cardinal

kariert (kah-*reert*) *adj* chequered

karmesinrot (kahr-may-*zeen*-rōat) *adj* crimson

Karneval (*kahr*-ner-vahl) *m* carnival

Karo (*kaa*-roa) *nt* (pl ~s) check

Karosserie (kah-ro-ser-*ree*) *f* (pl ~n) coachwork; motor body *Am*

Karotte (kah-*ro*-ter) *f* (pl ~n) carrot

Karpfen (*kahr*-pfern) *m* (pl ~) carp

Karren (*kah*-rern) *m* (pl ~) cart

Karriere (kah-rʸ*āy*-rer) *f* (pl ~n) career

Karte (kahr-ter) *f* (pl ~n) card; map; ticket

Kartoffel (kahr-*to*-ferl) *f* (pl ~n) potato

Karton (kahr-*tawng*) *m* (pl ~s) carton

Karussell (kah-roo-*sehl*) *nt* (pl ~s) merry-go-round

Kaschmir (*kahsh*-meer) *m* cashmere

Käse (*kai*-zer) *m* cheese

Kaserne (kah-*zehr*-ner) *f* (pl ~n) barracks *pl*

Kasino (kah-*zee*-noa) *nt* (pl ~s) casino

Kasperletheater (*kahss*-perr-ler-tay-*aa*-terr) *nt* (pl ~) puppet-show

Kasse (*kah*-ser) *f* (pl ~n) pay-desk; box-office

Kassierer (kah-*see*-rerr) *m* (pl ~) cashier

Kassiererin (kah-*see*-rer-rin) *f* (pl ~nen) cashier

Kastanie (kahss-*taa*-nʸer) *f* (pl ~n) chestnut

kastanienbraun (kahss-*taa*-nʸern-broun) *adj* auburn

Katakombe (kah-tah-*kom*-ber) *f* (pl ~n) catacomb

Katalog (kah-tah-*lōak*) *m* (pl ~e) catalogue

Katarrh (kah-*tahr*) *m* (pl ~e) catarrh

Katastrophe (kah-tahss-*trōa*-fer) *f* (pl ~n) catastrophe, disaster

Kategorie (kah-tay-goa-*ree*) *f* (pl ~n) category

Kater (*kaa*-terr) *m* hangover

Kathedrale (kah-tay-*draa*-ler) *f* (pl ~n) cathedral

katholisch (kah-*tōā*-lish) *adj* catholic

Katze (*kah*-tser) *f* (pl ~n) cat; pussy-cat

kauen (*kou*-ern) *v* chew

Kauf (kouf) *m* (pl ~̈e) purchase

kaufen (*kou*-fern) *v* *buy; purchase

Käufer (*koi*-ferr) *m* (pl ~) buyer, purchaser

Kaufhaus (*kouf*-houss) *nt* (pl ~̈er) department store

Kaufmann (*kouf*-mahn) *m* (pl -leute) dealer; merchant

Kaufpreis (*kouf*-prighss) *m* (pl ~e) purchase price

Kaugummi (*kou*-goo-mi) *m* chewing-gum

kaum (koum) *adv* hardly, scarcely, barely

Kaution (kou-*tsⁱōān*) *f* (pl ~en) bail

Kaviar (*kaa*-vi-ahr) *m* caviar

Kegelbahn (*kāy*-gerl-baan) *f* (pl ~en) bowling alley

Kegeln (*kāy*-gerln) *nt* bowling

Kehle (*kāy*-ler) *f* (pl ~n) throat

kehren (*kāy*-rern) *v* turn

Kehrseite (*kāyr*-zigh-ter) *f* (pl ~n) reverse

Keil (kighl) *m* (pl ~e) wedge

Keim (kighm) *m* (pl ~e) germ

kein (kighn) *pron* no

keiner (*kigh*-nerr) *pron* none; ~ **von beiden** neither

keinesfalls (*kigh*-nerss-fahls) *adv* by no means

keineswegs (*kigh*-nerss-vāyks) *adv* by no means

Keks (kāyks) *m* (pl ~e) biscuit; cookie *nAm*; cracker *nAm*

Keller (*keh*-lerr) *m* (pl ~) cellar

Kellermeister (*keh*-lerr-mighss-terr) *m* (pl ~) wine-waiter

Kellner (*kehl*-nerr) *m* (pl ~) waiter; bartender, barman

Kellnerin (*kehl*-ner-rin) *f* (pl ~nen) waitress

Kenia (*kāy*-nⁱah) Kenya

***kennen** (*keh*-nern) *v* *know

Kenner (*keh*-nerr) *m* (pl ~) connoisseur

Kenntnis (*kehnt*-niss) *f* (pl ~se) knowledge

Kennzeichen (*kehn*-tsigh-khern) *nt* (pl ~) characteristic, feature; registration number; licence number *Am*

kennzeichnen (*kehn*-tsighkh-nern) *v* mark

Keramik (kay-*raa*-mik) *f* (pl ~en) ceramics *pl*

Kerl (kehrl) *m* (pl ~e) chap, fellow

Kern (kehrn) *m* (pl ~e) essence; heart, core; pip, stone; nucleus; **Kern-** nuclear

Kernenergie (*kehrn*-ay-nehr-gee) *f* nuclear energy

Kerngehäuse (*kehrn*-ger-hoi-zer) *nt* (pl ~) core

Kerosin (kay-roa-*zeen*) *nt* kerosene

Kerze (*kehr*-tser) *f* (pl ~n) candle

Kessel (*keh*-serl) *m* (pl ~) kettle

Kette (*keh*-ter) *f* (pl ~n) chain

keuchen (*koi*-khern) *v* pant

Keule (*koi*-ler) *f* (pl ~n) club

keusch (koish) *adj* chaste

Khaki (*kaa*-ki) *nt* khaki

kichern (*ki*-kherrn) *v* giggle, chuckle

Kiebitz (*kee*-bits) *m* (pl ~e) pewit

Kiefer (*kee*-ferr) *m* (pl ~) jaw

Kiel (keel) *m* (pl ~e) keel

Kieme (*kee*-mer) *f* (pl ~n) gill

Kies (keess) *m* gravel

Kieselstein (*kee*-zerl-shtighn) *m* (pl ~e) pebble

Kilo (*kee*-loa) *nt* (pl ~s) kilogram

Kilometer (ki-loa-*māy*-terr) *m* (pl ~) kilometre

Kilometerzahl (ki-loa-*māy*-terr-tsaal) *f*

distance in kilometres

Kind (kint) *nt* (pl ~er) child; kid; **kleines ~** tot

Kindergarten (*kin*-derr-gahr-tern) *m* (pl ~̈) kindergarten

Kinderkrippe (*kin*-derr-kri-per) *f* (pl ~n) nursery

Kinderlähmung (*kin*-derr-lai-moong) *f* polio

Kindermädchen (*kin*-derr-mait-khern) *nt* (pl ~) nurse

Kinderwagen (*kin*-derr-vaa-gern) *m* (pl ~) pram; baby carriage *Am*

Kinderzimmer (*kin*-derr-tsi-merr) *nt* (pl ~) nursery

Kinn (kin) *nt* chin

Kino (*kee*-noa) *nt* (pl ~s) cinema; pictures; movie theater *Am*, movies *Am*

Kiosk (ki-*osk*) *m* (pl ~e) kiosk

Kirche (*keer*-kher) *f* (pl ~n) chapel, church

Kirchhof (*keerkh*-hōāf) *m* (pl ~̈e) graveyard, churchyard

Kirchspiel (*keerkh*-shpeel) *nt* (pl ~e) parish

Kirchturm (*keerkh*-toorm) *m* (pl ~̈e) steeple

Kirmes (*keer*-mehss) *f* (pl ~sen) fair

Kirsche (*keer*-sher) *f* (pl ~n) cherry

Kissen (*ki*-sern) *nt* (pl ~) cushion; pillow

Kissenbezug (*ki*-sern-ber-tsōōk) *m* (pl ~̈e) pillow-case

Kiste (*kiss*-ter) *f* (pl ~n) crate

kitzeln (*ki*-tserln) *v* tickle

Klage (*klaa*-ger) *f* (pl ~n) complaint

klagen (*klaa*-gern) *v* complain

Klammer (*klah*-merr) *f* (pl ~n) clamp

Klang (klahng) *m* (pl ~̈e) sound; tone

Klaps (klahps) *m* (pl ~e) smack

klar (klaar) *adj* clear; pure; serene

klären (*klai*-rern) *v* clarify

klarstellen (*klaar*-shteh-lern) *v* clarify

Klasse (*klah*-ser) *f* (pl ~n) class; form

Klassenkamerad (*klah*-sern-kah-mer-raat) *m* (pl ~en) class-mate

Klassenzimmer (*klah*-sern-tsi-merr) *nt* (pl ~) classroom

klassisch (*klah*-sish) *adj* classical

klatschen (*klah*-chern) *v* clap

Klatschmohn (*klahch*-mōān) *m* (pl ~e) poppy

Klaue (*klou*-er) *f* (pl ~n) claw

Klausel (*klou*-zerl) *f* (pl ~n) clause, stipulation

Klavier (klah-*veer*) *nt* (pl ~e) piano

Klebealbum (*klāy*-ber-ahl-boom) *nt* (pl -alben) scrap-book

kleben (*klāy*-bern) *v* *stick; paste

Klebestreifen (*klāy*-ber-shtrigh-fern) *m* (pl ~) adhesive tape

klebrig (*klāy*-brikh) *adj* sticky

Klebstoff (*klāyp*-shtof) *m* (pl ~e) gum

Klecks (klehks) *m* (pl ~e) stain, spot, blot

Klee (klāy) *m* clover

Kleeblatt (*klāy*-blaht) *nt* (pl ~̈er) shamrock

Kleid (klight) *nt* (pl ~er) dress; frock, robe, gown; **Kleider** clothes *pl*

kleiden (*kligh*-dern) *v* suit; **sich ~** dress

Kleiderbügel (*kligh*-derr-bēw-gerl) *m* (pl ~) coat-hanger

Kleiderbürste (*kligh*-derr-bewrs-ter) *f* (pl ~n) clothes-brush

Kleiderhaken (*kligh*-derr-haa-kern) *m* (pl ~) peg

Kleiderschrank (*kligh*-derr-shrahngk) *m* (pl ~̈e) wardrobe

Kleidung (*kligh*-doong) *f* clothes *pl*

klein (klighn) *adj* little, small; minor, petty, short

Kleingeld (*klighn*-gehlt) *nt* petty cash, change

Kleinhandel (*klighn*-hahn-derl) *m* retail trade

Kleinhändler (*klighn*-hehn-dlerr) *m* (pl ~) retailer

Kleinkind (*klighn*-kint) *nt* (pl ~er) toddler

kleinlich (*klighn*-likh) *adj* stingy

Kleinod (*klighn*-ōat) *nt* (pl ~e) gem

Klemme (*kleh*-mer) *f* (pl ~n) clamp

klettern (*kleh*-terrn) *v* climb

Klient (kli-*ehnt*) *m* (pl ~en) customer, client

Klima (*klee*-mah) *nt* climate

Klimaanlage (*klee*-mah-ahn-laa-ger) *f* (pl ~n) air-conditioning

klimatisiert (kli-mah-ti-*zeert*) *adj* air-conditioned

Klinge (*kling*-er) *f* (pl ~n) blade

Klingel (*kling*-erl) *f* (pl ~n) bell

****klingen** (*kling*-ern) *v* sound

Klinik (*klee*-nik) *f* (pl ~en) clinic; hospital

Klippe (*kli*-per) *f* (pl ~n) cliff

Klopfen (*klo*-pfern) *nt* knock, tap

klopfen (*klo*-pfern) *v* knock

Kloster (*klōass*-terr) *nt* (pl ~̈) cloister; convent; monastery

Klotz (klots) *m* (pl ~̈e) block; log

Klub (kloop) *m* (pl ~s) club

klug (klōōk) *adj* bright, clever

Klumpen (*kloom*-pern) *m* (pl ~) chunk; lump

klumpig (*kloom*-pikh) *adj* lumpy

knapp (knahp) *adj* scarce; tight; concise

Knappheit (*knahp*-hight) *f* shortage

****kneifen** (*knigh*-fern) *v* pinch

Kneifzange (*knighf*-tsahng-er) *f* (pl ~n) pincers *pl*

Kneipe (*knigh*-per) *f* (pl ~n) pub

Knie (knee) *nt* (pl ~) knee

knien (*knee*-ern) *v* *kneel

Kniescheibe (*knee*-shigh-ber) *f* (pl ~n) kneecap

Kniff (knif) *m* (pl ~e) trick

knirschen (*kneer*-shern) *v* creak

Knoblauch (*knōāp*-loukh) *m* garlic

Knochen (*kno*-khern) *m* (pl ~) bone

Knopf (knopf) *m* (pl ~̈e) button; knob

knöpfen (*knur*-pfern) *v* button

Knopfloch (*knopf*-lokh) *nt* (pl ~̈er) buttonhole

Knorpel (*knor*-perl) *m* cartilage

Knospe (*knoss*-per) *f* (pl ~n) bud

Knoten (*knōā*-tern) *m* (pl ~) knot

knoten (*knōā*-tern) *v* knot, tie

Knotenpunkt (*knōā*-tern-poongkt) *m* (pl ~e) junction

knuffen (*knoo*-fern) *v* punch

Knüppel (*knew*-perl) *m* (pl ~) cudgel, club

knusprig (*knooss*-prikh) *adj* crisp

Koch (kokh) *m* (pl ~̈e) cook

Kochbuch (*kokh*-bōōkh) *nt* (pl ~̈er) cookery-book; cookbook *nAm*

kochen (*ko*-khern) *v* cook; boil

Kocher (*ko*-kherr) *m* (pl ~) cooker

Kode (kōāt) *m* (pl ~s) code

Köder (*kūr*-derr) *m* (pl ~) bait

Koffein (ko-fay-*een*) *nt* caffeine

koffeinfrei (ko-fay-*een*-frigh) *adj* decaffeinated

Koffer (*ko*-ferr) *m* (pl ~) case, bag; trunk

Kofferraum (*ko*-ferr-roum) *m* (pl ~̈e) boot; trunk *nAm*

Kognak (*ko*-nᵞahk) *m* cognac

Kohl (kōāl) *m* cabbage

Kohle (*kōā*-ler) *f* (pl ~n) coal

Kohlepapier (*kōā*-ler-pah-peer) *nt* carbon paper

Koje (*kōā*-Yer) *f* (pl ~n) bunk, berth

Kokain (koa-kah-*een*) *nt* cocaine

Kokosnuß (*kōā*-koss-nooss) *f* (pl -nüsse) coconut

Kolben (*kol*-bern) *m* (pl ~) piston

Kolbenring (*kol*-bern-ring) *m* (pl ~e) piston ring

Kolbenstange (*kol*-bern-shtahng-er) *f*

(pl ~n) piston-rod

Kollege (ko-*lāy*-ger) *m* (pl ~n) colleague

Kollekteur (ko-lehk-*tūr*) *m* (pl ~e) collector

Kollektion (ko-lehk-tsʸ*ōān*) *f* (pl ~en) collection

kollektiv (ko-lehk-*teef*) *adj* collective

Kolonie (koa-loa-*nee*) *f* (pl ~n) colony

Kolonne (koa-*lo*-ner) *f* (pl ~n) column

Kolumbianer (koa-loom-*bʸaa*-nerr) *m* (pl ~) Colombian

kolumbianisch (koa-loom-*bʸaa*-nish) *adj* Colombian

Kolumbien (koa-*loom*-bʸern) Colombia

Koma (*kōā*-mah) *nt* coma

Kombination (kom-bi-nah-tsʸ*ōān*) *f* (pl ~en) combination

kombinieren (kom-bi-*nee*-rern) *v* combine

Komfort (kom-*fōar*) *m* comfort

Komiker (*kōā*-mi-kerr) *m* (pl ~) comedian

komisch (*kōā*-mish) *adj* funny, comic; strange, queer

Komma (*ko*-mah) *nt* (pl ~ta) comma

*****kommen** (*ko*-mern) *v* *come; ~ *lassen** *send for

Kommentar (ko-mehn-*taar*) *m* (pl ~e) comment

kommentieren (ko-mehn-*tee*-rern) *v* comment

kommerziell (ko-mehr-tsʸ*ehl*) *adj* commercial

Kommission (ko-mi-sʸ*ōān*) *f* (pl ~en) commission; committee

Kommode (ko-*mōā*-der) *f* (pl ~n) bureau *nAm*; chest of drawers

Kommune (ko-*mōō*-ner) *f* (pl ~n) commune

Kommunikation (ko-moo-ni-kah-tsʸ*ōān*) *f* communication

Kommunismus (ko-moo-*niss*-mooss)

m communism

Kommunist (ko-moo-*nist*) *m* (pl ~en) communist

Komödie (ko-*mūr*-dʸer) *f* (pl ~n) comedy

kompakt (kom-*pahkt*) *adj* compact

Kompaß (*kom*-pahss) *m* (pl -passe) compass

Kompetenz (kom-pay-*tehnts*) *f* (pl ~en) capacity

Komplex (kom-*plehks*) *m* (pl ~e) complex

Kompliment (kom-pli-*mehnt*) *nt* (pl ~e) compliment

kompliziert (kom-pli-*tseert*) *adj* complicated

Komplott (kom-*plot*) *nt* (pl ~e) plot, intrigue

Komponist (kom-poa-*nist*) *m* (pl ~en) composer

Komposition (kom-poa-zi-tsʸ*ōān*) *f* (pl ~en) composition

Konditor (kon-*dee*-tor) *m* (pl ~en) confectioner

Konditorei (kon-di-toa-*righ*) *f* (pl ~en) pastry shop

Konferenz (kon-fay-*rehnts*) *f* (pl ~en) conference

Konflikt (kon-*flikt*) *m* (pl ~e) conflict

Kongreß (kon-*grehss*) *m* (pl -gresse) congress

König (*kūr*-nikh) *m* (pl ~e) king

Königin (*kūr*-ni-gin) *f* (pl ~nen) queen

königlich (*kūr*-nik-likh) *adj* royal

Königreich (*kūr*-nik-righkh) *nt* (pl ~e) kingdom

konkret (kon-*krait*) *adj* concrete

Konkurrent (kon-koo-*rehnt*) *m* (pl ~en) competitor; rival

Konkurrenz (kon-koo-*rehnts*) *f* competition; rivalry

*****können** (*kur*-nern) *v* *can; *be able to; *might

konservativ (kon-zehr-vah-*teef*) *adj*

conservative

Konservatorium (kon-zehr-vah-*tōā*-r^yoom) *f* (pl -rien) music academy

Konserven (kon-*zehr*-vern) *fpl* tinned food

Konstruktion (kon-strook-*ts^yōān*) *f* (pl ~en) construction

Konsul (*kon*-zool) *m* (pl ~n) consul

Konsulat (kon-zoo-*laat*) *nt* (pl ~e) consulate

Konsultation (kon-zool-tah-*ts^yōān*) *f* (pl ~en) consultation

konsultieren (kon-zool-*tee*-rern) *v* consult

Konsument (kon-zoo-*mehnt*) *m* (pl ~en) consumer

Kontakt (kon-*tahkt*) *m* (pl ~e) touch, contact

Kontaktlinsen (kon-*tahkt*-lin-zern) *fpl* contact lenses

Kontinent (kon-ti-*nehnt*) *m* (pl ~e) continent

kontinental (kon-ti-nehn-*taal*) *adj* continental

Konto (*kon*-toa) *nt* (pl -ten) account

Kontrast (kon-*trahst*) *m* (pl ~e) contrast

Kontrollabschnitt (kon-*trol*-ahp-shnit) *m* (pl ~e) counterfoil, stub

Kontrolle (kon-*tro*-ler) *f* (pl ~n) control, inspection; supervision

kontrollieren (kon-troa-*lee*-rern) *v* control, check

konvertieren (kon-vehr-*tee*-rern) *v* convert

Konzentration (kon-tsehn-trah-*ts^yōān*) *f* (pl ~en) concentration

konzentrieren (kon-tsehn-*tree*-rern) *v* concentrate

Konzern (kon-*tsehrn*) *m* (pl ~e) concern

Konzert (kon-*tsehrt*) *nt* (pl ~e) concert

Konzertsaal (kon-*tsehrt*-zaal) *m* (pl -säle) concert hall

Konzession (kon-tseh-*s^yōān*) *f* (pl ~en) concession; licence, permission

konzessionieren (kon-tseh-s^yoa-*nee*-rern) *v* license

kooperativ (koa-oa-pay-rah-*teef*) *adj* co-operative

koordinieren (koa-or-di-*nee*-rern) *v* co-ordinate

Koordinierung (koa-or-di-*nee*-roong) *f* co-ordination

Kopf (kopf) *m* (pl ~̈e) head

Kopfkissen (*kopf*-ki-sern) *nt* (pl ~) pillow

Kopfschmerzen (*kopf*-shmehr-tsern) *mpl* headache

Kopie (koa-*pee*) *f* (pl ~n) copy

kopieren (koa-*pee*-rern) *v* copy

Koralle (koa-*rah*-ler) *f* (pl ~n) coral

Korb (korp) *m* (pl ~̈e) basket

Kordel (*kor*-derl) *f* (pl ~n) tape

Kordsamt (*kort*-zahmt) *m* corduroy

Korinthe (koa-*rin*-ter) *f* (pl ~n) currant

Korken (*kor*-kern) *m* (pl ~) cork

Korkenzieher (*kor*-kern-tsee-err) *m* (pl ~) corkscrew

Korn (korn) *nt* (pl ~̈er) corn, grain

Kornfeld (*korn*-fehlt) *nt* (pl ~er) cornfield

Körper (*kurr*-perr) *m* (pl ~) body

körperbehindert (*kurr*-perr-ber-hin-derrt) *adj* disabled

korpulent (kor-poo-*lehnt*) *adj* corpulent, stout

korrekt (ko-*rehkt*) *adj* correct

Korrespondent (ko-rehss-pon-*dehnt*) *m* (pl ~en) correspondent

Korrespondenz (ko-rehss-pon-*dehnts*) *f* correspondence

korrespondieren (ko-rehss-pon-*dee*-rern) *v* correspond

korrigieren (ko-ri-*gee*-rern) *v* correct

korrupt (ko-*roopt*) *adj* corrupt

Korsett (kor-*zeht*) *nt* (pl ~s) corset

Kosmetika (koss-*máy*-ti-kah) *ntpl* cosmetics *pl*

Kost (kost) *f* fare; food

kostbar (*kost*-baar) *adj* expensive, valuable

Kosten (*koss*-tern) *pl* cost

kosten (*koss*-tern) *v* *cost; taste

kostenlos (*koss*-tern-lōass) *adj* free of charge

Kostgänger (*kost*-gehng-err) *m* (pl ~) boarder

köstlich (*kurst*-likh) *adj* delicious; delightful

kostspielig (*kost*-shpee-likh) *adj* expensive

Kotelett (kot-*leht*) *nt* (pl ~e) cutlet, chop; **Koteletten** sideburns *pl*

Kotflügel (*kōat*-flēw-gerl) *m* (pl ~) mud-guard

Krabbe (*krah*-ber) *f* (pl ~n) crab; prawn

Krach (krahkh) *m* (pl ~e) noise; row

Krachen (*krah*-khern) *nt* crack

krachen (*krah*-khern) *v* crack

Kraft (krahft) *f* (pl ~e) force, strength; power; energy

Kraftfahrer (*krahft*-faa-rerr) *m* (pl ~) motorist

kräftig (*krehf*-tikh) *adj* strong

Kraftwagen (*krahft*-vaa-gern) *m* (pl ~) motor-car

Kraftwerk (*krahft*-vehrk) *nt* (pl ~e) power-station

Kragen (*kraa*-gern) *m* (pl ~) collar

Kragenknopf (*kraa*-gern-knopf) *m* (pl ~e) collar stud

Krähe (*krai*-er) *f* (pl ~n) crow

Krampf (krahmpf) *m* (pl ~e) convulsion; cramp

Krampfader (*krahmpf*-aa-derr) *f* (pl ~n) varicose vein

Kran (kraan) *m* (pl ~e) crane

krank (krahngk) *adj* sick, ill

kränken (*krehng*-kern) *v* offend, *hurt, injure

Krankenhaus (*krahng*-kern-houss) *nt* (pl ~er) hospital

Krankensaal (*krahng*-kern-zaal) *m* (pl -säle) infirmary

Krankenschwester (*krahng*-kern-shvehss-terr) *f* (pl ~n) nurse

Krankenwagen (*krahng*-kern-vaa-gern) *m* (pl ~) ambulance

Krankheit (*krahngk*-hight) *f* (pl ~en) sickness, illness, disease; ailment

Krater (*kraa*-terr) *m* (pl ~) crater

kratzen (*krah*-tsern) *v* scratch

Kratzer (*krah*-tserr) *m* (pl ~) scratch

Kraul (kroul) *m* crawl

Kraut (krout) *nt* (pl ~er) herb

Krawatte (krah-*vah*-ter) *f* (pl ~n) necktie, tie

Krebs (krāyps) *m* cancer

Kredit (kray-*deet*) *m* (pl ~e) credit

kreditieren (kray-di-*tee*-rern) *v* credit

Kreditkarte (kray-*deet*-kahr-ter) *f* (pl ~n) credit card; charge plate *Am*

Kreide (*krigh*-der) *f* chalk

Kreis (krighss) *m* (pl ~e) circle; ring, sphere

kreischen (*krigh*-shern) *v* shriek, scream

Kreislauf (*krighss*-louf) *m* circulation; cycle

Krem (krāym) *f* (pl ~s) cream

kremfarben (*krāym*-fahr-bern) *adj* cream

Kreuz (kroits) *nt* (pl ~e) cross

Kreuzfahrt (*kroits*-faart) *f* (pl ~en) cruise

kreuzigen (*kroi*-tsi-gern) *v* crucify

Kreuzigung (*kroi*-tsi-goong) *f* (pl ~en) crucifixion

Kreuzung (*kroi*-tsoong) *f* (pl ~en) crossing, crossroads, intersection

Kreuzzug (*kroits*-tsōok) *m* (pl ~e) crusade

Kricket (*kri*-kert) nt cricket

*kriechen (*kree*-khern) v *creep, crawl

Krieg (kreek) m (pl ~e) war

kriegen (*kree*-gern) v *get

Kriegsgefangene (*kreeks*-ger-fahng-er-ner) m (pl ~n) prisoner of war

Kriegsmacht (*kreeks*-mahkht) f (pl ~e) military force

Kriegsschiff (*kreeks*-shif) nt (pl ~e) man-of-war

Kriminalität (kri-mi-nah-li-*tait*) f criminality

Kriminalroman (kri-mi-*naal*-roa-maan) m (pl ~e) detective story

kriminell (kri-mi-*nehl*) adj criminal

Krippe (*kri*-per) f (pl ~n) manger

Krise (*kree*-zer) f (pl ~n) crisis

Kristall (kriss-*tahl*) nt crystal

kristallen (kriss-*tah*-lern) adj crystal

Kritik (kri-*teek*) f (pl ~en) criticism

Kritiker (*kree*-ti-kerr) m (pl ~) critic

kritisch (*kree*-tish) adj critical

kritisieren (kri-ti-*zee*-rern) v criticize

Krokodil (kroa-koa-*deel*) nt (pl ~e) crocodile

Krone (*krōa*-ner) f (pl ~n) crown

krönen (*krūr*-nern) v crown

Kröte (*krūr*-ter) f (pl ~n) toad

Krücke (*krew*-ker) f (pl ~n) crutch

Krug (krōok) m (pl ~e) pitcher, jug, jar

Krümel (*krēw*-merl) m (pl ~) crumb

krumm (kroom) adj curved, bent; crooked

Krümmung (*krew*-moong) f (pl ~en) bend

Kruste (*krooss*-ter) f (pl ~n) crust

Kruzifix (kroo-tsi-*fiks*) nt (pl ~e) crucifix

Kuba (*kōo*-bah) Cuba

Kubaner (koo-*baa*-nerr) m (pl ~) Cuban

kubanisch (koo-*baa*-nish) adj Cuban

Kubus (*kōo*-booss) m (pl Kuben) cube

Küche (*kew*-kher) f (pl ~n) kitchen

Kuchen (*kōo*-khern) m (pl ~) cake

Küchenchef (*kew*-khern-shehf) m (pl ~s) chef

Kuckuck (*koo*-kook) m (pl ~e) cuckoo

Kugel (*kōo*-gerl) f (pl ~n) sphere; bullet

Kugelschreiber (*kōo*-gerl-shrigh-berr) m (pl ~) ballpoint-pen, Biro

Kuh (kōo) f (pl ~e) cow

Kuhhaut (*kōo*-hout) f (pl ~e) cowhide

kühl (kewl) adj cool; chilly

Kühlschrank (*kewl*-shrahngk) m (pl ~e) fridge, refrigerator

Kühlsystem (*kewl*-zewss-tāym) nt cooling system

kühn (kewn) adj bold

Kühnheit (*kewn*-hight) f nerve

Küken (*kew*-kern) nt (pl ~) chicken

kultivieren (kool-ti-*vee*-rern) v cultivate

kultiviert (kool-ti-*veert*) adj cultured

Kultur (kool-*tōor*) f (pl ~en) culture

Kummer (*koo*-merr) m sorrow, grief

kümmern (*kew*-merrn) v mind; **sich ~ um** look after, *take care of

Kunde (*koon*-der) m (pl ~n) customer, client

Kundgebung (*koont*-gāy-boong) f (pl ~en) demonstration

Kunst (koonst) f (pl ~e) art; **die schönen Künste** fine arts

Kunstakademie (*koonst*-ah-kah-day-mee) f (pl ~n) art school

Kunstausstellung (*koonst*-ouss-shteh-loong) f (pl ~en) art exhibition

Kunstgalerie (*koonst*-gah-ler-ree) f (pl ~n) art gallery

Kunstgeschichte (*koonst*-ger-shikh-ter) f art history

Kunstgewerbe (*koonst*-ger-vehr-ber)

nt arts and crafts

Künstler (*kewnst*-lerr) *m* (pl ~) artist

Künstlerin (*kewnst*-ler-rin) *f* (pl ~nen) artist

künstlerisch (*kewnst*-ler-rish) *adj* artistic

künstlich (*kewnst*-likh) *adj* artificial

Kunstsammlung (*koonst*-zahm-loong) *f* (pl ~en) art collection

Kunstseide (*koonst*-zigh-der) *f* rayon

Kunststoff (*koonst*-shtof) *m* (pl ~e) plastic; **Kunststoff-** plastic

Kunstwerk (*koonst*-vehrk) *nt* (pl ~e) work of art

Kupfer (*koo*-pferr) *nt* copper

Kupon (koo-*pawng*) *m* (pl ~s) coupon

Kuppel (*koo*-perl) *f* (pl ~n) dome

Kupplung (*koop*-loong) *f* (pl ~en) clutch

Kur (kōōr) *f* (pl ~en) cure

Kurbelgehäuse (*koor*-berl-ger-hoi-zer) *nt* (pl ~) crankcase

Kurbelwelle (*koor*-berl-veh-ler) *f* (pl ~n) crankshaft

Kurpfuscher (*kōōr*-pfoo-sherr) *m* (pl ~) quack

Kurs (koors) *m* (pl ~e) rate of exchange; course

Kürschner (*kewrsh*-nerr) *m* (pl ~) furrier

Kursivschrift (koor-*zeef*-shrift) *f* italics *pl*

Kursus (*koor*-zooss) *m* (pl Kurse) course

Kurve (*koor*-ver) *f* (pl ~n) curve, turning, bend

kurz (koorts) *adj* short; brief; **in kurzem** shortly

in Kürze (in *kewr*-tser) soon

kurzgefaßt (*koorts*-ger-fahst) *adj* concise

Kurzlehrgang (*koorts*-lāyr-gahng) *m* (pl ~e) intensive course

kürzlich (*kewrts*-likh) *adv* recently,

lately

Kurzschluß (*koorts*-shlooss) *m* short circuit

kurzsichtig (*koorts*-zikh-tikh) *adj* short-sighted

Kurzwarengeschäft (*koorts*-vaa-rern-ger-shehft) *nt* (pl ~e) haberdashery

Kuß (kooss) *m* (pl Küsse) kiss

küssen (*kew*-sern) *v* kiss

Küste (*kewss*-ter) *f* (pl ~n) coast, shore; seaside

Küster (*kewss*-terr) *m* (pl ~) sexton

Kutsche (*koo*-cher) *f* (pl ~n) carriage, coach

L

labil (lah-*beel*) *adj* unstable

Laboratorium (lah-boa-rah-*tōā*-r[v]oom) *nt* (pl -rien) laboratory

Labyrinth (lah-bew-*rint*) *nt* (pl ~e) labyrinth

Lächeln (*leh*-kherln) *nt* smile

lächeln (*leh*-kherln) *v* smile

Lachen (*lah*-khern) *nt* laugh

lachen (*lah*-khern) *v* laugh

lächerlich (*leh*-kherr-likh) *adj* ridiculous; ludicrous

lachhaft (*lahkh*-hahft) *adj* ludicrous

Lachs (lahks) *m* (pl ~e) salmon

Lack (lahk) *m* (pl ~e) lacquer; varnish

lackieren (lah-*kee*-rern) *v* varnish

Laden (*laa*-dern) *m* (pl ~) store

*laden (*laa*-dern) *v* load; charge

Ladeninhaber (*laa*-dern-in-haa-berr) *m* (pl ~) shopkeeper

Ladentisch (*laa*-dern-tish) *m* (pl ~e) counter

Laderaum (*laa*-der-roum) *m* (pl ~e) hold

Ladung (*laa*-doong) *f* (pl ~en) freight,

charge, cargo

Lage (*laa*-ger) *f* (pl ~n) location; situation; position, site

Lager (*laa*-gerr) *nt* (pl ~) warehouse, depot; camp

Lagerhaus (*laa*-gerr-houss) *nt* (pl ~̈er) store-house

lagern (*laa*-gerrn) *v* store

Lagerraum (*laa*-gerr-roum) *m* (pl ~̈e) depository

Lagerung (*laa*-ger-roong) *f* storage

Lagune (lah-*gōō*-ner) *f* (pl ~n) lagoon

lahm (laam) *adj* lame

lähmen (*lai*-mern) *v* paralise

Laib (lighb) *m* (pl ~e) loaf

Laie (*ligh*-er) *m* (pl ~n) layman

Laken (*laa*-kern) *nt* (pl ~) sheet

Lakritze (lah-*kri*-tser) *f* liquorice

Lamm (lahm) *nt* (pl ~̈er) lamb

Lammfleisch (*lahm*-flighsh) *nt* lamb

Lampe (*lahm*-per) *f* (pl ~n) lamp

Lampenschirm (*lahm*-pern-sheerm) *m* (pl ~e) lampshade

Land (lahnt) *nt* (pl ~̈er) country, land; **an ~** ashore; **an ~** ***gehen** land; disembark

landen (*lahn*-dern) *v* land; disembark

Landenge (*lahnt*-ehng-er) *f* (pl ~n) isthmus

Landesgrenze (*lahn*-derss-grehn-tser) *f* (pl ~n) boundary

Landhaus (*lahnt*-houss) *nt* (pl ~̈er) country house

Landkarte (*lahnt*-kahr-ter) *f* (pl ~n) map

ländlich (*lehnt*-likh) *adj* rustic, rural

Landmarke (*lahnt*-mahr-ker) *f* (pl ~en) landmark

Landschaft (*lahnt*-shahft) *f* (pl ~en) countryside; landscape, scenery

Landsitz (*lahnt*-zits) *m* (pl ~e) estate

Landsmann (*lahnts*-mahn) *m* (pl -leute) countryman

Landstraße (*lahnt*-shtraa-ser) *f* (pl ~n) highway

Landstreicher (*lahnt*-shtrigh-kherr) *m* (pl ~) tramp

Landstreicherei (lahnt-shtrigh-kher-*righ*) *f* vagrancy

Landwirtschaft (*lahnt*-veert-shahft) *f* agriculture; **Landwirtschafts-** agrarian

Landzunge (*lahnt*-tsoong-er) *f* (pl ~n) headland

lang (lahng) *adj* long; tall; **lange** *adv* long

Länge (*lehng*-er) *f* length; **der ~ nach** lengthways

Längengrad (*lehng*-ern-graat) *m* (pl ~e) longitude

länglich (*lehng*-likh) *adj* oblong

langsam (*lahng*-zaam) *adj* slow

Langspielplatte (*lahng*-shpeel-plah-ter) *f* (pl ~n) long-playing record

langweilen (*lahng*-vigh-lern) *v* bore; annoy

Langweiler (*lahng*-vigh-lerr) *m* (pl ~) bore

langweilig (*lahng*-vigh-likh) *adj* dull, boring; unpleasant

langwierig (*lahng*-vee-rikh) *adj* long

Lappen (*lah*-pern) *m* (pl ~) cloth

Lärm (lehrm) *m* noise

lärmend (*lehr*-mernt) *adj* noisy

***lassen** (*lah*-sern) *v* *let; *leave, allow to

lässig (*leh*-sikh) *adj* easy-going

Last (lahst) *f* (pl ~en) burden; charge, load; trouble

lästig (*lehss*-tikh) *adj* troublesome, inconvenient; annoying

Lastwagen (*lahst*-vaa-gern) *m* (pl ~) lorry; truck *nAm*

Lateinamerika (lah-*tighn*-ah-māy-ri-kah) Latin America

lateinamerikanisch (lah-*tighn*-ah-may-ri-kaa-nish) *adj* Latin-American

Laterne (lah-*tehr*-ner) *f* (pl ~n) lantern

Laternenpfahl (lah-*tehr*-nern-pfaal) *m* (pl ̈-e) lamp-post

Lauf (louf) *m* (pl ̈-e) course

Laufbahn (*louf*-baan) *f* career

***laufen** (*lou*-fern) *v* *run

Laufplanke (*louf*-plahng-ker) *f* (pl ~n) gangway

Laune (*lou*-ner) *f* (pl ~n) spirit, mood; whim, fancy

Laus (louss) *f* (pl ̈-e) louse

laut (lout) *adj* loud; *adv* aloud

läuten (*loi*-tern) *v* *ring

Lautsprecher (*lout*-shpreh-kherr) *m* (pl ~) loud-speaker

lauwarm (*lou*-vahrm) *adj* tepid, lukewarm

Lawine (lah-*vee*-ner) *f* (pl ~n) avalanche

Leben (*lay*-bern) *nt* (pl ~) life; lifetime; **am ~** alive

leben (*lay*-bern) *v* live

lebend (*lay*-bernt) *adj* live, alive

Lebensmittel (*lay*-berns-mi-terl) *pl* groceries *pl*

Lebensmittelgeschäft (*lay*-berns-mi-terl-ger-shehft) *nt* (pl ~e) grocer's

Lebensmittelhändler (*lay*-berns-mi-terl-hehn-dlerr) *m* (pl ~) grocer

Lebensstandard (*lay*-berns-shtahn-dahrt) *m* standard of living

Lebensversicherung (*lay*-berns-fehr-zi-kher-roong) *f* (pl ~en) life insurance

Leber (*lay*-berr) *f* (pl ~n) liver

lebhaft (*layp*-hahft) *adj* brisk, vivid, lively, active

Leck (lehk) *nt* (pl ~s) leak

leck (lehk) *adj* leaky

lecken (*leh*-kern) *v* leak; lick

lecker (*leh*-kerr) *adj* appetizing; delicious, good, tasty

Leckerbissen (*leh*-kerr-bi-sern) *m* (pl ~) delicacy

Leder (*lay*-derr) *nt* leather; **Leder-** leather

ledern (*lay*-derrn) *adj* leather

ledig (*lay*-dikh) *adj* single

leer (layr) *adj* empty; blank

leeren (*lay*-rern) *v* empty

Leerung (*lay*-roong) *f* (pl ~en) collection

Legalisierung (lay-gah-li-*zee*-roong) *f* legalization

legen (*lay*-gern) *v* *lay, *put

lehnen (*lay*-nern) *v* *lean

Lehnstuhl (*layn*-shtool) *m* (pl ̈-e) armchair, easy chair

Lehrbuch (*layr*-bookh) *nt* (pl ̈-er) textbook

Lehre (*lay*-rer) *f* (pl ~n) teachings *pl*

lehren (*lay*-rern) *v* *teach

Lehrer (*lay*-rerr) *m* (pl ~) schoolteacher, schoolmaster, master; teacher; instructor

Lehrgang (*layr*-gahng) *m* (pl ̈-e) course

lehrreich (*layr*-righkh) *adj* instructive

Leib (lighp) *m* (pl ~er) body

Leibwache (*lighp*-vah-kher) *f* (pl ~n) bodyguard

Leiche (*ligh*-kher) *f* (pl ~n) corpse

leicht (lighkht) *adj* light; gentle, slight

Leichtigkeit (*lighkh*-tikh-kight) *f* ease

Leid (light) *nt* sorrow, grief; affliction

Leiden (*ligh*-dern) *nt* (pl ~) ailment; suffering

***leiden** (*ligh*-dern) *v* suffer

Leidenschaft (*ligh*-dern-shahft) *f* (pl ~en) passion

leidenschaftlich (*ligh*-dern-shahft-likh) *adj* passionate

leider (*ligh*-derr) *adv* unfortunately

leidlich (*light*-likh) *adv* fairly, quite

Leierkasten (*ligh*-err-kahss-tern) *m* (pl ̈-) street-organ

***leihen** (*ligh*-ern) *v* *lend

Leim (lighm) *m* glue

Leine (*ligh*-ner) *f* (pl ~n) cord; lead;

leash

Leinen (*ligh*-nern) *nt* linen

leise (*ligh*-zer) *adj* low; gentle

Leiste (*lighss*-ter) *f* (pl ~n) groin

leisten (*lighss*-tern) *v* achieve; offer; **sich** ~ afford

Leistung (*lighss*-toong) *f* (pl ~en) achievement

leistungsfähig (*lighss*-toongs-fai-ikh) *adj* efficient

Leistungsfähigkeit (*lighss*-toongs-fai-ikh-kight) *f* (pl ~en) capacity

leiten (*ligh*-tern) *v* head

Leiter[1] (*ligh*-terr) *m* (pl ~) leader

Leiter[2] (*ligh*-terr) *f* (pl ~n) ladder

Leitplanke (*light*-plahng-ker) *f* (pl ~n) crash barrier

Leitung (*ligh*-toong) *f* (pl ~en) lead

Lektion (lehk-*ts*ⁿ*ōan*) *f* (pl ~en) lesson

Lenksäule (*lehngk*-zoi-ler) *f* (pl ~n) steering-column

Lenz (lehnts) *m* spring

Lepra (*lā*ȳ-prah) *f* leprosy

Lerche (*lehr*-kher) *f* (pl ~n) lark

lernen (*lehr*-nern) *v* *learn; **auswendig** ~ memorize

Leselampe (*lā*ȳ-zer-lahm-per) *f* (pl ~n) reading-lamp

***lesen** (*lā*ȳ-zern) *v* *read

leserlich (*lā*ȳ-zerr-likh) *adj* legible

Lesesaal (*lā*ȳ-zer-zaal) *m* (pl -säle) reading-room

letzt (lehtst) *adj* last; ultimate, final; past

leuchten (*loikh*-tern) *v* *shine; **leuchtend** bright; luminous

Leuchtturm (*loikht*-toorm) *m* (pl ⁓e) lighthouse

leugnen (*loi*-gnern) *v* deny

Leute (*loi*-ter) *pl* people *pl*

Libanese (li-bah-*nā*ȳ-zer) *m* (pl ~n) Lebanese

libanesisch (li-bah-*nā*ȳ-zish) *adj* Lebanese

Libanon (*lee*-bah-non) Lebanon

liberal (li-bay-*raal*) *adj* liberal

Liberia (li-*bā*ȳ-rʸah) Liberia

Liberier (li-*bā*ȳ-rʸerr) *m* (pl ~) Liberian

liberisch (li-*bā*ȳ-rish) *adj* Liberian

Licht (likht) *nt* (pl ~er) light

Lichtbild (*likht*-bilt) *nt* (pl ~er) photograph

Lichtung (*likh*-toong) *f* (pl ~en) clearing

lieb (leep) *adj* dear; affectionate, sweet

Liebe (*lee*-ber) *f* love

lieben (*lee*-bern) *v* love

lieber (*lee*-berr) *adv* sooner, rather

Liebesgeschichte (*lee*-berss-ger-shikh-ter) *f* (pl ~n) love-story

Liebhaber (*leep*-haa-berr) *m* (pl ~) lover

Liebhaberei (leep-haa-ber-*righ*) *f* (pl ~en) hobby

liebkosen (*leep*-kōa-zern) *v* hug

Liebling (*leep*-ling) *m* (pl ~e) darling, sweetheart; favourite; pet; **Lieblings-** favourite; pet

Liebreiz (*leep*-rights) *m* charm

Liebschaft (*leep*-shahft) *f* (pl ~en) affair

Lied (leet) *nt* (pl ~er) song; tune

Lieferauto (*lee*-ferr-ou-toa) *nt* (pl ~s) van

liefern (*lee*-ferrn) *v* furnish, supply, provide

Lieferung (*lee*-fer-roong) *f* (pl ~en) supply; delivery

Lieferwagen (*lee*-ferr-vaa-gern) *m* (pl ~) delivery van, pick-up van

Liege (*lee*-ger) *f* (pl ~n) camp-bed; cot *nAm*

***liegen** (*lee*-gern) *v* *lie

Liegestuhl (*lee*-ger-shtōōl) *m* (pl ⁓e) deck chair

Likör (li-*kū*rr) *m* (pl ~e) liqueur

Lilie (*lee*-l^Yer) *f* (pl ~n) lily

Limonade (li-moa-*naa*-der) *f* (pl ~n) lemonade

Limone (li-*mōa*-ner) *f* (pl ~n) lime

Linde (*lin*-der) *f* (pl ~n) lime

Lindenbaum (*lin*-dern-boum) *m* (pl ~e) limetree

Lineal (li-nay-*aal*) *nt* (pl ~e) ruler

Linie (*lee*-n^Yer) *f* (pl ~n) line

Linienschiff (*lee*-n^Yern-shif) *nt* (pl ~e) liner

linke (*ling*-ker) *adj* left-hand, left

linkshändig (*lingks*-hehn-dikh) *adj* left-handed

Linse (*lin*-zer) *f* (pl ~n) lens

Lippe (*li*-per) *f* (pl ~n) lip

Lippensalbe (*li*-pern-zahl-ber) *f* (pl ~n) lipsalve

Lippenstift (*li*-pern-shtift) *m* (pl ~e) lipstick

List (list) *f* (pl ~en) artifice, ruse

Liste (*liss*-ter) *f* (pl ~n) list

listig (*liss*-tikh) *adj* cunning, sly

Liter (*lee*-terr) *m* (pl ~) litre

literarisch (li-tay-*raa*-rish) *adj* literary

Literatur (li-tay-rah-*tōōr*) *f* literature

Lizenz (li-*tsehnts*) *f* (pl ~en) licence

Lob (lōap) *nt* praise ; glory

loben (*lōa*-bern) *v* praise

Loch (lokh) *nt* (pl ~er) hole

Locke (*lo*-ker) *f* (pl ~n) curl

locken (*lo*-kern) *v* curl

Lockenwickler (*lo*-kern-vi-klerr) *m* (pl ~) curler

lockern (*lo*-kerrn) *v* loosen

lockig (*lo*-kikh) *adj* curly

Löffel (*lur*-ferl) *m* (pl ~) spoon

Logik (*lōa*-gik) *f* logic

logisch (*lōa*-gish) *adj* logical

Lohn (lōan) *m* (pl ~e) wages *pl*, salary, pay

sich lohnen (*lōa*-nern) *be worthwhile ; *pay

Lohnerhöhung (*lōan*-ehr-hūr-oong) *f*

(pl ~en) raise *nAm*

lokal (loa-*kaal*) *adj* local

Lokomotive (loa-koa-moa-*tee*-ver) *f* (pl ~n) engine, locomotive

Los (lōass) *nt* (pl ~e) lot

löschen (*lur*-shern) *v* extinguish

Löschpapier (*lursh*-pah-peer) *nt* blotting paper

lose (*lōa*-zer) *adj* loose

Lösegeld (*lūr*-zer-gehlt) *nt* (pl ~er) ransom

lösen (*lūr*-zern) *v* solve

löslich (*lūrss*-likh) *adj* soluble

losmachen (*lōass*-mah-khern) *v* detach

Lösung (*lūr*-zoong) *f* (pl ~en) solution

Losungswort (*lōa*-zoongs-vort) *nt* (pl ~er) password

löten (*lūr*-tern) *v* solder

Lötkolben (*lūrt*-kol-bern) *m* (pl ~) soldering-iron

Lotse (*lōa*-tser) *m* (pl ~n) pilot

Lötstelle (*lūrt*-shteh-ler) *f* (pl ~n) joint

Lotterie (lo-ter-*ree*) *f* (pl ~n) lottery

Löwe (*lūr*-ver) *m* (pl ~n) lion

Löwenzahn (*lūr*-vern-tsaan) *m* dandelion

loyal (lwah-^Y*aal*) *adj* loyal

Lücke (*lew*-ker) *f* (pl ~n) gap

Luft (looft) *f* (pl ~e) air ; sky ; breath

luftdicht (*looft*-dikht) *adj* airtight

Luftdruck (*looft*-drook) *m* atmospheric pressure

lüften (*lewf*-tern) *v* air, ventilate

Luftfilter (*looft*-fil-terr) *m* (pl ~) air-filter

luftig (*loof*-tikh) *adj* airy

Luftkrankheit (*looft*-krahngk-hight) *f* air-sickness

Luftpost (*looft*-post) *f* airmail

Lüftung (*lewf*-toong) *f* ventilation

Luftzug (*looft*-tsōōk) *m* draught

Lüge (*lēw*-ger) *f* (pl ~n) lie

*lügen (*lēw*-gern) *v* lie

Luke (*lōō*-ker) *f* (pl ~n) hatch ; porthole

Lumpen (*loom*-pern) *m* (pl ~) rag

Lunge (*loong*-er) *f* (pl ~n) lung

Lungenentzündung (*loong*-ern-ehnt-tsewn-doong) *f* pneumonia

Lunte (*loon*-ter) *f* (pl ~n) fuse

Lust (loost) *f* desire; zest; ~ * **haben zu** *feel like, fancy

lustig (*looss*-tikh) *adj* gay

Lustspiel (*loost*-shpeel) *nt* (pl ~e) comedy

lutschen (*loo*-chern) *v* suck

luxuriös (loo-ksoo-r^y*ūrss*) *adj* luxurious

Luxus (*loo*-ksooss) *m* luxury

M

machen (*mah*-khern) *v* *make; *have; cause to

Macht (mahkht) *f* (pl ᵕe) power; force, might

Machtbefugnis (*mahkht*-ber-fōōk-niss) *f* (pl ~se) authority

mächtig (*mehkh*-tikh) *adj* powerful, mighty

machtlos (*mahkh*-lōass) *adj* powerless

Mädchen (*mait*-khern) *nt* (pl ~) girl

Mädchenname (*mait*-khern-naa-mer) *m* (pl ~n) maiden name

Magen (*maa*-gern) *m* (pl ᵕ) stomach

Magengeschwür (*maa*-gern-ger-shvēwr) *nt* (pl ~e) gastric ulcer

Magenschmerzen (*maa*-gern-shmehr-tsern) *mpl* stomach-ache

Magenverstimmung (*maa*-gern-fehr-shti-moong) *f* indigestion

mager (*maa*-gerr) *adj* thin; lean

Magie (mah-*gee*) *f* magic

Magnet (mah-*gnāyt*) *m* (pl ~en) magneto

magnetisch (mah-*gnāy*-tish) *adj* magnetic

Mahl (maal) *nt* (pl ᵕer) meal

mahlen (*maa*-lern) *v* *grind

Mahlzeit (*maal*-tsight) *f* (pl ~en) meal

Mai (migh) May

Mais (mighss) *m* maize

Maiskolben (*mighss*-kol-bern) *m* (pl ~) corn on the cob

Major (mah-*^yōar*) *m* (pl ~e) major

Makel (*maa*-kerl) *m* (pl ~) blot

Makler (*maa*-klerr) *m* (pl ~) broker

Makrele (mah-*krāy*-ler) *f* (pl ~n) mackerel

Mal (maal) *nt* (pl ~e) time

mal (maal) times

malaiisch (mah-*ligh*-ish) *adj* Malaysian

Malaria (mah-*laa*-r^yah) *f* malaria

Malaysia (mah-*ligh*-z^yah) Malaysia

malen (*maa*-lern) *v* paint

Maler (*maa*-lerr) *m* (pl ~) painter

malerisch (*maa*-ler-rish) *adj* picturesque, scenic

Malkasten (*maal*-kahss-tern) *m* (pl ᵕ) paint-box

Mammut (*mah*-moot) *nt* (pl ~e) mammoth

man (mahn) *pron* one

manche (*mahn*-kher) *pron* some

manchmal (*mahnkh*-maal) *adv* sometimes

Mandarine (mahn-dah-*ree*-ner) *f* (pl ~n) mandarin, tangerine

Mandat (mahn-*daat*) *nt* (pl ~e) mandate

Mandel (*mahn*-derl) *f* (pl ~n) almond; **Mandeln** tonsils *pl*

Mandelentzündung (*mahn*-derl-ehnt-tsewn-doong) *f* tonsilitis

Mangel (*mahng*-erl) *m* (pl ᵕ) want, lack, scarcity, shortage; deficiency, fault

mangelhaft (*mahng*-erl-hahft) *adj* defective; faulty

mangeln (*mahng*-erln) *v* fail; lack

Manieren (mah-*nee*-rern) *fpl* manners *pl*

Maniküre (mah-ni-*kēw*-rer) *f* (pl ~n) manicure

maniküren (mah-ni-*kēw*-rern) *v* manicure

Mann (mahn) *m* (pl ˜er) man; husband

Mannequin (mah-ner-*kang*) *nt* (pl ~s) model, mannequin

männlich (*mehn*-likh) *adj* male; masculine

Mannschaft (*mahn*-shahft) *f* (pl ~en) team

Manschette (mahn-*sheh*-ter) *f* (pl ~n) cuff

Manschettenknöpfe (mahn-*sheh*-tern-knur-pfer) *mpl* cuff-links *pl*

Mantel (*mahn*-terl) *m* (pl ˜) coat, overcoat

Manuskript (mah-noo-*skript*) *nt* (pl ~e) manuscript

Märchen (*mair*-khern) *nt* (pl ~) fairy-tale

Margarine (mahr-gah-*ree*-ner) *f* margarine

Marine (mah-*ree*-ner) *f* navy; **Marine**-naval

maritim (mah-ri-*teem*) *adj* maritime

Mark (mahrk) *nt* marrow

Marke (*mahr*-ker) *f* (pl ~n) brand

Markenautomat (*mahr*-kern-ou-toa-maat) *m* (pl ~en) stamp machine

Markise (mahr-*kee*-zer) *f* (pl ~n) awning

Markstein (*mahrk*-shtighn) *m* (pl ~e) landmark

Markt (mahrkt) *m* (pl ˜e) market

Marktplatz (*mahrkt*-plahts) *m* (pl ˜e) market-place

Marmelade (mahr-mer-*laa*-der) *f* (pl ~n) marmalade; jam

Marmor (*mahr*-mor) *m* marble

Marokkaner (mah-ro-*kaa*-nerr) *m* (pl ~) Moroccan

marokkanisch (mah-ro-*kaa*-nish) *adj* Moroccan

Marokko (mah-*ro*-koa) Morocco

Marsch (mahrsh) *m* (pl ˜e) march

marschieren (mahr-*shee*-rern) *v* march

Marter (*mahr*-terr) *f* (pl ~n) torture

martern (*mahr*-terrn) *v* torture

Märtyrer (*mehr*-tew-rerr) *m* (pl ~) martyr

März (mehrts) March

Masche (*mah*-sher) *f* (pl ~n) mesh

Maschine (mah-*shee*-ner) *f* (pl ~n) machine; engine; aircraft; ~ **schreiben* type

Masern (*maa*-zerrn) *pl* measles

Maske (*mahss*-ker) *f* (pl ~n) mask

Maß (maass) *nt* (pl ~e) measure; **nach** ~ tailor-made

Massage (mah-*saa*-zher) *f* (pl ~n) massage

Masse (*mah*-ser) *f* (pl ~n) bulk; crowd

Massenproduktion (*mah*-sern-proa-dook-tsᵞōan) *f* mass production

Masseur (mah-*sūr*) *m* (pl ~e) masseur

massieren (mah-*see*-rern) *v* massage

mäßig (*mai*-sikh) *adj* moderate

massiv (mah-*seef*) *adj* solid, massive

Maßnahme (*maass*-naa-mer) *f* (pl ~n) measure

Maßstab (*maass*-shtaap) *m* (pl ˜e) scale; standard

Mast (mahst) *m* (pl ~e) mast

Mastdarm (*mahst*-dahrm) *m* (pl ˜e) rectum

Material (mah-tay-rᵞaal) *nt* (pl ~ien) material

Materie (mah-*tāȳ*-rᵞer) *f* (pl ~n) matter

materiell (mah-tay-rᵞehl) *adj* material

Mathematik (mah-tay-mah-*teek*) *f*

mathematics

mathematisch (mah-tay-*maa*-tish) *adj* mathematical

Matratze (mah-*trah*-tser) *f* (pl ~n) mattress

Mätresse (meh-*treh*-ser) *f* (pl ~n) mistress

Matrose (mah-*trōā*-zer) *m* (pl ~n) sailor, seaman

Matsch (mahch) *m* slush

matt (maht) *adj* mat; dull, dim

Matte (*mah*-ter) *f* (pl ~n) mat

Mauer (*mou*-err) *f* (pl ~n) wall

mauern (*mou*-errn) *v* *lay bricks

Maul (moul) *nt* (pl ~er) mouth

Maulbeere (*moul*-bāy-rer) *f* (pl ~n) mulberry

Maulesel (*moul*-āy-zerl) *m* (pl ~) mule

Maultier (*moul*-teer) *nt* (pl ~e) mule

Maurer (*mou*-rerr) *m* (pl ~) bricklayer

Maus (mouss) *f* (pl ~e) mouse

Mausoleum (mou-zoa-*lāy*-oom) *nt* (pl -leen) mausoleum

Mechaniker (may-*khaa*-ni-kerr) *m* (pl ~) mechanic

mechanisch (may-*khaa*-nish) *adj* mechanical

Mechanismus (may-khah-*niss*-mooss) *m* (pl -men) mechanism; machinery

Medaille (may-*dah*-l^{y}er) *f* (pl ~n) medal

meditieren (may-di-*tee*-rern) *v* meditate

Medizin (may-di-*tseen*) *f* medicine

medizinisch (may-di-*tsee*-nish) *adj* medical

Meer (māyr) *nt* (pl ~e) sea

Meeräsche (*māyr*-eh-sher) *f* (pl ~n) mullet

Meeresküste (*māy*-rerss-kewss-ter) *f* (pl ~n) sea-coast, seashore

Meerrettich (*māyr*-reh-tikh) *m* horse-radish

Meerschweinchen (*māyr*-shvighn-

khern) *nt* (pl ~) guinea-pig

Meerwasser (*māyr*-vah-serr) *nt* sea-water

Mehl (māyl) *nt* flour

mehr (māyr) *adv* more; **etwas ~** some more; **nicht ~** no longer

mehrere (*māy*-rer-rer) *pron* several

Mehrheit (*māyr*-hight) *f* (pl ~en) majority; bulk

Mehrzahl (*māyr*-tsaal) *f* plural

* **meiden** (*migh*-dern) *v* avoid

Meile (*migh*-ler) *f* (pl ~n) mile

Meilenstand (*migh*-lern-shtahnt) *m* mileage

Meilenstein (*migh*-lern-shtighn) *m* (pl ~e) milestone

mein (mighn) *pron* my

Meineid (*mighn*-ight) *m* (pl ~e) perjury

meinen (*migh*-nern) *v* *mean

Meinung (*migh*-noong) *f* (pl ~en) view, opinion

Meißel (*migh*-serl) *m* (pl ~) chisel

meist (mighst) *adj* most

meistens (*migh*-sterns) *adv* mostly

Meister (*mighss*-terr) *m* (pl ~) champion; master

Meisterstück (*mighss*-terr-shtewk) *nt* (pl ~e) masterpiece

melden (*mehl*-dern) *v* report

Meldung (*mehl*-doong) *f* (pl ~en) report; mention

meliert (*may*-leert) *adj* mixed

Melodie (may-loa-*dee*) *f* (pl ~n) melody; tune

melodisch (may-*lōā*-dish) *adj* tuneful

Melodrama (may-loa-*draa*-mah) *nt* (pl -dramen) melodrama

Melone (may-*lōā*-ner) *f* (pl ~n) melon

Membran (mehm-*braan*) *f* (pl ~en) diaphragm

Memorandum (may-moa-*rahn*-doom) *nt* (pl -den) memo

Menge (*mehng*-er) *f* (pl ~n) amount;

plenty, lot; crowd, mass

Mensch (mehnsh) m (pl ~en) man; human being

Menschheit (mehnsh-hight) f humanity, mankind

menschlich (mehnsh-likh) adj human

Menstruation (mehns-troo-ah-tsʸōān) f menstruation

Merkbuch (mehrk-bōōkh) nt (pl ̈er) diary

merken (mehr-kern) v notice

Merkmal (mehrk-maal) nt (pl ~e) indication

merkwürdig (mehrk-vewr-dikh) adj remarkable; singular

Messe (meh-ser) f (pl ~n) fair; Mass

*****messen** (meh-sern) v measure

Messer (meh-serr) nt (pl ~) knife; m gauge

Messing (meh-sing) nt brass

Messingwaren (meh-sing-vaa-rern) fpl brassware

Metall (may-tahl) nt (pl ~e) metal

metallisch (may-tah-lish) adj metal

Meter (māy-terr) nt (pl ~) metre

Methode (may-tōā-der) f (pl ~n) method

methodisch (may-tōā-dish) adj methodical

metrisch (māy-trish) adj metric

Metzger (mehts-gerr) m (pl ~) butcher

Meuterei (moi-ter-righ) f (pl ~en) mutiny

Mexikaner (meh-ksi-kaa-nerr) m (pl ~) Mexican

mexikanisch (meh-ksi-kaa-nish) adj Mexican

Mexiko (meh-ksi-koa) Mexico

mich (mikh) pron me; myself

Miete (mee-ter) f (pl ~n) rent

mieten (mee-tern) v hire, rent; lease; engage

Mieter (mee-terr) m (pl ~) tenant

Mietvertrag (meet-fehr-traak) m (pl ̈e) lease

Migräne (mi-grai-ner) f migraine

Mikrophon (mi-kroa-fōān) nt (pl ~e) microphone

Milch (milkh) f milk

milchig (mil-khikh) adj milky

Milchmann (milkh-mahn) m (pl ̈er) milkman

mild (milt) adj mild; mellow

mildern (mil-derrn) v soften

Milieu (mi-lʸūr) nt (pl ~s) milieu

militärisch (mi-li-tai-rish) adj military

Million (mi-lʸōān) f (pl ~en) million

Millionär (mi-lʸoa-nair) m (pl ~e) millionaire

Minderheit (min-derr-hight) f (pl ~en) minority

minderjährig (min-derr-ʸai-rikh) adj under age

Minderjährige (min-derr-ʸai-ri-ger) m (pl ~n) minor

minderwertig (min-derr-vāyr-tikh) adj inferior

mindest (min-derst) adj least

Mineral (mi-ner-raal) nt (pl ~e) mineral

Mineralwasser (mi-ner-raal-vah-serr) nt mineral water

Miniatur (mi-nʸah-tōōr) f (pl ~en) miniature

Minimum (mi-ni-moom) nt minimum

Minister (mi-niss-terr) m (pl ~) minister

Ministerium (mi-niss-tāy-rʸoom) nt (pl -rien) ministry

Ministerpräsident (mi-niss-terr-preh-zi-dehnt) m (pl ~en) Prime Minister

Minute (mi-nōō-ter) f (pl ~n) minute

Minze (min-tser) f (pl ~n) mint

mir (meer) pron me

mischen (mi-shern) v mix; shuffle

Mischung (mi-shoong) f (pl ~en) mixture

mißbilligen (miss-*bi*-li-gern) v disapprove

Mißbrauch (*miss*-broukh) m (pl ∼e) misuse, abuse

Mißerfolg (*miss*-ehr-folk) m (pl ∼e) failure

* **mißfallen** (miss-*fah*-lern) v displease

Mißgeschick (*miss*-ger-shik) nt (pl ∼e) misfortune; disaster

mißgestaltet (*miss*-ger-shtahl-tert) adj deformed

mißgönnen (miss-*gur*-nern) v grudge

mißlich (*miss*-likh) adj delicate

Mißtrauen (*miss*-trou-ern) nt suspicion

mißtrauen (miss-*trou*-ern) v mistrust

mißtrauisch (*miss*-trou-ish) adj suspicious

Mißverständnis (*miss*-fehr-shtehnt-niss) nt (pl ∼se) misunderstanding

* **mißverstehen** (*miss*-fehr-shtay-ern) v *misunderstand

Misthaufen (*mist*-hou-fern) m (pl ∼) dunghill

mit (mit) prep with; by

Mitarbeit (*mit*-ahr-bight) f co-operation

* **mitbringen** (*mit*-bring-ern) v *bring

mitfühlend (*mit*-few-lernt) adj sympathetic

Mitgefühl (*mit*-ger-fewl) nt sympathy

Mitglied (*mit*-gleet) nt (pl ∼er) associate, member

Mitgliedschaft (*mit*-gleet-shahft) f membership

Mitleid (*mit*-light) nt pity; ∼ *haben mit pity

* **mitnehmen** (*mit*-nay-mern) v *take along; exhaust

Mitschuldige (*mit*-shool-di-ger) m (pl ∼n) accessary

Mittag (*mi*-taak) m noon, midday

Mittagessen (*mi*-taak-eh-sern) nt lunch; luncheon, dinner

Mitte (*mi*-ter) f midst, middle

mitteilen (*mit*-tigh-lern) v communicate, notify, inform

Mitteilung (*mit*-tigh-loong) f (pl ∼en) communication, information

Mittel (*mi*-terl) nt (pl ∼) means; remedy; **antiseptisches** ∼ antiseptic; **empfängnisverhütendes** ∼ contraceptive

Mittelalter (*mi*-terl-ahl-terr) nt Middle Ages

mittelalterlich (*mi*-terl-ahl-terr-likh) adj mediaeval

mittelmäßig (*mi*-terl-mai-sikh) adj medium; moderate

Mittelmeer (*mi*-terl-mayr) nt Mediterranean

Mittelpunkt (*mi*-terl-poongkt) m (pl ∼e) centre

Mittelstand (*mi*-terl-shtahnt) m middle class

mitten in (*mi*-tern in) in the middle of

Mitternacht (*mi*-terr-nahkht) f midnight

mittler (*mit*-ler-rer) adj middle, medium

mittlerweile (mit-lerr-*vigh*-ler) adv in the meantime, meanwhile

Mittwoch (*mit*-vokh) m Wednesday

mitzählen (*mit*-tsai-lern) v count

Mixer (*mi*-kserr) m (pl ∼) mixer

Möbel (*mur*-berl) ntpl furniture

mobil (moa-*beel*) adj mobile

möblieren (mur-*blee*-rern) v furnish

Mode (*moa*-der) f (pl ∼n) fashion

Modell (moa-*dehl*) nt (pl ∼e) model

modellieren (moa-deh-*lee*-rern) v model

modern (moa-*dehrn*) adj modern; fashionable

modifizieren (moa-di-fi-*tsee*-rern) v modify

Modistin (moa-*diss*-tin) f (pl ∼nen) milliner

*mögen (*mūr*-gern) *v* like, fancy; *may

möglich (*mūrk*-likh) *adj* possible; eventual

Möglichkeit (*mūrk*-likh-kight) *f* (pl ~en) possibility

Mohair (moa-*hair*) *m* mohair

Mohn (mōan) *m* (pl ~e) poppy

Mohrrübe (*mōar*-rēw-ber) *f* (pl ~n) carrot

Molkerei (mol-ker-*righ*) *f* (pl ~en) dairy

mollig (*mo*-likh) *adj* plump

Moment (moa-*mehnt*) *m* (pl ~e) moment

Monarch (moa-*nahrkh*) *m* (pl ~en) ruler, monarch

Monarchie (moa-nahr-*khee*) *f* (pl ~n) monarchy

Monat (*mōa*-naht) *m* (pl ~e) month

monatlich (*mōa*-naht-likh) *adj* monthly

Monatsheft (*mōa*-nahts-hehft) *nt* (pl ~e) monthly magazine

Mönch (murnkh) *m* (pl ~e) monk

Mond (mōant) *m* (pl ~e) moon

Mondlicht (*mōant*-likht) *nt* moonlight

monetär (moa-nay-*tair*) *adj* monetary

Monolog (moa-noa-*lōag*) *m* (pl ~e) monologue

Monopol (moa-noa-*pōal*) *nt* (pl ~e) monopoly

monoton (moa-noa-*tōan*) *adj* monotonous

Montag (*mōan*-taak) *m* Monday

Monteur (mon-*tūrr*) *m* (pl ~e) mechanic

montieren (mon-*tee*-rern) *v* assemble

Monument (moa-noo-*mehnt*) *nt* (pl ~e) monument

Moor (mōar) *nt* (pl ~e) moor

Moorhuhn (*mōar*-hōon) *nt* (pl ¨er) grouse

Moos (mōass) *nt* (pl ~e) moss

Moped (*mōa*-peht) *nt* (pl ~s) moped; motorbike *nAm*

Moral (moa-*raal*) *f* moral; morality

moralisch (moa-*raa*-lish) *adj* moral

Morast (moa-*rahst*) *m* swamp

Mord (mort) *m* (pl ~e) murder, assassination

morden (*mor*-dern) *v* murder

Mörder (*murr*-derr) *m* (pl ~) murderer

Morgen (*mor*-gern) *m* (pl ~) morning

morgen (*mor*-gern) *adv* tomorrow

Morgenausgabe (*mor*-gern-ouss-gaa-ber) *f* (pl ~n) morning edition

Morgendämmerung (*mor*-gern-deh-mer-roong) *f* dawn

Morgenrock (*mor*-gern-rok) *m* (pl ¨e) dressing-gown

morgens (*mor*-gerns) *adv* in the morning

Morgenzeitung (*mor*-gern-tsigh-toong) *f* (pl ~en) morning paper

Morphium (*mor*-fᵞoom) *nt* morphine, morphia

Mosaik (moa-zah-*eek*) *nt* (pl ~en) mosaic

Moschee (mo-*shāy*) *f* (pl ~n) mosque

Moskito (moss-*kee*-toa) *m* (pl ~s) mosquito

Moskitonetz (moss-*kee*-toa-nehts) *nt* (pl ~e) mosquito-net

Motel (moa-*tehl*) *nt* (pl ~s) motel

Motiv (moa-*teef*) *nt* (pl ~e) motive; pattern

Motor (*mōa*-tor) *m* (pl ~en) engine, motor

Motorboot (*mōa*-tor-bōat) *nt* (pl ~e) motor-boat

Motorhaube (*mōa*-tor-hou-ber) *f* (pl ~n) bonnet; hood *nAm*

Motorrad (*mōa*-tor-raat) *nt* (pl ¨er) motor-cycle

Motorroller (*mōa*-tor-ro-lerr) *m* (pl ~) scooter

Motorschiff (*mōa*-tor-shif) *nt* (pl ~e)

launch

Motte (*mo*-ter) *f* (pl ~n) moth

Möwe (*mūr*-ver) *f* (pl ~n) gull

Mücke (*mew*-ker) *f* (pl ~n) mosquito

müde (*mew*-der) *adj* tired; weary

Mühe (*mew*-er) *f* (pl ~n) trouble; difficulty, pains; **sich** ~ ***geben** bother

Mühle (*mew*-ler) *f* (pl ~n) mill

Müll (mewl) *m* garbage, trash

Müller (*mew*-lerr) *m* (pl ~) miller

Multiplikation (mool-ti-pli-kah-*tsʸōan*) *f* (pl ~en) multiplication

multiplizieren (mool-ti-pli-*tsee*-rern) *v* multiply

Mumm (moom) *m* guts

Mumps (moomps) *m* mumps

Mund (moont) *m* (pl ~er) mouth

Mundart (*moont*-ahrt) *f* (pl ~en) dialect

mündig (*mewn*-dikh) *adj* of age

mündlich (*mewnt*-likh) *adj* oral, verbal

Mündung (*mewn*-doong) *f* (pl ~en) mouth

Mundwasser (*moont*-vah-serr) *nt* mouthwash

Münze (*mewn*-tser) *f* (pl ~n) coin; token

Münzwäscherei (*mewnts*-veh-sher-righ) *f* (pl ~en) launderette

Murmel (*moor*-merl) *f* (pl ~n) marble

murren (*moo*-rern) *v* grumble

Muschel (*moo*-sherl) *f* (pl ~n) seashell, shell; mussel

Museum (moo-*zāʸ*-oom) *nt* (pl Museen) museum

Musical (*mʸōō*-zi-kerl) *nt* (pl ~s) musical comedy

Musik (moo-*zeek*) *f* music

musikalisch (moo-zi-*kaa*-lish) *adj* musical

Musiker (*mōō*-zi-kerr) *m* (pl ~) musician

Musikinstrument (moo-*zeek*-in-stroo-

mehnt) *nt* (pl ~e) musical instrument

Muskatnuß (mooss-*kaat*-nooss) *f* (pl -nüsse) nutmeg

Muskel (*mooss*-kerl) *m* (pl ~n) muscle

muskulös (mooss-koo-*lūrss*) *adj* muscular

Muße (*mōō*-ser) *f* leisure

Musselin (moo-ser-*leen*) *m* muslin

*müssen (*mew*-sern) *v* *must; need to, *have to, *be obliged to, *should; *be bound to

müßig (*mēw*-sikh) *adj* idle

Muster (*mooss*-terr) *nt* (pl ~) pattern; sample

Mut (mōōt) *m* courage

mutig (*mōō*-tikh) *adj* brave, courageous; plucky

Mutter (*moo*-terr) *f* (pl ~) mother

Muttersprache (*moo*-terr-shpraa-kher) *f* native language, mother tongue

Mütze (*mew*-tser) *f* (pl ~n) cap

Mythos (*mēw*-toss) *m* (pl Mythen) myth

N

Nabel (*naa*-berl) *m* (pl ~) navel

nach (naakh) *prep* to; towards, for; at; after; **unterwegs** ~ bound for

nachahmen (*naakh*-aa-mern) *v* copy; imitate

Nachahmung (*naakh*-aa-moong) *f* imitation

Nachbar (*nahkh*-baar) *m* (pl ~n) neighbour

Nachbarschaft (*nahkh*-baar-shahft) *f* (pl ~en) neighbourhood; vicinity

nachdem (naakh-*dāym*) *conj* after

*nachdenken (*naakh*-dehng-kern) *v* *think

nachdenklich (*naakh*-dehngk-likh) *adj*

thoughtful

nachfolgen (*naakh*-fol-gern) *v* succeed

Nachfrage (*naakh*-fraa-ger) *f* (pl ~n) demand; inquiry

nachfragen (*naakh*-fraa-gern) *v* inquire

*nachgeben (*naakh*-gay-bern) *v* *give in, indulge

nachher (naakh-*hayr*) *adv* afterwards

Nachkomme (*naakh*-ko-mer) *m* (pl ~n) descendant

nachlässig (*naakh*-leh-sikh) *adj* neglectful, careless

nachmachen (*naakh*-mah-khern) *v* imitate

Nachmittag (*naakh*-mi-taak) *m* (pl ~e) afternoon

Nachname (*naakh*-naa-mer) *m* family name

nachprüfen (*naakh*-prew-fern) *v* verify

Nachricht (*naakh*-rikht) *f* (pl ~en) message; information; **Nachrichten** news; tidings *pl*

Nachsaison (*naakh*-zeh-zawng) *f* low season

*nachsenden (*naakh*-zehn-dern) *v* forward

nachspüren (*naakh*-shpew-rern) *v* trace

nächst (naikhst) *adj* next, following

nachstreben (*naakh*-shtray-bern) *v* pursue

nachsuchen (*naakh*-zoo-khern) *v* look up

Nacht (nahkht) *f* (pl ~e) night; **bei ~** by night; **über ~** overnight

Nachteil (*naakh*-tighl) *m* (pl ~e) disadvantage

nachteilig (*naakh*-tigh-likh) *adj* harmful

Nachtflug (*nahkht*-flook) *m* (pl ~e) night flight

Nachthemd (*nahkht*-hehmt) *nt* (pl ~en) nightdress

Nachtigall (*nahkh*-ti-gahl) *f* (pl ~en) nightingale

Nachtisch (*naakh*-tish) *m* (pl ~e) dessert, sweet

Nachtklub (*nahkht*-kloop) *m* (pl ~s) cabaret

Nachtkrem (*nahkht*-kraym) *f* (pl ~s) night-cream

nächtlich (*nehkht*-likh) *adj* nightly

Nachtlokal (*nahkht*-loa-kaal) *nt* (pl ~e) nightclub

Nachttarif (*nahkht*-tah-reef) *m* (pl ~e) night rate

Nachtzug (*nahkht*-tsook) *m* (pl ~e) night train

Nacken (*nah*-kern) *m* (pl ~) nape of the neck

nackt (nahkt) *adj* naked; nude, bare

Nadel (*naa*-derl) *f* (pl ~n) needle

Nagel (*naa*-gerl) *m* (pl ~) nail

Nagelbürste (*naa*-gerl-bewrs-ter) *f* (pl ~n) nailbrush

Nagelfeile (*naa*-gerl-figh-ler) *f* (pl ~n) nail-file

Nagellack (*naa*-gerl-lahk) *m* nail-polish

nagelneu (*naa*-gerl-noi) *adj* brand-new

Nagelschere (*naa*-gerl-shay-rer) *f* (pl ~n) nail-scissors *pl*

Nähe (*nay*-er) *f* vicinity

nahe (*naa*-er) *adj* nearby, near; close

nähen (*nai*-ern) *v* sew; sew up

sich nähern (*nai*-errn) approach

nahezu (*naa*-er-tsoo) *adv* practically

Nähmaschine (*nai*-mah-shee-ner) *f* (pl ~n) sewing-machine

nahrhaft (*naar*-hahft) *adj* nutritious, nourishing

Nahrung (*naa*-roong) *f* food

Nahrungsmittel (*naa*-roongs-mi-terl) *ntpl* foodstuffs *pl*

Nahrungsmittelvergiftung (*naa*-roongs-mi-terl-fehr-gif-toong) *f* food poisoning

Naht (naat) f (pl ⁓e) seam

nahtlos (naat-lōass) adj seamless

Nahverkehrszug (naa-fehr-kāyrs-tsōōk) m (pl ⁓e) local train

naiv (nah-eef) adj naïve

Name (naa-mer) m (pl ⁓n) name; fame; denomination; **im Namen von** on behalf of, in the name of

nämlich (naim-likh) adv namely

Narbe (nahr-ber) f (pl ⁓n) scar

Narkose (nahr-kōā-zer) f narcosis

Narr (nahr) m (pl ⁓en) fool

närrisch (neh-rish) adj foolish

Narzisse (nahr-tsi-ser) f (pl ⁓n) daffodil

Nascherei (nah-sher-righ) f (pl ⁓en) candy nAm

Nase (naa-zer) f (pl ⁓n) nose

Nasenbluten (naa-zern-blōō-tern) nt nosebleed

Nasenloch (naa-zern-lokh) nt (pl ⁓er) nostril

Nashorn (naass-horn) nt (pl ⁓er) rhinoceros

naß (nahss) adj wet; damp, moist

Nation (nah-tsʸōān) f (pl ⁓en) nation

national (nah-tsʸoa-naal) adj national

Nationalhymne (nah-tsʸoa-naal-hewm-ner) f (pl ⁓n) national anthem

nationalisieren (nah-tsʸoa-nah-li-zee-rern) v nationalize

Natur (nah-tōōr) f nature

natürlich (nah-tewr-likh) adj natural; adv naturally

Naturschutzpark (nah-tōōr-shoots-pahrk) m (pl ⁓s) national park

Naturwissenschaft (nah-tōōr-vi-sern-shahft) f physics

Navigation (nah-vi-gah-tsʸōān) f navigation

Nebel (nāy-berl) m (pl ⁓) fog, mist; haze

nebelig (nāy-ber-likh) adj foggy, misty

Nebellampe (nāy-berl-lahm-per) f (pl ⁓n) foglamp

neben (nāy-bern) prep next to, beside

nebenan (nāy-bern-ahn) adv next-door

Nebenanschluß (nāy-bern-ahn-shlooss) m (pl -schlüsse) extension

Nebenbedeutung (nāy-bern-ber-doi-toong) f (pl ⁓en) connotation

Nebenfluß (nāy-bern-flooss) m (pl -flüsse) tributary

Nebengebäude (nāy-bern-ger-boi-der) nt (pl ⁓) annex

nebensächlich (nāy-bern-zehkh-likh) adj additional

necken (neh-kern) v tease

Neffe (neh-fer) m (pl ⁓n) nephew

Negativ (nay-gah-teef) nt (pl ⁓e) negative

negativ (nay-gah-teef) adj negative

Neger (nāy-gerr) m (pl ⁓) Negro

Negligé (nay-gli-zhāy) nt (pl ⁓s) negligee

***nehmen** (nāy-mern) v *take; *catch

Neid (night) m envy

neidisch (nigh-dish) adj envious

neigen (nigh-gern) v *be inclined to; tend; **sich ⁓** slant

Neigung (nigh-goong) f (pl ⁓en) incline; inclination, tendency

nein (nighn) no

***nennen** (neh-nern) v call; name; mention

Neon (nāy-on) nt neon

Nerv (nehrf) m (pl ⁓en) nerve

nervös (nehr-vŭrss) adj nervous

Nerz (nehrts) m (pl ⁓e) mink

Nest (nehst) nt (pl ⁓er) nest

nett (neht) adj nice, pleasant, kind; neat

netto (neh-toa) adj net

Netz (nehts) nt (pl ⁓e) net; network

Netzhaut (nehts-hout) f retina

neu (noi) adj new

Neuerwerbung (*noi*-ehr-vehr-boong) *f* (pl ~en) acquisition

Neugier (*noi*-geer) *f* curiosity

neugierig (*noi*-gee-rikh) *adj* curious, inquisitive

Neuigkeit (*noi*-ikh-kight) *f* (pl ~en) news

Neujahr (*noi*-ⁱaar) New Year

neulich (*noi*-likh) *adv* recently

neun (noin) *num* nine

neunte (*noin*-ter) *num* ninth

neunzehn (*noin*-tsāȳn) *num* nineteen

neunzehnte (*noin*-tsāȳn-ter) *num* nineteenth

neunzig (*noin*-tsikh) *num* ninety

Neuralgie (noi-rahl-*gee*) *f* neuralgia

Neurose (noi-*rōā*-zer) *f* (pl ~n) neurosis

Neuseeland (*noi*-zāȳ-lahnt) New Zealand

neutral (noi-*traal*) *adj* neutral

nicht (nikht) *adv* not

Nichte (*nikh*-ter) *f* (pl ~n) niece

nichtig (*nikh*-tikh) *adj* void

nichts (nikhts) *pron* nothing; nil

nichtsdestoweniger (nikhts-dehss-toa-*vāȳ*-ni-gerr) *adv* nevertheless

nichtssagend (*nikhts*-zaa-gernt) *adj* insignificant

Nickel (*ni*-kerl) *m* nickel

Nicken (*ni*-kern) *nt* nod

nicken (*ni*-kern) *v* nod

nie (nee) *adv* never

nieder (*nee*-derr) *adv* down; over

niedergeschlagen (*nee*-derr-ger-shlaa-gern) *adj* depressed; down, low, sad, blue

Niedergeschlagenheit (*nee*-derr-ger-shlaa-gern-hight) *f* depression

Niederlage (*nee*-derr-laa-ger) *f* (pl ~n) defeat

Niederlande (*nee*-derr-lahn-der) *fpl* the Netherlands

Niederländer (*nee*-derr-lehn-derr) *m*

(pl ~) Dutchman

niederländisch (*nee*-derr-lehn-dish) *adj* Dutch

sich *niederlassen (*nee*-derr-lah-sern) settle down

sich niederlegen (*nee*-derr-lāȳ-gern) **lie down

*niederreißen (*nee*-derr-righ-sern) *v* demolish

Niederschläge (*nee*-derr-shlai-ger) *mpl* precipitation

*niederschlagen (*nee*-derr-shlaa-gern) *v* knock down

niederträchtig (*nee*-derr-trehkh-tikh) *adj* foul, mean

niedrig (*nee*-drikh) *adj* low

niemals (*nee*-maals) *adv* never

niemand (*nee*-mahnt) *pron* nobody, no one

Niere (*nee*-rer) *f* (pl ~n) kidney

niesen (*nee*-zern) *v* sneeze

Nigeria (ni-*gāȳ*-rⁱah) Nigeria

Nigerianer (ni-gay-rⁱaa-nerr) *m* (pl ~) Nigerian

nigerianisch (ni-gay-rⁱaa-nish) *adj* Nigerian

Nikotin (ni-koa-*teen*) *nt* nicotine

nirgends (*neer*-gernts) *adv* nowhere

Niveau (ni-*vōā*) *nt* (pl ~s) level

nivellieren (ni-veh-*lee*-rern) *v* level

noch (nokh) *adv* still; yet; ~ **ein** another; ~ **einmal** once more; **weder** ... ~ neither ... nor

nochmals (*nokh*-maals) *adv* again

Nockenwelle (*no*-kern-veh-ler) *f* (pl ~n) camshaft

nominell (noa-mi-*nehl*) *adj* nominal

Nonne (*no*-ner) *f* (pl ~n) nun

Nonnenkloster (*no*-nern-klōáss-terr) *nt* (pl ˜) nunnery

Norden (*nor*-dern) *m* north

nördlich (*nurrt*-likh) *adj* northern, northerly, north

Nordosten (nort-*oss*-tern) *m* north-east

Nordpol (*nort*-pōal) *m* North Pole

Nordwesten (nort-*vehss*-tern) *m* north-west

Norm (norm) *f* (pl ~en) standard

normal (nor-*maal*) *adj* normal; regular

Norwegen (*nor*-vāy-gern) Norway

Norweger (*nor*-vāy-gerr) *m* (pl ~) Norwegian

norwegisch (*nor*-vāy-gish) *adj* Norwegian

Not (nōat) *f* (pl ~e) distress, misery; need

Notar (noa-*taar*) *m* (pl ~e) notary

Notausgang (*nōat*-ouss-gahng) *m* (pl ~e) emergency exit

Notfall (*nōat*-fahl) *m* (pl ~e) emergency

nötig (*nūr*-tikh) *adj* necessary; ~ *haben need

Notiz (noa-*teets*) *f* (pl ~en) note

Notizblock (noa-*teets*-blok) *m* (pl ~e) writing-pad

Notizbuch (noa-*teets*-bōokh) *nt* (pl ~er) notebook

Notlage (*nōat*-laa-ger) *f* emergency

Notsignal (*nōat*-zi-gnaal) *nt* (pl ~e) distress signal

Nottreppe (*nōat*-treh-per) *f* (pl ~n) fire-escape

notwendig (*nōat*-vehn-dikh) *adj* necessary

Notwendigkeit (*nōat*-vehn-dikh-kight) *f* (pl ~en) need, necessity

Nougat (*nōo*-gaht) *m* nougat

November (noa-*vehm*-berr) November

Nuance (new-*ahng*-ser) *f* (pl ~n) nuance

nüchtern (*newkh*-terrn) *adj* matter-of-fact; sober

nuklear (noo-klay-*aar*) *adj* nuclear

Null (nool) *f* (pl ~en) nought; zero

Nummer (*noo*-merr) *f* (pl ~n) number; size; act

Nummernschild (*noo*-merrn-shilt) *nt* (pl ~er) registration plate; licence plate *Am*

nun (nōon) *adv* now

nur (nōōr) *adv* merely; only, exclusively

Nuß (nooss) *f* (pl Nüsse) nut

Nußknacker (*nooss*-knah-kerr) *m* (pl ~) nutcrackers *pl*

Nußschale (*nooss*-shaa-ler) *f* (pl ~n) nutshell

Nutzen (*noo*-tsern) *m* profit, benefit; interest; utility, use

nützen (*new*-tsern) *v* *be of use

nützlich (*newts*-likh) *adj* useful

nutzlos (*noots*-lōass) *adj* useless; idle

Nylon (*nigh*-lon) *nt* nylon

O

Oase (oa-*aa*-zer) *f* (pl ~n) oasis

ob (op) *conj* whether; ~ ... **oder** whether ... or

Obdach (*op*-dahkh) *nt* cover

oben (*ōa*-bern) *adv* above; upstairs; overhead; **nach** ~ up; upstairs; ~ **auf** on top of

Ober (*ōa*-berr) *m* (pl ~) waiter

ober (*ōa*-berr) *adj* superior, upper; **Ober-** chief

Oberdeck (*ōa*-berr-dehk) *nt* main deck

Oberfläche (*ōa*-berr-fleh-kher) *f* (pl ~n) surface

oberflächlich (*ōa*-berr-flehkh-likh) *adj* superficial

oberhalb (*ōa*-berr-hahlp) *prep* over

Oberkellner (*ōa*-berr-kehl-nerr) *m* (pl ~) head-waiter

Oberschenkel (*ōa*-berr-shehng-kerl) *m* (pl ~) thigh

Oberseite (*ōa*-berr-zigh-ter) *f* (pl ~n)

top side

Oberst (*ōā*-berrst) *m* (pl ~en) colonel

oberst (*ōā*-berrst) *adj* top

obgleich (op-*glighkh*) *conj* although, though

Obhut (*op*-hōōt) *f* custody

Objekt (op-*Yehkt*) *nt* (pl ~e) object

objektiv (op-Yehk-*teef*) *adj* objective

Oblate (oa-*blaa*-ter) *f* (pl ~n) wafer

Obligation (oa-bli-gah-ts*Yōān*) *f* (pl ~en) bond

obligatorisch (oa-bli-gah-*tōā*-rish) *adj* compulsory, obligatory

Observation (op-zehr-vah-ts*Yōān*) *f* (pl ~en) observation

Observatorium (op-zehr-vah-*tōā*-rYoom) *nt* (pl -rien) observatory

observieren (op-zehr-*vee*-rern) *v* observe

obskur (ops-*kōōr*) *adj* obscure

Obst (*ōā*pst) *nt* fruit

Obstgarten (*ōā*pst-gahr-tern) *m* (pl ~̈) orchard

Obstipation (op-sti-pah-ts*Yōān*) *f* constipation

obszön (ops-*tsȫrn*) *adj* obscene

Obus (*ōā*-booss) *m* (pl ~se) trolley-bus

obwohl (op-*vōāl*) *conj* although, though

Ochse (*o*-kser) *m* (pl ~n) ox

oder (*ōā*-derr) *conj* or

Ofen (*ōā*-fern) *m* (pl ~̈) stove; furnace

offen (*o*-fern) *adj* open

offenbaren (o-fern-*baa*-rern) *v* reveal

offenherzig (o-fern-hehr-tsikh) *adj* open

offensichtlich (*o*-fern-zikht-likh) *adj* obvious, apparent, evident

offensiv (o-fehn-*zeef*) *adj* offensive

Offensive (o-fehn-*zee*-ver) *f* (pl ~n) offensive

öffentlich (*ur*-fernt-likh) *adj* public

offiziell (o-fi-ts*Yehl*) *adj* official

Offizier (o-fi-*tseer*) *m* (pl ~e) officer

offiziös (o-fi-ts*Yūrss*) *adj* unofficial

öffnen (*urf*-nern) *v* open

Öffnung (*urf*-noong) *f* (pl ~en) opening

Öffnungszeiten (*urf*-noongs-tsigh-tern) *fpl* business hours

oft (oft) *adv* often; frequently

ohne (*ōā*-ner) *prep* without

ohnehin (*ōā*-ner-*hin*) *adv* anyway

Ohr (*ōār*) *nt* (pl ~en) ear

Ohrenschmerzen (*ōā*-rern-shmehr-tsern) *mpl* earache

Ohrring (*ōār*-ring) *m* (pl ~e) earring

Oktober (ok-*tōā*-berr) October

Öl (*ūl*) *nt* (pl ~e) oil

Öldruck (*ūl*-drook) *m* oil pressure

ölen (*ūr*-lern) *v* lubricate

Ölfilter (*ūr*-fil-terr) *nt* (pl ~) oil filter

Ölgemälde (*ūr*-ger-mail-der) *nt* (pl ~) oil-painting

ölig (*ūr*-likh) *adj* oily

Olive (oa-*lee*-ver) *f* (pl ~n) olive

Olivenöl (oa-*lee*-vern-ūrl) *nt* olive oil

Ölquelle (*ūrl*-kveh-ler) *f* (pl ~n) oil-well

Ölraffinerie (*ūrl*-rah-fi-ner-ree) *f* (pl ~n) oil-refinery

Oma (*ōā*-mah) *f* (pl ~s) grandmother

Onkel (*ong*-kerl) *m* (pl ~) uncle

Onyx (*ōā*-newks) *m* (pl ~e) onyx

Opa (*ōā*-pah) *m* (pl ~s) grandfather, granddad

Opal (oa-*paal*) *m* (pl ~e) opal

Oper (*ōā*-perr) *f* (pl ~n) opera

Operation (oa-pay-rah-ts*Yōān*) *f* (pl ~en) operation; surgery

Operette (oa-pay-*reh*-ter) *f* (pl ~n) operetta

operieren (oa-pay-*ree*-rern) *v* operate

Opernglas (*ōā*-perrn-glaass) *nt* (pl ~̈er) binoculars *pl*

Opernhaus (*ōā*-perrn-houss) *nt* (pl

~er) opera house

Opfer (*o*-pferr) *nt* (pl ~) sacrifice; casualty, victim

Opposition (o-poa-zi-*tsУ ōān*) *f* opposition

Optiker (*op*-ti-kerr) *m* (pl ~) optician

Optimismus (op-ti-*miss*-mooss) *m* optimism

Optimist (op-ti-*mist*) *m* (pl ~en) optimist

optimistisch (op-ti-*miss*-tish) *adj* optimistic

orange (oa-*rahng*-zher) *adj* orange

Orchester (or-*kehss*-terr) *nt* (pl ~) orchestra

Orden (*or*-dern) *m* (pl ~) congregation

ordentlich (*or*-dernt-likh) *adj* tidy

ordinär (or-di-*nair*) *adj* vulgar

ordnen (*or*-dnern) *v* arrange; sort

Ordnung (*or*-dnoong) *f* order; method, system; **in ~** in order; **in Ordnung!** okay!

Organ (or-*gaan*) *nt* (pl ~e) organ

Organisation (or-gah-ni-zah-*tsУ ōān*) *f* (pl ~en) organization

organisch (or-*gaa*-nish) *adj* organic

organisieren (or-gah-ni-*zee*-rern) *v* organize

Orgel (*or*-gerl) *f* (pl ~n) organ

Orient (*ōā*-ri-ehnt) *m* Orient

orientalisch (oa-ri-ehn-*taa*-lish) *adj* oriental

sich orientieren (oa-ri-ehn-*tee*-rern) orientate

originell (oa-ri-gi-*nehl*) *adj* original

Orlon (*or*-lon) *nt* orlon

ornamental (or-nah-mehn-*taal*) *adj* ornamental

Ort (ort) *m* (pl ~e) place

orthodox (or-toa-*doks*) *adj* orthodox

örtlich (*urrt*-likh) *adj* local; regional

Örtlichkeit (*urrt*-likh-kight) *f* (pl ~en) locality

Ortsansässige (*orts*-ahn-zeh-si-ger) *m* (pl ~n) resident

Ortsgespräch (*orts*-ger-shpraikh) *nt* (pl ~e) local call

Ortsnetzkennzahl (*orts*-nehts-kehn-tsaal) *f* area code

Osten (*oss*-tern) *m* east

Ostern (*ōāss*-terrn) Easter

Österreich (*ūrss*-ter-righkh) Austria

Österreicher (*ūrss*-ter-righ-kherr) *m* (pl ~) Austrian

österreichisch (*ūr*-ster-righ-khish) *adj* Austrian

östlich (*urst*-likh) *adj* eastern, easterly

Ouvertüre (oo-vehr-*teū*-rer) *f* (pl ~n) overture

oval (oa-*vaal*) *adj* oval

Ozean (*ōā*-tsay-aan) *m* (pl ~e) ocean

P

Paar (paar) *nt* (pl ~e) pair; couple

Pacht (pahkht) *f* lease

Päckchen (*pehk*-khern) *nt* (pl ~) packet

packen (*pah*-kern) *v* pack

Packkorb (*pahk*-korp) *m* (pl ~e) hamper

Packpapier (*pahk*-pah-peer) *nt* wrapping paper

Paddel (*pah*-derl) *nt* (pl ~) paddle

Paket (pah-*kāyt*) *nt* (pl ~e) parcel, package

Pakistan (*paa*-kiss-taan) Pakistan

Pakistaner (paa-kiss-*taa*-nerr) *m* (pl ~) Pakistani

pakistanisch (paa-kiss-*taa*-nish) *adj* Pakistani

Palast (pah-*lahst*) *m* (pl ~e) palace

Palme (*pahl*-mer) *f* (pl ~n) palm

Pampelmuse (pahm-perl-*mōō*-zer) *f* (pl ~n) grapefruit

Paneel (pah-*nāȳl*) *nt* (pl ~e) panel

Panik (*paa*-nik) *f* panic

Panne (*pah*-ner) *f* (pl ~n) break-down; **eine ~ *haben** *break down

Pantoffel (pahn-*to*-ferl) *m* (pl ~n) slipper

Papagei (pah-pah-*gigh*) *m* (pl ~e) parrot

Papier (pah-*peer*) *nt* paper

papieren (pah-*pee*-rern) *adj* paper

Papierkorb (pah-*peer*-korp) *m* (pl ~e) wastepaper-basket

Papierserviette (pah-*peer*-zehr-vᵛeh-ter) *f* (pl ~n) paper napkin

Papiertaschentuch (pah-*peer*-tah-shern-tōōkh) *nt* (pl ~er) tissue

Pappe (*pah*-per) *f* cardboard; **Papp-cardboard**

Papst (paapst) *m* (pl ~e) pope

Parade (pah-*raa*-der) *f* (pl ~n) parade; review

parallel (pah-rah-*lāȳl*) *adj* parallel

Parallele (pah-rah-*lāȳ*-ler) *f* (pl ~n) parallel

Parfüm (pahr-*feȳm*) *nt* (pl ~s) scent; perfume

Park (pahrk) *m* (pl ~s) park

parken (*pahr*-kern) *v* park; **Parken verboten** no parking

Parkgebühr (*pahrk*-ger-beȳr) *f* (pl ~en) parking fee

Parkleuchte (*pahrk*-loikh-ter) *f* (pl ~n) parking light

Parkplatz (*pahrk*-plahts) *m* (pl ~e) car park, parking lot *Am*

Parkuhr (*pahrk*-ōōr) *f* (pl ~en) parking meter

Parkzone (*pahrk*-tsōa-ner) *f* (pl ~n) parking zone

Parlament (pahr-lah-*mehnt*) *nt* (pl ~e) parliament

parlamentarisch (pahr-lah-mehn-*taa*-rish) *adj* parliamentary

Partei (pahr-*tigh*) *f* (pl ~en) party;
side

parteiisch (pahr-*tigh*-ish) *adj* partial

Partie (pahr-*tee*) *f* (pl ~n) batch

Partner (*pahrt*-nerr) *m* (pl ~) associate; partner

Party (*paar*-ti) *f* (pl -ties) party

Parzelle (pahr-*tseh*-ler) *f* (pl ~n) plot

Paß (pahss) *m* (pl Pässe) passport

Passagier (pah-sah-*zheer*) *m* (pl ~e) passenger

Passant (pah-*sahnt*) *m* (pl ~en) passer-by

passen (*pah*-sern) *v* fit; suit; ~ **zu** match

passend (*pah*-sernt) *adj* adequate, proper; convenient

passieren (pah-*see*-rern) *v* pass; happen

Passion (pah-sᵛōan) *f* passion

passiv (*pah*-seef) *adj* passive

Paßkontrolle (*pahss*-kon-tro-ler) *f* (pl ~n) passport control

Paßphoto (*pahss*-fōa-toa) *nt* (pl ~s) passport photograph

Paste (*pahss*-ter) *f* (pl ~n) paste

Pastor (*pahss*-tor) *m* (pl ~en) rector, clergyman

Pate (*paa*-ter) *m* (pl ~n) godfather

Patent (pah-*tehnt*) *nt* (pl ~e) patent

Pater (*paa*-terr) *m* (pl ~) father

Patient (pah-tsᵛehnt) *m* (pl ~en) patient

Patriot (pah-tri-*ōat*) *m* (pl ~en) patriot

Patrone (pah-*trōa*-ner) *f* (pl ~n) cartridge

patrouillieren (pah-trool-ᵛee-rern) *v* patrol

Pauschalsumme (pou-*shaal*-zoo-mer) *f* (pl ~n) lump sum

Pause (*pou*-zer) *f* (pl ~n) pause; break, interval, intermission

pausieren (pou-*zee*-rern) *v* pause

Pavillon (*pah*-vi-lᵛawng) *m* (pl ~s) pavilion

Pazifismus (pah-tsi-*fiss*-mooss) *m* pacifism

Pazifist (pah-tsi-*fist*) *m* (pl ~en) pacifist

pazifistisch (pah-tsi-*fiss*-tish) *adj* pacifist

Pech (pehkh) *nt* bad luck

Pedal (pay-*daal*) *nt* (pl ~en) pedal

Peddigrohr (*peh*-dig-rōar) *nt* rattan

peinlich (*pighn*-likh) *adj* embarrassing, awkward

Peitsche (*pigh*-cher) *f* (pl ~n) whip

Pelikan (*pāy*-li-kaan) *m* (pl ~e) pelican

Pelz (pehlts) *m* (pl ~e) fur

Pelzmantel (*pehlts*-mahn-terl) *m* (pl ~) fur coat

Pelzwerk (*pehlts*-vehrk) *nt* furs

Pendler (*pehn*-dlerr) *m* (pl ~) commuter

Penicillin (pay-ni-tsi-*leen*) *nt* penicillin

Pension (pahng-sʸ*ōan*) *f* (pl ~en) board; boarding-house; pension

pensioniert (pahng-sʸoa-*neert*) *adj* retired

Perfektion (pehr-fehk-*tsʸōan*) *f* perfection

periodisch (pay-rʸ*ōa*-dish) *adj* periodical

Perle (*pehr*-ler) *f* (pl ~n) pearl; bead

perlend (*pehr*-lernt) *adj* sparkling

Perlmutt (*pehrl*-moot) *nt* mother-of-pearl

Perser (*pehr*-zerr) *m* (pl ~) Persian

Persien (*pehr*-zʸern) Persia

persisch (*pehr*-zish) *adj* Persian

Person (pehr-*zōan*) *f* (pl ~en) person; pro ~ per person

Personal (pehr-zoa-*naal*) *nt* staff, personnel

Personalbeschreibung (pehr-zoa-naal-ber-shrigh-boong) *f* (pl ~en) description

Personenzug (pehr-*zōa*-nern-tsōok) *m* (pl ~e) passenger train

persönlich (pehr-*zūrn*-likh) *adj* personal, private

Persönlichkeit (pehr-*zūrn*-likh-kight) *f* (pl ~en) personality

Perspektive (pehr-spehk-*tee*-ver) *f* (pl ~n) perspective

Perücke (peh-*rew*-ker) *f* (pl ~n) wig

Pessimismus (peh-si-*miss*-mooss) *m* pessimism

Pessimist (peh-si-*mist*) *m* (pl ~en) pessimist

pessimistisch (peh-si-*miss*-tish) *adj* pessimistic

Petersilie (pay-terr-*zee*-lʸer) *f* parsley

Petroleum (pay-*trōa*-lay-oom) *nt* petroleum, oil; paraffin

Pfad (pfaat) *m* (pl ~e) trail, lane, path

Pfadfinder (*pfaat*-fin-derr) *m* (pl ~) boy scout, scout

Pfadfinderin (*pfaat*-fin-der-rin) *f* (pl ~nen) girl guide

Pfand (pfahnt) *nt* (pl ~er) security; deposit

Pfandleiher (*pfahnt*-ligh-err) *m* (pl ~) pawnbroker

Pfanne (*pfah*-ner) *f* (pl ~n) saucepan, pan

Pfarre (*pfah*-rer) *f* (pl ~n) rectory

Pfarrer (*pfah*-rerr) *m* (pl ~) clergyman; rector, parson

Pfarrhaus (*pfahr*-houss) *nt* (pl ~er) vicarage, parsonage

Pfau (pfou) *m* (pl ~en) peacock

Pfeffer (*pfeh*-ferr) *m* pepper

Pfefferminze (*pfeh*-ferr-min-tser) *f* peppermint

Pfeife (*pfigh*-fer) *f* (pl ~n) pipe; whistle

***pfeifen** (*pfigh*-fern) *v* whistle

Pfeifenreiniger (*pfigh*-fern-righ-ni-gerr) *m* (pl ~) pipe cleaner

Pfeil (pfighl) *m* (pl ~e) arrow

Pfeiler (*pfigh*-lerr) *m* (pl ~) column, pillar

Pferd (pfāyrt) *nt* (pl ~e) horse

Pferderennen (*pfāyr*-der-reh-nern) *nt* (pl ~) horserace

Pferdestärke (*pfāyr*-der-shtehr-ker) *f* (pl ~n) horsepower

Pfingsten (*pfings*-tern) Whitsun

Pfirsich (*pfeer*-zikh) *m* (pl ~e) peach

Pflanze (*pflahn*-tser) *f* (pl ~n) plant

pflanzen (*pflahn*-tsern) *v* plant

Pflaster (*pflahss*-terr) *nt* (pl ~) plaster; pavement

pflastern (*pflahss*-terrn) *v* pave

Pflaume (*pflou*-mer) *f* (pl ~n) plum

Pflege (*pflāy*-ger) *f* care

Pflegeeltern (*pflāy*-ger-ehl-terrn) *pl* foster-parents *pl*

pflegen (*pflāy*-gern) *v* nurse; tend; would

Pflicht (pflikht) *f* (pl ~en) duty

pflücken (*pflew*-kern) *v* pick

Pflug (pflook) *m* (pl ~e) plough

pflügen (*pflēw*-gern) *v* plough

Pförtner (*pfurrt*-nerr) *m* (pl ~) porter

Pfosten (*pfoss*-tern) *m* (pl ~) pole, post

Pfote (*pfōā*-ter) *f* (pl ~n) paw

pfui! (pfoo^ee) shame!

Pfund (pfoont) *nt* (pl ~e) pound

Pfütze (*pfew*-tser) *f* (pl ~n) puddle

Phantasie (fahn-tah-*see*) *f* fancy

phantastisch (fahn-*tahss*-tish) *adj* fantastic

Phase (*faa*-zer) *f* (pl ~n) stage; phase

Philippine (fi-li-*pee*-ner) *m* (pl ~n) Filipino

Philippinen (fi-li-*pee*-nern) *pl* Philippines *pl*

philippinisch (fi-li-*pee*-nish) *adj* Philippine

Philosoph (fi-loa-*zōāf*) *m* (pl ~en) philosopher

Philosophie (fi-loa-soa-*fee*) *f* (pl ~n) philosophy

phonetisch (foa-*nāy*-tish) *adj* phonetic

Photo (*fōā*-toa) *nt* (pl ~s) photo

Photogeschäft (*fōā*-toa-ger-shehft) *nt* (pl ~e) camera shop

Photograph (foa-toa-*graaf*) *m* (pl ~en) photographer

Photographie (foa-toa-grah-*fee*) *f* photography

photographieren (foa-toa-grah-*fee*-rern) *v* photograph

Photokopie (foa-toa-koa-*pee*) *f* (pl ~n) photostat

Physik (few-*zeek*) *f* physics

Physiker (*fēw*-zi-kerr) *m* (pl ~) physicist

Physiologie (few-z^yoa-loa-*gee*) *f* physiology

physisch (*fēw*-zish) *adj* physical

Pianist (p^yah-*nist*) *m* (pl ~en) pianist

Pickel (*pi*-kerl) *m* (pl ~) pimple

Pickles (*pi*-kerls) *pl* pickles *pl*

Picknick (*pik*-nik) *nt* picnic

picknicken (*pik*-ni-kern) *v* picnic

Pier (peer) *m* (pl ~s) pier, jetty

pikant (pi-*kahnt*) *adj* spicy, savoury

Pilger (*pil*-gerr) *m* (pl ~) pilgrim

Pilgerfahrt (*pil*-gerr-faart) *f* (pl ~en) pilgrimage

Pille (*pi*-ler) *f* (pl ~n) pill

Pilot (pi-*lōāt*) *m* (pl ~en) pilot

Pilz (pilts) *m* (pl ~e) mushroom; toadstool

Pinguin (ping-goo-*een*) *m* (pl ~e) penguin

Pinsel (*pin*-zerl) *m* (pl ~) brush, paint-brush

Pinzette (pin-*tseh*-ter) *f* (pl ~n) tweezers *pl*

Pionier (pi-oa-*neer*) *m* (pl ~e) pioneer

Pistole (piss-*tōā*-ler) *f* (pl ~n) pistol

pittoresk (pi-toa-*rehsk*) *adj* picturesque

plädieren (pleh-*dee*-rern) *v* plead

Plage (*plaa*-ger) *f* (pl ~n) plague

Plakat (plah-*kaat*) *nt* (pl ~e) poster, placard

Plan (plaan) *m* (pl ˜e) plan; scheme, project; map; schedule

Plane (*plaa*-ner) *f* (pl ~n) tarpaulin

planen (*plaa*-nern) *v* plan

Planet (plah-*nāyt*) *m* (pl ~en) planet

Planetarium (plah-nay-*taa*-r^yoom) *nt* (pl -rien) planetarium

Plantage (plahn-*taa*-zher) *f* (pl ~n) plantation

Plappermaul (*plah*-perr-moul) *nt* (pl ˜er) chatterbox

Platin (plah-*teen*) *nt* platinum

platt (plaht) *adj* level

Platte (*plah*-ter) *f* (pl ~n) plate, sheet; dish

Plattenspieler (*plah*-tern-shpee-lerr) *m* (pl ~) record-player

Platz (plahts) *m* (pl ˜e) spot; seat; room; square

Platzanweiser (*plahts*-ahn-vigh-zerr) *m* (pl ~) usher

Platzanweiserin (*plahts*-ahn-vigh-zer-rin) *f* (pl ~nen) usherette

plaudern (*plou*-derrn) *v* chat

Plombe (*plom*-ber) *f* (pl ~n) filling

Plötze (*plur*-tser) *f* (pl ~n) roach

plötzlich (*plurts*-likh) *adj* sudden; *adv* suddenly

Plunder (*ploon*-derr) *m* junk

plus (plooss) *adv* plus

pneumatisch (pnoi-*maa*-tish) *adj* pneumatic

pochen (*po*-khern) *v* tap

Pocken (*po*-kern) *fpl* smallpox

Pokal (poa-*kaal*) *m* (pl ~e) cup

Pole (*pōa*-ler) *m* (pl ~n) Pole

Polen (*pōa*-lern) Poland

Police (poa-*lee*-ser) *f* (pl ~n) policy

polieren (poa-*lee*-rern) *v* polish

Polio (*pōa*-l^yoa) *f* polio

Politik (poa-li-*teek*) *f* politics; policy

Politiker (poa-*lee*-ti-kerr) *m* (pl ~) politician

politisch (poa-*lee*-tish) *adj* political

Polizei (poa-li-*tsigh*) *f* police *pl*

Polizeiwache (poa-li-*tsigh*-vah-kher) *f* (pl ~n) police-station

Polizist (poa-li-*tsist*) *m* (pl ~en) policeman

polnisch (*pol*-nish) *adj* Polish

Polster (*pols*-terr) *nt* (pl ~) pad

polstern (*pols*-terrn) *v* upholster

Polyp (poa-*lēwp*) *m* (pl ~en) octopus

Pommes frites (pom-*frit*) chips

Pony (*po*-ni) *nt* (pl ~s) pony

Popelin (poa-per-*leen*) *m* poplin

Popmusik (*pop*-moo-zeek) *f* pop music

Portier (por-*t^yāy*) *m* (pl ~s) doorman, door-keeper

Portion (por-ts^y*ōan*) *f* (pl ~en) helping, portion

Porto (*por*-toa) *nt* postage

portofrei (*por*-toa-frigh) *adj* postage paid

Porträt (por-*trai*) *nt* (pl ~s) portrait

Portugal (*por*-too-gahl) Portugal

Portugiese (por-too-*gee*-zer) *m* (pl ~n) Portuguese

portugiesisch (por-too-*gee*-zish) *adj* Portuguese

Porzellan (por-tser-*laan*) *nt* porcelain, china

Position (poa-zi-ts^y*ōan*) *f* (pl ~en) position

Positiv (*pōa*-zi-teef) *nt* (pl ~e) positive

positiv (*pōa*-zi-teef) *adj* positive

Posse (*po*-ser) *f* (pl ~n) farce

Post (post) *f* post, mail

Postamt (*post*-ahmt) *nt* (pl ˜er) post-office

Postanweisung (*post*-ahn-vigh-zoong) *f* (pl ~en) postal order; mail order *Am*

Postbote (*post*-bōa-ter) *m* (pl ~n) postman

Postdienst (*post*-deenst) *m* postal service

Posten (*poss*-tern) *m* (pl ~) item; post

Postkarte (*post*-kahr-ter) *f* (pl ~n) postcard, card

postlagernd (*post*-laa-gerrnt) *adj* poste restante

Postleitzahl (*post*-light-tsaal) *f* (pl ~en) zip code *Am*

Pracht (prahkht) *f* splendour

prächtig (*prehkh*-tikh) *adj* magnificent; glorious, splendid, gorgeous, superb, wonderful, fine

Präfix (*preh*-fiks) *nt* (pl ~e) prefix

prahlen (*praa*-lern) *v* boast

praktisch (*prahk*-tish) *adj* practical

Praline (prah-*lee*-ner) *f* (pl ~n) chocolate

Prämie (*prai*-mᵛer) *f* (pl ~n) premium

Präposition (preh-poa-zi-*tsᵛōān*) *f* (pl ~en) preposition

Präsent (preh-*zehnt*) *nt* (pl ~e) present

Präsident (preh-zi-*dehnt*) *m* (pl ~en) president

Praxis (*prah*-ksiss) *f* practice

präzis (preh-*tseess*) *adj* precise, exact

predigen (*prāy*-di-gern) *v* preach

Predigt (*prāy*-dikht) *f* (pl ~en) sermon

Preis (prighss) *m* (pl ~e) cost, pricelist; award, prize; **den ~ festsetzen** price

Preisgericht (*prighss*-ger-rikht) *nt* (pl ~e) jury

Preisliste (*prighss*-liss-ter) *f* (pl ~n) price list

Preisnachlaß (*prighss*-naakh-lahss) *m* (pl -lässe) reduction

Preissenkung (*prighss*-sehng-koong) *f* (pl ~en) slump

Premierminister (prer-*mᵛāy*-mi-niss-terr) *m* (pl ~) premier

Presse (*preh*-ser) *f* press

Pressekonferenz (*preh*-ser-kon-fay-rehnts) *f* (pl ~en) press conference

Prestige (prehss-*tee*-zher) *nt* prestige

Priester (*preess*-terr) *m* (pl ~) priest

prima (*pree*-mah) *adj* first-rate

Prinz (prints) *m* (pl ~en) prince

Prinzessin (prin-*tseh*-sin) *f* (pl ~nen) princess

Prinzip (prin-*tseep*) *nt* (pl ~ien) principle

Priorität (pri-oa-ri-*tait*) *f* (pl ~en) priority

privat (pri-*vaat*) *adj* private

Privatleben (pri-*vaat*-lāy-bern) *nt* privacy

Probe (*prōā*-ber) *f* (pl ~n) test; rehearsal

proben (*prōā*-bern) *v* rehearse

probieren (proa-*bee*-rern) *v* try, attempt

Problem (proa-*blāym*) *nt* (pl ~e) problem; question

Produkt (proa-*dookt*) *nt* (pl ~e) product

Produktion (proa-dook-*tsᵛōān*) *f* production

Produzent (proa-doo-*tsehnt*) *m* (pl ~en) producer

Professor (proa-*feh*-sor) *m* (pl ~en) professor

profitieren (proa-fi-*tee*-rern) *v* profit, benefit

Programm (proa-*grahm*) *nt* (pl ~e) programme

progressiv (proa-greh-*seef*) *adj* progressive

Projekt (proa-ᵛ*ehkt*) *nt* (pl ~e) project

proklamieren (proa-klah-*mee*-rern) *v* proclaim

Promenade (proa-mer-*naa*-der) *f* (pl ~n) esplanade, promenade

Propaganda (proa-pah-*gahn*-dah) *f* propaganda

Propeller (proa-*peh*-lerr) *m* (pl ~) propeller

Prophet (proa-*fāyt*) *m* (pl ~en) prophet

proportional (proa-por-ts^yoa-*naal*) *adj* proportional

Prospekt (proa-*spehkt*) *m* (pl ~e) prospectus

Prostituierte (proa-sti-too-*eer*-ter) *f* (pl ~n) prostitute

Protein (proa-tay-*een*) *nt* (pl ~e) protein

Protest (proa-*tehst*) *m* (pl ~e) protest

protestantisch (proa-tehss-*tahn*-tish) *adj* Protestant

protestieren (proa-tehss-*tee*-rern) *v* protest

Protokoll (proa-toa-*kol*) *nt* (pl ~e) minutes

Provinz (proa-*vints*) *f* (pl ~en) province

provinziell (proa-vin-ts^y*ehl*) *adj* provincial

Prozent (proa-*tsehnt*) *nt* (pl ~e) percent

Prozentsatz (proa-*tsehnt*-zahts) *m* (pl ~e) percentage

Prozeß (proa-*tsehss*) *m* (pl -zesse) lawsuit, process

Prozession (proa-tseh-s^y*ōān*) *f* (pl ~en) procession

prüfen (*prēw*-fern) *v* check, examine; test

Prügel (*prēw*-gerl) *pl* spanking

Psychiater (psew-khi-*aa*-terr) *m* (pl ~) psychiatrist

psychisch (*psēw*-khish) *adj* psychic

Psychoanalytiker (psew-khoa-ah-nah-*lēw*-ti-kerr) *m* (pl ~) analyst, psychoanalyst

Psychologe (psew-khoa-*lōā*-ger) *m* (pl ~n) psychologist

Psychologie (psew-khoa-loa-*gee*) *f* psychology

psychologisch (psew-khoa-*lōā*-gish)

adj psychological

Publikum (*pōō*-bli-koom) *nt* audience, public

Puder (*pōō*-derr) *m* powder

Puderdose (*pōō*-derr-dōā-zer) *f* (pl ~n) powder compact

Puderquaste (*pōō*-derr-kvahss-ter) *f* powder-puff

Pullmanwagen (*pool*-mahn-vaa-gern) *m* (pl ~) Pullman

Pullover (poo-*lōā*-verr) *m* (pl ~) pullover

Puls (pools) *m* (pl ~e) pulse

Pulsschlag (*pools*-shlaak) *m* pulse

Pult (poolt) *nt* (pl ~e) desk

Pumpe (*poom*-per) *f* (pl ~n) pump

pumpen (*poom*-pern) *v* pump

Punkt (poongkt) *m* (pl ~e) point; full stop, period; item, issue

pünktlich (*pewngkt*-likh) *adj* punctual

Puppe (*poo*-per) *f* (pl ~n) doll

purpur (*poor*-poor) *adj* purple

Putz (poots) *m* plaster

putzen (*poo*-tsern) *v* brush

Puzzlespiel (*pah*-zerl-shpeel) *nt* (pl ~e) jigsaw puzzle

Pyjama (pi-*zhaa*-mah) *m* (pl ~s) pyjamas *pl*

Q

Quadrat (kvah-*draat*) *nt* (pl ~e) square

quadratisch (kvah-*draa*-tish) *adj* square

Qual (kvaal) *f* (pl ~en) torment

quälen (*kvai*-lern) *v* torment

qualifiziert (kvah-li-fi-*tseert*) *adj* qualified

Qualität (kvah-li-*tait*) *f* (pl ~en) quality

Qualle (*kvah*-ler) *f* (pl ~n) jelly-fish

Quantität (kvahn-ti-*tait*) f (pl ~en) quantity

Quarantäne (kah-rahn-*tai*-ner) f quarantine

Quartal (kvahr-*taal*) nt (pl ~e) quarter

Quatsch (kvahch) m rubbish

quatschen (*kvah*-chern) v talk rubbish

Quecksilber (*kvehk*-zil-berr) nt mercury

Quelle (*kveh*-ler) f (pl ~n) source, spring, well; fountain

quer (kvayr) adv athwart

quetschen (*kveh*-chern) v bruise

Quetschung (*kveh*-choong) f (pl ~en) bruise

Quittung (*kvi*-toong) f (pl ~en) receipt

Quote (*kvoa*-ter) f (pl ~n) quota

R

Rabatt (rah-*baht*) m (pl ~e) reduction, rebate, discount

Rabe (*raa*-ber) m (pl ~n) raven

Rache (*rah*-kher) f revenge

Rad (raat) nt (pl ~er) wheel; cycle, bicycle

Radfahrer (*raat*-faa-rerr) m (pl ~) cyclist

Radiergummi (rah-*deer*-goo-mi) m (pl ~s) eraser, rubber

Radierung (rah-*dee*-roong) f (pl ~en) etching

radikal (rah-di-*kaal*) adj radical

Radio (*raa*-dᵞoa) nt (pl ~s) radio

Raffinerie (rah-fi-ner-*ree*) f (pl ~n) refinery

Rahmen (*raa*-mern) m (pl ~) frame

Rakete (rah-*kay*-ter) f (pl ~n) rocket

Rampe (*rahm*-per) f (pl ~n) ramp

Rand (rahnt) m (pl ~er) brim, edge, border; margin; verge; rim

Randstein (*rahnt*-shtighn) m curb

Rang (rahng) m (pl ~e) grade, rank

ranzig (*rahn*-tsikh) adj rancid

Rarität (rah-ri-*tait*) f (pl ~en) curio

rasch (rahsh) adj fast

Rasen (*raa*-zern) m (pl ~) lawn

rasen (*raa*-zern) v rage; *speed

rasend (*raa*-zernt) adj furious

Rasierapparat (rah-*zeer*-ah-pah-raat) m (pl ~e) electric razor; safety-razor; shaver

sich rasieren (rah-*zee*-rern) shave

Rasierklinge (rah-*zeer*-kling-er) f (pl ~n) razor-blade

Rasierkrem (rah-*zeer*-kraym) f (pl ~s) shaving-cream

Rasierpinsel (rah-*zeer*-pin-zerl) m (pl ~) shaving-brush

Rasierseife (rah-*zeer*-zigh-fer) f (pl ~n) shaving-soap

Rasierwasser (rah-*zeer*-vah-serr) nt aftershave lotion

raspeln (*rahss*-perln) v grate

Rasse (*rah*-ser) f (pl ~n) race; breed; **Rassen-** racial

Rast (rahst) f rest

Rat (raat) m (pl ~e) advice, counsel; council, board

*raten (*raa*-tern) v guess; advise

Ratenzahlung (*raa*-tern-tsaa-loong) f (pl ~en) instalment

Ratgeber (*raat*-gay-berr) m (pl ~) counsellor

Rathaus (*raat*-houss) nt (pl ~er) town hall

Ration (rah-tsᵞ*oan*) f (pl ~en) ration

Rätsel (*rai*-tserl) nt (pl ~) riddle, puzzle; mystery, enigma

rätselhaft (*rai*-tserl-hahft) adj mysterious

Ratsmitglied (*raats*-mit-gleet) nt (pl ~er) councillor

Ratte (*rah*-ter) f (pl ~n) rat

Raub (roup) m robbery

rauben (*rou*-bern) *v* rob

Räuber (*roi*-berr) *m* (pl ~) robber

Raubtier (*roup*-teer) *nt* (pl ~e) beast of prey

Rauch (roukh) *m* smoke

rauchen (*rou*-khern) *v* smoke; **Rauchen verboten** no smoking

Raucher (*rou*-kherr) *m* (pl ~) smoker

Raucherabteil (*rou*-kherr-ahp-tighl) *nt* (pl ~e) smoking-compartment, smoker

Rauchzimmer (roukh-tsi-merr) *nt* (pl ~) smoking-room

rauh (rou) *adj* bleak; harsh; hoarse

Raum (roum) *m* (pl ̈e) space, room

räumen (*roi*-mern) *v* vacate

Rauschgift (*roush*-gift) *nt* (pl ~e) narcotic

Reaktion (ray-ahk-*ts*ʸ*ōan*) *f* (pl ~en) reaction

realisieren (ray-ah-li-*zee*-rern) *v* realize

rebellieren (ray-beh-*lee*-rern) *v* revolt

Rebhuhn (*rehp*-hōon) *nt* (pl ̈er) partridge

Rechenmaschine (*reh*-khern-mah-shee-ner) *f* (pl ~n) adding-machine

Rechnen (*rehkh*-nern) *nt* arithmetic

rechnen (*rehkh*-nern) *v* reckon

Rechnung (*rehkh*-noong) *f* (pl ~en) bill; check *nAm*

Recht (rehkht) *nt* (pl ~e) right; law, justice; **mit ~** rightly

recht (rehkht) *adj* right; right-hand; *adv* fairly, rather; **~ *haben*** be right

Rechteck (*rehkht*-ehk) *nt* (pl ~e) rectangle, oblong

rechteckig (*rehkht*-eh-kikh) *adj* rectangular

rechtlich (*rehkht*-likh) *adj* legal

rechtmäßig (*rehkht*-mai-sikh) *adj* legitimate

Rechtsanwalt (*rehkhts*-ahn-vahlt) *m* (pl ̈e) lawyer; barrister

rechtschaffen (*rehkht*-shah-fern) *adj* honourable

Rechtschreibung (*rehkht*-shrigh-boong) *f* spelling

rechtswidrig (*rehkhts*-vee-drikh) *adj* unlawful

rechtzeitig (*rehkht*-tsigh-tikh) *adv* in time

Redakteur (ray-dahk-*tūrr*) *m* (pl ~e) editor

Rede (*rāy*-der) *f* (pl ~n) speech

reden (*rāy*-dern) *v* talk

Redewendung (*rāy*-der-vehn-doong) *f* (pl ~en) phrase

redlich (*rāyt*-likh) *adj* right, fair

reduzieren (ray-doo-*tsee*-rern) *v* reduce

Reeder (*rāy*-derr) *m* (pl ~) shipowner

Referenz (ray-fay-*rehnts*) *f* (pl ~en) reference

Reflektor (ray-*flehk*-tor) *m* (pl ~en) reflector

Reformation (ray-for-mah-*ts*ʸ*ōan*) *f* reformation

Regal (ray-*gaal*) *nt* (pl ~e) shelf

Regatta (ray-*gah*-tah) *f* (pl Regatten) regatta

Regel (*rāy*-gerl) *f* (pl ~n) rule; **in der ~** as a rule

regelmäßig (*rāy*-gerl-mai-sikh) *adj* regular

regeln (*rāy*-gerln) *v* regulate; settle

Regelung (*rāy*-ger-loong) *f* (pl ~en) regulation; arrangement, settlement

Regen (*rāy*-gern) *m* rain

Regenbogen (*rāy*-gern-bōa-gern) *m* (pl ̈) rainbow

Regenguß (*rāy*-gern-gooss) *m* (pl -güsse) downpour

Regenmantel (*rāy*-gern-mahn-terl) *m* (pl ̈) mackintosh, raincoat

Regenschauer (*rāy*-gern-shou-err) *m* (pl ~) shower

Regenschirm (*rāy*-gern-sheerm) *m* (pl

~e) umbrella

Regie (ray-*zhee*) f direction

regieren (ray-*gee*-rern) v govern; rule, reign

Regierung (ray-*gee*-roong) f (pl ~en) government; rule

Regime (ray-*zheem*) nt (pl ~s) régime

Regisseur (ray-zhi-*surr*) m (pl ~e) director

regnen (*rāy*-gnern) v rain

regnerisch (*rāy*-gner-rish) adj rainy

regulieren (ray-goo-*lee*-rern) v adjust

Rehabilitation (ray-hah-bi-li-tah-ts^y*ōān*) f rehabilitation

rehbraun (*rāy*-broun) adj fawn

Rehkalb (*rāy*-kahlp) nt (pl ~er) fawn

Reibe (*righ*-ber) f (pl ~n) grater

*** reiben** (*righ*-bern) v rub

Reibung (*righ*-boong) f (pl ~en) friction

Reich (righkh) nt (pl ~e) empire; kingdom; **Reichs-** imperial

reich (righkh) adj rich; wealthy

reichen (*righ*-khern) v suffice; pass

reichlich (*righkh*-likh) adj plentiful, abundant

Reichtum (*righkh*-tēw-merr) m (pl ~er) riches pl, wealth

reif (righf) adj ripe, mature

Reife (*righ*-fer) f maturity

Reifen (*righ*-fern) m (pl ~) tyre, tire

Reifendruck (*righ*-fern-drook) m tyre pressure

Reifenpanne (*righ*-fern-pah-ner) f (pl ~n) blow-out, puncture, flat tyre

Reihe (*righ*-er) f (pl ~n) line, row; file, rank; turn

Reihenfolge (*righ*-ern-fol-ger) f order, sequence

Reiher (*righ*-err) m (pl ~) heron

Reim (righm) m (pl ~e) rhyme

rein (righn) adj clean; pure; sheer

Reinemachen (*righ*-ner-mah-khern) nt cleaning

reinigen (*righ*-ni-gern) v clean; **chemisch** ~ dry-clean

Reinigung (*righ*-ni-goong) f (pl ~en) cleaning; **chemische** ~ dry-cleaner's

Reinigungsmittel (*righ*-ni-goongs-mi-terl) nt (pl ~) cleaning fluid; detergent

Reis (righss) m rice

Reise (*righ*-zer) f (pl ~n) voyage, journey; trip

Reisebüro (*righ*-zer-bew-rōā) nt (pl ~s) travel agency

Reisebus (*righ*-zer-booss) m (pl ~se) coach

Reisegeschwindigkeit (*righ*-zer-ger-shvin-dikh-kight) f cruising speed

reisen (*righ*-zern) v travel

Reisende (*righ*-zern-der) m (pl ~n) traveller

Reiseplan (*righ*-zer-plaan) m (pl ~e) itinerary

Reisescheck (*righ*-zer-shehk) m (pl ~s) traveller's cheque

Reisespesen (*righ*-zer-shpāy-zern) pl travelling expenses

Reiseversicherung (*righ*-zer-fehr-zi-kher-roong) f travel insurance

*** reißen** (*righ*-sern) v *tear

Reißnagel (*righss*-naa-gerl) m (pl ~) thumbtack nAm

Reißverschluß (*righss*-fehr-shlooss) m (pl -verschlüsse) zipper, zip

Reißzwecke (*righss*-tsveh-ker) f (pl ~n) drawing-pin

*** reiten** (*righ*-tern) v *ride

Reiter (*righ*-terr) m (pl ~) rider, horseman

Reitschule (*right*-shōō-ler) f (pl ~n) riding-school

Reitsport (*right*-shport) m riding

Reiz (rights) m (pl ~e) attraction; glamour

reizbar (*rights*-baar) adj quick-tempered, irritable

reizen (*righ*-tsern) v irritate

reizend (*righ*-tsernt) adj adorable, graceful

Reizmittel (*rights*-mi-terl) nt (pl ~) stimulant

Reklame (ray-*klaa*-mer) f (pl ~n) publicity

Rekord (ray-*kort*) m (pl ~e) record

Rekrut (ray-*krōōt*) m (pl ~en) recruit

relativ (ray-lah-*teef*) adj comparative, relative

Relief (ray-*lʸehf*) nt (pl ~s) relief

Religion (ray-li-*gʸōan*) f (pl ~en) religion

religiös (ray-li-*gʸūrss*) adj religious

Reliquie (ray-*lee*-kvi-er) f (pl ~n) relic

Ren (rehn) nt (pl ~s) reindeer

Rennbahn (*rehn*-baan) f (pl ~en) race-course, race-track

Rennen (*reh*-nern) nt (pl ~) race

*rennen (*reh*-nern) v *run

Rennpferd (*rehn*-pfāyrt) nt (pl ~e) race-horse

rentabel (rehn-*taa*-berl) adj paying

Rente (*rehn*-ter) f (pl ~n) pension

Reparatur (ray-pah-rah-*tōōr*) f (pl ~en) reparation

reparieren (ray-pah-*ree*-rern) v repair

Repertoire (ray-pehr-*twaar*) nt (pl ~s) repertory

repräsentativ (ray-preh-zehn-tah-*teef*) adj representative

Reproduktion (ray-proa-dook-*tsʸōan*) f (pl ~en) reproduction

reproduzieren (ray-proa-doo-*tsee*-rern) v reproduce

Reptil (rehp-*teel*) nt (pl ~e) reptile

Republik (ray-poo-*bleek*) f (pl ~en) republic

republikanisch (ray-poo-bli-*kaa*-nish) adj republican

Reserve (ray-*zehr*-ver) f (pl ~n) reserve

Reserverad (ray-*zehr*-ver-raat) nt (pl ~er) spare wheel

reservieren (ray-zehr-*vee*-rern) v reserve; book

reserviert (ray-zehr-*veert*) adj reserved

Reservierung (ray-zehr-*vee*-roong) f (pl ~en) reservation; booking

Reservoir (ray-zehr-*vwaar*) nt (pl ~s) reservoir

resolut (ray-zoa-*lōōt*) adj resolute

Respekt (ray-*spehkt*) m esteem, regard, respect

Rest (rehst) m (pl ~e) rest; remainder, remnant

Restaurant (rehss-toa-*rahng*) nt (pl ~s) restaurant

Restbestand (*rehst*-ber-shtahnt) m (pl ~e) remainder

Resultat (ray-zool-*taat*) nt (pl ~e) issue

retten (*reh*-tern) v rescue, save

Retter (*reh*-terr) m (pl ~) saviour

Rettich (*reh*-tikh) m (pl ~e) radish

Rettung (*reh*-toong) f (pl ~en) rescue

Rettungsgürtel (*reh*-toongs-gewr-terl) m (pl ~) lifebelt

Reue (*roi*-er) f repentance

Revolution (ray-voa-loo-tsʸōan) f (pl ~en) revolution

revolutionär (ray-voa-loo-tsʸoa-*nair*) adj revolutionary

Revolver (ray-*vol*-verr) m (pl ~) revolver, gun

Rezept (ray-*tsehpt*) nt (pl ~e) recipe; prescription

Rezeption (ray-tsehp-*tsʸōan*) f reception office

Rhabarber (rah-*bahr*-berr) m rhubarb

Rheumatismus (roi-mah-*tiss*-mooss) m rheumatism

Rhythmus (*rewt*-mooss) m (pl -men) rhythm

richten (*rikh*-tern) v direct; fix; ~ **auf** aim at

Richter (*rikh*-terr) *m* (pl ~) judge; magistrate

richtig (*rikh*-tikh) *adj* right, correct, just; proper, appropriate

Richtigkeit (*rikh*-tikh-kight) *f* correctness

Richtlinie (*rikht*-lee-nᵞer) *f* (pl ~n) directive

Richtung (*rikh*-toong) *f* (pl ~en) direction; way

***riechen** (*ree*-khern) *v* *smell

Riegel (*ree*-gerl) *m* (pl ~) bolt

Riemen (*ree*-mern) *m* (pl ~) strap

Riese (*ree*-zer) *m* (pl ~n) giant

riesenhaft (*ree*-zern-hahft) *adj* gigantic

riesig (*ree*-zikh) *adj* enormous, huge

Riff (rif) *nt* (pl ~e) reef

Rille (*ri*-ler) *f* (pl ~n) groove

Rinde (*rin*-der) *f* (pl ~n) bark

Rindfleisch (*rint*-flighsh) *nt* beef

Ring (ring) *m* (pl ~e) ring

Ringen (*ring*-ern) *nt* struggle

***ringen** (*ring*-ern) *v* struggle

Rippe (*ri*-per) *f* (pl ~n) rib

Risiko (*ree*-zi-koa) *nt* (pl ~s) risk; chance, hazard

riskant (riss-*kahnt*) *adj* risky

Riß (riss) *m* (pl Risse) crack; tear; cave

Ritter (*ri*-terr) *m* (pl ~) knight

Rivale (ri-*vaa*-ler) *m* (pl ~n) rival

rivalisieren (ri-vah-li-*zee*-rern) *v* rival

Rivalität (ri-vah-li-*tait*) *f* rivalry

Robbe (*ro*-ber) *f* (pl ~n) seal

robust (roa-*boost*) *adj* robust

Rock (rok) *m* (pl ~̈e) skirt

Rockaufschlag (*rok*-ouf-shlaak) *m* (pl ~̈e) lapel

Rogen (*rōa*-gern) *m* roe

roh (rōa) *adj* raw

Rohmaterial (*rōa*-mah-tay-rᵞaal) *nt* (pl ~ien) raw material

Rohr (rōar) *nt* (pl ~e) tube, pipe; cane

Röhre (*rūr*-rer) *f* (pl ~n) tube

Rolle (*ro*-ler) *f* (pl ~n) roll; pulley

rollen (*ro*-lern) *v* roll

Roller (*ro*-lerr) *m* (pl ~) scooter

Rollstuhl (*rol*-shtōol) *m* (pl ~̈e) wheelchair

Rolltreppe (*roal*-treh-per) *f* (pl ~n) escalator

Roman (roa-*maan*) *m* (pl ~e) novel

Romanschriftsteller (roa-*maan*-shrift-shteh-lerr) *m* (pl ~) novelist

romantisch (roa-*mahn*-tish) *adj* romantic

Romanze (roa-*mahn*-tser) *f* (pl ~n) romance

römisch-katholisch (*rūr*-mish-kah-tōa-lish) *adj* Roman Catholic

röntgen (*rurnt*-gern) *v* X-ray

Röntgenbild (*rurnt*-gern-bilt) *nt* (pl ~er) X-ray

rosa (*rōa*-zah-rōat) *adj* rose, pink

Rose (*rōa*-zer) *f* (pl ~n) rose

Rosenkohl (*rōa*-zern-kōal) *m* sprouts *pl*

Rosenkranz (*rōa*-zern-krahnts) *m* (pl ~̈e) rosary, beads *pl*

Rosine (roa-*zee*-ner) *f* (pl ~n) raisin

Rost[1] (rost) *m* rust

Rost[2] (rost) *m* (pl ~e) grate

rösten (*rūrss*-tern) *v* roast

rostig (*ross*-tikh) *adj* rusty

rot (rōat) *adj* red

Rotkehlchen (*rōat*-kāyl-khern) *nt* (pl ~) robin

Rotwild (*rōat*-vilt) *nt* deer

Rouge (rōozh) *nt* rouge

Roulett (roo-*leht*) *nt* roulette

Route (*rōo*-ter) *f* (pl ~n) route

Routine (roo-*tee*-ner) *f* routine

Rübe (*rēw*-ber) *f* (pl ~n) beet

Rubin (roo-*been*) *m* (pl ~e) ruby

Rubrik (roo-*breek*) *f* (pl ~en) column

Ruck (rook) *m* (pl ~e) tug, wrench

Rücken (*rew*-kern) *m* (pl ~) back

Rückenschmerzen (*rew*-kern-shmehr-tsern) *mpl* backache

Rückfahrt (*rewk*-faart) *f* return journey; **Hin- und ~** round trip *Am*

Rückflug (*rewk*-flŏŏk) *m* (pl ~̈e) return flight

Rückgang (*rewk*-gahng) *m* recession, depression

Rückgrat (*rewk*-graat) *nt* (pl ~e) spine, backbone

Rückkehr (*rewk*-kāyr) *f* return

Rücklicht (*rewk*-likht) *nt* (pl ~er) tail-light

Rückreise (*rewk*-righ-zer) *f* return journey

Rucksack (*rook*-zahk) *m* (pl ~̈e) rucksack; knapsack

Rückschlag (*rewk*-shlaak) *m* (pl ~̈e) reverse

Rücksicht (*rewk*-zikht) *f* consideration

rücksichtsvoll (*rewk*-zikhts-fol) *adj* considerate

rückständig (*rewk*-shtehn-dikh) *adj* overdue

Rücktritt (*rewk*-trit) *m* resignation

rückvergüten (*rewk*-fehr-gēw-tern) *v* refund

Rückvergütung (*rewk*-fehr-gēw-toong) *f* (pl ~en) refund

rückwärts (*rewk*-vehrts) *adv* backwards; **~ *fahren** reverse

Rückwärtsgang (*rewk*-vehrts-gahng) *m* reverse

Rückweg (*rewk*-vāyk) *m* way back

Rückzahlung (*rewk*-tsaa-loong) *f* (pl ~en) repayment

Ruder (*rŏŏ*-derr) *nt* (pl ~) helm; oar

Ruderboot (*rŏŏ*-derr-bŏāt) *nt* (pl ~e) rowing-boat

rudern (*rŏŏ*-derrn) *v* row

Ruf (rŏŏf) *m* (pl ~e) call; cry, scream; fame, reputation

*rufen (*rŏŏ*-fern) *v* call; cry, shout

Ruhe (*rŏŏ*-er) *f* quiet

ruhelos (*rŏŏ*-er-lŏāss) *adj* restless

Ruhelosigkeit (*rŏŏ*-er-lŏā-zikh-kight) *f* unrest

ruhen (*rŏŏ*-ern) *v* rest

ruhig (*rŏŏ*-ikh) *adj* calm; tranquil, quiet, serene; restful

Ruhm (rŏŏm) *m* celebrity, fame; glory

Ruhr (rŏŏr) *f* dysentery

rühren (*rēw*-rern) *v* stir; move

rührend (*rēw*-rernt) *adj* touching

Rührung (*rēw*-roong) *f* emotion

Ruine (roo-*ee*-ner) *f* (pl ~n) ruins

ruinieren (roo-i-*nee*-rern) *v* ruin

Rumäne (roo-*mai*-ner) *m* (pl ~n) Rumanian

Rumänien (roo-*mai*-nᵞern) Rumania

rumänisch (roo-*mai*-nish) *adj* Rumanian

rund (roont) *adj* round

Runde (*roon*-der) *f* (pl ~n) round

Rundfunk (*roont*-foongk) *m* wireless

rundherum (*roont*-heh-room) *adv* around

Rundreise (*roont*-righ-zer) *f* (pl ~n) tour

Russe (*roo*-ser) *m* (pl ~n) Russian

russisch (*roo*-sish) *adj* Russian

Rußland (*rooss*-lahnt) Russia

Rüstung (*rewss*-toong) *f* (pl ~en) armour

Rutschbahn (*rooch*-baan) *f* (pl ~en) slide

S

Saal (zaal) *m* (pl Säle) hall

Saalwärter (*zaal*-vehr-terr) *m* (pl ~) custodian

Saccharin (zah-khah-*reen*) *nt* saccharin

Sache (*zah*-kher) *f* (pl ~en) matter;

cause

sachlich (*zahkh*-likh) *adj* down-to-earth; substantial

sächlich (*zehkh*-likh) *adj* neuter

Sachverständige (*zahkh*-fehr-shtehn-di-ger) *m* (pl ~n) expert

Sack (zahk) *m* (pl ~e) sack; bag

Sackgasse (*zahk*-gah-ser) *f* (pl ~n) cul-de-sac

säen (*zai*-ern) *v* *sow

Safe (sāyf) *m* (pl ~s) safe

Saft (zahft) *m* (pl ~e) juice

saftig (*zahf*-tikh) *adj* juicy

Säge (*zai*-ger) *f* (pl ~n) saw

Sägemehl (*zai*-ger-māyl) *nt* sawdust

Sägemühle (*zai*-ger-mēw-ler) *f* (pl ~n) saw-mill

sagen (*zaa*-gern) *v* *say; *tell

Sahne (*zaa*-ner) *f* cream

Sahnebonbon (*zaa*-ner-bawng-bawng) *m* (pl ~s) toffee

sahnig (*zaa*-nikh) *adj* creamy

Saison (zeh-*zawng*) *f* (pl ~s) season; **außer ~** off season

Saite (*zigh*-ter) *f* (pl ~n) string

Salat (zah-*laat*) *m* (pl ~e) salad; lettuce

Salatöl (zah-*laat*-ūrl) *nt* (pl ~e) salad-oil

Salbe (*zahl*-ber) *f* (pl ~n) salve, ointment

Saldo (*zahl*-doa) *m* (pl Salden) balance

Salmiakgeist (zahl-*m*ʸ*ahk*-gighst) *m* ammonia

Salon (zah-*lawng*) *m* (pl ~s) salon

Salz (zahlts) *nt* salt

Salzfäßchen (*zahlts*-fehss-khern) *nt* (pl ~) salt-cellar

salzig (*zahl*-tsikh) *adj* salty

Samen (*zaa*-mern) *m* (pl ~) seed

sammeln (*zah*-merln) *v* collect; gather

Sammler (*zahm*-lerr) *m* (pl ~) collector

Sammlung (*zahm*-loong) *f* (pl ~en) collection

Samt (zahmt) *m* velvet

Sanatorium (zah-nah-*tōa*-rʸoom) *nt* (pl -rien) sanatorium

Sand (zahnt) *m* sand

Sandale (zahn-*daa*-ler) *f* (pl ~n) sandal

sandig (*zahn*-dikh) *adj* sandy

sanft (zahnft) *adj* gentle

Sänger (*zehng*-err) *m* (pl ~) vocalist, singer

sanitär (zah-ni-*tair*) *adj* sanitary

Saphir (*zaa*-feer) *m* (pl ~e) sapphire

Sardelle (zahr-*deh*-ler) *f* (pl ~n) anchovy

Sardine (zahr-*dee*-ner) *f* (pl ~n) sardine

Satellit (zah-teh-*leet*) *m* (pl ~en) satellite

Satin (sah-*tang*) *m* satin

satt (zaht) *adj* satisfied

Sattel (*zah*-terl) *m* (pl ~) saddle

Satz (zahts) *m* (pl ~e) sentence; set; rate

sauber (*zou*-berr) *adj* clean

säubern (*zoi*-berrn) *v* clean

Saudi-Arabien (zou-di-ah-*raa*-bʸern) Saudi Arabia

saudiarabisch (zou-di-ah-*raa*-bish) *adj* Saudi Arabian

sauer (*zou*-err) *adj* sour

Sauerstoff (*zou*-err-shtof) *m* oxygen

Säugetier (*zoi*-ger-teer) *nt* (pl ~e) mammal

Säugling (*zoik*-ling) *m* (pl ~e) infant

Säule (*zoi*-ler) *f* (pl ~n) pillar, column

Saum (zoum) *m* (pl ~e) hem

Sauna (*zou*-nah) *f* (pl ~s) sauna

Säure (*zoi*-rer) *f* (pl ~n) acid

schaben (*shaa*-bern) *v* scrape

Schach (shahkh) *nt* chess; **Schach!** check!

Schachbrett (*shahkh*-breht) *nt* (pl

~er) checkerboard *nAm*

Schachtel (*shahkh*-terl) *f* (pl ~n) box

schade! (shaa-der) what a pity!

Schädel (*shai*-derl) *m* (pl ~) skull

Schaden (*shaa*-dern) *m* (pl ~̈) damage; harm, mischief

schaden (*shaa*-dern) *v* harm

Schadenersatz (*shaa*-dern-ehr-zahts) *m* compensation, indemnity

schadhaft (*shaat*-hahft) *adj* defective

schädlich (*shait*-likh) *adj* harmful, hurtful

Schaf (shaaf) *nt* (pl ~e) sheep

***schaffen** (*shah*-fern) *v* create; *make

Schaffner (*shahf*-nerr) *m* (pl ~) conductor; ticket collector

Schal (shaal) *m* (pl ~s) scarf, shawl

Schale (*shaa*-ler) *f* (pl ~n) bowl; skin, peel; shell

schälen (*shai*-lern) *v* peel

Schalentier (*shaa*-lern-teer) *nt* (pl ~e) shellfish

Schalk (shahlk) *m* (pl ~e) rascal

Schall (shahl) *m* (pl ~e) sound

schalldicht (*shahl*-dikht) *adj* soundproof

Schallplatte (*shahl*-plah-ter) *f* (pl ~n) record, disc

Schaltbrett (*shahlt*-breht) *nt* (pl ~er) switchboard

schalten (*shahl*-tern) *v* change gear

Schalter (*shahl*-terr) *m* (pl ~) switch; counter

Schaltjahr (*shahlt*-Yaar) *nt* leap-year

sich schämen (*shai*-mern) *be ashamed

Schande (*shahn*-der) *f* disgrace, shame

scharf (shahrf) *adj* sharp; keen

schärfen (*shehr*-fern) *v* sharpen

Scharfrichter (*shahrf*-rikh-terr) *m* (pl ~) executioner

scharlachrot (*shahr*-lahkh-rōat) *adj* scarlet

Scharlatan (*shahr*-lah-taan) *m* (pl ~e) quack

Scharm (shahrm) *m* charm

Scharnier (shahr-*neer*) *nt* (pl ~e) hinge

Schatten (*shah*-tern) *m* (pl ~) shade; shadow

schattig (*shah*-tikh) *adj* shady

Schatz (shahts) *m* (pl ~̈e) treasure; darling, sweetheart

Schatzamt (*shahts*-ahmt) *nt* treasury

schätzen (*sheh*-tsern) *v* appreciate; estimate, value; esteem

Schätzung (*sheh*-tsoong) *f* appreciation

Schauder (*shou*-derr) *m* horror; shudder

schauen (*shou*-ern) *v* look

Schauer (*shou*-err) *m* (pl ~) shower

Schaufel (*shou*-ferl) *f* (pl ~n) spade, shovel

Schaufenster (*shou*-fehns-terr) *nt* (pl ~) shop-window

Schaukel (*shou*-kerl) *f* (pl ~n) swing

schaukeln (*shou*-kerln) *v* *swing; rock

Schaum (shoum) *m* froth, lather; foam

schäumen (*shoi*-mern) *v* foam

Schaumgummi (*shoum*-goo-mi) *m* foam-rubber

Schauspiel (*shou*-shpeel) *nt* (pl ~e) spectacle; play

Schauspieler (*shou*-shpee-lerr) *m* (pl ~) actor; comedian

Schauspielerin (*shou*-shpee-ler-rin) *f* (pl ~nen) actress

Schauspielhaus (*shou*-shpeel-houss) *nt* (pl ~̈er) theatre

Scheck (shehk) *m* (pl ~s) cheque; check *nAm*

Scheckbuch (*shehk*-bōokh) *nt* (pl ~̈er) cheque-book; check-book *nAm*

Scheibe (*shigh*-ber) *f* (pl ~n) disc;

pane

Scheibenwischer (*shigh*-bern-vi-sherr) *m* (pl ~) windscreen wiper; windshield wiper *Am*

* **scheiden** (*shigh*-dern) *v* divorce

Scheidewand (*shigh*-der-vahnt) *f* (pl ˜e) partition

Scheideweg (*shigh*-der-vāyk) *m* (pl ~e) road fork

Scheidung (*shigh*-doong) *f* (pl ~en) divorce

Schein (shighn) *m* (pl ~e) shine; appearance; certificate; note

scheinbar (*shighn*-baar) *adj* apparent

* **scheinen** (*shigh*-nern) *v* look, appear, seem

scheinheilig (*shighn*-high-likh) *adj* hypocritical

Scheinwerfer (*shighn*-vehr-ferr) *m* (pl ~) headlight, headlamp; spotlight, searchlight

Scheitel (*shigh*-terl) *m* (pl ~) parting

Schellfisch (*shehl*-fish) *m* (pl ~e) haddock

Schelm (shehlm) *m* (pl ~e) rascal

schelmisch (*shehl*-mish) *adj* mischievous

Schema (*shāy*-mah) *nt* (pl ~ta) scheme; diagram

Schenke (*shehng*-ker) *f* (pl ~n) tavern

schenken (*shehng*-kern) *v* pour

Schenkung (*shehng*-koong) *f* (pl ~en) donation

Schere (*shāy*-rer) *f* (pl ~n) scissors *pl*

scheu (shoi) *adj* shy

scheuern (*shoi*-errn) *v* scrub

Scheune (*shoi*-ner) *f* (pl ~n) barn

scheußlich (*shoiss*-likh) *adj* horrible

Schi (shee) *m* (pl ~er) ski; ~ * **laufen** ski

Schicht (shikht) *f* (pl ~en) layer; shift; gang

schicken (*shi*-kern) *v* *send

Schicksal (*shik*-zaal) *nt* destiny, fate

* **schieben** (*shee*-bern) *v* push

Schiebetür (*shee*-ber-teẇr) *f* (pl ~en) sliding door

Schiedsrichter (*sheets*-rikh-terr) *m* (pl ~) umpire

schief (sheef) *adj* slanting

Schiefer (*shee*-ferr) *m* slate

schielend (*shee*-lernt) *adj* cross-eyed

Schiene (*shee*-ner) *f* (pl ~n) splint

Schienenweg (*shee*-nern-vāyk) *m* (pl ~e) railroad *nAm*

* **schießen** (*shee*-sern) *v* *shoot, fire

Schießpulver (*sheess*-pool-ferr) *nt* gunpowder

Schiff (shif) *nt* (pl ~e) boat, ship; vessel

Schiffahrt (*shif*-faart) *f* navigation

Schiffahrtslinie (*shif*-faarts-lee-nᵛer) *f* (pl ~n) shipping line

Schiffswerft (*shifs*-vehrft) *f* (pl ~en) shipyard

Schihose (*shee*-hōa-zer) *f* (pl ~n) ski pants

Schilauf (*shee*-louf) *m* skiing

Schiläufer (*shee*-loi-ferr) *m* (pl ~) skier

Schildkröte (*shilt*-krūr-ter) *f* (pl ~n) turtle

Schilfrohr (*shilf*-rōar) *nt* (pl ~e) reed

Schilift (*shee*-lift) *m* (pl ~e) ski-lift

Schimmel (*shi*-merl) *m* mildew

schimmelig (*shi*-mer-likh) *adj* mouldy

schimpfen (*shim*-pfern) *v* scold

Schinken (*shing*-kern) *m* (pl ~) ham

Schirm (sheerm) *m* (pl ~e) screen

Schischuhe (*shee*-shōō-er) *mpl* ski boots

Schisprung (*shee*-shproong) *m* (pl ˜e) ski-jump

Schistöcke (*shee*-shtur-ker) *mpl* ski sticks; ski poles *Am*

Schlacht (shlahkht) *f* (pl ~en) battle

Schlaf (shlaaf) *m* sleep; **im ~** asleep; **Schläfchen** *nt* nap

Schläfe (*shlai*-fer) *f* (pl ~n) temple

*schlafen (*shlaa*-fern) *v* *sleep

schlaff (shlahf) *adj* limp

schlaflos (*shlaaf*-lōass) *adj* sleepless

Schlaflosigkeit (*shlaaf*-lōa-zikh-kight) *f* insomnia

Schlafmittel (*shlaaf*-mi-terl) *nt* (pl ~) sleeping-pill

schläfrig (*shlaif*-rikh) *adj* sleepy

Schlafsaal (*shlaaf*-zaal) *m* (pl -säle) dormitory

Schlafsack (*shlaaf*-zahk) *m* (pl ~̈e) sleeping-bag

Schlafwagen (*shlaaf*-vaa-gern) *m* (pl ~) sleeping-car

Schlafwagenbett (*shlaaf*-vaa-gern-beht) *nt* (pl ~en) berth

Schlafzimmer (*shlaaf*-tsi-merr) *nt* (pl ~) bedroom

Schlag (shlaak) *m* (pl ~̈e) blow, slap; bump

Schlaganfall (*shlaak*-ahn-fahl) *m* (pl ~̈e) stroke

*schlagen (*shlaa*-gern) *v* *hit, slap; *strike, *beat; thump, bump; smack; whip; **sich** ~ *fight

Schlager (*shlaa*-gerr) *m* (pl ~) hit

Schläger (*shlai*-gerr) *m* (pl ~) racquet

Schlagwort (*shlaak*-vort) *nt* (pl ~̈er) slogan

Schlagzeile (*shlaak*-tsigh-ler) *f* (pl ~n) headline

Schlamm (shlahm) *m* mud

schlammig (*shlah*-mikh) *adj* muddy

schlampig (*shlahm*-pikh) *adj* sloppy

Schlange (*shlahng*-er) *f* (pl ~n) snake; queue; ~ *stehen queue; stand in line *Am*

schlank (shlahngk) *adj* slim, slender

schlau (shlou) *adj* bright, clever

Schlauch (shloukh) *m* (pl ~̈e) inner tube

schlecht (shlehkht) *adj* bad; ill, evil; **schlechter** *adj* worse; **schlechtest**
adj worst

Schleier (*shligh*-err) *m* (pl ~) veil

*schleifen (*shligh*-fern) *v* sharpen

schleppen (*shleh*-pern) *v* drag; haul, tug, tow

Schlepper (*shleh*-perr) *m* (pl ~) tug

schleudern (*shloi*-derrn) *v* *throw; skid

Schleuse (*shloi*-zer) *f* (pl ~n) lock, sluice

schlicht (shlikht) *adj* simple, plain

*schließen (*shlee*-sern) *v* close, *shut; fasten; **in sich** ~ imply

schließlich (*shleess*-likh) *adv* at last

schlimm (shlim) *adj* bad

Schlinge (*shling*-er) *f* (pl ~n) loop

Schlitten (*shli*-tern) *m* (pl ~) sledge; sleigh

Schlittschuh (*shlit*-shōō) *m* (pl ~e) skate

Schlittschuhbahn (*shlit*-shōō-baan) *f* (pl ~en) skating-rink

Schlitz (shlits) *m* (pl ~e) slot; fly

Schloß (shloss) *nt* (pl Schlösser) lock; castle

Schlucht (shlookht) *f* (pl ~en) gorge

Schluckauf (*shlook*-ouf) *m* hiccup

Schlückchen (*shlewk*-khern) *nt* (pl ~) sip

schlucken (*shloo*-kern) *v* swallow

Schlüpfer (*shlew*-pferr) *m* (pl ~) panties *pl*

schlüpfrig (*shlewpf*-rikh) *adj* slippery

Schluß (shlooss) *m* (pl Schlüsse) end, finish; conclusion

Schlüssel (*shlew*-serl) *m* (pl ~) key

Schlüsselbein (*shlew*-serl-bighn) *nt* (pl ~e) collarbone

Schlüsselloch (*shlew*-serl-lokh) *nt* (pl ~̈er) keyhole

Schlußfolgerung (*shlooss*-fol-ger-roong) *f* (pl ~en) conclusion

Schlußlicht (*shlooss*-likht) *nt* (pl ~er) rear-light

Schlußverkauf (*shlooss*-fehr-kouf) *m* sales

schmackhaft (*schmahk*-hahft) *adj* enjoyable, savoury, tasty

schmal (shmaal) *adj* narrow

Schmalz (shmahlts) *m* tear-jerker

schmecken (*shmeh*-kern) *v* taste

* **schmelzen** (*shmehl*-tsern) *v* melt

Schmerz (shmehrts) *m* (pl ~en) ache, pain

schmerzen (*shmehr*-tsern) *v* ache

schmerzhaft (*shmehrts*-hahft) *adj* sore, painful

schmerzlos (*shmehrts*-lōass) *adj* painless

Schmetterling (*shmeh*-terr-ling) *m* (pl ~e) butterfly

Schmetterlingsstil (*shmeh*-terr-lings-shteel) *m* butterfly stroke

Schmied (shmeet) *m* (pl ~e) smith, blacksmith

schmieren (*shmee*-rern) *v* grease; lubricate

schmierig (*shmee*-rikh) *adj* dirty

Schmieröl (*shmeer*-ürl) *nt* (pl ~e) lubrication oil

Schmiersystem (*shmeer*-zewss-tāym) *nt* lubrication system

Schmierung (*shmee*-roong) *f* (pl ~en) lubrication

Schminke (*shming*-ker) *f* (pl ~n) make-up

Schmirgelpapier (*shmeer*-gerl-pah-peer) *nt* sandpaper

Schmuck (shmook) *m* jewellery

schmuggeln (*shmoo*-gerln) *v* smuggle

Schmutz (shmoots) *m* dirt

schmutzig (*shmoo*-tsikh) *adj* dirty; foul, filthy

Schnabel (*shnaa*-berl) *m* (pl ~̈) beak; nozzle

Schnalle (*shnah*-ler) *f* (pl ~n) buckle

Schnappschuß (*shnahp*-shooss) *m* (pl -schüsse) snapshot

schnarchen (*shnahr*-khern) *v* snore

Schnauze (*shnou*-tser) *f* (pl ~n) snout

Schnecke (*shneh*-ker) *f* (pl ~n) snail

Schnee (shnāy) *m* snow

schneebedeckt (*shnāy*-ber-dehkt) *adj* snowy

Schneesturm (*shnāy*-shtoorm) *m* (pl ~̈e) blizzard, snowstorm

* **schneiden** (*shnigh*-dern) *v* *cut

Schneider (*shnigh*-derr) *m* (pl ~) tailor

Schneiderin (*shnigh*-der-rin) *f* (pl ~nen) dressmaker

schneien (*shnigh*-ern) *v* snow

schnell (shnehl) *adj* fast; quick, rapid; **zu ~** *fahren *speed

Schnelligkeit (*shneh*-likh-kight) *f* speed

Schnellkochtopf (*shnehl*-kokh-topf) *m* (pl ~̈e) pressure-cooker

Schnellzug (*shnehl*-tsōōk) *m* (pl ~̈e) express train

Schnitt (shnit) *m* (pl ~e) cut

Schnitte (*shni*-ter) *f* (pl ~n) slice

Schnittlauch (*shnit*-loukh) *m* chives *pl*

schnitzen (*shni*-tsern) *v* carve

Schnitzerei (shni-tser-*righ*) *f* (pl ~en) carving

Schnorchel (*shnor*-kherl) *m* (pl ~) snorkel

Schnupfen (*shnoo*-pfern) *m* cold

Schnur (shnōōr) *f* (pl ~̈e) string; line, twine

Schnurrbart (*shnoor*-baart) *m* (pl ~̈e) moustache

Schnürsenkel (*shnēwr*-zehng-kerl) *m* (pl ~) lace, shoe-lace

Schock (shok) *m* (pl ~s) shock

schockieren (sho-*kee*-rern) *v* shock

Schokolade (shoa-koa-*laa*-der) *f* chocolate

Scholle (*sho*-ler) *f* (pl ~n) plaice

schon (shōan) *adv* already

schön (*shurn*) *adj* beautiful; pretty, fine

Schönheit (*shurn*-hight) *f* beauty

Schönheitsmittel (*shurn*-hights-mi-terl) *ntpl* cosmetics *pl*

Schönheitssalon (*shurn*-hights-zah-lawng) *m* (pl ~s) beauty salon, beauty parlour

Schornstein (*shorn*-shtighn) *m* (pl ~e) chimney

Schotte (*sho*-ter) *m* (pl ~n) Scot

schottisch (*sho*-tish) *adj* Scottish, Scotch

Schottland (*shot*-lahnt) Scotland

schräg (shraik) *adj* slanting

Schramme (*shrah*-mer) *f* (pl ~n) graze, scratch

Schrank (shrahngk) *m* (pl ~e) cupboard

Schranke (*shrahng*-ker) *f* (pl ~n) barrier; **in Schranken *halten** restrain

Schraube (*shrou*-ber) *f* (pl ~n) screw; propeller

schrauben (*shrou*-bern) *v* screw

Schraubenmutter (*shrou*-bern-moo-terr) *f* (pl ~n) nut

Schraubenschlüssel (*shrou*-bern-shlew-serl) *m* (pl ~) spanner, wrench

Schraubenzieher (*shrou*-bern-tsee-err) *m* (pl ~) screw-driver

Schreck (shrehk) *m* fright, scare

schrecklich (*shrehk*-likh) *adj* frightful, horrible, dreadful, awful, terrible

Schrei (shrigh) *m* (pl ~e) cry, scream, yell, shout

Schreibblock (*shrighp*-blok) *m* (pl ~e) writing-pad, pad

***schreiben** (*shrigh*-bern) *v* *write

Schreiber (*shrigh*-berr) *m* (pl ~) clerk

Schreibmaschine (*shrighp*-mah-shee-ner) *f* (pl ~n) typewriter

Schreibmaschinenpapier (*shrighp*-mah-shee-nern-pah-peer) *nt* typing paper

Schreibpapier (*shrighp*-pah-peer) *nt* notepaper, writing-paper

Schreibtisch (*shrighp*-tish) *m* (pl ~e) bureau, desk

Schreibwaren (*shrighp*-vaa-rern) *fpl* stationery

Schreibwarenhandlung (*shrighp*-vaa-rern-hahn-dloong) *f* (pl ~en) stationer's

***schreien** (*shrigh*-ern) *v* cry, scream, yell, shout

Schrein (shrighn) *m* (pl ~e) shrine

schriftlich (*shrift*-likh) *adj* written; *adv* in writing

Schriftsteller (*shrift*-shteh-lerr) *m* (pl ~) writer

Schritt (shrit) *m* (pl ~e) pace; step; move; ~ *halten mit *keep up with

schroff (shrof) *adj* steep

schrumpfen (*shroom*-pfern) *v* *shrink

Schub (shoop) *m* (pl ~e) push

Schubkarren (*shoop*-kah-rern) *m* (pl ~) wheelbarrow

Schublade (*shoop*-laa-der) *f* (pl ~n) drawer

schüchtern (*shewkh*-terrn) *adj* timid, shy

Schüchternheit (*shewkh*-terrn-hight) *f* timidity, shyness

Schuft (shooft) *m* (pl ~e) bastard; villain

Schuh (shoo) *m* (pl ~e) shoe

Schuhgeschäft (*shoo*-ger-shehft) *nt* (pl ~e) shoe-shop

Schuhkrem (*shoo*-kraym) *f* (pl ~s) shoe polish

Schuhmacher (*shoo*-mah-kherr) *m* (pl ~) shoemaker

Schuhwerk (*shoo*-vehrk) *nt* footwear

Schulbank (*shool*-bahngk) *f* (pl ~e) desk

Schuld (shoolt) *f* (pl ~en) guilt, blame; debt

schulden (*shool*-dern) v owe

schuldig (*shool*-dikh) adj guilty; due; ~ *sein owe

Schuldirektor (*shool*-di-rehk-tor) m (pl ~en) headmaster, head teacher

Schule (*shoo*-ler) f (pl ~n) school; college; höhere ~ secondary school

Schüler (*shew*-lerr) m (pl ~) scholar, pupil; schoolboy

Schülerin (*shew*-ler-rin) f (pl ~nen) schoolgirl

Schullehrer (*shool*-lay-rerr) m (pl ~) teacher

Schulleiter (*shool*-ligh-terr) m (pl ~) headmaster, head teacher, principal

Schultasche (*shool*-tah-sher) f (pl ~n) satchel

Schulter (*shool*-terr) f (pl ~n) shoulder

Schuppe (*shoo*-per) f (pl ~n) scale; **Schuppen** fpl dandruff; m shed

Schürze (*shewr*-tser) f (pl ~n) apron

Schuß (shooss) m (pl Schüsse) shot

Schüssel (*shew*-serl) f (pl ~n) dish; basin

Schutt (shoot) m litter

schütteln (*shew*-terln) v *shake

Schutz (shoots) m protection; cover, shelter

Schutzbrille (*shoots*-bri-ler) f (pl ~n) goggles pl

schützen (*shew*-tsern) v protect; shelter

Schutzmann (*shoots*-mahn) m (pl ~er) policeman

Schutzmarke (*shoots*-mahr-ker) f (pl ~n) trademark

schwach (shvahkh) adj weak, feeble, faint; poor; dim

Schwäche (*shveh*-kher) f (pl ~n) weakness

Schwager (*shvaa*-gerr) m (pl ~) brother-in-law

Schwägerin (*shvai*-ger-rin) f (pl ~nen) sister-in-law

Schwalbe (*shvahl*-ber) f (pl ~n) swallow

Schwamm (shvahm) m (pl ~e) sponge

Schwan (shvaan) m (pl ~e) swan

schwanger (*shvahng*-err) adj pregnant

Schwanz (shvahnts) m (pl ~e) tail

schwänzen (*shvehn*-tsern) v play truant

schwarz (shvahrts) adj black

Schwarzmarkt (*shvahrts*-mahrkt) m black market

schwatzen (*shvah*-tsern) v chat

Schwede (*shvay*-der) m (pl ~n) Swede

Schweden (*shvay*-dern) Sweden

schwedisch (*shvay*-dish) adj Swedish

*schweigen** (*shvigh*-gern) v *keep quiet, *be silent; **schweigend** silent; **zum Schweigen *bringen** silence

Schwein (shvighn) nt (pl ~e) pig

Schweinefleisch (*shvigh*-ner-flighsh) nt pork

Schweinsleder (*shvighns*-lay-derr) nt pigskin

Schweiß (shvighss) m perspiration; sweat

schweißen (*shvigh*-sern) v weld

Schweiz (shvights) f Switzerland

Schweizer (*shvigh*-tserr) m (pl ~) Swiss

schweizerisch (*shvigh*-tser-rish) adj Swiss

Schwelle (*shveh*-ler) f (pl ~n) threshold

*schwellen** (*shveh*-lern) v *swell

schwer (shvayr) adj heavy; difficult

schwerfällig (*shvayr*-feh-likh) adj slow

Schwerkraft (*shvayr*-krahft) f gravity

Schwermut (*shvayr*-moot) f melancholy

Schwert (shvayrt) nt (pl ~er) sword

Schwester (*shvehss*-terr) *f* (pl ~n) sister; nurse

Schwiegereltern (*shvee*-gerr-ehl-terrn) *pl* parents-in-law *pl*

Schwiegermutter (*shvee*-gerr-moo-terr) *f* (pl ~̈) mother-in-law

Schwiegersohn (*shvee*-gerr-zōan) *m* (pl ~̈e) son-in-law

Schwiegervater (*shvee*-gerr-faa-terr) *m* (pl ~̈) father-in-law

Schwiele (*shvee*-ler) *f* (pl ~n) callus

schwierig (*shvee*-rikh) *adj* hard, difficult

Schwierigkeit (*shvee*-rikh-kight) *f* (pl ~en) difficulty

Schwimmbad (*shvim*-baat) *nt* (pl ~̈er) swimming pool

*****schwimmen** (*shvi*-mern) *v* *swim; float

Schwimmer (*shvi*-merr) *m* (pl ~) swimmer; float

Schwimmsport (*shvim*-shport) *m* swimming

Schwindel (*shvin*-derl) *m* dizziness; fraud

Schwindelanfall (*shvin*-derl-ahn-fahl) *m* (pl ~̈e) vertigo

Schwindelgefühl (*shvin*-derl-ger-fewl) *nt* giddiness

schwindlig (*shvin*-dlikh) *adj* giddy, dizzy

Schwingung (*shving*-oong) *f* (pl ~en) vibration

Schwitzbad (*shvits*-baat) *nt* (pl ~̈er) Turkish bath

schwitzen (*shvi*-tsern) *v* perspire, sweat

*****schwören** (*shvūr*-rern) *v* *swear; vow

sechs (zehks) *num* six

sechste (*zehks*-ter) *num* sixth

sechzehn (*zehkh*-tsāyn) *num* sixteen

sechzehnte (*zehkh*-tsāyn-ter) *num* sixteenth

sechzig (*zehkh*-tsikh) *num* sixty

Sediment (zay-di-*mehnt*) *nt* (pl ~e) deposit

See (zāy) *m* (pl ~n) lake; *f* sea

Seebad (*zāy*-baat) *nt* (pl ~̈er) seaside resort

Seehafen (*zāy*-haa-fern) *m* (pl ~̈) seaport

Seehund (*zāy*-hoont) *m* (pl ~e) seal

Seeigel (*zāy*-ee-gerl) *m* (pl ~) sea-urchin

Seejungfrau (*zāy*-Yoong-frou) *f* (pl ~en) mermaid

Seekarte (*zāy*-kahr-ter) *f* (pl ~n) chart

seekrank (*zāy*-krahngk) *adj* seasick

Seekrankheit (*zāy*-krahngk-hight) *f* seasickness

Seele (*zāy*-ler) *f* (pl ~n) soul

Seemöwe (*zāy*-mūr-ver) *f* (pl ~n) seagull

Seeräuber (*zāy*-roi-berr) *m* (pl ~) pirate

Seereise (*zāy*-righ-zer) *f* (pl ~n) cruise

Seevogel (*zāy*-fōa-gerl) *m* (pl ~̈) seabird

Seezunge (*zāy*-tsoong-er) *f* (pl ~n) sole

Segel (*zāy*-gerl) *nt* (pl ~) sail

Segelboot (*zāy*-gerl-bōat) *nt* (pl ~e) sailing-boat

Segelflugzeug (*zāy*-gerl-flōok-tsoik) *nt* (pl ~e) glider

Segelklub (*zāy*-gerl-kloop) *m* (pl ~s) yacht-club

Segelsport (*zāy*-gerl-shport) *m* yachting

Segeltuch (*zāy*-gerl-tōokh) *nt* canvas

Segen (*zāy*-gern) *m* blessing

segnen (*zāy*-gnern) *v* bless

*****sehen** (*zāy*-ern) *v* *see; notice; ~ *lassen* *show

Sehenswürdigkeit (*zāy*-erns-vewr-dikh-kight) *f* (pl ~en) sight

Sehne (*zāy*-ner) *f* (pl ~n) sinew, ten-

don
sich sehnen nach (*zāy*-nern) long for
Sehnsucht (*zāyn*-zookht) *f* (pl ⁓e)
longing
sehr (*zāyr*) *adv* quite, very
seicht (zighkht) *adj* shallow
Seide (*zigh*-der) *f* silk
seiden (*zigh*-dern) *adj* silken
Seife (*zigh*-fer) *f* (pl ⁓n) soap
Seifenpulver (*zigh*-fern-pool-ferr) *nt*
soap powder
Seil (zighl) *nt* (pl ⁓e) rope, cord
sein (zighn) *pron* his
* **sein** (zighn) *v* *be
seit (zight) *prep* since
seitdem (zight-*dāym*) *conj* since
Seite (*zigh*-ter) *f* (pl ⁓n) way, side;
page; **zur** ⁓ aside
Seitenlicht (*zigh*-tern-likht) *nt* (pl ⁓er)
sidelight
Seitenschiff (*zigh*-tern-shif) *nt* (pl ⁓e)
aisle
Seitenstraße (*zigh*-tern-shtraa-ser) *f*
(pl ⁓n) side-street
seither (zight-*hāyr*) *adv* since
seitwärts (*zight*-vehrts) *adv* sideways
Sekretär (zay-kray-*tair*) *m* (pl ⁓e) secretary; clerk
Sekretärin (zay-kray-*tai*-rin) *f* (pl
⁓nen) secretary
Sekt (zehkt) *m* champagne
Sekunde (zay-*koon*-der) *f* (pl ⁓n) second
selb (zehlb) *pron* same
selbst (zehlpst) *pron* myself; yourself; himself; herself; oneself; ourselves; yourselves; themselves
selbständig (*zehlp*-shtehn-dikh) *adj* independent; self-employed
Selbstbedienung (*zehlpst*-ber-dee-
noong) *f* self-service
Selbstbedienungsrestaurant
(*zehlpst*-ber-dee-noongs-rehss-toa-
rahng) *nt* (pl ⁓s) cafeteria, self-ser-

vice restaurant
selbstgemacht (*zehlpst*-ger-mahkht)
adj home-made
Selbstklebeband (*zehlpst*-klāy-ber-
bahnt) *nt* scotch tape
Selbstlaut (*zehlpst*-lout) *m* (pl ⁓e)
vowel
selbstlos (*zehlpst*-lōass) *adj* unselfish
Selbstmord (*zehlpst*-mort) *m* (pl ⁓e)
suicide
Selbstsucht (*zehlpst*-zookht) *f* selfishness
selbstsüchtig (*zehlpst*-zewkh-tikh) *adj*
selfish
selbstverständlich (*zehlpst*-fehr-
shtehnt-likh) *adj* self-evident; *adv*
naturally, of course
Selbstverwaltung (*zehlpst*-fehr-vahl-
toong) *f* self-government
Sellerie (*zeh*-ler-ree) *m* celery
selten (*zehl*-tern) *adj* rare; uncommon, infrequent; *adv* seldom, rarely
Selterswasser (*zehl*-terrs-vah-serr) *nt*
soda-water
seltsam (*zehlt*-zaam) *adj* curious, odd,
quaint
Senat (zay-*naat*) *m* senate
Senator (zay-*naa*-tor) *m* (pl ⁓en)
senator
* **senden** (*zehn*-dern) *v* *send; transmit, *broadcast
Sender (*zehn*-derr) *m* (pl ⁓) transmitter
Sendung (*zehn*-doong) *f* (pl ⁓en) consignment; transmission, broadcast
Senf (zehnf) *m* mustard
senil (zay-*neel*) *adj* senile
senken (*zehng*-kern) *v* *cut
senkrecht (*zehngk*-rehkht) *adj* vertical,
perpendicular
Sensation (zehn-zah-*ts^yōān*) *f* (pl ⁓en)
sensation
sensationell (zehn-zah-ts^yoa-*nehl*) *adj*
sensational

sentimental (zehn-ti-mehn-*taal*) *adj* sentimental

September (zehp-*tehm*-berr) September

septisch (*zehp*-tish) *adj* septic

Serie (*zāy*-r^{y}er) *f* (pl ~n) series

seriös (zay-r^{y}ūss) *adj* serious

Serum (*zāy*-room) *nt* (pl Seren) serum

Serviette (zehr-v^{y}eh-ter) *f* (pl ~n) napkin, serviette

Sessel (*zeh*-serl) *m* (pl ~) chair, arm-chair

setzen (*zeh*-tsern) *v* place; *lay, *put; **sich ~** *sit down

Sex (zehks) *m* sex

Sexualität (zeh-ksoo-ah-li-*tait*) *f* sexuality

sexuell (zeh-ksoo-*ehl*) *adj* sexual

Shampoo (shehm-*pōō*) *nt* shampoo

Siam (*zee*-ahm) Siam

Siamese (z^{y}ah-*māy*-zer) *m* (pl ~n) Siamese

siamesisch (z^{y}ah-*māy*-zish) *adj* Siamese

sich (zikh) *pron* himself; herself; themselves

sicher (*zi*-kherr) *adj* safe, secure; sure

Sicherheit (*zi*-kherr-hight) *f* safety, security

Sicherheitsgurt (*zi*-kherr-hights-goort) *m* (pl ~e) seat-belt; safety-belt

Sicherheitsnadel (*zi*-kherr-hights-naa-derl) *f* (pl ~n) safety-pin

sicherlich (*zi*-kherr-likh) *adv* surely

Sicherung (*zi*-kher-roong) *f* (pl ~en) fuse

Sicht (zikht) *f* sight

sichtbar (*zikht*-baar) *adj* visible

Sichtweite (*zikht*-vigh-ter) *f* visibility

Sie (zee) *pron* you

sie (zee) *pron* she; her; they; them

Sieb (zeep) *nt* (pl ~e) sieve

sieben[1] (*zee*-bern) *v* sift, sieve; strain

sieben[2] (*zee*-bern) *num* seven

siebente (*zee*-bern-ter) *num* seventh

siebzehn (*zeep*-tsāyn) *num* seventeen

siebzehnte (*zeep*-tsāyn-ter) *num* seventeenth

siebzig (*zeep*-tsikh) *num* seventy

Sieg (zeek) *m* (pl ~e) victory

Siegel (*zee*-gerl) *nt* (pl ~) seal

Sieger (*zee*-gerr) *m* (pl ~) winner

Signal (zi-*gnaal*) *nt* (pl ~e) signal

signalisieren (zi-gnah-li-*zee*-rern) *v* signal

Silbe (*zil*-ber) *f* (pl ~n) syllable

Silber (*zil*-berr) *nt* silver; silverware

silbern (*zil*-berrn) *adj* silver

Silberschmied (*zil*-berr-shmeet) *m* (pl ~e) silversmith

***singen** (*zing*-ern) *v* *sing

***sinken** (*zing*-kern) *v* *sink

Sinn (zin) *m* (pl ~e) sense

sinnlos (*zin*-lōass) *adj* meaningless

Siphon (zi-*fawng*) *m* (pl ~s) siphon, syphon

Sirene (zi-*rāy*-ner) *f* (pl ~n) siren

Sirup (*zee*-roop) *m* syrup

Sitte (*zi*-ter) *f* (pl ~n) custom; **Sitten** morals

Sittich (*zi*-tikh) *m* (pl ~e) parakeet

sittlich (*zit*-likh) *adj* moral

Sitz (zits) *m* (pl ~e) seat

***sitzen** (*zi*-tsern) *v* *sit

Sitzung (*zi*-tsoong) *f* (pl ~en) session

Skandal (skahn-*daal*) *m* (pl ~e) scandal

Skandinavien (skahn-di-*naa*-v^{y}ern) Scandinavia

Skandinavier (skahn-di-*naa*-v^{y}err) *m* (pl ~) Scandinavian

skandinavisch (skahn-di-*naa*-vish) *adj* Scandinavian

Skelett (skay-*leht*) *nt* (pl ~e) skeleton

Skizze (*ski*-tser) *f* (pl ~n) sketch

Skizzenbuch (*ski*-tsern-bōōkh) *nt* (pl ~er) sketch-book

skizzieren (ski-*tsee*-rern) *v* sketch

Sklave (*sklaa*-ver) *m* (pl ~n) slave
Skulptur (skoolp-*toor*) *f* (pl ~en) sculpture
Slip (slip) *m* (pl ~s) briefs *pl*
Smaragd (smah-*rahkt*) *m* (pl ~e) emerald
Smoking (*smoa*-king) *m* (pl ~s) dinner-jacket; tuxedo *nAm*
Snackbar (*snehk*-baar) *f* (pl ~s) snack-bar
so (zoa) *adv* so; such; thus; ~ **daß** so that
sobald als (zoa-*bahlt* ahls) as soon as
Socke (*zo*-ker) *f* (pl ~n) sock
Sodawasser (*zoa*-dah-vah-serr) *nt* soda-water
Sodbrennen (*zoat*-breh-nern) *nt* heartburn
soeben (zoa-*ay*-bern) *adv* just now
Sofa (*zoa*-fah) *nt* (pl ~s) sofa
sofort (zoa-*fort*) *adv* at once; presently, straight away, immediately, instantly
sofortig (zoa-*for*-tikh) *adj* prompt
sogar (zoa-*gaar*) *adv* even
sogenannt (*zoa*-ger-nahnt) *adj* so-called
sogleich (zoa-*glighkh*) *adv* presently, immediately
Sohle (*zoa*-ler) *f* (pl ~n) sole
Sohn (zoan) *m* (pl ~e) son
solch (zolkh) *pron* such
Soldat (zol-*daat*) *m* (pl ~en) soldier
solide (zoa-*lee*-der) *adj* firm
Solistenkonzert (zoa-*liss*-tern-kontsehrt) *nt* (pl ~e) recital
Soll (zol) *nt* debit
sollen (*zo*-lern) *v* *ought to, *shall
Sommer (*zo*-merr) *m* (pl ~) summer
Sommerhaus (*zo*-merr-houss) *nt* (pl ~er) cottage
Sommerzeit (*zo*-merr-tsight) *f* summer time
sonderbar (*zon*-derr-baar) *adj* funny,

odd, peculiar; queer
sondern (*zon*-derrn) *conj* but
Sonnabend (*zon*-aa-bernt) *m* Saturday
Sonne (*zo*-ner) *f* (pl ~n) sun
sich sonnen (*zo*-nern) sunbathe
Sonnenaufgang (*zo*-nern-ouf-gahng) *m* (pl ~e) sunrise
Sonnenbrand (*zo*-nern-brahnt) *m* sunburn
Sonnenbrille (*zo*-nern-bri-ler) *f* (pl ~n) sun-glasses *pl*
Sonnenlicht (*zo*-nern-likht) *nt* sunlight
Sonnenöl (*zo*-nern-url) *nt* suntan oil
Sonnenschein (*zo*-nern-shighn) *m* sunshine
Sonnenschirm (*zo*-nern-sheerm) *m* (pl ~e) sunshade
Sonnenstich (*zo*-nern-shtikh) *m* sunstroke
Sonnenuntergang (*zo*-nern-oon-terrgahng) *m* (pl ~e) sunset
sonnig (*zo*-nikh) *adj* sunny
Sonntag (*zon*-taak) *m* Sunday
sonst (zonst) *adv* otherwise; else
Sorge (*zor*-ger) *f* (pl ~n) care; trouble, concern, worry
sorgen für (*zor*-gern) see to, attend to, *take care of; **sich sorgen um** care about
sorgfältig (*zork*-fehl-tikh) *adj* neat; careful; thorough
Sorte (*zor*-ter) *f* (pl ~n) sort, kind
sortieren (zor-*tee*-rern) *v* sort, assort
Sortiment (zor-ti-*mehnt*) *nt* (pl ~e) assortment
Soße (*zoa*-ser) *f* (pl ~n) sauce
sowjetisch (zo-v'eh-tish) *adj* Soviet
Sowjetunion (zo-v'eht-oo-n'oan) *f* Soviet Union
sowohl ... als auch (zoa-*voal* ... ahls oukh) both ... and
sozial (zoa-ts'aal) *adj* social
Sozialismus (zoa-ts'ah-*liss*-mooss) *m* socialism

Sozialist (zoa-t^ysah-*list*) *m* (pl ~en) socialist

sozialistisch (zoa-ts^yah-*liss*-tish) *adj* socialist

spähen (*shpai*-ern) *v* peep

Spalt (shpahlt) *m* (pl ~e) chink; chasm

Spalte (*shpahl*-ter) *f* (pl ~n) cleft; column

spalten (*shpahl*-tern) *v* *split

Spanien (*shpaa*-n^yern) Spain

Spanier (*shpaa*-n^yerr) *m* (pl ~) Spaniard

spanisch (*shpaa*-nish) *adj* Spanish

spannen (*shpah*-nern) *v* tighten

Spannkraft (*shpahn*-krahft) *f* elasticity

Spannung (*shpah*-noong) *f* (pl ~en) pressure; stress, tension; voltage

sparen (*shpaa*-rern) *v* save, economize

Spargel (*shpahr*-gerl) *m* asparagus

Sparkasse (*shpaar*-kah-ser) *f* (pl ~n) savings bank

sparsam (*shpaar*-zaam) *adj* economical; thrifty

Spaß (shpaass) *m* fun, pleasure

spaßig (*shpaa*-sikh) *adj* funny, humorous

spät (shpait) *adj* late; **später** afterwards

Spaten (*shpaa*-tern) *m* (pl ~) spade

spazieren (shpah-*tsee*-rern) *v* walk

Spaziergang (shpah-*tseer*-gahng) *m* (pl ~̈e) walk

Spaziergänger (shpah-*tseer*-gehng-err) *m* (pl ~) walker

Spazierstock (shpah-*tseer*-shtok) *m* (pl ~̈e) walking-stick

Speck (shpehk) *m* bacon

Speer (shpā_yr) *m* (pl ~e) spear

Speiche (*shpigh*-kher) *f* (pl ~n) spoke

Speichel (*shpigh*-kherl) *m* spit

Speise (*shpigh*-zer) *f* (pl ~n) fare

Speisekammer (*shpigh*-zer-kah-merr) *f* (pl ~n) larder

Speisekarte (*shpigh*-zer-kahr-ter) *f* (pl ~en) menu

speisen (*shpigh*-zern) *v* *eat

Speisesaal (*shpigh*-zer-zaal) *m* (pl -säle) dining-room

Speisewagen (*shpigh*-zer-vaa-gern) *m* (pl ~) dining-car

Speisezimmer (*shpigh*-zer-tsi-merr) *nt* (pl ~) dining-room

spekulieren (shpay-koo-*lee*-rern) *v* speculate

Spende (*shpehn*-der) *f* (pl ~n) donation

spenden (*shpehn*-dern) *v* donate

Sperling (*shpehr*-ling) *m* (pl ~e) sparrow

sperren (*shpeh*-rern) *v* block

Sperrsitz (*shpehrr*-zits) *m* (pl ~e) stall

sich spezialisieren (shpay-ts^yah-li-*zee*-rern) specialize

Spezialist (shpay-ts^yah-*list*) *m* (pl ~en) specialist

Spezialität (shpay-ts^yah-li-*tait*) *f* (pl ~en) speciality

speziell (shpay-ts^y*ehl*) *adj* special; peculiar; *adv* in particular

spezifisch (shpay-*tsee*-fish) *adj* specific

Spiegel (*shpee*-gerl) *m* (pl ~) looking-glass, mirror

Spiegelbild (*shpee*-gerl-bilt) *nt* (pl ~er) reflection

Spiegelung (*shpee*-ger-loong) *f* (pl ~en) reflection

Spiel (shpeel) *nt* (pl ~e) game; play; match

spielen (*shpee*-lern) *v* play; act

Spieler (*shpee*-lerr) *m* (pl ~) player

Spielkarte (*shpeel*-kahr-ter) *f* (pl ~n) playing-card

Spielmarke (*shpeel*-mahr-ker) *f* (pl ~n) chip

Spielplatz (*shpeel*-plahts) *m* (pl ~̈e) playground, recreation ground

Spielstand (*shpeel*-shtahnt) *m* score

Spielwarenladen (*shpeel*-vaa-rern-laa-dern) *m* (pl ~) toyshop

Spielzeug (*shpeel*-tsoik) *nt* (pl ~e) toy

spießbürgerlich (*shpeess*-bewr-gerr-likh) *adj* bourgeois

Spinat (shpi-*naat*) *m* spinach

Spinne (*shpi*-ner) *f* (pl ~n) spider

*****spinnen** (*shpi*-nern) *v* *spin

Spinnwebe (*shpin*-vāy-ber) *f* (pl ~n) spider's web, cobweb

Spion (shpi-*ōan*) *m* (pl ~e) spy

Spirituosen (shpi-ri-too-*ōa*-zern) *pl* spirits, liquor

Spirituosenladen (shpi-ri-too-*ōa*-zern-laa-dern) *m* (pl ~) off-licence

Spirituskocher (*shpee*-ri-tooss-ko-kherr) *m* (pl ~) spirit stove

spitz (shpits) *adj* pointed

Spitze (*shpi*-tser) *f* (pl ~n) point; peak; top; tip; spire; lace

Spitzhacke (*shpits*-hah-ker) *f* (pl ~n) pick-axe

Spitzname (*shpits*-naa-mer) *m* (pl ~n) nickname

Splitter (*shpli*-terr) *m* (pl ~) splinter; chip

Sport (shport) *m* (pl ~e) sport

Sportjacke (*shport*-ʸah-ker) *f* (pl ~n) sports-jacket, blazer

Sportkleidung (*shport*-kligh-doong) *f* sportswear

Sportler (*shport*-lerr) *m* (pl ~) sportsman

Sportwagen (*shport*-vaa-gern) *m* (pl ~) sports-car

Spott (shpot) *m* mockery

Sprache (*shpraa*-kher) *f* (pl ~n) speech; language

Sprachführer (*shpraakh*-fēw-rerr) *m* (pl ~) phrase-book

Sprachlabor (*shpraakh*-lah-bōar) *nt* (pl ~e) language laboratory

sprachlos (*shpraakh*-lōass) *adj* speechless

Spray (sprāy) *nt* (pl ~s) atomizer

*****sprechen** (*shpreh*-khern) *v* *speak, talk

Sprechstunde (*shprehkh*-shtoon-der) *f* (pl ~n) consultation hours

Sprechzimmer (*shprehkh*-tsi-merr) *nt* (pl ~) surgery

Sprengstoff (*shprehng*-shtof) *m* (pl ~e) explosive

Sprichwort (*shprikh*-vort) *nt* (pl ~er) proverb

Springbrunnen (*shpring*-broo-nern) *m* (pl ~) fountain

*****springen** (*shpring*-ern) *v* jump; *leap

Spritze (*shpri*-tser) *f* (pl ~n) shot; syringe

Sprühregen (*shprēw*-rāy-gern) *m* drizzle

Sprung (shproong) *m* (pl ~e) leap, jump

Spucke (*shpoo*-ker) *f* spit

spucken (*shpoo*-kern) *v* *spit

Spule (*shpoō*-ler) *f* (pl ~n) spool

spülen (*shpēw*-lern) *v* rinse

Spülung (*shpēw*-loong) *f* (pl ~en) rinse

Spur (shpōor) *f* (pl ~en) trace

spüren (*shpēw*-rern) *v* sense

Staat (shtaat) *m* (pl ~en) state; **Staats-** national

Staatsangehörige (*shtaats*-ahn-ger-hūr-ri-ger) *m* (pl ~n) subject

Staatsangehörigkeit (*shtaats*-ahn-ger-hūr-rikh-kight) *f* nationality; citizenship

Staatsbeamte (*shtaats*-ber-ahm-ter) *m* (pl ~n) civil servant

Staatsmann (*shtaats*-mahn) *m* (pl ~er) statesman

Staatsoberhaupt (*shtaats*-ōa-berr-houpt) *nt* (pl ~er) head of state

stabil (shtah-*beel*) *adj* stable

Stachelbeere (*shtah*-kherl-bāy-rer) *f* (pl ~n) gooseberry

Stachelschwein (*shtah*-kherl-shvighn) *m* (pl ~e) porcupine

Stadion (*shtaa*-dʸon) *nt* (pl -dien) stadium

Stadium (*shtaa*-dʸoom) *nt* (pl -dien) stage

Stadt (shtaht) *f* (pl ~̈e) town; city

Städter (*shtai*-terr) *mpl* townspeople pl

städtisch (*shteh*-tish) *adj* urban; municipal

Stadtverwaltung (*shtaht*-fehr-vahl-toong) *f* (pl ~en) municipality

Stadtviertel (*shtaht*-feer-terl) *nt* (pl ~) quarter

Stadtzentrum (*shtaht*-tsehn-troom) *nt* (pl -zentren) town centre

Stahl (shtaal) *m* steel; **nichtrostender** ~ stainless steel

Stahlkammer (*shtaal*-kah-merr) *f* (pl ~n) vault

Stall (shtahl) *m* (pl ~̈e) stable

Stamm (shtahm) *m* (pl ~̈e) trunk; tribe

stammeln (*shtah*-merln) *v* falter

stämmig (*shteh*-mikh) *adj* stout

stampfen (*shtahm*-pfern) *v* stamp

Stand (shtahnt) *m* (pl ~̈e) stand, stall; level

Standbild (*shtahnt*-bilt) *nt* (pl ~er) statue

standhaft (*shtahnt*-hahft) *adj* steadfast

Standpunkt (*shtahnt*-poongkt) *m* (pl ~e) point of view

Stange (*shtahng*-er) *f* (pl ~n) rod; bar; carton

Stanniol (shtah-nʸōāl) *nt* tinfoil

Stapel (*shtaa*-perl) *m* (pl ~) stack; heap

Stapellauf (*shtaa*-perl-louf) *m* launching

Star (shtaar) *m* (pl ~e) starling

stark (shtahrk) *adj* powerful, strong; solid

Stärke (*shtehr*-ker) *f* strength; starch

stärken (*shtehr*-kern) *v* starch

Stärkungsmittel (*shtehr*-koongs-mi-terl) *nt* (pl ~) tonic

starr (shtahr) *adj* numb

starren (*shtah*-rern) *v* gaze, stare

starrköpfig (*shtahr*-kur-pfikh) *adj* head-strong, obstinate; pig-headed

Start (shtahrt) *m* take-off

Startbahn (*shtahrt*-baan) *f* (pl ~en) runway

starten (*shtahr*-tern) *v* *take off

Stationsvorsteher (shtah-tsʸōāns-fōār-shtāy-err) *m* (pl ~) station-master

Statistik (shtah-*tiss*-tik) *f* (pl ~en) statistics *pl*

statt (shtaht) *prep* instead of

***stattfinden** (*shtaht*-fin-dern) *v* *take place

stattlich (*shtaht*-likh) *adj* handsome

Staub (shtoup) *m* dust

staubig (*shtou*-bikh) *adj* dusty

staubsaugen (*shtoup*-zou-gern) *v* hoover; vacuum *vAm*

Staubsauger (*shtoup*-zou-gerr) *m* (pl ~) vacuum cleaner

Steak (stāyk) *nt* (pl ~s) steak

Stechen (*shteh*-khern) *nt* stitch

***stechen** (*shteh*-khern) *v* prick; *sting

stecken (*shteh*-kern) *v* *put

Steckenpferd (*shteh*-kern-pfāyrt) *nt* (pl ~e) hobby-horse; hobby

Stecker (*shteh*-kerr) *m* (pl ~) plug

Stecknadel (*shtehk*-naa-derl) *f* (pl ~n) pin

***stehen** (*shtāy*-ern) *v* *stand; **gut** ~ *become

***stehlen** (*shtāy*-lern) *v* *steal

steif (shtighf) *adj* stiff

Steigbügel (*shtighk*-bēw-gerl) *m* (pl ~) stirrup

***steigen** (*shtigh*-gern) *v* *rise; climb

Steigung (*shtigh*-goong) *f* (pl ~en) rise; ascent

steil (shtighl) *adj* steep

Stein (shtighn) *m* (pl ~e) stone

Steinbruch (shtighn-brookh) *m* (pl ~e) quarry

steinern (shtigh-nerrn) *adj* stone

Steingarnele (shtighn-gahr-nāy-ler) *f* (pl ~n) prawn

Steingut (shtighn-gōot) *nt* earthenware, crockery; faience

Stelle (shteh-ler) *f* (pl ~n) spot; station; passage; **wunde** ~ sore

stellen (shteh-lern) *v* *put; place, *lay, *set

Stellung (shteh-loong) *f* (pl ~en) position; job

Stellvertreter (shtehl-fehr-trāy-terr) *m* (pl ~) substitute; deputy

Stempel (shtehm-perl) *m* (pl ~) stamp

Stenograph (shtay-noa-*graaf*) *m* (pl ~en) stenographer

Stenographie (shtay-noa-grah-*fee*) *f* shorthand

Stenotypistin (shtay-noa-tew-*piss*-tin) *f* (pl ~nen) typist

Steppdecke (shtehp-deh-ker) *f* (pl ~n) quilt

***sterben** (shtehr-bern) *v* die; depart

sterblich (shtehrp-likh) *adj* mortal

steril (shtay-*reel*) *adj* sterile

sterilisieren (shtay-ri-li-*zee*-rern) *v* sterilize

Stern (shtehrn) *m* (pl ~e) star

stetig (shtāy-tikh) *adj* even

Steuer (shtoi-err) *f* (pl ~n) tax

Steuerbord (shtoi-err-bort) *nt* starboard

steuerfrei (shtoi-err-frigh) *adj* tax-free

Steuermann (shtoi-err-mahn) *m* (pl ~er) helmsman, steersman

steuern (shtoi-errn) *v* navigate

Steuerrad (shtoi-err-raat) *nt* steering-wheel

Steuerruder (shtoi-err-rōo-derr) *nt* (pl ~) rudder

Stich (shtikh) *m* (pl ~e) sting; bite; stitch; engraving, picture, print

sticken (shti-kern) *v* embroider

Stickerei (shti-ker-*righ*) *f* (pl ~en) embroidery

stickig (shti-kikh) *adj* stuffy

Stickstoff (shtik-shtof) *m* nitrogen

Stiefel (shtee-ferl) *m* (pl ~) boot

Stiefkind (shteef-kint) *nt* (pl ~er) stepchild

Stiefmutter (shteef-moo-terr) *f* (pl ~) stepmother

Stiefvater (shteef-faa-terr) *m* (pl ~) stepfather

Stiel (shteel) *m* (pl ~e) handle; stem

Stier (shteer) *m* (pl ~e) bull

Stierkampf (shteer-kahmpf) *m* (pl ~e) bullfight

Stierkampfarena (shteer-kahmpf-ah-rāy-nah) *f* (pl -arenen) bullring

stiften (shtif-tern) *v* found

Stiftung (shtif-toong) *f* (pl ~en) foundation

Stil (shteel) *m* (pl ~e) style

still (shtil) *adj* silent; still, calm, quiet

Stille (shti-ler) *f* silence; stillness, quiet

stillen (shti-lern) *v* nurse

Stille Ozean (shti-ler ōā-tsay-aan) Pacific Ocean

stillstehend (shtil-shtāy-ernt) *adj* stationary

Stimme (shti-mer) *f* (pl ~n) voice; vote

stimmen (shti-mern) *v* vote

Stimmung (shti-moong) *f* (pl ~en) spirits, mood; atmosphere.

***stinken** (shting-kern) *v* *smell; *stink

Stipendium (shti-*pehn*-dʸoom) *nt* (pl -dien) grant, scholarship

Stirn (shteern) *f* forehead

Stock (shtok) *m* (pl ~e) stick; cane

Stockwerk (shtok-vehrk) *nt* (pl ~e)

storey, floor

Stoff (shtof) *m* (pl ~e) matter; fabric; theme

stofflich (*shtof*-likh) *adj* material

stöhnen (*shtūr*-nern) *v* moan, groan

Stola (*shtōā*-lah) *f* (pl ~s) stole

stolpern (*shtol*-perrn) *v* stumble

Stolz (shtolts) *m* pride

stolz (shtolts) *adj* proud

stopfen (*shto*-pfern) *v* darn

Stopfgarn (*shtopf*-gahrn) *nt* darning wool

Stöpsel (*shtur*-pserl) *m* (pl ~) cork, stopper

Storch (shtorkh) *m* (pl ~e) stork

stören (*shtūr*-rern) *v* disturb; upset

Störung (*shtūr*-roong) *f* (pl ~en) disturbance

Stoß (shtōāss) *m* (pl ~e) bump; push

Stoßdämpfer (*shtōāss*-dehm-pferr) *m* (pl ~) shock absorber

* **stoßen** (*shtōā*-sern) *v* bump; push; kick

Stoßstange (*shtōāss*-shtahng-er) *f* (pl ~n) bumper, fender

Strafe (*shtraa*-fer) *f* (pl ~n) punishment, penalty

strafen (*shtraa*-fern) *v* punish

straffen (*shtrah*-fern) *v* tighten

Strafrecht (*shtraaf*-rehkht) *nt* criminal law

Strafstoß (*shtraaf*-shtōāss) *m* (pl ~e) penalty kick

Strahl (shtraal) *m* (pl ~en) beam, ray; squirt, spout, jet

strahlen (*shtraa*-lern) *v* *shine

Strahlturbine (*shtraal*-toor-bee-ner) *f* (pl ~n) turbojet

stramm (shtrahm) *adj* tight

Strand (shtrahnt) *m* (pl ~e) beach

Straße (*shtraa*-ser) *f* (pl ~n) road, street

Straßenarbeiten (*shtraa*-sern-ahr-bigh-tern) *fpl* road up

Straßenbahn (*shtraa*-sern-baan) *f* (pl ~en) tram; streetcar *nAm*

Straßenkreuzung (*shtraa*-sern-kroi-tsoong) *f* (pl ~en) junction

Straßennetz (*shtraa*-sern-nehts) *nt* (pl ~e) road system

Straßenseite (*shtraa*-sern-zigh-ter) *f* (pl ~n) roadside

Strauch (shtroukh) *m* (pl ~er) shrub

Strauß¹ (shtrouss) *m* (pl ~e) bunch, bouquet

Strauß² (shtrouss) *m* (pl ~e) ostrich

streben (*shtrāy*-bern) *v* aspire

strebsam (*shtrāyp*-zaam) *adj* ambitious

Strecke (*shtreh*-ker) *f* (pl ~n) stretch

* **streichen** (*shtrigh*-khern) *v* lower; *strike

Streichholz (*shtrighkh*-holts) *nt* (pl ~er) match

Streichholzschachtel (*shtrighkh*-holts-shahkh-terl) *f* (pl ~n) match-box

Streife (*shtrigh*-fer) *f* (pl ~n) patrol

Streifen (*shtrigh*-fern) *m* (pl ~) strip; stripe

Streik (shtrighk) *m* (pl ~s) strike

streiken (*shtrigh*-kern) *v* *strike

Streit (shtright) *m* quarrel; strife, contest; fight, battle; Streit- controversial

* **streiten** (*shtrigh*-tern) *v* quarrel; dispute, argue

Streitigkeit (*shtrigh*-tikh-kight) *f* (pl ~en) dispute

Streitkräfte (*shtright*-krehf-ter) *pl* armed forces

streitsüchtig (*shtright*-zewkh-tikh) *adj* rowdy

streng (shtrehng) *adj* strict; harsh, severe

Strich (shtrikh) *m* (pl ~e) line

Strichpunkt (*shtrikh*-poongkt) *m* (pl ~e) semi-colon

stricken (*shtri*-kern) *v* *knit

Stroh (shtrōa) *nt* straw

Strohdach (shtrōa-dahkh) *nt* (pl ̈er) thatched roof

Strom (shtrōam) *m* (pl ̈e) current

stromabwärts (shtrōam-*ahp*-vehrts) *adv* downstream

stromaufwärts (shtrōam-*ouf*-vehrts) *adv* upstream

strömen (shtrūr-mern) *v* flow; stream

Stromschnelle (shtrōam-shneh-ler) *f* (pl ~n) rapids *pl*

Strömung (shtrūr-moong) *f* (pl ~en) current

Stromverteiler (shtrōam-fehr-tigh-lerr) *m* distributor

Strophe (shtrōa-fer) *f* (pl ~n) stanza

Struktur (shtrook-*tōor*) *f* (pl ~en) structure; texture, fabric

Strumpf (shtroompf) *m* (pl ̈e) stocking; **elastische Strümpfe** support hose

Strumpfhose (shtroompf-hōa-zer) *f* (pl ~n) panty-hose

Stück (shtewk) *nt* (pl ~e) piece; part; lump, morsel

Stückchen (shtewk-khern) *nt* (pl ~) scrap, bit

Student (shtoo-*dehnt*) *m* (pl ~en) student

Studentin (shtoo-*dehn*-tin) *f* (pl ~nen) student

Studienrat (shtōo-dᵛern-raat) *m* (pl ̈e) master

studieren (shtoo-dee-rern) *v* study

Studium (shtōo-dᵛoom) *nt* (pl -dien) study

Stufe (shtōo-fer) *f* (pl ~n) step

Stuhl (shtōol) *m* (pl ̈e) chair

stumm (shtoom) *adj* mute; dumb

stumpf (shtoompf) *adj* blunt; dull

Stunde (shtoon-der) *f* (pl ~n) hour

stündlich (shtewnt-likh) *adj* hourly

Sturm (shtoorm) *m* (pl ̈e) gale, storm

stürmen (shtewr-mern) *v* dash

stürmisch (shtewr-mish) *adj* stormy

Sturmlaterne (shtoorm-lah-tehr-ner) *f* (pl ~n) hurricane lamp

Sturz (shtoorts) *m* (pl ̈e) fall

Stute (shtōo-ter) *f* (pl ~n) mare

stutzen (shtoo-tsern) *v* trim

stützen (shtew-tsern) *v* support; *hold up

Suaheli (swah-*hāy*-li) *nt* Swahili

Subjekt (zoop-ᵛehkt) *nt* (pl ~e) subject

Substantiv (zoop-stahn-teef) *nt* (pl ~e) noun

Substanz (zoop-*stahnts*) *f* (pl ~en) substance

subtil (zoop-*teel*) *adj* subtle

subtrahieren (zoop-trah-*hee*-rern) *v* subtract

Subvention (zoop-vehn-ts᷈ōan) *f* (pl ~en) subsidy

Suche (zōo-kher) *f* search

suchen (zōo-khern) *v* look for; *seek, search; hunt for

Sucher (zōo-kherr) *m* view-finder

Südafrika (zewt-aa-fri-kah) South Africa

Süden (zew-dern) *m* south

südlich (zewt-likh) *adj* southern, southerly

Südosten (zewt-*oss*-tern) *m* south-east

Südpol (zewt-pōal) *m* South Pole

Südwesten (zewt-*vehss*-tern) *m* south-west

Summe (zoo-mer) *f* (pl ~n) sum; amount

summen (zoo-mern) *v* hum

Sumpf (zoompf) *m* (pl ̈e) bog, marsh

sumpfig (zoom-pfikh) *adj* marshy

Sünde (zewn-der) *f* (pl ~n) sin

Sündenbock (zewn-dern-bok) *m* (pl ̈e) scapegoat

Superlativ (zōo-pehr-lah-teef) *m* superlative

Supermarkt (*zōo*-pehr-mahrkt) *m* (pl ⁓e) supermarket

Suppe (*zoo*-per) *f* (pl ⁓n) soup

Suppenlöffel (*zoo*-pern-lur-ferl) *m* (pl ⁓) soup-spoon

Suppenteller (*zoo*-pern-teh-lerr) *m* (pl ⁓) soup-plate

suspendieren (zooss-pehn-*dee*-rern) *v* suspend

süß (zēwss) *adj* sweet

süßen (*zēw*-sern) *v* sweeten

Süßigkeiten (*zēw*-sikh-kigh-tern) *fpl* sweets; candy *nAm*

Süßwarengeschäft (*zēwss*-vaa-rern-ger-shehft) *nt* (pl ⁓e) sweetshop; candy store *Am*

Süßwasser (*zēwss*-vah-serr) *nt* fresh water

Sweater (*svāy*-terr) *m* (pl ⁓) sweater

Symbol (zewm-*bōal*) *nt* (pl ⁓e) symbol

Sympathie (zewm-pah-*tee*) *f* sympathy

sympathisch (zewm-*paa*-tish) *adj* nice, sympathetic

Symphonie (zewm-foa-*nee*) *f* (pl ⁓n) symphony

Symptom (zewmp-*tōam*) *nt* (pl ⁓e) symptom

Synagoge (zew-nah-*gōa*-ger) *f* (pl ⁓n) synagogue

Synonym (zew-noa-*nēwm*) *nt* (pl ⁓e) synonym

synthetisch (zewn-*tāy*-tish) *adj* synthetic

Syrer (*zēw*-rerr) *m* (pl ⁓) Syrian

Syrien (*zēw*-r-ʸern) Syria

syrisch (*zēw*-rish) *adj* Syrian

System (zewss-*tāym*) *nt* (pl ⁓e) system

systematisch (zewss-tay-*maa*-tish) *adj* systematic

Szene (*stsāy*-ner) *f* (pl ⁓n) scene

T

Tabak (*taa*-bahk) *m* tobacco; pipe tobacco

Tabakhändler (*taa*-bahk-hehn-dlerr) *m* (pl ⁓) tobacconist

Tabakladen (*taa*-bahk-laa-dern) *m* (pl ⁓) tobacconist's

Tabaksbeutel (*taa*-bahks-boi-terl) *m* (pl ⁓) tobacco pouch

Tabelle (tah-*beh*-ler) *f* (pl ⁓n) chart, table

Tablett (tah-*bleht*) *nt* (pl ⁓s) tray

Tablette (tah-*bleh*-ter) *f* (pl ⁓n) tablet

Tabu (tah-*bōo*) *nt* (pl ⁓s) taboo

tadellos (*taa*-derl-lōass) *adj* faultless

tadeln (*taa*-derln) *v* reprimand

Tafel (*taa*-ferl) (pl ⁓n) board

Täfelung (*tai*-fer-loong) *f* panelling

Tag (taak) *m* (pl ⁓e) day; **bei Tage** by day; **eines Tages** some day; **guten Tag!** hello!; **pro ⁓** per day; **vierzehn Tage** fortnight

Tagebuch (*taa*-ger-bōokh) *nt* (pl ⁓er) diary

Tagesanbruch (*taa*-gerss-ahn-brookh) *m* daybreak, dawn

Tagesausflug (*taa*-gerss-ouss-flōok) *m* (pl ⁓e) day trip

Tageslicht (*taa*-gerss-likht) *nt* daylight

Tagesordnung (*taa*-gerss-or-dnoong) *f* (pl ⁓en) agenda

Tageszeitung (*taa*-gerss-tsigh-toong) *f* (pl ⁓en) daily

täglich (*taik*-likh) *adj* daily

Tagung (*taa*-goong) *f* (pl ⁓en) congress

Taille (tah-*l*ʸer) *f* (pl ⁓n) waist

Taktik (*tahk*-tik) *f* (pl ⁓en) tactics *pl*

Tal (taal) *nt* (pl ⁓er) valley

Talent (tah-*lehnt*) *nt* (pl ⁓e) faculty, talent

Talkpuder (*tahlk*-pōo-derr) *m* talc powder

Tampon (tahng-*pawng*) *m* (pl ~s) tampon

Tank (tahngk) *m* (pl ~s) tank

tanken (*tahng*-kern) *v* tank

Tankschiff (*tahngk*-shif) *nt* (pl ~e) tanker

Tankstelle (*tahngk*-shteh-ler) *f* (pl ~n) petrol station, service station, filling station ; gas station *Am*

Tanne (*tah*-ner) *f* (pl ~n) fir-tree

Tante (*tahn*-ter) *f* (pl ~n) aunt

Tanz (tahnts) *m* (pl ~e) dance

tanzen (*tahn*-tsern) *v* dance

Tapete (tah-*pāy*-ter) *f* (pl ~n) wallpaper

tapfer (*tah*-pferr) *adj* courageous, brave

Tapferkeit (*tah*-pferr-kight) *f* courage

Tarif (tah-*reef*) *m* (pl ~e) tariff, rate

Tasche (*tah*-sher) *f* (pl ~n) bag ; pocket

Taschenbuch (*tah*-shern-bōokh) *nt* (pl -bücher) paperback

Taschenkamm (*tah*-shern-kahm) *m* (pl ~e) pocket-comb

Taschenlampe (*tah*-shern-lahm-per) *f* (pl ~n) torch, flash-light

Taschenmesser (*tah*-shern-meh-serr) *nt* (pl ~) pocket-knife, penknife

Taschentuch (*tah*-shern-tōokh) *nt* (pl ~er) handkerchief

Taschenuhr (*tah*-shern-ōor) *f* (pl ~en) pocket-watch

Tasse (*tah*-ser) *f* (pl ~n) cup

Tastsinn (*tahst*-zin) *m* touch

Tat (taat) *f* (pl ~en) deed, act

Tätigkeit (*tai*-tikh-kight) *f* (pl ~en) work ; employment

Tatsache (*taat*-zah-kher) *f* (pl ~n) fact

tatsächlich (taat-*zehkh*-likh) *adj* actual, factual ; *adv* as a matter of fact, actually, in fact, in effect ; really

Tau (tou) *m* dew

taub (toup) *adj* deaf

Taube (*tou*-ber) *f* (pl ~n) pigeon

tauchen (*tou*-khern) *v* dive

Tauchsieder (*toukh*-zee-derr) *m* (pl ~) immersion heater

tauen (*tou*-ern) *v* thaw

Taufe (*tou*-fer) *f* (pl ~n) baptism, christening

taufen (*tou*-fern) *v* baptize, christen

tauglich (*touk*-likh) *adj* fit

Tausch (toush) *m* exchange

tauschen (*tou*-shern) *v* swap

sich täuschen (*toi*-shern) *be mistaken

Täuschung (*toi*-shoong) *f* (pl ~en) illusion

tausend (*tou*-zernt) *num* thousand

Tauwetter (*tou*-veh-terr) *nt* thaw

Taxameter (tah-ksah-*māy*-terr) *m* (pl ~) taxi-meter

Taxi (*tah*-ksi) *nt* (pl ~s) cab, taxi

Taxichauffeur (*tah*-ksi-sho-fūrr) *m* (pl ~e) taxi-driver

Taxifahrer (*tah*-ksi-faa-rerr) *m* (pl ~) cab-driver

Taxistand (*tah*-ksi-shtahnt) *m* (pl ~e) taxi rank ; taxi stand *Am*

Team (teem) *nt* (pl ~s) team

Technik (*taykh*-nik) *f* (pl ~en) technique

Techniker (*tehkh*-ni-kerr) *m* (pl ~) technician

technisch (*tehkh*-nish) *adj* technical

Technologie (tehkh-noa-loa-*gee*) *f* technology

Tee (tāy) *m* tea

Teekanne (*tāy*-kah-ner) *f* (pl ~n) tea-pot

Teelöffel (*tāy*-lur-ferl) *m* (pl ~) teaspoon

Teenager (*teen*-ay-jerr) *m* (pl ~) teenager

Teer (tāyr) *m* tar

Teeservice (tāy-zehr-veess) *nt* tea-set

Teestube (tāy-shtōō-ber) *f* (pl ~n) tea-shop

Teestunde (tāy-shtoon-der) *f* tea

Teetasse (tāy-tah-ser) *f* (pl ~n) teacup

Teich (tighkh) *m* (pl ~e) pond

Teig (tighk) *m* dough; batter

Teil (tighl) *m* (pl ~e) part; share; volume

teilen (tigh-lern) *v* divide; share

Teilhaber (tighl-haa-berr) *m* (pl ~) associate, partner

Teilnahme (tighl-naa-mer) *f* attendance

* **teilnehmen** (tighl-nāy-mern) *v* participate

Teilnehmer (tighl-nāy-merr) *m* (pl ~) participant

teils (tighls) *adv* partly

Teilung (tigh-loong) *f* (pl ~en) division

teilweise (tighl-vigh-zer) *adj* partial; *adv* partly

Teilzahlungskauf (tighl-tsaa-loongs-kouf) *m* (pl ~e) hire-purchase

Teint (tang) *m* complexion

Telegramm (tay-lay-*grahm*) *nt* (pl ~e) cable, telegram

telegraphieren (tay-lay-grah-*fee*-rern) *v* cable, telegraph

Teleobjektiv (tāy-lay-op-Yehk-teef) *nt* (pl ~e) telephoto lens

Telepathie (tay-lay-pah-*tee*) *f* telepathy

Telephon (tay-lay-*fōan*) *nt* (pl ~e) telephone

Telephonanruf (tay-lay-*fōan*-ahn-rōof) *m* (pl ~e) telephone call

Telephonbuch (tay-lay-*fōan*-bōokh) *nt* (pl ~er) telephone directory; telephone book *Am*

Telephonhörer (tay-lay-*fōan*-hūr-rerr) *m* (pl ~) receiver

telephonieren (tay-lay-foa-*nee*-rern) *v* phone

Telephonistin (tay-lay-foa-*niss*-tin) *f* (pl ~nen) operator, telephonist, telephone operator

Telephonzentrale (tay-lay-*fōan*-tsehn-traa-ler) *f* (pl ~n) telephone exchange

Telex (tāy-lehks) *nt* (pl ~e) telex

Teller (teh-lerr) *m* (pl ~) plate, dish

Tempel (tehm-perl) *m* (pl ~) temple

Temperatur (tehm-pay-rah-*tōor*) *f* (pl ~en) temperature

Tempo (tehm-poa) *nt* pace

Tendenz (tehn-*dehnts*) *f* (pl ~en) tendency

Tennis (teh-niss) *nt* tennis

Tennisplatz (teh-niss-plahts) *m* (pl ~e) tennis-court

Tennisschuhe (teh-niss-shōō-er) *mpl* tennis shoes

Teppich (teh-pikh) *m* (pl ~e) carpet

Termin (tehr-*meen*) *m* (pl ~e) term

Terpentin (tehr-pehn-*teen*) *nt* turpentine

Terrasse (teh-*rah*-ser) *f* (pl ~n) terrace

Terror (teh-ror) *m* terrorism

Terrorismus (teh-ro-*riss*-mooss) *m* terrorism

Terrorist (teh-ro-*rist*) *m* (pl ~en) terrorist

Terylene (teh-ri-lāyn) *nt* terylene

Test (tehst) *m* (pl ~s) test

Testament (tehss-tah-*mehnt*) *nt* (pl ~e) will

testen (tehss-tern) *v* test

teuer (toi-err) *adj* expensive; dear, precious

Teufel (toi-ferl) *m* (pl ~) devil

Text (tehkst) *m* (pl ~e) text

Textilien (tehks-*tee*-lYern) *pl* textile

Thailand (tigh-lahnt) Thailand

Thailänder (tigh-lehn-derr) *m* (pl ~) Thai

thailändisch (*tigh*-lehn-dish) *adj* Thai

Theater (tay-*aa*-terr) *nt* (pl ~) theatre; drama

Thema (*tāy*-mah) *nt* (pl Themen) topic; theme

Theologie (tay-oa-loa-*gee*) *f* theology

theoretisch (tay-oa-*rāy*-tish) *adj* theoretical

Theorie (tay-oa-*ree*) *f* (pl ~n) theory

Therapie (tay-rah-*pee*) *f* (pl ~n) therapy

Thermometer (tehr-moa-*māy*-terr) *nt* (pl ~) thermometer

Thermosflasche (*tehr*-moss-flah-sher) *f* (pl ~n) thermos flask, vacuum flask

Thermostat (tehr-moa-*staat*) *m* (pl ~en) thermostat

These (*tāy*-zer) *f* (pl ~n) thesis

Thron (trōan) *m* (pl ~e) throne

Thunfisch (*tōōn*-fish) *m* (pl ~e) tuna

Thymian (tēw-mᵞaan) *m* thyme

Tief (teef) *nt* depression

tief (teef) *adj* deep; low

Tiefe (*tee*-fer) *f* (pl ~n) depth

Tiefkühltruhe (*teef*-kēwl-trōō-er) *f* (pl ~n) deep-freeze

Tiefland (*teef*-lahnt) *nt* lowlands *pl*

tiefsinnig (*teef*-zi-nikh) *adj* profound

Tier (teer) *nt* (pl ~e) beast, animal

Tierarzt (*teer*-ahrtst) *m* (pl ~e) veterinary surgeon

Tierkreis (*teer*-krighss) *m* zodiac

Tiger (*tee*-gerr) *m* (pl ~) tiger

tilgen (*til*-gern) *v* *pay off

Tinte (*tin*-ter) *f* (pl ~n) ink

tippen (*ti*-pern) *v* type

Tisch (tish) *m* (pl ~e) table

Tischler (*tish*-lerr) *m* (pl ~) carpenter

Tischtennis (*tish*-teh-niss) *nt* ping-pong, table tennis

Tischtuch (*tish*-tōōkh) *nt* (pl ~er) table-cloth

Titel (*tee*-terl) *m* (pl ~) title; degree

Toast (tōast) *m* (pl ~e) toast

Toben (*tōā*-bern) *nt* rage

Tochter (*tokh*-terr) *f* (pl ~) daughter

Tod (tōāt) *m* death

Todesstrafe (*tōā*-derss-shtraa-fer) *f* death penalty

tödlich (*tūrt*-likh) *adj* mortal, fatal

Toilette (twah-*leh*-ter) *f* (pl ~n) lavatory, toilet; washroom *nAm*

Toilettenartikel (twah-*leh*-tern-ahr-tee-kerl) *mpl* toiletry

Toilettennecessaire (twah-*leh*-tern-nay-seh-sair) *nt* (pl ~s) toilet case

Toilettenpapier (twah-*leh*-tern-pah-peer) *nt* toilet-paper

Toilettenraum (twah-*leh*-tern-roum) *m* (pl ~e) bathroom

toll (tol) *adj* mad

Tollwut (*tol*-vōōt) *f* rabies

Tomate (toa-*maa*-ter) *f* (pl ~n) tomato

Ton[1] (tōan) *m* (pl ~e) tone; note

Ton[2] (tōan) *m* clay

Tonbandgerät (*tōān*-bahnt-ger-rait) *nt* (pl ~e) recorder, tape-recorder

Tonleiter (*tōān*-ligh-terr) *f* (pl ~n) scale

Tonne (*to*-ner) *f* (pl ~n) barrel; ton, cask

Topf (topf) *m* (pl ~e) pot

Töpferware (*tur*-pferr-vaa-rer) *f* (pl ~n) ceramics *pl*, pottery, crockery

Tor[1] (tōar) *nt* (pl ~e) gate; goal

Tor[2] (tōar) *m* (pl ~en) fool

Torheit (*tōār*-hight) *f* (pl ~en) fad

töricht (*tūr*-rikht) *adj* foolish, silly

Torte (tor-ter) *f* (pl ~n) cake

Torwart (*tōār*-vahrt) *m* (pl ~e) goalkeeper

tot (tōāt) *adj* dead

total (toa-*taal*) *adj* total

Totalisator (toa-tah-li-*zaa*-tor) *m* (pl ~en) totalizator

totalitär (toa-tah-li-*tair*) *adj* totalitarian

töten (_tūr_-tern) v kill

Toupet (too-_pāy_) nt (pl ~s) hair piece

Tourist (too-_rist_) m (pl ~en) tourist

Touristenklasse (too-_riss_-tern-klah-ser) f tourist class

toxisch (_to_-ksish) adj toxic

Tracht (trahkht) f (pl ~en) national dress

Tradition (trah-di-ts^y_ōan_) f (pl ~en) tradition

traditionell (trah-di-ts^yoa-_nehl_) adj traditional

tragbar (_traak_-baar) adj portable

träge (_trai_-ger) adj slack

*tragen (_traa_-gern) v carry; *bear; *wear

Träger (_trai_-gerr) m (pl ~) porter

tragisch (_traa_-gish) adj tragic

Tragödie (trah-_gūr_-d^yer) f (pl ~n) tragedy

Trainer (_trai_-nerr) m (pl ~) coach

trainieren (trai-_nee_-rern) v drill

Traktor (_trahk_-tor) m (pl ~en) tractor

Träne (_trai_-ner) f (pl ~n) tear

Transaktion (trahns-ahk-ts^y_ōan_) f (pl ~en) deal, transaction

transatlantisch (trahns-aht-_lahn_-tish) adj transatlantic

Transformator (trahns-for-_maa_-tor) m (pl ~en) transformer

Transpiration (trahns-pi-rah-ts^y_ōan_) f perspiration

transpirieren (trahns-pi-_ree_-rern) v perspire

Transport (trahns-_port_) m (pl ~e) transportation

transportieren (trahns-por-_tee_-rern) v transport

Tratsch (traach) m gossip

tratschen (_traa_-chern) v gossip

Tratte (_trah_-ter) f (pl ~n) draft

Trauben (_trou_-bern) fpl grapes pl

sich trauen (_trou_-ern) dare

Trauer (_trou_-err) f mourning

Trauerspiel (_trou_-err-shpeel) nt (pl ~e) drama

Traum (troum) m (pl ~̈e) dream

träumen (_troi_-mern) v *dream

traurig (_trou_-rikh) adj sad

Traurigkeit (_trou_-rikh-kight) f sadness

Treffen (_treh_-fern) nt (pl ~) meeting

*treffen (_treh_-fern) v *hit; *meet

treffend (_treh_-fernt) adj striking

Treffpunkt (_trehf_-poongkt) m (pl ~e) meeting-place

*treiben (_trigh_-bern) v press, *drive; *do; float

Treibhaus (_trighp_-houss) nt (pl ~̈er) greenhouse

Treibkraft (_trighp_-krahft) f driving force

trennen (_treh_-nern) v separate, part; divide; disconnect

Trennung (_treh_-noong) f (pl ~en) division

Treppe (_treh_-per) f (pl ~n) stairs pl, staircase

Treppengeländer (_treh_-pern-ger-lehn-derr) nt (pl ~) banisters pl

*treten (_trāy_-tern) v step; kick

treu (troi) adj true, faithful

Tribüne (tri-_bew_-ner) f (pl ~n) stand

Trichter (_trikh_-terr) m (pl ~) funnel

Trichtermündung (_trikh_-terr-mewn-doong) f (pl ~en) estuary

Trick (trik) m (pl ~s) trick

Trikot (tri-_kōa_) nt (pl ~s) tights pl

trinkbar (_tringk_-baar) adj for drinking

*trinken (_tring_-kern) v *drink

Trinkgeld (_tringk_-gehlt) nt (pl ~er) tip, gratuity

Trinkspruch (_tringk_-shprookh) m (pl ~̈e) toast

Trinkwasser (_tringk_-vah-serr) nt drinking-water

Tritt (trit) m (pl ~e) step; kick

Triumph (tri-_oomf_) m triumph

triumphieren (tri-oom-_fee_-rern) v triumph; **triumphierend** triumphant

trocken (*tro*-kern) *adj* dry

trockenlegen (*tro*-kern-*lay*-gern) *v* drain

trocknen (*tro*-knern) *v* dry

Trockner (*tro*-knerr) *m* (pl ~) dryer

Trommel (*tro*-merl) *f* (pl ~n) drum

Trommelfell (*tro*-merl-fehl) *nt* eardrum

Trompete (trom-*pay*-ter) *f* (pl ~n) trumpet

Tropen (*tröa*-pern) *pl* tropics *pl*

Tropfen (*tro*-pfern) *m* (pl ~) drop

tropisch (*tröa*-pish) *adj* tropical

Trost (tröast) *m* comfort

trösten (*trürss*-tern) *v* comfort

Trostpreis (*tröast*-prighss) *m* (pl ~e) consolation prize

trotz (trots) *prep* despite, in spite of

trotzdem (*trots*-daym) *conj* nevertheless

trübe (*trew*-ber) *adj* dim

trübsinnig (*trewp*-zi-nikh) *adj* sad

Truhe (*tröo*-er) *f* (pl ~n) chest

Truppen (*troo*-pern) *fpl* troops *pl*

Truthahn (*tröot*-haan) *m* (pl ~e) turkey

Tscheche (*cheh*-kher) *m* (pl ~n) Czech

tschechisch (*cheh*-khish) *adj* Czech

Tschechoslowakei (cheh-khoa-sloa-vah-*kigh*) *f* Czechoslowakia

Tube (*töo*-ber) *f* (pl ~n) tube

Tuberkulose (too-behr-koo-*löa*-zer) *f* tuberculosis

Tuch (töokh) *nt* (pl ~e) cloth

Tuchhändler (*töokh*-hehn-dlerr) *m* (pl ~) draper

tüchtig (*tewkh*-tikh) *adj* capable

Tuchwaren (*töokh*-vaa-rern) *fpl* drapery

Tugend (*töo*-gernt) *f* (pl ~en) virtue

Tulpe (*tool*-per) *f* (pl ~n) tulip

Tumor (*töo*-mor) *m* (pl ~en) tumour

Tumult (too-*moolt*) *m* racket

***tun** (töon) *v* *do

Tunesien (too-*nay*-z^{y}ern) Tunisia

Tunesier (too-*nay*-z^{y}err) *m* (pl ~) Tunisian

tunesisch (too-*nay*-zish) *adj* Tunisian

Tunika (*töo*-ni-kah) *f* (pl -ken) tunic

Tunnel (*too*-nerl) *m* (pl ~) tunnel

Tür (tewr) *f* (pl ~en) door

Turbine (toor-*bee*-ner) *f* (pl ~n) turbine

Türke (*tewr*-ker) *m* (pl ~n) Turk

Türkei (tewr-*kigh*) Turkey

türkisch (*tewr*-kish) *adj* Turkish

Türklingel (*tewr*-kling-erl) *f* (pl ~n) doorbell

Turm (toorm) *m* (pl ~e) tower

Turnen (*toor*-nern) *nt* gymnastics *pl*

Turner (*toor*-nerr) *m* (pl ~) gymnast

Turnhalle (*toorn*-hah-ler) *f* (pl ~n) gymnasium

Turnhose (*toorn*-höa-zer) *f* (pl ~n) trunks *pl*

Turnier (toor-*neer*) *nt* (pl ~e) tournament

Turnschuhe (*toorn*-shöo-er) *mpl* plimsolls *pl*, gym shoes; sneakers *plAm*

Tüte (*tew*-ter) *f* (pl ~n) paper bag

Tweed (tweet) *m* tweed

Typ (tewp) *m* (pl ~en) type

Typhus (*tew*-fooss) *m* typhoid

typisch (*tew*-pish) *adj* typical

Tyrann (tew-*rahn*) *m* (pl ~en) tyrant

U

U-Bahn (*öo*-baan) *f* (pl ~en) underground

Übel (*ew*-berl) *nt* (pl ~n) harm, evil

übel (*ew*-berl) *adj* sick

Übelkeit (*ew*-berl-kight) *f* (pl ~en) nausea, sickness

*übelnehmen (ew-berl-náy-mern) v resent

übelriechend (ew-berl-ree-khernt) adj smelly

üben (ew-bern) v exercise; sich ~ practise

über (ew-berr) prep over; above; across; about; via; ~ ... hinaus beyond

überall (ew-berr-ahl) adv everywhere; throughout, anywhere

überarbeiten (ew-berr-ahr-bigh-tern) v revise; sich ~ overwork

Überarbeitung (ew-berr-ahr-bigh-toong) f (pl ~en) revision

Überbleibsel (ew-berr-blighp-serl) nt (pl ~) remainder, remnant

überdies (ew-berr-deess) adv furthermore, besides

überdrüssig (ew-berr-drew-sikh) adj weary; fed up with, tired of

übereilt (ew-berr-ighlt) adj rash

Übereinkunft (ew-berr-ighn-koonft) f (pl ~e) settlement

übereinstimmen (ew-berr-ighn-shti-mern) v agree; correspond; nicht ~ disagree

Übereinstimmung (ew-berr-ighn-shti-moong) f agreement; in ~ mit according to

Überfahrt (ew-berr-faart) f crossing, passage

Überfall (ew-berr-fahl) m (pl ~le) hold-up

überfällig (ew-berr-feh-likh) adj overdue

Überfluß (ew-berr-flooss) m abundance

überflüssig (ew-berr-flew-sikh) adj redundant, superfluous

überführen (ew-berr-few-rern) v convict

Überführung (ew-berr-few-roong) f (pl ~en) conviction

überfüllt (ew-berr-fewlt) adj crowded

Übergabe (ew-berr-gaa-ber) f surrender

Übergang (ew-berr-gahng) m (pl ~e) transition; crossing

*übergeben (ew-berr-gáy-bern) v hand; commit; sich ~ vomit

*übergehen (ew-berr-gáy-ern) v skip

Übergewicht (ew-berr-ger-vikht) nt overweight

Übergröße (ew-berr-grü-ser) f (pl ~n) outsize

überhaupt (ew-berr-houpt) adv at all

überheblich (ew-berr-háyp-likh) adj presumptuous

überholen (ew-berr-hóa-lern) v *overtake; pass; overhaul; Überholen verboten no overtaking; no passing Am

Überleben (ew-berr-láy-bern) nt survival

überleben (ew-berr-láy-bern) v survive

überlegen (ew-berr-láy-gern) v *think over; deliberate; adj superior

übermorgen (ew-berr-mor-gern) adv the day after tomorrow

übermüdet (ew-berr-méw-dert) adj over-tired

übermütig (ew-berr-méw-tikh) adj presumptuous

*übernehmen (ew-berr-náy-mern) v *take over; *take charge of

überragend (ew-berr-ráa-gernt) adj superior; superlative

überraschen (ew-berr-ráh-shern) v surprise

Überraschung (ew-berr-ráh-shoong) f (pl ~en) surprise

überreden (ew-berr-ráy-dern) v persuade

überreichen (ew-berr-righ-khern) v *give

Überrest (ew-berr-rehst) m (pl ~e) remnant

Überrock (ēw-berr-rok) m (pl ~̈e) top-coat

*überschreiten (ēw-berr-shrigh-tern) v exceed

Überschrift (ēw-berr-shrift) f (pl ~en) heading

Überschuß (ēw-berr-shooss) m (pl -schüsse) surplus

überschüssig (ēw-berr-shew-sikh) adj spare

Überschwemmung (ēw-berr-shveh-moong) f (pl ~en) flood

überschwenglich (ēw-berr-shvehng-likh) adj exuberant

überseeisch (ēw-berr-zāy-ish) adj overseas

*übersehen (ēw-berr-zāy-ern) v overlook

übersetzen (ēw-berr-zeh-tsern) v translate

Übersetzer (ēw-berr-zeh-tserr) m (pl ~) translator

Übersetzung (ēw-berr-zeh-tsoong) f (pl ~en) translation; version

Übersicht (ēw-berr-zikht) f (pl ~en) survey

überspannt (ēw-berr-shpahnt) adj overstrung; eccentric

*übertragen (ēw-berr-traa-gern) v transfer

*übertreffen (ēw-berr-treh-fern) v *outdo, exceed

*übertreiben (ēw-berr-trigh-bern) v exaggerate

übertrieben (ēw-berr-tree-bern) adj extravagant; excessive

übervoll (ēw-berr-fol) adj chock-full

überwachen (ēw-berr-vah-khern) v watch; patrol

überwachsen (ēw-berr-vah-ksern) adj overgrown

überwältigen (ēw-berr-vehl-ti-gern) v overwhelm

*überweisen (ēw-berr-vigh-zern) v re-mit

Überweisung (ēw-berr-vigh-zoong) f (pl ~en) remittance

*überwinden (ēw-berr-vin-dern) v *overcome

überzeugen (ēw-berr-tsoi-gern) v convince, persuade

Überzeugung (ēw-berr-tsoi-goong) f (pl ~en) conviction, persuasion

*überziehen (ēw-berr-tsee-ern) v upholster

Überzieher (ēw-berr-tsee-err) m (pl ~) coat

üblich (ēwp-likh) adj customary, common; simple; frequent

übrig (ēw-brikh) adj remaining

*übrigbleiben (ēw-brikh-bligh-bern) v remain

übrigens (ēw-bri-gerns) adv by the way, besides

Übung (ēw-boong) f (pl ~en) exercise

Ufer (ōō-ferr) nt (pl ~) bank, shore

Uferschnecke (ōō-ferr-shneh-ker) f (pl ~n) winkle

Uhr (ōōr) f (pl ~en) clock; watch; **um ... ~** at ... o'clock

Uhrband (ōōr-bahnt) nt (pl ~̈er) watch-strap

Uhrmacher (ōōr-mah-kherr) m (pl ~) watch-maker

Ulk (oolk) m fun

Ulme (ool-mer) f (pl ~n) elm

ultraviolett (ool-trah-vi-oa-leht) adj ultraviolet

um (oom) prep round, around; ~ ... **herum** round, around; ~ **zu** to, in order to

umarmen (oom-ahr-mern) v embrace; hug

Umarmung (oom-ahr-moong) f (pl ~en) embrace; hug

*umbringen (oom-bring-ern) v kill

umdrehen (oom-drāy-ern) v turn; invert; **sich ~** turn round

Umdrehung (*oom*-drāy-oong) *f* (pl ~en) revolution

Umfang (*oom*-fahng) *m* bulk

umfangreich (*oom*-fahng-righkh) *adj* bulky, big; extensive

umfassen (oom-*fah*-sern) *v* comprise, contain

umfassend (oom-*fah*-sernt) *adj* comprehensive, extensive

Umfrage (*oom*-fraa-ger) *f* (pl ~n) enquiry

Umgang (*oom*-gahng) *m* intercourse

***umgeben** (oom-*gāy*-bern) *v* surround

Umgebung (oom-*gāy*-boong) *f* environment, surroundings *pl*; setting

***umgehen** (oom-*gāy*-ern) *v* by-pass; ~ **mit** associate with

Umgehungsstraße (oom-*gāy*-oongs-shtraa-ser) *f* (pl ~n) by-pass

umgekehrt (*oom*-ger-kāyrt) *adj* reverse; *adv* upside-down

Umhang (*oom*-hahng) *m* (pl ~̈e) cloak; cape

umher (oom-*hāyr*) *adv* about

umherschweifen (oom-*hāyr*-shvigh-fern) *v* roam, wander

umherwandern (oom-*hāyr*-vahn-derrn) *v* wander

umherziehend (oom-*hāyr*-tsee-ernt) *adj* itinerant

umkehren (*oom*-kāy-rer) *v* turn round; turn back

Umkleidekabine (*oom*-kligh-der-kah-bee-ner) *f* (pl ~n) cabin

***umkommen** (*oom*-ko-mern) *v* perish

Umkreis (*oom*-krighss) *m* radius

umkreisen (oom-*krigh*-zern) *v* circle

Umlauf (*oom*-louf) *m* circulation

Umleitung (*oom*-ligh-toong) *f* (pl ~en) detour; diversion

umliegend (*oom*-lee-gernt) *adj* surrounding

umrechnen (*oom*-rehkh-nern) *v* convert

Umrechnungstabelle (*oom*-rehkh-noongs-tah-beh-ler) *f* (pl ~n) conversion chart

umringen (oom-*ring*-ern) *v* surround

Umriß (*oom*-riss) *m* (pl Umrisse) outline, contour

Umsatz (*oom*-zahts) *m* (pl ~̈e) turnover

Umsatzsteuer (*oom*-zahts-shtoi-err) *f* turnover tax

Umschlag (*oom*-shlaak) *m* (pl ~̈e) cover, jacket

Umschlagtuch (*oom*-shlaak-tōokh) *nt* (pl ~er) shawl

***umschließen** (oom-*shlee*-sern) *v* encircle

Umschwung (*oom*-shvoong) *m* reverse

umsonst (oom-*zonst*) *adv* gratis; in vain

Umstand (*oom*-shtahnt) *m* (pl ~̈e) circumstance; condition

***umsteigen** (*oom*-shtigh-gern) *v* change

umstritten (oom-*shtri*-tern) *adj* controversial

Umweg (*oom*-vāyk) *m* (pl ~e) detour

Umwelt (*oom*-vehlt) *f* environment

***umwenden** (*oom*-vehn-dern) *v* turn over

***umziehen** (*oom*-tsee-ern) *v* move; **sich** ~ change

Umzug (*oom*-tsōok) *m* (pl ~̈e) parade; move

unabhängig (*oon*-ahp-hehng-ikh) *adj* independent

Unabhängigkeit (*oon*-ahp-hehng-ikh-kight) *f* independence

unabsichtlich (*oon*-ahp-zikht-likh) *adj* unintentional

unähnlich (*oon*-ain-likh) *adj* unlike

unangebracht (*oon*-ahn-ger-brahkht) *adj* misplaced

unangenehm (*oon*-ahn-ger-nāym) *adj* unpleasant, disagreeable; nasty

unannehmbar (oon-ahn-*nāym*-baar) *adj* unacceptable

Unannehmlichkeit (*oon*-ahn-nāym-likh-kight) *f* (pl ~en) inconvenience

unanständig (*oon*-ahn-shtehn-dikh) *adj* indecent

unartig (*oon*-ahr-tikh) *adj* naughty

unauffällig (*oon*-ouf-feh-likh) *adj* inconspicuous

unaufhörlich (*oon*-ouf-hūrr-likh) *adj* continual

unbeantwortet (*oon*-ber-ahnt-vor-tert) *adj* unanswered

unbedeutend (*oon*-ber-doi-ternt) *adj* insignificant; petty

unbedingt (*oon*-ber-dingt) *adv* without fail

unbefriedigend (*oon*-ber-free-di-gernt) *adj* unsatisfactory

unbefugt (*oon*-ber-fōōkt) *adj* unauthorized

unbegreiflich (*oon*-ber-grighf-likh) *adj* puzzling

unbegrenzt (*oon*-ber-grehntst) *adj* unlimited

unbekannt (*oon*-ber-kahnt) *adj* unknown; unfamiliar

Unbekannte (*oon*-ber-kahn-ter) *m* (pl ~n) stranger

unbekümmert (*oon*-ber-kew-merrt) *adj* carefree

unbeliebt (*oon*-ber-leept) *adj* unpopular

Unbequemlichkeit (*oon*-ber-kvāym-likh-kight) *f* (pl ~en) inconvenience

unbeschädigt (*oon*-ber-shai-dikht) *adj* whole

unbescheiden (*oon*-ber-shigh-dern) *adj* immodest

unbeschränkt (*oon*-ber-shrehngkt) *adj* unlimited

unbesetzt (*oon*-ber-zehtst) *adj* unoccupied

unbesonnen (*oon*-ber-zo-nern) *adj* rash

unbestimmt (*oon*-ber-shtimt) *adj* indefinite

unbewohnbar (*oon*-ber-vōan-baar) *adj* uninhabitable

unbewohnt (*oon*-ber-vōant) *adj* uninhabited

unbewußt (*oon*-ber-voost) *adj* unaware

unbillig (*oon*-bi-likh) *adj* unfair

und (oont) *conj* and; ~ **so weiter** etcetera

undankbar (*oon*-dahngk-baar) *adj* ungrateful

undeutlich (*oon*-doit-likh) *adj* vague

uneben (*oon*-āy-bern) *adj* uneven

unecht (*oon*-ehkht) *adj* false

unehrlich (*oon*-āyr-likh) *adj* crooked, dishonest

unempfindlich (*oon*-ehm-pfint-likh) *adj* insensitive

unendlich (*oon*-*ehnt*-likh) *adj* infinite, endless; immense

unentbehrlich (oon-ehnt-*bāyr*-likh) *adj* essential

unentgeltlich (oon-ehnt-*gehlt*-likh) *adj* free of charge

unerfahren (*oon*-ehr-faa-rern) *adj* inexperienced

unerfreulich (*oon*-ehr-froi-likh) *adj* unpleasant

unerheblich (*oon*-ehr-hāyp-likh) *adj* insignificant

unerklärlich (*oon*-ehr-*klair*-likh) *adj* unaccountable

unermeßlich (*oon*-ehr-*mehss*-likh) *adj* immense, vast

unerschwinglich (oon-ehr-*shving*-likh) *adj* prohibitive

unerträglich (oon-ehr-*traik*-likh) *adj* unbearable, intolerable

unerwartet (*oon*-ehr-vahr-tert) *adj* unexpected

unerwünscht (*oon*-ehr-vewnsht) *adj*

undesirable

unfähig (*oon*-fai-ikh) *adj* unable, incompetent, incapable

Unfall (*oon*-fahl) *m* (pl ~e) accident

Unfallstation (*oon*-fahl-shtah-ts^yoān) *f* (pl ~en) first-aid post

unfaßbar (*oon*-fahss-baar) *adj* inconceivable

unfreundlich (*oon*-froint-likh) *adj* unkind, unfriendly

Unfug (*oon*-fook) *m* nuisance; mischief

ungangbar (*oon*-gahng-baar) *adj* impassable

Ungar (*oong*-gahr) *m* (pl ~n) Hungarian

ungarisch (*oong*-gah-rish) *adj* Hungarian

Ungarn (*oong*-gahrn) Hungary

ungeachtet (*oon*-ger-ahkh-tert) *prep* in spite of

ungebildet (*oon*-ger-bil-dert) *adj* uneducated

ungebräuchlich (*oon*-ger-broikh-likh) *adj* unusual

ungeduldig (*oon*-ger-dool-dikh) *adj* impatient

ungeeignet (*oon*-ger-igh-gnert) *adj* unsuitable

ungefähr (*oon*-ger-fair) *adv* approximately

ungehalten (*oon*-ger-hahl-tern) *adj* cross

ungeheuer (*oon*-ger-hoi-err) *adj* tremendous, enormous, huge, immense

ungelegen (*oon*-ger-lāy-gern) *adj* inconvenient

ungelernt (*oon*-ger-lehrnt) *adj* unskilled

ungemütlich (*oon*-ger-mēwt-likh) *adj* uncomfortable

ungenau (*oon*-ger-nou) *adj* incorrect, inaccurate

ungenießbar (*oon*-ger-neess-baar) *adj*

inedible

ungenügend (*oon*-ger-nēw-gernt) *adj* insufficient

ungerade (*oon*-ger-raa-der) *adj* odd

ungerecht (*oon*-ger-rehkht) *adj* unjust, unfair

ungeschickt (*oon*-ger-shikt) *adj* clumsy, awkward

ungeschützt (*oon*-ger-shewtst) *adj* unprotected

ungesetzlich (*oon*-ger-zehts-likh) *adj* illegal

ungesund (*oon*-ger-zoont) *adj* unsound, unhealthy

ungewiß (*oon*-ger-viss) *adj* doubtful

ungewöhnlich (*oon*-ger-vūrn-likh) *adj* uncommon, unusual; exceptional

ungewohnt (*oon*-ger-vōant) *adj* unaccustomed

ungezogen (*oon*-ger-tsōā-gern) *adj* naughty, bad

Ungezwungenheit (*oon*-ger-tsvoong-ern-hight) *f* ease

unglaublich (oon-*gloup*-likh) *adj* incredible

ungleich (*oon*-glighkh) *adj* unequal; uneven

Unglück (*oon*-glewk) *nt* (pl ~e) misfortune; accident; calamity

unglücklich (*oon*-glewk-likh) *adj* unlucky; unhappy, unfortunate

unglücklicherweise (*oon*-glewk-li-kherr-vigh-zer) *adv* unfortunately

ungültig (*oon*-gewl-tikh) *adj* invalid

ungünstig (*oon*-gewns-tikh) *adj* unfavourable

Unheil (*oon*-highl) *nt* disaster; mischief

unheilbar (*oon*-highl-baar) *adj* incurable

unheilvoll (*oon*-highl-fol) *adj* sinister; fatal

unheimlich (*oon*-highm-likh) *adj* scary, creepy

unhöflich (*oon*-hŭrf-likh) *adj* impolite

Uniform (oo-ni-*form*) *f* (pl ~en) uniform

Union (oo-*nʸōan*) *f* (pl ~en) union

universal (oo-ni-vehr-*zaal*) *adj* universal

Universität (oo-ni-vehr-zi-*tait*) *f* (pl ~en) university

unklar (*oon*-klaar) *adj* obscure

Unkosten (*oon*-koss-tern) *pl* expenses *pl*

Unkraut (*oon*-krout) *nt* (pl ˉer) weed

unkultiviert (*oon*-kool-ti-veert) *adj* uncultivated

unlängst (*oon*-lehngst) *adv* lately

unleserlich (*oon*-lāy-zerr-likh) *adj* illegible

unliebenswürdig (*oon*-lee-berns-vewr-dikh) *adj* unkind

unmittelbar (*oon*-mi-terl-baar) *adj* direct; immediate

unmöbliert (*oon*-mur-bleert) *adj* unfurnished

unmöglich (*oon*-mŭrk-likh) *adj* impossible

unnötig (*oon*-nŭr-tikh) *adj* unnecessary

unnütz (*oon*-newts) *adj* vain

unordentlich (*oon*-or-dehnt-likh) *adj* slovenly, untidy

Unordnung (*oon*-or-dnoong) *f* disorder; mess; **in ~ *bringen** mess up

unparteiisch (*oon*-pahr-tigh-ish) *adj* impartial

unpassend (*oon*-pah-sernt) *adj* improper

unpersönlich (*oon*-pehr-zŭrn-likh) *adj* impersonal

unpopulär (*oon*-poa-poo-lair) *adj* unpopular

unqualifiziert (*oon*-kvah-li-fi-tseert) *adj* unqualified

Unrecht (*oon*-rehkht) *nt* injustice; wrong; ~ ***tun** wrong

unrecht (*oon*-rehkht) *adj* wrong; ~ ***haben** *be wrong

unregelmäßig (*oon*-rāy-gerl-mai-sikh) *adj* irregular

unrein (*oon*-righn) *adj* unclean

unrichtig (*oon*-rikh-tikh) *adj* incorrect

Unruhe (*oon*-rōō-er) *f* unrest

unruhig (*oon*-rōō-ikh) *adj* uneasy, restless

uns (oons) *pron* us; ourselves

unschätzbar (*oon*-shehts-baar) *adj* priceless

Unschuld (*oon*-shoolt) *f* innocence

unschuldig (*oon*-shool-dikh) *adj* innocent

unser (*oon*-zerr) *pron* our

unsicher (*oon*-zi-kherr) *adj* unsafe; uncertain

unsichtbar (*oon*-zikht-baar) *adj* invisible

Unsinn (*oon*-zin) *m* nonsense, rubbish

unsinnig (*oon*-zi-nikh) *adj* senseless

unstet (*oon*-shtāyt) *adj* unsteady

unsympathisch (*oon*-zewm-paa-tish) *adj* unpleasant

untauglich (*oon*-touk-likh) *adj* unfit

unten (*oon*-tern) *adv* beneath, below; underneath; downstairs; **nach ~** downwards

unter (*oon*-terr) *prep* under; beneath, below; among, amid; *adj* inferior; **Unter-** subordinate; ~ **anderem** among other things

*unterbrechen (oon-terr-*breh*-khern) *v* interrupt

Unterbrechung (oon-terr-*breh*-khoong) *f* (pl ~en) interruption

*unterbringen (*oon*-terr-bring-ern) *v* accommodate

unterdrücken (oon-terr-*drew*-kern) *v* oppress; suppress

Unterernährung (*oon*-terr-ehr-nai-roong) *f* malnutrition

Untergang (*oon*-terr-gahng) *m* ruin, destruction

untergeordnet (*oon*-terr-ger-or-dnert) *adj* subordinate; minor, secondary

Untergeschoß (*oon*-terr-ger-shoss) *nt* basement

Untergrundbahn (*oon*-terr-groont-baan) *f* (pl ~en) subway *nAm*

unterhalb (*oon*-terr-hahlp) *prep* under, below

Unterhalt (*oon*-terr-hahlt) *m* livelihood; upkeep

***unterhalten** (*oon*-terr-*hahl*-tern) *v* entertain, amuse

unterhaltsam (*oon*-terr-*hahlt*-zaam) *adj* entertaining, amusing

Unterhaltung (*oon*-terr-*hahl*-toong) *f* (pl ~en) conversation; entertainment, amusement

Unterhemd (*oon*-terr-hehmt) *nt* (pl ~en) undershirt

Unterhose (*oon*-terr-hōa-zer) *f* (pl ~n) pants *pl*; briefs *pl*, drawers, knickers *pl*; shorts *plAm*; underpants *plAm*

unterirdisch (*oon*-terr-eer-dish) *adj* underground

Unterkunft (*oon*-terr-koonft) *f* (pl ¨e) accommodation; lodgings *pl*

Untermieter (*oon*-terr-mee-terr) *m* (pl ~) lodger

Unternehmen (oon-terr-*nāȳ*-mern) *nt* (pl ~) enterprise, business; concern, company

***unternehmen** (oon-terr-*nāȳ*-mern) *v* *undertake

Unternehmer (oon-terr-*nāȳ*-merr) *m* (pl ~) contractor

Unternehmung (oon-terr-*nāȳ*-moong) *f* (pl ~en) undertaking

Unterredung (oon-terr-*rāȳ*-doong) *f* (pl ~en) interview

Unterricht (*oon*-terr-rikht) *m* tuition

unterrichten (oon-terr-*rikh*-tern) *v*

*teach

Unterrock (*oon*-terr-rok) *m* (pl ¨e) slip

unterschätzen (oon-terr-*sheh*-tsern) *v* underestimate

***unterscheiden** (oon-terr-*shigh*-dern) *v* distinguish; **sich ~** differ

Unterscheidung (oon-terr-*shigh*-doong) *f* distinction

Unterschied (*oon*-terr-sheet) *m* (pl ~e) difference, distinction; contrast

***unterschreiben** (oon-terr-*shrigh*-bern) *v* sign

Unterschrift (*oon*-terr-shrift) *f* (pl ~en) signature

unterst (*oon*-terrst) *adj* bottom

***unterstreichen** (oon-terr-*shtrigh*-khern) *v* underline

Unterströmung (*oon*-terr-shtrūr-moong) *f* undercurrent

unterstützen (oon-terr-*shtew*-tsern) *v* support; assist, aid

Unterstützung (oon-terr-*shtew*-tsoong) *f* (pl ~en) support; assistance, relief

untersuchen (oon-terr-*zōō*-khern) *v* enquire, investigate

Untersuchung (oon-terr-*zōō*-khoong) *f* (pl ~en) enquiry, investigation, inquiry; check-up, examination

Untertasse (*oon*-terr-tah-ser) *f* (pl ~n) saucer

Untertitel (*oon*-terr-tee-terl) *m* (pl ~) subtitle

Unterwäsche (*oon*-terr-veh-sher) *fpl* underwear

***unterweisen** (oon-terr-*vigh*-zern) *v* instruct

Unterweisung (oon-terr-*vigh*-zoong) *f* instruction

***unterwerfen** (oon-terr-*vehr*-fern) *v* subject; **sich ~** submit; **unterworfen** liable to

unterzeichnen (oon-terr-*tsighkh*-nern) *v* sign

Unterzeichnete (oon-terr-*tsighkh*-ner-ter) *m* (pl ~n) undersigned

untreu (*oon*-troi) *adj* unfaithful

unüberlegt (*oon*-ēw-berr-lāykt) *adj* unwise

unübertroffen (*oon*-ēw-berr-tro-fern) *adj* unsurpassed

ununterbrochen (*oon*-oon-terr-bro-khern) *adj* continuous

unverdient (*oon*-fehr-deent) *adj* unearned

unverletzt (*oon*-fehr-lehtst) *adj* unhurt

unvermeidlich (oon-fehr-*might*-likh) *adj* unavoidable, inevitable

unvernünftig (*oon*-fehr-newnf-tikh) *adj* unreasonable

unverschämt (*oon*-fehr-shaimt) *adj* impudent, impertinent, insolent

Unverschämtheit (*oon*-fehr-shaimt-hight) *f* impertinence, insolence

unversehrt (*oon*-fehr-zāyrt) *adj* unbroken; intact

unverzüglich (oon-fehr-*tsēw*k-likh) *adj* prompt; *adv* immediately, instantly

unvollkommen (*oon*-fol-ko-mern) *adj* imperfect

unvollständig (*oon*-fol-shtehn-dikh) *adj* incomplete

unvorhergesehen (*oon*-fōar-hāyr-ger-zāy-ern) *adj* unexpected

unwahr (*oon*-vaar) *adj* untrue, false

unwahrscheinlich (*oon*-vaar-shighn-likh) *adj* unlikely, improbable

Unwetter (*oon*-veh-terr) *nt* (pl ~) tempest

unwichtig (*oon*-vikh-tikh) *adj* unimportant

unwiderruflich (*oon*-vee-derr-rōof-likh) *adj* irrevocable

unwillig (*oon*-vi-likh) *adj* unwilling

unwissend (*oon*-vi-sernt) *adj* ignorant

unwohl (*oon*-vōal) *adj* unwell

unzerbrechlich (*oon*-tsehr-brehkh-likh) *adj* unbreakable

unzufrieden (*oon*-tsoo-free-dern) *adj* dissatisfied, discontented

unzugänglich (*oon*-tsōō-gerng-likh) *adj* inaccessible

unzulänglich (*oon*-tsōō-lehng-likh) *adj* inadequate

Unzulänglichkeit (*oon*-tsōō-lehng-likh-kight) *f* (pl ~en) shortcoming

unzuverlässig (*oon*-tsōō-vehr-leh-sikh) *adj* untrustworthy, unreliable

unzweckmäßig (*oon*-tsvehk-mai-sikh) *adj* inefficient

uralt (*ōōr*-ahlt) *adj* ancient

Urin (oo-*reen*) *m* urine

Urkunde (*ōōr*-koon-der) *f* (pl ~n) certificate, document

Urlaub (*ōōr*-loup) *m* (pl ~e) holiday; leave; **auf ~** on holiday

Ursache (*ōōr*-zah-kher) *f* (pl ~n) cause; reason

Ursprung (*ōōr*-shproong) *m* (pl ~e) origin

ursprünglich (*ōōr*-shprewng-likh) *adj* original

Urteil (*oor*-tighl) *nt* (pl ~e) judgment; sentence, verdict

urteilen (*oor*-tigh-lern) *v* judge

Urteilsspruch (*oor*-tighls-shprookh) *m* (pl ~e) verdict

Uruguay (oo-roo-*gvigh*) Uruguay

uruguayisch (oo-roo-*gvigh*-ish) *adj* Uruguayan

Urwald (*ōōr*-vahlt) *m* (pl ~er) jungle

V

Vagabund (vah-gah-*boont*) *m* (pl ~en) tramp

vage (*vaa*-ger) *adj* faint

Vakanz (vah-*kahnts*) *f* (pl ~en) vacancy

Vakuum (*vaa*-koo-oom) *nt* (pl Vakua)

vacuum

Vanille (vah-*ni*-l^yer) *f* vanilla

Varietétheater (vah-ri-ay-*tāy*-tay-aa-terr) *nt* (pl ~) music-hall, variety theatre

Varietévorstellung (vah-ri-ay-*tāy*-fōar-shteh-loong) *f* (pl ~en) variety show

variieren (vah-ri-*ee*-rern) *v* vary

Vase (*vaa*-zer) *f* (pl ~n) vase

Vaseline (vah-say-*lee*-ner) *f* vaseline

Vater (*faa*-terr) *m* (pl ¨) father; dad

Vaterland (*faa*-terr-lahnt) *nt* native country; fatherland

Vati (*faa*-ti) *m* daddy

Vegetarier (vay-gay-*taa*-r^yerr) *m* (pl ~) vegetarian

Vegetation (vay-gay-tah-ts^y*ōan*) *f* (pl ~en) vegetation

Veilchen (*fighl*-khern) *nt* (pl ~) violet

Venezolaner (vay-nay-tsoa-*laa*-nerr) *m* (pl ~) Venezuelan

venezolanisch (vay-nay-tsoa-*laa*-nish) *adj* Venezuelan

Venezuela (vay-nay-tsoo-*āy*-lah) Venezuela

Ventil (vehn-*teel*) *nt* (pl ~e) valve

Ventilation (vehn-ti-lah-ts^y*ōan*) *f* (pl ~en) ventilation

Ventilator (vehn-ti-*laa*-tor) *m* (pl ~en) fan, ventilator

Ventilatorriemen (vehn-ti-*laa*-tor-ree-mern) *m* (pl ~) fan belt

ventilieren (vehn-ti-*lee*-rern) *v* ventilate

Verabredung (fehr-*ahp*-rāy-doong) *f* (pl ~en) appointment; date, engagement

verabreichen (fehr-*ahp*-righ-khern) *v* administer

verachten (fehr-*ahkh*-tern) *v* despise, scorn

Verachtung (fehr-*ahkh*-toong) *f* scorn, contempt

veraltet (fehr-*ahl*-tert) *adj* ancient; out of date

Veranda (vay-*rahn*-dah) *f* (pl -den) veranda

veränderlich (fehr-*ehn*-derr-likh) *adj* variable

verändern (fehr-*ehn*-derrn) *v* alter; vary

Veränderung (fehr-*ehn*-der-roong) *f* (pl ~en) alteration; variation

verängstigt (fehr-*ehngs*-tikht) *adj* frightened

verantwortlich (fehr-*ahnt*-vort-likh) *adj* responsible; liable

Verantwortlichkeit (fehr-*ahnt*-vort-likh-kight) *f* responsibility; liability

verausgaben (fehr-*ouss*-gaa-bern) *v* *spend

Verband (fehr-*bahnt*) *m* (pl ¨e) bandage; federation

Verbandskasten (fehr-*bahnts*-kahss-tern) *m* (pl ¨) first-aid kit

Verbannte (fehr-*bahn*-ter) *m* (pl ~n) exile

Verbannung (fehr-*bah*-noong) *f* exile

***verbergen** (fehr-*behr*-gern) *v* *hide; conceal

verbessern (fehr-*beh*-serrn) *v* improve; correct

Verbesserung (fehr-*beh*-ser-roong) *f* (pl ~en) improvement; correction

***verbieten** (fehr-*bee*-tern) *v* *forbid, prohibit

***verbinden** (fehr-*bin*-dern) *v* link, join, connect; combine; dress

Verbindung (fehr-*bin*-doong) *f* (pl ~en) link; connection; relation; **sich in ~ setzen mit** contact

verblassen (fehr-*blah*-sern) *v* fade

verblüffen (fehr-*blew*-fern) *v* astonish; overwhelm

Verbot (fehr-*bōat*) *nt* (pl ~e) prohibition

verboten (fehr-*bōā*-tern) *adj* prohibited

verbrauchen (fehr-*brou*-khern) *v* use up

Verbraucher (fehr-*brou*-kherr) *m* (pl ~) consumer

Verbrauchssteuer (fehr-*broukhs*-shtoi-err) *f* purchase tax ; sales tax

Verbrechen (fehr-*breh*-khern) *nt* (pl ~) crime

Verbrecher (fehr-*breh*-kherr) *m* (pl ~) criminal

verbrecherisch (fehr-*breh*-kher-rish) *adj* criminal

verbreiten (fehr-*brigh*-tern) *v* *shed

***verbrennen** (fehr-*breh*-nern) *v* *burn ; cremate

***verbringen** (fehr-*bring*-ern) *v* *spend

verbunden (fehr-*boon*-dern) *adj* joint

Verbündete (fehr-*bewn*-der-ter) *m* (pl ~n) associate

Verdacht (fehr-*dahkht*) *m* suspicion

verdächtig (fehr-*dehkh*-tikh) *adj* suspicious

Verdächtige (fehr-*dehkh*-ti-ger) *m* (pl ~n) suspect

verdächtigen (fehr-*dehkh*-ti-gern) *v* suspect

verdampfen (fehr-*dahm*-pfern) *v* evaporate

verdanken (fehr-*dahng*-kern) *v* owe

verdauen (fehr-*dou*-ern) *v* digest

verdaulich (fehr-*dou*-likh) *adj* digestible

Verdauung (fehr-*dou*-oong) *f* digestion

verdecken (fehr-*deh*-kern) *v* cover

***verderben** (fehr-*dehr*-bern) *v* *spoil ; **leicht verderblich** perishable

verdicken (fehr-*di*-kern) *v* thicken

verdienen (fehr-*dee*-nern) *v* earn, *make ; deserve, merit

Verdienst (fehr-*deenst*) *nt* (pl ~e) merit ; *m* earnings *pl*

verdorben (fehr-*dor*-bern) *adj* rotten

verdrehen (fehr-*drāy*-ern) *v* wrench

Verdruß (fehr-*drooss*) *m* annoyance

verdünnen (fehr-*dew*-nern) *v* dilute

verehren (fehr-*āy*-rern) *v* worship

Verein (fehr-*ighn*) *m* (pl ~e) society, club

vereinigen (fehr-*igh*-ni-gern) *v* unite ; join ; **Vereinigte Staaten** United States, the States

Vereinigung (fehr-*igh*-ni-goong) *f* (pl ~en) association ; union

Verfahren (fehr-*faa*-rern) *nt* (pl ~) procedure ; process

***verfahren** (fehr-*faa*-rern) *v* proceed

verfallen (fehr-*fah*-lern) *adj* expired

***verfallen** (fehr-*fah*-lern) *v* expire

sich verfärben (fehr-*fehr*-bern) discolour

verfärbt (fehr-*fehrpt*) *adj* discoloured

Verfasser (fehr-*fah*-serr) *m* (pl ~) author

Verfassung (fehr-*fah*-soong) *f* condition

Verfechter (fehr-*fehkh*-terr) *m* (pl ~) champion

verfluchen (fehr-*flōō*-khern) *v* curse

verfolgen (fehr-*fol*-gern) *v* carry on ; chase, pursue

verfügbar (fehr-*fewk*-baar) *adj* available

verfügen über (fehr-*few*-gern) dispose of

Verfügung (fehr-*few*-goong) *f* disposal

verführen (fehr-*few*-rern) *v* seduce

vergangen (fehr-*gahng*-ern) *adj* past

Vergangenheit (fehr-*gahng*-ern-hight) *f* past

Vergaser (fehr-*gaa*-zerr) *m* (pl ~) carburettor

vergebens (fehr-*gāy*-berns) *adv* in vain

sich vergegenwärtigen (fehr-*gāy*-gern-*vehr*-ti-gern) realize

Vergehen (fehr-*gāy*-ern) *nt* (pl ~) offence

***vergehen** (fehr-*gāy*-ern) *v* pass; **sich ~** offend

***vergessen** (fehr-*geh*-sern) *v* *forget

vergeßlich (fehr-*gehss*-likh) *adj* forgetful

vergeuden (fehr-*goi*-dern) *v* waste

vergewaltigen (fehr-ger-*vahl*-ti-gern) *v* assault, rape

sich vergewissern (fehr-ger-*vi*-serrn) *v* ascertain

***vergießen** (fehr-*gee*-sern) *v* *shed

vergiften (fehr-*gif*-tern) *v* poison

Vergleich (fehr-*glighkh*) *m* (pl ~e) comparison; compromise, settlement

***vergleichen** (fehr-*gligh*-khern) *v* compare

Vergnügen (fehr-*gnēw*-gern) *nt* (pl ~) fun, pleasure; amusement; **mit ~** gladly

vergoldet (fehr-*gol*-dert) *adj* gilt

vergrößern (fehr-*grūr*-serrn) *v* enlarge; increase

Vergrößerung (fehr-*grūr*-ser-roong) *f* (pl ~en) enlargement

Vergrößerungsglas (fehr-*grūr*-ser-roongs-glaass) *nt* (pl ~er) magnifying glass

vergüten (fehr-*gēw*-tern) *v* *make good

verhaften (fehr-*hahf*-tern) *v* arrest

Verhaftung (fehr-*hahf*-toong) *f* (pl ~en) arrest

Verhältnis (fehr-*hehlt*-niss) *nt* (pl ~se) proportion; affair

verhältnismäßig (fehr-*hehlt*-niss-mai-sikh) *adj* relative

verhandeln (fehr-*hahn*-derln) *v* negotiate

Verhandlung (fehr-*hahn*-dloong) *f* (pl ~en) negotiation

Verhängnis (fehr-*hehng*-niss) *nt* destiny

verhängnisvoll (fehr-*hehng*-niss-fol) *adj* ominous; fatal

verhätscheln (fehr-*heh*-cherln) *v* cuddle

verheerend (fehr-*hāy*-rernt) *adj* disastrous

verhindern (fehr-*hin*-derrn) *v* prevent

Verhör (fehr-*hūr*) *nt* (pl ~e) interrogation, examination

verhören (fehr-*hūr*-rern) *v* interrogate

verhüten (fehr-*hēw*-tern) *v* prevent

verirrt (fehr-*eert*) *adj* lost

verjagen (fehr-*Yaa*-gern) *v* chase

Verkauf (fehr-*kouf*) *m* (pl ~e) sale

verkaufen (fehr-*kou*-fern) *v* *sell; **im kleinen ~** retail; **zu ~** for sale

Verkäufer (fehr-*koi*-ferr) *m* (pl ~) salesman; shop assistant

Verkäuferin (fehr-*koi*-fer-rin) *f* (pl ~nen) salesgirl

verkäuflich (fehr-*koif*-likh) *adj* saleable

Verkehr (fehr-*kāyr*) *m* traffic

verkehren mit (fehr-*kāy*-rern) mix with

Verkehrsampel (fehr-*kāyrs*-ahm-perl) *f* (pl ~n) traffic light

verkehrsreich (fehr-*kāyrs*-righkh) *adj* busy

Verkehrsstauung (fehr-*kāyrs*-shtou-oong) *f* (pl ~en) traffic jam, jam

Verkehrsverein (fehr-*kāyrs*-fehr-ighn) *m* tourist office

verkehrt (fehr-*kāyrt*) *adj* false; *adv* inside out

sich verkleiden (fehr-*kligh*-dern) disguise

Verkleidung (fehr-*kligh*-doong) *f* (pl ~en) disguise

verkrüppelt (fehr-*krew*-perlt) *adj* crippled

verkürzen (fehr-*kewr*-tsern) *v* shorten

Verlangen (fehr-*lahng*-ern) *nt* desire

verlangen (fehr-*lahng*-ern) v desire; demand; charge

verlängern (fehr-*lehng*-errn) v lengthen, extend; renew

Verlängerung (fehr-*lehng*-er-roong) f (pl ~en) extension

Verlängerungsschnur (fehr-*lehng*-er-roongs-shnōōr) f (pl ~e) extension cord

verlangsamen (fehr-*lahng*-zaa-mern) v slow down

verlassen (fehr-*lah*-sern) adj desert

*verlassen** (fehr-*lah*-sern) v *leave; desert; **sich ~ auf** rely on

verlegen (fehr-*lāy*-gern) v *mislay; adj embarrassed; **in Verlegenheit *bringen** embarrass

Verleger (fehr-*lāy*-gerr) m (pl ~) publisher

*verleihen** (fehr-*ligh*-ern) v grant

verlernen (fehr-*lehr*-nern) v unlearn

verletzbar (fehr-*lehts*-baar) adj vulnerable

verletzen (fehr-*leh*-tsern) v *hurt, injure; wound

Verletzung (fehr-*leh*-tsoong) f (pl ~en) injury; violation

Verleumdung (fehr-*loim*-doong) f (pl ~en) slander

verliebt (fehr-*leept*) adj in love

*verlieren** (fehr-*lee*-rern) v *lose

verlobt (fehr-*lōapt*) adj engaged

Verlobte (fehr-*lōap*-ter) m (pl ~n) fiancé; f fiancée

Verlobung (fehr-*lōa*-boong) f (pl ~en) engagement

Verlobungsring (fehr-*lōa*-boongs-ring) m (pl ~e) engagement ring

Verlust (fehr-*loost*) m (pl ~e) loss

*vermeiden** (fehr-*migh*-dern) v avoid

Vermerk (fehr-*mehrk*) m (pl ~e) note

Vermerkhäkchen (fehr-*mehrk*-haik-khern) nt (pl ~) tick

vermieten (fehr-*mee*-tern) v *let; lease; **zu ~** for hire

vermindern (fehr-*min*-derrn) v lessen, decrease, reduce

vermischt (fehr-*misht*) adj miscellaneous

Vermißte (fehr-*miss*-ter) m (pl ~n) missing person

vermitteln (fehr-*mi*-terln) v mediate

Vermittler (fehr-*mit*-lerr) m (pl ~) mediator; intermediary

Vermögen (fehr-*mūr*-gern) nt (pl ~) ability; fortune

vermuten (fehr-*mōō*-tern) v suspect; guess, suppose

vermutlich (fehr-*mōōt*-likh) adj presumable, probable

Vermutung (fehr-*mōō*-toong) f (pl ~en) guess

vernachlässigen (fehr-*naakh*-leh-si-gern) v neglect

Vernachlässigung (fehr-*naakh*-leh-si-goong) f (pl ~en) neglect

verneinend (fehr-*nigh*-nernt) adj negative

vernichten (fehr-*nikh*-tern) v destroy; wreck

Vernunft (fehr-*noonft*) f sense, reason

vernünftig (fehr-*newnf*-tikh) adj reasonable

veröffentlichen (fehr-*ur*-fernt-li-khern) v publish

Veröffentlichung (fehr-*ur*-fernt-li-khoong) f (pl ~en) publication

verpachten (fehr-*pahkh*-tern) v lease

Verpackung (fehr-*pah*-koong) f (pl ~en) packing

verpassen (fehr-*pah*-sern) v miss

verpfänden (fehr-*pfehn*-dern) v pawn

verpflichten (fehr-*pflikh*-tern) v oblige; **sich ~** engage; **verpflichtet *sein zu** *be obliged to

Verpflichtung (fehr-*pflikh*-toong) f (pl ~en) engagement

Verrat (fehr-*raat*) m treason

*verraten (fehr-*raa*-tern) *v* betray;
*give away

Verräter (fehr-*rai*-terr) *m* (pl ~) traitor

verrenkt (fehr-*rehngkt*) *adj* dislocated

verrichten (fehr-*rikh*-tern) *v* perform

verrückt (fehr-*rewkt*) *adj* mad, crazy;
idiotic

Vers (fehrs) *m* (pl ~e) verse

versagen (fehr-*zaa*-gern) *v* fail; deny

versammeln (fehr-*zah*-merln) *v* assemble; **sich ~** gather

Versammlung (fehr-*zahm*-loong) *f* (pl
~en) assembly, meeting; rally

Versand (fehr-*zahnt*) *m* expedition

verschaffen (fehr-*shah*-fern) *v* furnish

verschicken (fehr-*shi*-kern) *v* dispatch

*verschieben (fehr-*shee*-bern) *v* adjourn, *put off

verschieden (fehr-*shee*-dern) *adj* different, distinct; varied; **verschiedene** various; ~ ***sein** vary

*verschießen (fehr-*shee*-sern) *v* fade

*verschlafen (fehr-*shlaa*-fern) *v* *oversleep

*verschließen (fehr-*shlee*-sern) *v* lock

*verschlingen (fehr-*shling*-ern) *v*
swallow

verschlissen (fehr-*shli*-sern) *adj*
threadbare

Verschluß (fehr-*shlooss*) *m* (pl -
schlüsse) fastener

Verschmutzung (fehr-*shmoo*-tsoong) *f*
pollution

*verschreiben (fehr-*shrigh*-bern) *v*
prescribe

verschütten (fehr-*shew*-tern) *v* *spill

verschwenderisch (fehr-*shvehn*-der-
rish) *adj* wasteful, lavish

Verschwendung (fehr-*shvehn*-doong) *f*
waste

*verschwinden (fehr-*shvin*-dern) *v*
disappear, vanish

sich *verschwören (fehr-*shvūr*-rern)
conspire

Verschwörung (fehr-*shvūr*-roong) *f* (pl
~en) plot

Versehen (fehr-*zāy*-ern) *nt* (pl ~)
oversight; mistake

*versehen mit (fehr-*zāy*-ern) furnish
with

*versenden (fehr-*zehn*-dern) *v* despatch; ship

versetzen (fehr-*zeh*-tsern) *v* move

versichern (fehr-*zi*-kherrn) *v* assure;
insure

Versicherung (fehr-*zi*-kher-roong) *f* (pl
~en) insurance

Versicherungspolice (fehr-*zi*-kher-
roongs-poa-lee-ser) *f* (pl ~n) insurance policy

Versöhnung (fehr-*zūr*-noong) *f* (pl
~en) reconciliation

versorgen (fehr-*zor*-gern) *v* look after

verspätet (fehr-*shpai*-tert) *adj* late

versperren (fehr-*shpeh*-rern) *v* block

verspotten (fehr-*shpo*-tern) *v* mock

Versprechen (fehr-*shpreh*-khern) *nt* (pl
~) promise

*versprechen (fehr-*shpreh*-khern) *v*
promise

Verstand (fehr-*shtahnt*) *m* brain; wits
pl, sense, intellect, reason

verständig (fehr-*shtehn*-dikh) *adj* sensible

Verständigung (fehr-*shtehn*-di-goong)
f understanding

verstauchen (fehr-*shtou*-khern) *v*
sprain

Verstauchung (fehr-*shtou*-khoong) *f*
(pl ~en) sprain

verstecken (fehr-*shteh*-kern) *v* *hide

*verstehen (fehr-*shtāy*-ern) *v* *understand; *take; conceive

Versteigerung (fehr-*shtigh*-ger-roong)
f (pl ~en) auction

sich verstellen (fehr-*shteh*-lern) pretend

verstimmen (fehr-*shti*-mern) *v* displease

verstopft (fehr-*shtopft*) *adj* constipated

Verstopfung (fehr-*shto*-pfoong) *f* constipation

verstorben (fehr-*shtor*-bern) *adj* dead

Verstoß (fehr-*shtōass*) *m* offence

verstreuen (fehr-*shtroi*-ern) *v* scatter

Versuch (fehr-*zōōkh*) *m* (pl ~e) try, attempt; trial, experiment

versuchen (fehr-*zōō*-khern) *v* try, attempt; tempt

Versuchung (fehr-*zōō*-khoong) *f* (pl ~en) temptation

verteidigen (fehr-*tigh*-di-gern) *v* defend

Verteidigung (fehr-*tigh*-di-goong) *f* defence

Verteidigungsrede (fehr-*tigh*-di-goongs-rāy-der) *f* (pl ~n) plea

verteilen (fehr-*tigh*-lern) *v* divide; distribute

Vertrag (fehr-*traak*) *m* (pl ~e) agreement; contract; treaty

Vertrauen (fehr-*trou*-ern) *nt* confidence; trust, faith

vertrauen (fehr-*trou*-ern) *v* trust

vertraulich (fehr-*trou*-likh) *adj* confidential; familiar

vertraut (fehr-*trout*) *adj* familiar

*****vertreiben** (fehr-*trigh*-bern) *v* chase

*****vertreten** (fehr-*trāy*-tern) *v* represent

Vertreter (fehr-*trāy*-terr) *m* (pl ~) agent

Vertretung (fehr-*trāy*-toong) *f* (pl ~en) representation; agency

verüben (fehr-*eūw*-bern) *v* commit

Verunreinigung (fehr-*oon*-righ-ni-goong) *f* pollution

verursachen (fehr-*ōōr*-zah-khern) *v* cause

verurteilen (fehr-*oor*-tigh-lern) *v* sentence

Verurteilte (fehr-*oor*-tighl-ter) *m* (pl ~n) convict

verwalten (fehr-*vahl*-tern) *v* manage

Verwaltung (fehr-*vahl*-toong) *f* (pl ~en) administration; management, direction; rule, government; **Verwaltungs-** administrative

Verwaltungsrecht (fehr-*vahl*-toongs-rehkht) *nt* administrative law

verwandeln (fehr-*vahn*-derln) *v* transform; **sich ~ in** turn into

verwandt (fehr-*vahnt*) *adj* related

Verwandte (fehr-*vahn*-ter) *m* (pl ~n) relative, relation

Verwandtschaft (fehr-*vahnt*-shahft) *f* family

verwechseln (fehr-*veh*-kserln) *v* *mistake

verweigern (fehr-*vigh*-gerrn) *v* deny, refuse

Verweigerung (fehr-*vigh*-ger-roong) *f* (pl ~en) refusal

verweilen (fehr-*vigh*-lern) *v* stay

Verweis (fehr-*vighss*) *m* (pl ~e) reference

*****verweisen auf** (fehr-*vigh*-zern) refer to

*****verwenden** (fehr-*vehn*-dern) *v* employ; apply

*****verwerfen** (fehr-*vehr*-fern) *v* turn down, reject

verwickelt (fehr-*vi*-kerlt) *adj* complicated, complex

verwirklichen (fehr-*veerk*-li-khern) *v* realize

verwirren (fehr-*vi*-rern) *v* confuse; embarrass

Verwirrung (fehr-*vi*-roong) *f* confusion; disturbance

verwöhnen (fehr-*vūr*-nern) *v* *spoil

verwunden (fehr-*voon*-dern) *v* wound

verwundern (fehr-*voon*-derrn) *v* amaze

Verwunderung (fehr-*voon*-der-roong) *f* wonder

Verwundung (fehr-*voon*-doong) *f* (pl

~en) injury

verzaubern (fehr-*tsou*-berrn) *v* bewitch

Verzeichnis (fehr-*tsighkh*-niss) *nt* (pl ~se) index

***verzeihen** (fehr-*tsigh*-ern) *v* *forgive; excuse

Verzeihung (fehr-*tsigh*-oong) *f* pardon; **Verzeihung!** sorry!

Verzierung (fehr-*tsee*-roong) *f* (pl ~en) ornament

verzögern (fehr-*tsūr*-gerrn) *v* delay; slow down

Verzögerung (fehr-*tsūr*-ger-roong) *f* (pl ~en) delay

verzollen (fehr-*tso*-lern) *v* declare

Verzückung (fehr-*tsew*-koong) *f* ecstasy

verzweifeln (fehr-*tsvigh*-ferln) *v* despair

verzweifelt (fehr-*tsvigh*-ferlt) *adj* desperate

Verzweiflung (fehr-*tsvigh*-floong) *f* despair

Vestibül (vehss-ti-*bēwl*) *nt* (pl ~e) lobby

Vetter (*feh*-terr) *m* (pl ~n) cousin

Viadukt (vi-ah-*dookt*) *m* (pl ~e) viaduct

vibrieren (vi-*bree*-rern) *v* vibrate

Vieh (fee) *nt* cattle *pl*

viel (feel) *adj* much, many; *adv* much, far

vielleicht (fi-*lighkht*) *adv* maybe, perhaps

vielmehr (feel-*māyr*) *adv* rather

vielseitig (*feel*-zigh-tikh) *adj* all-round

vier (feer) *num* four

vierte (*feer*-ter) *num* fourth

Viertel (*feer*-terl) *nt* (pl ~) quarter

vierteljährlich (*feer*-terl-ᵞair-likh) *adj* quarterly

Viertelstunde (feer-terl-*shtoon*-der) *f* (pl ~n) quarter of an hour

vierzehn (*feer*-tsāyn) *num* fourteen

vierzehnte (*feer*-tsāyn-ter) *num* fourteenth

vierzig (*feer*-tsikh) *num* forty

Vikar (vi-*kaar*) *m* (pl ~e) vicar

Villa (*vi*-lah) *f* (pl Villen) villa

violett (vi-oa-*leht*) *adj* violet

Visitenkarte (vi-*zee*-tern-kahr-ter) *f* (pl ~n) visiting-card

visitieren (vi-zi-*tee*-rern) *v* search

Visum (*vee*-zoom) *nt* (pl Visa) visa

Vitamin (vi-tah-*meen*) *nt* (pl ~e) vitamin

Vitrine (vi-*tree*-ner) *f* (pl ~n) showcase

Vizepräsident (*fee*-tser-preh-zi-dehnt) *m* (pl ~en) vice-president

Vogel (*fōā*-gerl) *m* (pl ~͏̈) bird

Vokabular (voa-kah-boo-*laar*) *nt* vocabulary

vokal (voa-*kaal*) *adj* vocal

Volk (folk) *nt* (pl ~͏̈er) people; nation, folk; **Volks-** national; popular; vulgar

Volkslied (*folks*-leet) *nt* (pl ~er) folk song

Volksschullehrer (*folks*-shōōl-lāy-rerr) *m* (pl ~) schoolmaster, teacher

Volkstanz (*folks*-tahnts) *m* (pl ~͏̈e) folk-dance

Volkswirt (*folks*-veert) *m* (pl ~e) economist

voll (fol) *adj* full; crowded; **brechend ~** chock-full

vollbesetzt (*fol*-ber-zehtst) *adj* full up

vollblütig (*fol*-blēw-tikh) *adj* thoroughbred

vollenden (fol-*ehn*-dern) *v* accomplish; complete

vollfüllen (*fol*-few-lern) *v* fill up

völlig (*fur*-likh) *adj* utter; *adv* completely, absolutely, quite

vollkommen (fol-*ko*-mern) *adj* perfect; *adv* completely

Vollkommenheit (fol-*ko*-mern-hight) *f*

perfection

Vollkornbrot (*fol*-korn-brōāt) *nt* wholemeal bread

Vollpension (*fol*-pahng-s^yōān) *f* full board, board and lodging, bed and board

vollständig (*fol*-shtehn-dikh) *adj* complete, whole

*vollziehen** (fol-*tsee*-ern) *v* execute; **vollziehend** *adj* executive

Volt (volt) *nt* volt

Volumen (voa-*lōō*-mern) *nt* (pl ~) volume

von (fon) *prep* of; from, off; by; with; ~ ... an from, as from; ~ nun an henceforth

vor (fōar) *prep* before; ahead of, in front of; to; ~ allem essentially

*vorangehen** (foa-*rahn*-gāy-ern) *v* precede

Voranschlag (*fōar*-ahn-shlaak) *m* (pl ~e) estimate; budget

voraus (foa-*rouss*) *adv* forward; im ~ in advance

vorausbezahlt (foa-*rouss*-ber-tsaalt) *adj* prepaid

voraussagen (foa-*rouss*-zaa-gern) *v* forecast

voraussetzen (foa-*rouss*-zeh-tsern) *v* assume; **vorausgesetzt daß** provided that

Vorbehalt (*fōar*-ber-hahlt) *m* (pl ~e) qualification

vorbei (foar-*bigh*) *adv* over; an ... ~ past

*vorbeifahren** (foar-*bigh*-faa-rern) *v* pass *vAm*

*vorbeigehen** (foar-*bigh*-gāy-ern) *v* pass by

vorbereiten (*fōar*-ber-righ-tern) *v* prepare; arrange

Vorbereitung (*fōar*-ber-righ-toong) *f* (pl ~en) preparation

vorbestellen (*fōar*-ber-shteh-lern) *v* reserve

vorbeugend (*fōar*-boi-gernt) *adj* preventive

Vorbildung (*fōar*-bil-doong) *f* background

*vorbringen** (*fōar*-bring-ern) *v* *bring up

Vordergrund (*for*-derr-groont) *m* foreground

Vorderseite (*for*-derr-zigh-ter) *f* front

Vorfahr (*fōar*-faar) *m* (pl ~en) ancestor

Vorfahrtsrecht (*fōar*-faarts-rehkht) *nt* right of way

Vorfall (*fōar*-fahl) *m* (pl ~e) event

vorführen (*fōar*-few-rern) *v* exhibit

Vorgang (*fōar*-gahng) *m* (pl ~e) process

Vorgänger (*fōar*-gehng-err) *m* (pl ~) predecessor

*vorgeben** (*fōar*-gāy-bern) *v* pretend

Vorgehen (*fōar*-gāy-ern) *nt* policy

*vorgehen** (*fōar*-gāy-ern) *v* act

vorgestern (*fōar*-gehss-terrn) *adv* the day before yesterday

vorhanden (*fōar*-hahn-dern) *adj* available

Vorhang (*fōar*-hahng) *m* (pl ~e) curtain

Vorhängeschloß (*fōar*-hehng-er-shloss) *nt* (pl -schlösser) padlock

vorher (*fōar*-hāyr) *adv* in advance, before

vorhergehend (*fōar*-hāyr-gāy-ernt) *adj* previous, preceding, last

Vorhersage (*fōar*-hāyr-zaa-ger) *f* (pl ~n) forecast

vorhersagen (*fōar*-hāyr-zaa-gern) *v* predict

*vorhersehen** (*fōar*-hāyr-zāy-ern) *v* anticipate

vorig (*fōa*-rikh) *adj* previous, past

*vorkommen** (*fōar*-ko-mern) *v* occur

Vorladung (*fōar*-laa-doong) *f* (pl ~en)

summons

vorläufig (*fōar*-loi-fikh) *adj* provisional, temporary; preliminary

Vorleger (*fōar*-lāy-gerr) *m* (pl ~) rug

Vorlesung (*fōar*-lāy-zoong) *f* (pl ~en) lecture

vormals (*fōar*-maals) *adv* formerly

Vormittag (*fōar*-mi-taak) *m* (pl ~e) morning

Vormund (*fōar*-moont) *m* (pl ~e) tutor, guardian

Vormundschaft (*fōar*-moont-shahft) *f* custody

Vorname (*fōar*-naa-mer) *m* (pl ~n) first name, Christian name

vornehm (*fōar*-nāym) *adj* distinguished

Vorort (*fōar*-ort) *m* (pl ~e) suburb

Vorrang (*fōar*-rahng) *m* priority

Vorrat (*fōar*-raat) *m* (pl ~e) stock, store; provisions *pl*, supply

vorrätig (*fōar*-rai-tikh) *adj* available; ~ *haben stock

Vorrecht (*fōar*-rehkht) *nt* (pl ~e) privilege

Vorrichtung (*fōar*-rikh-toong) *f* (pl ~en) appliance, apparatus

*vorschießen (*fōar*-shee-sern) *v* advance

Vorschlag (*fōar*-shlaak) *m* (pl ~e) proposition, proposal, suggestion

*vorschlagen (*fōar*-shlaa-gern) *v* suggest, propose

Vorschrift (*fōar*-shrift) *f* (pl ~en) regulation

Vorschuß (*fōar*-shooss) *m* (pl -schüsse) advance

sich *vorsehen (*fōar*-zāy-ern) look out

Vorsicht (*fōar*-zikht) *f* caution; precaution

vorsichtig (*fōar*-zikh-tikh) *adj* careful; cautious

Vorsichtsmaßnahme (*fōar*-zikhts-maass-naa-mer) *f* (pl ~n) precaution

Vorsitzende (*fōar*-zi-tsern-der) *m* (pl ~n) chairman, president

Vorspeise (*fōar*-shpigh-zer) *f* (pl ~n) hors-d'œuvre

Vorsprung (*fōar*-shproong) *m* lead

Vorstadt (*fōar*-shtaht) *f* (pl ~e) suburb

vorstädtisch (*fōar*-shteh-tish) *adj* suburban

Vorstand (*fōar*-shtahnt) *m* (pl ~e) direction

vorstellen (*fōar*-shteh-lern) *v* present, introduce; represent; **sich ~** fancy, imagine; conceive

Vorstellung (*fōar*-shteh-loong) *f* introduction; conception, idea; show

Vorteil (*foar*-tighl) *m* (pl ~e) advantage; profit, benefit

vorteilhaft (*foar*-tighl-hahft) *adj* advantageous; cheap

Vortrag (*fōar*-traak) *m* (pl ~e) lecture

Vorurteil (*fōar*-oor-tighl) *nt* (pl ~e) prejudice

Vorverkaufskasse (*fōar*-fehr-koufs-kah-ser) *f* (pl ~n) box-office

Vorwand (*fōar*-vahnt) *m* (pl ~e) pretext, pretence

vorwärts (*fōar*-vehrts) *adv* ahead, forward, onwards

*vorwärtskommen (*fōar*-vehrts-ko-mern) *v* *get on

*vorwerfen (*fōar*-vehr-fern) *v* reproach; blame

Vorwurf (*fōar*-voorf) *m* (pl ~e) reproach; blame

vorzeitig (*fōar*-tsigh-tikh) *adj* premature

*vorziehen (*fōar*-tsee-ern) *v* prefer

Vorzug (*fōar*-tsōok) *m* (pl ~e) preference

vorzüglich (fōar-*tsēwk*-likh) *adj* first-rate

Vulkan (vool-*kaan*) *m* (pl ~e) volcano

W

Waage (*vaa*-ger) *f* (pl ~n) scales *pl*, weighing-machine

waagerecht (*vaa*-ger-rehkht) *adj* horizontal

wach (vahkh) *adj* awake; ~ *werden wake up

Wache (*vah*-kher) *f* (pl ~n) guard

Wachs (vahks) *nt* wax

wachsam (*vahkh*-zaam) *adj* vigilant

*wachsen (vah-ksern) *v* *grow

Wachsfigurenkabinett (*vahks*-fi-gōō-rern-kah-bi-neht) *nt* (pl ~e) waxworks *pl*

Wachtel (*vahkh*-terl) *f* (pl ~n) quail

Wächter (*vehkh*-terr) *m* (pl ~) warden

wacklig (*vahk*-likh) *adj* unsteady, shaky, ramshackle

Wade (*vaa*-der) *f* (pl ~n) calf

Waffe (*vah*-fer) *f* (pl ~n) weapon, arm

Waffel (*vah*-ferl) *f* (pl ~n) waffle

wagehalsig (*vaa*-ger-hahl-zikh) *adj* daring

Wagen (*vaa*-gern) *m* (pl ~) car; carriage, coach; cart; passenger car *Am*

wagen (*vaa*-gern) *v* dare; risk, venture

Wagenheber (*vaa*-gern-hāy-berr) *m* (pl ~) jack

Waggon (vah-*gawng*) *m* (pl ~s) waggon

Wahl (vaal) *f* (pl ~en) choice; pick, selection; election

wählen (*vai*-lern) *v* pick, *choose; elect

wählerisch (*vai*-ler-rish) *adj* particular

Wahlkreis (*vaal*-krighss) *m* (pl ~e) constituency

Wahlrecht (*vaal*-rehkht) *nt* franchise; suffrage

Wahlspruch (*vaal*-shprookh) *m* (pl ~e) slogan

Wahnsinn (*vaan*-zin) *m* madness

wahnsinnig (*vaan*-zi-nikh) *adj* crazy, insane

wahr (vaar) *adj* true; very

während (*vai*-rernt) *prep* for, during; *conj* while

wahrhaft (*vaar*-hahft) *adj* truthful

Wahrheit (*vaar*-hight) *f* (pl ~en) truth

wahrnehmbar (*vaar*-nāym-baar) *adj* noticeable, perceptible

*wahrnehmen (*vaar*-nāy-mern) *v* perceive; note

wahrscheinlich (vaar-*shighn*-likh) *adj* likely, probable; *adv* probably

Währung (*vai*-roong) *f* (pl ~en) currency; **fremde** ~ foreign currency

Währungseinheit (*vai*-roongs-ighn-hight) *f* (pl ~en) monetary unit

Waise (*vigh*-zer) *f* (pl ~n) orphan

Wal (vaal) *m* (pl ~e) whale

Wald (vahlt) *m* (pl ~er) forest, wood

Waldung (*vahl*-doong) *f* (pl ~en) woodland

Wallgraben (*vahl*-graa-bern) *m* (pl ~) moat

Walnuß (*vahl*-nooss) *f* (pl -nüsse) walnut

Walzer (*vahl*-tserr) *m* (pl ~) waltz

Wand (vahnt) *f* (pl ~e) wall

wandern (*vahn*-dern) *v* tramp, hike

Wandschrank (*vahnt*-shrahngk) *m* (pl ~e) closet

Wandtafel (*vahnt*-taa-ferl) *f* (pl ~n) blackboard

Wandteppich (*vahnt*-teh-pikh) *m* (pl ~e) tapestry

Wange (*vahng*-er) *f* (pl ~n) cheek

wankelmütig (*vahng*-kehl-mēw-tikh) *adj* unsteady

wanken (*vahng*-kern) *v* falter

wann (vahn) *adv* when; ~ **immer** whenever

Wanze (*vahn*-tser) *f* (pl ~n) bug

Ware (*vaa*-rer) *f* (pl ~n) merchandise; **Waren** wares *pl*, goods *pl*

Warenhaus (*vaa*-rern-houss) *nt* (pl ~er) drugstore *nAm*

warm (vahrm) *adj* hot, warm

Wärme (*vehr*-mer) *f* warmth; heat

wärmen (*vehr*-mern) *v* warm

Wärmflasche (*vehrm*-flah-sher) *f* (pl ~n) hot-water bottle

warnen (*vahr*-nern) *v* warn; caution

Warnung (*vahr*-noong) *f* (pl ~en) warning

Warteliste (*vahr*-ter-liss-ter) *f* (pl ~n) waiting-list

warten (*vahr*-tern) *v* wait; ~ **auf** await

Wärter (*vehr*-terr) *m* (pl ~) attendant

Wartezimmer (*vahr*-ter-tsi-merr) *nt* (pl ~) waiting-room

warum (vah-*room*) *adv* why

was (vahss) *pron* what; some; ~ ... **betrifft** as regards; ~ **auch immer** whatever

waschbar (*vahsh*-baar) *adj* washable

Waschbecken (*vahsh*-beh-kern) *nt* (pl ~) wash-basin

Wäsche (*veh*-sher) *f* washing, laundry; linen

waschecht (*vahsh*-ehkht) *adj* fast-dyed

Waschen (*vah*-shern) *nt* washing

*waschen (*vah*-shern) *v* wash

Wäscherei (veh-sher-*righ*) *f* (pl ~en) laundry

Waschmaschine (*vahsh*-mah-shee-ner) *f* (pl ~n) washing-machine

Waschpulver (*vahsh*-pool-ferr) *nt* (pl ~) washing-powder

Waschtisch (*vahsh*-tish) *m* (pl ~e) wash-stand

Wasser (*vah*-serr) *nt* water; **fließendes** ~ running water

wasserdicht (*vah*-serr-dikht) *adj* waterproof, rainproof

Wasserfall (*vah*-serr-fahl) *m* (pl ~e) waterfall

Wasserfarbe (*vah*-serr-fahr-ber) *f* (pl ~n) water-colour

Wasserhahn (*vah*-serr-haan) *m* (pl ~e) faucet *nAm*

Wasserlauf (*vah*-serr-louf) *m* (pl ~e) stream

Wassermelone (*vah*-serr-may-lōā-ner) *f* (pl ~n) watermelon

Wasserpumpe (*vah*-serr-poom-per) *f* (pl ~n) water pump

Wasserschi (*vah*-serr-shee) *m* (pl ~er) water ski

Wasserstoff (*vah*-serr-shtof) *m* hydrogen

Wasserstoffsuperoxyd (vah-serr-shtof-zōō-pehr-o-ksewt) *nt* peroxide

Wasserstraße (*vah*-serr-shtraa-ser) *f* (pl ~n) waterway

Wasserwaage (*vah*-serr-vaa-ger) *f* (pl ~n) level

waten (*vaa*-tern) *v* wade

Watte (*vah*-ter) *f* cotton-wool

weben (*vāy*-bern) *v* *weave

Weber (*vāy*-berr) *m* (pl ~) weaver

Wechsel (*vehk*-serl) *m* (pl ~) transition, change; exchange

Wechselgeld (*veh*-kserl-gehlt) *nt* change

Wechselkurs (*veh*-kserl-koors) *m* (pl ~e) exchange rate

wechseln (*veh*-kserln) *v* change, exchange; switch; vary

wechselseitig (*veh*-kserl-zigh-tikh) *adj* mutual

Wechselstrom (*veh*-kserl-shtrōām) *m* alternating current

Wechselstube (*veh*-kserl-shtōō-ber) *f* (pl ~n) money exchange, exchange office

wecken (*veh*-kern) *v* *wake, *awake

Wecker (*veh*-kerr) *m* (pl ~) alarm-clock

Weg (vāyk) *m* (pl ~e) way; drive

weg (vehk) *adv* away; lost; off

Wegegeld (vāy-ger-gehlt) *nt* toll

wegen (vāy-gern) *prep* because of; for, on account of

*weggehen** (vehk-gāy-ern) *v* depart, *leave; *go away

weglegen (vehk-lāy-gern) *v* *put away

*wegnehmen** (vehk-nāy-mern) *v* *take away

Wegrand (vāyk-rahnt) *m* (pl ~er) wayside

Wegweiser (vāyk-vigh-zerr) *m* (pl ~) milepost, signpost

wegwerfbar (vehk-vehrf-baar) *adj* disposable

Wehen (vāy-ern) *fpl* labour

wehen (vāy-ern) *v* *blow

weh *tun (vāy tōōn) *hurt

weiblich (vighp-likh) *adj* female; feminine

weich (vighkh) *adj* soft

weichen (vigh-khern) *v* soak

Weide (vigh-der) *f* (pl ~n) pasture

weiden (vigh-dern) *v* graze

Weihnachten (vigh-nahkh-tern) Xmas, Christmas

Weihrauch (vigh-roukh) *m* incense

weil (vighl) *conj* because; as

Weile (vigh-ler) *f* while

Weiler (vigh-lerr) *m* (pl ~) hamlet

Wein (vighn) *m* (pl ~e) wine

Weinberg (vighn-behrk) *m* (pl ~e) vineyard

weinen (vigh-nern) *v* *weep, cry

Weinhändler (vighn-hehn-dlerr) *m* (pl ~) wine-merchant

Weinkarte (vighn-kahr-ter) *f* (pl ~n) wine-list

Weinkeller (vighn-keh-lerr) *m* (pl ~) wine-cellar

Weinlese (vighn-lāy-zer) *f* vintage

Weinrebe (vighn-rāy-ber) *f* (pl ~n)

vine

Weise (vigh-zer) *f* (pl ~n) way, fashion, manner

weise (vigh-zer) *adj* wise

*weisen** (vigh-zern) *v* direct

Weisheit (vighss-hight) *f* (pl ~en) wisdom

weiß (vighss) *adj* white

Weißfisch (vighss-fish) *m* (pl ~e) whiting

weit (vight) *adj* broad; wide, vast; **bei weitem** by far

weiter (vigh-terr) *adj* further; **und so ~** and so on

*weitergehen** (vigh-terr-gāy-ern) *v* *go on

Weizen (vigh-tsern) *m* wheat

welcher (vehl-kherr) *pron* who; which; **~ auch immer** whichever

Welle (veh-ler) *f* (pl ~n) wave

Wellenlänge (veh-lern-lehng-er) *f* (pl ~n) wave-length

Wellenreiterbrett (veh-lern-righ-terr-breht) *nt* (pl ~er) surf-board

wellig (veh-likh) *adj* wavy, undulating

Welt (vehlt) *f* world

Weltall (vehlt-ahl) *nt* universe

weltberühmt (vehlt-ber-rēwmt) *adj* world-famous

Weltkrieg (vehlt-kreek) *m* (pl ~e) world war

weltumfassend (vehlt-oom-fah-sernt) *adj* global

weltweit (vehlt-vight) *adj* world-wide

wem (vāym) *pron* whom

*wenden** (vehn-dern) *v* turn

Wendepunkt (vehn-der-poongkt) *m* (pl ~e) turning-point

Wendung (vehn-doong) *f* (pl ~en) turn

wenig (vāy-nikh) *adj* little; few

weniger (vāy-ni-gerr) *adj* minus; *adv* less

wenigstens (vāy-nikhs-terns) *adv* at

least

wenn (vehn) *conj* if; when; ~ **auch** though

wer (vayr) *pron* who; ~ **auch immer** whoever

Werbesendung (vehr-ber-zehn-doong) *f* (pl ~en) commercial

Werbung (vehr-boong) *f* (pl ~en) advertising

*__werden__ (vayr-dern) *v* *will, *shall; *become; *go, *get, *grow

*__werfen__ (vehr-fern) *v* *throw; toss, *cast

Werk (vehrk) *nt* (pl ~e) deed; work; works *pl*

Werkmeister (vehrk-mighss-terr) *m* (pl ~) foreman

Werkstatt (vehrk-shtaht) *f* (pl ˜en) workshop

Werktag (vehrk-taak) *m* (pl ~e) working day

Werkzeug (vehrk-tsoik) *nt* (pl ~e) tool; utensil, implement

Werkzeugtasche (vehrk-tsoik-tah-sher) *f* (pl ~n) tool kit

Wert (vayrt) *m* (pl ~e) worth, value

wert (vayrt) *adj* dear; ~ *sein* *be worth

wertlos (vayrt-lōass) *adj* worthless

Wertsachen (vayrt-zah-khern) *fpl* valuables *pl*

wertvoll (vayrt-fol) *adj* valuable

Wesen (vay-zern) *nt* (pl ~) being; essence

Wesensart (vay-zerns-aart) *f* nature

wesentlich (vay-zernt-likh) *adj* essential; vital

Wespe (vehss-per) *f* (pl ~n) wasp

Weste (vehss-ter) *f* (pl ~n) waistcoat, vest *nAm*

Westen (vehss-tern) *m* west

westlich (vehst-likh) *adj* westerly; western

Wettbewerb (veht-ber-vehrp) *m* (pl

~e) competition, contest

Wette (veh-ter) *f* (pl ~n) bet

wetteifern (veht-igh-ferrn) *v* compete

wetten (veh-tern) *v* *bet

Wetter (veh-terr) *nt* weather

Wetterbericht (veh-terr-ber-rikht) *m* (pl ~e) weather forecast

Wettlauf (veht-louf) *m* (pl ˜e) race

wichtig (vikh-tikh) *adj* important; **wichtigste** principal, main

Wichtigkeit (vikh-tikh-kight) *f* importance

Wichtigtuerei (vikh-tikh-tōō-er-righ) *f* fuss

Widerhall (vee-derr-hahl) *m* echo

widerlich (vee-derr-likh) *adj* disgusting

*__widerrufen__ (vee-derr-rōō-fern) *v* recall; cancel

sich widersetzen (vee-derr-zeh-tsern) oppose

widersinnig (vee-derr-zi-nikh) *adj* absurd

widerspiegeln (vee-derr-shpee-gerln) *v* reflect

*__widersprechen__ (vee-derr-shpreh-khern) *v* contradict; **widersprechend** contradictory

Widerspruch (vee-derr-shprookh) *m* (pl ˜e) objection

Widerstand (vee-derr-shtahnt) *m* resistance

Widerstandsfähigkeit (vee-derr-shtahnts-fai-ikh-kight) *f* stamina

widerwärtig (vee-derr-vehr-tikh) *adj* revolting, repulsive, repellent

Widerwille (vee-derr-vi-ler) *m* aversion, dislike

widmen (vit-mern) *v* dedicate; devote

widrig (vee-drikh) *adj* nasty

wie (vee) *adv* how; *conj* like, like, such as; as; ~ **auch immer** any way

wieder (vee-derr) *adv* again; **hin und** ~ now and then

*wiederaufnehmen (vee-derr-*ouf*-nāy-mern) v resume

wiedererlangen (vee-derr-ehr-lahng-ern) v recover

wiedererstatten (vee-derr-ehr-shtah-tern) v reimburse

Wiederherstellung (vee-derr-*hāyr*-shteh-loong) f reparation; revival

wiederholen (vee-derr-*hōa*-lern) v repeat

Wiederholung (vee-derr-*hōa*-loong) f (pl ~en) repetition

auf Wiedersehen! (ouf vee-derr-*zāy*-ern) good-bye!

wiedervereinigen (vee-derr-fehr-igh-ni-gern) v reunite

Wiederverkäufer (vee-derr-fehr-koi-ferr) m (pl ~) retailer

Wiege (vee-ger) f (pl ~n) cradle

*wiegen (vee-gern) v weigh

Wiese (vee-zer) f (pl ~n) meadow

wieviel (vi-*feel*) adv how much; how many

Wild (vilt) nt game

wild (vilt) adj wild; savage, fierce

wildern (vil-derrn) v poach

Wildleder (vilt-lāy-derr) nt suede

Wildpark (vilt-pahrk) m (pl ~s) game reserve

Wille (vi-ler) m will

Willenskraft (vi-lerns-krahft) f will-power

willig (vi-likh) adj willing, co-operative

Willkommen (vil-ko-mern) nt welcome

willkommen (vil-ko-mern) adj welcome

willkürlich (vil-kewr-likh) adj arbitrary

Wimperntusche (vim-perrn-too-sher) f (pl ~n) mascara

Wind (vint) m (pl ~e) wind

Windel (vin-derl) f (pl ~n) nappy, diaper nAm

*winden (vin-dern) v *wind; twist

Windhund (vint-hoont) m (pl ~e) greyhound

windig (vin-dikh) adj windy, gusty

Windmühle (vint-mēw-ler) f (pl ~n) windmill

Windpocken (vint-po-kern) fpl chickenpox

Windschutzscheibe (vint-shoots-shigh-ber) f (pl ~n) windscreen; windshield nAm

Windstoß (vint-shtōass) m (pl ~e) gust, blow

Wink (vingk) m (pl ~e) sign

Winkel (ving-kerl) m (pl ~) angle

winken (ving-kern) v wave

Winker (ving-kerr) m (pl ~) trafficator; directional signal Am

Winter (vin-terr) m (pl ~) winter

Wintersport (vin-terr-shport) m winter sports

winzig (vin-tsikh) adj tiny, minute

Wippe (vi-per) f (pl ~n) seesaw

wir (veer) pron we

wirbeln (veer-berln) v *spin

Wirbelsturm (veer-berl-shtoorm) m (pl ~e) hurricane

wirken (veer-kern) v operate

wirklich (veerk-likh) adj actual, real; true, substantial, very; adv indeed, really

Wirklichkeit (veerk-likh-kight) f reality

wirksam (veerk-zaam) adj effective

Wirkung (veer-koong) f (pl ~en) effect; consequence

wirkungsvoll (veer-koongs-fol) adj effective

Wirkwaren (veerk-vaa-rern) fpl hosiery

Wirrwarr (veer-vahr) m muddle

Wirt (veert) m (pl ~e) landlord

Wirtin (veer-tin) f (pl ~nen) landlady

Wirtschaft (veert-shahft) f economy

wirtschaftlich (veert-shahft-likh) adj

economic

Wirtshaus (*veerts*-houss) *nt* (pl ⁓er) public house; pub

*****wissen** (*vi*-sern) *v* *****know**

Wissenschaft (*vi*-sern-shahft) *f* (pl ⁓en) science

Wissenschaftler (*vi*-sern-shahft-lerr) *m* (pl ⁓) scientist

wissenschaftlich (*vi*-sern-shahft-likh) *adj* scientific

Witwe (*vit*-ver) *f* (pl ⁓n) widow

Witwer (*vit*-verr) *m* (pl ⁓) widower

Witz (vits) *m* (pl ⁓e) joke

witzig (*vi*-tsikh) *adj* humorous

wo (voa) *adv* where; *conj* where; ⁓ **auch immer** anywhere; ⁓ **immer** wherever

Woche (*vo*-kher) *f* (pl ⁓n) week

Wochenende (*vo*-khern-ehn-der) *nt* (pl ⁓n) weekend

Wochenschau (*vo*-khern-shou) *f* (pl ⁓en) newsreel

Wochentag (*vo*-khern-taak) *m* (pl ⁓e) weekday

wöchentlich (*vur*-khernt-likh) *adj* weekly

Wohlbefinden (*voal*-ber-fin-dern) *nt* welfare; ease

wohlbegründet (*voal*-ber-grewn-dert) *adj* well-founded

wohlhabend (*voal*-haa-bernt) *adj* prosperous; well-to-do

wohlschmeckend (*voal*-shmeh-kernt) *adj* nice

Wohlstand (*voal*-shtahnt) *m* prosperity

Wohltätigkeit (*voal*-tai-tikh-kight) *f* charity

Wohlwollen (*voal*-vo-lern) *nt* goodwill

Wohnblock (*voan*-blok) *m* (pl ⁓e) block of flats

Wohnboot (*voan*-boat) *nt* (pl ⁓e) houseboat

wohnen (*voa*-nern) *v* live, reside

Wohngebäude (*voan*-ger-boi-der) *nt* (pl ⁓) apartment house *Am*

wohnhaft (*voan*-hahft) *adj* resident

Wohnsitz (*voan*-zits) *m* (pl ⁓e) domicile, residence

Wohnung (*voa*-noong) *f* (pl ⁓en) house; flat; apartment *nAm*

Wohnwagen (*voan*-vaa-gern) *m* (pl ⁓) trailer *nAm*, caravan

Wohnzimmer (*voan*-tsi-merr) *nt* (pl ⁓) living-room, sitting-room

Wolf (volf) *m* (pl ⁓e) wolf

Wolke (*vol*-ker) *f* (pl ⁓n) cloud

Wolkenbruch (*vol*-kern-brookh) *m* (pl ⁓e) cloud-burst

Wolkenkratzer (*vol*-kern-krah-tserr) *m* (pl ⁓) skyscraper

Wolle (*vo*-ler) *f* wool

wollen (*vo*-lern) *adj* woollen

*****wollen** (*vo*-lern) *v* want, *****will**

Wolljacke (*vol*-Yah-ker) *f* (pl ⁓n) cardigan

Wollpullover (*vol*-poo-loa-verr) *m* (pl ⁓) jersey

Wollust (*vo*-loost) *f* lust

Wonne (*vo*-ner) *f* (pl ⁓n) delight, joy

Wort (vort) *nt* (pl ⁓er) word

Wörterbuch (*vurr*-terr-bookh) *nt* (pl ⁓er) dictionary

Wörterverzeichnis (*vurr*-terr-fehr-tsighkh-niss) *nt* (pl ⁓se) vocabulary

Wortschatz (*vort*-shahts) *m* vocabulary

Wortwechsel (*vort*-veh-kserl) *m* (pl ⁓) argument

wozu (voa-*tsoo*) *adv* what for

Wrack (vrahk) *nt* (pl ⁓s) wreck

Wuchs (vooks) *m* growth

wund (voont) *adj* sore

Wunde (*voon*-der) *f* (pl ⁓n) wound

Wunder (*voon*-derr) *nt* (pl ⁓) miracle; wonder, marvel

wunderbar (*voon*-derr-baar) *adj* marvellous; lovely, wonderful, swell;

miraculous

wunderlich (*voon*-derr-likh) *adj* queer

sich wundern (*voon*-derrn) marvel

Wunsch (voonsh) *m* (pl ¨e) wish; desire

wünschen (*vewn*-shern) *v* wish; want, desire

wünschenswert (*vewn*-sherns-vāyrt) *adj* desirable

würdevoll (*vewr*-der-fol) *adj* dignified

würdig (*vewr*-dikh) *adj* worthy of

Wurf (voorf) *m* (pl ¨e) throw; cast; litter

Würfel (*vewr*-ferl) *m* (pl ~) cube

Wurm (voorm) *m* (pl ¨er) worm

Wurst (voorst) *f* (pl ¨e) sausage

Wurzel (*voor*-tserl) *f* (pl ~n) root

würzen (*vewr*-tsern) *v* flavour

wüst (vēwst) *adj* desert; wild, fierce

Wüste (*vēwss*-ter) *f* (pl ~n) desert

Wut (vōōt) *f* anger, rage, temper; passion

wüten (*vēw*-tern) *v* rage

wütend (*vēw*-ternt) *adj* furious, mad

Z

zäh (tsai) *adj* tough

Zahl (tsaal) *f* (pl ~en) number; figure

zahlen (*tsaa*-lern) *v* *pay

zählen (*tsai*-lern) *v* count

Zähler (*tsai*-lerr) *m* (pl ~) meter

Zahlmeister (*tsaal*-mighss-terr) *m* (pl ~) treasurer

zahlreich (*tsaal*-righkh) *adj* numerous

Zahlungsempfänger (*tsaa*-loongs-ehm-pfehng-err) *m* (pl ~) payee

zahlungsunfähig (*tsaa*-loongs-oon-fai-ikh) *adj* bankrupt

Zahlwort (*tsaal*-vort) *nt* (pl ¨er) numeral

zahm (tsaam) *adj* tame

zähmen (*tsai*-mern) *v* tame

Zahn (tsaan) *m* (pl ¨e) tooth

Zahnarzt (*tsaan*-ahrtst) *m* (pl ¨e) dentist

Zahnbürste (*tsaan*-bewrs-ter) *f* (pl ~n) toothbrush

Zahnfleisch (*tsaan*-flighsh) *nt* gum

Zahnpaste (*tsaan*-pahss-ter) *f* (pl ~n) toothpaste

Zahnpulver (*tsaan*-pool-ferr) *nt* toothpowder

Zahnstocher (*tsaan*-shto-kherr) *m* (pl ~) toothpick

Zahnweh (*tsaan*-vāy) *nt* toothache

Zange (*tsahng*-er) *f* (pl ~n) pliers *pl*; tongs *pl*

Zank (tsahngk) *m* quarrel, dispute

zanken (*tsahng*-kern) *v* quarrel

Zäpfchen (*tsehpf*-khern) *nt* (pl ~) suppository

zart (tsaart) *adj* gentle, delicate, tender

zärtlich (*tsairt*-likh) *adj* tender; affectionate

Zauber (*tsou*-berr) *m* spell; **Zauber-** magic

Zauberei (tsou-ber-*righ*) *f* magic

Zauberer (*tsou*-ber-rerr) *m* (pl ~) magician

zauberhaft (*tsou*-berr-hahft) *adj* enchanting

Zaun (tsoun) *m* (pl ¨e) fence

Zebra (*tsāy*-brah) *nt* (pl ~s) zebra

Zebrastreifen (*tsāy*-brah-shtrigh-fern) *m* (pl ~) crosswalk *nAm*

Zehe (*tsāy*-er) *f* (pl ~n) toe

zehn (tsāyn) *num* ten

zehnte (*tsāy*n-ter) *num* tenth

Zeichen (*tsigh*-khern) *nt* (pl ~) sign; signal; mark; token

Zeichentrickfilm (*tsigh*-khern-trik-film) *m* (pl ¨e) cartoon

zeichnen (*tsighkh*-nern) *v* *draw, sketch; mark

Zeichnung (*tsighkh*-noong) *f* (pl ~en) drawing, sketch

Zeigefinger (*tsigh*-ger-fing-err) *m* (pl ~) index finger

zeigen (*tsigh*-gern) *v* *show; display; point, point out, indicate; prove; **sich ~** appear

Zeile (*tsigh*-ler) *f* (pl ~n) line

Zeit (tsight) *f* (pl ~en) time; **in letzter ~** lately

Zeitabschnitt (*tsight*-ahp-shnit) *m* (pl ~e) period

Zeitgenosse (*tsight*-ger-no-ser) *m* (pl ~n) contemporary

zeitgenössisch (*tsight*-ger-nur-sish) *adj* contemporary

Zeitraum (*tsight*-roum) *m* (pl ~e) period

Zeitschrift (*tsight*-shrift) *f* (pl ~en) periodical; magazine, journal, review

zeitsparend (*tsight*-shpaa-rernt) *adj* time-saving

Zeitung (*tsigh*-toong) *f* (pl ~en) newspaper, paper

Zeitungshändler (*tsigh*-toongs-hehn-dlerr) *m* (pl ~) newsagent

Zeitungsstand (*tsigh*-toongs-shtahnt) *m* (pl ~e) newsstand

zeitweilig (*tsight*-vigh-likh) *adj* temporary

Zeitwort (*tsight*-vort) *nt* (pl ~er) verb

Zelle (*tseh*-ler) *f* (pl ~n) cell; booth

Zellophan (tseh-loa-*faan*) *nt* cellophane

Zelt (tsehlt) *nt* (pl ~e) tent

zelten (*tsehl*-tern) *v* camp

Zeltplatz (*tsehlt*-plahts) *m* (pl ~e) camping site

Zement (tsay-*mehnt*) *m* cement

Zenit (tsay-*neet*) *m* zenith

Zensur (tsehn-*zoor*) *f* (pl ~en) mark; censorship

Zentimeter (tsehn-ti-*māy*-terr) *m* (pl ~) centimetre

zentral (tsehn-*traal*) *adj* central

Zentralheizung (tsehn-*traal*-high-tsoong) *f* (pl ~en) central heating

zentralisieren (tsehn-trah-li-*zee*-rern) *v* centralize

Zentrum (*tsehn*-troom) *nt* (pl -tren) centre

zerbrechlich (tsehr-*brehkh*-likh) *adj* fragile

zerfasern (tsehr-*faa*-zerrn) *v* fray

zerhacken (tsehr-*hah*-kern) *v* mince

zerknittern (tsehr-*kni*-terrn) *v* crease

zerlegen (tsehr-*lāy*-gern) *v* carve; analyse

***zerreiben** (tsehr-*righ*-bern) *v* *grind

***zerreißen** (tsehr-*righ*-sern) *v* rip

zerstampfen (tsehr-*shtahm*-pfern) *v* mash

Zerstäuber (tsehr-*shtoi*-berr) *m* (pl ~) atomizer

zerstören (tsehr-*shtūr*-rern) *v* destroy

Zerstörung (tsehr-*shtūr*-roong) *f* destruction

Zettel (*tseh*-terl) *m* (pl ~) piece of paper; ticket, note; form

Zeuge (*tsoi*-ger) *m* (pl ~n) witness

Zeugnis (*tsoik*-niss) *nt* (pl ~se) certificate

Ziege (*tsee*-ger) *f* (pl ~n) goat

Ziegel (*tsee*-gerl) *m* (pl ~) brick

Ziegelstein (*tsee*-gerl-shtighn) *m* (pl ~e) brick

Ziegenbock (*tsee*-gern-bok) *m* (pl ~e) goat

Ziegenleder (*tsee*-gern-lāy-derr) *nt* kid

***ziehen** (*tsee*-ern) *v* pull; *draw

Ziehung (*tsee*-oong) *f* (pl ~en) draw

Ziel (tseel) *nt* (pl ~e) aim; goal, object, target

zielen auf (*tsee*-lern) *v* aim at

Ziellinie (*tseel*-lee-nⁿer) *f* (pl ~n) finish

Zielscheibe (*tseel*-shigh-ber) *f* (pl ~n)

mark; target

ziemlich (*tseem*-likh) *adv* pretty, fairly, rather; somewhat, quite

Ziffer (*tsi*-ferr) *f* (pl ~n) digit; number

Zigarette (tsi-gah-*reh*-ter) *f* (pl ~n) cigarette

Zigarettenetui (tsi-gah-*reh*-tern-eht-vi) *nt* (pl ~s) cigarette-case

Zigarettenspitze (tsi-gah-*reh*-tern-shpi-tser) *f* (pl ~n) cigarette-holder

Zigarettentabak (tsi-gah-*reh*-tern-taa-bahk) *m* cigarette tobacco

Zigarre (tsi-*gah*-rer) *f* (pl ~n) cigar

Zigarrenladen (tsi-*gah*-rern-laa-dern) *m* (pl ~̈) cigar shop

Zigeuner (tsi-*goi*-nerr) *m* (pl ~) gipsy

Zimmer (*tsi*-merr) *nt* (pl ~) room; chamber; ~ **mit Frühstück** bed and breakfast; ~ **mit Vollpension** room and board

Zimmerbedienung (*tsi*-merr-ber-dee-noong) *f* room service

Zimmerflucht (*tsi*-merr-flookht) *f* suite

Zimmermädchen (*tsi*-merr-mait-khern) *nt* (pl ~) chambermaid

Zimmertemperatur (*tsi*-merr-tehm-pay-rah-tōōr) *f* room temperature

Zimt (tsimt) *m* cinnamon

Zink (tsingk) *nt* zinc

Zinn (*tsi*-tern) *nt* tin, pewter

Zins (tsins) *m* (pl ~en) interest

Zirkus (*tseer*-kooss) *m* (pl ~se) circus

Zirkusarena (*tseer*-kooss-ah-rāy-nah) *f* (pl -arenen) ring

Zitat (tsi-*taat*) *nt* (pl ~e) quotation

zitieren (tsi-*tee*-rern) *v* quote

Zitrone (tsi-*trōa*-ner) *f* (pl ~n) lemon

zittern (*tsi*-terrn) *v* tremble, shiver

zivil (tsi-*veel*) *adj* civil

Zivilisation (tsi-vi-li-zah-ts^y*ōan*) *f* (pl ~en) civilization

zivilisiert (*tsi*-vi-li-*zeert*) *adj* civilized

Zivilist (tsi-vi-*list*) *m* (pl ~en) civilian

Zivilrecht (tsi-*veel*-rehkht) *nt* civil law

zögern (*tsūr*-gerrn) *v* hesitate

Zölibat (tsur-li-*baat*) *nt* celibacy

Zoll (tsol) *m* (pl ~̈e) Customs duty

Zollbehörde (*tsol*-ber-hūrr-der) *f* (pl ~n) Customs *pl*

zollfrei (*tsol*-frigh) *adj* duty-free

Zöllner (*tsurl*-nerr) *m* (pl ~) Customs officer

zollpflichtig (*tsol*-pflikh-tikh) *adj* dutiable

Zone (*tsōā*-ner) *f* (pl ~n) zone

Zoo (tsōā) *m* (pl ~s) zoo

Zoologie (tsoa-oa-loa-*gee*) *f* zoology

Zorn (tsorn) *m* anger

zornig (*tsor*-nikh) *adj* angry

zu (tsōō) *prep* to; towards; *adv* too; closed, shut

Zubehör (*tsōō*-ber-hūrr) *nt* (pl ~e) accessories *pl*

zubereiten (*tsōō*-ber-righ-tern) *v* cook

züchten (*tsewkh*-tern) *v* *breed, raise; *grow

Zucker (*tsoo*-kerr) *m* sugar; **Stück** ~ lump of sugar

Zuckerkrankheit (*tsoo*-kerr-krahngk-hight) *f* diabetes

***zuerkennen** (*tsōō*-ehr-keh-nern) *v* award

zuerst (tsoo-*āyrst*) *adv* at first

Zufall (*tsōō*-fahl) *m* (pl ~̈e) chance; luck

zufällig (*tsōō*-feh-likh) *adj* accidental, casual, incidental; *adv* by chance

zufrieden (tsoo-*free*-dern) *adj* satisfied; happy, content

zufriedenstellen (tsoo-*free*-dern-shteh-lern) *v* satisfy

Zufuhr (*tsōō*-fōōr) *f* supply

Zug (tsōōk) *m* (pl ~̈e) train; procession; move; trait; **durchgehender** ~ through train

Zugang (*tsōō*-gahng) *m* entry; approach

zugänglich (*tsōō*-gehng-likh) *adj* accessible

Zugbrücke (*tsōōk*-brew-ker) *f* (pl ~n) drawbridge

*__zugeben__ (*tsōō*-gāy-bern) *v* admit, acknowledge

zügeln (*tsēw*-gerln) *v* curb

Zugeständnis (*tsōō*-ger-shtehnt-niss) *nt* (pl ~se) concession

zugetan (*tsōō*-ger-taan) *adj* attached to

zugleich (tsoo-*glighkh*) *adv* at the same time

zugunsten (tsoo-*goons*-tern) *prep* on behalf of

zuhören (*tsōō*-hūr-rern) *v* listen

Zuhörer (*tsōō*-hūr-rerr) *m* (pl ~) listener, auditor

Zuhörerraum (*tsōō*-hūr-rerr-roum) *m* (pl ~e) auditorium

zujubeln (*tsōō-Yōō*-berln) *v* cheer

Zukunft (*tsōō*-koonft) *f* future

zukünftig (*tsōō*-kewnf-tikh) *adj* future

Zulage (*tsōō*-laa-ger) *f* (pl ~n) allowance

Zulassung (*tsōō*-lah-soong) *f* (pl ~en) admission

zuletzt (tsoo-*lehtst*) *adv* at last

zumachen (*tsōō*-mah-khern) *v* close

zumindest (tsoo-*min*-derst) *adv* at least

Zunahme (*tsōō*-naa-mer) *f* increase

Zündkerze (*tsewnt*-kehr-tser) *f* (pl ~n) sparking-plug

Zündung (*tsewn*-doong) *f* (pl ~en) ignition; ignition coil

*__zunehmen__ (*tsōō*-nāy-mern) *v* increase; **zunehmend** progressive

Zuneigung (*tsōō*-nigh-goong) *f* affection

Zunge (*tsoong*-er) *f* (pl ~n) tongue

zurichten (*tsōō*-rikh-tern) *v* cook

zurück (tsoo-*rewk*) *adv* back

*__zurückbringen__ (tsoo-*rewk*-bring-ern) *v* *bring back

*__zurückgehen__ (tsoo-*rewk*-gāy-ern) *v* *go back; *get back

*__zurückhalten__ (tsoo-*rewk*-hahl-tern) *v* restrain

zurückkehren (tsoo-*rewk*-kāy-rern) *v* return

*__zurückkommen__ (tsoo-*rewk*-ko-mern) *v* return

*__zurücklassen__ (tsoo-*rewk*-lah-sern) *v* *leave behind

*__zurückrufen__ (tsoo-*rewk*-rōō-fern) *v* recall

zurückschicken (tsoo-*rewk*-shi-kern) *v* *send back

*__zurücksenden__ (tsoo-*rewk*-zehn-dern) *v* *send back

*__zurücktreten__ (tsoo-*rewk*-trāy-tern) *v* resign

*__zurückweisen__ (tsoo-*rewk*-vigh-zern) *v* reject

zurückzahlen (tsoo-*rewk*-tsaa-lern) *v* *repay, reimburse

*__zurückziehen__ (tsoo-*rewk*-tsee-ern) *v* *withdraw

zusammen (tsoo-*zah*-mern) *adv* together

Zusammenarbeit (tsoo-*zah*-mern-ahr-bight) *f* co-operation

*__zusammenbinden__ (tsoo-*zah*-mern-bin-dern) *v* bundle

*__zusammenbrechen__ (tsoo-*zah*-mern-breh-khern) *v* collapse

*__zusammenfallen__ (tsoo-*zah*-mern-fah-lern) *v* coincide

zusammenfalten (tsoo-*zah*-mern-fahl-tern) *v* fold

Zusammenfassung (tsoo-*zah*-mern-fah-soong) *f* (pl ~en) résumé, summary

zusammenfügen (tsoo-*zah*-mern-fēw-gern) *v* join

Zusammenhang (tsoo-*zah*-mern-hahng) *m* (pl ~e) connection; coherence

Zusammenkunft (tsoo-*zah*-mern-koonft) *f* (pl ~e) assembly

zusammensetzen (tsoo-*zah*-mern-zeh-tsern) *v* assemble

Zusammensetzung (tsoo-*zah*-mern-zeh-tsoong) *f* (pl ~en) composition

zusammenstellen (tsoo-*zah*-mern-shteh-lern) *v* compile; compose, *make up

Zusammenstoß (tsoo-*zah*-mern-shtōass) *m* (pl ~e) collision; crash

*__zusammenstoßen__ (tsoo-*zah*-mern-shtōa-sern) *v* bump; crash, collide

Zusammensturz (tsoo-*zah*-mern-shtoorts) *m* ruination

Zusammentreffen (tsoo-*zah*-mern-treh-fern) *nt* concurrence

*__zusammenziehen__ (tsoo-*zah*-mern-tsee-ern) *v* tighten

zusätzlich (tsōō-zehts-likh) *adj* additional, extra

Zuschauer (tsōō-shou-err) *m* (pl ~) spectator

Zuschlag (tsōō-shlaak) *m* (pl ~e) surcharge

*__zuschlagen__ (tsōō-shlaa-gern) *v* slam; *strike

zuschreiben (tsōō-shrigh-bern) *v* assign to

Zuschuß (tsōō-shooss) *m* (pl Zuschüsse) grant

Zustand (tsōō-shtahnt) *m* (pl ~e) state, condition

zustande *bringen (tsoo-*shtahn*-der *bring*-ern) effect; accomplish

Zustellung (tsōō-shteh-loong) *f* delivery

zustimmen (tsōō-shti-mern) *v* agree; consent

Zustimmung (tsōō-shti-moong) *f* consent; approval

Zutat (tsōō-taat) *f* (pl ~en) ingredient

zuteilen (tsōō-tigh-lern) *v* allot

Zutritt (tsōō-trit) *m* entrance, admittance, access

zuverlässig (tsōō-fehr-leh-sikh) *adj* trustworthy, reliable; sound

zuversichtlich (tsōō-fehr-zikht-likh) *adj* confident

zuviel (tsoo-*feel*) *pron* too much

zuvor (tsoo-*fōar*) *adv* before

*__zuvorkommen__ (tsoo-*fōar*-ko-mern) *v* anticipate

zuvorkommend (tsoo-*fōar*-ko-mernt) *adj* thoughtful

*__zuweisen__ (tsōō-vigh-zern) *v* assign to

Zuweisung (tsōō-vigh-zoong) *f* (pl ~en) assignment

sich *zuziehen (tsōō-tsee-ern) contract

zwanglos (tsvahng-lōass) *adj* casual

zwangsweise (tsvahngs-vigh-zer) *adv* by force

zwanzig (tsvahn-tsikh) *num* twenty

zwanzigste (tsvahn-tsikhs-ter) *num* twentieth

Zweck (tsvehk) *m* (pl ~e) purpose; objective, design

zweckmäßig (tsvehk-mai-sikh) *adj* appropriate; efficient

zwei (tsvigh) *num* two

zweideutig (tsvigh-doi-tikh) *adj* ambiguous

Zweifel (tsvigh-ferl) *m* (pl ~) doubt; ohne ~ without doubt

zweifelhaft (tsvigh-ferl-hahft) *adj* doubtful

zweifellos (tsvigh-ferl-lōass) *adv* undoubtedly

zweifeln (tsvigh-ferln) *v* doubt

Zweig (tsvighk) *m* (pl ~e) twig

Zweigstelle (tsvighk-shteh-ler) *f* (pl ~n) branch

zweimal (tsvigh-maal) *adv* twice

zweisprachig (tsvigh-shpraa-khikh) *adj* bilingual

zweite (tsvigh-ter) *num* second

zweiteilig (tsvigh-tigh-likh) *adj* two-piece

Zwerg (tsvehrk) *m* (pl ~e) dwarf

Zwiebel (*tsvee*-berl) *f* (pl ~n) onion; bulb

Zwielicht (*tsvee*-likht) *nt* twilight

Zwillinge (*tsvi*-li-nger) *mpl* twins *pl*

*****zwingen** (*tsving*-ern) *v* force; compel

Zwirn (tsveern) *m* thread

zwischen (*tsvi*-shern) *prep* between; among, amid

Zwischenfall (*tsvi*-shern-fahl) *m* (pl ~e) incident

Zwischenraum (*tsvi*-shern-roum) *m* (pl ~e) space

Zwischenspiel (*tsvi*-shern-shpeel) *nt* (pl ~e) interlude

Zwischenstock (*tsvi*-shern-shtok) *m* (pl ~e) mezzanine

Zwischenzeit (*tsvi*-shern-tsight) *f* interim

zwölf (tsvurlf) *num* twelve

zwölfte (*tsvurlf*-ter) *num* twelfth

Zyklus (*tsew*-klooss) *m* (pl Zyklen) cycle

Zylinder (tsi-*lin*-derr) *m* (pl ~) cylinder

Zylinderkopf (tsi-*lin*-derr-kopf) *m* (pl ~e) cylinder head

Menu Reader

Food

Aal eel

Abendbrot, Abendessen evening meal, supper

Allgäuer Bergkäse hard cheese from Bavaria resembling *Emmentaler*

Allgäuer Rahmkäse a mild and creamy Bavarian cheese

Altenburger a mild, soft goat's milk cheese

Ananas pineapple

Anis aniseed

~**brot** aniseed-flavoured cake or biscuit

Apfel apple

Apfelsine orange

Appenzeller (Käse) slightly bitter, fully flavoured cheese

Appetithäppchen, Appetitschnittchen appetizer, canapé

Aprikose apricot

Artischocke artichoke

Artischockenboden artichoke bottom

Aubergine aubergine (US eggplant)

Auflauf 1) soufflé 2) a meat, fish, fowl, fruit or vegetable dish which is oven-browned

Aufschnitt cold meat (US cold cuts)

Auster oyster

Backforelle baked trout

Backhähnchen, Backhendl, Backhuhn fried chicken

Backobst dried fruit

Backpflaume prune

Backsteinkäse strong cheese from Bavaria resembling *Limburger*

Banane banana

Barsch perch

Bauernbrot rye or wholemeal bread

Bauernfrühstück breakfast usually consisting of eggs, bacon and potatoes

Bauernomelett diced bacon and onion omelet

Bauernschmaus sauerkraut garnished with bacon, smoked pork, sausages and dumplings or potatoes

Bauernsuppe a thick soup of sliced frankfurters and cabbage

Baumnuß walnut

Bayerische Leberknödel veal-liver dumplings, served with sauerkraut

Bedienung (nicht) (e)inbegriffen service (not) included

Beere berry

Beilage side dish, sometimes a garnish

belegtes Brot/Brötchen roll with any of a variety of garnishes

Berliner (Pfannkuchen) jam-filled doughnut (US jelly donut)

Berliner Luft dessert made of eggs and lemon, served with raspberry juice

Berner Platte a mound of sauerkraut or French beans liberally garnished with smoked pork chops, boiled bacon and beef, sausages, tongue, ham and boiled potatoes

Beuschel heart, kidney and liver of calf or lamb in a slightly sour sauce

Bienenstich cake with honey and almonds

Bierrettich black radish, generally cut, salted and served with beer

Biersuppe a sweet, spicy soup made on beer

Birchermus, Birchermüsli uncooked oats with raw, shredded fruit, chopped nuts in milk or yoghurt

Birne pear

Bischofsbrot fruit-nut cake

Biskuitrolle Swiss roll; jelly and butter-cream roll

Bismarckhering pickled herring, seasoned with onions

blau word to designate fish freshly poached

Blaubeere bilberry (US blueberry)

Blaukraut red cabbage

Blumenkohl cauliflower

Blutwurst black pudding (US blood sausage)

Bockwurst boiled sausage

Bohne bean

Bouillon broth, consommé

Brachse, Brasse bream

Bratapfel baked apple

Braten roast, joint
~ **soße** gravy

Bratfisch fried fish

Brathähnchen, Brathendl, Brathuhn roast chicken

Bratkartoffel fried potato

Bratwurst fried sausage

Braunschweiger Kuchen rich cake with fruit and almonds

Brei porridge, mash, purée

Brezel salted, knot-shaped roll (US pretzel)

Bries, Brieschen, Briesel sweetbread

Brombeere blackberry

Brot bread
~ **suppe** broth with stale bread

Brötchen roll

Brühe broth, consommé

Brunnenkresse watercress

Brüsseler Endivie chicory (US endive)

Brust breast
~ **stück** brisket

Bückling bloater

Bulette meat- or fishball

Bündnerfleisch cured, dried beef served in very thin slices

Butt(e) brill

Champignon button mushroom

Chicorée chicory (US endive)

Cornichon small gherkin (US pickle)

Dampfnudel steamed sweet dumpling, served warm with vanilla sauce

Dattel date

deutsches Beefsteak hamburger, sometimes topped with a fried egg

doppeltes Lendenstück a thick fillet of beef (US tenderloin)

Dörrobst dried fruit

Dorsch cod

Dotterkäse cheese made from skimmed milk and egg-yolk

durchgebraten well-done

Egli perch

Ei egg

~ **dotter,** ~ **gelb** egg-yolk

~ **schnee** beaten egg-white

~ **weiß** egg-white

Eierauflauf egg soufflé

Eierkuchen pancake

Eierschwamm(erl) chanterelle mushroom

eingemacht preserved (of fruit or vegetables)

Eintopf stew, usually of meat and vegetables

Eis ice, ice-cream

~ **bombe** ice-cream dessert

~ **krem** ice-cream

Eisbein mit Sauerkraut pickled pig's knuckle with sauerkraut

Emmentaler (Käse) a semi-hard, robust Swiss cheese with holes

Endivie endive (US chicory)

Ente duck

Erbse pea

Erdbeere strawberry

Erdnuß peanut

errötende Jungfrau raspberries with cream

Essig vinegar

~ **gurke** gherkin (US pickle)

Eßkastanie chestnut

Extraaufschlag extra charge, supplementary charge

Fadennudel thin noodle, vermicelli

falscher Hase a meat loaf of beef and pork

Fasan pheasant

Faschiertes minced meat

faschiertes Laibchen meatball

Feige fig

Felchen variety of lake trout

Fenchel fennel

fester Preis, zu festem Preis fixed price

Filet fillet

~ **Stroganoff** thin slices of beef cooked in a sauce of sour cream, mustard and onions

Fisch fish

~ **klößchen** fishball

~ **schüssel** casserole of fish and diced bacon

Fladen pancake

Flädle, Flädli thin strips of pancake added to soup

flambiert flambé (food set aflame with brandy)

Flammeri a pudding made of rice or semolina and served with stewed fruit or vanilla custard

Fleisch meat

~ **käse** seasoned meat loaf made of beef and other minced meats

~ **kloß** meat dumpling

~ **roulade,** ~ **vogel** slice of meat rolled around a stuffing and braised; veal bird

Flunder flounder

Forelle trout

Frankfurter (Würstchen) frankfurter (sausage)

Frikadelle a meat, fowl or fish dumpling

Frikassee fricassée, stew

frisch fresh

Frischling young wild boar

Froschschenkel frogs' legs

Frucht fruit

Frühlingssuppe soup with diced spring vegetables

Frühstück breakfast

Frühstückskäse a strong cheese with a smooth texture
Frühstücksspeck smoked bacon
Füllung stuffing, filling, forcemeat
Fürst-Pückler-Eis(bombe) chocolate, vanilla and strawberry ice-cream dessert
Gabelfrühstück brunch
Gans goose
Gänseklein goose giblets
Garnele shrimp
Garnitur garnish
Gebäck pastry
gebacken baked
gebraten roasted, fried
gedämpft steamed
Gedeck meal at a set price
gedünstet braised, steamed
Geflügel fowl
  ~**klein** giblets
Gefrorenes ice-cream
gefüllt stuffed
gegrillt grilled
gehackt minced or chopped
Gehacktes minced meat
gekocht cooked, boiled
Gelee 1) aspic 2) jelly 3) jam
gemischt mixed
Gemüse vegetable
gepökelt pickled
geräuchert smoked
Gericht dish
geröstet roasted
Gerste barley
gesalzen salted
geschmort stewed, braised
Geschnetzeltes meat cut into thin, small slices
Geselchtes cured and smoked pork
gesotten simmered, boiled
gespickt larded
gesülzt jellied, in aspic
Gewürz spice

~**gurke** gherkin (US pickle)
~**kuchen** spice cake
~**nelke** clove
gewürzt spiced, hot
Gipfel crescent-shaped roll
Gittertorte almond cake or tart with a raspberry topping
Gitzi kid
Glace ice-cream
Glattbutt brill
Gnagi cured pig's knuckle
Götterspeise fruit jelly dessert (US Jell-O)
Granat prawn
~**apfel** pomegranate
gratiniert oven-browned, gratinéed
Graubrot brown bread (US black bread)
Graupensuppe barley soup
Greyerzer (Käse) Gruyère, a cheese rich in flavour, smooth in texture
Griebenwurst a larded frying sausage
Grieß semolina
grilliert grilled
Gröstl grated, fried potatoes with pieces of meat
Gründling gudgeon
grüne Bohne French bean (US green bean)
Grünkohl kale
Gugelhopf, Gugelhupf a moulded cake with a hole in the centre; usually with almonds and raisins
Güggeli spring chicken
Gulasch goulash
Gurke cucumber, gherkin
Hachse knuckle, shank
Hackbraten meat loaf of beef and pork
Hackfleisch minced meat

Haferbrei oatmeal, porridge

Haferflocken rolled oats

Hähnchen spring chicken

halb half

~ **gar** rare (US underdone)

Hamme ham

Hammel(fleisch) mutton

Handkäse cheese made from sour milk, with a pungent aroma

Haschee hash

Hase hare

Hasenpfeffer jugged hare

Haselnuß hazelnut

Hauptgericht main course

hausgemacht, von Haus home-made

Hausmannskost plain food

Haxe knuckle, shank

Hecht pike

Hefekranz ring-shaped cake

Heidelbeere bilberry (US blueberry)

Heilbutt halibut

heiß very warm (hot)

Hering herring

~ **Hausfrauenart** herring fillets with onions in sour cream

Heringskartoffeln a casserole of layers of herring and potatoes

Heringskönig John Dory (fish)

Herz heart

Himbeere raspberry

Himmel und Erde slices of black pudding served with mashed potatoes and apple sauce

Hirn brains

Hirsch stag (venison)

Hirse millet

hohe Rippe roast ribs of beef

Holsteiner Schnitzel breaded veal cutlet served with vegetables and topped with a fried egg

Honig honey

Hörnchen crescent-shaped roll

Huhn chicken

Hühnchen chicken

Hühnerklein chicken giblets

Hummer lobster

Husarenfleisch braised beef, veal and pork fillets, with sweet peppers, onions and sour cream

Hutzelbrot bread made of prunes and other dried fruit

Imbiß snack

Ingwer ginger

italienischer Salat finely sliced veal, salami, tomatoes, anchovies, cucumber and celery in mayonnaise

(nach) Jägerart sautéed with mushrooms and sometimes onions

Jakobsmuschel scallop

Johannisbeere redcurrant

jung young, spring

Jungfernbraten roast pork with bacon

Kabeljau cod

Kaisergranat Norway lobster, Dublin Bay prawn

Kaiserschmarren delicious, fluffy pancakes with raisins served with a compote or chocolate sauce

Kalb(fleisch) veal

Kalbsbries veal sweetbread

Kalbskopf calf's head

Kalbsmilch veal sweetbread

Kalbsnierenbraten roast veal stuffed with kidneys

Kaldaunen tripe

kalt cold

Kaltschale chilled fruit soup

Kammuschel scallop

kandierte Frucht crystallized fruit (US candied fruit)

Kaninchen rabbit

Kapaun capon

Kaper caper
Karamelkrem caramel custard
Karfiol cauliflower
Karotte carrot
Karpfen carp
Kartoffel potato
~**puffer** potato fritter
Käse cheese
~**platte** cheese board
~**stange** cheese straw, cheese stick
Kasseler Rippenspeer smoked pork chops, often served with sauerkraut
Kastanie chestnut
Katenrauchschinken country-style smoked ham
Katenwurst country-style smoked sausage
Katzenjammer cold slices of beef in mayonnaise with cucumbers or gherkins
Kaviar caviar
Keks biscuit (US cookie)
Kerbel chervil
Kesselfleisch boiled pork served with vegetables
Keule leg, haunch
Kieler Sprotte smoked sprat
Kipfel crescent-shaped roll
Kirsche cherry
Kitz kid
Kliesche dab
Klops meatball
Kloß dumpling
Klößchen small dumpling
Kluftsteak rumpsteak
Knackwurst a lightly garlic-flavoured sausage, generally boiled
Knoblauch garlic
Knochen bone
~**schinken** cured ham
Knödel dumpling

Knöpfli thick noodle
Kohl cabbage
~**rabi**, ~**rübe** turnip
~**roulade** cabbage leaves stuffed with minced meat
Kompott stewed fruit, compote
Konfitüre jam
Königinpastetchen vol-au-vent; puff-pastry shell filled with diced chicken and mushrooms
Königinsuppe creamy chicken soup with pieces of chicken breast
Königsberger Klops cooked meatball in white caper sauce
Kopfsalat green salad, lettuce
Korinthe currant
Kotelett chop, cutlet
Krabbe crab
Kraftbrühe broth, consommé
Krainer spiced pork sausage
Kranzkuchen ring-shaped cake
Krapfen 1) fritter 2) jam-filled doughnut (US jelly donut)
Krauskohl kale
Kraut cabbage
Kräutersoße herb dressing
Krautsalat coleslaw
Krautstiel white beet, Swiss chard
Krautwickel stuffed cabbage
Krebs freshwater crayfish
Krem cream, custard
~**schnitte** custard slice (US napoleon)
Kren horse-radish
~**fleisch** pork stew with vegetables and horse-radish
Kresse cress
Krustentier shellfish
Kuchen cake
Kukuruz maize (US corn)
Kümmel caraway
Kürbis pumpkin
Kuttelfleck, Kutteln tripe

Labskaus thick stew of minced, marinated meat with mashed potatoes

Lachs salmon

~**forelle** salmon trout

Lamm(fleisch) lamb

Languste spiny lobster, crawfish

Lattich lettuce

Lauch leek

Leber liver

~**käse** seasoned meat loaf made of minced liver, pork and bacon

Lebkuchen gingerbread

Leckerli honey-flavoured ginger biscuit

legiert thickened, usually with egg-yolk (refers to sauces or soups)

Leipziger Allerlei spring carrots, peas and asparagus (sometimes with mushrooms)

Lende loin

Lendenbraten roast tenderloin

Lendenstück fillet of beef (US tenderloin)

Limburger (Käse) a semi-soft, strong-smelling whole-milk cheese

Linse lentil

Linzer Torte almond cake or tart with a raspberry-jam topping

Löwenzahn young dandelion green, usually prepared as salad

Lunge light (lung of an animal)

Mahlzeit meal

Mainauer (Käse) semi-hard, full-cream round cheese with a red rind and yellow interior

Mainzer Rippchen pork chop

Mais maize (US corn)

Makrele mackerel

Makrone macaroon

Mandarine mandarin

Mandel almond

Mangold white beet, Swiss chard

Marille apricot

mariniert marinated, pickled

Mark (bone) marrow

Marmelade jam

Marone chestnut

Mastente fattened duckling

Masthühnchen broiler, spring chicken

Matjeshering slightly salted young herring

Matrosenbrot a sandwich with chopped, hard-boiled eggs, anchovies and seasoning

Maulbeere mulberry

Maultasche a kind of ravioli filled with meat, vegetables and seasoning

Meerrettich horse-radish

Mehlnockerl small dumpling

Mehlsuppe brown-flour soup

Melone melon

Menü meal at a set price

Meringe(l) meringue

Mettwurst spiced and smoked pork sausage, usually for spreading on bread

Miesmuschel mussel

Milke sweetbread

Mirabelle small yellow plum

Mittagessen midday meal, lunch

Mohn poppy

Möhre, Mohrrübe carrot

Mondseer (Käse) whole-milk yellow cheese with a moist texture

Morchel morel mushroom

Morgenessen breakfast

Morgenrötesuppe thick soup of meat, tapioca, tomatoes and chicken stock

Mostrich mustard

Mus stewed fruit, purée, mash

Muschel mussel

Muskat(nuß) nutmeg

Nachspeise, Nachtisch dessert, sweet

naturell plain

Nelke clove

Nidel, Nidle cream

Niere kidney

Nierenstück loin

Nockerl small dumpling

Nudel noodle

Nürnberger Bratwurst frying sausage made of veal and pork

Nuß 1) nut 2) approx. rumpsteak

Obst fruit

~**salat** fruit salad

Ochs(enfleisch) beef

Ochsenauge fried egg (US sunny side up)

Ochsenmaulsalat ox muzzle salad

Ochsenschwanz oxtail

Ohr ear

Öl oil

Omelett(e) omelet

Palatschinken pancake usually filled with jam or cheese, sometimes served with a hot chocolate and nut topping

Pampelmuse grapefruit

paniert breaded

Paprikaschote sweet pepper

Paradeis(er), Paradiesapfel tomato

Pastetchen filled puff-pastry case

Pastete pastry, pie

Patisserie pastry

Pellkartoffel potato boiled in its jacket

Perlgraupe pearl barley

Petersilie parsley

Pfahlmuschel mussel

Pfannkuchen pancake

Pfeffer pepper

~**kuchen** very spicy gingerbread

~**nuß** ginger(bread)-nut

~**schote** hot pepper

Pfifferling chanterelle mushroom

Pfirsich peach

~ **Melba** peach-halves poached in syrup, served over vanilla ice-cream, topped with raspberry sauce and whipped cream

Pflaume plum

Pichelsteiner (Fleisch) meat and vegetable stew

pikant spiced, highly seasoned

Pilz mushroom

Platte platter

Plätzchen biscuit (US cookie)

Plätzli scallop, cutlet

pochiert poached

Pökelfleisch marinated meat

Pomeranzensoße sauce of bitter oranges, wine and brandy, usually served with duck

Pommes frites chips (US french fries)

Porree leek

Poulet chicken

Praline praline; chocolate with a sweet filling

Preiselbeere cranberry

Preßkopf brawn (US headcheese)

Printe honey-flavoured biscuit (US cookie)

Pudding custard, pudding

Püree mash, purée

Puter turkey

Quargel a small, round cheese, slightly acid and salty

Quark(käse) fresh white cheese

Quitte quince

Radieschen radish

Ragout stew

Rahm cream

Rande beetroot

Räucheraal smoked eel

Räucherhering smoked herring

Räucherlachs smoked salmon

Räucherspeck smoked bacon

Rebhuhn partridge

Rechnung bill (US check)

Regensburger a highly spiced and smoked sausage

Reh deer, venison

~ **pfeffer** jugged venison, fried and braised in its marinade, served with sour cream

Reibekuchen potato pancake

Reibkäse grated cheese

Reis rice

~ **fleisch** veal braised with rice, tomatoes and other vegetables

Rettich black radish

Rhabarber rhubarb

Ribisel redcurrant

Rinderbrust brisket of beef

Rind(fleisch) beef

Rippe rib

Rippchen, Rippenspeer, Rippenstück, Rippli chop (usually smoked pork)

Rochen skate, ray

Rogen roe (generally cod's roe)

Roggenbrot rye bread

roh raw

Rohkost uncooked vegetables, vegetarian food

Rohschinken cured ham

Rollmops soused herring fillet rolled around chopped onions or gherkins

Rosenkohl brussels sprout

Rosine raisin

Rosmarin rosemary

Rostbraten rumpsteak

Rösti grated, fried (US hashed-brown) potatoes

Röstkartoffel roast potato

rote Beete/Rübe beetroot

rote Grütze fruit jelly served with cream

Rotkohl, Rotkraut red cabbage

Rotzunge lemon sole

Roulade beef olives; usually thin slices of beef, stuffed, rolled and braised

Rücken chine, saddle

Rüebli carrot

Rührei scrambled egg

russische Eier Russian eggs; egg-halves topped with caviar, served with remoulade sauce

Sachertorte rich chocolate layer cake with jam filling

Safran saffron

Saft juice

Sahne cream

Saibling char

Saitenwurst a variety of frankfurter or wiener sausage

Salat salad

Salbei sage

Salm salmon

Salz salt

~ **fleisch** salted meat

~ **gurke** pickled cucumber

~ **kartoffel** boiled potato

Salzburger Nockerl dumpling made of beaten egg-yolks, egg-whites, sugar and flour, fried in butter

Sandmuschel clam

Sardelle anchovy

Sardellenring rolled anchovy

Sardine sardine, pilchard

Sattel chine, saddle

Saubohne broad bean

sauer sour

Sauerampfer sorrel

Sauerbraten pot roast marinated with herbs

Schalentier shellfish

Schalotte shallot

Schaschlik chunks of meat, slices

of kidneys and bacon, grilled then braised in a spicy sauce of tomatoes, onions and bacon

Schaumrolle puff-pastry rolls filled with whipped cream or custard

Scheibe slice

Schellfisch haddock

Schildkrötensuppe turtle soup

Schillerlocke pastry cornet with vanilla cream filling

Schinken ham

~ **brot** ham sandwich, usually open(-faced)

Schlachtplatte cold meat, liver sausage and sauerkraut

Schlagobers, Schlagrahm, Schlagsahne whipped cream

Schlegel leg, haunch

Schleie tench

Schmelzkäse a soft and pungent cheese, usually for spreading on bread

Schmorbraten pot roast

Schmorfleisch meat stew

Schnecke 1) cinnamon roll 2) snail

Schnepfe snipe

Schnittbohne sliced French bean

Schnitte slice, cut

Schnittlauch chive

Schnitzel cutlet

Schokolade chocolate

Scholle plaice

Schulter shoulder

Schwamm(erl) mushroom

schwarze Johannisbeere/Ribisel blackcurrant

Schwarzwälder Kirschtorte a chocolate layer cake filled with cream and cherries, flavoured with *Kirsch*

Schwarzwälder Schinken a variety of smoked ham from the Black Forest

Schwarzwurzel salsify

Schwein(efleisch) pork

Seezunge sole

Selchfleisch smoked pork

Sellerie celery

Semmel roll

~ **brösel** breadcrumbs

~ **knödel** dumpling made of diced white bread

Senf mustard

Siedfleisch boiled meat

Soße sauce, gravy

Spanferkel suck(l)ing pig

spanische Soße a brown sauce with herbs

Spargel asparagus

Spätzle, Spätzli thick noodle

Speck bacon

~ **knödel** dumpling made with bacon, eggs and white bread

Speise food

~ **eis** ice-cream

~ **karte** menu, bill of fare

Spekulatius spiced biscuit (US cookie)

Spezialität speciality

~ **des Hauses** chef's speciality

~ **des Tages** day's speciality

Spiegelei fried egg (US sunny side up)

(am) Spieß (on the) spit

Spinat spinach

Sprossenkohl brussels sprout

Sprotte sprat

Stachelbeere gooseberry

Steckrübe turnip

Steinbuscher (Käse) semi-hard creamy cheese; strong and slightly bitter

Steinbutt turbot

Steingarnele prawn

Steinpilz boletus mushroom

Stelze knuckle of pork

Stierenauge fried egg (US sunny side up)

Stock mashed potatoes

~**fisch** stockfish, dried cod

Stollen loaf cake with raisins, almonds, nuts and candied lemon peel

Stoßsuppe caraway soup

Stotzen leg, haunch

Strammer Max slice of bread or sandwich with spiced minced pork (sometimes sausage or ham) served with fried eggs and onions

Streichkäse any soft cheese spread, with different flavours

Streuselkuchen coffee cake with a topping made of butter, sugar, flour and cinnamon

Strudel paper-thin layers of pastry filled with apple slices, nuts, raisins and jam or honey

Stück piece, slice

Sülze 1) jellied, in aspic 2) brawn (US headcheese)

Suppe soup

süß sweet

~**sauer** sweet-and-sour (of sauces)

Süßigkeit sweet (US candy)

Süßspeise dessert, pudding

Tagesgericht day's special

Tagessuppe day's soup

Tascherl pastry turnover with meat, cheese or jam filling

Tatar raw, spiced minced beef

Tatarenbrot open(-faced) sandwich with *Tatar*

Taube pigeon (US squab)

Teigwaren macaroni, noodles, spaghetti

Teller plate, dish

~**gericht** one-course meal

Thunfisch tunny (US tuna)

Thymian thyme

Tilsiter (Käse) semi-hard cheese, mildly pungent

Tomate tomato

Topfen fresh white cheese

~**strudel** flaky pastry filled with creamed, vanilla-flavoured white cheese, rolled and baked

Topfkuchen moulded cake with raisins

Törtchen small tart or cake

Torte layer cake, usually rich

Traube grape

Trüffel truffle

Truthahn turkey

Tunke sauce, gravy

Türkenkorn maize (US corn)

Vanille vanilla

verlorenes Ei poached egg

Voressen meat stew

Vorspeise starter, first course

Wacholderbeere juniper berry

Wachtel quail

Waffel waffle

Walnuß walnut

Wassermelone watermelon

Weinbeere, Weintraube grape

Weinkarte wine list

Weinkraut white cabbage, often braised with apples and simmered in wine

weiße Bohne haricot bean (US navy bean)

Weißbrot white bread

Weißkäse fresh white cheese

Weißkohl, Weißkraut white cabbage

Weißwurst sausage made of veal and bacon, flavoured with parsley, onion and lemon peel

Weizen wheat

Welschkorn maize (US corn)

Westfälischer Schinken a well-known variety of cured and smoked ham

Wiener Schnitzel breaded veal cutlet

Wiener Würstchen, Wienerli wiener, frankfurter (sausage)

Wild(bret) game, venison

Wildente wild duck

Wildschwein wild boar

Wilstermarschkäse semi-hard cheese, similar to *Tilsiter*

Windbeutel cream puff

Wirsing(kohl) savoy cabbage

Wittling whiting

Wurst sausage

Würstchen small sausage

würzig spiced

Zander pike-perch

Zervelat(wurst) a seasoned and smoked sausage made of pork, beef and bacon

Zichorie chicory (US endive)

Ziege goat

Zimt cinnamon

Zitrone lemon

Zucker sugar

Zunge tongue

Zutat (added) ingredient

Zwetsch(g)e plum

Zwiebel onion

~**fleisch** beef sautéed with onions

~**wurst** liver and onion sausage

Zwischenrippenstück approx. rib-eye steak, entrecôte

Drinks

Abfüllung bottled, from wine brought directly from the grower

Abzug wine bottled on the estate or at the vineyard where the grapes were grown, e.g., *Schloßabzug, Kellerabzug*

Ahr the region, named after its tributary of the Rhine, has the continent's northernmost vineyards; the red wine—pale, delicious with a fine aroma—is the best in Germany, which produces little red wine; try it around the towns of Ahrweiler, Neuenahr and Walporzheim

Apfelmost apple cider

Apfelsaft apple juice

Apfelwein apple cider with a high

alcoholic content

Aprikosenlikör apricot liqueur

Auslese wine produced from choice grapes

Baden this wine-producing region is situated in the southwestern part of Germany with Switzerland to the south and Alsace, France, to the west; vineyards are especially found on the outskirts of the Black Forest facing the valley of the Rhine: some examples of the wine are *Kaiserstuhl*, produced at the foot of a one-time volcano to the west of Freiburg, *Markgräfler, Mauerwein* and *Seewein* from the Lake of Constance

Beerenauslese wine produced

from choice, very mature grapes resulting in a dessert wine

Bier beer
  dunkles ~ dark
  helles ~ light, lager

Bock(bier) a beer with a high malt content

Branntwein brandy, spirits

Brauner coffee with milk
  kleiner ~ small cup of coffee with milk

Danziger Goldwasser a caraway seed-flavoured liqueur flecked with tiny golden leaves

Doppelkorn spirit distilled from grain

Dornkaat a grain-distilled spirit, slightly flavoured with juniper berries

Eierlikör egg liqueur

Eiskaffee iced coffee

Enzian spirit distilled from gentian root

Exportbier a beer with a higher hops content than lager beer

Flasche bottle

Flaschenbier bottled beer

Franken Franconia; the best vineyards of this wine-producing region around the River Main are situated in the vicinity of Iphofen, Escherndorf, Randersacker, Rödelsee and Würzburg; Franconian white wine is dry, strong and full-bodied; Würzburg produces one of the area's best wines under the name *Steinwein*

Fruchtsaft fruit juice

Gewächs used together with the year on the label of quality wines

gezuckert sugar added, sweetened

Glühwein mulled wine

Himbeergeist spirit distilled from raspberries

Kabinett a term indicating that a wine is of high quality

Kaffee coffee
  ~ **Hag** caffeine-free
  ~ **mit Sahne (und Zucker)** with cream (and sugar)
  ~ **mit Schlag(obers)** served with whipped cream
  schwarzer ~ black

Kakao cocoa

Kapuziner coffee with whipped cream and grated chocolate

Kirsch(wasser) spirit distilled from cherries

Klosterlikör herb liqueur

Kognak cognac

Korn(branntwein) spirit distilled from grain

Kümmel(branntwein) caraway-flavoured spirit

Likör liqueur, cordial

Limonade 1) soft drink 2) lemon drink

Lindenblütentee lime-blossom tea

Malzbier malt beer, with a low alcoholic content

Märzenbier beer with a high alcoholic content, brewed in March

Maß(krug) a large beer mug holding 1 litre (about 1 quart)

Milch milk
  ~**kaffee** half coffee and half hot milk
  ~**mix** milk shake

Mineralwasser mineral water

Mosel(–Saar–Ruwer) the official name of the Moselle region; the best Moselle wine is produced in only a part of the region, the mid-Moselle Valley which runs from Trittenheim to Traben-Trarbach; the best vineyards are those of Bernkastel, Braune-berg, Graach, Piesport, Wehlen and Zeltingen

Most must, young wine

Nahe a wine-producing region, named after its tributary of the River Rhine, in the vicinity of Bad Kreuznach; its white wine is full-bodied and may be compared to the best wine of Rhenish Hesse; the most celebrated vineyard is Schloß Böckelheim, owned by the state; other excellent wine is produced in the vicinity of Bad Kreuznach, Bretzenheim, Münster, Nieder-hausen, Norheim, Roxheim, Winzerheim

Naturwein unblended, unsweetened wine

Österreich Austria; very little of its wine is exported; the red—mainly from Burgenland—is not especially notable and is usually drunk only locally; probably the best-known Austrian wine is *Gumpoldskirchner*, produced to the south of Vienna, a good white wine which generations of Viennese have enjoyed; along the banks of the River Danube to the west of Vienna, good white wine is produced in the Wachau area (e.g., *Dürn-steiner, Loibner, Kremser);* in the immediate vicinity of the Austrian capital, table wine is produced (e.g., *Nußberger, Grinzinger, Badener)* of which the best is sometimes exported

Perlwein white, semi-sparkling wine

Pfalz Palatinate; in good years this region is often first among West Germany's wine-producing regions in terms of production, predominantly of white wine; in medieval times, the Palatinate gained a reputation for being "the wine cellar of the Holy Roman Empire"; today's Palatinate is bounded on the north by Rhenish Hesse, to the east by the River Rhine, to the south and west by Alsace, and Saarland; some examples *Dürkheimer, Forster, Deidesheimer, Ruppertsberger* for white, *Dürkheimer* also for red

Pils(e)ner beer with a particularly strong aroma of hops

Pfefferminztee peppermint tea

Pflümli(wasser) spirit distilled from plums

Portwein port (wine)

Rhein Rhine wine is produced in five regions in the Rhine valley offering the country's best white wines

Rheingau region situated at the foot of the Taunus Mountains facing the River Rhine; its best wines are dessert wines which can be compared to fine Sauternes; a good red wine is produced in Aßmannshausen

Rheinhessen Rhenish Hesse, of which Mainz is the capital; no less than 155 villages are dedicated to wine production; some produce wines of exceptional quality (Alsheim, Bingen, Bodenheim, Dienheim, Guntersblum, Ingelheim, Nackenheim, Nierstein, Oppenheim and Worms); wine of lesser quality is sold under the name of *Liebfrau(en)milch*

Schillerwein rosé wine

Schloß castle, denotes a wine estate

Schnaps brandy, spirits

Schokolade chocolate

Schweiz Switzerland; the most notable wines (both red and white) are produced in French- and Italian-speaking cantons; German-speaking cantons produce mostly light red wines

Sekt sparkling wine similar to Champagne

Sirup syrup

Sodawasser soda water

Spätlese wine produced from grapes picked late in the season, often resulting in full-bodied wine

Spezialbier more strongly brewed beer than *Vollbier*

Sprudel(wasser) soda water

Starkbier strong beer with a high malt content

Steinhäger juniper-flavoured spirit

Tee tea
 ~ **mit Milch** with milk
 ~ **mit Zitrone** with lemon

trocken dry

Trockenbeerenauslese wine produced from specially selected overripe grapes; usually results in a rich, full-bodied dessert wine

ungezuckert unsweetened

verbessert in reference to wine, "improved" or sweetened

Viertel $\frac{1}{4}$ litre (about $\frac{1}{2}$ pint) of wine

Vollbier the typical German beer with an alcoholic content of 3–4%

Wachstum used on a wine label with the name of the grower, guarantees natural wine

Wasser water

Wein wine
 Rot~ red
 Schaum~ sparkling
 Süß~ dessert
 Weiß~ white

Weinbrand brandy distilled from wine

Weißbier light beer brewed from wheat

Wermut vermouth

Württemberg wine from this region, rarely exported, must be drunk very young; the term *Schillerwein* is employed in the region to denote rosé wine; best wine is produced at Cannstatt, Feuerbach, Untertürckheim; *Stettener Brotwasser* is a noted wine

Zitronensaft lemon squash (US lemon soda)

Zwetschgenwasser spirit distilled from plums

German Irregular Verbs

The following list contains the most common strong and irregular verbs. In parentheses, we have given the irregular forms of the present tense, generally the second and the third persons singular (when they change their stem). If a compound verb or a verb with a prefix (*ab-, an-, auf-, aus-, be-, bei-, ein-, emp-, ent-, er-, mit-, nach-, um-, ver-, vor-, zer-, zu-*, etc.) is not listed, its forms may be found by looking up the simple verb.

Infinitive	*Past*	*Past Participle*	
backen (bäckst, bäckt)	backte/buk	gebacken	*bake*
befehlen (befiehlst, befiehlt)	befahl	befohlen	*(give an) order*
beginnen	begann	begonnen	*begin*
beißen	biß	gebissen	*bite*
bergen (birgst, birgt)	barg	geborgen	*salvage*
bersten (birst, birst)	barst	geborsten	*burst*
bewegen	bewog	bewogen	*induce*
biegen	bog	gebogen	*bend*
bieten	bot	geboten	*offer*
binden	band	gebunden	*bind*
bitten	bat	gebeten	*request*
blasen (bläst, bläst)	blies	geblasen	*blow*
bleiben	blieb	geblieben	*remain*
braten (brätst, brät)	briet	gebraten	*roast*
brechen (brichst, bricht)	brach	gebrochen	*break*
brennen	brannte	gebrannt	*burn*
bringen	brachte	gebracht	*bring*
denken	dachte	gedacht	*think*
dringen	drang	gedrungen	*penetrate*
dürfen (darf, darfst, darf)	durfte	gedurft	*be allowed*
empfehlen (empfiehlst, empfiehlt)	empfahl	empfohlen	*recommend*
essen (ißt, ißt)	aß	gegessen	*eat*
fahren (fährst, fährt)	fuhr	gefahren	*go, drive*
fallen (fällst, fällt)	fiel	gefallen	*fall*
fangen (fängst, fängt)	fing	gefangen	*catch*
fechten (fichst, ficht)	focht	gefochten	*fence*
finden	fand	gefunden	*find*
flechten (flichtst, flicht)	flocht	geflochten	*plait*
fliegen	flog	geflogen	*fly*
fliehen	floh	geflohen	*flee*
fließen	floß	geflossen	*flow*
fressen (frißt, frißt)	fraß	gefressen	*eat (animals)*
frieren	fror	gefroren	*freeze*
gären	gor/ gärte	gegoren/ gegärt	*ferment*
geben (gibst, gibt)	gab	gegeben	*give*
gedeihen	gedieh	gediehen	*prosper*
gehen	ging	gegangen	*go*

gelingen[1]	gelang	gelungen	*succeed*
gelten (giltst, gilt)	galt	gegolten	*be valid*
genesen	genas	genesen	*convalesce*
genießen	genoß	genossen	*enjoy*
geschehen[1] (geschieht)	geschah	geschehen	*happen*
gewinnen	gewann	gewonnen	*win*
gießen	goß	gegossen	*pour*
gleichen	glich	geglichen	*resemble*
gleiten	glitt	geglitten	*glide*
graben (gräbst, gräbt)	grub	gegraben	*dig*
greifen	griff	gegriffen	*seize*
haben (hast, hat)	hatte	gehabt	*have*
halten (hältst, hält)	hielt	gehalten	*hold*
hängen	hing	gehangen	*be suspended*
hauen	hieb	gehauen	*hit, cut*
heben	hob	gehoben	*lift*
heißen	hieß	geheißen	*be called*
helfen (hilfst, hilft)	half	geholfen	*help*
kennen	kannte	gekannt	*know*
klingen	klang	geklungen	*sound*
kneifen	kniff	gekniffen	*pinch*
kommen	kam	gekommen	*come*
können (kann, kannst, kann)	konnte	gekonnt	*can*
kriechen	kroch	gekrochen	*crawl*
laden (lädst, lädt)	lud	geladen	*load*
lassen (läßt, läßt)	ließ	gelassen	*let, leave*
laufen (läufst, läuft)	lief	gelaufen	*run*
leiden	litt	gelitten	*suffer*
leihen	lieh	geliehen	*lend*
lesen (liest, liest)	las	gelesen	*read*
liegen	lag	gelegen	*lie, rest*
lügen	log	gelogen	*tell a lie*
mahlen	mahlte	gemahlen	*grind*
meiden	mied	gemieden	*avoid*
messen (mißt, mißt)	maß	gemessen	*measure*
mißlingen	mißlang	mißlungen	*fail*
mögen (mag, magst, mag)	mochte	gemocht	*want, like*
müssen (muß, mußt, muß)	mußte	gemußt	*must*
nehmen (nimmst, nimmt)	nahm	genommen	*take*
nennen	nannte	genannt	*name*
pfeifen	pfiff	gepfiffen	*whistle*
raten (rätst, rät)	riet	geraten	*counsel*
reiben	rieb	gerieben	*rub*
reißen	riß	gerissen	*tear*
reiten	ritt	geritten	*ride*
rennen	rannte	gerannt	*run*
riechen	roch	gerochen	*smell*
ringen	rang	gerungen	*struggle*

---

[1] impersonal

rinnen	rann	geronnen	*flow, run*
rufen	rief	gerufen	*call*
saufen (säufst, säuft)	soff	gesoffen	*drink (animals)*
schaffen	schuf	geschaffen	*create*
schallen	schallte/	geschallt	*resound*
	scholl		
scheiden	schied	geschieden	*separate*
scheinen	schien	geschienen	*shine, seem*
schieben	schob	geschoben	*push*
schießen	schoß	geschossen	*shoot*
schlafen (schläfst, schläft)	schlief	geschlafen	*sleep*
schlagen (schlägst, schlägt)	schlug	geschlagen	*beat*
schleichen	schlich	geschlichen	*creep*
schleifen	schliff	geschliffen	*sharpen*
schließen	schloß	geschlossen	*close*
schlingen	schlang	geschlungen	*twine*
schmeißen	schmiß	geschmissen	*hurl*
schmelzen (schmilzt, schmilzt)	schmolz	geschmolzen	*melt*
schneiden	schnitt	geschnitten	*cut*
schrecken[1] (schrickst, schrickt)	schrak	geschrocken	*frighten*
schreiben	schrieb	geschrieben	*write*
schreien	schrie	geschrie(e)n	*scream*
schreiten	schritt	geschritten	*stride*
schweigen	schwieg	geschwiegen	*be silent*
schwellen (schwillst, schwillt)	schwoll	geschwollen	*swell*
schwimmen	schwamm	geschwommen	*swim*
schwinden	schwand	geschwunden	*diminish*
schwingen	schwang	geschwungen	*swing*
schwören	schwor	geschworen	*swear*
sehen	sah	gesehen	*see*
sein (bin, bist, ist, sind, seid, sind)	war	gewesen	*be*
senden	sandte	gesandt	*send*
sieden	sott	gesotten	*boil*
singen	sang	gesungen	*sing*
sinken	sank	gesunken	*sink*
sinnen	sann	gesonnen	*meditate*
sitzen	saß	gesessen	*sit*
sollen (soll, sollst, soll)	sollte	gesollt	*must, shall*
spinnen	spann	gesponnen	*spin*
sprechen (sprichst, spricht)	sprach	gesprochen	*speak*
springen	sprang	gesprungen	*jump*
stechen (stichst, sticht)	stach	gestochen	*prick*
stehen	stand	gestanden	*stand*
stehlen (stiehlst, stiehlt)	stahl	gestohlen	*steal*
steigen	stieg	gestiegen	*mount*
sterben (stirbst, stirbt)	starb	gestorben	*die*
stinken	stank	gestunken	*stink*

---

[1] only used with prefixes

stoßen (stößt, stößt)	stieß	gestoßen	*push*
streichen	strich	gestrichen	*stroke*
streiten	stritt	gestritten	*quarrel*
tragen (trägst, trägt)	trug	getragen	*carry*
treffen (triffst, trifft)	traf	getroffen	*het, meet*
treiben	trieb	getrieben	*drive, push*
treten (trittst, tritt)	trat	getreten	*tread*
triefen	troff/triefte	getroffen/ getrieft	*drip*
trinken	trank	getrunken	*drink*
trügen	trog	getrogen	*deceive*
tun (tue, tust, tut)	tat	getan	*do*
verderben (verdirbst, verdirbt)	verdarb	verdorben	*spoil*
verdrießen	verdroß	verdrossen	*annoy*
vergessen (vergißt, vergißt)	vergaß	vergessen	*forget*
verlieren	verlor	verloren	*lose*
verzeihen	verzieh	verziehen	*forgive*
wachsen (wächst, wächst)	wuchs	gewachsen	*grow*
wägen	wog	gewogen	*consider*
waschen (wäschst, wäscht)	wusch	gewaschen	*wash*
weben	wob/webte	gewoben/ gewebt	*weave*
weichen	wich	gewichen	*yield*
weisen	wies	gewiesen	*indicate*
wenden	wandte/ wendete	gewandt/ gewendet	*turn*
werben (wirbst, wirbt)	warb	geworben	*recruit*
werden (wirst, wird)	wurde	geworden	*become*
werfen (wirfst, wirft)	warf	geworfen	*throw*
wiegen	wog	gewogen	*weigh*
winden	wand	gewunden	*wind, twist*
wissen (weiß, weißt, weiß)	wußte	gewußt	*know*
wollen (will, willst, will)	wollte	gewollt	*want*
ziehen	zog	gezogen	*pull*
zwingen	zwang	gezwungen	*force*

German Abbreviations

Abf.	*Abfahrt*	departure
Abs.	*Absender*	sender
ACS	*Automobil-Club der Schweiz*	Automobile Association of Switzerland
ADAC	*Allgemeiner Deutscher Automobil-Club*	German Automobile Association
AG	*Aktiengesellschaft*	Ltd., Inc.
Ank.	*Ankunft*	arrival
Anm.	*Anmerkung*	remark
AvD	*Automobilclub von Deutschland*	Automobile Association of Germany
Bhf.	*Bahnhof*	train station
Bez.	*Bezirk*	district
BRD	*Bundesrepublik Deutschland*	Federal Republic of Germany
b.w.	*bitte wenden*	please turn over
bzw.	*beziehungsweise*	respectively
DB	*Deutsche Bundesbahn*	German Federal Railways
DBP	*Deutsche Bundespost*	German Federal Post Office
DDR	*Deutsche Demokratische Republik*	German Democratic Republic
d.h.	*das heißt*	i.e.
DIN	*Deutsche Industrie-Norm*	German Industrial Standards
DM	*Deutsche Mark*	(West) German mark
d.M.	*dieses Monats*	inst., of this month
D-Zug	*Durchgangszug*	through train
EG	*Europäische Gemeinschaften*	EC, European Community
EWG	*Europäische Wirtschafts-gemeinschaft*	EEC, European Economic Community
E-Zug	*Eilzug*	express train
Ffm.	*Frankfurt am Main*	Frankfurt, West Germany
fl.W.	*fließendes Wasser*	running water
Fr.	*Franken; Frau*	franc; Mrs.
Frl.	*Fräulein*	Miss
g	*Groschen*	1/100 of a schilling
Gebr.	*Gebrüder*	brothers
gefl.	*gefälligst*	please, kindly
GmbH	*Gesellschaft mit beschränkter Haftung*	limited liability company
Hbf.	*Hauptbahnhof*	main railway station

Hr.	*Herr*	Mr.
Ing.	*Ingenieur*	engineer
Inh.	*Inhaber; Inhalt*	proprietor; contents
Kfm.	*Kaufmann*	merchant
Kfz	*Kraftfahrzeug*	motor vehicle
KG	*Kommanditgesellschaft*	limited partnership
Lkw	*Lastkraftwagen*	lorry, truck
MEZ	*Mitteleuropäische Zeit*	Central European Time
MwSt	*Mehrwertsteuer*	VAT, value added tax
n. Chr.	*nach Christus*	A.D.
ÖAMTC	*Österreichischer Automobil-, Motorrad- und Touringclub*	Austrian Automobile, Motorcycle and Touring Association
OB	*Oberbürgermeister*	mayor (of a large city)
ÖBB	*Österreichische Bundesbahnen*	Austrian Federal Railways
OHG	*Offene Handelsgesellschaft*	ordinary partnership
Pf	*Pfennig*	1/100 of a mark
Pfd.	*Pfund*	pound (weight)
Pkw	*Personenkraftwagen*	automobile
PS	*Pferdestärke*	hp, horsepower
PTT	*Post, Telefon, Telegraf*	Post and Telecommunications
Rp.	*Rappen*	1/100 of a franc
S	*Schilling*	Austrian schilling
SBB	*Schweizerische Bundesbahnen*	Swiss Federal Railways
Str.	*Straße*	street
TCS	*Touring-Club der Schweiz*	Swiss Touring Association
u. a.	*unter anderem*	among other things
U-Bahn	*Untergrundbahn*	underground (GB), subway (US)
ü. d. M.	*über dem Meeresspiegel*	above sea level
UKW	*Ultrakurzwelle*	FM (radio)
ung.	*ungefähr*	approximately
UNO	*Vereinte Nationen*	United Nations
usw.	*und so weiter*	etc., and so on
u. U.	*unter Umständen*	in certain cases
v. Chr.	*vor Christus*	B.C.
vgl.	*vergleiche*	compare
v. H.	*vom Hundert*	per cent
Wwe.	*Witwe*	widow
z. B.	*zum Beispiel*	e.g.
z. H.	*zu Händen*	to the attention of
z. Z.	*zur Zeit*	at present

Numerals

Cardinal numbers		Ordinal numbers	
0	null	1.	erste
1	eins	2.	zweite
2	zwei	3.	dritte
3	drei	4.	vierte
4	vier	5.	fünfte
5	fünf	6.	sechste
6	sechs	7.	sieb(en)te
7	sieben	8.	achte
8	acht	9.	neunte
9	neun	10.	zehnte
10	zehn	11.	elfte
11	elf	12.	zwölfte
12	zwölf	13.	dreizehnte
13	dreizehn	14.	vierzehnte
14	vierzehn	15.	fünfzehnte
15	fünfzehn	16.	sechzehnte
16	sechzehn	17.	siebzehnte
17	siebzehn	18.	achtzehnte
18	achtzehn	19.	neunzehnte
19	neunzehn	20.	zwanzigste
20	zwanzig	21.	einundzwanzigste
21	einundzwanzig	22.	zweiundzwanzigste
22	zweiundzwanzig	23.	dreiundzwanzigste
23	dreiundzwanzig	24.	vierundzwanzigste
30	dreißig	25.	fünfundzwanzigste
40	vierzig	26.	sechsundzwanzigste
50	fünfzig	27.	siebenundzwanzigste
60	sechzig	28.	achtundzwanzigste
70	siebzig	29.	neunundzwanzigste
80	achtzig	30.	dreißigste
90	neunzig	40.	vierzigste
100	(ein)hundert	50.	fünfzigste
101	hundert(und)eins	60.	sechzigste
230	zweihundert(und)dreißig	70.	siebzigste
538	fünfhundert(und) achtunddreißig	80.	achtzigste
		90.	neunzigste
1 000	(ein)tausend	100.	(ein)hundertste
10 000	zehntausend	230.	zweihundert(und)- dreißigste
100 000	(ein)hunderttausend		
1 000 000	eine Million	1 000.	(ein)tausendste

Time

Although official time in Germany, Austria and Switzerland is based on the 24-hour clock, the 12-hour system is used in conversation.

If you want to indicate a.m. or p.m., add *morgens, nachmittags* or *abends*.

Thus:

acht Uhr morgens	8 a.m.
zwei Uhr nachmittags	2 p.m.
acht Uhr abends	8 p.m.

Days of the Week

Sonntag	Sunday	*Donnerstag*	Thursday
Montag	Monday	*Freitag*	Friday
Dienstag	Tuesday	*Samstag,*	Saturday
Mittwoch	Wednesday	*Sonnabend*	

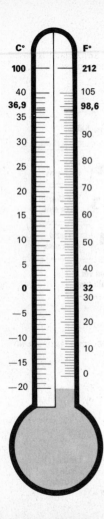

Conversion tables/ Umrechnungstabellen

Metres and Feet

The figure in the middle stands for both metres and feet, e.g. 1 metre = 3.281 ft. and 1 foot = 0.30 m.

Meter und Fuß

Die Zahlen in der Mitte gelten zugleich für Meter und Fuß, z.B. 1 Meter = 3,281 Fuß; 1 Fuß = 0,30 Meter.

Metres/Meter		Feet/Fuß
0.30	**1**	3.281
0.61	**2**	6.563
0.91	**3**	9.843
1.22	**4**	13.124
1.52	**5**	16.403
1.83	**6**	19.686
2.13	**7**	22.967
2.44	**8**	26.248
2.74	**9**	29.529
3.05	**10**	32.810
3.66	**12**	39.372
4.27	**14**	45.934
6.10	**20**	65.620
7.62	**25**	82.023
15.24	**50**	164.046
22.86	**75**	246.069
30.48	**100**	328.092

Temperature

To convert Centigrade to Fahrenheit, multiply by 1.8 and add 32.
To convert Fahrenheit to Centigrade, subtract 32 from Fahrenheit and divide by 1.8.

Temperatur

Um Celsius in Fahrenheit umzurechnen, multiplizieren Sie den Celsiuswert mit 1,8 und zählen zum Ergebnis 32 hinzu.
Um Fahrenheit in Celsius umzurechnen, ziehen Sie vom Fahrenheitwert 32 ab und dividieren die Summe durch 1,8.

Some Basic Phrases

Nützliche Redewendungen

Please.	Bitte.
Thank you very much.	Vielen Dank.
Don't mention it.	Gern geschehen.
Good morning.	Guten Morgen.
Good afternoon.	Guten Tag *(nachmittags)*.
Good evening.	Guten Abend.
Good night.	Gute Nacht.
Good-bye.	Auf Wiedersehen.
See you later.	Bis bald.
Where is/Where are...?	Wo ist/Wo sind...?
What do you call this?	Wie heißt dies?
What does that mean?	Was bedeutet das?
Do you speak English?	Sprechen Sie Englisch?
Do you speak German?	Sprechen Sie Deutsch?
Do you speak French?	Sprechen Sie Französisch?
Do you speak Spanish?	Sprechen Sie Spanisch?
Do you speak Italian?	Sprechen Sie Italienisch?
Could you speak more slowly, please?	Könnten Sie bitte etwas langsamer sprechen?
I don't understand.	Ich verstehe nicht.
Can I have...?	Kann ich... haben?
Can you show me...?	Können Sie mir... zeigen?
Can you tell me...?	Können Sie mir sagen...?
Can you help me, please?	Können Sie mir bitte helfen?
I'd like...	Ich hätte gern...
We'd like...	Wir hätten gern...
Please give me...	Geben Sie mir bitte...
Please bring me...	Bringen Sie mir bitte...
I'm hungry.	Ich habe Hunger.
I'm thirsty.	Ich habe Durst.
I'm lost.	Ich habe mich verirrt.
Hurry up!	Beeilen Sie sich!

There is/There are...	Es gibt...
There isn't/There aren't...	Es gibt keinen, keine, kein/Es gibt keine...

Arrival — Ankunft

Your passport, please.	Ihren Paß, bitte.
Have you anything to declare?	Haben Sie etwas zu verzollen?
No, nothing at all.	Nein, gar nichts.
Can you help me with my luggage, please?	Können Sie mir mit meinem Gepäck helfen, bitte?
Where's the bus to the centre of town, please?	Wo ist der Bus zum Stadtzentrum, bitte?
This way, please.	Hier durch, bitte.
Where can I get a taxi?	Wo finde ich ein Taxi?
What's the fare to...?	Was kostet es bis...?
Take me to this address, please.	Fahren Sie mich bitte zu dieser Adresse.
I'm in a hurry.	Ich habe es eilig.

Hotel — Hotel

My name is...	Mein Name ist...
Have you a reservation?	Haben Sie vorbestellt?
I'd like a room with a bath.	Ich hätte gern ein Zimmer mit Bad.
What's the price per night?	Wieviel kostet es pro Nacht?
May I see the room?	Kann ich das Zimmer sehen?
What's my room number, please?	Welche Zimmernummer habe ich, bitte?
There's no hot water.	Es kommt kein warmes Wasser.
May I see the manager, please?	Kann ich bitte den Direktor sprechen?
Did anyone telephone me?	Hat mich jemand angerufen?
Is there any mail for me?	Ist Post für mich da?
May I have my bill (check), please?	Kann ich bitte meine Rechnung haben?

Eating out | Gaststätten

Eating out	Gaststätten
Do you have a fixed-price menu?	Haben Sie ein Menü?
May I see the menu?	Kann ich die Speisekarte sehen?
May we have an ashtray, please?	Können wir bitte einen Aschenbecher haben?
Where's the toilet, please?	Wo ist die Toilette, bitte?
I'd like an hors d'œuvre (starter).	Ich hätte gern eine Vorspeise.
Have you any soup?	Haben Sie Suppe?
I'd like some fish.	Ich hätte gern Fisch.
What kind of fish do you have?	Was für Fisch haben Sie?
I'd like a steak.	Ich hätte gern ein Beefsteak.
What vegetables have you got?	Was für Gemüse haben Sie?
Nothing more, thanks.	Nein danke, nichts mehr.
What would you like to drink?	Was möchten Sie gern trinken?
I'll have a beer, please.	Ich nehme ein Bier, bitte.
I'd like a bottle of wine.	Ich möchte eine Flasche Wein.
May I have the bill (check), please?	Die Rechnung, bitte.
Is service included?	Ist Bedienung inbegriffen?
Thank you, that was a very good meal.	Danke, das Essen war sehr gut.

Travelling | Reisen

Travelling	Reisen
Where's the railway station, please?	Wo ist der Bahnhof, bitte?
Where's the ticket office, please?	Wo ist der Fahrkartenschalter, bitte?
I'd like a ticket to…	Ich möchte eine Fahrkarte nach..
First or second class?	Erste oder zweite Klasse?
First class, please.	Erste Klasse, bitte.
Single or return (one way or roundtrip)?	Einfach oder hin und zurück?
Do I have to change trains?	Muß ich umsteigen?
What platform does the train for… leave from?	Auf welchem Bahnsteig fährt der Zug nach … ab?

Where's the nearest underground (subway) station?

Wo ist die nächste U-Bahn-Station?

Where's the bus station, please?

Wo ist der Busbahnhof, bitte?

When's the first bus to...?

Wann fährt der erste Bus nach...?

Please let me off at the next stop.

Bitte lassen Sie mich an der nächsten Haltestelle aussteigen.

Relaxing

Unterhaltung

What's on at the cinema (movies)?

Was gibt es im Kino zu sehen?

What time does the film begin?

Wann beginnt der Film?

Are there any tickets for tonight?

Gibt es noch Karten für heute abend?

Where can we go dancing?

Wohin können wir tanzen gehen?

Meeting people

Bekanntschaft schließen

How do you do.

Guten Tag.

How are you?

Wie geht es Ihnen?

Very well, thank you And you?

Sehr gut, danke. Und Ihnen?

May I introduce...?

Darf ich Ihnen... vorstellen?

My name is...

Ich heiße...

I'm very pleased to meet you.

Sehr erfreut.

How long have you been here?

Wie lange sind Sie schon hier?

It was nice meeting you.

Es war mir ein Vergnügen.

Do you mind if I smoke?

Stört es Sie, wenn ich rauche?

Do you have a light, please?

Haben Sie Feuer, bitte?

May I get you a drink?

Darf ich Ihnen etwas zu trinken bestellen?

May I invite you for dinner tonight?

Darf ich Sie heute abend zum Essen einladen?

Where shall we meet?

Wo treffen wir uns?

Shops, stores and services

Läden, Geschäfte usw.

Where's the nearest bank, please?

Wo ist die nächste Bank, bitte?

Where can I cash some travellers' cheques?

Wo kann ich Reiseschecks einlösen?

Can you give me some small change, please?	Können Sie mir bitte Kleingeld geben?
Where's the nearest chemist's (pharmacy)?	Wo ist die nächste Apotheke?
How do I get there?	Wie komme ich dorthin?
Is it within walking distance?	Kann man zu Fuß gehen?
Can you help me, please?	Können Sie mir helfen, bitte?
How much is this? And that?	Wieviel kostet dies? Und das?
It's not quite what I want.	Es ist nicht ganz das, was ich möchte.
I like it.	Es gefällt mir.
Can you recommend something for sunburn?	Können Sie mir etwas gegen Sonnenbrand empfehlen?
I'd like a haircut, please.	Ich möchte mir das Haar schneiden lassen, bitte.
I'd like a manicure, please.	Ich möchte eine Maniküre, bitte.

Street directions

Wo? Wohin?

Can you show me on the map where I am?	Können Sie mir auf der Karte zeigen, wo ich bin?
You are on the wrong road.	Sie sind auf der falschen Straße.
Go/Walk straight ahead.	Fahren/Gehen Sie geradeaus.
It's on the left/on the right.	Es ist linker Hand/rechter Hand.

Emergencies

Im Notfall

Call a doctor quickly.	Rufen Sie schnell einen Arzt.
Call an ambulance.	Rufen Sie einen Krankenwagen.
Please call the police.	Rufen Sie bitte die Polizei.

englisch-deutsch

english-german

Erläuterungen

Die Gestaltung des Wörterverzeichnisses wird allen praktischen Anforderungen gerecht. Unnötige sprachwissenschaftliche Angaben wurden weggelassen. Alle Eintragungen sind alphabetisch geordnet, egal ob das Stichwort in einem Wort, mit Bindestrich oder als zwei oder mehr Wörter geschrieben wird. Die einzige Ausnahme von dieser Regel bilden einige idiomatische Wendungen, deren wichtigstes Wortglied als Stichwort dient. Untergeordnete Eintragungen wie übliche Redewendungen oder festgelegte Ausdrücke sind ebenfalls alphabetisch geordnet.

Jedem Stichwort folgt eine Aussprachebezeichnung (siehe Erklärung der Lautschrift). Der Umschrift folgt gegebenenfalls die Angabe der Wortart. Kann eine Vokabel mehreren Wortarten angehören, so stehen die Wortbedeutungen nach der Angabe der entsprechenden Wortart.

Die unregelmäßige Pluralform der Substantive wird im gegebenen Falle angeführt. Der Plural steht außerdem nach einigen Wörtern, deren Mehrzahlbildung nicht offensichtlich ist.

Soll eine Eintragung wiederholt werden (auch in unregelmäßigen Pluralformen), so vertritt die Tilde (~) die ganze vorangegangene Eintragung.

Ein waagrechter Strich vertritt den Teil einer Eintragung vor der abweichenden, ausgeschriebenen Wortendung.

Ein Sternchen (*) vor einem Verb bedeutet, daß es unregelmäßig konjugiert wird (siehe Tabelle der unregelmäßigen Verben).

Dieses Wörterbuch folgt der britischen Rechtschreibung. Alle Wörter und Wortbedeutungen, die in erster Linie dem amerikanischen Sprachkreis zugerechnet werden, sind entsprechend gekennzeichnet (siehe Tabelle der im Wörterverzeichnis verwandten Abkürzungen).

Abkürzungen

adj	Adjektiv	*ntpl*	Neutrum Plural
adv	Adverb	*num*	Numerale
Am	Amerikanisch	*p*	Präteritum
art	Artikel	*pl*	Plural
conj	Konjunktion	*plAm*	Plural (amerikanisch)
f	Femininum	*pp*	Partizip Perfekt
fpl	Femininum Plural	*pr*	Präsens
m	Maskulinum	*pref*	Präfix
mpl	Maskulinum Plural	*prep*	Präposition
n	Substantiv	*pron*	Pronomen
nAm	Substantiv (amerikanisch)	*v*	Verb
nt	Neutrum	*vAm*	Verb (amerikanisch)

Aussprache

In diesem Teil des Wörterbuchs ist zu jedem Stichwort die Aussprache in Internationaler Lautschrift (IPA) angegeben. Jedes einzelne Zeichen dieser Umschrift steht für einen ganz bestimmten Laut. Zeichen, die hier nicht erklärt sind, werden ungefähr wie die entsprechenden Buchstaben im Deutschen ausgesprochen.

Konsonanten

ð	wie s in Rose, aber gelispelt
ŋ	wie ng in Ring
r	schwer zu beschreiben! Die Zunge ist ungefähr in der gleichen Stellung wie bei ʒ (siehe unten), aber viel tiefer, und die Lippen sind eher in einer neutralen Stellung
s	immer wie in es
ʃ	wie sch in rasch
θ	wie s in es, aber gelispelt
v	wie w in wo
w	ein flüchtiger u-Laut, ungefähr wie in Ritual
z	wie s in Rose
ʒ	wie g in Etage

Vokale

ɑː	wie aa in Saal
æ	zwischen a in hat und ä in nächste
ʌ	ähnlich wie a in hat
e	wie e in fest
ɛ	wie e in best, aber mit der Zunge etwas tiefer
ə	wie e in haben, aber mit gedehnten Lippen (ungerundet)
əː	eher wie ö in lösen, aber mit gedehnten Lippen (ungerundet)
ɔ	wie o in Post

1) Ein Doppelpunkt (ː) bezeichnet die Länge des vorhergehenden Vokals.

2) Einige aus dem Französischen entlehnte Wörter enthalten nasale Vokale, die durch eine Tilde über dem Vokal bezeichnet werden (z.B. ã). Sie werden gleichzeitig durch Mund und Nase ausgesprochen.

Diphthonge

Ein Diphthong besteht aus zwei Vokalen, von denen der eine stärker (betont) und der andere schwächer (unbetont) ist und die zusammen als »gleitender« Laut ausgesprochen werden, wie z.B. **ai** in M**ai**. Im Englischen ist der zweite Vokal immer der schwächere. Manchmal folgt auf einen Diphthong noch ein [ə], wodurch der zweite Vokal etwas weiter abgeschwächt wird. Folgende Diphthonge sind zu beachten:

ei   nicht wie in **eins**! Der erste Laut ist **e** wie in fest

ou   ungerundetes **ö** mit folgendem flüchtigem **u**-Laut

Betonung

Das Zeichen (') steht vor der Silbe mit Hauptton, (ˌ) vor einer Silbe mit Nebenton.

Amerikanische Aussprache

Unsere Umschrift gibt die übliche britische Aussprache an. Die amerikanische weicht davon in einigen Punkten ab (wobei es noch bedeutende regionale Unterschiede gibt). Hier einige der auffallendsten Abweichungen:

1) Im Gegensatz zum britischen Englisch wird **r** auch vor einem Konsonanten und am Wortende ausgesprochen.

2) In vielen Wörtern (z.B. *ask*, *castle*, *laugh* usw.) wird [ɑ:] zu [æ:].

3) Den [ɔ]-Laut spricht der Amerikaner [ɑ], vielfach auch [ɔ:].

4) In Wörtern wie *duty*, *tune*, *new* usw. entfällt oft der [j]-Laut vor [u:].

5) Schließlich werden eine Anzahl von Wörtern anders betont.

A

a [ei,ə] *art* (an) ein *art*

abbey ['æbi] *n* Abtei *f*

abbreviation [ə,bri:vi'eiʃən] *n* Abkürzung *f*

aberration [,æbə'reiʃən] *n* Abweichung *f*

ability [ə'biləti] *n* Fähigkeit *f*; Vermögen *nt*

able ['eibəl] *adj* imstande; fähig; *be ~ to imstande *sein zu; *können

abnormal [æb'nɔ:məl] *adj* abnorm

aboard [ə'bɔ:d] *adv* an Bord

abolish [ə'bɔliʃ] *v* abschaffen

abortion [ə'bɔ:ʃən] *n* Abortus *m*

about [ə'baut] *prep* über; betreffs, hinsichtlich; um; *adv* etwa; umher, herum

above [ə'bʌv] *prep* über; *adv* oben

abroad [ə'brɔ:d] *adv* ins Ausland, im Ausland

abscess ['æbses] *n* Abszeß *m*

absence ['æbsəns] *n* Abwesenheit *f*

absent ['æbsənt] *adj* abwesend

absolutely ['æbsəlu:tli] *adv* völlig

abstain from [əb'stein] sich *enthalten

abstract ['æbstrækt] *adj* abstrakt

absurd [əb'sə:d] *adj* absurd, widersinnig

abundance [ə'bʌndəns] *n* Überfluß *m*

abundant [ə'bʌndənt] *adj* reichlich

abuse [ə'bju:s] *n* Mißbrauch *m*

abyss [ə'bis] *n* Abgrund *m*

academy [ə'kædəmi] *n* Akademie *f*

accelerate [ək'seləreit] *v* beschleunigen

accelerator [ək'seləreitə] *n* Gaspedal *nt*

accent ['æksənt] *n* Akzent *m*; Betonung *f*

accept [ək'sept] *v* *annehmen; akzeptieren

access ['ækses] *n* Zutritt *m*

accessary [ək'sesəri] *n* Mitschuldige *m*

accessible [ək'sesəbəl] *adj* zugänglich

accessories [ək'sesəriz] *pl* Zubehör *nt*

accident ['æksidənt] *n* Unglück *nt*, Unfall *m*

accidental [,æksi'dentəl] *adj* zufällig

accommodate [ə'kɔmədeit] *v* *unterbringen

accommodation [ə,kɔmə'deiʃən] *n* Unterkunft *f*

accompany [ə'kʌmpəni] *v* begleiten

accomplish [ə'kʌmpliʃ] *v* vollenden; zustande *bringen

in accordance with [in ə'kɔ:dəns wið] gemäß

according to [ə'kɔ:diŋ tu:] gemäß; in Übereinstimmung mit

account [ə'kaunt] *n* Konto *nt*; Bericht *m*; ~ for Rechenschaft ablegen über; on ~ of wegen

accountable [ə'kauntəbəl] *adj* erklärbar

accurate ['ækjurət] *adj* genau

accuse [ə'kju:z] *v* beschuldigen; anklagen

accused [ə'kju:zd] *n* Angeklagte *m*

accustom [ə'kʌstəm] *v* gewöhnen; **accustomed** gewöhnt, gewohnt

ache [eik] *v* schmerzen; *n* Schmerz *m*

achieve [ə'tʃi:v] *v* erreichen; leisten

achievement [ə'tʃi:vmənt] *n* Leistung *f*

acid ['æsid] *n* Säure *f*

acknowledge [ək'nɔlidʒ] *v* *erkennen; *zugeben; bestätigen

acne ['ækni] *n* Akne *f*

acorn ['eikɔ:n] *n* Eichel *f*

acquaintance [ə'kweintəns] *n* Bekanntschaft *f*, Bekannte *m*

acquire [ə'kwaiə] *v* *erwerben

acquisition [,ækwi'ziʃən] *n* Neuerwerbung *f*

acquittal [ə'kwitəl] *n* Freispruch *m*

across [ə'krɔs] *prep* über; jenseits; *adv* drüben

act [ækt] *n* Tat *f*; Akt *m*; Nummer *f*; *v* *vorgehen, handeln; sich *benehmen; spielen

action ['ækʃən] *n* Aktion *f*, Handlung *f*

active ['æktiv] *adj* aktiv; lebhaft

activity [æk'tivəti] *n* Aktivität *f*

actor ['æktə] *n* Schauspieler *m*

actress ['æktris] *n* Schauspielerin *f*

actual ['æktʃuəl] *adj* tatsächlich, wirklich

actually ['æktʃuəli] *adv* tatsächlich

acute [ə'kju:t] *adj* akut

adapt [ə'dæpt] *v* anpassen

add [æd] *v* addieren; hinzufügen

adding-machine ['ædiŋməʃi:n] *n* Rechenmaschine *f*

addition [ə'diʃən] *n* Addition *f*; Hinzufügung *f*

additional [ə'diʃənəl] *adj* zusätzlich;

nebensächlich

address [ə'dres] *n* Anschrift *f*; *v* adressieren; *ansprechen

addressee [,ædre'si:] *n* Adressat *m*

adequate ['ædikwət] *adj* angemessen; entsprechend, passend

adjective ['ædʒiktiv] *n* Eigenschaftswort *nt*

adjourn [ə'dʒə:n] *v* *verschieben

adjust [ə'dʒʌst] *v* regulieren; anpassen

administer [əd'ministə] *v* verabreichen

administration [əd,mini'streiʃən] *n* Verwaltung *f*

administrative [əd'ministrətiv] *adj* administrativ; Verwaltungs-; ~ **law** Verwaltungsrecht *nt*

admiral ['ædmərəl] *n* Admiral *m*

admiration [,ædmə'reiʃən] *n* Bewunderung *f*

admire [əd'maiə] *v* bewundern

admission [əd'miʃən] *n* Eintritt *m*; Zulassung *f*

admit [əd'mit] *v* *einlassen; einräumen, *zugeben

admittance [əd'mitəns] *n* Zutritt *m*; **no** ~ kein Eingang

adopt [ə'dɔpt] *v* adoptieren; *annehmen

adorable [ə'dɔ:rəbəl] *adj* reizend

adult ['ædʌlt] *n* Erwachsene *m*; *adj* erwachsen

advance [əd'va:ns] *n* Fortschritt *m*; Vorschuß *m*; *v* *fortschreiten; *vorschießen; **in** ~ im voraus, vorher

advanced [əd'va:nst] *adj* fortgeschritten

advantage [əd'va:ntidʒ] *n* Vorteil *m*

advantageous [,ædvən'teidʒəs] *adj* vorteilhaft

adventure [əd'ventʃə] *n* Abenteuer *nt*

adverb ['ædvə:b] *n* Adverb *nt*

advertisement [əd'və:tismənt] *n* Anzeige *f*

advertising ['ædvətaizin] n Werbung f

advice [əd'vais] n Empfehlung f, Rat m

advise [əd'vaiz] v *empfehlen, *raten

advocate ['ædvəkət] n Anhänger m

aerial ['cəriəl] n Antenne f

aeroplane ['cərəplein] n Flugzeug nt

affair [ə'fcə] n Angelegenheit f; Verhältnis nt, Liebschaft f

affect [ə'fekt] v beeinflussen; sich *beziehen auf

affected [ə'fektid] adj geziert

affection [ə'fekʃən] n Erkrankung f; Zuneigung f

affectionate [ə'fekʃənit] adj lieb, zärtlich

affiliated [ə'filieitid] adj angegliedert

affirmative [ə'fə:mətiv] adj bejahend

affliction [ə'flikʃən] n Leid nt

afford [ə'fɔ:d] v sich leisten

afraid [ə'freid] adj ängstlich, bange; *be ~ Angst *haben

Africa ['æfrikə] Afrika

African ['æfrikən] adj afrikanisch; n Afrikaner m

after ['ɑ:ftə] prep nach; hinter; conj nachdem

afternoon [,ɑ:ftə'nu:n] n Nachmittag m; **this ~** heute nachmittag

afterwards ['ɑ:ftəwədz] adv später; hernach, nachher

again [ə'gen] adv wieder; nochmals; **~ and again** immer wieder

against [ə'genst] prep gegen

age [eidʒ] n Alter nt; **of ~** mündig; **under ~** minderjährig

aged ['eidʒid] adj bejahrt; alt

agency ['eidʒənsi] n Agentur f; Dienststelle f; Vertretung f

agenda [ə'dʒendə] n Tagesordnung f

agent ['eidʒənt] n Agent m, Vertreter m

aggressive [ə'gresiv] adj aggressiv

ago [ə'gou] adv her

agrarian [ə'grcəriən] adj agrarisch, Landwirtschafts-

agree [ə'gri:] v übereinstimmen; zustimmen

agreeable [ə'gri:əbəl] adj angenehm

agreement [ə'gri:mənt] n Vertrag m; Akkord m, Abkommen nt; Übereinstimmung f

agriculture ['ægrikʌltʃə] n Landwirtschaft f

ahead [ə'hed] adv vorwärts; **~ of** vor; ***go ~** *fortfahren; **straight ~** geradeaus

aid [eid] n Hilfe f; v unterstützen, *helfen

ailment ['eilmənt] n Leiden nt; Krankheit f

aim [eim] n Ziel nt; **~ at** richten auf, zielen auf; beabsichtigen, bezwecken

air [cə] n Luft f; v lüften

air-conditioning ['cəkən,diʃəniŋ] n Klimaanlage f; **air-conditioned** adj klimatisiert

aircraft ['cəkrɑ:ft] n (pl ~) Flugzeug nt; Maschine f

airfield ['cəfi:ld] n Flugplatz m

air-filter ['cə,filtə] n Luftfilter m

airline ['cəlain] n Fluglinie f

airmail ['cəmeil] n Luftpost f

airplane ['cəplein] nAm Flugzeug nt

airport ['cəpɔ:t] n Flughafen m

air-sickness ['cə,siknəs] n Luftkrankheit f

airtight ['cətait] adj luftdicht

airy ['cəri] adj luftig

aisle [ail] n Seitenschiff nt; Gang m

alarm [ə'lɑ:m] n Alarm m; v alarmieren

alarm-clock [ə'lɑ:mklɔk] n Wecker m

album ['ælbəm] n Album nt

alcohol ['ælkəhɔl] n Alkohol m

alcoholic [,ælkə'hɔlik] adj alkoholisch

ale [eil] n Bier nt

algebra ['ældʒibrə] n Algebra f

Algeria [æl'dʒiəriə] Algerien

Algerian [æl'dʒiəriən] adj algerisch; n Algerier m

alien ['eiliən] n Ausländer m; Fremdling m; adj ausländisch

alike [ə'laik] adj gleich, ähnlich

alimony ['æliməni] n Alimente ntpl

alive [ə'laiv] adj am Leben, lebend

all [ɔːl] adj all, alle; ~ in alles inbegriffen; ~ right! gut!; at ~ überhaupt

allergy ['ælədʒi] n Allergie f

alley ['æli] n Gasse f

alliance [ə'laiəns] n Bündnis nt

Allies ['ælaiz] pl Alliierten mpl

allot [ə'lɔt] v zuteilen

allow [ə'lau] v gestatten, bewilligen, erlauben; ~ to *lassen; *be allowed erlaubt *sein; *be allowed to *dürfen

allowance [ə'lauəns] n Zulage f

all-round [ˌɔːl'raund] adj vielseitig

almanac ['ɔːlmənæk] n Almanach m

almond ['aːmənd] n Mandel f

almost ['ɔːlmoust] adv beinahe; fast

alone [ə'loun] adv allein

along [ə'lɔŋ] prep entlang

aloud [ə'laud] adv laut

alphabet ['ælfəbet] n Alphabet nt

already [ɔːl'redi] adv bereits, schon

also ['ɔːlsou] adv auch; gleichfalls, ebenfalls

altar ['ɔːltə] n Altar m

alter ['ɔːltə] v ändern, verändern

alteration [ˌɔːltə'reiʃən] n Veränderung f, Änderung f

alternate [ɔːl'təːnət] adj abwechselnd

alternative [ɔːl'təːnətiv] n Alternative f

although [ɔːl'ðou] conj obgleich, obwohl

altitude ['æltitjuːd] n Höhe f

alto ['æltou] n (pl ~s) Alt m

altogether [ˌɔːltə'geðə] adv gänzlich; insgesamt

always ['ɔːlweiz] adv immer

am [æm] v (pr be)

amaze [ə'meiz] v verwundern, erstaunen

amazement [ə'meizmənt] n Erstaunen nt

ambassador [æm'bæsədə] n Botschafter m

amber ['æmbə] n Bernstein m

ambiguous [æm'bigjuəs] adj doppelsinnig; zweideutig

ambitious [æm'biʃəs] adj strebsam; ehrgeizig

ambulance ['æmbjuləns] n Krankenwagen m, Ambulanz f

ambush ['æmbuʃ] n Hinterhalt m

America [ə'merikə] Amerika

American [ə'merikən] adj amerikanisch; n Amerikaner m

amethyst ['æmiθist] n Amethyst m

amid [ə'mid] prep unter; zwischen, inmitten

ammonia [ə'mouniə] n Salmiakgeist m

amnesty ['æmnisti] n Amnestie f

among [ə'mʌŋ] prep unter; zwischen, inmitten; ~ other things unter anderem

amount [ə'maunt] n Menge f; Summe f, Betrag m; ~ to *betragen

amuse [ə'mjuːz] v *unterhalten, amüsieren

amusement [ə'mjuːzmənt] n Vergnügen nt, Unterhaltung f

amusing [ə'mjuːziŋ] adj unterhaltsam

anaemia [ə'niːmiə] n Blutarmut f

anaesthesia [ˌænis'θiːziə] n Betäubung f

anaesthetic [ˌænis'θetik] n Betäubungsmittel nt

analyse ['ænəlaiz] v zerlegen, analysieren

analysis [ə'næləsis] n (pl -ses) Analyse

f

analyst ['ænəlist] *n* Analytiker *m*; Psychoanalytiker *m*

anarchy ['ænəki] *n* Anarchie *f*

anatomy [ə'nætəmi] *n* Anatomie *f*

ancestor ['ænsestə] *n* Vorfahr *m*

anchor ['æŋkə] *n* Anker *m*

anchovy ['æntʃəvi] *n* Sardelle *f*

ancient ['einʃənt] *adj* alt; altmodisch, veraltet; uralt

and [ænd, ənd] *conj* und

angel ['eindʒəl] *n* Engel *m*

anger ['æŋgə] *n* Ärger *m*, Zorn *m*; Wut *f*

angle ['æŋgəl] *v* angeln; *n* Winkel *m*

angry ['æŋgri] *adj* zornig, böse

animal ['æniməl] *n* Tier *nt*

ankle ['æŋkəl] *n* Fußknöchel *m*

annex[1] ['æneks] *n* Nebengebäude *nt*; Anhang *m*

annex[2] [ə'neks] *v* einverleiben

anniversary [,æni'vɔ:səri] *n* Jahrestag *m*

announce [ə'nauns] *v* bekanntmachen, ankündigen

announcement [ə'naunsmənt] *n* Bekanntmachung *f*, Ankündigung *f*

annoy [ə'nɔi] *v* irritieren, ärgern; langweilen

annoyance [ə'nɔiəns] *n* Verdruß *m*

annoying [ə'nɔiiŋ] *adj* lästig, ärgerlich

annual ['ænjuəl] *adj* jährlich; *n* Jahrbuch *nt*

per annum [pər 'ænəm] jährlich

anonymous [ə'nɔniməs] *adj* anonym

another [ə'nʌðə] *adj* noch ein; ein anderer

answer ['ɑ:nsə] *v* antworten; beantworten; *n* Antwort *f*

ant [ænt] *n* Ameise *f*

anthology [æn'θɔlədʒi] *n* Anthologie *f*

antibiotic [,æntibai'ɔtik] *n* Antibiotikum *nt*

anticipate [æn'tisipeit] *v* erwarten,

*vorhersehen; *zuvorkommen

antifreeze ['æntifri:z] *n* Gefrierschutzmittel *nt*

antipathy [æn'tipəθi] *n* Abneigung *f*

antique [æn'ti:k] *adj* antik; *n* Antiquität *f*; ~ **dealer** Antiquitätenhändler *m*

antiquity [æn'tikwəti] *n* Altertum *nt*; **antiquities** *pl* Altertümer

antiseptic [,ænti'septik] *n* antiseptisches Mittel

antlers ['æntləz] *pl* Geweih *nt*

anxiety [æŋ'zaiəti] *n* Besorgtheit *f*

anxious ['æŋkʃəs] *adj* bestrebt; besorgt

any ['eni] *adj* irgendein

anybody ['enibɔdi] *pron* irgend jemand

anyhow ['enihau] *adv* irgendwie

anyone ['eniwʌn] *pron* jedermann

anything ['eniθiŋ] *pron* irgend etwas

anyway ['eniwei] *adv* ohnehin

anywhere ['eniwɛə] *adv* wo auch immer; überall

apart [ə'pɑ:t] *adv* gesondert, getrennt; ~ **from** abgesehen von

apartment [ə'pɑ:tmənt] *nAm* Appartement *nt*, Wohnung *f*; Etage *f*; ~ **house** *Am* Wohngebäude *nt*

aperitif [ə'perətiv] *n* Aperitif *m*

apologize [ə'pɔlədʒaiz] *v* sich entschuldigen

apology [ə'pɔlədʒi] *n* Entschuldigung *f*

apparatus [,æpə'reitəs] *n* Vorrichtung *f*, Apparat *m*

apparent [ə'pærənt] *adj* scheinbar; offensichtlich

apparently [ə'pærəntli] *adv* anscheinend; offensichtlich

apparition [,æpə'riʃən] *n* Erscheinung *f*

appeal [ə'pi:l] *n* Appell *m*

appear [ə'piə] *v* *scheinen; sich zeigen; *erscheinen; *auftreten appearance [ə'piərəns] n Erscheinung f; Erscheinen nt; Auftritt m

appendicitis [ə‚pendi'saitis] n Blinddarmentzündung f

appendix [ə'pendiks] n (pl -dices, -dixes) Blinddarm m

appetite ['æpətait] n Eßlust f, Appetit m

appetizer ['æpətaizə] n Appetithappen m

appetizing ['æpətaiziŋ] adj lecker

applause [ə'plɔ:z] n Beifall m

apple ['æpəl] n Apfel m

appliance [ə'plaiəns] n Vorrichtung f, Gerät nt

application [‚æpli'keiʃən] n Anwendung f; Gesuch nt; Bewerbung f

apply [ə'plai] v *verwenden; gebrauchen; sich *bewerben; *gelten

appoint [ə'pɔint] v anstellen; *ernennen

appointment [ə'pɔintmənt] n Verabredung f; Ernennung f

appreciate [ə'pri:ʃieit] v schätzen

appreciation [ə‚pri:ʃi'eiʃən] n Schätzung f

approach [ə'prout∫] v sich nähern; n Behandlungsweise f; Zugang m

appropriate [ə'proupriət] adj richtig, zweckmäßig, geeignet, angemessen

approval [ə'pru:vəl] n Billigung f; Zustimmung f, Einverständnis nt; on ~ zur Ansicht

approve [ə'pru:v] v genehmigen, bejahen; ~ of billigen

approximate [ə'prɔksimət] adj annähernd

approximately [ə'prɔksimətli] adv etwa, ungefähr

apricot ['eiprikɔt] n Aprikose f

April ['eiprəl] April

apron ['eiprən] n Schürze f

Arab ['ærəb] adj arabisch; n Araber m

arbitrary ['a:bitrəri] adj willkürlich

arcade [a:'keid] n Bogengang m, Arkade f

arch [a:t∫] n Bogen m; Gewölbe nt

archaeologist [‚a:ki'ɔlədʒist] n Archäologe m

archaeology [‚a:ki'ɔlədʒi] n Altertumskunde f, Archäologie f

archbishop [‚a:t∫'biʃəp] n Erzbischof m

arched [a:t∫t] adj bogenförmig

architect ['a:kitekt] n Architekt m

architecture ['a:kitekt∫ə] n Baukunst f, Architektur f

archives ['a:kaivz] pl Archiv nt

are [a:] v (pr be)

area ['εəriə] n Gegend f; Gebiet nt; Fläche f; ~ code Ortsnetzkennzahl f

Argentina [‚a:dʒən'ti:nə] Argentinien

Argentinian [‚a:dʒən'tiniən] adj argentinisch; n Argentinier m

argue ['a:gju:] v argumentieren, erörtern, diskutieren; *streiten

argument ['a:gjumənt] n Argument nt; Auseinandersetzung f; Wortwechsel m

arid ['ærid] adj dürr

*arise [ə'raiz] v sich *erheben, *entstehen

arithmetic [ə'riθmətik] n Rechnen nt

arm [a:m] n Arm m; Waffe f; Armlehne f; v bewaffnen

armchair ['a:mt∫εə] n Sessel m, Lehnstuhl m

armed [a:md] adj bewaffnet; ~ forces Streitkräfte pl

armour ['a:mə] n Rüstung f

army ['a:mi] n Armee f

aroma [ə'roumə] n Aroma nt

around [ə'raund] prep um, um ... herum; adv rundherum

arrange [ə'reindʒ] v ordnen; vorbereiten

arrangement [ə'reindʒmənt] n Regelung f

arrest [ə'rest] v verhaften; n Festnahme f, Verhaftung f

arrival [ə'raivəl] n Ankunft f; Eintreffen nt

arrive [ə'raiv] v *ankommen, *eintreffen

arrow ['ærou] n Pfeil m

art [ɑ:t] n Kunst f; Fertigkeit f; ~ collection Kunstsammlung f; ~ exhibition Kunstausstellung f; ~ gallery Kunstgalerie f; ~ history Kunstgeschichte f; arts and crafts Kunstgewerbe nt; ~ school Kunstakademie f

artery ['ɑ:təri] n Arterie f

artichoke ['ɑ:titʃouk] n Artischocke f

article ['ɑ:tikəl] n Gegenstand m; Artikel m

artifice ['ɑ:tifis] n List f

artificial [,ɑ:ti'fiʃəl] adj künstlich

artist ['ɑ:tist] n Künstler m; Künstlerin f

artistic [ɑ:'tistik] adj künstlerisch

as [æz] conj wie; ebenso; da, weil; ~ from von ... an; ab; ~ if als ob

asbestos [æz'bestəs] n Asbest m

ascend [ə'send] v *aufsteigen; *hinaufsteigen; *besteigen

ascent [ə'sent] n Steigung f; Aufstieg m

ascertain [,æsə'tein] v feststellen; sich vergewissern, ermitteln

ash [æʃ] n Asche f

ashamed [ə'ʃeimd] adj beschämt; *be ~ sich schämen

ashore [ə'ʃɔ:] adv ans Land, an Land

ashtray ['æʃtrei] n Aschenbecher m

Asia ['eiʃə] Asien

Asian ['eiʃən] adj asiatisch; n Asiate m

aside [ə'said] adv zur Seite, beiseite

ask [ɑ:sk] v fragen; *bitten; *einladen

asleep [ə'sli:p] adj im Schlaf

asparagus [ə'spærəgəs] n Spargel m

aspect ['æspekt] n Aspekt m

asphalt ['æsfælt] n Asphalt m

aspire [ə'spaiə] v streben

aspirin ['æspərin] n Aspirin nt

ass [æs] n Esel m

assassination [ə,sæsi'neiʃən] n Mord m

assault [ə'sɔ:lt] v *angreifen; vergewaltigen

assemble [ə'sembəl] v versammeln; zusammensetzen, montieren

assembly [ə'sembli] n Versammlung f, Zusammenkunft f

assignment [ə'sainmənt] n Zuweisung f

assign to [ə'sain] *zuweisen; zuschreiben

assist [ə'sist] v unterstützen, *helfen; ~ at beiwohnen

assistance [ə'sistəns] n Hilfe f; Unterstützung f, Beistand m

assistant [ə'sistənt] n Assistent m

associate [ə'souʃiət] n Partner m, Teilhaber m; Verbündete m; Mitglied nt; v assoziieren; ~ with *umgehen mit

association [ə,sousi'eiʃən] n Vereinigung f

assort [ə'sɔ:t] v sortieren

assortment [ə'sɔ:tmənt] n Auswahl f, Sortiment nt

assume [ə'sju:m] v *annehmen, voraussetzen

assure [ə'ʃuə] v versichern

asthma ['æsmə] n Asthma nt

astonish [ə'stɔniʃ] v verblüffen

astonishing [ə'stɔniʃiŋ] adj erstaunlich

astonishment [ə'stɔniʃmənt] n Erstaunen nt

astronomy [ə'strɔnəmi] n Astronomie f

asylum [ə'sailəm] n Asyl nt; Anstalt f,

Heim *nt*

at [æt] *prep* in, bei, auf; nach

ate [et] *v* (p eat)

atheist ['eiθiist] *n* Atheist *m*

athlete ['æθli:t] *n* Athlet *m*

athletics [æθ'letiks] *pl* Athletik *f*

Atlantic [ət'læntik] Atlantik *m*

atmosphere ['ætməsfiə] *n* Atmosphäre *f*; Stimmung *f*

atom ['ætəm] *n* Atom *nt*

atomic [ə'tɔmik] *adj* atomar; Atom-

atomizer ['ætəmaizə] *n* Zerstäuber *m*; Spray *nt*

attach [ə'tætʃ] *v* befestigen; anheften; beifügen; attached to zugetan

attack [ə'tæk] *v* *angreifen; *n* Angriff *m*

attain [ə'tein] *v* erreichen

attainable [ə'teinəbəl] *adj* erreichbar

attempt [ə'tempt] *v* probieren, versuchen; *n* Versuch *m*

attend [ə'tend] *v* beiwohnen; ~ on bedienen; ~ to sorgen für, sich beschäftigen mit; beachten, *achtgeben auf

attendance [ə'tendəns] *n* Teilnahme *f*

attendant [ə'tendənt] *n* Wärter *m*

attention [ə'tenʃən] *n* Aufmerksamkeit *f*; *pay ~ aufpassen

attentive [ə'tentiv] *adj* aufmerksam

attic ['ætik] *n* Boden *m*

attitude ['ætitju:d] *n* Einstellung *f*

attorney [ə'tə:ni] *n* Anwalt *m*

attract [ə'trækt] *v* *anziehen

attraction [ə'trækʃən] *n* Attraktion *f*; Anziehung *f*, Reiz *m*

attractive [ə'træktiv] *adj* anziehend

auburn ['ɔ:bən] *adj* kastanienbraun

auction ['ɔ:kʃən] *n* Versteigerung *f*

audible ['ɔ:dibəl] *adj* hörbar

audience ['ɔ:diəns] *n* Publikum *nt*

auditor ['ɔ:ditə] *n* Zuhörer *m*

auditorium [,ɔ:di'tɔ:riəm] *n* Zuhörerraum *m*

August ['ɔ:gəst] August

aunt [ɑ:nt] *n* Tante *f*

Australia [ə'streiliə] Australien

Australian [ə'streiliən] *adj* australisch; *n* Australier *m*

Austria ['ɔstriə] Österreich

Austrian ['ɔstriən] *adj* österreichisch; *n* Österreicher *m*

authentic [ɔ:'θentik] *adj* authentisch; echt

author ['ɔ:θə] *n* Verfasser *m*, Autor *m*

authoritarian [ɔ:,θɔri'teəriən] *adj* autoritär

authority [ɔ:'θɔrəti] *n* Befugnis *f*; Machtbefugnis *f*; authorities *pl* Behörde *f*

authorization [,ɔ:θərai'zeiʃən] *n* Ermächtigung *f*; Genehmigung *f*

automatic [,ɔ:tə'mætik] *adj* automatisch

automation [,ɔ:tə'meiʃən] *n* Automatisierung *f*

automobile [ɔ:'təməbi:l] *n* Auto *nt*; ~ club Automobilklub *m*

autonomous [ɔ:'tɔnəməs] *adj* autonom

autopsy ['ɔ:tɔpsi] *n* Autopsie *f*

autumn ['ɔ:təm] *n* Herbst *m*

available [ə'veiləbəl] *adj* vorrätig, vorhanden, verfügbar

avalanche ['ævəlɑ:nʃ] *n* Lawine *f*

avaricious [,ævə'riʃəs] *adj* geizig

avenue ['ævənju:] *n* Allee *f*

average ['ævəridʒ] *adj* durchschnittlich; *n* Durchschnitt *m*; on the ~ durchschnittlich

averse [ə'və:s] *adj* abgeneigt

aversion [ə'və:ʃən] *n* Widerwille *m*

avert [ə'və:t] *v* abwenden

avoid [ə'vɔid] *v* *vermeiden; *meiden

await [ə'weit] *v* warten auf, erwarten

awake [ə'weik] *adj* wach

*awake [ə'weik] *v* wecken

award [ə'wɔ:d] *n* Preis *m*; *v* *zuerkennen

aware [ə'wɛə] *adj* bewußt

away [ə'wei] *adv* weg; ***go ~** *weggehen

awful ['ɔ:fəl] *adj* furchtbar, schrecklich

awkward ['ɔ:kwəd] *adj* peinlich; ungeschickt

awning ['ɔ:niŋ] *n* Markise *f*

axe [æks] *n* Beil *nt*

axle ['æksəl] *n* Achse *f*

B

baby ['beibi] *n* Baby *nt*; **~ carriage** *Am* Kinderwagen *m*

babysitter ['beibi,sitə] *n* Babysitter *m*

bachelor ['bætʃələ] *n* Junggeselle *m*

back [bæk] *n* Rücken *m*; *adv* zurück; ***go ~** *zurückgehen

backache ['bækeik] *n* Rückenschmerzen *mpl*

backbone ['bækboun] *n* Rückgrat *nt*

background ['bækgraund] *n* Hintergrund *m*; Vorbildung *f*

backwards ['bækwədz] *adv* rückwärts

bacon ['beikən] *n* Speck *m*

bacterium [bæk'ti:riəm] *n* (pl -ria) Bakterie *f*

bad [bæd] *adj* schlecht; ernsthaft, schlimm; ungezogen

bag [bæg] *n* Sack *m*; Tasche *f*, Handtasche *f*; Koffer *m*

baggage ['bægidʒ] *n* Gepäck *nt*; **~ deposit office** *Am* Gepäckaufbewahrung *f*; **hand ~** *Am* Handgepäck *nt*

bail [beil] *n* Kaution *f*

bailiff ['beilif] *n* Gerichtsvollzieher *m*

bait [beit] *n* Köder *m*

bake [beik] *v* backen

baker ['beikə] *n* Bäcker *m*

bakery ['beikəri] *n* Bäckerei *f*

balance ['bæləns] *n* Gleichgewicht *nt*; Bilanz *f*; Saldo *m*

balcony ['bælkəni] *n* Balkon *m*

bald [bɔ:ld] *adj* kahl

ball [bɔ:l] *n* Ball *m*

ballet ['bælei] *n* Ballett *nt*

balloon [bə'lu:n] *n* Ballon *m*

ballpoint-pen ['bɔ:lpɔintpen] *n* Kugelschreiber *m*

ballroom ['bɔ:lru:m] *n* Ballsaal *m*

bamboo [bæm'bu:] *n* (pl ~s) Bambus *m*

banana [bə'nɑ:nə] *n* Banane *f*

band [bænd] *n* Kapelle *f*; Band *nt*

bandage ['bændidʒ] *n* Verband *m*

bandit ['bændit] *n* Bandit *m*

bangle ['bæŋgəl] *n* Armreif *m*

banisters ['bænistəz] *pl* Treppengeländer *nt*

bank [bæŋk] *n* Ufer *nt*; Bank *f*; *v* deponieren; **~ account** Bankkonto *nt*

banknote ['bæŋknout] *n* Banknote *f*

bank-rate ['bæŋkreit] *n* Diskontsatz *m*

bankrupt ['bæŋkrʌpt] *adj* zahlungsunfähig, bankrott

banner ['bænə] *n* Banner *nt*

banquet ['bæŋkwit] *n* Festmahl *nt*

banqueting-hall ['bæŋkwitiŋhɔ:l] *n* Bankettsaal *m*

baptism ['bæptizəm] *n* Taufe *f*

baptize [bæp'taiz] *v* taufen

bar [bɑ:] *n* Bar *f*; Stange *f*

barber ['bɑ:bə] *n* Friseur *m*

bare [bɛə] *adj* nackt, bloß; kahl

barely ['bɛəli] *adv* kaum

bargain ['bɑ:gin] *n* Gelegenheitskauf *m*; *v* handeln

baritone ['bæritoun] *n* Bariton *m*

bark [bɑ:k] *n* Rinde *f*; *v* bellen

barley ['bɑ:li] *n* Gerste *f*

barmaid ['bɑ:meid] *n* Bardame *f*

barman ['bɑ:mən] *n* (pl -men) Kellner *m*

barn [bɑ:n] *n* Scheune *f*

barometer [bə'rɔmitə] *n* Barometer *nt*

baroque [bə'rɔk] *adj* barock

barracks ['bærəks] *pl* Kaserne *f*

barrel ['bærəl] *n* Tonne *f*, Faß *nt*

barrier ['bæriə] *n* Schranke *f*

barrister ['bæristə] *n* Rechtsanwalt *m*

bartender ['bɑː,tendə] *n* Kellner *m*

base [beis] *n* Basis *f*; Grundlage *f*; *v* gründen

baseball ['beisbɔːl] *n* Baseball *m*

basement ['beismənt] *n* Untergeschoß *nt*

basic ['beisik] *adj* grundlegend

basilica [bə'zilikə] *n* Basilika *f*

basin ['beisən] *n* Schüssel *f*, Becken *nt*

basis ['beisis] *n* (pl bases) Grundlage *f*, Basis *f*

basket ['bɑːskit] *n* Korb *m*

bass[1] [beis] *n* Baß *m*

bass[2] [bæs] *n* (pl ~) Barsch *m*

bastard ['bɑːstəd] *n* Bastard *m*; Schuft *m*

batch [bætʃ] *n* Partie *f*

bath [bɑːθ] *n* Bad *nt*; ~ **salts** Badesalz *nt*; ~ **towel** Badetuch *nt*

bathe [beið] *v* baden

bathing-cap ['beiðiŋkæp] *n* Bademütze *f*

bathing-suit ['beiðiŋsuːt] *n* Badeanzug *m*; Badehose *f*

bathing-trunks ['beiðiŋtrʌŋks] *n* Badehose *f*

bathrobe ['bɑːθroub] *n* Bademantel *m*

bathroom ['bɑːθruːm] *n* Badezimmer *nt*; Toilettenraum *m*

batter ['bætə] *n* Teig *m*

battery ['bætəri] *n* Batterie *f*; Akku *m*

battle ['bætəl] *n* Schlacht *f*; Streit *m*, Kampf *m*; *v* kämpfen

bay [bei] *n* Bucht *f*; *v* bellen

* **be** [biː] *v* *sein

beach [biːtʃ] *n* Strand *m*; **nudist ~** FKK-Strand *m*

bead [biːd] *n* Perle *f*; **beads** *pl* Halsband *nt*; Rosenkranz *m*

beak [biːk] *n* Schnabel *m*

beam [biːm] *n* Strahl *m*; Balken *m*

bean [biːn] *n* Bohne *f*

bear [bɛə] *n* Bär *m*

* **bear** [bɛə] *v* *tragen; dulden; *ertragen

beard [biəd] *n* Bart *m*

bearer ['bɛərə] *n* Inhaber *m*

beast [biːst] *n* Tier *nt*; ~ **of prey** Raubtier *nt*

* **beat** [biːt] *v* *schlagen; besiegen

beautiful ['bjuːtifəl] *adj* schön

beauty ['bjuːti] *n* Schönheit *f*; ~ **parlour** Schönheitssalon *m*; ~ **salon** Schönheitssalon *m*; ~ **treatment** kosmetische Behandlung

beaver ['biːvə] *n* Biber *m*

because [bi'kɔz] *conj* weil; da; ~ **of** aufgrund, wegen

* **become** [bi'kʌm] *v* *werden; gut *stehen

bed [bed] *n* Bett *nt*; ~ **and board** Vollpension *f*; ~ **and breakfast** Zimmer mit Frühstück

bedding ['bediŋ] *n* Bettzeug *nt*

bedroom ['bedruːm] *n* Schlafzimmer *nt*

bee [biː] *n* Biene *f*

beech [biːtʃ] *n* Buche *f*

beef [biːf] *n* Rindfleisch *nt*

beehive ['biːhaiv] *n* Bienenkorb *m*

been [biːn] *v* (pp be)

beer [biə] *n* Bier *nt*

beet [biːt] *n* Rübe *f*

beetle ['biːtəl] *n* Käfer *m*

beetroot ['biːtruːt] *n* Bete *f*

before [bi'fɔː] *prep* vor; *conj* bevor; *adv* vorher; eher, zuvor

beg [beg] *v* betteln; anflehen; *bitten

beggar ['begə] *n* Bettler *m*

* **begin** [bi'gin] *v* *beginnen; *anfangen

beginner [bi'ginə] *n* Anfänger *m*

beginning [bi'giniŋ] n Beginn m; Anfang m

on behalf of [ɔn bi'haːf ɔv] im Namen von; zugunsten

behave [bi'heiv] v sich *benehmen

behaviour [bi'heivjə] n Betragen nt

behind [bi'haind] prep hinter; adv hinten

beige [beiʒ] adj beige

being ['biːiŋ] n Wesen nt

Belgian ['beldʒən] adj belgisch; n Belgier m

Belgium ['beldʒəm] Belgien

belief [bi'liːf] n Glaube m

believe [bi'liːv] v glauben

bell [bel] n Glocke f; Klingel f

bellboy ['belbɔi] n Hotelpage m

belly ['beli] n Bauch m

belong [bi'lɔŋ] v gehören

belongings [bi'lɔŋiŋz] pl Habe f

beloved [bi'lʌvd] adj geliebt

below [bi'lou] prep unterhalb; unter; adv unten

belt [belt] n Gürtel m; **garter** ~ Am Hüfthalter m

bench [bentʃ] n Bank f

bend [bend] n Kurve f, Biegung f; Krümmung f

*bend [bend] v *biegen; ~ **down** sich bücken

beneath [bi'niːθ] prep unter; adv unten

benefit ['benifit] n Gewinn m, Nutzen m; Vorteil m; v profitieren

bent [bent] adj (pp bend) krumm

beret ['berei] n Baskenmütze f

berry ['beri] n Beere f

berth [bəːθ] n Schlafwagenbett nt; Koje f

beside [bi'said] prep neben

besides [bi'saidz] adv überdies; übrigens; prep außer

best [best] adj best

bet [bet] n Wette f; Einsatz m

*bet [bet] v wetten

betray [bi'trei] v *verraten

better ['betə] adj besser

between [bi'twiːn] prep zwischen

beverage ['bevəridʒ] n Getränk nt

beware [bi'weə] v sich in Acht *nehmen, sich hüten

bewitch [bi'witʃ] v behexen, verzaubern

beyond [bi'jɔnd] prep über ... hinaus; jenseits; außer; adv jenseits

bible ['baibəl] n Bibel f

bicycle ['baisikəl] n Fahrrad nt; Rad nt

big [big] adj groß; umfangreich; dick; bedeutend

bile [bail] n Galle f

bilingual [bai'liŋgwəl] adj zweisprachig

bill [bil] n Rechnung f; v fakturieren

billiards ['biljədz] pl Billard nt

*bind [baind] v *binden

binding ['baindiŋ] n Einband m

binoculars [bi'nɔkjələz] pl Feldstecher m; Opernglas nt

biology [bai'ɔlədʒi] n Biologie f

birch [bəːtʃ] n Birke f

bird [bəːd] n Vogel m

Biro ['bairou] n Kugelschreiber m

birth [bəːθ] n Geburt f

birthday ['bəːθdei] n Geburtstag m

biscuit ['biskit] n Keks m

bishop ['biʃəp] n Bischof m

bit [bit] n Stückchen n; bißchen

bitch [bitʃ] n Hündin f

bite [bait] n Bissen m; Biß m; Stich m

*bite [bait] v *beißen

bitter ['bitə] adj bitter

black [blæk] adj schwarz; ~ **market** Schwarzmarkt m

blackberry ['blækbəri] n Brombeere f

blackbird ['blækbəːd] n Amsel f

blackboard ['blækbɔːd] n Wandtafel f

black-currant [ˌblæk'kʌrənt] n Johannisbeere f

blackmail ['blækmeil] n Erpressung f; v erpressen

blacksmith ['blæksmiθ] n Schmied m

bladder ['blædə] n Blase f

blade [bleid] n Klinge f; ~ **of grass** Grashalm m

blame [bleim] n Schuld f; Vorwurf m; v *vorwerfen, beschuldigen

blank [blæŋk] adj leer

blanket ['blæŋkit] n Decke f

blast [bla:st] n Explosion f

blazer ['bleizə] n Sportjacke f, Blazer m

bleach [bli:tʃ] v bleichen

bleak [bli:k] adj rauh

*****bleed** [bli:d] v bluten; aussaugen

bless [bles] v segnen

blessing ['blesiŋ] n Segen m

blind [blaind] n Jalousie f; adj blind; v blenden

blister ['blistə] n Blase f

blizzard ['blizəd] n Schneesturm m

block [blɔk] v versperren, blockieren, sperren; n Klotz m; ~ **of flats** Wohnblock m

blonde [blɔnd] n Blondine f

blood [blʌd] n Blut nt; ~ **pressure** Blutdruck m

blood-poisoning ['blʌd,pɔizəniŋ] n Blutvergiftung f

blood-vessel ['blʌd,vesəl] n Blutgefäß nt

blot [blɔt] n Klecks m; Makel m; **blotting paper** Löschpapier nt

blouse [blauz] n Bluse f

blow [blou] n Schlag m; Windstoß m

*****blow** [blou] v *blasen; wehen

blow-out ['blouaut] n Reifenpanne f

blue [blu:] adj blau; niedergeschlagen

blunt [blʌnt] adj stumpf

blush [blʌʃ] v erröten

board [bɔ:d] n Brett nt; Tafel; Pension f; Rat m; ~ **and lodging** Voll-

pension f

boarder ['bɔ:də] n Kostgänger m

boarding-house ['bɔ:diŋhaus] n Pension f

boarding-school ['bɔ:diŋsku:l] n Internat nt

boast [boust] v prahlen

boat [bout] n Schiff nt, Boot nt

body ['bɔdi] n Körper m; Leib m

bodyguard ['bɔdiga:d] n Leibwache f

bog [bɔg] n Sumpf m

boil [bɔil] v kochen; n Furunkel m

bold [bould] adj kühn; frech

Bolivia [bə'liviə] Bolivien

Bolivian [bə'liviən] adj bolivianisch; n Bolivianer m

bolt [boult] n Riegel m; Bolzen m

bomb [bɔm] n Bombe f; v bombardieren

bond [bɔnd] n Obligation f

bone [boun] n Bein nt, Knochen m; Gräte f; v entbeinen

bonnet ['bɔnit] n Motorhaube f

book [buk] n Buch nt; v reservieren, buchen; *einschreiben, *eintragen

booking ['bukiŋ] n Einschreibung f, Reservierung f

bookseller ['buk,selə] n Buchhändler m

bookstand ['bukstænd] n Bücherstand m

bookstore ['bukstɔ:] n Buchladen m, Buchhandlung f

boot [bu:t] n Stiefel m; Kofferraum m

booth [bu:ð] n Bude f; Zelle f

border ['bɔ:də] n Grenze f; Rand m

bore¹ [bɔ:] v langweilen; bohren; n Langweiler m

bore² [bɔ:] v (p bear)

boring ['bɔ:riŋ] adj langweilig

born [bɔ:n] adj geboren

borrow ['bɔrou] v borgen; *entleihen

bosom ['buzəm] n Brust f; Busen m

boss [bɔs] n Chef m

botany ['bɔtəni] n Botanik f

both [bouθ] adj beide; **both ... and** sowohl ... als auch

bother ['bɔðə] v belästigen; sich Mühe *geben; n Belästigung f

bottle ['bɔtl] n Flasche f; ~ **opener** Flaschenöffner m; **hot-water** ~ Wärmflasche f

bottleneck ['bɔtlnek] n Engpaß m

bottom ['bɔtəm] n Boden m; Hintern m, Gesäß nt; adj unterst

bough [bau] n Ast m

bought [bɔ:t] v (p, pp buy)

boulder ['bouldə] n Felsblock m

bound [baund] n Grenze f; *be ~ to *müssen; ~ **for** unterwegs nach

boundary ['baundəri] n Grenze f; Landesgrenze f

bouquet [bu'kei] n Strauß m

bourgeois ['buəʒwa:] adj spießbürgerlich

boutique [bu'ti:k] n Boutique f

bow[1] [bau] v beugen

bow[2] [bou] n Bogen m; ~ **tie** Fliege f

bowels [bauəlz] pl Därme, Eingeweide pl

bowl [boul] n Schale f

bowling ['bouliŋ] n Bowling nt, Kegeln nt; ~ **alley** Kegelbahn f

box[1] [bɔks] v boxen; **boxing match** Boxkampf m

box[2] [bɔks] n Schachtel f

box-office ['bɔks,ɔfis] n Vorverkaufskasse f, Kasse f

boy [bɔi] n Junge m; Bursche m, Bub m; Diener m; ~ **scout** Pfadfinder m

bra [bra:] n BH m, Büstenhalter m

bracelet ['breislit] n Armband nt

braces ['breisiz] pl Hosenträger mpl

brain [brein] n Gehirn nt; Verstand m

brain-wave ['breinweiv] n Geistesblitz m

brake [breik] n Bremse f; ~ **drum** Bremstrommel f; ~ **lights** Bremslichter ntpl

branch [bra:ntʃ] n Ast m; Zweigstelle f

brand [brænd] n Marke f; Brandmarke f

brand-new [,brænd'nju:] adj nagelneu

brass [bra:s] n Messing nt; ~ **band** n Blaskapelle f

brassiere ['bræziə] n Beha m, Büstenhalter m

brassware ['bra:sweə] n Messingwaren fpl

brave [breiv] adj mutig, tapfer; beherzt

Brazil [brə'zil] Brasilien

Brazilian [brə'ziljən] adj brasilianisch; n Brasilianer m

breach [bri:tʃ] n Bresche f

bread [bred] n Brot nt; **wholemeal** ~ Vollkornbrot nt

breadth [bredθ] n Breite f

break [breik] n Bruch m; Pause f

*break** [breik] v *brechen; ~ **down** eine Panne *haben; aufgliedern

breakdown ['breikdaun] n Betriebsstörung f, Panne f

breakfast ['brekfəst] n Frühstück nt

bream [bri:m] n (pl ~) Brassen m

breast [brest] n Brust f

breaststroke ['breststrouk] n Brustschwimmen nt

breath [breθ] n Atem m; Luft f

breathe [bri:ð] v atmen

breathing ['bri:ðiŋ] n Atmung f

breed [bri:d] n Rasse f; Gattung f

*breed** [bri:d] v züchten

breeze [bri:z] n Brise f

brew [bru:] v brauen

brewery ['bru:əri] n Brauerei f

bribe [braib] v *bestechen

bribery ['braibəri] n Bestechung f

brick [brik] n Ziegelstein m, Ziegel m

bricklayer ['brikleiə] *n* Maurer *m*

bride [braid] *n* Braut *f*

bridegroom ['braidgru:m] *n* Bräutigam *m*

bridge [bridʒ] *n* Brücke *f*; Bridge *nt*

brief [bri:f] *adj* kurz; bündig

briefcase ['bri:fkeis] *n* Aktentasche *f*

briefs [bri:fs] *pl* Slip *m*, Unterhose *f*

bright [brait] *adj* hell; leuchtend; schlau, klug

brill [bril] *n* Glattbutt *m*

brilliant ['briljənt] *adj* glänzend; brillant

brim [brim] *n* Rand *m*

***bring** [briŋ] *v* *bringen; *mitbringen; ~ **back** *zurückbringen; ~ **up** *erziehen, *großziehen; *vorbringen

brisk [brisk] *adj* lebhaft

Britain ['britən] England

British ['britiʃ] *adj* britisch; englisch

Briton ['britən] *n* Brite *m*; Engländer *m*

broad [brɔ:d] *adj* breit; ausgedehnt, weit; global

broadcast ['brɔ:dka:st] *n* Sendung *f*

***broadcast** ['brɔ:dka:st] *v* *senden

brochure ['brouʃuə] *n* Broschüre *f*

broke¹ [brouk] *v* (p break)

broke² [brouk] *adj* blank

broken ['broukən] *adj* (pp break) kaputt, entzwei

broker ['broukə] *n* Makler *m*

bronchitis [brɔŋ'kaitis] *n* Bronchitis *f*

bronze [brɔnz] *n* Bronze *f*; *adj* bronzen

brooch [broutʃ] *n* Brosche *f*

brook [bruk] *n* Bach *m*

broom [bru:m] *n* Besen *m*

brothel ['brɔθəl] *n* Bordell *nt*

brother ['brʌðə] *n* Bruder *m*

brother-in-law ['brʌðərinlɔ:] *n* (pl brothers-) Schwager *m*

brought [brɔ:t] *v* (p, pp bring)

brown [braun] *adj* braun

bruise [bru:z] *n* blauer Fleck, Quetschung *f*; *v* quetschen

brunette [bru:'net] *n* Brünette *f*

brush [brʌʃ] *n* Bürste *f*; Pinsel *m*; *v* putzen, bürsten

brutal ['bru:təl] *adj* brutal

bubble ['bʌbəl] *n* Blase *f*

bucket ['bʌkit] *n* Eimer *m*

buckle ['bʌkəl] *n* Schnalle *f*

bud [bʌd] *n* Knospe *f*

budget ['bʌdʒit] *n* Voranschlag *m*, Budget *nt*

buffet ['bufei] *n* Büfett *nt*

bug [bʌg] *n* Wanze *f*; Käfer *m*; *nAm* Insekt *nt*

***build** [bild] *v* bauen

building ['bildiŋ] *n* Gebäude *nt*

bulb [bʌlb] *n* Zwiebel *f*; Blumenzwiebel *f*; **light** ~ Glühbirne *f*

Bulgaria [bʌl'gɛəriə] Bulgarien

Bulgarian [bʌl'gɛəriən] *adj* bulgarisch; *n* Bulgare *m*

bulk [bʌlk] *n* Umfang *m*; Masse *f*; Mehrheit *f*

bulky ['bʌlki] *adj* dick, umfangreich

bull [bul] *n* Stier *m*

bullet ['bulit] *n* Kugel *f*

bullfight ['bulfait] *n* Stierkampf *m*

bullring ['bulriŋ] *n* Stierkampfarena *f*

bump [bʌmp] *v* *stoßen; *zusammenstoßen; *schlagen; *n* Schlag *m*, Stoß *m*

bumper ['bʌmpə] *n* Stoßstange *f*

bumpy ['bʌmpi] *adj* holperig

bun [bʌn] *n* Brötchen *nt*

bunch [bʌntʃ] *n* Strauß *m*; Haufen *m*

bundle ['bʌndəl] *n* Bündel *nt*; *v* *zusammenbinden, bündeln

bunk [bʌŋk] *n* Koje *f*

buoy [bɔi] *n* Boje *f*

burden ['bə:dən] *n* Last *f*

bureau ['bjuərou] *n* (pl ~x, ~s) Schreibtisch *m*; *nAm* Kommode *f*

bureaucracy [bjuə'rɔkrəsi] *n* Bürokratie *f*
burglar ['bə:glə] *n* Einbrecher *m*
burgle ['bə:gəl] *v* *einbrechen
burial ['beriəl] *n* Bestattung *f*, Begräbnis *nt*
burn [bə:n] *n* Brandwunde *f*
*****burn** [bə:n] *v* *brennen; *verbrennen; *anbrennen
*****burst** [bə:st] *v* *bersten
bury ['beri] *v* beerdigen; *begraben
bus [bʌs] *n* Bus *m*
bush [buʃ] *n* Busch *m*
business ['biznəs] *n* Handel *m*, Gewerbe *nt*; Unternehmen *nt*, Geschäft *nt*; Beschäftigung *f*; Angelegenheit *f*; ~ **hours** Öffnungszeiten *fpl*, Geschäftszeit *f*; ~ **trip** Geschäftsreise *f*; **on** ~ geschäftlich
business-like ['biznislaik] *adj* geschäftsmäßig
businessman ['biznəsmən] *n* (pl -men) Geschäftsmann *m*
bust [bʌst] *n* Büste *f*
bustle ['bʌsəl] *n* Geschäftigkeit *f*
busy ['bizi] *adj* beschäftigt; verkehrsreich
but [bʌt] *conj* aber; jedoch; *prep* außer
butcher ['butʃə] *n* Fleischer *m*
butter ['bʌtə] *n* Butter *f*
butterfly ['bʌtəflai] *n* Schmetterling *m*; ~ **stroke** Schmetterlingsstil *m*
buttock ['bʌtək] *n* Hinterbacke *f*
button ['bʌtən] *n* Knopf *m*; *v* knöpfen
buttonhole ['bʌtənhoul] *n* Knopfloch *nt*
*****buy** [bai] *v* kaufen; *erwerben
buyer ['baiə] *n* Käufer *m*
by [bai] *prep* von, durch; mit; bei
by-pass ['baipɑ:s] *n* Umgehungsstraße *f*; *v* *umgehen

C

cab [kæb] *n* Taxi *nt*
cabaret ['kæbərei] *n* Kabarett *nt*; Nachtklub *m*
cabbage ['kæbidʒ] *n* Kohl *m*
cab-driver ['kæb,draivə] *n* Taxifahrer *m*
cabin ['kæbin] *n* Kabine *f*; Hütte *f*; Umkleidekabine *f*; Kajüte *f*
cabinet ['kæbinət] *n* Kabinett *nt*
cable ['keibəl] *n* Kabel *nt*; Telegramm *nt*; *v* telegraphieren
cadre ['kɑ:də] *n* Kader *m*
café ['kæfei] *n* Café *nt*
cafeteria [,kæfə'tiəriə] *n* Selbstbedienungsrestaurant *nt*
caffeine ['kæfi:n] *n* Koffein *nt*
cage [keidʒ] *n* Käfig *m*
cake [keik] *n* Kuchen *m*; Torte *f*, Gebäck *nt*
calamity [kə'læməti] *n* Unglück *nt*, Kalamität *f*
calcium ['kælsiəm] *n* Kalzium *nt*
calculate ['kælkjuleit] *v* berechnen, ausrechnen
calculation [,kælkju'leiʃən] *n* Kalkulation *f*
calendar ['kæləndə] *n* Kalender *m*
calf [kɑ:f] *n* (pl calves) Kalb *nt*; Wade *f*; ~ **skin** Kalbleder *nt*
call [kɔ:l] *v* *rufen; *nennen; *anrufen; *n* Ruf *m*; Besuch *m*; Anruf *m*; *****be called** *heißen; ~ **names** ausschimpfen; ~ **on** besuchen; ~ **up** *Am* *anrufen
callus ['kæləs] *n* Schwiele *f*
calm [kɑ:m] *adj* ruhig, still; ~ **down** beruhigen
calorie ['kæləri] *n* Kalorie *f*
Calvinism ['kælvinizəm] *n* Kalvinismus *m*

came [keim] v (p come)

camel ['kæməl] n Kamel nt

cameo ['kæmiou] n (pl ~s) Kamee f

camera ['kæmərə] n Kamera f; ~ shop Photogeschäft nt

camp [kæmp] n Lager nt; v zelten

campaign [kæm'pein] n Kampagne f

camp-bed [,kæmp'bed] n Liege f, Feldbett nt

camper ['kæmpə] n Camper m

camping ['kæmpiŋ] n Camping nt; ~ site Zeltplatz m, Campingplatz m

camshaft ['kæmʃɑ:ft] n Nockenwelle f

can [kæn] n Büchse f; ~ opener Büchsenöffner m

*can [kæn] v *können

Canada ['kænədə] Kanada

Canadian [kə'neidiən] adj kanadisch; n Kanadier m

canal [kə'næl] n Kanal m

canary [kə'nɛəri] n Kanarienvogel m

cancel ['kænsəl] v annullieren; *widerrufen

cancellation [,kænsə'leiʃən] n Annullierung f

cancer ['kænsə] n Krebs m

candelabrum [,kændə'lɑ:brəm] n (pl -bra) Armleuchter m

candidate ['kændidət] n Kandidat m, Bewerber m

candle ['kændəl] n Kerze f

candy ['kændi] nAm Bonbon m; Süßigkeiten fpl, Nascherei f; ~ store Am Süßwarengeschäft nt

cane [kein] n Rohr nt; Stock m

canister ['kænistə] n Dose f

canoe [kə'nu:] n Kanu nt

canteen [kæn'ti:n] n Kantine f

canvas ['kænvəs] n Segeltuch nt

cap [kæp] n Mütze f

capable ['keipəbəl] adj tüchtig, fähig

capacity [kə'pæsəti] n Fähigkeit f; Leistungsfähigkeit f; Kompetenz f

cape [keip] n Umhang m; Kap nt

capital ['kæpitəl] n Hauptstadt f; Kapital nt; adj bedeutend, Haupt-; ~ letter Großbuchstabe m

capitalism ['kæpitəlizəm] n Kapitalismus m

capitulation [kə,pitju'leiʃən] n Kapitulation f

capsule ['kæpsju:l] n Kapsel f

captain ['kæptin] n Kapitän m; Flugkapitän m

capture ['kæptʃə] v *gefangennehmen, *fangen; *einnehmen; n Festnahme f; Einnahme f

car [kɑ:] n Wagen m; ~ hire Autovermietung f; ~ park Parkplatz m; ~ rental Am Autovermietung f

carafe [kə'ræf] n Karaffe f

caramel ['kærəməl] n Karamelle f

carat ['kærət] n Karat nt

caravan ['kærəvæn] n Wohnwagen m

carburettor [,kɑ:bju'retə] n Vergaser m

card [kɑ:d] n Karte f; Postkarte f

cardboard ['kɑ:dbɔ:d] n Pappe f; adj Papp-

cardigan ['kɑ:digən] n Wolljacke f

cardinal ['kɑ:dinəl] n Kardinal m; adj Kardinal-, hauptsächlich

care [kɛə] n Pflege f; Sorge f; ~ about sich sorgen um; ~ for gern *haben; *take ~ of sorgen für, sich kümmern um

career [kə'riə] n Laufbahn f, Karriere f

carefree ['kɛəfri:] adj unbekümmert

careful ['kɛəfəl] adj vorsichtig; sorgfältig, genau

careless ['kɛələs] adj gedankenlos, nachlässig

caretaker ['kɛə,teikə] n Hausmeister m

cargo ['kɑ:gou] n (pl ~es) Ladung f, Fracht f

carnival ['kɑ:nivəl] n Karneval m

carp [kɑ:p] n (pl ~) Karpfen m

carpenter ['ka:pintə] n Tischler m

carpet ['ka:pit] n Teppich m

carriage ['kæridʒ] n Wagen m; Kutsche f

carriageway ['kæridʒwei] n Fahrbahn f

carrot ['kærət] n Mohrrübe f, Karotte f

carry ['kæri] v *tragen; führen; ~ on verfolgen; *fortfahren; ~ out durchführen

carry-cot ['kærikɔt] n Baby-Tragetasche f

cart [ka:t] n Karren m, Wagen m

cartilage ['ka:tilidʒ] n Knorpel m

carton ['ka:tən] n Karton m; Stange f

cartoon [ka:'tu:n] n Zeichentrickfilm m

cartridge ['ka:tridʒ] n Patrone f

carve [ka:v] v zerlegen; einkerben, schnitzen

carving ['ka:viŋ] n Schnitzerei f

case [keis] n Fall m; Koffer m; Etui nt; attaché ~ Aktentasche f; in ~ falls; in ~ of im Fall

cash [kæʃ] n Bargeld nt; v zu Gelde machen, *einnehmen, einkassieren

cashier [kæ'ʃiə] n Kassierer m; Kassiererin f

cashmere ['kæʃmiə] n Kaschmir m

casino [kə'si:nou] n (pl ~s) Kasino nt

cask [ka:sk] n Tonne f, Faß nt

cast [ka:st] n Wurf m

*cast [ka:st] v *werfen; cast iron Gußeisen nt

castle ['ka:səl] n Schloß nt, Burg f

casual ['kæʒuəl] adj zwanglos; beiläufig, zufällig

casualty ['kæʒuəlti] n Opfer nt

cat [kæt] n Katze f

catacomb ['kætəkoum] n Katakombe f

catalogue ['kætəlɔg] n Katalog m

catarrh [kə'ta:] n Katarrh m

catastrophe [kə'tæstrəfi] n Katastrophe f

*catch [kætʃ] v *fangen; *ergreifen; erwischen; *nehmen, erreichen

category ['kætigəri] n Kategorie f

cathedral [kə'θi:drəl] n Dom m, Kathedrale f

catholic ['kæθəlik] adj katholisch

cattle ['kætəl] pl Vieh nt

caught [kɔ:t] v (p, pp catch)

cauliflower ['kɔliflauə] n Blumenkohl m

cause [kɔ:z] v verursachen; anrichten; n Ursache f; Grund m, Anlaß m; Sache f; ~ to machen

causeway ['kɔ:zwei] n Chaussee f

caution ['kɔ:ʃən] n Vorsicht f; v warnen

cautious ['kɔ:ʃəs] adj vorsichtig

cave [keiv] n Höhle f; Riß m

cavern ['kævən] n Höhle f

caviar ['kævia:] n Kaviar m

cavity ['kævəti] n Höhlung f

cease [si:s] v aufhören

ceiling ['si:liŋ] n Decke f

celebrate ['selibreit] v feiern

celebration [,seli'breiʃən] n Feier f

celebrity [si'lebrəti] n Ruhm m

celery ['seləri] n Sellerie m

celibacy ['selibəsi] n Zölibat nt

cell [sel] n Zelle f

cellar ['selə] n Keller m

cellophane ['seləfein] n Zellophan nt

cement [si'ment] n Zement m

cemetery ['semitri] n Friedhof m

censorship ['sensəʃip] n Zensur f

centigrade ['sentigreid] adj Celsius

centimetre ['sentimi:tə] n Zentimeter m

central ['sentrəl] adj zentral; ~ heating Zentralheizung f; ~ station Hauptbahnhof m

centralize ['sentrəlaiz] v zentralisieren

centre ['sentə] n Zentrum nt; Mittelpunkt m

century ['sentʃəri] n Jahrhundert nt
ceramics [si'ræmiks] pl Töpferware f, Keramik f
ceremony ['serəməni] n Feierlichkeit f
certain ['sə:tən] adj bestimmt; gewiß
certificate [sə'tifikət] n Bescheinigung f; Attest nt, Urkunde f, Diplom nt, Zeugnis nt
chain [tʃein] n Kette f
chair [tʃeə] n Stuhl m; Sessel m
chairman ['tʃeəmən] n (pl -men) Vorsitzende m
chalet ['ʃælei] n Chalet nt
chalk [tʃɔ:k] n Kreide f
challenge ['tʃæləndʒ] v herausfordern; n Herausforderung f
chamber ['tʃeimbə] n Zimmer nt
chambermaid ['tʃeimbəmeid] n Zimmermädchen nt
champagne [ʃæm'pein] n Sekt m
champion ['tʃæmpjən] n Meister m; Verfechter m
chance [tʃa:ns] n Zufall m; Chance f, Gelegenheit f; Risiko nt; by ~ zufällig
change [tʃeindʒ] v abändern, ändern; wechseln; sich *umziehen; *umsteigen; n Änderung f; Kleingeld nt, Wechselgeld nt
channel ['tʃænəl] n Kanal m; English Channel Ärmelkanal m
chaos ['keiɔs] n Chaos nt
chaotic [kei'ɔtik] adj chaotisch
chap [tʃæp] n Kerl m
chapel ['tʃæpəl] n Kirche f, Kapelle f
chaplain ['tʃæplin] n Kaplan m
character ['kærəktə] n Charakter m
characteristic [,kærəktə'ristik] adj bezeichnend, charakteristisch; n Kennzeichen nt; Charakterzug m
characterize ['kærəktəraiz] v charakterisieren
charcoal ['tʃa:koul] n Holzkohle f
charge [tʃa:dʒ] v verlangen; belasten;

anklagen; *laden; n Gebühr f; Belastung f, Ladung f, Last f; Anklage f; ~ plate Am Kreditkarte f; free of ~ unentgeltlich; in ~ of beauftragt mit; *take ~ of *übernehmen
charity ['tʃærəti] n Wohltätigkeit f
charm [tʃa:m] n Liebreiz m, Scharm m; Amulett nt
charming ['tʃa:miŋ] adj charmant
chart [tʃa:t] n Tabelle f; Diagramm nt; Seekarte f; conversion ~ Umrechnungstabelle f
chase [tʃeis] v verfolgen; *vertreiben, verjagen; n Jagd f
chasm ['kæzəm] n Spalt m
chassis ['ʃæsi] n (pl ~) Fahrgestell nt
chaste [tʃeist] adj keusch
chat [tʃæt] v plaudern, schwatzen; n Geschwätz nt, Geplauder nt
chatterbox ['tʃætəbɔks] n Plappermaul nt
chauffeur ['ʃoufə] n Chauffeur m
cheap [tʃi:p] adj billig; vorteilhaft
cheat [tʃi:t] v *betrügen; beschwindeln
check [tʃek] v kontrollieren, prüfen; n Karo nt; nAm Rechnung f; Scheck m; check! Schach!; ~ in sich anmelden; ~ out sich abmelden
check-book ['tʃekbuk] nAm Scheckbuch nt
checkerboard ['tʃekəbɔ:d] nAm Schachbrett nt
checkers ['tʃekəz] plAm Damespiel nt
checkroom ['tʃekru:m] nAm Garderobe f
check-up ['tʃekʌp] n Untersuchung f
cheek [tʃi:k] n Wange f
cheek-bone ['tʃi:kboun] n Backenknochen m
cheer [tʃiə] v zujubeln; ~ up aufheitern
cheerful ['tʃiəfəl] adj fröhlich, heiter

cheese [tʃi:z] n Käse m

chef [ʃef] n Küchenchef m

chemical ['kemikəl] adj chemisch

chemist ['kemist] n Apotheker m; chemist's Apotheke f; Drogerie f

chemistry ['kemistri] n Chemie f

cheque [tʃek] n Scheck m

cheque-book ['tʃekbuk] n Scheckbuch nt

chequered ['tʃekəd] adj kariert, gewürfelt

cherry ['tʃeri] n Kirsche f

chess [tʃes] n Schach nt

chest [tʃest] n Brust f; Brustkasten m; Truhe f; ~ of drawers Kommode f

chestnut ['tʃesnʌt] n Kastanie f

chew [tʃu:] v kauen

chewing-gum ['tʃu:ingʌm] n Kaugummi m

chicken ['tʃikin] n Huhn nt; Küken nt

chickenpox ['tʃikinpɔks] n Windpocken fpl

chief [tʃi:f] n Haupt nt; adj Ober-, Haupt-

chieftain ['tʃi:ftən] n Häuptling m

chilblain ['tʃilblein] n Frostbeule f

child [tʃaild] n (pl children) Kind nt

childbirth ['tʃaildbə:θ] n Entbindung f

childhood ['tʃaildhud] n Jugend f

Chile ['tʃili] Chile

Chilean ['tʃiliən] adj chilenisch; n Chilene m

chill [tʃil] n Frösteln nt

chilly ['tʃili] adj kühl

chimes [tʃaimz] pl Glockenspiel nt

chimney ['tʃimni] n Schornstein m

chin [tʃin] n Kinn nt

China ['tʃainə] China

china ['tʃainə] n Porzellan nt

Chinese [tʃai'ni:z] adj chinesisch; n Chinese m

chink [tʃiŋk] n Spalt m

chip [tʃip] n Splitter m; Spielmarke f; v *abschneiden, absplittern; chips Pommes frites

chiropodist [ki'rɔpədist] n Fußpfleger m

chisel ['tʃizəl] n Meißel m

chives [tʃaivz] pl Schnittlauch m

chlorine ['klɔ:ri:n] n Chlor nt

chock-full ['tʃɔk'ful] adj übervoll, brechend voll

chocolate ['tʃɔklət] n Schokolade f; Praline f

choice [tʃɔis] n Wahl f; Auswahl f

choir [kwaiə] n Chor m

choke [tʃouk] v ersticken; erwürgen; n Choke m

*choose [tʃu:z] v wählen

chop [tʃɔp] n Kotelett nt; v hacken

Christ [kraist] Christus

christen ['krisən] v taufen

christening ['krisəniŋ] n Taufe f

Christian ['kristʃən] adj christlich; n Christ m; ~ name Vorname m

Christmas ['krisməs] Weihnachten

chromium ['kroumiəm] n Chrom nt

chronic ['krɔnik] adj chronisch

chronological [,krɔnə'lɔdʒikəl] adj chronologisch

chuckle ['tʃʌkəl] v kichern

chunk [tʃʌŋk] n Klumpen m

church [tʃə:tʃ] n Kirche f

churchyard ['tʃə:tʃjɑ:d] n Kirchhof m

cigar [si'gɑ:] n Zigarre f; ~ shop Zigarrenladen m

cigarette [,sigə'ret] n Zigarette f

cigarette-case [,sigə'retkeis] n Zigarettenetui nt

cigarette-holder [,sigə'ret,houldə] n Zigarettenspitze f

cigarette-lighter [,sigə'ret,laitə] n Feuerzeug nt

cinema ['sinəmə] n Kino nt

cinnamon ['sinəmən] n Zimt m

circle ['sə:kəl] n Kreis m; Balkon m;

v *einschließen, umkreisen

circulation [,sə:kju'leiʃən] *n* Kreislauf *m*; Umlauf *m*

circumstance ['sə:kəmstæns] *n* Umstand *m*

circus ['sə:kəs] *n* Zirkus *m*

citizen ['sitizən] *n* Bürger *m*

citizenship ['sitizənʃip] *n* Staatsangehörigkeit *f*

city ['siti] *n* Stadt *f*

civic ['sivik] *adj* Bürger-

civil ['sivəl] *adj* zivil; höflich; ~ **law** Zivilrecht *nt*; ~ **servant** Staatsbeamte *m*

civilian [si'viljən] *adj* Bürger-; *n* Zivilist *m*

civilization [,sivəlai'zeiʃən] *n* Zivilisation *f*

civilized ['sivəlaizd] *adj* zivilisiert

claim [kleim] *v* fordern, beanspruchen; behaupten; *n* Forderung *f*, Anspruch *m*

clamp [klæmp] *n* Klemme *f*; Klammer *f*

clap [klæp] *v* klatschen

clarify ['klærifai] *v* klarstellen, klären

class [klɑ:s] *n* Klasse *f*

classical ['klæsikəl] *adj* klassisch

classify ['klæsifai] *v* einteilen

class-mate ['klɑ:smeit] *n* Klassenkamerad *m*

classroom ['klɑ:sru:m] *n* Klassenzimmer *nt*

clause [klɔ:z] *n* Klausel *f*

claw [klɔ:] *n* Klaue *f*

clay [klei] *n* Ton *m*

clean [kli:n] *adj* rein, sauber; *v* säubern, reinigen

cleaning ['kli:niŋ] *n* Reinemachen *nt*, Reinigung *f*; ~ **fluid** Reinigungsmittel *nt*

clear [kliə] *adj* klar; deutlich; *v* aufräumen

clearing ['kliəriŋ] *n* Lichtung *f*

cleft [kleft] *n* Spalte *f*

clergyman ['klə:dʒimən] *n* (pl -men) Pastor *m*, Pfarrer *m*; Geistliche *m*

clerk [klɑ:k] *n* Büroangestellte *m*, Beamte *m*; Schreiber *m*; Sekretär *m*

clever ['klevə] *adj* intelligent; schlau, gescheit, klug

client ['klaiənt] *n* Kunde *m*; Klient *m*

cliff [klif] *n* Klippe *f*

climate ['klaimit] *n* Klima *nt*

climb [klaim] *v* klettern; *steigen; *n* Aufstieg *m*

clinic ['klinik] *n* Klinik *f*

cloak [klouk] *n* Umhang *m*

cloakroom ['kloukru:m] *n* Garderobe *f*

clock [klɔk] *n* Uhr *f*; **at ... o'clock** um ... Uhr

cloister ['klɔistə] *n* Kloster *nt*

close[1] [klouz] *v* zumachen, *schließen; **closed** *adj* zu, geschlossen

close[2] [klous] *adj* nahe

closet ['klɔzit] *n* Wandschrank *m*; *nAm* Garderobenschrank *m*

cloth [klɔθ] *n* Tuch *nt*; Lappen *m*

clothes [klouðz] *pl* Kleidung *f*, Kleider

clothes-brush ['klouðzbrʌʃ] *n* Kleiderbürste *f*

clothing ['klouðiŋ] *n* Kleidung *f*

cloud [klaud] *n* Wolke *f*; **clouds** Bewölkung *f*

cloud-burst ['klaudbə:st] *n* Wolkenbruch *m*

cloudy ['klaudi] *adj* bewölkt

clover ['klouvə] *n* Klee *m*

clown [klaun] *n* Clown *m*

club [klʌb] *n* Klub *m*; Verein *m*; Keule *f*, Knüppel *m*

clumsy ['klʌmzi] *adj* ungeschickt

clutch [klʌtʃ] *n* Kupplung *f*; Griff *m*

coach [koutʃ] *n* Reisebus *m*; Wagen *m*; Kutsche *f*; Trainer *m*

coachwork ['koutʃwə:k] *n* Karosserie *f*

coagulate [kou'ægjuleit] *v* *gerinnen

coal [koul] n Kohle f

coarse [kɔ:s] adj grob; gemein

coast [koust] n Küste f

coat [kout] n Überzieher m, Mantel m

coat-hanger ['kout,hæŋə] n Kleiderbügel m

cobweb ['kɔbweb] n Spinnwebe f

cocaine [kou'kein] n Kokain nt

cock [kɔk] n Hahn m

cocktail ['kɔkteil] n Cocktail m

coconut ['koukənʌt] n Kokosnuß f

cod [kɔd] n (pl ~) Kabeljau m

code [koud] n Kode m

coffee ['kɔfi] n Kaffee m

cognac ['kɔnjæk] n Kognak m

coherence [kou'hiərəns] n Zusammenhang m

coin [kɔin] n Münze f

coincide [,kouin'said] v *zusammenfallen

cold [kould] adj kalt; n Kälte f; Erkältung f; catch a ~ sich erkälten

collapse [kə'læps] v *zusammenbrechen

collar ['kɔlə] n Halsband nt; Kragen m; ~ stud Kragenknopf m

collarbone ['kɔləboun] n Schlüsselbein nt

colleague ['kɔli:g] n Kollege m

collect [kə'lekt] v sammeln; holen, abholen; einsammeln

collection [kə'lekʃən] n Kollektion f, Sammlung f; Leerung f

collective [kə'lektiv] adj kollektiv

collector [kə'lektə] n Sammler m; Kollekteur m

college ['kɔlidʒ] n höhere Lehranstalt; Schule f

collide [kə'laid] v *zusammenstoßen

collision [kə'liʒən] n Zusammenstoß m

Colombia [kə'lɔmbiə] Kolumbien

Colombian [kə'lɔmbiən] adj kolumbianisch; n Kolumbianer m

colonel ['kə:nəl] n Oberst m

colony ['kɔləni] n Kolonie f

colour ['kʌlə] n Farbe f; v färben; ~ film Farbfilm m

colourant ['kʌlərənt] n Färbemittel nt

colour-blind ['kʌləblaind] adj farbenblind

coloured ['kʌləd] adj farbig

colourful ['kʌləfəl] adj bunt, farbenfroh

column ['kɔləm] n Pfeiler m, Säule f; Spalte f; Rubrik f; Kolonne f

coma ['koumə] n Koma nt

comb [koum] v kämmen; n Kamm m

combat ['kɔmbæt] n Kampf m, Gefecht nt; v bekämpfen, kämpfen

combination [,kɔmbi'neiʃən] n Kombination f

combine [kəm'bain] v kombinieren; *verbinden

*come [kʌm] v *kommen; ~ across begegnen; *finden

comedian [kə'mi:diən] n Schauspieler m; Komiker m

comedy ['kɔmədi] n Lustspiel nt, Komödie f; musical ~ Musical nt

comfort ['kʌmfət] n Bequemlichkeit f, Behaglichkeit f, Komfort m; Trost m; v trösten

comfortable ['kʌmfətəbəl] adj bequem

comic ['kɔmik] adj komisch

comics ['kɔmiks] pl Comics pl

coming ['kʌmiŋ] n Ankunft f

comma ['kɔmə] n Komma nt

command [kə'mɑ:nd] v *befehlen; n Befehl m

commander [kə'mɑ:ndə] n Befehlshaber m

commemoration [kə,memə'reiʃən] n Gedenkfeier f

commence [kə'mens] v *anfangen

comment ['kɔment] n Kommentar m; v kommentieren

commerce ['kɔməːs] *n* Handel *m*

commercial [kə'məːʃəl] *adj* Handels-, kommerziell; *n* Werbesendung *f*; ~ **law** Handelsrecht *m*

commission [kə'miʃən] *n* Kommission *f*

commit [kə'mit] *v* *übergeben, anvertrauen; verüben, *begehen

committee [kə'miti] *n* Kommission *f*, Ausschuß *m*

common ['kɔmən] *adj* gemeinsam; üblich, allgemein; gewöhnlich

commune ['kɔmjuːn] *n* Kommune *f*

communicate [kə'mjuːnikeit] *v* mitteilen

communication [kə,mjuːni'keiʃən] *n* Kommunikation *f*; Mitteilung *f*

communiqué [kə'mjuːnikei] *n* Bekanntmachung *f*

communism ['kɔmjunizəm] *n* Kommunismus *m*

communist ['kɔmjunist] *n* Kommunist *m*

community [kə'mjuːnəti] *n* Gemeinschaft *f*, Gemeinde *f*

commuter [kə'mjuːtə] *n* Pendler *m*

compact ['kɔmpækt] *adj* kompakt

companion [kəm'pænjən] *n* Gefährte *m*

company ['kʌmpəni] *n* Gesellschaft *f*; Firma *f*, Unternehmen *nt*

comparative [kəm'pærətiv] *adj* relativ

compare [kəm'pɛə] *v* *vergleichen

comparison [kəm'pærisən] *n* Vergleich *m*

compartment [kəm'pɑːtmənt] *n* Abteil *nt*

compass ['kʌmpəs] *n* Kompaß *m*

compel [kəm'pel] *v* *zwingen

compensate ['kɔmpənseit] *v* *ausgleichen

compensation [,kɔmpən'seiʃən] *n* Ausgleich *m*; Schadenersatz *m*

compete [kəm'piːt] *v* wetteifern

competition [,kɔmpə'tiʃən] *n* Wettbewerb *m*; Konkurrenz *f*

competitor [kəm'petitə] *n* Konkurrent *m*

compile [kəm'pail] *v* zusammenstellen

complain [kəm'plein] *v* sich beschweren

complaint [kəm'pleint] *n* Beschwerde *f*; **complaints book** Beschwerdebuch *nt*

complete [kəm'pliːt] *adj* ganz, vollständig; *v* vollenden

completely [kəm'pliːtli] *adv* vollkommen, gänzlich, völlig

complex ['kɔmpleks] *n* Komplex *m*; *adj* verwickelt

complexion [kəm'plekʃən] *n* Teint *m*

complicated ['kɔmplikeitid] *adj* kompliziert, verwickelt

compliment ['kɔmplimənt] *n* Kompliment *nt*; *v* gratulieren, beglückwünschen

compose [kəm'pouz] *v* zusammenstellen

composer [kəm'pouzə] *n* Komponist *m*

composition [,kɔmpə'ziʃən] *n* Komposition *f*; Zusammensetzung *f*

comprehensive [,kɔmpri'hensiv] *adj* umfassend

comprise [kəm'praiz] *v* umfassen, *einschließen

compromise ['kɔmprəmaiz] *n* Vergleich *m*

compulsory [kəm'pʌlsəri] *adj* obligatorisch

comrade ['kɔmreid] *n* Genosse *m*

conceal [kən'siːl] *v* *verbergen

conceited [kən'siːtid] *adj* eingebildet

conceive [kən'siːv] *v* auffassen, *verstehen; sich vorstellen

concentrate ['kɔnsəntreit] *v* konzentrieren

concentration [,kɔnsən'treiʃən] *n* Konzentration f

conception [kən'sepʃən] n Vorstellung f; Empfängnis f

concern [kən'sə:n] v *angehen, *betreffen; n Sorge f; Angelegenheit f; Unternehmen nt, Konzern m

concerned [kən'sə:nd] adj besorgt; beteiligt

concerning [kən'sə:niŋ] prep hinsichtlich, betreffs

concert ['kɔnsət] n Konzert nt; ~ **hall** Konzertsaal m

concession [kən'seʃən] n Konzession f; Zugeständnis nt

concierge [,kõsi'eəʒ] n Hausmeister m

concise [kən'sais] adj kurzgefaßt, knapp

conclusion [kən'klu:ʒən] n Schlußfolgerung f, Schluß m

concrete ['kɔnkri:t] adj konkret; n Beton m

concurrence [kən'kʌrəns] n Zusammentreffen nt

concussion [kən'kʌʃən] n Gehirnerschütterung f

condition [kən'diʃən] n Bedingung f; Zustand m, Verfassung f; Umstand m

conditional [kən'diʃənəl] adj bedingt

conduct¹ ['kɔndʌkt] n Betragen nt

conduct² [kən'dʌkt] v führen; begleiten; dirigieren

conductor [kən'dʌktə] n Schaffner m; Dirigent m

confectioner [kən'fekʃənə] n Konditor m

conference ['kɔnfərəns] n Konferenz f

confess [kən'fes] v *gestehen; beichten; *bekennen

confession [kən'feʃən] n Geständnis nt; Beichte f

confidence ['kɔnfidəns] n Vertrauen nt

confident ['kɔnfidənt] adj zuversichtlich

confidential [,kɔnfi'denʃəl] adj vertraulich

confirm [kən'fə:m] v bestätigen

confirmation [,kɔnfə'meiʃən] n Bestätigung f

confiscate ['kɔnfiskeit] v *einziehen, beschlagnahmen

conflict ['kɔnflikt] n Konflikt m

confuse [kən'fju:z] v verwirren

confusion [kən'fju:ʒən] n Verwirrung f

congratulate [kən'grætʃuleit] v gratulieren, beglückwünschen

congratulation [kən,grætʃu'leiʃən] n Beglückwünschung f, Glückwunsch m

congregation [,kɔŋgri'geiʃən] n Gemeinde f; Orden m, Bruderschaft f

congress ['kɔŋgres] n Kongreß m; Tagung f

connect [kə'nekt] v *verbinden; *anschließen

connection [kə'nekʃən] n Beziehung f; Zusammenhang m; Verbindung f, Anschluß m

connoisseur [,kɔnə'sə:] n Kenner m

connotation [,kɔnə'teiʃən] n Nebenbedeutung f

conquer ['kɔŋkə] v erobern; besiegen

conqueror ['kɔŋkərə] n Eroberer m

conquest ['kɔŋkwest] n Eroberung f

conscience ['kɔnʃəns] n Gewissen nt

conscious ['kɔnʃəs] adj bewußt

consciousness ['kɔnʃəsnəs] n Bewußtsein nt

conscript ['kɔnskript] n Dienstpflichtige m

consent [kən'sent] v einwilligen; zustimmen; n Einwilligung f, Zustimmung f

consequence ['kɔnsikwəns] n Wirkung f, Folge f

consequently ['kɔnsikwəntli] adv folglich

conservative [kən'sə:vətiv] adj erhaltend, konservativ

consider [kən'sidə] v betrachten; *erwägen; der Ansicht *sein, *finden

considerable [kən'sidərəbəl] adj beträchtlich; beachtlich, bedeutend

considerate [kən'sidərət] adj rücksichtsvoll

consideration [kən,sidə'reiʃən] n Erwägung f; Rücksicht f, Beachtung f

considering [kən'sidəriŋ] prep in Anbetracht

consignment [kən'sainmənt] n Sendung f

consist of [kən'sist] *bestehen aus

conspire [kən'spaiə] v sich *verschwören

constant ['kɔnstənt] adj beständig

constipated ['kɔnstipeitid] adj verstopft

constipation [,kɔnsti'peiʃən] n Obstipation f, Verstopfung f

constituency [kən'stitʃuənsi] n Wahlkreis m

constitution [,kɔnsti'tju:ʃən] n Grundgesetz nt

construct [kən'strʌkt] v bauen; aufbauen, errichten

construction [kən'strʌkʃən] n Konstruktion f; Bau m; Gebäude nt

consul ['kɔnsəl] n Konsul m

consulate ['kɔnsjulət] n Konsulat nt

consult [kən'sʌlt] v konsultieren

consultation [,kɔnsəl'teiʃən] n Konsultation f; ~ hours Sprechstunde f

consumer [kən'sju:mə] n Verbraucher m, Konsument m

contact ['kɔntækt] n Kontakt m; Berührung f; v sich in Verbindung setzen mit; ~ lenses Kontaktlinsen fpl

contagious [kən'teidʒəs] adj ansteckend

contain [kən'tein] v *enthalten; umfassen

container [kən'teinə] n Behälter m; Container m

contemporary [kən'tempərəri] adj zeitgenössisch; damalig; n Zeitgenosse m

contempt [kən'tempt] n Verachtung f, Geringschätzung f

content [kən'tent] adj zufrieden

contents ['kɔntents] pl Inhalt m

contest ['kɔntest] n Streit m; Wettbewerb m

continent ['kɔntinənt] n Kontinent m, Erdteil m; Festland nt

continental [,kɔnti'nentəl] adj kontinental

continual [kən'tinjuəl] adj unaufhörlich; **continually** adv fortwährend

continue [kən'tinju:] v fortsetzen; *fortfahren, fortdauern

continuous [kən'tinjuəs] adj fortlaufend, anhaltend, ununterbrochen

contour ['kɔntuə] n Umriß m

contraceptive [,kɔntrə'septiv] n empfängnisverhütendes Mittel

contract[1] ['kɔntrækt] n Vertrag m

contract[2] [kən'trækt] v sich *zuziehen

contractor [kən'træktə] n Unternehmer m

contradict [,kɔntrə'dikt] v *widersprechen

contradictory [,kɔntrə'diktəri] adj widersprechend

contrary ['kɔntrəri] n Gegenteil nt; adj entgegengesetzt; **on the** ~ im Gegenteil

contrast ['kɔntrɑ:st] n Kontrast m; Unterschied m, Gegensatz m

contribution [,kɔntri'bju:ʃən] n Beitrag m

control [kən'troul] n Kontrolle f; v kontrollieren

controversial [,kɔntrə'və:ʃəl] adj Streit-, umstritten

convenience [kən'vi:njəns] n Bequemlichkeit f

convenient [kən'vi:njənt] *adj* bequem; angemessen, geeignet, passend

convent ['kɔnvənt] *n* Kloster *nt*

conversation [,kɔnvə'seiʃən] *n* Unterhaltung f, Gespräch *nt*

convert [kən'və:t] *v* bekehren; umrechnen, konvertieren

convict[1] [kən'vikt] *v* überführen

convict[2] ['kɔnvikt] *n* Verurteilte *m*

conviction [kən'vikʃən] *n* Überzeugung f; Überführung f

convince [kən'vins] *v* überzeugen

convulsion [kən'vʌlʃən] *n* Krampf *m*

cook [kuk] *n* Koch *m*; *v* kochen; zubereiten, zurichten

cookbook ['kukbuk] *nAm* Kochbuch *nt*

cooker ['kukə] *n* Kocher *m*; **gas ~** Gasherd *m*

cookery-book ['kukəribuk] *n* Kochbuch *nt*

cookie ['kuki] *nAm* Keks *m*

cool [ku:l] *adj* kühl; **cooling system** Kühlsystem *nt*

co-operation [kou,ɔpə'reiʃən] *n* Zusammenarbeit f; Mitarbeit f

co-operative [kou'ɔpərətiv] *adj* kooperativ; willig, bereitwillig; *n* Genossenschaft f

co-ordinate [kou'ɔ:dineit] *v* koordinieren

co-ordination [kou,ɔ:di'neiʃən] *n* Koordinierung f

copper ['kɔpə] *n* Kupfer *nt*

copy ['kɔpi] *n* Kopie f; Abschrift f; Exemplar *nt*; *v* kopieren; nachahmen; **carbon ~** Durchschlag *m*

coral ['kɔrəl] *n* Koralle f

cord [kɔ:d] *n* Seil *nt*; Leine f

cordial ['kɔ:diəl] *adj* herzlich

corduroy ['kɔ:dərɔi] *n* Kordsamt *m*

core [kɔ:] *n* Kern *m*; Kerngehäuse *nt*

cork [kɔ:k] *n* Korken *m*; Stöpsel *m*

corkscrew ['kɔ:kskru:] *n* Korkenzieher *m*

corn [kɔ:n] *n* Korn *nt*; Getreide *nt*; Hühnerauge *nt*; **~ on the cob** Maiskolben *m*

corner ['kɔ:nə] *n* Ecke f

cornfield ['kɔ:nfi:ld] *n* Kornfeld *nt*

corpse [kɔ:ps] *n* Leiche f

corpulent ['kɔ:pjulənt] *adj* korpulent; beleibt, dick

correct [kə'rekt] *adj* genau, korrekt, richtig; *v* korrigieren, verbessern

correction [kə'rekʃən] *n* Berichtigung f; Verbesserung f

correctness [kə'rektnəs] *n* Richtigkeit f

correspond [,kɔri'spɔnd] *v* korrespondieren; übereinstimmen

correspondence [,kɔri'spɔndəns] *n* Korrespondenz f, Briefwechsel *m*

correspondent [,kɔri'spɔndənt] *n* Korrespondent *m*

corridor ['kɔridɔ:] *n* Flur *m*

corrupt [kə'rʌpt] *adj* korrupt; *v* *be-stechen

corruption [kə'rʌpʃən] *n* Bestechung f

corset ['kɔ:sit] *n* Korsett *nt*

cosmetics [kɔz'metiks] *pl* Kosmetika *ntpl*, Schönheitsmittel *ntpl*

cost [kɔst] *n* Kosten *pl*; Preis *m*

***cost** [kɔst] *v* kosten

cosy ['kouzi] *adj* gemütlich, behaglich

cot [kɔt] *nAm* Liege f

cottage ['kɔtidʒ] *n* Sommerhaus *nt*

cotton ['kɔtən] *n* Baumwolle f; Baumwoll-

cotton-wool ['kɔtənwul] *n* Watte f

couch [kautʃ] *n* Couch f

cough [kɔf] *n* Husten *m*; *v* husten

could [kud] *v* (p can)

council ['kaunsəl] *n* Rat *m*

councillor ['kaunsələ] *n* Ratsmitglied *nt*

counsel ['kaunsəl] *n* Rat *m*

counsellor ['kaunsələ] n Ratgeber m

count [kaunt] v zählen; addieren; mitzählen; *halten für; n Graf m

counter ['kauntə] n Ladentisch m; Schalter m

counterfeit ['kauntəfi:t] v fälschen

counterfoil ['kauntəfɔil] n Kontrollabschnitt m

counterpane ['kauntəpein] n Bettdecke f

countess ['kauntis] n Gräfin f

country ['kʌntri] n Land nt; Gegend f; ~ house Landhaus nt

countryman ['kʌntrimən] n (pl -men) Landsmann m

countryside ['kʌntrisaid] n Landschaft f

county ['kaunti] n Grafschaft f

couple ['kʌpəl] n Paar nt

coupon ['ku:pɔn] n Kupon m; Bezugsschein m

courage ['kʌridʒ] n Tapferkeit f, Mut m

courageous [kə'reidʒəs] adj tapfer, mutig

course [kɔ:s] n Kurs m; Gang m; Lauf m; Lehrgang m, Kursus m; intensive ~ Kurzlehrgang m; of ~ allerdings, selbstverständlich

court [kɔ:t] n Gericht nt; Hof m

courteous ['kɔ:tiəs] adj höflich

cousin ['kʌzən] n Base f, Vetter m

cover ['kʌvə] v bedecken, verdecken; n Obdach nt, Schutz m; Deckel m; Umschlag m; ~ charge Gedeckkosten pl

cow [kau] n Kuh f

coward ['kauəd] n Feigling m

cowardly ['kauədli] adj feige

cow-hide ['kauhaid] n Kuhhaut f

crab [kræb] n Krabbe f

crack [kræk] n Krachen nt; Riß m; v krachen; *brechen, *bersten

cracker ['krækə] nAm Keks m

cradle ['kreidəl] n Wiege f

cramp [kræmp] n Krampf m

crane [krein] n Kran m

crankcase ['kræŋkkeis] n Kurbelgehäuse nt

crankshaft ['kræŋkʃɑ:ft] n Kurbelwelle f

crash [kræʃ] n Zusammenstoß m; v *zusammenstoßen; abstürzen; ~ barrier Leitplanke f

crate [kreit] n Kiste f

crater ['kreitə] n Krater m

crawl [krɔ:l] v *kriechen; n Kraul m

craze [kreiz] n Fimmel m

crazy ['kreizi] adj verrückt; wahnsinnig

creak [kri:k] v knirschen

cream [kri:m] n Krem f; Sahne f; adj kremfarben

creamy ['kri:mi] adj sahnig

crease [kri:s] v zerknittern; n Falte f

create [kri'eit] v *schaffen; erschaffen

creature ['kri:tʃə] n Geschöpf nt

credible ['kredibəl] adj glaubwürdig

credit ['kredit] n Kredit m; v kreditieren; ~ card Kreditkarte f

creditor ['kreditə] n Gläubiger m

credulous ['kredjuləs] adj gutgläubig

creek [kri:k] n Bucht f

*creep [kri:p] v *kriechen

creepy ['kri:pi] adj unheimlich, gruselig

cremate [kri'meit] v *verbrennen

cremation [kri'meiʃən] n Einäscherung f

crew [kru:] n Besatzung f

cricket ['krikit] n Kricket nt; Grille f

crime [kraim] n Verbrechen nt

criminal ['kriminəl] n Delinquent m, Verbrecher m; adj verbrecherisch, kriminell; ~ law Strafrecht nt

criminality [,krimi'næləti] n Kriminalität f

crimson ['krimzən] adj karmesinrot

crippled ['krɪpəld] adj verkrüppelt

crisis ['kraɪsɪs] n (pl crises) Krise f

crisp [krɪsp] adj knusprig

critic ['krɪtɪk] n Kritiker m

critical ['krɪtɪkəl] adj kritisch; entscheidend, heikel, bedenklich

criticism ['krɪtɪsɪzəm] n Kritik f

criticize ['krɪtɪsaɪz] v kritisieren

crochet ['krəʊʃeɪ] v häkeln

crockery ['krɒkəri] n Steingut nt, Töpferware f

crocodile ['krɒkədaɪl] n Krokodil nt

crooked ['krʊkɪd] adj verdreht, krumm; unehrlich

crop [krɒp] n Ernte f

cross [krɒs] v *hinübergehen; adj ungehalten, böse; n Kreuz nt

cross-eyed ['krɒsaɪd] adj schielend

crossing ['krɒsɪŋ] n Überfahrt f; Kreuzung f; Übergang m; Bahnübergang m

crossroads ['krɒsrəʊdz] n Kreuzung f

crosswalk ['krɒswɔːk] nAm Zebrastreifen m

crow [krəʊ] n Krähe f

crowbar ['krəʊbɑː] n Brecheisen nt

crowd [kraʊd] n Masse f, Menge f

crowded ['kraʊdɪd] adj voll; überfüllt

crown [kraʊn] n Krone f; v krönen; bekrönen

crucifix ['kruːsɪfɪks] n Kruzifix nt

crucifixion [ˌkruːsɪ'fɪkʃən] n Kreuzigung f

crucify ['kruːsɪfaɪ] v kreuzigen

cruel [krʊəl] adj grausam

cruise [kruːz] n Kreuzfahrt f, Seereise f

crumb [krʌm] n Krümel m

crusade [kruː'seɪd] n Kreuzzug m

crust [krʌst] n Kruste f

crutch [krʌtʃ] n Krücke f

cry [kraɪ] v weinen; *schreien; *rufen; n Aufschrei m, Schrei m; Ruf m

crystal ['krɪstəl] n Kristall nt; adj kristallen

Cuba ['kjuːbə] Kuba

Cuban ['kjuːbən] adj kubanisch; n Kubaner m

cube [kjuːb] n Kubus m; Würfel m

cuckoo ['kʊkuː] n Kuckuck m

cucumber ['kjuːkəmbə] n Gurke f

cuddle ['kʌdəl] v verhätscheln

cudgel ['kʌdʒəl] n Knüppel m

cuff [kʌf] n Manschette f

cuff-links ['kʌflɪŋks] pl Manschettenknöpfe mpl

cul-de-sac ['kʌldəsæk] n Sackgasse f

cultivate ['kʌltɪveɪt] v bebauen; anbauen, kultivieren

culture ['kʌltʃə] n Kultur f

cultured ['kʌltʃəd] adj kultiviert

cunning ['kʌnɪŋ] adj listig

cup [kʌp] n Tasse f; Pokal m

cupboard ['kʌbəd] n Schrank m

curb [kɜːb] n Randstein m; v zügeln

cure [kjʊə] v heilen; n Kur f; Genesung f

curio ['kjʊərɪəʊ] n (pl ~s) Rarität f

curiosity [ˌkjʊərɪ'ɒsəti] n Neugier f

curious ['kjʊərɪəs] adj gespannt, neugierig; seltsam

curl [kɜːl] v locken; n Locke f

curler ['kɜːlə] n Lockenwickler m

curling-tongs ['kɜːlɪŋtɒŋz] pl Brennschere f

curly ['kɜːli] adj lockig

currant ['kʌrənt] n Korinthe f; Beere f

currency ['kʌrənsi] n Währung f; foreign ~ fremde Währung

current ['kʌrənt] n Strömung f; Strom m; adj gangbar, gegenwärtig; alternating ~ Wechselstrom m; direct ~ Gleichstrom m

curry ['kʌri] n Curry m

curse [kɜːs] v fluchen; verfluchen; n Fluch m

curtain ['kɜːtən] n Vorhang m

curve [kə:v] n Kurve f; Biegung f

curved [kə:vd] adj krumm, gekrümmt

cushion ['kuʃən] n Kissen nt

custodian [kʌ'stoudiən] n Saalwärter m

custody ['kʌstədi] n Haft f; Obhut f; Vormundschaft f

custom ['kʌstəm] n Gewohnheit f; Sitte f

customary ['kʌstəməri] adj üblich, gewöhnlich

customer ['kʌstəmə] n Kunde m; Klient m

Customs ['kʌstəmz] pl Zollbehörde f; ~ **duty** Zoll m; ~ **officer** Zöllner m

cut [kʌt] n Einschnitt m; Schnitt m

*cut [kʌt] v *schneiden; senken; ~ **off** *abschneiden; abschalten

cutlery ['kʌtləri] n Besteck nt

cutlet ['kʌtlət] n Kotelett nt

cycle ['saikəl] n Rad nt; Fahrrad nt; Kreislauf m, Zyklus m

cyclist ['saiklist] n Radfahrer m

cylinder ['silində] n Zylinder m; ~ **head** Zylinderkopf m

cystitis [si'staitis] n Blasenentzündung f

Czech [tʃek] adj tschechisch; n Tscheche m

Czechoslovakia [,tʃekəslə'va:kiə] Tschechoslowakei f

D

dad [dæd] n Vater m

daddy ['dædi] n Vati m

daffodil ['dæfədil] n Narzisse f

daily ['deili] adj alltäglich, täglich; n Tageszeitung f

dairy ['dɛəri] n Molkerei f

dam [dæm] n Damm m; Deich m

damage ['dæmidʒ] n Schaden m; v beschädigen

damp [dæmp] adj feucht; naß; n Feuchtigkeit f; v befeuchten

dance [dɑ:ns] v tanzen; n Tanz m

dandelion ['dændilaiən] n Löwenzahn m

dandruff ['dændrəf] n Schuppen

Dane [dein] n Däne m

danger ['deindʒə] n Gefahr f

dangerous ['deindʒərəs] adj gefährlich

Danish ['deiniʃ] adj dänisch

dare [dɛə] v sich trauen, wagen; herausfordern

daring ['dɛəriŋ] adj wagehalsig

dark [dɑ:k] adj finster, dunkel; n Dunkelheit f, Finsternis f

darling ['dɑ:liŋ] n Schatz m, Liebling m

darn [dɑ:n] v stopfen

dash [dæʃ] v stürmen; n Gedankenstrich m

dashboard ['dæʃbɔ:d] n Armaturenbrett nt

data ['deitə] pl Angabe f

date¹ [deit] n Datum nt; Verabredung f; v datieren; **out of** ~ veraltet

date² [deit] n Dattel f

daughter ['dɔ:tə] n Tochter f

dawn [dɔ:n] n Morgendämmerung f; Tagesanbruch m

day [dei] n Tag m; **by** ~ bei Tage; ~ **trip** Tagesausflug m; **per** ~ pro Tag; **the** ~ **before yesterday** vorgestern

daybreak ['deibreik] n Tagesanbruch m

daylight ['deilait] n Tageslicht nt

dead [ded] adj tot; verstorben

deaf [def] adj taub

deal [di:l] n Transaktion f, Geschäft nt

*deal [di:l] v austeilen; ~ **with** v sich

befassen mit; Geschäfte machen mit

dealer ['di:lə] n Kaufmann m, Händler m

dear [diə] adj lieb; teuer; wert

death [deθ] n Tod m; ~ **penalty** Todesstrafe f

debate [di'beit] n Debatte f

debit ['debit] n Soll nt

debt [det] n Schuld f

decaffeinated [di:'kæfineitid] adj koffeinfrei

deceit [di'si:t] n Betrug m

deceive [di'si:v] v *betrügen

December [di'sembə] Dezember

decency ['di:sənsi] n Anstand m

decent ['di:sənt] adj anständig

decide [di'said] v *beschließen, sich *entschließen, *entscheiden

decision [di'siʒən] n Beschluß m, Entscheidung f

deck [dek] n Deck nt; ~ **cabin** Deckkajüte f; ~ **chair** Liegestuhl m

declaration [,deklə'reiʃən] n Erklärung f

declare [di'kleə] v erklären; *angeben; verzollen

decoration [,dekə'reiʃən] n Dekoration f

decrease [di:'kri:s] v vermindern; *abnehmen; n Abnahme f

dedicate ['dedikeit] v widmen

deduce [di'dju:s] v ableiten

deduct [di'dʌkt] v *abziehen

deed [di:d] n Handlung f, Tat f

deep [di:p] adj tief

deep-freeze [,di:p'fri:z] n Tiefkühltruhe f

deer [diə] n (pl ~) Rotwild nt

defeat [di'fi:t] v besiegen; n Niederlage f

defective [di'fektiv] adj schadhaft, mangelhaft

defence [di'fens] n Verteidigung f;

Abwehr f

defend [di'fend] v verteidigen

deficiency [di'fiʃənsi] n Mangel m

deficit ['defisit] n Defizit nt

define [di'fain] v definieren, bestimmen

definite ['definit] adj bestimmt

definition [,defi'niʃən] n Bestimmung f, Definition f

deformed [di'fɔ:md] adj mißgestaltet, entstellt

degree [di'gri:] n Grad m; Titel m

delay [di'lei] v verzögern; *aufschieben; n Aufenthalt m, Verzögerung f; Aufschub m

delegate ['deligət] n Abgesandte m

delegation [,deli'geiʃən] n Delegation f, Abordnung f

deliberate¹ [di'libəreit] v beratschlagen, überlegen

deliberate² [di'libərət] adj absichtlich

deliberation [di,libə'reiʃən] n Erörterung f, Beratung f

delicacy ['delikəsi] n Leckerbissen m

delicate ['delikət] adj fein; zart; mißlich

delicatessen [,delikə'tesən] n Feinkost f; Feinkostgeschäft nt

delicious [di'liʃəs] adj lecker, köstlich

delight [di'lait] n Genuß m, Wonne f; v entzücken

delightful [di'laitfəl] adj köstlich, entzückend

deliver [di'livə] v abliefern, ausliefern; erlösen

delivery [di'livəri] n Zustellung f, Lieferung f; Entbindung f; Erlösung f; ~ **van** Lieferwagen m

demand [di'mɑ:nd] v verlangen, fordern; n Forderung f; Nachfrage f

democracy [di'mɔkrəsi] n Demokratie f

democratic [,demə'krætik] adj demokratisch

demolish [di'mɔliʃ] v *niederreißen
demolition [,demə'liʃən] n Abbruch m
demonstrate ['demənstreit] v *beweisen; demonstrieren
demonstration [,demən'streiʃən] n Demonstration f; Kundgebung f
den [den] n Höhle f
Denmark ['denma:k] Dänemark
denomination [di,nɔmi'neiʃən] n Benennung f
dense [dens] adj dicht
dent [dent] n Beule f
dentist ['dentist] n Zahnarzt m
denture ['dentʃə] n Gebiß nt
deny [di'nai] v leugnen; versagen, verweigern, *enthalten
deodorant [di:'oudərənt] n Deodorant nt
depart [di'pa:t] v *weggehen, abreisen; *sterben
department [di'pa:tmənt] n Abteilung f; ~ store Kaufhaus nt
departure [di'pa:tʃə] n Abreise f, Abfahrt f
dependant [di'pendənt] adj abhängig
depend on [di'pend] *abhängen von
deposit [di'pɔzit] n Bank-Einlage f; Pfand nt; Sediment nt, Ablagerung f; v hinterlegen
depository [di'pɔzitəri] n Lagerraum m
depot ['depou] n Lager nt; nAm Bahnhof m
depress [di'pres] v deprimieren
depressed [di'prest] adj niedergeschlagen
depression [di'preʃən] n Niedergeschlagenheit f; Tief nt; Rückgang m
deprive of [di'praiv] *entnehmen
depth [depθ] n Tiefe f
deputy ['depjuti] n Abgeordnete m; Stellvertreter m
descend [di'send] v *herabsteigen

descendant [di'sendənt] n Nachkomme m
descent [di'sent] n Abstieg m
describe [di'skraib] v *beschreiben
description [di'skripʃən] n Beschreibung f; Personalbeschreibung f
desert[1] ['dezət] n Wüste f; adj wüst, verlassen
desert[2] [di'zə:t] v desertieren; *verlassen
deserve [di'zə:v] v verdienen
design [di'zain] v *entwerfen; n Entwurf m; Zweck m
designate ['dezigneit] v *anweisen
desirable [di'zaiərəbəl] adj begehrenswert, wünschenswert
desire [di'zaiə] n Wunsch m; Lust f, Verlangen nt; v begehren, verlangen, wünschen
desk [desk] n Schreibtisch m; Pult nt; Schulbank f
despair [di'spɛə] n Verzweiflung f; v verzweifeln
despatch [di'spætʃ] v *versenden
desperate ['despərət] adj verzweifelt
despise [di'spaiz] v verachten
despite [di'spait] prep trotz
dessert [di'zə:t] n Nachtisch m
destination [,desti'neiʃən] n Bestimmungsort m
destine ['destin] v bestimmen
destiny ['destini] n Verhängnis nt, Schicksal nt
destroy [di'strɔi] v zerstören, vernichten
destruction [di'strʌkʃən] n Zerstörung f; Untergang m
detach [di'tætʃ] v losmachen
detail ['di:teil] n Einzelheit f
detailed ['di:teild] adj ausführlich, eingehend
detect [di'tekt] v entdecken
detective [di'tektiv] n Detektiv m; ~ story Kriminalroman m

detergent [di'tə:dʒənt] n Reinigungsmittel nt

determine [di'tə:min] v festsetzen, bestimmen

determined [di'tə:mind] adj entschlossen

detour ['di:tuə] n Umweg m; Umleitung f

devaluation [,di:vælju'eiʃən] n Abwertung f

devalue [,di:'vælju:] v entwerten

develop [di'veləp] v entwickeln

development [di'veləpmənt] n Entwicklung f

deviate ['di:vieit] v *abweichen

devil ['devəl] n Teufel m

devise [di'vaiz] v *ausdenken

devote [di'vout] v widmen

dew [dju:] n Tau m

diabetes [,daiə'bi:ti:z] n Diabetes m,
Zuckerkrankheit f

diabetic [,daiə'betik] n Diabetiker m

diagnose [,daiəg'nouz] v diagnostizieren; feststellen

diagnosis [,daiəg'nousis] n (pl -ses)
Diagnose f

diagonal [dai'ægənəl] n Diagonale f;
adj diagonal

diagram ['daiəgræm] n Schema nt;
graphische Darstellung

dialect ['daiəlekt] n Mundart f

diamond ['daiəmənd] n Diamant m

diaper ['daiəpə] nAm Windel f

diaphragm ['daiəfræm] n Membran f

diarrhoea [daiə'riə] n Durchfall m

diary ['daiəri] n Merkbuch nt; Tagebuch nt

dictaphone ['diktəfoun] n Diktiergerät
nt

dictate [dik'teit] v diktieren

dictation [dik'teiʃən] n Diktat nt

dictator [dik'teitə] n Diktator m

dictionary ['dikʃənəri] n Wörterbuch
nt

did [did] v (p do)

die [dai] v *sterben

diesel ['di:zəl] n Diesel m

diet ['daiət] n Diät f

differ ['difə] v sich *unterscheiden

difference ['difərəns] n Unterschied m

different ['difərənt] adj verschieden;
ander

difficult ['difikəlt] adj schwierig;
schwer

difficulty ['difikəlti] n Schwierigkeit f;
Mühe f

*dig [dig] v *graben

digest [di'dʒest] v verdauen

digestible [di'dʒestəbəl] adj verdaulich

digestion [di'dʒestʃən] n Verdauung f

digit ['didʒit] n Ziffer f

dignified ['dignifaid] adj würdevoll

dike [daik] n Deich m; Damm m

dilapidated [di'læpideitid] adj baufällig

diligence ['dilidʒəns] n Fleiß m, Eifer
m

diligent ['dilidʒənt] adj fleißig, eifrig

dilute [dai'lju:t] v verdünnen

dim [dim] adj trübe, matt; dunkel,
schwach

dine [dain] v zu Abend *essen

dinghy ['diŋgi] n Jolle f

dining-car ['dainiŋka:] n Speisewagen
m

dining-room ['dainiŋru:m] n Speisezimmer nt; Speisesaal m

dinner ['dinə] n Hauptmahlzeit f;
Abendessen nt, Mittagessen nt

dinner-jacket ['dinə,dʒækit] n Smoking
m

dinner-service ['dinə,sə:vis] n Eßservice nt

diphtheria [dif'θiəriə] n Diphtherie f

diploma [di'ploumə] n Diplom nt

diplomat ['dipləmæt] n Diplomat m

direct [di'rekt] adj unmittelbar, direkt;
v richten; *weisen; führen

direction [di'rekʃən] n Richtung f;

Anweisung f; Regie f; Verwaltung f, Vorstand m; **directional signal** Am Winker m; **directions for use** Gebrauchsanweisung f

directive [di'rektiv] n Richtlinie f

director [di'rektə] n Direktor m; Regisseur m

dirt [də:t] n Schmutz m

dirty ['də:ti] adj schmierig, dreckig, schmutzig

disabled [di'seibəld] adj körperbehindert, invalide

disadvantage [,disəd'va:ntidʒ] n Nachteil m

disagree [,disə'gri:] v uneins *sein, nicht übereinstimmen

disagreeable [,disə'gri:əbəl] adj unangenehm

disappear [,disə'piə] v *verschwinden

disappoint [,disə'pɔint] v enttäuschen

disappointment [,disə'pɔintmənt] n Enttäuschung f

disapprove [,disə'pru:v] v mißbilligen

disaster [di'za:stə] n Katastrophe f; Mißgeschick nt, Unheil nt

disastrous [di'za:strəs] adj verheerend

disc [disk] n Scheibe f; Schallplatte f; **slipped** ~ Hernie f

discard [di'ska:d] v ausrangieren

discharge [dis'tʃa:dʒ] v *entladen, *ausladen; ~ **of** *entbinden von

discipline ['disiplin] n Disziplin f

discolour [di'skʌlə] v sich verfärben

disconnect [,diskə'nekt] v trennen; ausschalten

discontented [,diskən'tentid] adj unzufrieden

discontinue [,diskən'tinju:] v einstellen, aufhören mit

discount ['diskaunt] n Rabatt m

discover [di'skʌvə] v entdecken

discovery [di'skʌvəri] n Entdeckung f

discuss [di'skʌs] v erörtern; diskutieren

discussion [di'skʌʃən] n Diskussion f; Gespräch nt, Besprechung f, Auseinandersetzung f

disease [di'zi:z] n Krankheit f

disembark [,disim'ba:k] v an Land *gehen, landen

disgrace [dis'greis] n Schande f

disguise [dis'gaiz] v sich verkleiden; n Verkleidung f

disgusting [dis'gʌstiŋ] adj widerlich, ekelhaft

dish [diʃ] n Teller m; Platte f, Schüssel f; Gericht nt

dishonest [di'sɔnist] adj unehrlich

disinfect [,disin'fekt] v desinfizieren

disinfectant [,disin'fektənt] n Desinfektionsmittel nt

dislike [di'slaik] v nicht ausstehen *können, nicht *mögen; n Abneigung f, Widerwille m, Antipathie f

dislocated ['disləkeitid] adj verrenkt

dismiss [dis'mis] v fortschicken; *entlassen

disorder [di'sɔ:də] n Unordnung f

dispatch [di'spætʃ] v verschicken, abfertigen

display [di'splei] v auslegen; zeigen; n Ausstellung f, Auslage f

displease [di'spli:z] v verstimmen, *mißfallen

disposable [di'spouzəbəl] adj wegwerfbar

disposal [di'spouzəl] n Verfügung f

dispose of [di'spouz] verfügen über

dispute [di'spju:t] n Auseinandersetzung f; Zank m, Streitigkeit f; v *streiten, *bestreiten

dissatisfied [di'sætisfaid] adj unzufrieden

dissolve [di'zɔlv] v auflösen

dissuade from [di'sweid] *abraten

distance ['distəns] n Entfernung f; ~ **in kilometres** Kilometerzahl f

distant ['distənt] adj entfernt

distinct [di'stiŋkt] *adj* deutlich; verschieden

distinction [di'stiŋkʃən] *n* Unterscheidung *f*, Unterschied *m*

distinguish [di'stiŋgwiʃ] *v* *unterscheiden

distinguished [di'stiŋgwiʃt] *adj* vornehm

distress [di'stres] *n* Not *f*; ~ **signal** Notsignal *nt*

distribute [di'stribju:t] *v* verteilen

distributor [di'stribjutə] *n* Generalvertreter *m*; Stromverteiler *m*

district ['distrikt] *n* Bezirk *m*; Gegend *f*

disturb [di'stə:b] *v* stören

disturbance [di'stə:bəns] *n* Störung *f*; Verwirrung *f*

ditch [ditʃ] *n* Graben *m*

dive [daiv] *v* tauchen

diversion [dai'və:ʃən] *n* Umleitung *f*; Ablenkung *f*

divide [di'vaid] *v* teilen; verteilen; trennen

divine [di'vain] *adj* göttlich

division [di'viʒən] *n* Teilung *f*; Trennung *f*; Abteilung *f*

divorce [di'vɔ:s] *n* Scheidung *f*; *v* *scheiden

dizziness ['dizinəs] *n* Schwindel *m*

dizzy ['dizi] *adj* schwindlig

***do** [du:] *v* *tun; genügen

dock [dɔk] *n* Dock *nt*; Kai *m*; *v* anlegen

docker ['dɔkə] *n* Hafenarbeiter *m*

doctor ['dɔktə] *n* Doktor *m*, Arzt *m*

document ['dɔkjumənt] *n* Urkunde *f*

dog [dɔg] *n* Hund *m*

dogged ['dɔgid] *adj* hartnäckig

doll [dɔl] *n* Puppe *f*

dome [doum] *n* Kuppel *f*

domestic [də'mestik] *adj* häuslich; inländisch; *n* Diener *m*

domicile ['dɔmisail] *n* Wohnsitz *m*

domination [,dɔmi'neiʃən] *n* Herrschaft *f*

dominion [də'minjən] *n* Herrschaft *f*

donate [dou'neit] *v* spenden

donation [dou'neiʃən] *n* Spende *f*, Schenkung *f*

done [dʌn] *v* (pp do)

donkey ['dɔŋki] *n* Esel *m*

donor ['dounə] *n* Donator *m*

door [dɔ:] *n* Tür *f*; **revolving** ~ Drehtür *f*; **sliding** ~ Schiebetür *f*

doorbell ['dɔ:bel] *n* Türklingel *f*

door-keeper ['dɔ:,ki:pə] *n* Portier *m*

doorman ['dɔ:mən] *n* (pl -men) Portier *m*

dormitory ['dɔ:mitri] *n* Schlafsaal *m*

dose [dous] *n* Dosis *f*

dot [dɔt] *n* Punkt *m*

double ['dʌbəl] *adj* doppelt

doubt [daut] *v* bezweifeln, zweifeln; *n* Zweifel *m*; **without** ~ ohne Zweifel

doubtful ['dautfəl] *adj* zweifelhaft; ungewiß

dough [dou] *n* Teig *m*

down[1] [daun] *adv* herab; hinab, herunter, nieder; *adj* niedergeschlagen; *prep* entlang, hinab; ~ **payment** Anzahlung *f*

down[2] [daun] *n* Daune *f*

downpour ['daunpɔ:] *n* Regenguß *m*

downstairs [,daun'stɛəz] *adv* hinunter, unten

downstream [,daun'stri:m] *adv* stromabwärts

down-to-earth [,dauntu'ə:θ] *adj* sachlich

downwards ['daunwədz] *adv* nach unten, abwärts

dozen ['dʌzən] *n* (pl ~, ~s) Dutzend *nt*

draft [drɑ:ft] *n* Tratte *f*

drag [dræg] *v* schleppen

dragon ['drægən] *n* Drache *m*

drain [drein] *v* trockenlegen; entwässern; n Abfluß m

drama ['drɑːmə] n Drama nt; Trauerspiel nt; Theater nt

dramatic [drə'mætik] adj dramatisch

dramatist ['dræmətist] n Dramatiker m

drank [dræŋk] v (p drink)

draper ['dreipə] n Tuchhändler m

drapery ['dreipəri] n Tuchwaren fpl

draught [drɑːft] n Luftzug m; **draughts** Damespiel nt

draught-board ['drɑːftbɔːd] n Damebrett nt

draw [drɔː] n Ziehung f

***draw** [drɔː] v zeichnen; *ziehen; *abheben; ~ **up** abfassen

drawbridge ['drɔːbridʒ] n Zugbrücke f

drawer ['drɔːə] n Schublade f; **drawers** Unterhose f

drawing ['drɔːiŋ] n Zeichnung f

drawing-pin ['drɔːiŋpin] n Reißzwecke f

drawing-room ['drɔːiŋruːm] n Empfangszimmer nt

dread [dred] v befürchten; n Angst f

dreadful ['dredfəl] adj schrecklich, furchtbar

dream [driːm] n Traum m

***dream** [driːm] v träumen

dress [dres] v ankleiden; sich kleiden, sich ankleiden; *verbinden; n Kleid m

dressing-gown ['dresiŋgaun] n Morgenrock m

dressing-room ['dresiŋruːm] n Ankleideraum nt

dressing-table ['dresiŋˌteibəl] n Frisierkommode f

dressmaker ['dresˌmeikə] n Schneiderin f

drill [dril] v bohren; trainieren; n Bohrer m

drink [driŋk] n Aperitif m, Drink m

***drink** [driŋk] v *trinken

drinking-water ['driŋkiŋˌwɔːtə] n Trinkwasser nt

drip-dry [ˌdrip'drai] adj bügelfrei

drive [draiv] n Weg m; Fahrt f

***drive** [draiv] v *fahren

driver ['draivə] n Fahrer m

drizzle ['drizəl] n Sprühregen m

drop [drɔp] v fallen *lassen; n Tropfen m

drought [draut] n Dürre f

drown [draun] v *ertrinken; *be **drowned** *ertrinken

drug [drʌg] n Droge f; Arznei f

drugstore ['drʌgstɔː] nAm Drogerie f, Apotheke f; Warenhaus nt

drum [drʌm] n Trommel f

drunk [drʌŋk] adj (pp drink) betrunken

dry [drai] adj trocken; v trocknen; abtrocknen

dry-clean [ˌdrai'kliːn] v chemisch reinigen

dry-cleaner's [ˌdrai'kliːnəz] n chemische Reinigung

dryer ['draiə] n Trockner m

duchess [dʌtʃis] n Herzogin f

duck [dʌk] n Ente f

due [djuː] adj erwartet; schuldig; fällig

dues [djuːz] pl Gebühren

dug [dʌg] v (p, pp dig)

duke [djuːk] n Herzog m

dull [dʌl] adj langweilig; matt; stumpf

dumb [dʌm] adj stumm; blöde, dumm

dune [djuːn] n Düne f

dung [dʌŋ] n Dünger m

dunghill ['dʌŋhil] n Misthaufen m

duration [dju'reifən] n Dauer f

during ['djuəriŋ] prep während

dusk [dʌsk] n Abenddämmerung f

dust [dʌst] n Staub m

dustbin ['dʌstbin] n Abfalleimer m

dusty ['dʌsti] adj staubig

Dutch [dʌtʃ] adj niederländisch, holländisch

Dutchman ['dʌtʃmən] *n* (pl -men) Niederländer *m*, Holländer *m*

dutiable ['dju:tiəbəl] *adj* zollpflichtig

duty ['dju:ti] *n* Pflicht *f*; Aufgabe *f*; Einfuhrzoll *m*; **Customs ~** Zoll *m*

duty-free [,dju:ti'fri:] *adj* zollfrei

dwarf [dwɔ:f] *n* Zwerg *m*

dye [dai] *v* färben; *n* Farbe *f*

dynamo ['dainəmou] *n* (pl ~s) Dynamo *m*

dysentery ['disəntri] *n* Ruhr *f*

E

each [i:tʃ] *adj* jeder; **~ other** einander

eager ['i:gə] *adj* begierig

eagle ['i:gəl] *n* Adler *m*

ear [iə] *n* Ohr *nt*

earache ['iəreik] *n* Ohrenschmerzen *mpl*

ear-drum ['iədrʌm] *n* Trommelfell *nt*

earl [ə:l] *n* Graf *m*

early ['ə:li] *adj* früh

earn [ə:n] *v* verdienen

earnest ['ə:nist] *n* Ernst *m*

earnings ['ə:niŋz] *pl* Einnahmen, Verdienst *m*

earring ['iəriŋ] *n* Ohrring *m*

earth [ə:θ] *n* Erde *f*; Boden *m*

earthenware ['ə:θənwεə] *n* Steingut *nt*

earthquake ['ə:θkweik] *n* Erdbeben *nt*

ease [i:z] *n* Ungezwungenheit *f*, Leichtigkeit *f*; Wohlbefinden *nt*

east [i:st] *n* Osten *m*

Easter ['i:stə] Ostern

easterly ['i:stəli] *adj* östlich

eastern ['i:stən] *adj* östlich

easy ['i:zi] *adj* bequem; behaglich; **~ chair** Lehnstuhl *m*

easy-going ['i:zi,gouiŋ] *adj* lässig

***eat** [i:t] *v* *essen; speisen

eavesdrop ['i:vzdrɔp] *v* abhorchen

ebony ['ebəni] *n* Ebenholz *nt*

eccentric [ik'sentrik] *adj* überspannt

echo ['ekou] *n* (pl ~es) Widerhall *m*, Echo *nt*

eclipse [i'klips] *n* Finsternis *f*

economic [,i:kə'nɔmik] *adj* wirtschaftlich

economical [,i:kə'nɔmikəl] *adj* sparsam

economist [i'kɔnəmist] *n* Volkswirt *m*

economize [i'kɔnəmaiz] *v* sparen

economy [i'kɔnəmi] *n* Wirtschaft *f*

ecstasy ['ekstəzi] *n* Verzückung *f*

Ecuador ['ekwadɔ:] Ekuador

Ecuadorian [,ekwə'dɔ:riən] *n* Ekuadorianer *m*

eczema ['eksimə] *n* Ekzem *nt*

edge [edʒ] *n* Kante *f*, Rand *m*

edible ['edibəl] *adj* eßbar

edition [i'diʃən] *n* Ausgabe *f*; **morning ~** Morgenausgabe *f*

editor ['editə] *n* Redakteur *m*

educate ['edʒukeit] *v* ausbilden

education [,edʒu'keiʃən] *n* Erziehung *f*

eel [i:l] *n* Aal *m*

effect [i'fekt] *n* Ergebnis *nt*, Wirkung *f*; *v* zustande *bringen; **in ~** tatsächlich

effective [i'fektiv] *adj* wirksam, wirkungsvoll

efficient [i'fiʃənt] *adj* leistungsfähig, zweckmäßig

effort ['efət] *n* Anstrengung *f*; Bemühung *f*

egg [eg] *n* Ei *nt*

egg-cup ['egkʌp] *n* Eierbecher *m*

eggplant ['egplɑ:nt] *n* Aubergine *f*

egg-yolk ['egjouk] *n* Eidotter *m*

egoistic [,egou'istik] *adj* egoistisch

Egypt ['i:dʒipt] Ägypten

Egyptian [i'dʒipʃən] *adj* ägyptisch; *n* Agypter *m*

eiderdown ['aidədaun] *n* Daunendecke *f*

eight [eit] *num* acht

eighteen [,ei'ti:n] *num* achtzehn

eighteenth [,ei'ti:nθ] *num* achtzehnte

eighth [eitθ] *num* achte

eighty ['eiti] *num* achtzig

either ['aiðə] *pron* einer von beiden; **either ... or** entweder ... oder

elaborate [i'læbəreit] *v* ausarbeiten

elastic [i'læstik] *adj* elastisch; dehnbar; Gummiband *nt*

elasticity [,elæ'stisəti] *n* Spannkraft *f*

elbow ['elbou] *n* Ellbogen *m*

elder ['eldə] *adj* älter

elderly ['eldəli] *adj* ältlich

eldest ['eldist] *adj* ältest

elect [i'lekt] *v* wählen

election [i'lekʃən] *n* Wahl *f*

electric [i'lektrik] *adj* elektrisch; ~ **razor** Rasierapparat *m*; ~ **cord** Kabel *nt*

electrician [,ilek'triʃən] *n* Elektriker *m*

electricity [,ilek'trisəti] *n* Elektrizität *f*

electronic [ilek'trɔnik] *adj* elektronisch

elegance ['eligəns] *n* Eleganz *f*

elegant ['eligənt] *adj* elegant

element ['elimənt] *n* Bestandteil *m*, Element *nt*

elephant ['elifənt] *n* Elefant *m*

elevator ['eliveitə] *nAm* Aufzug *m*

eleven [i'levən] *num* elf

eleventh [i'levənθ] *num* elfte

elf [elf] *n* (pl elves) Elfe *f*

eliminate [i'limineit] *v* beseitigen

elm [elm] *n* Ulme *f*

else [els] *adv* sonst

elsewhere [,el'sweə] *adv* anderswo

elucidate [i'lu:sideit] *v* erläutern

emancipation [i,mænsi'peiʃən] *n* Emanzipation *f*

embankment [im'bæŋkmənt] *n* Damm *m*

embargo [em'ba:gou] *n* (pl ~es) Embargo *nt*

embark [im'ba:k] *v* sich einschiffen; *einsteigen

embarkation [,emba:'keiʃən] *n* Einschiffung *f*

embarrass [im'bærəs] *v* verwirren; in Verlegenheit *bringen; hindern; **embarrassed** verlegen; **embarrassing** peinlich

embassy ['embəsi] *n* Botschaft *f*

emblem ['embləm] *n* Emblem *nt*

embrace [im'breis] *v* umarmen; *n* Umarmung *f*

embroider [im'brɔidə] *v* sticken

embroidery [im'brɔidəri] *n* Stickerei *f*

emerald ['emərəld] *n* Smaragd *m*

emergency [i'mə:dʒənsi] *n* Notfall *m*; Notlage *f*; ~ **exit** Notausgang *m*

emigrant ['emigrənt] *n* Auswanderer *m*

emigrate ['emigreit] *v* auswandern

emigration [,emi'greiʃən] *n* Auswanderung *f*

emotion [i'mouʃən] *n* Rührung *f*, Erregung *f*

emperor ['empərə] *n* Kaiser *m*

emphasize ['emfəsaiz] *v* betonen

empire ['empaiə] *n* Kaiserreich *nt*, Reich *nt*

employ [im'plɔi] *v* beschäftigen; *verwenden

employee [,emplɔi'i:] *n* Arbeitnehmer *m*, Angestellte *m*

employer [im'plɔiə] *n* Arbeitgeber *m*

employment [im'plɔimənt] *n* Beschäftigung *f*, Tätigkeit *f*; ~ **exchange** Arbeitsamt *nt*

empress ['empris] *n* Kaiserin *f*

empty ['empti] *adj* leer; *v* leeren

enable [i'neibəl] *v* befähigen

enamel [i'næməl] *n* Email *f*

enamelled [i'næməld] *adj* emailliert

enchanting [in'tʃa:ntiŋ] *adj* zauberhaft, bezaubernd

encircle [in'sə:kəl] *v* einkreisen, *umschließen; *einschließen

enclose [in'klouz] v *beischließen, beilegen

enclosure [in'klouʒə] n Beilage f

encounter [in'kauntə] v begegnen; n Begegnung f

encourage [in'kʌridʒ] v ermutigen

encyclopaedia [en,saiklə'pi:diə] n Enzyklopädie f

end [end] n Schluß m, Ende nt; v beenden; enden

ending ['endiŋ] n Ende nt

endless ['endləs] adj unendlich

endorse [in'dɔ:s] v abzeichnen, indossieren

endure [in'djuə] v *ertragen

enemy ['enəmi] n Feind m

energetic [,enə'dʒetik] adj energisch

energy ['enədʒi] n Energie f; Kraft f

engage [in'geidʒ] v anstellen; mieten; sich verpflichten; **engaged** verlobt; beschäftigt, besetzt

engagement [in'geidʒmənt] n Verlobung f; Verpflichtung f; Verabredung f; ~ **ring** Verlobungsring m

engine ['endʒin] n Maschine f, Motor m; Lokomotive f

engineer [,endʒi'niə] n Ingenieur m

England ['iŋglənd] England

English ['iŋgliʃ] adj englisch

Englishman ['iŋgliʃmən] n (pl -men) Engländer m

engrave [iŋ'greiv] v gravieren

engraver [iŋ'greivə] n Graveur m

engraving [iŋ'greiviŋ] n Stich m

enigma [i'nigmə] n Rätsel nt

enjoy [in'dʒɔi] v *genießen

enjoyable [in'dʒɔiəbəl] adj erfreulich, gefällig, angenehm; schmackhaft

enjoyment [in'dʒɔimənt] n Genuß m

enlarge [in'la:dʒ] v vergrößern; erweitern

enlargement [in'la:dʒmənt] n Vergrößerung f

enormous [i'nɔ:məs] adj riesig, ungeheuer

enough [i'nʌf] adv genug; adj genügend

enquire [iŋ'kwaiə] v sich erkundigen; untersuchen

enquiry [iŋ'kwaiəri] n Erkundigung f; Untersuchung f; Umfrage f

enter ['entə] v *betreten, *eintreten; *einschreiben

enterprise ['entəpraiz] n Unternehmen nt

entertain [,entə'tein] v *unterhalten, amüsieren; bewirten

entertainer [,entə'teinə] n Conférencier m

entertaining [,entə'teiniŋ] adj unterhaltsam, amüsant

entertainment [,entə'teinmənt] n Amüsement nt, Unterhaltung f

enthusiasm [in'θju:ziæzəm] n Begeisterung f

enthusiastic [in,θju:zi'æstik] adj begeistert

entire [in'taiə] adj ganz

entirely [in'taiəli] adv ganz

entrance ['entrəns] n Eingang m; Zutritt m; Eintritt m

entrance-fee ['entrənsfi:] n Eintrittsgeld nt

entry ['entri] n Eingang m, Eintritt m; Zugang m; Eintragung f; **no ~** Eintritt verboten

envelope ['envəloup] n Briefumschlag m

envious ['enviəs] adj neidisch, eifersüchtig

environment [in'vaiərənmənt] n Umwelt f; Umgebung f

envoy ['envɔi] n Abgesandte m

envy ['envi] n Neid m; v beneiden

epic ['epik] n Epos nt; adj episch

epidemic [,epi'demik] n Epidemie f

epilepsy ['epilepsi] n Epilepsie f

epilogue ['epilɔg] n Epilog m

episode ['episoud] n Episode f
equal ['i:kwəl] adj gleich; v *gleichkommen
equality [i'kwɔləti] n Gleichheit f
equalize ['i:kwəlaiz] v *ausgleichen
equally ['i:kwəli] adv ebenso
equator [i'kweitə] n Äquator m
equip [i'kwip] v ausrüsten, ausstatten
equipment [i'kwipmənt] n Ausrüstung f
equivalent [i'kwivələnt] adj entsprechend, gleichwertig
eraser [i'reizə] n Radiergummi m
erect [i'rekt] v aufbauen, errichten, aufrichten; adj aufgerichtet, aufrecht
err [ə:] v sich irren; irren
errand ['erənd] n Botengang m
error ['erə] n Fehler m, Irrtum m
escalator ['eskəleitə] n Rolltreppe f
escape [i'skeip] v *entkommen; *fliehen, flüchten, *entgehen; n Flucht f
escort¹ ['eskɔ:t] n Geleit nt
escort² [i'skɔ:t] v eskortieren
especially [i'speʃəli] adv hauptsächlich, besonders
esplanade [,esplə'neid] n Promenade f
essay ['esei] n Essay m; Abhandlung f, Aufsatz m
essence ['esəns] n Essenz f; Kern m, Wesen nt
essential [i'senʃəl] adj unentbehrlich; grundlegend, wesentlich
essentially [i'senʃəli] adv vor allem
establish [i'stæbliʃ] v gründen; feststellen
estate [i'steit] n Landsitz m
esteem [i'sti:m] n Respekt m, Achtung f; v schätzen
estimate¹ ['estimeit] v veranschlagen, schätzen
estimate² ['estimət] n Voranschlag m
estuary ['estʃuəri] n Trichtermündung f

etcetera [et'setərə] und so weiter
etching ['etʃiŋ] n Radierung f
eternal [i'tə:nəl] adj ewig
eternity [i'tə:nəti] n Ewigkeit f
ether ['i:θə] n Äther m
Ethiopia [iθi'oupiə] Äthiopien
Ethiopian [iθi'oupiən] adj äthiopisch; n Äthiopier m
Europe ['juərəp] Europa
European [,juərə'pi:ən] adj europäisch; n Europäer m
evacuate [i'vækjueit] v evakuieren
evaluate [i'væljueit] v veranschlagen
evaporate [i'væpəreit] v verdampfen
even ['i:vən] adj glatt, eben, gleich; stetig; gerade; adv sogar
evening ['i:vniŋ] n Abend m; ~ **dress** Gesellschaftsanzug m
event [i'vent] n Ereignis nt; Vorfall m
eventual [i'ventʃuəl] adj möglich; endgültig
ever ['evə] adv jemals; immer
every ['evri] adj jeder
everybody ['evri,bɔdi] pron jedermann
everyday ['evridei] adj alltäglich
everyone ['evriwʌn] pron jeder, jedermann
everything ['evriθiŋ] pron alles
everywhere ['evriwɛə] adv überall
evidence ['evidəns] n Beweis m
evident ['evidənt] adj offensichtlich
evil ['i:vəl] n Übel nt; adj böse, schlecht
evolution [,i:və'lu:ʃən] n Evolution f
exact [ig'zækt] adj präzis, genau
exactly [ig'zæktli] adv genau
exaggerate [ig'zædʒəreit] v *übertreiben
examination [ig,zæmi'neiʃən] n Examen nt; Untersuchung f; Verhör nt
examine [ig'zæmin] v prüfen
example [ig'za:mpəl] n Beispiel nt; **for**

~ zum Beispiel

excavation [,ekskə'veiʃən] n Ausgrabung f

exceed [ik'si:d] v *überschreiten; *übertreffen

excel [ik'sel] v sich auszeichnen

excellent ['eksələnt] adj ausgezeichnet, hervorragend

except [ik'sept] prep ausgenommen, außer

exception [ik'sepʃən] n Ausnahme f

exceptional [ik'sepʃənəl] adj ungewöhnlich, außergewöhnlich

excerpt ['eksə:pt] n Auszug m

excess [ik'ses] n Ausschreitung f

excessive [ik'sesiv] adj übertrieben

exchange [iks'tʃeindʒ] v auswechseln, wechseln, austauschen; n Tausch m; Börse f; ~ **office** Wechselstube f; ~ **rate** Wechselkurs m

excite [ik'sait] v aufregen, erregen

excitement [ik'saitmənt] n Erregung f, Aufregung f

exciting [ik'saitiŋ] adj aufregend

exclaim [ik'skleim] v *ausrufen

exclamation [,eksklə'meiʃən] n Ausruf m

exclude [ik'sklu:d] v *ausschließen

exclusive [ik'sklu:siv] adj exklusiv

exclusively [ik'sklu:sivli] adv ausschließlich, nur

excursion [ik'skə:ʃən] n Ausflug m

excuse¹ [ik'skju:s] n Entschuldigung f

excuse² [ik'skju:z] v *verzeihen, entschuldigen

execute ['eksikju:t] v ausführen, *vollziehen

execution [,eksi'kju:ʃən] n Hinrichtung f

executioner [,eksi'kju:ʃənə] n Scharfrichter m

executive [ig'zekjutiv] adj vollziehend; n vollziehende Gewalt; Geschäftsführer m

exempt [ig'ʒempt] v befreien, *ausnehmen; adj befreit

exemption [ig'zempʃən] n Befreiung f

exercise ['eksəsaiz] n Übung f; Aufgabe f; v üben; ausüben

exhale [eks'heil] v ausatmen

exhaust [ig'zɔ:st] n Auspuff m; v verschöpfen; ~ **gases** Auspuffgase ntpl

exhibit [ig'zibit] v ausstellen; vorführen

exhibition [,eksi'biʃən] n Ausstellung f

exile ['eksail] n Verbannung f; Verbannte m

exist [ig'zist] v *bestehen

existence [ig'zistəns] n Dasein nt

exit ['eksit] n Ausgang m; Ausfahrt f

exotic [ig'zɔtik] adj exotisch

expand [ik'spænd] v ausbreiten; ausdehnen; entfalten

expect [ik'spekt] v erwarten

expectation [,ekspek'teiʃən] n Erwartung f

expedition [,ekspə'diʃən] n Versand m; Expedition f

expel [ik'spel] v *ausweisen

expenditure [ik'spenditʃə] n Aufwand m

expense [ik'spens] n Ausgabe f; ex-penses pl Unkosten pl

expensive [ik'spensiv] adj kostspielig, teuer; kostbar

experience [ik'spiəriəns] n Erfahrung f; v *erfahren, erleben; experienced erfahren

experiment [ik'sperimənt] n Versuch m, Experiment nt; v experimentieren

expert ['ekspə:t] n Fachmann m, Sachverständige m; adj fachkundig

expire [ik'spaiə] v *verfallen, aufhören, *ablaufen; ausatmen; expired verfallen

expiry [ik'spaiəri] n Fälligkeitstermin

m

explain [ik'splein] *v* erläutern, erklären

explanation [,eksplə'neiʃən] *n* Erläuterung *f*, Auslegung *f*, Erklärung *f*

explicit [ik'splisit] *adj* ausdrücklich

explode [ik'sploud] *v* explodieren

exploit [ik'sploit] *v* ausbeuten, ausnutzen

explore [ik'splɔ:] *v* erforschen

explosion [ik'splouʒən] *n* Explosion *f*

explosive [ik'splousiv] *adj* explosiv; *n* Sprengstoff *m*

export[1] [ik'spɔ:t] *v* ausführen, exportieren

export[2] ['ekspɔ:t] *n* Export *m*

exportation [,ekspɔ:'teiʃən] *n* Ausfuhr *f*

exports ['ekspɔ:ts] *pl* Ausfuhr *f*

exposition [,ekspə'ziʃən] *n* Ausstellung *f*

exposure [ik'spouʒə] *n* Aussetzung *f*; Belichtung *f*; ~ **meter** Belichtungsmesser *m*

express [ik'spres] *v* ausdrücken; Ausdruck *geben, äußern; *adj* Eilausdrücklich; ~ **train** Schnellzug *m*

expression [ik'spreʃən] *n* Ausdruck *m*; Äußerung *f*

exquisite [ik'skwizit] *adj* auserlesen

extend [ik'stend] *v* verlängern; erweitern; gewähren

extension [ik'stenʃən] *n* Verlängerung *f*; Ausdehnung *f*; Nebenanschluß *m*; ~ **cord** Verlängerungsschnur *f*

extensive [ik'stensiv] *adj* umfangreich; umfassend, ausgedehnt

extent [ik'stent] *n* Ausmaß *nt*

exterior [ek'stiəriə] *adj* äußerlich; *n* Außenseite *f*

external [ek'stə:nəl] *adj* äußerlich

extinguish [ik'stiŋgwiʃ] *v* löschen, auslöschen

extort [ik'stɔ:t] *v* erpressen

extortion [ik'stɔ:ʃən] *n* Erpressung *f*

extra ['ekstrə] *adj* zusätzlich

extract[1] [ik'strækt] *v* *ausziehen, *ausreißen

extract[2] ['ekstrækt] *n* Abschnitt *m*

extradite ['ekstrədait] *v* ausliefern

extraordinary [ik'strɔ:dənri] *adj* außerordentlich

extravagant [ik'strævəgənt] *adj* übertrieben, extravagant

extreme [ik'stri:m] *adj* extrem; höchst, äußerst; *n* Extrem *nt*

exuberant [ig'zju:bərənt] *adj* überschwenglich

eye [ai] *n* Auge *nt*

eyebrow ['aibrau] *n* Augenbraue *f*

eyelash ['ailæʃ] *n* Augenwimper *f*

eyelid ['ailid] *n* Augenlid *nt*

eye-pencil ['ai,pensəl] *n* Augenbrauenstift *m*

eye-shadow ['ai,ʃædou] *n* Augenschminke *f*

eye-witness ['ai,witnəs] *n* Augenzeuge *m*

F

fable ['feibəl] *n* Fabel *f*

fabric ['fæbrik] *n* Stoff *m*; Struktur *f*

façade [fə'sɑ:d] *n* Fassade *f*

face [feis] *n* Gesicht *nt*; *v* *gegenüberstehen; ~ **massage** Gesichtsmassage *f*; **facing** gegenüber

face-cream ['feiskri:m] *n* Gesichtskrem *f*

face-pack ['feispæk] *n* Gesichtspackung *f*

facility [fə'siləti] *n* Fazilität *f*

fact [fækt] *n* Tatsache *f*; **in** ~ tatsächlich

factor ['fæktə] *n* Faktor *m*

factory ['fæktəri] *n* Fabrik *f*

factual ['fæktʃuəl] *adj* tatsächlich

faculty ['fækəlti] *n* Gabe *f*; Begabung *f*, Talent *nt*, Fähigkeit *f*; Fakultät *f*

fad [fæd] *n* Torheit *f*

fade [feid] *v* verblassen, *verschießen

faience [fai'ū:s] *n* Steingut *nt*, Fayence *f*

fail [feil] *v* versagen; fehlen; mangeln; versäumen; *durchfallen; **without** ~ unbedingt

failure ['feiljə] *n* Mißerfolg *m*; Fehlschlag *m*

faint [feint] *v* ohnmächtig *werden; *adj* schwach, vage

fair [fɛə] *n* Kirmes *f*; Messe *f*; *adj* redlich, gerecht; blond; hübsch

fairly ['fɛəli] *adv* recht, leidlich, ziemlich

fairy ['fɛəri] *n* Fee *f*

fairytale ['fɛəriteil] *n* Märchen *nt*

faith [feiθ] *n* Glaube *m*; Vertrauen *nt*

faithful ['feiθful] *adj* treu

fake [feik] *n* Fälschung *f*

fall [fɔ:l] *n* Sturz *m*; *nAm* Herbst *m*
*fall [fɔ:l] *v* *fallen

false [fɔ:ls] *adj* falsch; verkehrt, unwahr, unecht; ~ **teeth** künstliches Gebiß

falter ['fɔ:ltə] *v* wanken; stammeln

fame [feim] *n* Name *m*, Ruhm *m*; Ruf *m*

familiar [fə'miljə] *adj* vertraut; vertraulich

family ['fæməli] *n* Familie *f*; Verwandtschaft *f*; ~ **name** Nachname *m*

famous ['feiməs] *adj* berühmt

fan [fæn] *n* Ventilator *m*; Fächer *m*; Fan *m*; ~ **belt** Ventilatorriemen *m*

fanatical [fə'nætikəl] *adj* fanatisch

fancy ['fænsi] *v* *mögen, Lust *haben zu; sich einbilden, sich vorstellen; *n* Laune *f*; Phantasie *f*

fantastic [fæn'tæstik] *adj* phantastisch

fantasy ['fæntəzi] *n* Einbildung *f*

far [fɑ:] *adj* fern; *adv* viel; **by** ~ bei weitem; **so** ~ bis jetzt

far-away ['fɑ:rəwei] *adj* entfernt

farce [fɑ:s] *n* Posse *f*

fare [fɛə] *n* Fahrgeld *nt*; Kost *f*, Speise *f*

farm [fɑ:m] *n* Bauernhof *m*

farmer ['fɑ:mə] *n* Bauer *m*; **farmer's wife** Bäuerin *f*

farmhouse ['fɑ:mhaus] *n* Bauernhaus *nt*

far-off ['fɑ:rɔf] *adj* abgelegen

fascinate ['fæsineit] *v* fesseln

fascism ['fæʃizəm] *n* Faschismus *m*

fascist ['fæʃist] *adj* faschistisch; *n* Faschist *m*

fashion ['fæʃən] *n* Mode *f*; Weise *f*

fashionable ['fæʃənəbəl] *adj* modern

fast [fɑ:st] *adj* rasch, schnell; fest

fast-dyed [,fɑ:st'daid] *adj* waschecht, farbecht

fasten ['fɑ:sən] *v* festmachen, befestigen; *schließen

fastener ['fɑ:sənə] *n* Verschluß *m*

fat [fæt] *adj* fett, dick; *n* Fett *nt*

fatal ['feitəl] *adj* unheilvoll, tödlich, verhängnisvoll

fate [feit] *n* Schicksal *nt*

father ['fɑ:ðə] *n* Vater *m*; Pater *m*

father-in-law ['fɑ:ðərinlɔ:] *n* (pl fathers-) Schwiegervater *m*

fatherland ['fɑ:ðələnd] *n* Vaterland *nt*

fatness ['fætnəs] *n* Fettheit *f*

fatty ['fæti] *adj* fettig

faucet ['fɔ:sit] *nAm* Wasserhahn *m*

fault [fɔ:lt] *n* Fehler *m*; Mangel *m*, Defekt *m*

faultless ['fɔ:ltləs] *adj* tadellos; einwandfrei

faulty ['fɔ:lti] *adj* mangelhaft, fehlerhaft

favour ['feivə] *n* Gefälligkeit *f*; *v* bevorrechten, begünstigen

favourable ['feivərəbəl] *adj* günstig

favourite ['feivərit] n Liebling m, Favorit m; adj Lieblings-

fawn [fɔ:n] adj rehbraun; n Rehkalb nt

fear [fiə] n Furcht f, Angst f; v fürchten

feasible ['fi:zəbəl] adj durchführbar

feast [fi:st] n Fest nt

feat [fi:t] n Glanzleistung f

feather ['feðə] n Feder f

feature ['fi:tʃə] n Kennzeichen nt; Gesichtszug m

February ['februəri] Februar

federal ['fedərəl] adj Bundes-

federation [,fedə'reiʃən] n Föderation f; Verband m

fee [fi:] n Honorar nt

feeble ['fi:bəl] adj schwach

***feed** [fi:d] v ernähren; **fed up with** überdrüssig

***feel** [fi:l] v fühlen; betasten; ~ **like** Lust *haben zu

feeling ['fi:liŋ] n Gefühl nt

fell [fel] v (p fall)

fellow ['felou] n Kerl m

felt[1] [felt] n Filz m

felt[2] [felt] v (p, pp feel)

female ['fi:meil] adj weiblich

feminine ['feminin] adj weiblich

fence [fens] n Zaun m; Gatter nt; v *fechten

fender ['fendə] n Stoßstange f

ferment [fə:'ment] v *gären

ferry-boat ['feribout] n Fährboot nt

fertile ['fə:tail] adj fruchtbar

festival ['festivəl] n Festival nt

festive ['festiv] adj festlich

fetch [fetʃ] v holen; abholen

feudal ['fju:dəl] adj feudal

fever ['fi:və] n Fieber nt

feverish ['fi:vəriʃ] adj fiebrig

few [fju:] adj wenig

fiancé [fi'ã:sei] n Verlobte m

fiancée [fi'ã:sei] n Verlobte f

fibre ['faibə] n Faser f

fiction ['fikʃən] n Fiktion f, Erdichtung f

field [fi:ld] n Acker m, Feld nt; Gebiet nt; ~ **glasses** Feldstecher m

fierce [fiəs] adj wild; wüst, heftig

fifteen [,fif'ti:n] num fünfzehn

fifteenth [,fif'ti:nθ] num fünfzehnte

fifth [fifθ] num fünfte

fifty ['fifti] num fünfzig

fig [fig] n Feige f

fight [fait] n Streit m, Kampf m

***fight** [fait] v sich *schlagen, kämpfen

figure ['figə] n Figur f, Gestalt f; Zahl f

file [fail] n Feile f; Akten; Reihe f

Filipino [,fili'pi:nou] n Philippine m

fill [fil] v füllen; ~ **in** ausfüllen; **filling station** Tankstelle f; ~ **out** Am ausfüllen; ~ **up** vollfüllen

filling ['filiŋ] n Plombe f; Füllung f

film [film] n Film m; v filmen

filter ['filtə] n Filter m

filthy ['filθi] adj dreckig, schmutzig

final ['fainəl] adj letzt

finance [fai'næns] v finanzieren

finances [fai'nænsiz] pl Finanzen pl

financial [fai'nænʃəl] adj finanziell

finch [fintʃ] n Fink m

***find** [faind] v *finden

fine [fain] n Geldstrafe f; adj fein; schön; ausgezeichnet, prächtig; ~ **arts** die schönen Künste

finger ['fiŋgə] n Finger m

fingerprint ['fiŋgəprint] n Fingerabdruck m

finish ['finiʃ] v fertigmachen, beenden; enden; n Schluß m; Ziellinie f; **finished** fertig; alle

Finland ['finlənd] Finnland

Finn [fin] n Finne m

Finnish ['finiʃ] adj finnisch

fire [faiə] n Feuer nt; Brand m; v *schießen, *entlassen fire-alarm ['faiərə,la:m] *n* Feueralarm *m*

fire-brigade ['faiəbri,geid] *n* Feuerwehr *f*

fire-escape ['faiəri,skeip] *n* Nottreppe *f*

fire-extinguisher ['faiərik,stiŋwiʃə] *n* Feuerlöscher *m*

fireplace ['faiəpleis] *n* Kamin *m*

fireproof ['faiəpru:f] *adj* feuersicher; feuerfest

firm [fə:m] *adj* fest; solide; *n* Firma *f*

first [fə:st] *num* erste; at ~ zuerst; anfangs; ~ name Vorname *m*

first-aid [,fə:st'eid] *n* erste Hilfe; ~ kit Verbandskasten *m*; ~ post Unfallstation *f*

first-class [,fə:st'kla:s] *adj* erstklassig

first-rate [,fə:st'reit] *adj* vorzüglich, erstrangig

fir-tree ['fə:tri:] *n* Tanne *f*

fish¹ [fiʃ] *n* (pl ~, ~es) Fisch *m*; ~ shop Fischhandlung *f*

fish² [fiʃ] *v* fischen; angeln; fishing gear Angelgeräte *ntpl*; fishing hook Angelhaken *m*; fishing industry Fischerei *f*; fishing licence Angelschein *m*; fishing line Angelschnur *f*; fishing net Fischnetz *nt*; fishing rod Angelrute *f*; fishing tackle Angelgeräte *ntpl*

fishbone ['fiʃboun] *n* Gräte *f*, Fischgräte *f*

fisherman ['fiʃəmən] *n* (pl -men) Fischer *m*

fist [fist] *n* Faust *f*

fit [fit] *adj* tauglich; *n* Anfall *m*; *v* passen; fitting room Anproberaum *m*

five [faiv] *num* fünf

fix [fiks] *v* richten

fixed [fikst] *adj* fest

fizz [fiz] *n* Brause *f*

fjord [fjɔ:d] *n* Fjord *m*

flag [flæg] *n* Fahne *f*

flame [fleim] *n* Flamme *f*

flamingo [flə'miŋgou] *n* (pl ~s, ~es) Flamingo *m*

flannel ['flænəl] *n* Flanell *m*

flash [flæʃ] *n* Blitz *m*

flash-bulb ['flæʃbʌlb] *n* Blitzlicht *nt*

flash-light ['flæʃlait] *n* Taschenlampe *f*

flask [fla:sk] *n* Flakon *nt*; thermos ~ Thermosflasche *f*

flat [flæt] *adj* eben, flach; *n* Wohnung *f*; ~ tyre Reifenpanne *f*

flavour ['fleivə] *n* Geschmack *m*; *v* würzen

fleet [fli:t] *n* Flotte *f*

flesh [fleʃ] *n* Fleisch *nt*

flew [flu:] *v* (p fly)

flex [fleks] *n* Kabel *nt*

flexible ['fleksibəl] *adj* geschmeidig; biegsam

flight [flait] *n* Flug *m*; charter ~ Charterflug *m*

flint [flint] *n* Feuerstein *m*

float [flout] *v* *schwimmen; *n* Schwimmer *m*

flock [flɔk] *n* Herde *f*

flood [flʌd] *n* Überschwemmung *f*; Flut *f*

floor [flɔ:] *n* Fußboden *m*; Geschoß *nt*, Stockwerk *nt*; ~ show Kabarett *nt*

florist ['flɔrist] *n* Blumenhändler *m*

flour [flauə] *n* Mehl *nt*

flow [flou] *v* strömen, *fließen

flower [flauə] *n* Blume *f*

flowerbed ['flauəbed] *n* Blumenbeet *nt*

flower-shop ['flauəʃɔp] *n* Blumenhandlung *f*

flown [floun] *v* (pp fly)

flu [flu:] *n* Grippe *f*

fluent ['flu:ənt] *adj* fließend

fluid ['flu:id] *adj* flüssig; *n* Flüssigkeit *f*

flute [flu:t] *n* Flöte *f*

fly [flai] *n* Fliege *f*; Schlitz *m*

*fly [flai] v *fliegen

foam [foum] n Schaum m; v schäumen

foam-rubber ['foum,rʌbə] n Schaumgummi m

focus ['foukəs] n Brennpunkt m

fog [fɔg] n Nebel m

foggy ['fɔgi] adj nebelig

foglamp ['fɔglæmp] n Nebellampe f

fold [fould] v falten; zusammenfalten; n Falte f

folk [fouk] n Volk nt; ~ **song** Volkslied nt

folk-dance ['foukdɑːns] n Volkstanz m

folklore ['fouklɔː] n Folklore f

follow ['fɔlou] v folgen; **following** adj nächst, folgend

*be fond of [biː fɔnd ɔv] gern *mögen

food [fuːd] n Nahrung f; Kost f, Essen nt; ~ **poisoning** Nahrungsmittelvergiftung f

foodstuffs ['fuːdstʌfs] pl Nahrungsmittel ntpl

fool [fuːl] n Tor m, Narr m; v zum besten *haben

foolish ['fuːliʃ] adj albern, töricht; närrisch

foot [fut] n (pl feet) Fuß m; ~ **powder** Fußpuder m; **on** ~ zu Fuß

football ['futbɔːl] n Fußball m; ~ **match** Fußballspiel nt

foot-brake ['futbreik] n Fußbremse f

footpath ['futpɑːθ] n Fußweg m

footwear ['futwɛə] n Schuhwerk nt

for [fɔː, fə] prep für; während; nach; wegen, aus; conj denn

*forbid [fə'bid] v *verbieten

force [fɔːs] v *zwingen; forcieren; n Macht f, Kraft f; Gewalt f; **by** ~ zwangsweise; **driving** ~ Treibkraft f

ford [fɔːd] n Furt f

forecast ['fɔːkɑːst] n Vorhersage f; v voraussagen

foreground ['fɔːgraund] n Vordergrund m

forehead ['fɔred] n Stirn f

foreign ['fɔrin] adj ausländisch; fremd

foreigner ['fɔrinə] n Fremde m; Ausländer m

foreman ['fɔːmən] n (pl -men) Werkmeister m

foremost ['fɔːmoust] adj erste

foresail ['fɔːseil] n Focksegel nt

forest ['fɔrist] n Forst m, Wald m

forester ['fɔristə] n Förster m

forge [fɔːdʒ] v fälschen

*forget [fə'get] v *vergessen

forgetful [fə'getfəl] adj vergeßlich

*forgive [fə'giv] v entschuldigen, *verzeihen

fork [fɔːk] n Gabel f; Gabelung f; v sich gabeln

form [fɔːm] n Form f; Formular nt; Klasse f; v formen

formal ['fɔːməl] adj förmlich

formality [fɔː'mæləti] n Formalität f

former ['fɔːmə] adj ehemalig; früher; **formerly** vormals, früher

formula ['fɔːmjulə] n (pl ~e, ~s) Formel f

fort [fɔːt] n Fort nt

fortnight ['fɔːtnait] n vierzehn Tage

fortress ['fɔːtris] n Festung f

fortunate ['fɔːtʃənət] adj glücklich

fortune ['fɔːtʃuːn] n Vermögen nt; Geschick nt, Glück nt

forty ['fɔːti] num vierzig

forward ['fɔːwəd] adv voraus, vorwärts; v *nachsenden

foster-parents ['fɔstə,pɛərənts] pl Pflegeeltern pl

fought [fɔːt] v (p, pp fight)

foul [faul] adj schmutzig; niederträchtig

found¹ [faund] v (p, pp find)

found² [faund] v gründen, errichten, stiften

foundation [faun'deiʃən] n Stiftung f; ~ **cream** Make-up-Unterlage

fountain ['fauntin] n Springbrunnen m; Quelle f

fountain-pen ['fauntinpen] n Füller m

four [fɔ:] num vier

fourteen [,fɔ:'ti:n] num vierzehn

fourteenth [,fɔ:'ti:nθ] num vierzehnte

fourth [fɔ:θ] num vierte

fowl [faul] n (pl ~s, ~) Geflügel nt

fox [fɔks] n Fuchs m

foyer ['fɔiei] n Foyer nt

fraction ['frækʃən] n Bruchstück nt

fracture ['fræktʃə] v *brechen; n Bruch m

fragile ['frædʒail] adj zerbrechlich

fragment ['frægmənt] n Fragment nt; Bruchstück nt

frame [freim] n Rahmen m; Gestell nt

France [frɑ:ns] Frankreich

franchise ['fræntʃaiz] n Wahlrecht nt

fraternity [frə'tə:nəti] n Brüderschaft f

fraud [frɔ:d] n Schwindel m, Betrug m

fray [frei] v zerfasern

free [fri:] adj frei; gratis; ~ **of charge** kostenlos; ~ **ticket** Freikarte f

freedom ['fri:dəm] n Freiheit f

***freeze** [fri:z] v *frieren; *gefrieren

freezing ['fri:ziŋ] adj eisig

freezing-point ['fri:ziŋpɔint] n Gefrierpunkt m

freight [freit] n Ladung f, Fracht f

freight-train ['freittrein] nAm Güterzug m

French [frentʃ] adj französisch

Frenchman ['frentʃmən] n (pl -men) Franzose m

frequency ['fri:kwənsi] n Frequenz f; Häufigkeit f

frequent ['fri:kwənt] adj üblich, häufig; **frequently** oft

fresh [freʃ] adj frisch; erfrischend; ~ **water** Süßwasser nt

friction ['frikʃən] n Reibung f

Friday ['fraidi] Freitag m

fridge [fridʒ] n Kühlschrank m

friend [frend] n Freund m; Freundin f

friendly ['frendli] adj freundlich; freundschaftlich

friendship ['frendʃip] n Freundschaft f

fright [frait] n Angst f, Schreck m

frighten ['fraitən] v *erschrecken

frightened ['fraitənd] adj verängstigt; *be ~ *erschrecken

frightful ['fraitfəl] adj fürchterlich, schrecklich

fringe [frindʒ] n Franse f

frock [frɔk] n Kleid nt

frog [frɔg] n Frosch m

from [frɔm] prep von; aus; von ... an

front [frʌnt] n Vorderseite f; **in ~ of** vor

frontier ['frʌntiə] n Grenze f

frost [frɔst] n Frost m

froth [frɔθ] n Schaum m

frozen ['frouzən] adj gefroren; ~ **food** Gefrierwaren fpl

fruit [fru:t] n Obst nt; Frucht f

fry [frai] v *braten

frying-pan ['fraiiŋpæn] n Bratpfanne f

fuel ['fju:əl] n Brennstoff m; Benzin nt; ~ **pump** Am Benzinpumpe f

full [ful] adj voll; ~ **board** Vollpension f; ~ **stop** Punkt m; ~ **up** vollbesetzt

fun [fʌn] n Vergnügen nt, Spaß m; Ulk m

function ['fʌŋkʃən] n Funktion f

fund [fʌnd] n Fonds m

fundamental [,fʌndə'mentəl] adj grundlegend

funeral ['fju:nərəl] n Begräbnis nt

funnel ['fʌnəl] n Trichter m

funny ['fʌni] adj spaßig, komisch; sonderbar

fur [fə:] n Pelz m; ~ **coat** Pelzmantel

m; **furs** Pelzwerk *nt*
furious ['fjuəriəs] *adj* rasend, wütend
furnace ['fə:nis] *n* Ofen *m*
furnish ['fə:niʃ] *v* liefern, verschaffen; möblieren, einrichten; ~ **with** *versehen mit
furniture ['fə:nitʃə] *n* Möbel *ntpl*
furrier ['fʌriə] *n* Kürschner *m*
further ['fə:ðə] *adj* ferner; weiter
furthermore ['fə:ðəmɔ:] *adv* überdies
furthest ['fə:ðist] *adj* entferntest
fuse [fju:z] *n* Sicherung *f*; Lunte *f*
fuss [fʌs] *n* Getue *nt*; Wichtigtuerei *f*
future ['fju:tʃə] *n* Zukunft *f*; *adj* zukünftig

G

gable ['geibəl] *n* Giebel *m*
gaiety ['geiəti] *n* Heiterkeit *f*, Fröhlichkeit *f*
gain [gein] *v* *gewinnen; *n* Gewinn *m*
gait [geit] *n* Gang *m*
gale [geil] *n* Sturm *m*
gall [gɔ:l] *n* Galle *f*; ~ **bladder** Gallenblase *f*
gallery ['gæləri] *n* Galerie *f*
gallop ['gæləp] *n* Galopp *m*
gallows ['gælouz] *pl* Galgen *m*
gallstone ['gɔ:lstoun] *n* Gallenstein *m*
game [geim] *n* Spiel *nt*; Wild *nt*; ~ **reserve** Wildpark *m*
gang [gæŋ] *n* Bande *f*; Schicht *f*
gangway ['gæŋwei] *n* Laufplanke *f*
gaol [dʒeil] *n* Gefängnis *nt*
gap [gæp] *n* Lücke *f*
garage ['gærɑ:ʒ] *n* Garage *f*; *v* einstellen
garbage ['gɑ:bidʒ] *n* Müll *m*, Abfall *m*
garden ['gɑ:dən] *n* Garten *m*; **public** ~ Anlage *f*; **zoological gardens**

zoologischer Garten
gardener ['gɑ:dənə] *n* Gärtner *m*
gargle ['gɑ:gəl] *v* gurgeln
garlic ['gɑ:lik] *n* Knoblauch *m*
gas [gæs] *n* Gas *nt*; *nAm* Benzin *nt*; ~ **cooker** Gasherd *m*; ~ **pump** *Am* Benzinpumpe *f*; ~ **station** *Am* Tankstelle *f*; ~ **stove** Gasofen *m*
gasoline ['gæsəli:n] *nAm* Benzin *nt*
gastric ['gæstrik] *adj* gastrisch; ~ **ulcer** Magengeschwür *nt*
gasworks ['gæswə:ks] *n* Gaswerk *nt*
gate [geit] *n* Tor *nt*
gather ['gæðə] *v* sammeln; sich versammeln; einholen
gauge [geidʒ] *n* Messer *m*
gauze [gɔ:z] *n* Gaze *f*
gave [geiv] *v* (p give)
gay [gei] *adj* lustig; bunt
gaze [geiz] *v* starren
gazetteer [,gæzə'tiə] *n* geographisches Lexikon
gear [giə] *n* Gang *m*; Ausrüstung *f*; **change** ~ schalten; ~ **lever** Gangschaltung *f*
gear-box ['giəbɔks] *n* Getriebe *nt*
gem [dʒem] *n* Juwel *nt*, Edelstein *m*; Kleinod *nt*
gender ['dʒendə] *n* Geschlecht *nt*
general ['dʒenərəl] *adj* allgemein; *n* General *m*; ~ **practitioner** praktischer Arzt; **in** ~ im allgemeinen
generate ['dʒenəreit] *v* erzeugen
generation [,dʒenə'reiʃən] *n* Generation *f*
generator ['dʒenəreitə] *n* Generator *m*
generosity [,dʒenə'rɔsəti] *n* Großmut *m*
generous ['dʒenərəs] *adj* freigebig, großzügig
genital ['dʒenitəl] *adj* geschlechtlich
genius ['dʒi:niəs] *n* Genie *nt*
gentle ['dʒentəl] *adj* sanft; zart, leicht;

behutsam
gentleman ['dʒentəlmən] n (pl -men)
Herr m
genuine ['dʒenjuin] adj echt
geography [dʒi'ɔgrəfi] n Erdkunde f
geology [dʒi'ɔlədʒi] n Geologie f
geometry [dʒi'ɔmətri] n Geometrie f
germ [dʒə:m] n Bazille f; Keim m
German ['dʒə:mən] adj deutsch; n
Deutsche m
Germany ['dʒə:məni] Deutschland
gesticulate [dʒi'stikjuleit] v gestikulieren
*get [get] v *bekommen; holen;
*werden; ~ **back** *zurückgehen; ~
off *aussteigen; ~ **on** *einsteigen;
*vorwärtskommen; ~ **up** *aufstehen
ghost [goust] n Geist m
giant ['dʒaiənt] n Riese m
giddiness ['gidinəs] n Schwindelgefühl
nt
giddy ['gidi] adj schwindlig
gift [gift] n Geschenk nt; Gabe f
gifted ['giftid] adj begabt
gigantic [dʒai'gæntik] adj riesenhaft
giggle ['gigəl] v kichern
gill [gil] n Kieme f
gilt [gilt] adj vergoldet
ginger ['dʒindʒə] n Ingwer m
gipsy ['dʒipsi] n Zigeuner m
girdle ['gə:dəl] n Hüfthalter m
girl [gə:l] n Mädchen nt; ~ **guide**
Pfadfinderin f
*give [giv] v *geben; überreichen; ~
away *verraten; ~ **in** *nachgeben;
~ **up** *aufgeben
glacier ['glæsiə] n Gletscher m
glad [glæd] adj erfreut, froh; **gladly**
mit Vergnügen, gerne
gladness ['glædnəs] n Freude f
glamorous ['glæmərəs] adj bezaubernd
glamour ['glæmə] n Reiz m
glance [glɑ:ns] n Blick m; v erblicken

gland [glænd] n Drüse f
glare [gleə] n grelles Licht; Glanz m
glaring ['gleəriŋ] adj blendend
glass [glɑ:s] n Glas nt; gläsern;
glasses Brille f; **magnifying** ~
Vergrößerungsglas nt
glaze [gleiz] v glasieren
glen [glen] n Bergschlucht f
glide [glaid] v *gleiten
glider ['glaidə] n Segelflugzeug nt
glimpse [glimps] n Blick m; v erblicken
global ['gloubəl] adj weltumfassend
globe [gloub] n Globus m, Erdball m
gloom [glu:m] n Düsterkeit f
gloomy ['glu:mi] adj düster
glorious ['glɔ:riəs] adj prächtig
glory ['glɔ:ri] n Ehre f, Ruhm m; Lob
nt
gloss [glɔs] n Glanz m
glossy ['glɔsi] adj glänzend
glove [glʌv] n Handschuh m
glow [glou] v glühen; n Glut f
glue [glu:] n Leim m
*go [gou] v *gehen; *werden; ~
ahead *fortfahren; ~ **away** *weggehen; ~ **back** *zurückgehen; ~
home *heimgehen; ~ **in** *hineingehen; ~ **on** *weitergehen, *fortfahren; ~ **out** *ausgehen; ~ **through**
durchmachen
goal [goul] n Ziel nt, Tor nt
goalkeeper ['goul,ki:pə] n Torwart m
goat [gout] n Ziegenbock m, Ziege f
god [gɔd] n Gott m
goddess ['gɔdis] n Göttin f
godfather ['gɔd,fa:ðə] n Pate m
goggles ['gɔgəlz] pl Schutzbrille f
gold [gould] n Gold nt; ~ **leaf** Blattgold nt
golden ['gouldən] adj golden
goldmine ['gouldmain] n Goldgrube f
goldsmith ['gouldsmiθ] n Goldschmied
m

golf [gɔlf] *n* Golf *nt*

golf-club ['gɔlfklʌb] *n* Golfklub *m*

golf-course ['gɔlfkɔːs] *n* Golfplatz *m*

golf-links ['gɔlfliŋks] *n* Golfplatz *m*

gondola ['gɔndələ] *n* Gondel *f*

gone [gɔn] *adv* (pp go) fort

good [gud] *adj* gut; lecker; brav, artig

good-bye! [,gud'bai] auf Wiedersehen!

good-humoured [,gud'hjuːməd] *adj* gutgelaunt

good-looking [,gud'lukiŋ] *adj* hübsch

good-natured [,gud'neitʃəd] *adj* gutmütig

goods [gudz] *pl* Waren, Güter *ntpl*; ~ **train** Güterzug *m*

good-tempered [,gud'tempəd] *adj* gutgelaunt

goodwill [,gud'wil] *n* Wohlwollen *nt*

goose [guːs] *n* (pl geese) Gans *f*

gooseberry ['guzbəri] *n* Stachelbeere *f*

goose-flesh ['guːsfleʃ] *n* Gänsehaut *f*

gorge [gɔːdʒ] *n* Schlucht *f*

gorgeous ['gɔːdʒəs] *adj* prächtig

gospel ['gɔspəl] *n* Evangelium *nt*

gossip ['gɔsip] *n* Tratsch *m*; *v* tratschen

got [gɔt] *v* (p, pp get)

gourmet ['guəmei] *n* Feinschmecker *m*

gout [gaut] *n* Gicht *f*

govern ['gʌvən] *v* regieren

governess ['gʌvənis] *n* Gouvernante *f*

government ['gʌvənmənt] *n* Verwaltung *f*, Regierung *f*

governor ['gʌvənə] *n* Gouverneur *m*

gown [gaun] *n* Kleid *nt*

grace [greis] *n* Anmut *f*; Gunst *f*, Gnade *f*

graceful ['greisfəl] *adj* reizend, anmutig

grade [greid] *n* Rang *m*; *v* einstufen

gradient ['greidiənt] *n* Gefälle *nt*

gradual ['grædʒuəl] *adj* allmählich

graduate ['grædʒueit] *v* ein Diplom erlangen

grain [grein] *n* Korn *nt*, Getreide *nt*

gram [græm] *n* Gramm *nt*

grammar ['græmə] *n* Grammatik *f*

grammatical [grə'mætikəl] *adj* grammatikalisch

gramophone ['græməfoun] *n* Grammophon *nt*

grand [grænd] *adj* großartig

granddad ['grændæd] *n* Opa *m*

granddaughter ['græn,dɔːtə] *n* Enkelin *f*

grandfather ['græn,faːðə] *n* Großvater *m*; Großpapa *m*, Opa *m*

grandmother ['græn,mʌðə] *n* Großmutter *f*; Großmama *f*, Oma *f*

grandparents ['græn,pɛərənts] *pl* Großeltern *pl*

grandson ['grænsʌn] *n* Enkel *m*

granite ['grænit] *n* Granit *m*

grant [graːnt] *v* bewilligen, *verleihen; gewähren; *n* Zuschuß *m*, Stipendium *nt*

grapefruit ['greipfruːt] *n* Pampelmuse *f*

grapes [greips] *pl* Trauben *fpl*

graph [græf] *n* Graphik *f*

graphic ['græfik] *adj* graphisch

grasp [graːsp] *v* *ergreifen; *n* Griff *m*

grass [graːs] *n* Gras *nt*

grasshopper ['graːs,hɔpə] *n* Heuschrecke *f*

grate [greit] *n* Rost *m*; *v* raspeln

grateful ['greitfəl] *adj* erkenntlich, dankbar

grater ['greitə] *n* Reibe *f*

gratis ['grætis] *adj* umsonst

gratitude ['grætitjuːd] *n* Dankbarkeit *f*

gratuity [grə'tjuːəti] *n* Trinkgeld *nt*

grave [greiv] *n* Grab *nt*; *adj* ernst

gravel ['grævəl] *n* Kies *m*

gravestone ['greivstoun] *n* Grabstein *m*

graveyard ['greivjaːd] *n* Kirchhof *m*

gravity ['grævəti] *n* Schwerkraft *f*;

Ernst m

gravy ['greivi] n Bratensoße f

graze [greiz] v weiden; n Schramme f

grease [gri:s] n Fett nt; v schmieren

greasy ['gri:si] adj fett, fettig

great [greit] adj groß; **Great Britain** Großbritannien

Greece [gri:s] Griechenland

greed [gri:d] n Gier f

greedy ['gri:di] adj gierig; gefräßig

Greek [gri:k] adj griechisch; n Grieche m

green [gri:n] adj grün; ~ **card** grüne Versicherungskarte

greengrocer ['gri:n,grousə] n Gemüsehändler m

greenhouse ['gri:nhaus] n Treibhaus nt, Gewächshaus nt

greens [gri:nz] pl Gemüse nt

greet [gri:t] v grüßen

greeting ['gri:tiŋ] n Gruß m

grey [grei] adj grau

greyhound ['greihaund] n Windhund m

grief [gri:f] n Leid nt; Betrübnis f, Kummer m

grieve [gri:v] v sich grämen

grill [gril] n Bratrost m; v grillen

grill-room ['grilru:m] n Grillroom m

grin [grin] v grinsen; n Grinsen nt

***grind** [graind] v mahlen; *zerreiben

grip [grip] v fassen; n Halt m, Griff m; nAm Handköfferchen nt

grit [grit] n Grus m

groan [groun] v stöhnen

grocer ['grousə] n Lebensmittelhändler m; **grocer's** Lebensmittelgeschäft nt

groceries ['grousəriz] pl Lebensmittel pl

groin [grɔin] n Leiste f

groove [gru:v] n Rille f

gross¹ [grous] n (pl ~) Gros nt

gross² [grous] adj grob; brutto

grotto ['grɔtou] n (pl ~es, ~s) Grotte f

ground¹ [graund] n Boden m, Grund m; ~ **floor** Erdgeschoß nt; **grounds** Grundstück nt

ground² [graund] v (p, pp grind)

group [gru:p] n Gruppe f

grouse [graus] n (pl ~) Moorhuhn nt

grove [grouv] n Hain m

***grow** [grou] v *wachsen; züchten; *werden

growl [graul] v brummen

grown-up ['grounʌp] adj erwachsen; n Erwachsene m

growth [grouθ] n Wuchs m; Geschwulst f

grudge [grʌdʒ] v mißgönnen

grumble ['grʌmbəl] v murren

guarantee [,gærən'ti:] n Garantie f; Bürgschaft f; v garantieren

guarantor [,gærən'tɔ:] n Bürge m

guard [gɑ:d] n Wache f; v bewachen

guardian ['gɑ:diən] n Vormund m

guess [ges] v *raten; *denken, vermuten; n Vermutung f

guest [gest] n Gast m

guest-house ['gesthaus] n Fremdenheim nt

guest-room ['gestru:m] n Gästezimmer nt

guide [gaid] n Führer m; v führen

guidebook ['gaidbuk] n Führer m

guide-dog ['gaiddɔg] n Blindenhund m

guilt [gilt] n Schuld f

guilty ['gilti] adj schuldig

guinea-pig ['ginipig] n Meerschweinchen nt

guitar [gi'tɑ:] n Gitarre f

gulf [gʌlf] n Golf m

gull [gʌl] n Möwe f

gum [gʌm] n Zahnfleisch nt; Gummi m; Klebstoff m

gun [gʌn] n Gewehr nt, Revolver m; Kanone f

gunpowder ['gʌn,paudə] n Schießpul-

ver *nt*
gust [gʌst] *n* Windstoß *m*
gusty ['gʌsti] *adj* windig
gut [gʌt] *n* Darm *m*; **guts** Mumm *m*
gutter ['gʌtə] *n* Gosse *f*
guy [gai] *n* Bursche *m*
gymnasium [dʒim'neiziəm] *n* (pl ~s, -sia) Turnhalle *f*
gymnast ['dʒimnæst] *n* Turner *m*
gymnastics [dʒim'næstiks] *pl* Turnen *nt*
gynaecologist [,gainə'kɔlədʒist] *n* Gynäkologe *m*, Frauenarzt *m*

H

haberdashery ['hæbədæʃəri] *n* Kurzwarengeschäft *nt*
habit ['hæbit] *n* Gewohnheit *f*
habitable ['hæbitəbəl] *adj* bewohnbar
habitual [hə'bitʃuəl] *adj* gewohnt
had [hæd] *v* (p, pp have)
haddock ['hædək] *n* (pl ~) Schellfisch *m*
haemorrhage ['heməridʒ] *n* Blutsturz *m*
haemorrhoids ['hemərɔidz] *pl* Hämorrhoiden *fpl*
hail [heil] *n* Hagel *m*
hair [hɛə] *n* Haar *nt*; ~ **cream** Haarkrem *f*; ~ **piece** Toupet *nt*; ~ **tonic** Haartonikum *nt*
hairbrush ['hɛəbrʌʃ] *n* Haarbürste *f*
haircut ['hɛəkʌt] *n* Haarschnitt *m*
hair-do ['hɛədu:] *n* Haartracht *f*, Frisur *f*
hairdresser ['hɛə,dresə] *n* Friseur *m*
hair-dryer ['hɛədraiə] *n* Fön *m*
hair-grip ['hɛəgrip] *n* Haarklemme *f*
hair-net ['hɛənet] *n* Haarnetz *nt*
hair-oil ['hɛərɔil] *n* Haaröl *nt*
hairpin ['hɛəpin] *n* Haarnadel *f*

hair-spray ['hɛəsprei] *n* Haarlack *m*
hairy ['hɛəri] *adj* haarig
half¹ [hɑ:f] *adj* halb
half² [hɑ:f] *n* (pl halves) Hälfte *f*
half-time [,hɑ:f'taim] *n* Halbzeit *f*
halfway [,hɑ:f'wei] *adv* halbwegs
halibut ['hælibət] *n* (pl ~) Heilbutt *m*
hall [hɔ:l] *n* Halle *f*; Saal *m*
halt [hɔ:lt] *v* *anhalten
halve [hɑ:v] *v* halbieren
ham [hæm] *n* Schinken *m*
hamlet ['hæmlət] *n* Weiler *m*
hammer ['hæmə] *n* Hammer *m*
hammock ['hæmək] *n* Hängematte *f*
hamper ['hæmpə] *n* Packkorb *m*
hand [hænd] *n* Hand *f*; *v* *übergeben; ~ **cream** Handkrem *f*
handbag ['hændbæg] *n* Handtasche *f*
handbook ['hændbuk] *n* Handbuch *nt*
hand-brake ['hændbreik] *n* Handbremse *f*
handcuffs ['hændkʌfs] *pl* Handschellen *fpl*
handful ['hændful] *n* Handvoll *f*
handicraft ['hændikrɑ:ft] *n* Handarbeit *f*; Handwerk *nt*
handkerchief ['hæŋkətʃif] *n* Taschentuch *nt*
handle ['hændəl] *n* Stiel *m*, Handgriff *m*; *v* handhaben; behandeln
hand-made [,hænd'meid] *adj* handgearbeitet
handshake ['hændʃeik] *n* Händedruck *m*
handsome ['hænsəm] *adj* stattlich
handwork ['hændwə:k] *n* Handarbeit *f*
handwriting ['hænd,raitiŋ] *n* Handschrift *f*
handy ['hændi] *adj* handlich
***hang** [hæŋ] *v* aufhängen; *hängen
hanger ['hæŋə] *n* Aufhänger *m*
hangover ['hæŋ,ouvə] *n* Kater *m*
happen ['hæpən] *v* *geschehen, passieren, sich ereignen

happening ['hæpəniŋ] n Ereignis nt

happiness ['hæpinəs] n Glück nt

happy ['hæpi] adj zufrieden, glücklich

harbour ['ha:bə] n Hafen m

hard [ha:d] adj hart; schwierig; hardly kaum

hardware ['ha:dweə] n Eisenwaren fpl; ~ store Eisenwarenhandlung f

hare [heə] n Hase m

harm [ha:m] n Schaden m; Übel nt, Böse nt; v schaden

harmful ['ha:mfəl] adj nachteilig, schädlich

harmless ['ha:mləs] adj harmlos

harmony ['ha:məni] n Harmonie f

harp [ha:p] n Harfe f

harpsichord ['ha:psikɔ:d] n Cembalo nt

harsh [ha:ʃ] adj rauh; streng; grausam

harvest ['ha:vist] n Ernte f

has [hæz] v (pr have)

haste [heist] n Hast f, Eile f

hasten ['heisən] v eilen

hasty ['heisti] adj hastig

hat [hæt] n Hut m; ~ rack Garderobenständer m

hatch [hætʃ] n Luke f

hate [heit] v hassen; n Haß m

hatred ['heitrid] n Haß m

haughty ['hɔ:ti] adj hochmütig

haul [hɔ:l] v schleppen

*have [hæv] v *haben; machen; ~ to *müssen

haversack ['hævəsæk] n Brotbeutel m

hawk [hɔ:k] n Habicht m; Falke m

hay [hei] n Heu nt; ~ fever Heuschnupfen m

hazard ['hæzəd] n Risiko nt

haze [heiz] n Dunst m; Nebel m

hazelnut ['heizəlnʌt] n Haselnuß f

hazy ['heizi] adj diesig

he [hi:] pron er

head [hed] n Kopf m; Haupt nt; v

leiten; ~ of state Staatsoberhaupt nt; ~ teacher Schulleiter m, Schuldirektor m

headache ['hedeik] n Kopfschmerzen mpl

heading ['hediŋ] n Überschrift f

headlamp ['hedlæmp] n Scheinwerfer m

headland ['hedlənd] n Landzunge f

headlight ['hedlait] n Scheinwerfer m

headline ['hedlain] n Schlagzeile f

headmaster [,hed'ma:stə] n Schulleiter m; Direktor m, Schuldirektor m

headquarters [,hed'kwɔ:təz] pl Hauptquartier nt

head-strong ['hedstrɔŋ] adj starrköpfig

head-waiter [,hed'weitə] n Oberkellner m

heal [hi:l] v heilen

health [helθ] n Gesundheit f; ~ centre Beratungsstelle f; ~ certificate Gesundheitsattest nt

healthy ['helθi] adj gesund

heap [hi:p] n Stapel m, Haufen m

*hear [hiə] v hören

hearing ['hiəriŋ] n Gehör nt

heart [ha:t] n Herz nt; Kern m; by ~ auswendig; ~ attack Herzschlag m

heartburn ['ha:tbə:n] n Sodbrennen nt

hearth [ha:θ] n Herd m

heartless ['ha:tləs] adj herzlos

hearty ['ha:ti] adj herzlich

heat [hi:t] n Wärme f, Hitze f; v heizen; heating pad Heizkissen nt

heater ['hi:tə] n Heizofen m; immersion ~ Tauchsieder m

heath [hi:θ] n Heide f

heathen ['hi:ðən] n Heide m; heidnisch

heather ['heðə] n Heidekraut nt

heating ['hi:tiŋ] n Heizung f

heaven ['hevən] n Himmel m

heavy ['hevi] adj schwer

Hebrew ['hi:bru:] n Hebräisch nt

hedge [hedʒ] n Hecke f

hedgehog ['hedʒhɔg] n Igel m

heel [hi:l] n Ferse f; Absatz m

height [hait] n Höhe f; Gipfel m, Höhepunkt m

hell [hel] n Hölle f

hello! [he'lou] hallo!; guten Tag!

helm [helm] n Ruder nt

helmet ['helmit] n Helm m

helmsman ['helmzmən] n Steuermann m

help [help] v *helfen; n Hilfe f

helper ['helpə] n Helfer m

helpful ['helpfəl] adj hilfreich

helping ['helpiŋ] n Portion f

hem [hem] n Saum m

hemp [hemp] n Hanf m

hen [hen] n Henne f; Huhn nt

henceforth [,hens'fɔ:θ] adv von nun an

her [hə:] pron sie, ihr

herb [hə:b] n Kraut nt

herd [hə:d] n Herde f

here [hiə] adv hier; ~ you are bitte

hereditary [hi'reditəri] adj erblich

hernia ['hə:niə] n Bruch m

hero ['hiərou] n (pl ~es) Held m

heron ['herən] n Reiher m

herring ['heriŋ] n (pl ~, ~s) Hering m

herself [hə:'self] pron sich; selbst

hesitate ['heziteit] v zögern

heterosexual [,hetərə'sekʃuəl] adj heterosexuell

hiccup ['hikʌp] n Schluckauf m

hide [haid] n Haut f

*hide [haid] v verstecken; *verbergen

hideous ['hidiəs] adj abscheulich

hierarchy ['haiərɑ:ki] n Hierarchie f

high [hai] adj hoch

highway ['haiwei] n Landstraße f; nAm Autobahn f

hijack ['haidʒæk] v kapern

hijacker ['haidʒækə] n Kaper m

hike [haik] v wandern

hill [hil] n Hügel m

hillock ['hilək] n Erhebung f

hillside ['hilsaid] n Hang m

hilly ['hili] adj hügelig

him [him] pron ihn, ihm

himself [him'self] pron sich; selbst

hinder ['hində] v hindern

hinge [hindʒ] n Scharnier nt

hip [hip] n Hüfte f

hire [haiə] v mieten; for ~ zu vermieten

hire-purchase [,haiə'pə:tʃəs] n Teilzahlungskauf m

his [hiz] adj sein

historian [hi'stɔ:riən] n Historiker m

historic [hi'stɔrik] adj historisch

historical [hi'stɔrikəl] adj geschichtlich

history ['histəri] n Geschichte f

hit [hit] n Schlager m

*hit [hit] v *schlagen; *treffen

hitchhike ['hitʃhaik] v per Anhalter *fahren

hitchhiker ['hitʃ,haikə] n Anhalter m

hoarse [hɔ:s] adj rauh, heiser

hobby ['hɔbi] n Liebhaberei f, Steckenpferd nt

hobby-horse ['hɔbihɔ:s] n Steckenpferd nt

hockey ['hɔki] n Hockey nt

hoist [hɔist] v *hochziehen

hold [hould] n Laderaum m

*hold [hould] v *festhalten, *halten; *freihalten; ~ on sich *festhalten; ~ up stützen

hold-up ['houldʌp] n Überfall m

hole [houl] n Grube f, Loch nt

holiday ['hɔlədi] n Urlaub m; Feiertag m; ~ camp Ferienlager nt; ~ resort Erholungsort m; on ~ auf Urlaub

Holland ['hɔlənd] Holland

hollow ['hɔlou] adj hohl

holy ['houli] adj heilig

homage ['hɔmidʒ] n Huldigung f

home [houm] *n* Heim *nt*; Haus *nt*; *adv* zu Hause, nach Hause; **at** ~ zu Hause

home-made [,houm'meid] *adj* selbstgemacht

homesickness ['houm,siknəs] *n* Heimweh *nt*

homosexual [,houmə'sekʃuəl] *adj* homosexuell

honest ['ɔnist] *adj* ehrlich; aufrichtig

honesty ['ɔnisti] *n* Ehrlichkeit *f*

honey ['hʌni] *n* Honig *m*

honeymoon ['hʌnimu:n] *n* Hochzeitsreise *f*, Flitterwochen *fpl*

honk [hʌŋk] *vAm* hupen

honour ['ɔnə] *n* Ehre *f*; *v* ehren, huldigen

honourable ['ɔnərəbəl] *adj* ehrenwert; rechtschaffen

hood [hud] *n* Kapuze *f*; *nAm* Motorhaube *f*

hoof [hu:f] *n* Huf *m*

hook [huk] *n* Haken *m*

hoot [hu:t] *v* hupen

hooter ['hu:tə] *n* Hupe *f*

hoover ['hu:və] *v* staubsaugen

hop[1] [hɔp] *v* hüpfen; *n* Hupf *m*

hop[2] [hɔp] *n* Hopfen *m*

hope [houp] *n* Hoffnung *f*; *v* hoffen

hopeful ['houpfəl] *adj* hoffnungsvoll

hopeless ['houpləs] *adj* hoffnungslos

horizon [hə'raizən] *n* Horizont *m*

horizontal [,hɔri'zɔntəl] *adj* waagerecht

horn [hɔ:n] *n* Horn *nt*; Horn *f*; Hupe *f*

horrible ['hɔribəl] *adj* entsetzlich; schrecklich, grauenhaft, scheußlich

horror ['hɔrə] *n* Schauder *m*, Entsetzen *nt*

hors-d'œuvre [ɔ:'də:vr] *n* Horsd'œuvre *nt*, Vorspeise *f*

horse [hɔ:s] *n* Pferd *nt*

horseman ['hɔ:smən] *n* (pl -men) Reiter *m*

horsepower ['hɔ:s,pauə] *n* Pferdestärke *f*

horserace ['hɔ:sreis] *n* Pferderennen *nt*

horseradish ['hɔ:s,rædiʃ] *n* Meerrettich *m*

horseshoe ['hɔ:sʃu:] *n* Hufeisen *nt*

horticulture ['hɔ:tikʌltʃə] *n* Gartenbau *m*

hosiery ['houʒəri] *n* Wirkwaren *fpl*

hospitable ['hɔspitəbəl] *adj* gastfreundlich

hospital ['hɔspitəl] *n* Klinik *f*, Krankenhaus *nt*

hospitality [,hɔspi'tæləti] *n* Gastfreundschaft *f*

host [houst] *n* Gastgeber *m*

hostage ['hɔstidʒ] *n* Geisel *f*

hostel ['hɔstəl] *n* Herberge *f*

hostess ['houstis] *n* Gastgeberin *f*

hostile ['hɔstail] *adj* feindlich

hot [hɔt] *adj* warm, heiß

hotel [hou'tel] *n* Hotel *nt*

hot-tempered [,hɔt'tempəd] *adj* jähzornig

hour [auə] *n* Stunde *f*

hourly ['auəli] *adj* stündlich

house [haus] *n* Haus *nt*; Wohnung *f*; Gebäude *nt*; ~ **agent** Häusermakler *m*; ~ **block** *Am* Häuserblock *m*; **public** ~ Wirtshaus *nt*

houseboat ['hausbout] *n* Wohnboot *nt*

household ['haushould] *n* Haushalt *m*

housekeeper ['haus,ki:pə] *n* Haushälterin *f*

housekeeping ['haus,ki:piŋ] *n* Hausarbeit *f*, Haushalt *m*

housemaid ['hausmeid] *n* Hausangestellte *f*

housewife ['hauswaif] *n* Hausfrau *f*

housework ['hauswə:k] *n* Haushaltsarbeiten *fpl*

how [hau] *adv* wie; ~ **many** wieviel; ~ **much** wieviel

however [hau'evə] *conj* dennoch, jedoch

hug [hʌg] *v* umarmen; liebkosen; *n*
Umarmung *f*

huge [hju:dʒ] *adj* gewaltig, ungeheuer,
riesig

hum [hʌm] *v* summen

human ['hju:mən] *adj* menschlich; ~
being Mensch *m*

humanity [hju'mænəti] *n* Menschheit *f*

humble ['hʌmbəl] *adj* bescheiden

humid ['hju:mid] *adj* feucht

humidity [hju'midəti] *n* Feuchtigkeit *f*

humorous ['hju:mərəs] *adj* spaßig, witzig, humorvoll

humour ['hju:mə] *n* Humor *m*

hundred ['hʌndrəd] *n* hundert

Hungarian [hʌŋ'gɛəriən] *adj* ungarisch; *n* Ungar *m*

Hungary ['hʌŋgəri] Ungarn

hunger ['hʌŋgə] *n* Hunger *m*

hungry ['hʌŋgri] *adj* hungrig

hunt [hʌnt] *v* jagen; *n* Jagd *f*; ~ for
suchen

hunter ['hʌntə] *n* Jäger *m*

hurricane ['hʌrikən] *n* Wirbelsturm
m; ~ lamp Sturmlaterne *f*

hurry ['hʌri] *v* sich beeilen, eilen; *n*
Eile *f*; in a ~ eilig

*hurt [hə:t] *v* weh *tun, verletzen;
kränken

hurtful ['hə:tfəl] *adj* schädlich

husband ['hʌzbənd] *n* Gatte *m*, Mann
m

hut [hʌt] *n* Hütte *f*

hydrogen ['haidrədʒən] *n* Wasserstoff
m

hygiene ['haidʒi:n] *n* Hygiene *f*

hygienic [hai'dʒi:nik] *adj* hygienisch

hymn [him] *n* Hymne *f*

hyphen ['haifən] *n* Bindestrich *m*

hypocrisy [hi'pɔkrəsi] *n* Heuchelei *f*

hypocrite ['hipəkrit] *n* Heuchler *m*

hypocritical [,hipə'kritikəl] *adj* heuchlerisch, hypokritisch, scheinheilig

hysterical [hi'sterikəl] *adj* hysterisch

I

I [ai] *pron* ich

ice [ais] *n* Eis *nt*

ice-bag ['aisbæg] *n* Eisbeutel *m*

ice-cream ['aiskri:m] *n* Eis *nt*

Iceland ['aislənd] Island

Icelander ['aisləndə] *n* Isländer *m*

Icelandic [ais'lændik] *adj* isländisch

icon ['aikɔn] *n* Ikone *f*

idea [ai'diə] *n* Idee *f*; Einfall *m*, Gedanke *m*; Vorstellung *f*, Anschauung *f*

ideal [ai'diəl] *adj* ideal; *n* Ideal *nt*

identical [ai'dentikəl] *adj* identisch

identification [ai,dentifi'keiʃən] *n* Identifizierung *f*

identify [ai'dentifai] *v* identifizieren

identity [ai'dentəti] *n* Identität *f*; ~
card Ausweis *m*

idiom ['idiəm] *n* Idiom *nt*

idiomatic [,idiə'mætik] *adj* idiomatisch

idiot ['idiət] *n* Idiot *m*

idiotic [,idi'ɔtik] *adj* verrückt

idle ['aidəl] *adj* müßig; faul; nutzlos

idol ['aidəl] *n* Abgott *m*; Idol *nt*

if [if] *conj* wenn; falls

ignition [ig'niʃən] *n* Zündung *f*; ~ coil
Zündung *f*

ignorant ['ignərənt] *adj* unwissend

ignore [ig'nɔ:] *v* ignorieren

ill [il] *adj* krank; schlecht; böse

illegal [i'li:gəl] *adj* illegal, ungesetzlich

illegible [i'ledʒəbəl] *adj* unleserlich

illiterate [i'litərət] *n* Analphabet *m*

illness ['ilnəs] *n* Krankheit *f*

illuminate [i'lu:mineit] *v* erleuchten

illumination [i,lu:mi'neiʃən] *n* Beleuchtung *f*

illusion [i'lu:ʒən] *n* Illusion *f*; Täuschung *f*

illustrate ['iləstreit] *v* illustrieren

illustration [,ilə'streifən] *n* Illustration *f*

image ['imidʒ] *n* Bild *nt*

imaginary [i'mædʒinəri] *adj* imaginär

imagination [i,mædʒi'neifən] *n* Einbildung *f*

imagine [i'mædʒin] *v* sich vorstellen; sich einbilden; sich *denken

imitate ['imiteit] *v* nachmachen, nachahmen

imitation [,imi'teifən] *n* Nachahmung *f*, Imitation *f*

immediate [i'mi:djət] *adj* unmittelbar

immediately [i'mi:djətli] *adv* unverzüglich, sogleich, sofort

immense [i'mens] *adj* unendlich, ungeheuer, unermeßlich

immigrant ['imigrənt] *n* Einwanderer *m*

immigrate ['imigreit] *v* einwandern

immigration [,imi'greifən] *n* Einwanderung *f*

immodest [i'mɔdist] *adj* unbescheiden

immunity [i'mju:nəti] *n* Immunität *f*

immunize ['imjunaiz] *v* immunisieren

impartial [im'pɑ:fəl] *adj* unparteiisch

impassable [im'pɑ:səbəl] *adj* ungangbar

impatient [im'peifənt] *adj* ungeduldig

impede [im'pi:d] *v* hindern

impediment [im'pedimənt] *n* Hindernis *nt*

imperfect [im'pə:fikt] *adj* unvollkommen

imperial [im'piəriəl] *adj* kaiserlich; Reichs-

impersonal [im'pə:sənəl] *adj* unpersönlich

impertinence [im'pə:tinəns] *n* Unverschämtheit *f*

impertinent [im'pə:tinənt] *adj* frech,

flegelhaft, unverschämt

implement¹ ['implimənt] *n* Werkzeug *nt*, Gerät *nt*

implement² ['impliment] *v* ausführen

imply [im'plai] *v* besagen; in sich *schließen

impolite [,impə'lait] *adj* unhöflich

import¹ [im'pɔ:t] *v* einführen, importieren

import² ['impɔ:t] *n* Importware *f*, Einfuhr *f*, Import *m*; ~ **duty** Einfuhrzoll *m*

importance [im'pɔ:təns] *n* Bedeutung *f*, Wichtigkeit *f*

important [im'pɔ:tənt] *adj* bedeutend, wichtig

importer [im'pɔ:tə] *n* Importeur *m*

imposing [im'pouziŋ] *adj* imposant

impossible [im'pɔsəbəl] *adj* unmöglich

impotence ['impətəns] *n* Impotenz *f*

impotent ['impətənt] *adj* impotent

impound [im'paund] *v* beschlagnahmen

impress [im'pres] *v* imponieren, beeindrucken

impression [im'prefən] *n* Eindruck *m*

impressive [im'presiv] *adj* eindrucksvoll

imprison [im'prizən] *v* inhaftieren

imprisonment [im'prizənmənt] *n* Haft *f*

improbable [im'prɔbəbəl] *adj* unwahrscheinlich

improper [im'prɔpə] *adj* unpassend

improve [im'pru:v] *v* verbessern

improvement [im'pru:vmənt] *n* Verbesserung *f*

improvise ['imprəvaiz] *v* improvisieren

impudent ['impjudənt] *adj* unverschämt

impulse ['impʌls] *n* Impuls *m*; Anregung *f*

impulsive [im'pʌlsiv] *adj* impulsiv

in [in] *prep* in; *adv* hinein

inaccessible [i,næk'sesəbəl] adj unzugänglich

inaccurate [i'nækjurət] adj ungenau

inadequate [i'nædikwət] adj unzulänglich

incapable [iŋ'keipəbəl] adj unfähig

incense ['insens] n Weihrauch m

incident ['insidənt] n Zwischenfall m

incidental [,insi'dentəl] adj zufällig

incite [in'sait] v anregen

inclination [,iŋkli'neiʃən] n Neigung f

incline [iŋ'klain] n Neigung f

inclined [iŋ'klaind] adj gewillt, geneigt; *be ~ to v neigen

include [iŋ'klu:d] v *enthalten, *einschließen

inclusive [iŋ'klu:siv] adj einschließlich

income ['iŋkəm] n Einkommen nt

income-tax ['iŋkəmtæks] n Einkommenssteuer f

incompetent [iŋ'kɔmpətənt] adj unfähig

incomplete [,inkəm'pli:t] adj unvollständig

inconceivable [,iŋkən'si:vəbəl] adj unfaßbar

inconspicuous [,iŋkən'spikjuəs] adj unauffällig

inconvenience [,iŋkən'vi:njəns] n Unbequemlichkeit f, Unannehmlichkeit f

inconvenient [,iŋkən'vi:njənt] adj ungelegen; lästig

incorrect [,iŋkə'rekt] adj ungenau, unrichtig

increase[1] [iŋ'kri:s] v vergrößern; *anwachsen, *zunehmen

increase[2] ['iŋkri:s] n Zunahme f; Erhöhung f

incredible [iŋ'kredəbəl] adj unglaublich

incurable [iŋ'kjuərəbəl] adj unheilbar

indecent [in'di:sənt] adj unanständig

indeed [in'di:d] adv wirklich

indefinite [in'definit] adj unbestimmt

indemnity [in'demnəti] n Entschädigung f, Schadenersatz m

independence [,indi'pendəns] n Unabhängigkeit f

independent [,indi'pendənt] adj unabhängig; selbständig

index ['indeks] n Verzeichnis nt, Index m; ~ finger Zeigefinger m

India ['indiə] Indien

Indian ['indiən] adj indisch; indianisch; n Inder m; Indianer m

indicate ['indikeit] v *angeben, zeigen

indication [,indi'keiʃən] n Merkmal nt, Anzeichen nt

indicator ['indikeitə] n Blinker m

indifferent [in'difərənt] adj gleichgültig

indigestion [,indi'dʒestʃən] n Magenverstimmung f

indignation [,indig'neiʃən] n Entrüstung f

indirect [,indi'rekt] adj indirekt

individual [,indi'vidʒuəl] adj einzeln, individuell; n Einzelne m, Individuum nt

Indonesia [,ində'ni:ziə] Indonesien

Indonesian [,ində'ni:ziən] adj indonesisch; n Indonesier m

indoor ['indɔ:] adj im Haus

indoors [,in'dɔ:z] adv im Haus

indulge [in'dʌldʒ] v *nachgeben

industrial [in'dʌstriəl] adj industriell; ~ area Industriegebiet nt

industrious [in'dʌstriəs] adj fleißig

industry ['indəstri] n Industrie f

inedible [i'nedibəl] adj ungenießbar

inefficient [,ini'fiʃənt] adj unzweckmäßig

inevitable [i'nevitəbəl] adj unvermeidlich

inexpensive [,inik'spensiv] adj billig

inexperienced [,inik'spiəriənst] adj unerfahren

infant ['infənt] n Säugling m

infantry ['infəntri] n Infanterie f

infect [in'fekt] v anstecken

infection [in'fekʃən] n Infektion f

infectious [in'fekʃəs] adj ansteckend

infer [in'fə:] v ableiten

inferior [in'fiəriə] adj geringer, minderwertig; unter

infinite ['infinət] adj unendlich

infinitive [in'finitiv] n Infinitiv m

infirmary [in'fə:məri] n Krankensaal m

inflammable [in'flæməbəl] adj entzündbar

inflammation [,infləʹmeiʃən] n Entzündung f

inflatable [in'fleitəbəl] adj aufblasbar

inflate [in'fleit] v aufblähen

inflation [in'fleiʃən] n Inflation f

influence ['influəns] n Einfluß m; v beeinflussen

influential [,influ'enʃəl] adj einflußreich

influenza [,influ'enzə] n Grippe f

inform [in'fɔ:m] v informieren; berichten, mitteilen

informal [in'fɔ:məl] adj informell

information [,infə'meiʃən] n Auskunft f; Nachricht f, Mitteilung f; ~ bureau Auskunftsbüro nt

infra-red [,infrə'red] adj infrarot

infrequent [in'fri:kwənt] adj selten

ingredient [iŋ'gri:diənt] n Zutat f, Bestandteil m

inhabit [in'hæbit] v bewohnen

inhabitable [in'hæbitəbəl] adj bewohnbar

inhabitant [in'hæbitənt] n Einwohner m; Bewohner m

inhale [in'heil] v einatmen

inherit [in'herit] v erben

inheritance [in'heritəns] n Erbschaft f

initial [i'niʃəl] adj Anfangs-, erste; n Anfangsbuchstabe m; v abzeichnen

initiative [i'niʃətiv] n Initiative f

inject [in'dʒekt] v einspritzen

injection [in'dʒekʃən] n Injektion f

injure ['indʒə] v verletzen; kränken

injury ['indʒəri] n Verletzung f; Verwundung f

injustice [in'dʒʌstis] n Unrecht nt

ink [iŋk] n Tinte f

inlet ['inlet] n Bucht f

inn [in] n Gasthof m

inner ['inə] adj inwendig; ~ tube Schlauch m

inn-keeper ['in,ki:pə] n Gastwirt m

innocence ['inəsəns] n Unschuld f

innocent ['inəsənt] adj unschuldig

inoculate [i'nɔkjuleit] v impfen

inoculation [i,nɔkju'leiʃən] n Impfung f

inquire [iŋ'kwaiə] v nachfragen, sich erkundigen

inquiry [iŋ'kwaiəri] n Frage f, Nachfrage f; Untersuchung f; ~ office Auskunftsbüro nt

inquisitive [iŋ'kwizətiv] adj neugierig

insane [in'sein] adj wahnsinnig

inscription [in'skripʃən] n Inschrift f

insect ['insekt] n Insekt nt; ~ repellent Insektenschutzmittel nt

insecticide [in'sektisaid] n Insektengift nt

insensitive [in'sensətiv] adj unempfindlich

insert [in'sə:t] v einfügen

inside [,in'said] n Innenseite f; adj inner; adv drinnen; im Innern; prep in, innerhalb; ~ out verkehrt; insides Eingeweide pl

insight ['insait] n Einsicht f

insignificant [,insig'nifikənt] adj unbedeutend; unerheblich, nichtssagend; belanglos

insist [in'sist] v *bestehen; beharren

insolence ['insələns] n Unverschämtheit f

insolent ['insələnt] adj frech, unverschämt

insomnia [in'sɔmniə] *n* Schlaflosigkeit *f*

inspect [in'spekt] *v* inspizieren

inspection [in'spekʃən] *n* Inspektion *f*; Kontrolle *f*

inspector [in'spektə] *n* Aufsichtsbeamte *m*

inspire [in'spaiə] *v* begeistern

install [in'stɔ:l] *v* installieren

installation [,instə'leiʃən] *n* Einrichtung *f*

instalment [in'stɔ:lmənt] *n* Ratenzahlung *f*

instance ['instəns] *n* Beispiel *nt*; Fall *m*; for ~ zum Beispiel

instant ['instənt] *n* Augenblick *m*

instantly ['instəntli] *adv* unverzüglich, augenblicklich, sofort

instead of [in'sted ɔv] anstatt

instinct ['instiŋkt] *n* Instinkt *m*

institute ['institju:t] *n* Institut *nt*; Anstalt *f*; *v* einrichten

institution [,insti'tju:ʃən] *n* Einrichtung *f*, Institution *f*

instruct [in'strʌkt] *v* *unterweisen

instruction [in'strʌkʃən] *n* Unterweisung *f*

instructive [in'strʌktiv] *adj* lehrreich

instructor [in'strʌktə] *n* Lehrer *m*

instrument ['instrumənt] *n* Instrument *nt*; musical ~ Musikinstrument *nt*

insufficient ['insə'fiʃənt] *adj* ungenügend

insulate ['insjuleit] *v* isolieren

insulation [,insju'leiʃən] *n* Isolation *f*

insulator ['insjuleitə] *n* Isolator *m*

insult¹ [in'sʌlt] *v* beleidigen

insult² ['insʌlt] *n* Beleidigung *f*

insurance [in'ʃuərəns] *n* Versicherung *f*; ~ policy Versicherungspolice *f*

insure [in'ʃuə] *v* versichern

intact [in'tækt] *adj* unversehrt

intellect ['intəlekt] *n* Intellekt *m*, Verstand *m*

intellectual [,intə'lektʃuəl] *adj* intellektuell

intelligence [in'telidʒəns] *n* Intelligenz *f*

intelligent [in'telidʒənt] *adj* intelligent

intend [in'tend] *v* beabsichtigen

intense [in'tens] *adj* intensiv; heftig

intention [in'tenʃən] *n* Absicht *f*

intentional [in'tenʃənəl] *adj* absichtlich

intercourse ['intəkɔ:s] *n* Umgang *m*

interest ['intrəst] *n* Interesse *nt*; Nutzen *m*; Zins *m*; *v* interessieren

interesting ['intrəstiŋ] *adj* interessant

interfere [,intə'fiə] *v* *einschreiten; ~ with sich einmischen

interference [,intə'fiərəns] *n* Eingreifen *nt*

interim ['intərim] *n* Zwischenzeit *f*

interior [in'tiəriə] *n* Innere *nt*

interlude ['intəlu:d] *n* Zwischenspiel *nt*

intermediary [,intə'mi:djəri] *n* Vermittler *m*

intermission [,intə'miʃən] *n* Pause *f*

internal [in'tə:nəl] *adj* inner, intern

international [,intə'næʃənəl] *adj* international

interpret [in'tə:prit] *v* dolmetschen; darstellen

interpreter [in'tə:pritə] *n* Dolmetscher *m*

interrogate [in'terəgeit] *v* verhören

interrogation [in,terə'geiʃən] *n* Verhör *nt*

interrogative [,intə'rɔgətiv] *adj* fragend

interrupt [,intə'rʌpt] *v* *unterbrechen

interruption [,intə'rʌpʃən] *n* Unterbrechung *f*

intersection [,intə'sekʃən] *n* Kreuzung *f*

interval ['intəvəl] *n* Pause *f*; Intervall *nt*

intervene [,intə'vi:n] *v* sich einmischen

interview ['intəvju:] n Unterredung f, Interview nt

intestine [in'testin] n Darm m; **intestines** Eingeweide pl

intimate ['intimət] adj intim

into ['intu] prep in

intolerable [in'tɔlərəbəl] adj unerträglich

intoxicated [in'tɔksikeitid] adj berauscht

intrigue [in'tri:g] n Komplott nt

introduce [,intrə'dju:s] v vorstellen; einführen

introduction [,intrə'dʌkʃən] n Vorstellung f; Einführung f

invade [in'veid] v *eindringen

invalid¹ [invəli:d] n Invalide m; adj invalide

invalid² [in'vælid] adj ungültig

invasion [in'veiʒən] n Einfall m, Invasion f

invent [in'vent] v *erfinden; *ersinnen

invention [in'venʃən] n Erfindung f

inventive [in'ventiv] adj erfinderisch

inventor [in'ventə] n Erfinder m

inventory ['invəntri] n Inventar nt

invert [in'və:t] v umdrehen

invest [in'vest] v investieren; anlegen

investigate [in'vestigeit] v untersuchen

investigation [in,vesti'geifən] n Untersuchung f

investment [in'vestmənt] n Investition f; Anlage f, Geldanlage f

investor [in'vestə] n Kapitalgeber m

invisible [in'vizəbəl] adj unsichtbar

invitation [,invi'teifən] n Einladung f

invite [in'vait] v auffordern, *einladen

invoice ['invɔis] n Faktur f

involve [in'vɔlv] v *einschließen; **involved** beteiligt

inwards ['inwədz] adv nach innen

iodine ['aiədi:n] n Jod nt

Iran [i'ra:n] Iran

Iranian [i'reiniən] adj iranisch; n Iranier m

Iraq [i'ra:k] Irak

Iraqi [i'ra:ki] adj irakisch ·

irascible [i'ræsibəl] adj jähzornig

Ireland ['aiələnd] Irland

Irish ['aiəriʃ] adj irisch

Irishman ['aiəriʃmən] n (pl -men) Ire m

iron ['aiən] n Eisen nt; Bügeleisen nt; eisern; v bügeln

ironical [ai'rɔnikəl] adj ironisch

ironworks ['aiənwə:ks] n Eisenhütte f

irony ['aiərəni] n Ironie f

irregular [i'regjulə] adj unregelmäßig

irreparable [i'repərəbəl] adj irreparabel

irrevocable [i'revəkəbəl] adj unwiderruflich

irritable ['iritəbəl] adj reizbar

irritate ['iriteit] v reizen, irritieren

is [iz] v (pr be)

island ['ailənd] n Insel f

isolate ['aisəleit] v isolieren

isolation [,aisə'leifən] n Isolation f; Isolierung f

Israel ['izreil] Israel

Israeli [iz'reili] adj israelisch; n Israeli m

issue ['iʃu:] v *ausgeben; n Ausgabe f, Auflage f; Frage f, Punkt m; Ergebnis nt, Resultat nt, Folge f, Abschluß m, Ende nt; Ausweg m

isthmus ['isməs] n Landenge f

it [it] pron es

Italian [i'tæljən] adj italienisch; n Italiener m

italics [i'tæliks] pl Kursivschrift f

Italy ['itəli] Italien

itch [itʃ] n Jucken nt; v jucken

item ['aitəm] n Posten m; Punkt m

itinerant [ai'tinərənt] adj umherziehend

itinerary [ai'tinərəri] n Reiseplan m

ivory ['aivəri] n Elfenbein nt

ivy ['aivi] n Efeu m

J

jack [dʒæk] n Wagenheber m

jacket ['dʒækit] n Jacke f, Jackett nt; Umschlag m

jade [dʒeid] n Jade m

jail [dʒeil] n Gefängnis nt

jailer ['dʒeilə] n Gefängniswärter m

jam [dʒæm] n Marmelade f; Verkehrsstauung f

janitor ['dʒænitə] n Hausmeister m

January ['dʒænjuəri] Januar

Japan [dʒə'pæn] Japan

Japanese [,dʒæpə'ni:z] adj japanisch; n Japaner m

jar [dʒɑ:] n Krug m

jaundice ['dʒɔ:ndis] n Gelbsucht f

jaw [dʒɔ:] n Kiefer m

jealous ['dʒeləs] adj eifersüchtig

jealousy ['dʒeləsi] n Eifersucht f

jeans [dʒi:nz] pl Bluejeans pl

jelly ['dʒeli] n Gelee nt

jelly-fish ['dʒelifiʃ] n Qualle f

jersey ['dʒə:zi] n Jersey m; Wollpullover m

jet [dʒet] n Strahl m; Düsenflugzeug nt

jetty ['dʒeti] n Pier m

Jew [dʒu:] n Jude m

jewel ['dʒu:əl] n Juwel nt

jeweller ['dʒu:ələ] n Juwelier m

jewellery ['dʒu:əlri] n Schmuck m

Jewish ['dʒu:iʃ] adj jüdisch

job [dʒɔb] n Arbeit f; Stellung f, Beschäftigung f

jockey ['dʒɔki] n Jockei m

join [dʒɔin] v *verbinden; sich beteiligen an, sich *anschließen; zusammenfügen, vereinigen

joint [dʒɔint] n Gelenk nt; Lötstelle f; adj verbunden, gemeinschaftlich

jointly ['dʒɔintli] adv gemeinsam

joke [dʒouk] n Witz m

jolly ['dʒɔli] adj fröhlich

Jordan ['dʒɔ:dən] Jordanien

Jordanian [dʒɔ:'deiniən] adj jordanisch; n Jordanier m

journal ['dʒə:nəl] n Zeitschrift f

journalism ['dʒə:nəlizəm] n Journalismus m

journalist ['dʒə:nəlist] n Journalist m

journey ['dʒə:ni] n Reise f

joy [dʒɔi] n Wonne f, Freude f

joyful ['dʒɔifəl] adj froh, freudig

jubilee ['dʒu:bili:] n Jubiläum nt

judge [dʒʌdʒ] n Richter m; v urteilen; beurteilen

judgment ['dʒʌdʒmənt] n Urteil nt

jug [dʒʌg] n Krug m

Jugoslav [ju:gə'slɑ:v] adj jugoslawisch; n Jugoslawe m

Jugoslavia [ju:gə'slɑ:viə] Jugoslawien

juice [dʒu:s] n Saft m

juicy ['dʒu:si] adj saftig

July [dʒu'lai] Juli

jump [dʒʌmp] v *springen; n Sprung m

jumper ['dʒʌmpə] n Jumper m

junction ['dʒʌŋkʃən] n Straßenkreuzung f; Knotenpunkt m

June [dʒu:n] Juni

jungle ['dʒʌŋgəl] n Urwald m, Dschungel m

junior ['dʒu:njə] adj jünger

junk [dʒʌŋk] n Plunder m

jury ['dʒuəri] n Preisgericht nt

just [dʒʌst] adj berechtigt, gerecht; richtig; adv gerade; genau

justice ['dʒʌstis] n Recht nt; Gerechtigkeit f

juvenile ['dʒu:vənail] adj jugendlich

K

kangaroo [ˌkæŋgəˈruː] *n* Känguruh *nt*
keel [kiːl] *n* Kiel *m*
keen [kiːn] *adj* begeistert; scharf
***keep** [kiːp] *v* *halten; bewahren;
*bleiben; ~ **away from** sich *fern-
halten von; ~ **off** nicht anrühren;
~ **on** *fortfahren mit; ~ **quiet**
*schweigen; ~ **up** ausharren; ~ **up
with** Schritt *halten mit
keg [keg] *n* Fäßchen *nt*
kennel [ˈkenəl] *n* Hundehütte *f*; Hundezwinger *m*
Kenya [ˈkenjə] Kenia
kerosene [ˈkerəsiːn] *n* Kerosin *nt*
kettle [ˈketəl] *n* Kessel *m*
key [kiː] *n* Schlüssel *m*
keyhole [ˈkiːhoul] *n* Schlüsselloch *nt*
khaki [ˈkɑːki] *n* Khaki *nt*
kick [kik] *v* *stoßen, *treten; *n* Tritt
m, Fußtritt *m*
kick-off [ˌkiˈkɔf] *n* Anstoß *m*
kid [kid] *n* Kind *nt*; Ziegenleder *nt*; *v*
foppen
kidney [ˈkidni] *n* Niere *f*
kill [kil] *v* *umbringen, töten
kilogram [ˈkiləgræm] *n* Kilo *nt*
kilometre [ˈkiləˌmiːtə] *n* Kilometer *m*
kind [kaind] *adj* nett, freundlich; gütig; *n* Sorte *f*
kindergarten [ˈkindəˌgɑːtən] *n* Kindergarten *m*
king [kiŋ] *n* König *m*
kingdom [ˈkiŋdəm] *n* Königreich *nt*;
Reich *nt*
kiosk [ˈkiːɔsk] *n* Kiosk *m*
kiss [kis] *n* Kuß *m*; *v* küssen
kit [kit] *n* Ausrüstung *f*
kitchen [ˈkitʃin] *n* Küche *f*; ~ **garden**
Gemüsegarten *m*

knapsack [ˈnæpsæk] *n* Rucksack *m*
knave [neiv] *n* Bube *m*
knee [niː] *n* Knie *nt*
kneecap [ˈniːkæp] *n* Kniescheibe *f*
***kneel** [niːl] *v* knien
knew [njuː] *v* (p know)
knickers [ˈnikəz] *pl* Unterhose *f*
knife [naif] *n* (pl knives) Messer *nt*
knight [nait] *n* Ritter *m*
***knit** [nit] *v* stricken
knob [nɔb] *n* Knopf *m*
knock [nɔk] *v* klopfen; *n* Klopfen *nt*;
~ **against** *zusammenstoßen mit;
~ **down** *niederschlagen
knot [nɔt] *n* Knoten *m*; *v* knoten
***know** [nou] *v* *wissen, *kennen
knowledge [ˈnɔlidʒ] *n* Kenntnis *f*
knuckle [ˈnʌkəl] *n* Fingergelenk *nt*

L

label [ˈleibəl] *n* Etikett *nt*; *v* beschriften
laboratory [ləˈbɔrətəri] *n* Laboratorium *nt*
labour [ˈleibə] *n* Arbeit *f*; Wehen *fpl*;
v sich abmühen; **labor permit** *Am*
Arbeitsbewilligung *f*
labourer [ˈleibərə] *n* Arbeiter *m*
labour-saving [ˈleibəˌseiviŋ] *adj* ar-
beitssparend
labyrinth [ˈlæbərinθ] *n* Labyrinth *nt*
lace [leis] *n* Spitze *f*; Schnürsenkel *m*
lack [læk] *n* Mangel *m*; *v* mangeln
lacquer [ˈlækə] *n* Lack *m*
lad [læd] *n* Junge *m*, Bursche *m*
ladder [ˈlædə] *n* Leiter *f*
lady [ˈleidi] *n* Dame *f*; **ladies' room**
Damentoilette *f*
lagoon [ləˈguːn] *n* Lagune *f*
lake [leik] *n* See *m*

lamb [læm] n Lamm nt; Lammfleisch nt

lame [leim] adj gelähmt, lahm

lamentable ['læməntəbəl] adj jämmerlich

lamp [læmp] n Lampe f

lamp-post ['læmppoust] n Laternenpfahl m

lampshade ['læmpʃeid] n Lampenschirm m

land [lænd] n Land nt; v landen; an Land *gehen

landlady ['lænd,leidi] n Wirtin f

landlord ['lændlɔ:d] n Hausbesitzer m; Wirt m

landmark ['lændmɑ:k] n Landmarke f; Markstein m

landscape ['lændskeip] n Landschaft f

lane [lein] n Gasse f, Pfad m; Fahrbahn f

language ['læŋgwidʒ] n Sprache f; ~ laboratory Sprachlabor nt

lantern ['læntən] n Laterne f

lapel [lə'pel] n Rockaufschlag m

larder ['lɑ:də] n Speisekammer f

large [lɑ:dʒ] adj groß; geräumig

lark [lɑ:k] n Lerche f

laryngitis [,lærin'dʒaitis] n Halsentzündung f

last [lɑ:st] adj letzt; vorhergehend; v dauern; at ~ endlich; schließlich, zuletzt

lasting ['lɑ:stiŋ] adj bleibend, dauerhaft

latchkey ['lætʃki:] n Hausschlüssel m

late [leit] adj spät; verspätet

lately ['leitli] adv in letzter Zeit, kürzlich, unlängst

lather ['lɑ:ðə] n Schaum m

Latin America ['lætin ə'merikə] Lateinamerika

Latin-American [,lætinə'merikən] adj lateinamerikanisch

latitude ['lætitju:d] n Breitengrad m

laugh [lɑ:f] v lachen; n Lachen nt

laughter ['lɑ:ftə] n Gelächter nt

launch [lɔ:ntʃ] v in Gang *bringen; *abschießen; n Motorschiff nt

launching ['lɔ:ntʃiŋ] n Stapellauf m

launderette [,lɔ:ndə'ret] n Münzwäscherei f

laundry ['lɔ:ndri] n Wäscherei f; Wäsche f

lavatory ['lævətəri] n Toilette f

lavish ['læviʃ] adj verschwenderisch

law [lɔ:] n Gesetz nt; Recht nt; ~ court Gerichtshof m

lawful ['lɔ:fəl] adj gesetzlich

lawn [lɔ:n] n Rasen m

lawsuit ['lɔ:su:t] n Prozeß m, Gerichtsverfahren nt

lawyer ['lɔ:jə] n Rechtsanwalt m; Jurist m

laxative ['læksətiv] n Abführmittel nt

*lay [lei] v stellen, setzen, legen; ~ bricks mauern

layer [leiə] n Schicht f

layman ['leimən] n Laie m

lazy ['leizi] adj faul

lead¹ [li:d] n Vorsprung m; Leitung f; Leine f

lead² [led] n Blei nt

*lead [li:d] v führen

leader ['li:də] n Anführer m, Leiter m

leadership ['li:dəʃip] n Führung f

leading ['li:diŋ] adj Haupt-, führend

leaf [li:f] n (pl leaves) Blatt nt

league [li:g] n Bund m

leak [li:k] v lecken; n Leck nt

leaky ['li:ki] adj leck

lean [li:n] adj mager

*lean [li:n] v lehnen

leap [li:p] n Sprung m

*leap [li:p] v *springen

leap-year ['li:pjiə] n Schaltjahr nt

*learn [lə:n] v lernen

learner ['lə:nə] n Anfänger m

lease [li:s] n Mietvertrag m; Pacht f;

v verpachtèn, vermieten; mieten

leash [li:ʃ] *n* Leine *f*

least [li:st] *adj* geringst, mindest; kleinst; **at ~** wenigstens; zumindest

leather ['leðə] *n* Leder *nt*; Leder-, ledern

leave [li:v] *n* Urlaub *m*

*leave [li:v] *v* *weggehen, *verlassen; *lassen; **~ behind** *zurücklassen; **~ out** *auslassen

Lebanese [,lebə'ni:z] *adj* libanesisch; *n* Libanese *m*

Lebanon ['lebənən] Libanon

lecture ['lektʃə] *n* Vorlesung *f*, Vortrag *m*

left¹ [left] *adj* linke

left² [left] *v* (p, pp leave)

left-hand ['lefthænd] *adj* linke

left-handed [,left'hændid] *adj* linkshändig

leg [leg] *n* Bein *nt*

legacy ['legəsi] *n* Erbschaft *f*

legal ['li:gəl] *adj* gesetzmäßig, gesetzlich; rechtlich

legalization [,li:gəlai'zeiʃən] *n* Legalisierung *f*

legation [li'geiʃən] *n* Gesandtschaft *f*

legible ['ledʒibəl] *adj* leserlich

legitimate [li'dʒitimət] *adj* rechtmäßig

leisure ['leʒə] *n* Muße *f*

lemon ['lemən] *n* Zitrone *f*

lemonade [,lemə'neid] *n* Limonade *f*

*lend [lend] *v* *leihen

length [leŋθ] *n* Länge *f*

lengthen ['leŋθən] *v* verlängern

lengthways ['leŋθweiz] *adv* der Länge nach

lens [lenz] *n* Linse *f*; **telephoto ~** Teleobjektiv *nt*; **zoom ~** Gummilinse *f*

leprosy ['leprəsi] *n* Lepra *f*

less [les] *adv* weniger

lessen ['lesən] *v* vermindern

lesson ['lesən] *n* Lektion *f*

*let [let] *v* *lassen; vermieten; **~ down** enttäuschen

letter ['letə] *n* Brief *m*; Buchstabe *m*; **~ of credit** Akkreditiv *nt*; **~ of recommendation** Empfehlungsschreiben *nt*

letter-box ['letəbɔks] *n* Briefkasten *m*

lettuce ['letis] *n* Salat *m*

level ['levəl] *adj* gleich; platt, flach, eben; *n* Stand *m*, Niveau *nt*; Wasserwaage *f*; *v* gleichmachen, nivellieren; **~ crossing** Bahnübergang *m*

lever ['li:və] *n* Hebel *m*

Levis ['li:vaiz] *pl* Bluejeans *pl*

liability [,laiə'biləti] *n* Verantwortlichkeit *f*

liable ['laiəbəl] *adj* verantwortlich; **~ to** unterworfen

liberal ['libərəl] *adj* liberal; großzügig, freigebig

liberation [,libə'reiʃən] *n* Befreiung *f*

Liberia [lai'biəriə] Liberia

Liberian [lai'biəriən] *adj* liberisch; *n* Liberier *m*

liberty ['libəti] *n* Freiheit *f*

library ['laibrəri] *n* Bibliothek *f*

licence ['laisəns] *n* Lizenz *f*; Konzession *f*; **driving ~** Führerschein *m*; **~ number** *Am* Kennzeichen *nt*; **~ plate** *Am* Nummernschild *nt*

license ['laisəns] *v* konzessionieren

lick [lik] *v* lecken

lid [lid] *n* Deckel *m*

lie [lai] *v* *lügen; *n* Lüge *f*

*lie [lai] *v* *liegen; **~ down** sich niederlegen

life [laif] *n* (pl lives) Leben *nt*; **~ insurance** Lebensversicherung *f*

lifebelt ['laifbelt] *n* Rettungsgürtel *m*

lifetime ['laiftaim] *n* Leben *nt*

lift [lift] *v* *aufheben, *heben; *n* Aufzug *m*

light [lait] *n* Licht *nt*; *adj* leicht; hell;

~ **bulb** Birne f
*light [lait] v anzünden
lighter ['laitə] n Anzünder m
lighthouse ['laithaus] n Leuchtturm m
lighting ['laitiŋ] n Beleuchtung f
lightning ['laitniŋ] n Blitz m
like [laik] v gern *mögen; gern *haben, *mögen; adj egal; conj wie
likely ['laikli] adj wahrscheinlich
like-minded [,laik'maindid] adj gleichgesinnt
likewise ['laikwaiz] adv ebenso, ebenfalls
lily ['lili] n Lilie f
limb [lim] n Glied nt
lime [laim] n Kalk m; Linde f; Limone f
limetree ['laimtri:] n Lindenbaum m
limit ['limit] n Grenze f; v beschränken
limp [limp] v hinken; adj schlaff
line [lain] n Zeile f; Strich m; Schnur f; Linie f; Reihe f; **stand in** ~ Am Schlange *stehen
linen ['linin] n Leinen nt; Wäsche f
liner ['lainə] n Linienschiff nt
lingerie ['lɔ̃ʒəri:] n Damenunterwäsche f
lining ['lainiŋ] n Futter nt
link [liŋk] v *verbinden; n Verbindung f; Glied nt
lion ['laiən] n Löwe m
lip [lip] n Lippe f
lipsalve ['lipsa:v] n Lippensalbe f
lipstick ['lipstik] n Lippenstift m
liqueur [li'kjuə] n Likör m
liquid ['likwid] adj flüssig; n Flüssigkeit f
liquor ['likə] n Spirituosen pl
liquorice ['likəris] n Lakritze f
list [list] n Liste f; v *eintragen
listen ['lisən] v anhören, zuhören
listener ['lisnə] n Zuhörer m
literary ['litrəri] adj literarisch

literature ['litrətʃə] n Literatur f
litre ['li:tə] n Liter m
litter ['litə] n Abfall m; Schutt m; Wurf m
little ['litəl] adj klein; wenig
live[1] [liv] v leben; wohnen
live[2] [laiv] adj lebend
livelihood ['laivlihud] n Unterhalt m
lively ['laivli] adj lebhaft
liver ['livə] n Leber f
living-room ['liviŋru:m] n Wohnzimmer nt
load [loud] n Last f; v *laden
loaf [louf] n (pl loaves) Laib m
loan [loun] n Anleihe f
lobby ['lɔbi] n Vestibül nt; Foyer nt
lobster ['lɔbstə] n Hummer m
local ['loukəl] adj lokal, örtlich; ~ **call** Ortsgespräch nt; ~ **train** Nahverkehrszug m
locality [lou'kæləti] n Örtlichkeit f
locate [lou'keit] v ausfindig machen
location [lou'keiʃən] n Lage f
lock [lɔk] v *verschließen; n Schloß nt; Schleuse f; ~ **up** einsperren
locomotive [,loukə'moutiv] n Lokomotive f
lodge [lɔdʒ] v beherbergen; n Jagdhaus nt
lodger ['lɔdʒə] n Untermieter m
lodgings ['lɔdʒiŋz] pl Unterkunft f
log [lɔg] n Klotz m
logic ['lɔdʒik] n Logik f
logical ['lɔdʒikəl] adj logisch
lonely ['lounli] adj einsam
long [lɔŋ] adj lang; langwierig; ~ **for** sich sehnen nach; **no longer** nicht mehr
longing ['lɔŋiŋ] n Sehnsucht f
longitude ['lɔndʒitju:d] n Längengrad m
look [luk] v gucken, schauen; *scheinen, *aussehen; n Blick m; Aussehen nt, Anblick m; ~ **after** versor-

gen, aufpassen auf, sich kümmern um; ~ **at** anschauen, *ansehen; ~ **for** suchen; ~ **out** *achtgeben, sich *vorsehen; ~ **up** nachsuchen

looking-glass ['lukiŋglɑ:s] n Spiegel m

loop [lu:p] n Schlinge f

loose [lu:s] adj lose

loosen ['lu:sən] v lockern

lord [lɔ:d] n Lord m

lorry ['lɔri] n Lastwagen m

*****lose** [lu:z] v einbüßen, *verlieren

loss [lɔs] n Verlust m

lost [lɔst] adj verirrt; weg; ~ **and found** Fundsachen fpl; ~ **property office** Fundbüro nt

lot [lɔt] n Los nt; Haufen m, Menge f

aftershave lotion Rasierwasser nt

lottery ['lɔtəri] n Lotterie f

loud [laud] adj laut

loud-speaker [,laud'spi:kə] n Lautsprecher m

lounge [laundʒ] n Gesellschaftsraum m

louse [laus] n (pl lice) Laus f

love [lʌv] v gern *haben, lieben; n Liebe f; **in** ~ verliebt

lovely ['lʌvli] adj herrlich, wunderbar, hübsch

lover ['lʌvə] n Liebhaber m

love-story ['lʌv,stɔ:ri] n Liebesgeschichte f

low [lou] adj niedrig; tief; niedergeschlagen; ~ **tide** Ebbe f

lower ['louə] v *herunterlassen; herabsetzen; *streichen; adj unter, niedrig

lowlands ['louləndz] pl Tiefland nt

loyal ['lɔiəl] adj loyal

lubricate ['lu:brikeit] v ölen, schmieren

lubrication [,lu:bri'keiʃən] n Schmierung f; ~ **oil** Schmieröl nt; ~ **system** Schmiersystem nt

luck [lʌk] n Glück nt; Zufall m; **bad** ~ Pech nt

lucky ['lʌki] adj glücklich; ~ **charm** Amulett nt

ludicrous ['lu:dikrəs] adj lächerlich, lachhaft

luggage ['lʌgidʒ] n Gepäck nt; **hand** ~ Handgepäck nt; **left** ~ **office** Gepäckaufbewahrung f; ~ **rack** Gepäcknetz nt; ~ **van** Gepäckwagen m

lukewarm ['lu:kwɔ:m] adj lauwarm

lumbago [lʌm'beigou] n Hexenschuß m

luminous ['lu:minəs] adj leuchtend

lump [lʌmp] n Brocken m, Klumpen m, Stück nt; Beule f; ~ **of sugar** Stück Zucker; ~ **sum** Pauschalsumme f

lumpy ['lʌmpi] adj klumpig

lunacy ['lu:nəsi] n Irrsinn m

lunatic ['lu:nətik] adj irrsinnig; n Irre m

lunch [lʌntʃ] n Imbiß m, Mittagessen nt

luncheon ['lʌntʃən] n Mittagessen nt

lung [lʌŋ] n Lunge f

lust [lʌst] n Wollust f

luxurious [lʌg'ʒuəriəs] adj luxuriös

luxury ['lʌkʃəri] n Luxus m

M

machine [mə'ʃi:n] n Apparat m, Maschine f

machinery [mə'ʃi:nəri] n Mechanismus m

mackerel ['mækrəl] n (pl ~) Makrele f

mackintosh ['mækintɔʃ] n Regenmantel m

mad [mæd] adj irre, toll, verrückt; wütend

madam ['mædəm] n gnädige Frau

madness ['mædnəs] n Wahnsinn m

magazine [,mægə'zi:n] n Zeitschrift f

magic ['mædʒik] n Zauberei f, Magie f; adj Zauber-

magician [mə'dʒiʃən] n Zauberer m

magistrate ['mædʒistreit] n Richter m

magnetic [mæg'netik] adj magnetisch

magneto [mæg'ni:tou] n (pl ~s) Magnet m

magnificent [mæg'nifisənt] adj prächtig; großartig, glänzend

magpie ['mægpai] n Elster f

maid [meid] n Dienstmädchen nt

maiden name ['meidən neim] Mädchenname m

mail [meil] n Post f; v *aufgeben; ~ order Am Postanweisung f

mailbox ['meilbɔks] nAm Briefkasten m

main [mein] adj Haupt-, wichtigste; größt; ~ deck Oberdeck nt; ~ line Hauptstrecke f; ~ road Hauptstraße f; ~ street Hauptstraße f

mainland ['meinlənd] n Festland nt

mainly ['meinli] adv hauptsächlich

mains [meinz] pl Hauptleitung f

maintain [mein'tein] v *aufrechterhalten

maintenance ['meintənəns] n Instandhaltung f

maize [meiz] n Mais m

major ['meidʒə] adj groß; Haupt-; größer; n Major m

majority [mə'dʒɔrəti] n Mehrheit f

*make [meik] v machen; verdienen; *schaffen; ~ do with sich *behelfen mit; ~ good vergüten; ~ up zusammenstellen

make-up ['meikʌp] n Schminke f

malaria [mə'leəriə] n Malaria f

Malaysia [mə'leiziə] Malaysia

Malaysian [mə'leiziən] adj malaiisch

male [meil] adj männlich

malicious [mə'liʃəs] adj boshaft

malignant [mə'lignənt] adj bösartig

mallet ['mælit] n Holzhammer m

malnutrition [,mælnju'triʃən] n Unterernährung f

mammal ['mæməl] n Säugetier nt

mammoth ['mæməθ] n Mammut nt

man [mæn] n (pl men) Mann m; Mensch m; men's room Herrentoilette f

manage ['mænidʒ] v verwalten; *gelingen

manageable ['mænidʒəbəl] adj handlich

management ['mænidʒmənt] n Verwaltung f; Führung f

manager ['mænidʒə] n Chef m, Direktor m

mandarin ['mændərin] n Mandarine f

mandate ['mændeit] n Mandat nt

manger ['meindʒə] n Krippe f

manicure ['mænikjuə] n Maniküre f; v maniküren

mankind [mæn'kaind] n Menschheit f

mannequin ['mænəkin] n Mannequin nt

manner ['mænə] n Art f, Weise f; manners pl Manieren fpl

man-of-war [,mænəv'wɔ:] n Kriegsschiff nt

manor-house ['mænəhaus] n Herrschaftshaus nt

mansion ['mænʃən] n Herrschaftshaus nt

manual ['mænjuəl] adj Hand-

manufacture [,mænju'fæktʃə] v herstellen, fabrizieren

manufacturer [,mænju'fæktʃərə] n Fabrikant m

manure [mə'njuə] n Dünger m

manuscript ['mænjuskript] n Manuskript nt

many ['meni] adj viel

map [mæp] n Karte f; Landkarte f; Plan m

maple ['meipəl] n Ahorn m

marble ['ma:bəl] *n* Marmor *m*; Murmel *f*

March [ma:tʃ] März

march [ma:tʃ] *v* marschieren; *n* Marsch *m*

mare [meə] *n* Stute *f*

margarine [,ma:dʒə'ri:n] *n* Margarine *f*

margin ['ma:dʒin] *n* Rand *m*

maritime ['mæritaim] *adj* maritim

mark [ma:k] *v* ankreuzen; bezeichnen, zeichnen; kennzeichnen; *n* Zeichen *nt*; Zensur *f*; Zielscheibe *f*

market ['ma:kit] *n* Markt *m*

market-place ['ma:kitpleis] *n* Marktplatz *m*

marmalade ['ma:məleid] *n* Marmelade *f*

marriage ['mæridʒ] *n* Ehe *f*

marrow ['mærou] *n* Mark *nt*

marry ['mæri] *v* heiraten; **married couple** Ehepaar *nt*

marsh [ma:ʃ] *n* Sumpf *m*

marshy ['ma:ʃi] *adj* sumpfig

martyr ['ma:tə] *n* Märtyrer *m*

marvel ['ma:vəl] *n* Wunder *nt*; *v* sich wundern

marvellous ['ma:vələs] *adj* wunderbar

mascara [mæ'ska:rə] *n* Wimperntusche *f*

masculine ['mæskjulin] *adj* männlich

mash [mæʃ] *v* zerstampfen

mask [ma:sk] *n* Maske *f*

Mass [mæs] *n* Messe *f*

mass [mæs] *n* Menge *f*; ~ **production** Massenproduktion *f*

massage ['mæsa:ʒ] *n* Massage *f*; *v* massieren

masseur [mæ'sə:] *n* Masseur *m*

massive ['mæsiv] *adj* massiv

mast [ma:st] *n* Mast *m*

master ['ma:stə] *n* Meister *m*; Studienrat *m*, Lehrer *m*; *v* beherrschen

masterpiece ['ma:stəpi:s] *n* Meister-

stück *nt*

mat [mæt] *n* Matte *f*; *adj* matt, glanzlos

match [mætʃ] *n* Streichholz *nt*; Spiel *nt*; *v* passen zu

match-box ['mætʃbɔks] *n* Streichholzschachtel *f*

material [mə'tiəriəl] *n* Material *nt*; *adj* stofflich, materiell

mathematical [,mæθə'mætikəl] *adj* mathematisch

mathematics [,mæθə'mætiks] *n* Mathematik *f*

matrimonial [,mætri'mouniəl] *adj* ehelich

matrimony ['mætriməni] *n* Ehe *f*

matter ['mætə] *n* Stoff *m*, Materie *f*; Sache *f*, Frage *f*; *v* von Bedeutung *sein; **as a** ~ **of fact** tatsächlich

matter-of-fact [,mætərəv'fækt] *adj* nüchtern

mattress ['mætrəs] *n* Matratze *f*

mature [mə'tjuə] *adj* reif

maturity [mə'tjuərəti] *n* Reife *f*

mausoleum [,mɔ:sə'li:əm] *n* Mausoleum *nt*

mauve [mouv] *adj* hellviolett

May [mei] Mai

* **may** [mei] *v* *mögen; *dürfen

maybe ['meibi:] *adv* vielleicht

mayor [meə] *n* Bürgermeister *m*

maze [meiz] *n* Irrgarten *m*

me [mi:] *pron* mich; mir

meadow ['medou] *n* Wiese *f*

meal [mi:l] *n* Mahl *nt*, Mahlzeit *f*

mean [mi:n] *adj* niederträchtig; *n* Durchschnitt *m*

* **mean** [mi:n] *v* bedeuten; meinen

meaning ['mi:niŋ] *n* Bedeutung *f*

meaningless ['mi:niŋləs] *adj* sinnlos

means [mi:nz] *n* Mittel *nt*; **by no** ~ keineswegs, keinesfalls

in the meantime [in ðə 'mi:ntaim] mittlerweile, inzwischen

meanwhile ['mi:nwail] *adv* inzwischen, mittlerweile

measles ['mi:zəlz] *n* Masern *pl*

measure ['meʒə] *v* *messen; *n* Maß *nt*; Maßnahme *f*

meat [mi:t] *n* Fleisch *nt*

mechanic [mi'kænik] *n* Monteur *m*, Mechaniker *m*

mechanical [mi'kænikəl] *adj* mechanisch

mechanism ['mekənizəm] *n* Mechanismus *m*

medal ['medəl] *n* Medaille *f*

mediaeval [,medi'i:vəl] *adj* mittelalterlich

mediate ['mi:dieit] *v* vermitteln

mediator ['mi:dieitə] *n* Vermittler *m*

medical ['medikəl] *adj* ärztlich, medizinisch

medicine ['medsin] *n* Medizin *f*

meditate ['mediteit] *v* meditieren

Mediterranean [,meditə'reiniən] Mittelmeer *nt*

medium ['mi:diəm] *adj* mittelmäßig, durchschnittlich, mittler

*meet [mi:t] *v* *treffen; begegnen

meeting ['mi:tiŋ] *n* Versammlung *f*, Treffen *nt*

meeting-place ['mi:tiŋpleis] *n* Treffpunkt *m*

melancholy ['melənkəli] *n* Schwermut *f*

mellow ['melou] *adj* mild

melodrama ['melə,dra:mə] *n* Melodrama *nt*

melody ['melədi] *n* Melodie *f*

melon ['melən] *n* Melone *f*

melt [melt] *v* *schmelzen

member ['membə] *n* Mitglied *nt*; **Member of Parliament** Abgeordnete *m*

membership ['membəʃip] *n* Mitgliedschaft *f*

memo ['memou] *n* (pl ~s) Memorandum *nt*

memorable ['memərəbəl] *adj* denkwürdig

memorial [mə'mɔ:riəl] *n* Denkmal *nt*

memorize ['meməraiz] *v* auswendig lernen

memory ['meməri] *n* Gedächtnis *nt*; Erinnerung *f*; Andenken *nt*

mend [mend] *v* flicken, ausbessern

menstruation [,menstru'eiʃən] *n* Menstruation *f*

mental ['mentəl] *adj* geistig

mention ['menʃən] *v* *nennen, erwähnen; *n* Meldung *f*, Erwähnung *f*

menu ['menju:] *n* Speisekarte *f*

merchandise ['mə:tʃəndaiz] *n* Handelsware *f*, Ware *f*

merchant ['mə:tʃənt] *n* Händler *m*, Kaufmann *m*

merciful ['mə:sifəl] *adj* barmherzig

mercury ['mə:kjuri] *n* Quecksilber *nt*

mercy ['mə:si] *n* Gnade *f*, Barmherzigkeit *f*

mere [miə] *adj* bloß

merely ['miəli] *adv* nur

merger ['mə:dʒə] *n* Fusion *f*

merit ['merit] *v* verdienen; *n* Verdienst *nt*

mermaid ['mə:meid] *n* Seejungfrau *f*

merry ['meri] *adj* fröhlich

merry-go-round ['merigou,raund] *n* Karussell *nt*

mesh [meʃ] *n* Masche *f*

mess [mes] *n* Durcheinander *nt*, Unordnung *f*; ~ **up** in Unordnung *bringen

message ['mesidʒ] *n* Nachricht *f*, Bescheid *m*

messenger ['mesindʒə] *n* Bote *m*

metal ['metəl] *n* Metall *nt*; metallisch

meter ['mi:tə] *n* Zähler *m*

method ['meθəd] *n* Methode *f*; Ordnung *f*

methodical [mə'θɔdikəl] *adj* metho-

disch
methylated spirits ['meθəleitid 'spirits]
Brennspiritus *m*
metre ['mi:tə] *n* Meter *nt*
metric ['metrik] *adj* metrisch
Mexican ['meksikən] *adj* mexikanisch;
n Mexikaner *m*
Mexico ['meksikou] Mexiko
mezzanine ['mezəni:n] *n* Zwischenstock *m*
microphone ['maikrəfoun] *n* Mikrophon *nt*
midday ['middei] *n* Mittag *m*
middle ['midəl] *n* Mitte *f*; *adj* mittler;
Middle Ages Mittelalter *nt*; ~
class Mittelstand *m*; **middle-class**
adj bürgerlich
midnight ['midnait] *n* Mitternacht *f*
midst [midst] *n* Mitte *f*
midsummer ['mid,sʌmə] *n* Hochsommer *m*
midwife ['midwaif] *n* (pl -wives) Hebamme *f*
might [mait] *n* Macht *f*
* **might** [mait] *v* *können
mighty ['maiti] *adj* mächtig
migraine ['migrein] *n* Migräne *f*
mild [maild] *adj* mild
mildew ['mildju] *n* Schimmel *m*
mile [mail] *n* Meile *f*
mileage ['mailidʒ] *n* Meilenstand *m*
milepost ['mailpoust] *n* Wegweiser *m*
milestone ['mailstoun] *n* Meilenstein
m
milieu ['mi:ljə:] *n* Milieu *nt*
military ['militəri] *adj* militärisch; ~
force Kriegsmacht *f*
milk [milk] *n* Milch *f*
milkman ['milkmən] *n* (pl -men)
Milchmann *m*
milk-shake ['milkʃeik] *n* Milkshake *m*
milky ['milki] *adj* milchig
mill [mil] *n* Mühle *f*; Fabrik *f*
miller ['milə] *n* Müller *m*

milliner ['milinə] *n* Modistin *f*
million ['miljən] *n* Million *f*
millionaire [,miljə'neə] *n* Millionär *m*
mince [mins] *v* zerhacken
mind [maind] *n* Geist *m*; *v* etwas einzuwenden *haben gegen; *achtge-
ben auf, kümmern, achten auf
mine [main] *n* Bergwerk *nt*
miner ['mainə] *n* Bergmann *m*
mineral ['minərəl] *n* Mineral *nt*; ~
water Mineralwasser *nt*
miniature ['minjətʃə] *n* Miniatur *f*
minimum ['miniməm] *n* Minimum *nt*
mining ['mainiŋ] *n* Bergbau *m*
minister ['ministə] *n* Minister *m*;
Geistliche *m*; **Prime Minister** Ministerpräsident *m*
ministry ['ministri] *n* Ministerium *nt*
mink [miŋk] *n* Nerz *m*
minor ['mainə] *adj* klein, gering, kleiner; untergeordnet; *n* Minderjährige *m*
minority [mai'nɔrəti] *n* Minderheit *f*
mint [mint] *n* Minze *f*
minus ['mainəs] *prep* weniger
minute¹ ['minit] *n* Minute *f*; **minutes**
Protokoll *n*
minute² [mai'nju:t] *adj* winzig
miracle ['mirəkəl] *n* Wunder *nt*
miraculous [mi'rækjuləs] *adj* wunderbar
mirror ['mirə] *n* Spiegel *m*
misbehave [,misbi'heiv] *v* sich schlecht
*benehmen
miscarriage [mis'kæridʒ] *n* Fehlgeburt
f
miscellaneous [,misə'leiniəs] *adj* vermischt
mischief ['mistʃif] *n* Unfug *m*; Unheil
nt, Schaden *m*
mischievous ['mistʃivəs] *adj* schelmisch
miserable ['mizərəbəl] *adj* erbärmlich,
elend

misery ['mɪzəri] n Jammer m, Elend nt; Not f

misfortune [mɪs'fɔ:tʃen] n Unglück nt, Mißgeschick nt

* **mislay** [mɪs'leɪ] v verlegen

misplaced [mɪs'pleɪst] adj unangebracht

mispronounce [,mɪsprə'naʊns] v falsch *aussprechen

miss¹ [mɪs] Fräulein nt

miss² [mɪs] v verpassen

missing ['mɪsɪŋ] adj fehlend; ~ person Vermißte m

mist [mɪst] n Nebel m

mistake [mɪ'steɪk] n Versehen nt, Irrtum m, Fehler m

* **mistake** [mɪ'steɪk] v verwechseln

mistaken [mɪ'steɪkən] adj falsch; *be ~ sich täuschen, sich irren

mister ['mɪstə] Herr m

mistress ['mɪstrəs] n Hausherrin f; Herrin f; Mätresse f

mistrust [mɪs'trʌst] v mißtrauen

misty ['mɪsti] adj nebelig

* **misunderstand** [,mɪsʌndə'stænd] v *mißverstehen

misunderstanding [,mɪsʌndə'stændɪŋ] n Mißverständnis nt

misuse [mɪs'ju:s] n Mißbrauch m

mittens ['mɪtənz] pl Fausthandschuhe mpl

mix [mɪks] v mischen; ~ with verkehren mit

mixed [mɪkst] adj meliert, gemischt

mixer ['mɪksə] n Mixer m

mixture ['mɪkstʃə] n Mischung f

moan [məʊn] v stöhnen

moat [məʊt] n Wallgraben m

mobile ['məʊbaɪl] adj mobil, beweglich

mock [mɔk] v verspotten

mockery ['mɔkəri] n Spott m

model ['mɔdəl] n Modell nt; Mannequin nt; v formen, modellieren

moderate ['mɔdərət] adj gemäßigt, mäßig; mittelmäßig

modern ['mɔdən] adj modern

modest ['mɔdɪst] adj bescheiden

modesty ['mɔdɪsti] n Bescheidenheit f

modify ['mɔdɪfaɪ] v modifizieren

mohair ['məʊheə] n Mohair m

moist [mɔɪst] adj naß, feucht

moisten ['mɔɪsən] v anfeuchten

moisture ['mɔɪstʃə] n Feuchtigkeit f; **moisturizing cream** Feuchtigkeitskrem f

molar ['məʊlə] n Backenzahn m

moment ['məʊmənt] n Moment m, Augenblick m

monarch ['mɔnək] n Monarch m

monarchy ['mɔnəki] n Monarchie f

monastery ['mɔnəstri] n Kloster nt

Monday ['mʌndi] Montag m

monetary ['mʌnɪtəri] adj monetär; ~ unit Währungseinheit f

money ['mʌni] n Geld nt; ~ exchange Wechselstube f; ~ order Anweisung f

monk [mʌŋk] n Mönch m

monkey ['mʌŋki] n Affe m

monologue ['mɔnəlɔg] n Monolog m

monopoly [mə'nɔpəli] n Monopol nt

monotonous [mə'nɔtənəs] adj monoton

month [mʌnθ] n Monat m

monthly ['mʌnθli] adj monatlich; ~ magazine Monatsheft nt

monument ['mɔnjumənt] n Monument nt, Denkmal nt

mood [mu:d] n Laune f, Stimmung f

moon [mu:n] n Mond m

moonlight ['mu:nlaɪt] n Mondlicht nt

moor [mʊə] n Heide f, Moor nt

moose [mu:s] n (pl ~, ~s) Elch m

moped [məʊped] n Moped nt

moral ['mɔrəl] n Moral f; adj sittlich, moralisch; **morals** Sitten

morality [mə'ræləti] n Moral f

more [mɔ:] adj mehr; **once** ~ noch

einmal

moreover [mɔːˈrouvə] *adv* ferner, außerdem

morning [ˈmɔːniŋ] *n* Morgen *m*; ~ **paper** Morgenzeitung *f*; **this** ~ heute morgen

Moroccan [məˈrɔkən] *adj* marokkanisch; *n* Marokkaner *m*

Morocco [məˈrɔkou] Marokko

morphia [ˈmɔːfiə] *n* Morphium *nt*

morphine [ˈmɔːfiːn] *n* Morphium *nt*

morsel [ˈmɔːsəl] *n* Stück *nt*

mortal [ˈmɔːtəl] *adj* tödlich, sterblich

mortgage [ˈmɔːgidʒ] *n* Hypothek *f*

mosaic [məˈzeiik] *n* Mosaik *nt*

mosque [mɔsk] *n* Moschee *f*

mosquito [məˈskiːtou] *n* (pl ~es) Mücke *f*; Moskito *m*

mosquito-net [məˈskiːtounet] *n* Moskitonetz *nt*

moss [mɔs] *n* Moos *nt*

most [moust] *adj* meist; **at** ~ allenfalls, höchstens; ~ **of all** besonders

mostly [ˈmoustli] *adv* meistens

motel [mouˈtel] *n* Motel *nt*

moth [mɔθ] *n* Motte *f*

mother [ˈmʌðə] *n* Mutter *f*; ~ **tongue** Muttersprache *f*

mother-in-law [ˈmʌðərinlɔː] *n* (pl mothers-) Schwiegermutter *f*

mother-of-pearl [ˌmʌðərəvˈpəːl] *n* Perlmutt *nt*

motion [ˈmouʃən] *n* Bewegung *f*; Antrag *m*

motive [ˈmoutiv] *n* Motiv *nt*

motor [ˈmoutə] *n* Motor *m*; *v* im Auto *fahren; ~ **body** *Am* Karosserie *f*; **starter** ~ Anlasser *m*

motorbike [ˈmoutəbaik] *nAm* Moped *nt*

motor-boat [ˈmoutəbout] *n* Motorboot *nt*

motor-car [ˈmoutəkaː] *n* Kraftwagen *m*

motor-cycle [ˈmoutəˌsaikəl] *n* Motorrad *nt*

motoring [ˈmoutəriŋ] *n* Automobilismus *m*

motorist [ˈmoutərist] *n* Autofahrer *m*

motorway [ˈmoutəwei] *n* Autobahn *f*

motto [ˈmotou] *n* (pl ~es, ~s) Devise *f*

mouldy [ˈmouldi] *adj* schimmelig

mound [maund] *n* Erhebung *f*

mount [maunt] *v* *besteigen; *n* Berg *m*

mountain [ˈmauntin] *n* Berg *m*; ~ **pass** Gebirgspaß *m*; ~ **range** Bergkette *f*

mountaineering [ˌmauntiˈniəriŋ] *n* Bergsteigen *nt*

mountainous [ˈmauntinəs] *adj* gebirgig

mourning [ˈmɔːniŋ] *n* Trauer *f*

mouse [maus] *n* (pl mice) Maus *f*

moustache [məˈstaːʃ] *n* Schnurrbart *m*

mouth [mauθ] *n* Mund *m*; Maul *nt*; Mündung *f*

mouthwash [ˈmauθwɔʃ] *n* Mundwasser *nt*

movable [ˈmuːvəbəl] *adj* beweglich

move [muːv] *v* bewegen; versetzen; *umziehen; rühren; *n* Zug *m*, Schritt *m*; Umzug *m*

movement [ˈmuːvmənt] *n* Bewegung *f*

movie [ˈmuːvi] *n* Film *m*; **movies** *Am* Kino *nt*; ~ **theater** *Am* Kino *nt*

much [mʌtʃ] *adj* viel; **as** ~ ebensoviel; ebensosehr

muck [mʌk] *n* Dreck *m*

mud [mʌd] *n* Schlamm *m*

muddle [ˈmʌdəl] *n* Wirrwarr *m*, Durcheinander *m*, Durcheinander *nt*; *v* *durcheinanderbringen

muddy [ˈmʌdi] *adj* schlammig

mud-guard [ˈmʌdgaːd] *n* Kotflügel *m*

muffler [ˈmʌflə] *nAm* Auspufftopf *m*

mug [mʌg] *n* Becher *m*

mulberry [ˈmʌlbəri] *n* Maulbeere *f*

mule [mju:l] *n* Maultier *nt*, Maulesel *m*

mullet ['mʌlit] *n* Meeräsche *f*

multiplication [ˌmʌltipli'keiʃən] *n* Multiplikation *f*

multiply ['mʌltiplai] *v* multiplizieren

mumps [mʌmps] *n* Mumps *m*

municipal [mju:'nisipəl] *adj* städtisch

municipality [mju:ˌnisi'pæləti] *n* Stadtverwaltung *f*

murder ['mə:də] *n* Mord *m* ; *v* morden

murderer ['mə:dərə] *n* Mörder *m*

muscle ['mʌsəl] *n* Muskel *m*

muscular ['mʌskjulə] *adj* muskulös

museum [mju:'zi:əm] *n* Museum *nt*

mushroom ['mʌʃru:m] *n* Champignon *m* ; Pilz *m*

music ['mju:zik] *n* Musik *f* ; ~ **academy** Konservatorium *f*

musical ['mju:zikəl] *adj* musikalisch ; *n* Musical *nt*

music-hall ['mju:zikhɔ:l] *n* Varietétheater *nt*

musician [mju:'ziʃən] *n* Musiker *m*

muslin ['mʌzlin] *n* Musselin *m*

mussel ['mʌsəl] *n* Muschel *f*

***must** [mʌst] *v* *müssen

mustard ['mʌstəd] *n* Senf *m*

mute [mju:t] *adj* stumm

mutiny ['mju:tini] *n* Meuterei *f*

mutton ['mʌtən] *n* Hammelfleisch *nt*

mutual ['mju:tʃuəl] *adj* wechselseitig, gegenseitig

my [mai] *adj* mein

myself [mai'self] *pron* mich ; selbst

mysterious [mi'stiəriəs] *adj* rätselhaft, geheimnisvoll

mystery ['mistəri] *n* Rätsel *nt*, Geheimnis *nt*

myth [miθ] *n* Mythos *m*

N

nail [neil] *n* Nagel *m*

nailbrush ['neilbrʌʃ] *n* Nagelbürste *f*

nail-file ['neilfail] *n* Nagelfeile *f*

nail-polish ['neilˌpɔliʃ] *n* Nagellack *m*

nail-scissors ['neilˌsizəz] *pl* Nagelschere *f*

naïve [na:'i:v] *adj* naiv

naked ['neikid] *adj* bloß, nackt ; kahl

name [neim] *n* Name *m* ; *v* *nennen ; **in the ~ of** im Namen von

namely ['neimli] *adv* nämlich

nap [næp] *n* Schläfchen *nt*

napkin ['næpkin] *n* Serviette *f*

nappy ['næpi] *n* Windel *f*

narcosis [na:'kousis] *n* (pl -ses) Narkose *f*

narcotic [na:'kɔtik] *n* Rauschgift *nt*

narrow ['nærou] *adj* eng, schmal

narrow-minded [ˌnærou'maindid] *adj* engstirnig

nasty ['na:sti] *adj* unangenehm, widrig ; garstig

nation ['neiʃən] *n* Nation *f* ; Volk *nt*

national ['næʃənəl] *adj* national ; Volks- ; Staats- ; ~ **anthem** Nationalhymne *f* ; ~ **dress** Tracht *f* ; ~ **park** Naturschutzpark *m*

nationality [ˌnæʃə'næləti] *n* Staatsangehörigkeit *f*

nationalize ['næʃənəlaiz] *v* nationalisieren

native ['neitiv] *n* Eingeborene *m* ; *adj* einheimisch ; ~ **country** Vaterland *nt*, Heimatland *nt* ; ~ **language** Muttersprache *f*

natural ['nætʃərəl] *adj* natürlich ; angeboren

naturally ['nætʃərəli] *adv* natürlich, selbstverständlich

nature ['neitʃə] *n* Natur *f* ; Wesensart

f

naughty ['nɔːti] *adj* ungezogen, unartig

nausea ['nɔːsiə] *n* Übelkeit *f*

naval ['neivəl] *adj* Marine-

navel ['neivəl] *n* Nabel *m*

navigable ['nævigəbəl] *adj* befahrbar

navigate ['nævigeit] *v* steuern

navigation [,nævi'geiʃən] *n* Navigation *f*; Schiffahrt *f*

navy ['neivi] *n* Marine *f*

near [niə] *prep* bei; *adj* nahe

nearby ['niəbai] *adj* nahe

nearly ['niəli] *adv* fast, beinahe

neat [niːt] *adj* nett, sorgfältig

necessary ['nesəsəri] *adj* nötig, notwendig

necessity [nə'sesəti] *n* Notwendigkeit *f*

neck [nek] *n* Hals *m*; **nape of the ~** Nacken *m*

necklace ['nekləs] *n* Halskette *f*

necktie ['nektai] *n* Krawatte *f*

need [niːd] *v* brauchen, nötig *haben; *n* Not *f*, Bedürfnis *nt*; Notwendigkeit *f*; **~ to** *müssen

needle ['niːdəl] *n* Nadel *f*

needlework ['niːdəlwəːk] *n* Handarbeit *f*

negative ['negətiv] *adj* verneinend, negativ; *n* Negativ *nt*

neglect [ni'glekt] *v* vernachlässigen; *n* Vernachlässigung *f*

neglectful [ni'glektfəl] *adj* nachlässig

negligee ['negliʒei] *n* Negligé *nt*

negotiate [ni'gouʃieit] *v* verhandeln

negotiation [ni,gouʃi'eiʃən] *n* Verhandlung *f*

Negro ['niːgrou] *n* (pl ~es) Neger *m*

neighbour ['neibə] *n* Nachbar *m*

neighbourhood ['neibəhud] *n* Nachbarschaft *f*

neighbouring ['neibəriŋ] *adj* benachbart

neither ['naiðə] *pron* keiner von beiden; **neither ... nor** weder ... noch

neon ['niːɔn] *n* Neon *nt*

nephew ['nefjuː] *n* Neffe *m*

nerve [nəːv] *n* Nerv *m*; Kühnheit *f*

nervous ['nəːvəs] *adj* nervös

nest [nest] *n* Nest *nt*

net [net] *n* Netz *nt*; *adj* netto

the Netherlands ['neðələndz] Niederlande *fpl*

network ['netwəːk] *n* Netz *nt*

neuralgia [njuə'rældʒə] *n* Neuralgie *f*

neurosis [njuə'rousis] *n* Neurose *f*

neuter ['njuːtə] *adj* sächlich

neutral ['njuːtrəl] *adj* neutral

never ['nevə] *adv* nie, niemals

nevertheless [,nevəðə'les] *adv* nichtsdestoweniger

new [njuː] *adj* neu; **New Year** Neujahr

news [njuːz] *n* Nachrichten, Neuigkeit *f*

newsagent ['njuː,zeidʒənt] *n* Zeitungshändler *m*

newspaper ['njuːz,peipə] *n* Zeitung *f*

newsreel ['njuːzriːl] *n* Wochenschau *f*

newsstand ['njuːzstænd] *n* Zeitungsstand *m*

New Zealand [njuː 'ziːlənd] Neuseeland

next [nekst] *adj* nächst; **~ to** neben

next-door [,nekst'dɔː] *adv* nebenan

nice [nais] *adj* nett, hübsch; wohlschmeckend; sympathisch

nickel ['nikəl] *n* Nickel *m*

nickname ['nikneim] *n* Spitzname *m*

nicotine ['nikətiːn] *n* Nikotin *nt*

niece [niːs] *n* Nichte *f*

Nigeria [nai'dʒiəriə] Nigeria

Nigerian [nai'dʒiəriən] *adj* nigerianisch; *n* Nigerianer *m*

night [nait] *n* Nacht *f*; Abend *m*; **by ~** bei Nacht; **~ flight** Nachtflug *m*; **~ rate** Nachttarif *m*; **~ train**

Nachtzug *m*

nightclub ['naitklʌb] *n* Nachtlokal *nt*

night-cream ['naitkri:m] *n* Nachtkrem *f*

nightdress ['naitdres] *n* Nachthemd *nt*

nightingale ['naitiŋgeil] *n* Nachtigall *f*

nightly ['naitli] *adj* nächtlich

nil [nil] nichts

nine [nain] *num* neun

nineteen [,nain'ti:n] *num* neunzehn

nineteenth [,nain'ti:nθ] *num* neunzehnte

ninety ['nainti] *num* neunzig

ninth [nainθ] *num* neunte

nitrogen ['naitrədʒən] *n* Stickstoff *m*

no [nou] nein; *adj* kein; ~ **one** niemand

nobility [nou'biləti] *n* Adel *m*

noble ['noubəl] *adj* adlig; edel

nobody ['noubədi] *pron* niemand

nod [nɔd] *n* Nicken *nt*; *v* nicken

noise [nɔiz] *n* Geräusch *nt*; Krach *m*, Lärm *m*

noisy ['nɔizi] *adj* lärmend; hellhörig

nominal ['nɔminəl] *adj* nominell

nominate ['nɔmineit] *v* *ernennen

nomination [,nɔmi'neiʃən] *n* Ernennung *f*

none [nʌn] *pron* keiner

nonsense ['nɔnsəns] *n* Unsinn *m*

noon [nu:n] *n* Mittag *m*

normal ['nɔ:məl] *adj* gewohnt, normal

north [nɔ:θ] *n* Norden *m*; *adj* nördlich; **North Pole** Nordpol *m*

north-east [,nɔ:θ'i:st] *n* Nordosten *m*

northerly ['nɔ:ðəli] *adj* nördlich

northern ['nɔ:ðən] *adj* nördlich

north-west [,nɔ:θ'west] *n* Nordwesten *m*

Norway ['nɔ:wei] *n* Norwegen

Norwegian [nɔ:'wi:dʒən] *adj* norwegisch; *n* Norweger *m*

nose [nouz] *n* Nase *f*

nosebleed ['nouzbli:d] *n* Nasenbluten

nt

nostril ['nɔstril] *n* Nasenloch *nt*

not [nɔt] *adv* nicht

notary ['noutəri] *n* Notar *m*

note [nout] *n* Aufzeichnung *f*, Notiz *f*; Vermerk *m*; Ton *m*; *v* anmerken; *wahrnehmen, bemerken

notebook ['noutbuk] *n* Notizbuch *nt*

noted ['noutid] *adj* berühmt

notepaper ['nout,peipə] *n* Schreibpapier *nt*, Briefpapier *nt*

nothing ['nʌθiŋ] *n* nichts

notice ['noutis] *v* feststellen, merken, bemerken; *sehen; *n* Anzeige *f*, Bericht *m*; Aufmerksamkeit *f*, Acht *f*

noticeable ['noutisəbəl] *adj* wahrnehmbar; bemerkenswert

notify ['noutifai] *v* mitteilen; benachrichtigen

notion ['nouʃən] *n* Begriff *m*, Ahnung *f*

notorious [nou'tɔ:riəs] *adj* berüchtigt

nougat ['nu:ga:] *n* Nougat *m*

nought [nɔ:t] *n* Null *f*

noun [naun] *n* Hauptwort *nt*, Substantiv *nt*

nourishing ['nʌriʃiŋ] *adj* nahrhaft

novel ['nɔvəl] *n* Roman *m*

novelist ['nɔvəlist] *n* Romanschriftsteller *m*

November [nou'vembə] November

now [nau] *adv* jetzt; ~ **and then** hin und wieder

nowadays ['nauədeiz] *adv* heutzutage

nowhere ['nouweə] *adv* nirgends

nozzle ['nɔzəl] *n* Schnabel *m*

nuance [nju:'ã:s] *n* Nuance *f*

nuclear ['nju:kliə] *adj* Kern-, nuklear; ~ **energy** Kernenergie *f*

nucleus ['nju:kliəs] *n* Kern *m*

nude [nju:d] *adj* nackt; *n* Akt *m*

nuisance ['nju:səns] *n* Unfug *m*

numb [nʌm] *adj* starr; erstarrt

number ['nʌmbə] *n* Nummer *f*; Ziffer

f, Zahl f; Anzahl f

numeral ['nju:mərəl] n Zahlwort nt

numerous ['nju:mərəs] adj zahlreich

nun [nʌn] n Nonne f

nunnery ['nʌnəri] n Nonnenkloster nt

nurse [nə:s] n Schwester f, Krankenschwester f; Kindermädchen nt; v pflegen; stillen

nursery ['nə:səri] n Kinderzimmer nt; Kinderkrippe f; Baumschule f

nut [nʌt] n Nuß f; Schraubenmutter f

nutcrackers ['nʌt,krækəz] pl Nußknacker m

nutmeg ['nʌtmeg] n Muskatnuß f

nutritious [nju:'triʃəs] adj nahrhaft

nutshell ['nʌtʃel] n Nußschale f

nylon ['nailɔn] n Nylon nt

O

oak [ouk] n Eiche f

oar [ɔ:] n Ruder nt

oasis [ou'eisis] n (pl oases) Oase f

oath [ouθ] n Eid m

oats [outs] pl Hafer m

obedience [ə'bi:diəns] n Gehorsam m

obedient [ə'bi:diənt] adj gehorsam

obey [ə'bei] v gehorchen

object[1] ['ɔbdʒikt] n Objekt nt; Gegenstand m; Ziel nt

object[2] [əb'dʒekt] v *einwenden; ~ to Einwand *erheben gegen

objection [əb'dʒekʃən] n Widerspruch m, Einwand m

objective [əb'dʒektiv] adj objektiv; n Zweck m

obligatory [ə'bligətəri] adj obligatorisch

oblige [ə'blaidʒ] v verpflichten; *be obliged to verpflichtet *sein zu; *müssen

obliging [ə'blaidʒiŋ] adj gefällig

oblong ['ɔblɔŋ] adj länglich; n Rechteck nt

obscene [əb'si:n] adj obszön

obscure [əb'skjuə] adj obskur, unklar, dunkel

observation [,ɔbzə'veiʃən] n Observation f, Beobachtung f

observatory [əb'zə:vətri] n Observatorium nt

observe [əb'zə:v] v observieren, beachten

obsession [əb'seʃən] n Besessenheit f

obstacle ['ɔbstəkəl] n Hindernis nt

obstinate ['ɔbstinət] adj starrköpfig; hartnäckig

obtain [əb'tein] v erlangen, *erhalten

obtainable [əb'teinəbəl] adj erhältlich

obvious ['ɔbviəs] adj offensichtlich

occasion [ə'keiʒən] n Gelegenheit f; Anlaß m

occasionally [ə'keiʒənəli] adv ab und zu, gelegentlich

occupant ['ɔkjupənt] n Inhaber m

occupation [,ɔkju'peiʃən] n Beschäftigung f; Besetzung f

occupy ['ɔkjupai] v *einnehmen, besetzen; occupied adj besetzt

occur [ə'kə:] v *geschehen, *vorkommen, sich ereignen

occurrence [ə'kʌrəns] n Ereignis nt

ocean ['ouʃən] n Ozean m

October [ɔk'toubə] Oktober

octopus ['ɔktəpəs] n Polyp m

oculist ['ɔkjulist] n Augenarzt m

odd [ɔd] adj seltsam, sonderbar; ungerade

odour ['oudə] n Geruch m

of [ɔv, əv] prep von

off [ɔf] adv ab; weg; prep von

offence [ə'fens] n Vergehen nt; Beleidigung f, Verstoß m

offend [ə'fend] v kränken, beleidigen; sich *vergehen

offensive [ə'fensiv] adj offensiv; beleidigend, anstößig; n Offensive f

offer ['ɔfə] v *anbieten; leisten; n Angebot nt

office ['ɔfis] n Dienstraum m, Büro nt; Amt nt; ~ **hours** Bürostunden fpl

officer ['ɔfisə] n Offizier m

official [ə'fiʃəl] adj offiziell

off-licence ['ɔf,laisəns] n Spirituosenladen m

often ['ɔfən] adv häufig, oft

oil [ɔil] n Öl nt; Petroleum nt; **fuel** ~ Heizöl nt; ~ **filter** Ölfilter nt; ~ **pressure** Öldruck m

oil-painting [,ɔil'peintiŋ] n Ölgemälde nt

oil-refinery ['ɔilri,fainəri] n Ölraffinerie f

oil-well ['ɔilwel] n Ölquelle f

oily ['ɔili] adj ölig

ointment ['ɔintmənt] n Salbe f

okay! [,ou'kei] in Ordnung!

old [ould] adj alt; ~ **age** Alter nt

old-fashioned [,ould'fæʃənd] adj altmodisch

olive ['ɔliv] n Olive f; ~ **oil** Olivenöl nt

omelette ['ɔmlət] n Eierkuchen m

ominous ['ɔminəs] adj verhängnisvoll

omit [ə'mit] v *auslassen

omnipotent [ɔm'nipətənt] adj allmächtig

on [ɔn] prep auf; an

once [wʌns] adv einst, einmal; **at** ~ sofort; ~ **more** noch einmal

oncoming ['ɔn,kʌmiŋ] adj entgegenkommend, herannahend

one [wʌn] num eins; pron man

oneself [wʌn'self] pron selbst

onion ['ʌnjən] n Zwiebel f

only ['ounli] adj einzig; adv nur, bloß; conj jedoch

onwards ['ɔnwədz] adv vorwärts

onyx ['ɔniks] n Onyx m

opal ['oupəl] n Opal m

open ['oupən] v öffnen; adj offen; offenherzig

opening ['oupəniŋ] n Öffnung f

opera ['ɔpərə] n Oper f; ~ **house** Opernhaus nt

operate ['ɔpəreit] v wirken, arbeiten; operieren

operation [,ɔpə'reiʃən] n Funktion f; Operation f

operator ['ɔpəreitə] n Telephonistin f

operetta [,ɔpə'retə] n Operette f

opinion [ə'pinjən] n Ansicht f, Meinung f

opponent [ə'pounənt] n Gegner m

opportunity [,ɔpə'tju:nəti] n Gelegenheit f

oppose [ə'pouz] v sich widersetzen

opposite ['ɔpəzit] prep gegenüber; adj gegensätzlich, entgegengesetzt

opposition [,ɔpə'ziʃən] n Opposition f

oppress [ə'pres] v bedrücken, unterdrücken

optician [ɔp'tiʃən] n Optiker m

optimism ['ɔptimizəm] n Optimismus m

optimist ['ɔptimist] n Optimist m

optimistic [,ɔpti'mistik] adj optimistisch

optional ['ɔpʃənəl] adj beliebig

or [ɔ:] conj oder

oral ['ɔ:rəl] adj mündlich

orange ['ɔrindʒ] n Apfelsine f; adj orange

orchard ['ɔ:tʃəd] n Obstgarten m

orchestra ['ɔ:kistrə] n Orchester nt

order ['ɔ:də] v *befehlen; bestellen; n Reihenfolge f, Ordnung f; Auftrag m, Befehl m; Bestellung f; **in** ~ in Ordnung; **in** ~ **to** um zu; **made to** ~ auf Bestellung gemacht; **out of** ~ funktionsunfähig; **postal** ~ Postanweisung f

order-form ['ɔ:dəfɔ:m] n Bestellzettel

m

ordinary ['ɔ:dənri] *adj* alltäglich, gewöhnlich

ore [ɔ:] *n* Erz *nt*

organ ['ɔ:gən] *n* Organ *nt*; Orgel *f*

organic [ɔ:'gænik] *adj* organisch

organization [,ɔ:gənai'zeiʃən] *n* Organisation *f*

organize ['ɔ:gənaiz] *v* organisieren

Orient ['ɔ:riənt] *n* Orient *m*

oriental [,ɔ:ri'entəl] *adj* orientalisch

orientate ['ɔ:riənteit] *v* sich orientieren

origin ['ɔridʒin] *n* Abstammung *f*, Ursprung *m*; Herkunft *f*

original [ə'ridʒinəl] *adj* ursprünglich, originell

originally [ə'ridʒinəli] *adv* anfänglich

orlon ['ɔ:lɔn] *n* Orlon *nt*

ornament ['ɔ:nəmənt] *n* Verzierung *f*

ornamental [,ɔ:nə'mentəl] *adj* ornamental

orphan ['ɔ:fən] *n* Waise *f*

orthodox ['ɔ:θədɔks] *adj* orthodox

ostrich ['ɔstritʃ] *n* Strauß *m*

other ['ʌðə] *adj* ander

otherwise ['ʌðəwaiz] *conj* sonst; *adv* anders

* **ought to** [ɔ:t] sollen

our [auə] *adj* unser

ourselves [auə'selvz] *pron* uns; selbst

out [aut] *adv* heraus, hinaus; ~ **of** außer, aus

outbreak ['autbreik] *n* Ausbruch *m*

outcome ['autkʌm] *n* Ergebnis *nt*

* **outdo** [,aut'du:] *v* *übertreffen

outdoors [,aut'dɔ:z] *adv* draußen

outer ['autə] *adj* äußer

outfit ['autfit] *n* Ausrüstung *f*

outline ['autlain] *n* Umriß *m*; *v* *umreißen

outlook ['autluk] *n* Aussicht *f*; Anschauung *f*

output ['autput] *n* Ausstoß *m*

outrage ['autreidʒ] *n* Gewaltakt *m*

outside [,aut'said] *adv* draußen; *prep* außerhalb; *n* Äußere *nt*, Außenseite *f*

outsize ['autsaiz] *n* Übergröße *f*

outskirts ['autskə:ts] *pl* Außenbezirke *mpl*

outstanding [,aut'stændiŋ] *adj* eminent, hervorragend

outward ['autwəd] *adj* äußer

outwards ['autwədz] *adv* nach draußen

oval ['ouvəl] *adj* oval

oven ['ʌvən] *n* Backofen *m*

over ['ouvə] *prep* oberhalb, über; *adv* über; nieder; *adj* vorbei; ~ **there** drüben

overall ['ouvərɔ:l] *adj* gesamt

overalls ['ouvərɔ:lz] *pl* Arbeitsanzug *m*

overcast ['ouvəka:st] *adj* bewölkt

overcoat ['ouvəkout] *n* Mantel *m*

* **overcome** [,ouvə'kʌm] *v* *überwinden

overdue [,ouvə'dju:] *adj* überfällig; rückständig

overgrown [,ouvə'groun] *adj* überwachsen

overhaul [,ouvə'hɔ:l] *v* überholen

overhead [,ouvə'hed] *adv* oben

overlook [,ouvə'luk] *v* *übersehen

overnight [,ouvə'nait] *adv* über Nacht

overseas [,ouvə'si:z] *adj* überseeisch

oversight ['ouvəsait] *n* Versehen *nt*

* **oversleep** [,ouvə'sli:p] *v* *verschlafen

overstrung [,ouvə'strʌŋ] *adj* überspannt

* **overtake** [,ouvə'teik] *v* überholen; **no overtaking** Überholen verboten

over-tired [,ouvə'taiəd] *adj* übermüdet

overture ['ouvətʃə] *n* Ouvertüre *f*

overweight ['ouvəweit] *n* Übergewicht *nt*

overwhelm [,ouvə'welm] *v* verblüffen, überwältigen

overwork [,ouvə'wə:k] *v* sich überarbeiten

owe [ou] v schuldig *sein, schulden; verdanken; **owing to** aufgrund, infolge

owl [aul] n Eule f

own [oun] v *besitzen; adj eigen

owner ['ounə] n Besitzer m, Eigentümer m

ox [ɔks] n (pl oxen) Ochse m

oxygen ['ɔksidʒən] n Sauerstoff m

oyster ['ɔistə] n Auster f

P

pace [peis] n Gang m; Schritt m; Tempo nt

Pacific Ocean [pə'sifik 'ouʃən] Stille Ozean

pacifism ['pæsifizəm] n Pazifismus m

pacifist ['pæsifist] n Pazifist m; pazifistisch

pack [pæk] v packen; ~ **up** einpacken

package ['pækidʒ] n Paket nt

packet ['pækit] n Päckchen nt

packing ['pækiŋ] n Verpackung f

pad [pæd] n Polster nt; Schreibblock m

paddle ['pædəl] n Paddel nt

padlock ['pædlɔk] n Vorhängeschloß nt

pagan ['peigən] adj heidnisch; n Heide m

page [peidʒ] n Blatt nt, Seite f

page-boy ['peidʒbɔi] n Hotelpage m

pail [peil] n Eimer m

pain [pein] n Schmerz m; **pains** Mühe f

painful ['peinfəl] adj schmerzhaft

painless ['peinləs] adj schmerzlos

paint [peint] n Farbe f; v malen; *anstreichen

paint-box ['peintbɔks] n Malkasten m

paint-brush ['peintbrʌʃ] n Pinsel m

painter ['peintə] n Maler m

painting ['peintiŋ] n Gemälde nt

pair [pɛə] n Paar nt

Pakistan [,pɑ:ki'stɑ:n] Pakistan

Pakistani [,pɑ:ki'stɑ:ni] adj pakistanisch; n Pakistaner m

palace ['pæləs] n Palast m

pale [peil] adj bleich; hell

palm [pɑ:m] n Palme f; Handfläche f

palpable ['pælpəbəl] adj fühlbar

palpitation [,pælpi'teiʃən] n Herzklopfen nt

pan [pæn] n Pfanne f

pane [pein] n Scheibe f

panel ['pænəl] n Paneel nt

panelling ['pænəliŋ] n Täfelung f

panic ['pænik] n Panik f

pant [pænt] v keuchen

panties ['pæntiz] pl Schlüpfer m

pants [pænts] pl Unterhose f; plAm Hose f

pant-suit ['pæntsu:t] n Hosenanzug m

panty-hose ['pæntihouz] n Strumpfhose f

paper ['peipə] n Papier nt; Zeitung f; papieren; **carbon** ~ Kohlepapier nt; ~ **bag** Tüte f; ~ **napkin** Papierserviette f; **typing** ~ Schreibmaschinenpapier nt; **wrapping** ~ Packpapier nt

paperback ['peipəbæk] n Taschenbuch nt

paper-knife ['peipənaif] n Brieföffner m

parade [pə'reid] n Parade f, Umzug m

paraffin ['pærəfin] n Petroleum nt

paragraph ['pærəgrɑ:f] n Absatz m

parakeet ['pærəki:t] n Sittich m

paralise ['pærəlaiz] v lähmen

parallel ['pærəlel] adj gleichlaufend, parallel; n Parallele f

parcel ['pɑ:səl] n Paket nt

pardon ['pɑ:dən] n Verzeihung f; Begnadigung f

parents ['pɛərənts] pl Eltern pl

parents-in-law ['pɛərəntsinlɔ:] pl Schwiegereltern pl

parish ['pærɪʃ] n Kirchspiel nt

park [pɑ:k] n Park m; v parken; **no parking** Parken verboten; **parking** Parkplatz m; **parking fee** Parkgebühr f; **parking light** Parkleuchte f; **parking lot** Am Parkplatz m; **parking meter** Parkuhr f; **parking zone** Parkzone f

parliament ['pɑ:ləmənt] n Parlament nt

parliamentary [ˌpɑ:lə'mentəri] adj parlamentarisch

parrot ['pærət] n Papagei m

parsley ['pɑ:sli] n Petersilie f

parson ['pɑ:sən] n Pfarrer m

parsonage ['pɑ:sənidʒ] n Pfarrhaus nt

part [pɑ:t] n Teil m; Stück nt; v trennen; **spare** ~ Ersatzteil nt

partial ['pɑ:ʃəl] adj teilweise; parteiisch

participant [pɑ:'tisipənt] n Teilnehmer m

participate [pɑ:'tisipeit] v *teilnehmen

particular [pə'tikjulə] adj besonder; wählerisch; **in** ~ speziell

parting ['pɑ:tiŋ] n Abschied m; Scheitel m

partition [pɑ:'tiʃən] n Scheidewand f

partly ['pɑ:tli] adv teils, teilweise

partner ['pɑ:tnə] n Partner m; Teilhaber m

partridge ['pɑ:tridʒ] n Rebhuhn nt

party ['pɑ:ti] n Partei f; Party f; Gruppe f

pass [pɑ:s] v *vergehen, passieren, überholen; reichen; *bestehen; vAm *vorbeifahren; **no passing** Am Überholen verboten; ~ **by** *vorbeigehen; ~ **through** durchqueren

passage ['pæsidʒ] n Durchgang m; Überfahrt f; Stelle f; Durchfahrt f

passenger ['pæsəndʒə] n Passagier m; ~ **car** Am Wagen m; ~ **train** Personenzug m

passer-by [ˌpɑ:sə'bai] n Passant m

passion ['pæʃən] n Leidenschaft f, Passion f; Wut f

passionate ['pæʃənət] adj leidenschaftlich

passive ['pæsiv] adj passiv

passport ['pɑ:spɔ:t] n Paß m; ~ **control** Paßkontrolle f; ~ **photograph** Paßphoto nt

password ['pɑ:swɔ:d] n Losungswort nt

past [pɑ:st] n Vergangenheit f; adj vorig, letzt, vergangen; prep entlang, an ... vorbei

paste [peist] n Paste f; v kleben

pastry ['peistri] n Gebäck nt; ~ **shop** Konditorei f

pasture ['pɑ:stʃə] n Weide f

patch [pætʃ] v flicken

patent ['peitənt] n Patent nt

path [pɑ:θ] n Pfad m

patience ['peiʃəns] n Geduld f

patient ['peiʃənt] adj geduldig; n Patient m

patriot ['peitriət] n Patriot m

patrol [pə'troul] n Streife f; v patrouillieren; überwachen

pattern ['pætən] n Motiv nt, Muster nt

pause [pɔ:z] n Pause f; v pausieren

pave [peiv] v pflastern

pavement ['peivmənt] n Bürgersteig m; Pflaster nt

pavilion [pə'viljən] n Pavillon m

paw [pɔ:] n Pfote f

pawn [pɔ:n] v verpfänden; n Bauer m

pawnbroker ['pɔ:nˌbroukə] n Pfandleiher m

pay [pei] n Gehalt nt, Lohn m

*pay [pei] v bezahlen, zahlen; sich lohnen; ~ **attention to** achten auf; **paying** rentabel; ~ **off** tilgen; ~ **on account** abzahlen

pay-desk ['peidesk] n Kasse f

payee [pei'i:] n Zahlungsempfänger m

payment ['peimənt] n Bezahlung f

pea [pi:] n Erbse f

peace [pi:s] n Frieden m

peaceful ['pi:sfəl] adj friedlich

peach [pi:tʃ] n Pfirsich m

peacock ['pi:kɔk] n Pfau m

peak [pi:k] n Gipfel m; Spitze f; ~ **hour** Hauptverkehrszeit f; ~ **season** Hochsaison f

peanut ['pi:nʌt] n Erdnuß f

pear [peə] n Birne f

pearl [pə:l] n Perle f

peasant ['pezənt] n Bauer m

pebble ['pebəl] n Kieselstein m

peculiar [pi'kju:ljə] adj eigentümlich; speziell, sonderbar

peculiarity [pi,kju:li'ærəti] n Eigentümlichkeit f

pedal ['pedəl] n Pedal nt

pedestrian [pi'destriən] n Fußgänger m; **no pedestrians** Fußgänger verboten; ~ **crossing** Fußgängerübergang m

pedicure ['pedikjuə] n Fußpfleger m

peel [pi:l] v schälen; n Schale f

peep [pi:p] v spähen

peg [peg] n Kleiderhaken m

pelican ['pelikən] n Pelikan m

pelvis ['pelvis] n Becken nt

pen [pen] n Feder f

penalty ['penəlti] n Buße f; Strafe f; ~ **kick** Strafstoß m

pencil ['pensəl] n Bleistift m

pencil-sharpener ['pensəl,ʃa:pnə] n Bleistiftspitzer m

pendant ['pendənt] n Anhänger m

penetrate ['penitreit] v *durchdringen

penguin ['peŋgwin] n Pinguin m

penicillin [,peni'silin] n Penicillin nt

peninsula [pə'ninsjulə] n Halbinsel f

penknife ['pennaif] n (pl -knives) Taschenmesser nt

pension[1] ['pā:siɔ:] n Pension f

pension[2] ['penʃən] n Rente f

people ['pi:pəl] pl Leute pl; n Volk nt

pepper ['pepə] n Pfeffer m

peppermint ['pepəmint] n Pfefferminze f

perceive [pə'si:v] v *wahrnehmen

percent [pə'sent] n Prozent nt

percentage [pə'sentidʒ] n Prozentsatz m

perceptible [pə'septibəl] adj wahrnehmbar

perception [pə'sepʃən] n Empfindung f

perch [pə:tʃ] (pl ~) Barsch m

percolator ['pə:kəleitə] n Kaffeemaschine f

perfect ['pə:fikt] adj vollkommen

perfection [pə'fekʃən] n Perfektion f, Vollkommenheit f

perform [pə'fɔ:m] v ausführen, verrichten

performance [pə'fɔ:məns] n Aufführung f

perfume ['pə:fju:m] n Parfüm nt

perhaps [pə'hæps] adv vielleicht

peril ['peril] n Gefahr f

perilous ['periləs] adj gefährlich

period ['piəriəd] n Zeitraum m, Zeitabschnitt m; Punkt m

periodical [,piəri'ɔdikəl] n Zeitschrift f; adj periodisch

perish ['periʃ] v *umkommen

perishable ['periʃəbəl] adj leicht verderblich

perjury ['pə:dʒəri] n Meineid m

permanent ['pə:mənənt] adj dauerhaft, dauernd; beständig, fest; ~ **press** mit Dauerbügelfalte; ~ **wave** Dauerwelle f

permission [pə'miʃən] *n* Erlaubnis *f*, Genehmigung *f*; Bewilligung *f*, Konzession *f*

permit[1] [pə'mit] *v* gestatten, erlauben

permit[2] ['pə:mit] *n* Genehmigung *f*

peroxide [pə'rɔksaid] *n* Wasserstoffsuperoxyd *nt*

perpendicular [,pə:pən'dikjulə] *adj* senkrecht

Persia ['pə:ʃə] Persien

Persian ['pə:ʃən] *adj* persisch; *n* Perser *m*

person ['pə:sən] *n* Person *f*; **per** ~ pro Person

personal ['pə:sənəl] *adj* persönlich

personality [,pə:sə'næləti] *n* Persönlichkeit *f*

personnel [,pə:sə'nel] *n* Personal *nt*

perspective [pə'spektiv] *n* Perspektive *f*

perspiration [,pə:spə'reiʃən] *n* Transpiration *f*, Schweiß *m*

perspire [pə'spaiə] *v* transpirieren, schwitzen

persuade [pə'sweid] *v* bereden, überreden; überzeugen

persuasion [pə'sweiʒən] *n* Überzeugung *f*

pessimism ['pesimizəm] *n* Pessimismus *m*

pessimist ['pesimist] *n* Pessimist *m*

pessimistic [,pesi'mistik] *adj* pessimistisch

pet [pet] *n* Haustier *nt*; Liebling *m*

petal ['petəl] *n* Blumenblatt *nt*

petition [pi'tiʃən] *n* Bittschrift *f*

petrol ['petrəl] *n* Benzin *nt*; ~ **pump** Benzinpumpe *f*; ~ **station** Tankstelle *f*; ~ **tank** Benzintank *m*

petroleum [pi'trouliəm] *n* Petroleum *nt*

petty ['peti] *adj* klein, unbedeutend, geringfügig; ~ **cash** Kleingeld *nt*

pewit ['pi:wit] *n* Kiebitz *m*

pewter ['pju:tə] *n* Zinn *nt*

phantom ['fæntəm] *n* Gespenst *nt*

pharmacology [,fɑ:mə'kɔlədʒi] *n* Arzneimittellehre *f*

pharmacy ['fɑ:məsi] *n* Apotheke *f*; Drogerie *f*

phase [feiz] *n* Phase *f*

pheasant ['fezənt] *n* Fasan *m*

Philippine ['filipain] *adj* philippinisch

Philippines ['filipi:nz] *pl* Philippinen *pl*

philosopher [fi'lɔsəfə] *n* Philosoph *m*

philosophy [fi'lɔsəfi] *n* Philosophie *f*

phone [foun] *n* Fernsprecher *m*; *v* *anrufen, telephonieren

phonetic [fə'netik] *adj* phonetisch

photo ['foutou] *n* (pl ~s) Photo *nt*

photograph ['foutəgrɑ:f] *n* Lichtbild *nt*; *v* photographieren

photographer [fə'tɔgrəfə] *n* Photograph *m*

photography [fə'tɔgrəfi] *n* Photographie *f*

photostat ['foutəstæt] *n* Photokopie *f*

phrase [freiz] *n* Redewendung *f*

phrase-book ['freizbuk] *n* Sprachführer *m*

physical ['fizikəl] *adj* physisch

physician [fi'ziʃən] *n* Arzt *m*

physicist ['fizisist] *n* Physiker *m*

physics ['fiziks] *n* Physik *f*, Naturwissenschaft *f*

physiology [,fizi'ɔlədʒi] *n* Physiologie *f*

pianist ['pi:ənist] *n* Pianist *m*

piano [pi'ænou] *n* Klavier *nt*; **grand** ~ Flügel *m*

pick [pik] *v* pflücken; wählen; *n* Wahl *f*; ~ **up** *aufnehmen; abholen; **pick-up van** Lieferwagen *m*

pick-axe ['pikæks] *n* Spitzhacke *f*

pickles ['pikəlz] *pl* Pickles *pl*

picnic ['piknik] *n* Picknick *nt*; *v* picknicken

picture ['piktʃə] *n* Gemälde *nt*; Abbildung f, Stich m; Bild nt; ~ **post-card** Ansichtskarte f; **pictures** Kino nt

picturesque [ˌpiktʃə'resk] adj pittoresk, malerisch

piece [pi:s] n Stück nt

pier [piə] n Pier m

pierce [piəs] v durchbohren

pig [pig] n Schwein nt

pigeon ['pidʒən] n Taube f

pig-headed [ˌpig'hedid] adj starrköpfig

piglet ['piglət] n Ferkel nt

pigskin ['pigskin] n Schweinsleder nt

pike [paik] n (pl ~) Hecht m

pile [pail] n Haufen m; v anhäufen; **piles** pl Hämorrhoiden fpl

pilgrim ['pilgrim] n Pilger m

pilgrimage ['pilgrimidʒ] n Pilgerfahrt f

pill [pil] n Pille f

pillar ['pilə] n Pfeiler m, Säule f

pillar-box ['piləbɔks] n Briefkasten m

pillow ['pilou] n Kissen nt, Kopfkissen nt

pillow-case ['piloukeis] n Kissenbezug m

pilot ['pailət] n Pilot m; Lotse m

pimple ['pimpəl] n Pickel m

pin [pin] n Stecknadel f; v feststecken; **bobby** ~ Am Haarklemme f

pincers ['pinsəz] pl Kneifzange f

pinch [pintʃ] v *kneifen

pineapple ['pai,næpəl] n Ananas f

ping-pong ['piŋpɔŋ] n Tischtennis nt

pink [piŋk] adj rosa

pioneer [ˌpaiə'niə] n Pionier m

pious ['paiəs] adj fromm

pip [pip] n Kern m

pipe [paip] n Pfeife f; Rohr nt; ~ **cleaner** Pfeifenreiniger m; ~ **tobacco** Tabak m

pirate ['paiərət] n Seeräuber m

pistol ['pistəl] n Pistole f

piston ['pistən] n Kolben m; ~ **ring** Kolbenring m

piston-rod ['pistənrɔd] n Kolbenstange f

pit [pit] n Grube f

pitcher ['pitʃə] n Krug m

pity ['piti] n Mitleid nt; v Mitleid *haben mit, bemitleiden; **what a pity!** schade!

placard ['plæka:d] n Plakat nt

place [pleis] n Ort m; v setzen, stellen; ~ **of birth** Geburtsort m; *take ~ *stattfinden

plague [pleig] n Plage f

plaice [pleis] (pl ~) Scholle f

plain [plein] adj deutlich; gewöhnlich, schlicht; n Ebene f

plan [plæn] n Plan m; Grundriß m; v planen

plane [plein] adj flach; n Flugzeug nt; ~ **crash** Flugzeugabsturz m

planet ['plænit] n Planet m

planetarium [ˌplæni'tɛəriəm] n Planetarium nt

plank [plæŋk] n Brett nt

plant [plɑ:nt] n Pflanze f; Betriebsanlage f; v pflanzen

plantation [plæn'teiʃən] n Plantage f

plaster ['plɑ:stə] n Putz m, Gips m; Pflaster nt, Heftpflaster nt

plastic ['plæstik] adj Kunststoff-; n Kunststoff m

plate [pleit] n Teller m; Platte f

plateau ['plætou] n (pl ~x, ~s) Hochebene f

platform ['plætfɔ:m] n Bahnsteig m; ~ **ticket** Bahnsteigkarte f

platinum ['plætinəm] n Platin nt

play [plei] v spielen; n Spiel nt; Schauspiel nt; **one-act** ~ Einakter m; ~ **truant** schwänzen

player [pleiə] n Spieler m

playground ['pleigraund] n Spielplatz m

playing-card ['pleiiŋka:d] n Spielkarte

f

playwright ['pleirait] *n* Bühnenautor *m*

plea [pli:] *n* Verteidigungsrede *f*

plead [pli:d] *v* plädieren

pleasant ['plezənt] *adj* angenehm, nett

please [pli:z] bitte; *v* *gefallen; **pleased** erfreut; **pleasing** angenehm

pleasure ['pleʒə] *n* Vergnügen *nt*, Spaß *m*, Freude *f*

plentiful ['plentifəl] *adj* reichlich

plenty ['plenti] *n* Fülle *f*; Menge *f*

pliers [plaiəz] *pl* Zange *f*

plimsolls ['plimsəlz] *pl* Turnschuhe *mpl*

plot [plɔt] *n* Verschwörung *f*, Komplott *nt*; Handlung *f*; Parzelle *f*

plough [plau] *n* Pflug *m*; *v* pflügen

plucky ['plʌki] *adj* mutig

plug [plʌg] *n* Stecker *m*; ~ **in** einstöpseln

plum [plʌm] *n* Pflaume *f*

plumber ['plʌmə] *n* Installateur *m*

plump [plʌmp] *adj* mollig

plural ['pluərəl] *n* Mehrzahl *f*

plus [plʌs] *prep* plus

pneumatic [nju:'mætik] *adj* pneumatisch

pneumonia [nju:'mouniə] *n* Lungenentzündung *f*

poach [poutʃ] *v* wildern

pocket ['pɔkit] *n* Tasche *f*

pocket-book ['pɔkitbuk] *n* Brieftasche *f*

pocket-comb ['pɔkitkoum] *n* Taschenkamm *m*

pocket-knife ['pɔkitnaif] *n* (pl -knives) Taschenmesser *nt*

pocket-watch ['pɔkitwɔtʃ] *n* Taschenuhr *f*

poem ['pouim] *n* Gedicht *nt*

poet ['pouit] *n* Dichter *m*

poetry ['pouitri] *n* Dichtung *f*

point [pɔint] *n* Punkt *m*; Spitze *f*; *v* zeigen; ~ **of view** Standpunkt *m*

pointed ['pɔintid] *adj* spitz

poison ['pɔizən] *n* Gift *nt*; *v* vergiften

poisonous ['pɔizənəs] *adj* giftig

Poland ['poulənd] Polen

Pole [poul] *n* Pole *m*

pole [poul] *n* Pfosten *m*

police [pə'li:s] *pl* Polizei *f*

policeman [pə'li:smən] *n* (pl -men) Schutzmann *m*, Polizist *m*

police-station [pə'li:s,steiʃən] *n* Polizeiwache *f*

policy ['pɔlisi] *n* Vorgehen *nt*, Politik *f*; Police *f*

polio ['pouliou] *n* Polio *f*, Kinderlähmung *f*

Polish ['pouliʃ] *adj* polnisch

polish ['pɔliʃ] *v* polieren

polite [pə'lait] *adj* höflich

political [pə'litikəl] *adj* politisch

politician [,pɔli'tiʃən] *n* Politiker *m*

politics ['pɔlitiks] *n* Politik *f*

pollution [pə'lu:ʃən] *n* Verschmutzung *f*, Verunreinigung *f*

pond [pɔnd] *n* Teich *m*

pony ['pouni] *n* Pony *nt*

poor [puə] *adj* arm; ärmlich; schwach

pope [poup] *n* Papst *m*

poplin ['pɔplin] *n* Popelin *m*

pop music [pɔp 'mju:zik] Popmusik *f*

poppy ['pɔpi] *n* Klatschmohn *m*; Mohn *m*

popular ['pɔpjulə] *adj* beliebt; Volks-

population [,pɔpju'leiʃən] *n* Bevölkerung *f*

populous ['pɔpjuləs] *adj* dicht bevölkert

porcelain ['pɔ:səlin] *n* Porzellan *nt*

porcupine ['pɔ:kjupain] *n* Stachelschwein *n*

pork [pɔ:k] *n* Schweinefleisch *nt*

port [pɔ:t] *n* Hafen *m*; Backbord *nt*

portable ['pɔ:təbəl] *adj* tragbar

porter ['pɔ:tə] *n* Träger *m*; Pförtner *m*

porthole ['pɔ:thoul] *n* Luke *f*

portion ['pɔ:ʃən] *n* Portion *f*

portrait ['pɔ:trit] *n* Porträt *nt*

Portugal ['pɔ:tjugəl] Portugal

Portuguese [,pɔ:tju'gi:z] *adj* portugiesisch; *n* Portugiese *m*

position [pə'ziʃən] *n* Position *f*; Lage *f*; Haltung *f*; Stellung *f*

positive ['pɔzətiv] *adj* positiv; *n* Positiv *nt*

possess [pə'zes] *v* *besitzen; **possessed** *adj* besessen

possession [pə'zeʃən] *n* Besitz *m*; **possessions** Habe *f*

possibility [,pɔsə'biləti] *n* Möglichkeit *f*

possible ['pɔsəbəl] *adj* möglich; eventuell

post [poust] *n* Pfosten *m*; Posten *m*; Post *f*; *v* *aufgeben; **post-office** Postamt *nt*

postage ['poustidʒ] *n* Porto *nt*; ~ **paid** portofrei; ~ **stamp** Briefmarke *f*

postcard ['poustkɑ:d] *n* Postkarte *f*; Ansichtskarte *f*

poster ['poustə] *n* Anschlagzettel *m*, Plakat *nt*

poste restante [poust re'stɑ:t] postlagernd

postman ['poustmən] *n* (pl -men) Postbote *m*

post-paid [,poust'peid] *adj* franko

postpone [pə'spoun] *v* *aufschieben

pot [pɔt] *n* Topf *m*

potato [pə'teitou] *n* (pl ~es) Kartoffel *f*

pottery ['pɔtəri] *n* Töpferware *f*

pouch [pautʃ] *n* Beutel *m*

poulterer ['poultərə] *n* Geflügelhändler *m*

poultry ['poultri] *n* Geflügel *nt*

pound [paund] *n* Pfund *nt*

pour [pɔ:] *v* einschenken, schenken, *gießen

poverty ['pɔvəti] *n* Armut *f*

powder ['paudə] *n* Puder *m*; ~ **compact** Puderdose *f*; **talc** ~ Talkpuder *m*

powder-puff ['paudəpʌf] *n* Puderquaste *f*

powder-room ['paudəru:m] *n* Damentoilette *f*

power [pauə] *n* Kraft *f*; Energie *f*; Macht *f*

powerful ['pauəfəl] *adj* mächtig; stark

powerless ['pauələs] *adj* machtlos

power-station ['pauə,steiʃən] *n* Kraftwerk *nt*

practical ['præktikəl] *adj* praktisch

practically ['præktikli] *adv* nahezu

practice ['præktis] *n* Praxis *f*

practise ['præktis] *v* ausüben; sich üben

praise [preiz] *v* loben; *n* Lob *nt*

pram [præm] *n* Kinderwagen *m*

prawn [prɔ:n] *n* Krabbe *f*, Steingarnele *f*

pray [prei] *v* beten

prayer [prɛə] *n* Gebet *nt*

preach [pri:tʃ] *v* predigen

precarious [pri'kɛəriəs] *adj* heikel

precaution [pri'kɔ:ʃən] *n* Vorsicht *f*; Vorsichtsmaßnahme *f*

precede [pri'si:d] *v* *vorangehen

preceding [pri'si:diŋ] *adj* vorhergehend

precious ['preʃəs] *adj* teuer

precipice ['presipiʃ] *n* Abgrund *m*

precipitation [pri,sipi'teiʃən] *n* Niederschläge *mpl*

precise [pri'sais] *adj* präzis, exakt, genau

predecessor ['pri:disesə] *n* Vorgänger *m*

predict [pri'dikt] *v* vorhersagen

prefer [pri'fə:] *v* *vorziehen

preferable ['prefərəbəl] *adj* vorzuziehend

preference ['prefərəns] *n* Vorzug *m*

prefix ['pri:fiks] *n* Präfix *nt*

pregnant ['pregnənt] *adj* schwanger

prejudice ['predʒədis] *n* Vorurteil *nt*

preliminary [pri'liminəri] *adj* einleitend; vorläufig

premature ['premətʃuə] *adj* vorzeitig

premier ['premiə] *n* Premierminister *m*

premises ['premisiz] *pl* Gebäude *nt*

premium ['pri:miəm] *n* Prämie *f*

prepaid [‚pri:'peid] *adj* vorausbezahlt

preparation [‚prepə'reiʃən] *n* Vorbereitung *f*

prepare [pri'peə] *v* vorbereiten; fertigmachen

prepared [pri'peəd] *adj* bereit

preposition [‚prepə'ziʃən] *n* Präposition *f*

prescribe [pri'skraib] *v* *verschreiben

prescription [pri'skripʃən] *n* Rezept *nt*

presence ['prezəns] *n* Anwesenheit *f*; Gegenwart *f*

present¹ ['prezənt] *n* Präsent *nt*, Geschenk *nt*; Gegenwart *f*; *adj* gegenwärtig; anwesend

present² [pri'zent] *v* vorstellen; *anbieten

presently ['prezəntli] *adv* sofort, sogleich

preservation [‚prezə'veiʃən] *n* Bewahrung *f*

preserve [pri'zə:v] *v* bewahren; einmachen

president ['prezidənt] *n* Präsident *m*; Vorsitzende *m*

press [pres] *n* Presse *f*; *v* drücken; bügeln; ~ **conference** Pressekonferenz *f*

pressing ['presiŋ] *adj* dringlich, dringend

pressure ['preʃə] *n* Druck *m*; Spannung *f*; **atmospheric** ~ Luftdruck

m

pressure-cooker ['preʃə,kukə] *n* Schnellkochtopf *m*

prestige [pre'sti:ʒ] *n* Prestige *nt*

presumable [pri'zju:məbəl] *adj* vermutlich

presumptuous [pri'zʌmpʃəs] *adj* übermütig; überheblich

pretence [pri'tens] *n* Vorwand *m*

pretend [pri'tend] *v* sich verstellen, *vorgeben

pretext ['pri:tekst] *n* Vorwand *m*

pretty ['priti] *adj* schön, hübsch; *adv* ziemlich, beträchtlich

prevent [pri'vent] *v* *anhalten, verhindern; verhüten

preventive [pri'ventiv] *adj* vorbeugend

previous ['pri:viəs] *adj* vorig, früher, vorhergehend

pre-war [‚pri:'wo:] *adj* Vorkriegs-

price [prais] *v* den Preis festsetzen; ~ **list** Preisliste *f*

priceless ['praisləs] *adj* unschätzbar

price-list ['prais‚list] *n* Preis *m*

prick [prik] *v* *stechen

pride [praid] *n* Stolz *m*

priest [pri:st] *n* Priester *m*

primary ['praiməri] *adj* Grund-; Anfangs-, hauptsächlich; elementar

prince [prins] *n* Prinz *m*

princess [prin'ses] *n* Prinzessin *f*

principal ['prinsəpəl] *adj* wichtigste; *n* Schulleiter *m*, Direktor *m*

principle ['prinsəpəl] *n* Grundsatz *m*, Prinzip *nt*

print [print] *v* drucken; *n* Abzug *m*; Stich *m*; **printed matter** Drucksache *f*

prior [praiə] *adj* früher

priority [prai'ɔrəti] *n* Priorität *f*, Vorrang *m*

prison ['prizən] *n* Gefängnis *nt*

prisoner ['prizənə] *n* Häftling *m*, Gefangene *m*; ~ **of war** Kriegsgefangene *m*

privacy ['praivəsi] *n* Privatleben *nt*

private ['praivit] *adj* privat; persönlich

privilege ['privilidʒ] *n* Vorrecht *nt*

prize [praiz] *n* Preis *m*; Belohnung *f*

probable ['prɔbəbəl] *adj* vermutlich, wahrscheinlich

probably ['prɔbəbli] *adv* wahrscheinlich

problem ['prɔbləm] *n* Problem *nt*; Frage *f*

procedure [prə'si:dʒə] *n* Verfahren *nt*

proceed [prə'si:d] *v* *fortfahren; *verfahren

process ['prouses] *n* Verfahren *nt*, Vorgang *m*; Prozeß *m*

procession [prə'sefən] *n* Prozession *f*, Zug *m*

proclaim [prə'kleim] *v* proklamieren

produce[1] [prə'dju:s] *v* herstellen

produce[2] ['prɔdju:s] *n* Erlös *m*, Ertrag *m*

producer [prə'dju:sə] *n* Produzent *m*

product ['prɔdʌkt] *n* Produkt *nt*

production [prə'dʌkfən] *n* Produktion *f*

profession [prə'fefən] *n* Fach *nt*, Beruf *m*

professional [prə'fefənəl] *adj* beruflich

professor [prə'fesə] *n* Professor *m*

profit ['prɔfit] *n* Vorteil *m*, Gewinn *m*; Nutzen *m*; *v* profitieren

profitable ['prɔfitəbəl] *adj* einträglich

profound [prə'faund] *adj* tiefsinnig

programme ['prougræm] *n* Programm *nt*

progress[1] ['prougres] *n* Fortschritt *m*

progress[2] [prə'gres] *v* *weiterkommen

progressive [prə'gresiv] *adj* fortschrittlich, progressiv; zunehmend

prohibit [prə'hibit] *v* *verbieten

prohibition [,proui'bifən] *n* Verbot *nt*

prohibitive [prə'hibitiv] *adj* unerschwinglich

project ['prɔdʒekt] *n* Plan *m*, Projekt *nt*

promenade [,prɔmə'nɑ:d] *n* Promenade *f*

promise ['prɔmis] *n* Versprechen *nt*; *v* *versprechen

promote [prə'mout] *v* fördern, befördern

promotion [prə'moufən] *n* Beförderung *f*

prompt [prɔmpt] *adj* sofortig, unverzüglich

pronoun ['prounaun] *n* Fürwort *nt*

pronounce [prə'nauns] *v* *aussprechen

pronunciation [,prənʌnsi'eifən] *n* Aussprache *f*

proof [pru:f] *n* Beweis *m*

propaganda [,prɔpə'gændə] *n* Propaganda *f*

propel [prə'pel] *v* *antreiben

propeller [prə'pelə] *n* Schraube *f*, Propeller *m*

proper ['prɔpə] *adj* richtig; gebührend, passend, angebracht, geeignet

property ['prɔpəti] *n* Besitz *m*, Eigentum *nt*; Eigenschaft *f*

prophet ['prɔfit] *n* Prophet *m*

proportion [prə'pɔ:fən] *n* Verhältnis *nt*

proportional [prə'pɔ:fənəl] *adj* proportional

proposal [prə'pouzəl] *n* Vorschlag *m*

propose [prə'pouz] *v* *vorschlagen

proposition [,prɔpə'zifən] *n* Vorschlag *m*

proprietor [prə'praiətə] *n* Eigentümer *m*

prospect ['prɔspekt] *n* Aussicht *f*

prospectus [prə'spektəs] *n* Prospekt *m*

prosperity [prə'sperəti] *n* Wohlstand *m*

prosperous ['prɔspərəs] *adj* wohlhabend

prostitute ['prɔstitju:t] *n* Prostituierte *f*

protect [prə'tekt] *v* schützen

protection [prə'tekʃən] *n* Schutz *m*

protein ['prouti:n] *n* Protein *nt*

protest[1] ['proutest] *n* Protest *m*

protest[2] [prə'test] *v* protestieren

Protestant ['prɔtistənt] *adj* protestantisch

proud [praud] *adj* stolz; hochmütig

prove [pru:v] *v* zeigen, *beweisen; sich herausstellen

proverb ['prɔvɜ:b] *n* Sprichwort *nt*

provide [prə'vaid] *v* liefern, beschaffen; **provided that** vorausgesetzt daß

province ['prɔvins] *n* Provinz *f*

provincial [prə'vinʃəl] *adj* provinziell

provisional [prə'viʒənəl] *adj* vorläufig

provisions [prə'viʒənz] *pl* Vorrat *m*

prune [pru:n] *n* Backpflaume *f*

psychiatrist [sai'kaiətrist] *n* Psychiater *m*

psychic ['saikik] *adj* psychisch

psychoanalyst [ˌsaikou'ænəlist] *n* Psychoanalytiker *m*

psychological [ˌsaikɔ'lɔdʒikəl] *adj* psychologisch

psychologist [sai'kɔlədʒist] *n* Psychologe *m*

psychology [sai'kɔlədʒi] *n* Psychologie *f*

pub [pʌb] *n* Wirtshaus *nt*; Kneipe *f*

public ['pʌblik] *adj* öffentlich; allgemein; *n* Publikum *nt*; ~ **garden** Anlage *f*; ~ **house** Wirtshaus *nt*

publication [ˌpʌbli'keiʃən] *n* Veröffentlichung *f*

publicity [pʌ'blisəti] *n* Reklame *f*

publish ['pʌbliʃ] *v* veröffentlichen, *herausgeben

publisher ['pʌbliʃə] *n* Verleger *m*

puddle ['pʌdəl] *n* Pfütze *f*

pull [pul] *v* *ziehen; ~ **out** *abfahren; ~ **up** *anhalten

pulley ['puli] *n* (pl ~s) Rolle *f*

Pullman ['pulmən] *n* Pullmanwagen *m*

pullover ['pu,louvə] *n* Pullover *m*

pulpit ['pulpit] *n* Kanzel *f*

pulse [pʌls] *n* Pulsschlag *m*, Puls *m*

pump [pʌmp] *n* Pumpe *f*; *v* pumpen

punch [pʌntʃ] *v* knuffen; *n* Faustschlag *m*

punctual ['pʌŋktʃuəl] *adj* genau, pünktlich

puncture ['pʌŋktʃə] *n* Reifenpanne *f*

punctured ['pʌŋktʃəd] *adj* durchstochen

punish ['pʌniʃ] *v* strafen

punishment ['pʌniʃmənt] *n* Strafe *f*

pupil ['pju:pəl] *n* Schüler *m*

puppet-show ['pʌpitʃou] *n* Kasperletheater *nt*

purchase ['pɜ:tʃəs] *v* kaufen; *n* Erwerb *m*, Kauf *m*; ~ **price** Kaufpreis *m*; ~ **tax** Verbrauchssteuer *f*

purchaser ['pɜ:tʃəsə] *n* Käufer *m*

pure [pjuə] *adj* klar, rein

purple ['pɜ:pəl] *adj* purpur

purpose ['pɜ:pəs] *n* Absicht *f*, Zweck *m*; **on** ~ absichtlich

purse [pɜ:s] *n* Börse *f*, Geldbeutel *m*

pursue [pə'sju:] *v* verfolgen; nachstreben

pus [pʌs] *n* Eiter *m*

push [puʃ] *n* Schub *m*, Stoß *m*; *v* *stoßen; *schieben; drängen

push-button ['puʃ,bʌtən] *n* Druckknopf *m*

*****put** [put] *v* setzen, legen, stellen; stecken; ~ **away** weglegen; ~ **off** *verschieben; ~ **on** *anziehen; ~ **out** auslöschen

puzzle ['pʌzəl] *n* Rätsel *nt*; *v* verwirren; **jigsaw** ~ Puzzlespiel *nt*

puzzling ['pʌzliŋ] *adj* unbegreiflich

pyjamas [pə'dʒɑ:məz] *pl* Pyjama *m*

Q

quack [kwæk] *n* Kurpfuscher *m*, Scharlatan *m*

quail [kweil] *n* (pl ~, ~s) Wachtel *f*

quaint [kweint] *adj* seltsam; altmodisch

qualification [,kwɔlifi'keiʃən] *n* Befähigung *f*; Vorbehalt *m*, Einschränkung *f*

qualified ['kwɔlifaid] *adj* qualifiziert; befugt

qualify ['kwɔlifai] *v* sich eignen

quality ['kwɔləti] *n* Qualität *f*; Eigenschaft *f*

quantity ['kwɔntəti] *n* Quantität *f*; Anzahl *f*

quarantine ['kwɔrənti:n] *n* Quarantäne *f*

quarrel ['kwɔrəl] *v* zanken, *streiten; *n* Streit *m*, Zank *m*

quarry ['kwɔri] *n* Steinbruch *m*

quarter ['kwɔ:tə] *n* Viertel *nt*; Quartal *nt*; Stadtviertel *nt*; ~ **of an hour** Viertelstunde *f*

quarterly ['kwɔ:təli] *adj* vierteljährlich

quay [ki:] *n* Kai *m*

queen [kwi:n] *n* Königin *f*

queer [kwiə] *adj* wunderlich, sonderbar; komisch

query ['kwiəri] *n* Frage *f*; *v* befragen; bezweifeln

question ['kwestʃən] *n* Frage *f*; Problem *nt*; *v* befragen; in Zweifel *ziehen; ~ **mark** Fragezeichen *nt*

queue [kju:] *n* Schlange *f*; *v* Schlange *stehen

quick [kwik] *adj* schnell

quick-tempered [,kwik'tempəd] *adj* reizbar

quiet ['kwaiət] *adj* still, ruhig, gelassen; *n* Stille *f*, Ruhe *f*

quilt [kwilt] *n* Steppdecke *f*

quinine [kwi'ni:n] *n* Chinin *nt*

quit [kwit] *v* aufhören mit, *aufgeben

quite [kwait] *adv* völlig, durchaus; leidlich, ziemlich, beträchtlich; sehr, ganz

quiz [kwiz] *n* (pl ~zes) Quiz *nt*

quota ['kwoutə] *n* Quote *f*

quotation [kwou'teiʃən] *n* Zitat *nt*; ~ **marks** Anführungszeichen *ntpl*

quote [kwout] *v* zitieren

R

rabbit ['ræbit] *n* Kaninchen *nt*

rabies ['reibiz] *n* Tollwut *f*

race [reis] *n* Wettlauf *m*, Rennen *nt*; Rasse *f*

race-course ['reiskɔ:s] *n* Rennbahn *f*

race-horse ['reishɔ:s] *n* Rennpferd *nt*

race-track ['reistræk] *n* Rennbahn *f*

racial ['reiʃəl] *adj* Rassen-

racket ['rækit] *n* Tumult *m*

racquet ['rækit] *n* Schläger *m*

radiator ['reidieitə] *n* Heizkörper *m*

radical ['rædikəl] *adj* radikal

radio ['reidiou] *n* Radio *nt*

radish ['rædiʃ] *n* Rettich *m*

radius ['reidiəs] *n* (pl radii) Umkreis *m*

raft [rɑ:ft] *n* Floß *nt*

rag [ræg] *n* Lumpen *m*

rage [reidʒ] *n* Toben *nt*, Wut *f*; *v* rasen, wüten

raid [reid] *n* Einfall *m*

rail [reil] *n* Brüstung *f*, Geländer *nt*

railing ['reiliŋ] *n* Gitter *nt*

railroad ['reilroud] *nAm* Schienenweg *m*, Eisenbahn *f*

railway ['reilwei] *n* Bahn *f*, Eisenbahn *f*

rain [rein] *n* Regen *m*; *v* regnen

rainbow ['reinbou] *n* Regenbogen *m*

raincoat ['reinkout] *n* Regenmantel *m*

rainproof ['reinpru:f] *adj* wasserdicht

rainy ['reini] *adj* regnerisch

raise [reiz] *v* *heben; erhöhen; *aufziehen, anbauen, züchten; *erheben; *nAm* Lohnerhöhung *f*, Erhöhung *f*

raisin ['reizən] *n* Rosine *f*

rake [reik] *n* Harke *f*

rally ['ræli] *n* Versammlung *f*

ramp [ræmp] *n* Rampe *f*

ramshackle ['ræm,ʃækəl] *adj* wacklig

rancid ['rænsid] *adj* ranzig

rang [ræŋ] *v* (p ring)

range [reindʒ] *n* Bereich *m*

range-finder ['reindʒ,faində] *n* Entfernungsmesser *m*

rank [ræŋk] *n* Rang *m*; Reihe *f*

ransom ['rænsəm] *n* Lösegeld *nt*

rape [reip] *v* vergewaltigen

rapid ['ræpid] *adj* schnell

rapids ['ræpidz] *pl* Stromschnelle *f*

rare [reə] *adj* selten

rarely ['reəli] *adv* selten

rascal ['rɑ:skəl] *n* Schalk *m*, Schelm *m*

rash [ræʃ] *n* Hautausschlag *m*, Ausschlag *m*; *adj* übereilt, unbesonnen

raspberry ['rɑ:zbəri] *n* Himbeere *f*

rat [ræt] *n* Ratte *f*

rate [reit] *n* Satz *m*, Tarif *m*; Geschwindigkeit *f*; **at any ~** jedenfalls, auf jeden Fall; **~ of exchange** Kurs *m*

rather ['rɑ:ðə] *adv* recht, ziemlich, vielmehr; lieber, eher

ration ['ræʃən] *n* Ration *f*

rattan [ræ'tæn] *n* Peddigrohr *nt*

raven ['reivən] *n* Rabe *m*

raw [rɔ:] *adj* roh; **~ material** Rohmaterial *nt*

ray [rei] *n* Strahl *m*

rayon ['reiən] *n* Kunstseide *f*

razor ['reizə] *n* Rasierapparat *m*

razor-blade ['reizəbleid] *n* Rasierklinge *f*

reach [ri:tʃ] *v* erreichen; *n* Bereich *m*

reaction [ri'ækʃən] *n* Reaktion *f*

***read** [ri:d] *v* *lesen

reading-lamp ['ri:diŋlæmp] *n* Leselampe *f*

reading-room ['ri:diŋru:m] *n* Lesesaal *m*

ready ['redi] *adj* fertig, bereit

ready-made [,redi'meid] *adj* Konfektions-

real [riəl] *adj* wirklich

reality [ri'æləti] *n* Wirklichkeit *f*

realizable ['riəlaizəbəl] *adj* ausführbar

realize ['riəlaiz] *v* sich vergegenwärtigen; realisieren, verwirklichen

really ['riəli] *adv* tatsächlich, wirklich; eigentlich

rear [riə] *n* Hinterseite *f*; *v* *großziehen

rear-light [riə'lait] *n* Schlußlicht *nt*

reason ['ri:zən] *n* Ursache *f*, Grund *m*; Verstand *m*, Vernunft *f*; *v* logisch *durchdenken

reasonable ['ri:zənəbəl] *adj* vernünftig; billig

reassure [,ri:ə'ʃuə] *v* beruhigen

rebate ['ri:beit] *n* Ermäßigung *f*, Rabatt *m*

rebellion [ri'beljən] *n* Aufstand *m*, Aufruhr *m*

recall [ri'kɔ:l] *v* sich erinnern; *zurückrufen; *widerrufen

receipt [ri'si:t] *n* Empfangsschein *m*, Quittung *f*; Empfang *m*

receive [ri'si:v] *v* *bekommen, *empfangen

receiver [ri'si:və] *n* Telephonhörer *m*

recent ['ri:sənt] *adj* jüngst

recently ['ri:səntli] *adv* kürzlich, neulich

reception [ri'sepʃən] *n* Empfang *m*; Aufnahme *f*; **~ office** Rezeption *f*

receptionist [ri'sepʃənist] *n* Empfangsdame f

recession [ri'seʃən] n Rückgang m

recipe ['resipi] n Rezept nt

recital [ri'saitəl] n Solistenkonzert nt

reckon ['rekən] v rechnen; *halten für; *denken

recognition [,rekəg'niʃən] n Anerkennung f

recognize ['rekəgnaiz] v *erkennen; *anerkennen

recollect [,rekə'lekt] v sich *entsinnen

recommence [,ri:kə'mens] v wieder *beginnen

recommend [,rekə'mend] v *anempfehlen, *empfehlen; *anraten

recommendation [,rekəmen'deiʃən] n Empfehlung f

reconciliation [,rekənsili'eiʃən] n Versöhnung f

record[1] ['rekɔ:d] n Schallplatte f; Rekord m; Akte f; **long-playing ~** Langspielplatte f

record[2] [ri'kɔ:d] v aufzeichnen

recorder [ri'kɔ:də] n Tonbandgerät nt

recording [ri'kɔ:diŋ] n Aufnahme f

record-player ['rekɔ:d,pleiə] n Grammophon nt, Plattenspieler m

recover [ri'kʌvə] v wiedererlangen; sich erholen; *genesen

recovery [ri'kʌvəri] n Genesung f, Erholung f

recreation [,rekri'eiʃən] n Erholung f; **~ ground** Spielplatz m

recruit [ri'kru:t] n Rekrut m

rectangle ['rektæŋgəl] n Rechteck nt

rectangular [rek'tæŋgjulə] adj rechteckig

rector ['rektə] n Pfarrer m, Pastor m

rectory ['rektəri] n Pfarre f

rectum ['rektəm] n Mastdarm m

red [red] adj rot

redeem [ri'di:m] v erlösen

reduce [ri'dju:s] v reduzieren, vermindern, herabsetzen

reduction [ri'dʌkʃən] n Rabatt m, Preisnachlaß m

redundant [ri'dʌndənt] adj überflüssig

reed [ri:d] n Schilfrohr nt

reef [ri:f] n Riff nt

reference ['refrəns] n Referenz f, Verweis m; Beziehung f; **with ~ to** hinsichtlich

refer to [ri'fə:] *verweisen auf

refill ['ri:fil] n Ersatzfüllung f

refinery [ri'fainəri] n Raffinerie f

reflect [ri'flekt] v widerspiegeln

reflection [ri'flekʃən] n Spiegelung f; Spiegelbild nt

reflector [ri'flektə] n Reflektor m

reformation [,refə'meiʃən] n Reformation f

refresh [ri'freʃ] v erfrischen

refreshment [ri'freʃmənt] n Erfrischung f

refrigerator [ri'fridʒəreitə] n Eisschrank m, Kühlschrank m

refund[1] [ri'fʌnd] v rückvergüten

refund[2] ['ri:fʌnd] n Rückvergütung f

refusal [ri'fju:zəl] n Verweigerung f

refuse[1] [ri'fju:z] v verweigern

refuse[2] ['refju:s] n Abfall m

regard [ri'ga:d] v ansehen; betrachten; n Respekt m; **as regards** hinsichtlich, in Bezug auf, was ... betrifft

regarding [ri'ga:diŋ] prep betreffs, hinsichtlich; in Anbetracht

regatta [ri'gætə] n Regatta f

régime [rei'ʒi:m] n Regime nt

region ['ri:dʒən] n Gegend f; Gebiet nt

regional ['ri:dʒənəl] adj örtlich

register ['redʒistə] v sich *einschreiben; *einschreiben; **registered letter** eingeschriebener Brief

registration [,redʒi'streiʃən] n Eintragung f; **~ form** Anmeldebogen m; **~ number** Kennzeichen nt; **~**

plate Nummernschild *nt*

regret [ri'gret] *v* bedauern; *n* Bedauern *nt*

regular ['regjulə] *adj* regelmäßig; gewohnt, normal

regulate ['regjuleit] *v* regeln

regulation [,regju'leiʃən] *n* Vorschrift *f*; Regelung *f*

rehabilitation [,ri:hə,bili'teiʃən] *n* Rehabilitation *f*

rehearsal [ri'hə:səl] *n* Probe *f*

rehearse [ri'hə:s] *v* proben

reign [rein] *n* Herrschaft *f*; *v* regieren

reimburse [,ri:im'bə:s] *v* zurückzahlen, wiedererstatten

reindeer ['reindiə] *n* (pl ~) Ren *nt*

reject [ri'dʒekt] *v* ablehnen, *zurückweisen; *verwerfen

relate [ri'leit] *v* erzählen

related [ri'leitid] *adj* verwandt

relation [ri'leiʃən] *n* Beziehung *f*, Verbindung *f*; Verwandte *m*

relative ['relətiv] *n* Verwandte *m*; *adj* verhältnismäßig, relativ

relax [ri'læks] *v* sich entspannen

relaxation [,rilæk'seiʃən] *n* Entspannung *f*

reliable [ri'laiəbəl] *adj* zuverlässig

relic ['relik] *n* Reliquie *f*

relief [ri'li:f] *n* Erleichterung *f*; Unterstützung *f*; Relief *nt*

relieve [ri'li:v] *v* erleichtern; ablösen

religion [ri'lidʒən] *n* Religion *f*

religious [ri'lidʒəs] *adj* religiös

rely on [ri'lai] sich *verlassen auf

remain [ri'mein] *v* *bleiben; *übrigbleiben

remainder [ri'meində] *n* Restbestand *m*, Überbleibsel *nt*, Rest *m*

remaining [ri'meiniŋ] *adj* übrig

remark [ri'ma:k] *n* Bemerkung *f*; *v* bemerken

remarkable [ri'ma:kəbəl] *adj* merkwürdig

remedy ['remədi] *n* Heilmittel *nt*; Mittel *nt*

remember [ri'membə] *v* sich erinnern; *behalten

remembrance [ri'membrəns] *n* Andenken *nt*, Erinnerung *f*

remind [ri'maind] *v* erinnern

remit [ri'mit] *v* *überweisen

remittance [ri'mitəns] *n* Überweisung *f*

remnant ['remnənt] *n* Überbleibsel *nt*, Rest *m*, Überrest *m*

remote [ri'mout] *adj* abgelegen, entfernt

removal [ri'mu:vəl] *n* Beseitigung *f*

remove [ri'mu:v] *v* beseitigen

remunerate [ri'mju:nəreit] *v* entschädigen

remuneration [ri,mju:nə'reiʃən] *n* Entlohnung *f*

renew [ri'nju:] *v* erneuern; verlängern

rent [rent] *v* mieten; *n* Miete *f*

repair [ri'peə] *v* reparieren; *n* Instandsetzung *f*

reparation [,repə'reiʃən] *n* Wiederherstellung *f*, Reparatur *f*

*repay [ri'pei] *v* zurückzahlen

repayment [ri'peimənt] *n* Rückzahlung *f*

repeat [ri'pi:t] *v* wiederholen

repellent [ri'pelənt] *adj* widerwärtig, abstoßend

repentance [ri'pentəns] *n* Reue *f*

repertory ['repətəri] *n* Repertoire *nt*

repetition [,repə'tiʃən] *n* Wiederholung *f*

replace [ri'pleis] *v* ersetzen

reply [ri'plai] *v* antworten; *n* Antwort *f*; in ~ als Antwort

report [ri'po:t] *v* berichten; melden; sich melden; *n* Meldung *f*, Bericht *m*

reporter [ri'po:tə] *n* Berichterstatter *m*

represent [,repri'zent] *v* *vertreten;

vorstellen

representation [,reprizen'teiʃən] n Vertretung f

representative [,repri'zentətiv] adj repräsentativ

reprimand ['reprimɑ:nd] v tadeln

reproach [ri'proutʃ] n Vorwurf m; v *vorwerfen

reproduce [,ri:prə'dju:s] v reproduzieren

reproduction [,ri:prə'dʌkʃən] n Reproduktion f

reptile ['reptail] n Reptil nt

republic [ri'pʌblik] n Republik f

republican [ri'pʌblikən] adj republikanisch

repulsive [ri'pʌlsiv] adj widerwärtig

reputation [,repju'teiʃən] n Ruf m; Ansehen nt

request [ri'kwest] n Bitte f; Gesuch nt; v *bitten

require [ri'kwaiə] v erfordern

requirement [ri'kwaiəmənt] n Erfordernis nt

requisite ['rekwizit] adj erforderlich

rescue ['reskju:] v retten; n Rettung f

research [ri'sə:tʃ] n Forschung f

resemblance [ri'zembləns] n Ähnlichkeit f

resemble [ri'zembəl] v *gleichen

resent [ri'zent] v *übelnehmen

reservation [,rezə'veiʃən] n Reservierung f

reserve [ri'zə:v] v reservieren; vorbestellen; n Reserve f

reserved [ri'zə:vd] adj reserviert

reservoir ['rezəvwɑ:] n Reservoir nt

reside [ri'zaid] v wohnen

residence ['rezidəns] n Wohnsitz m; ~ permit Aufenthaltsgenehmigung f

resident ['rezidənt] n Ortsansässige m; adj wohnhaft; intern

resign [ri'zain] v *zurücktreten

resignation [,rezig'neiʃən] n Rücktritt m

resin ['rezin] n Harz m

resist [ri'zist] v sich widersetzen

resistance [ri'zistəns] n Widerstand m

resolute ['rezəlu:t] adj resolut, entschlossen

respect [ri'spekt] n Respekt m; Ehrfurcht f, Achtung f, Ehrerbietung f; v achten

respectable [ri'spektəbəl] adj achtbar, ehrbar

respectful [ri'spektfəl] adj ehrerbietig

respective [ri'spektiv] adj jeweilig

respiration [,respə'reiʃən] n Atmung f

respite ['respait] n Aufschub m

responsibility [ri,spɔnsə'biləti] n Verantwortlichkeit f; Haftbarkeit f

responsible [ri'spɔnsəbəl] adj verantwortlich; haftbar

rest [rest] n Rast f; Rest m; v ausruhen, ruhen

restaurant ['restərɔ̃:] n Restaurant nt

restful ['restfəl] adj ruhig

rest-home ['resthoum] n Erholungsheim nt

restless ['restləs] adj unruhig; ruhelos

restrain [ri'strein] v in Schranken *halten, *zurückhalten

restriction [ri'strikʃən] n Einschränkung f

result [ri'zʌlt] n Ergebnis nt; Folge f; v sich *ergeben

resume [ri'zju:m] v *wiederaufnehmen

résumé ['rezjumei] n Zusammenfassung f

retail ['ri:teil] v im kleinen verkaufen; ~ trade Einzelhandel m, Kleinhandel m

retailer ['ri:teilə] n Einzelhändler m, Kleinhändler m; Wiederverkäufer m

retina ['retinə] n Netzhaut f

retired [ri'taiəd] adj pensioniert

return [ri'tə:n] v *zurückkommen, zurückkehren; n Rückkehr f; ~ **flight** Rückflug m; ~ **journey** Rückreise f, Rückfahrt f

reunite [,ri:ju:'nait] v wiedervereinigen

reveal [ri'vi:l] v offenbaren, enthüllen

revelation [,revə'leiʃən] n Enthüllung f

revenge [ri'vendʒ] n Rache f

revenue ['revənju:] n Einkünfte fpl, Einkommen nt

reverse [ri'və:s] n Gegenteil nt; Kehrseite f; Rückwärtsgang m; Umschwung m, Rückschlag m; adj umgekehrt; v rückwärts *fahren

review [ri'vju:] n Besprechung f; Zeitschrift f

revise [ri'vaiz] v überarbeiten

revision [ri'viʒən] n Überarbeitung f

revival [ri'vaivəl] n Wiederherstellung f

revolt [ri'voult] v rebellieren; n Aufstand m, Aufruhr m

revolting [ri'voultiŋ] adj widerwärtig, empörend, abstoßend

revolution [,revə'lu:ʃən] n Revolution f; Umdrehung f

revolutionary [,revə'lu:ʃənəri] adj revolutionär

revolver [ri'vɔlvə] n Revolver m

revue [ri'vju:] n Kabarett nt

reward [ri'wɔ:d] n Belohnung f; v belohnen

rheumatism ['ru:mətizəm] n Rheumatismus m

rhinoceros [rai'nɔsərəs] n (pl ~, ~es) Nashorn nt

rhubarb ['ru:bɑ:b] n Rhabarber m

rhyme [raim] n Reim m

rhythm ['riðəm] n Rhythmus m

rib [rib] n Rippe f

ribbon ['ribən] n Band nt

rice [rais] n Reis m

rich [ritʃ] adj reich

riches ['ritʃiz] pl Reichtum m

riddle ['ridəl] n Rätsel nt

ride [raid] n Fahrt f

*** ride** [raid] v *fahren; *reiten

rider ['raidə] n Reiter m

ridge [ridʒ] n Grat m

ridicule ['ridikju:l] v bespötteln

ridiculous [ri'dikjuləs] adj lächerlich

riding ['raidiŋ] n Reitsport m

riding-school ['raidiŋsku:l] n Reitschule f

rifle ['raifəl] v Gewehr nt

right [rait] n Recht nt; adj gut, richtig; recht; redlich, gerecht; **all right!** einverstanden!; *** be** ~ recht *haben; ~ **of way** Vorfahrtsrecht nt

righteous ['raitʃəs] adj gerecht

right-hand ['raithænd] adj recht

rightly ['raitli] adv mit Recht

rim [rim] n Felge f; Rand m

ring [riŋ] n Ring m; Kreis m; Zirkusarena f

*** ring** [riŋ] v läuten; ~ **up** *anrufen

rinse [rins] v spülen; n Spülung f

riot ['raiət] n Aufruhr m

rip [rip] v *zerreißen

ripe [raip] adj reif

rise [raiz] n Gehaltserhöhung f, Erhöhung f; Anhöhe f; Steigung f; Aufstieg m

*** rise** [raiz] v *aufstehen; *aufgehen; *steigen

rising ['raiziŋ] n Aufstand m

risk [risk] n Risiko nt; Gefahr f; v wagen

risky ['riski] adj gewagt, riskant

rival ['raivəl] n Rivale m; Konkurrent m; v rivalisieren

rivalry ['raivəlri] n Rivalität f; Konkurrenz f

river ['rivə] n Fluß m; ~ **bank** Flußufer nt

riverside ['rivəsaid] n Flußufer nt

roach [routʃ] n (pl ~) Plötze f

road [roud] *n* Straße *f*; ~ **fork** *n* Scheideweg *m*; ~ **map** Autokarte *f*; ~ **system** Straßennetz *nt*; ~ **up** Straßenarbeiten *fpl*

roadhouse ['roudhaus] *n* Gaststätte *f*

roadside ['roudsaid] *n* Straßenseite *f*; ~ **restaurant** Gaststätte *f*

roadway ['roudwei] *n Am* Fahrbahn *f*

roam [roum] *v* umherschweifen

roar [rɔ:] *v* heulen, brüllen; *n* Brüllen *nt*, Dröhnen *nt*

roast [roust] *v* *braten, rösten

rob [rɔb] *v* rauben

robber ['rɔbə] *n* Räuber *m*

robbery ['rɔbəri] *n* Raub *m*, Diebstahl *m*

robe [roub] *n* Kleid *nt*; Gewand *nt*

robin ['rɔbin] *n* Rotkehlchen *nt*

robust [rou'bʌst] *adj* robust

rock [rɔk] *n* Felsen *m*; *v* schaukeln

rocket ['rɔkit] *n* Rakete *f*

rocky ['rɔki] *adj* felsig

rod [rɔd] *n* Stange *f*

roe [rou] *n* Rogen *m*

roll [roul] *v* rollen; *n* Rolle *f*; Brötchen *nt*

Roman Catholic ['roumən 'kæθəlik] römisch-katholisch

romance [rə'mæns] *n* Romanze *f*

romantic [rə'mæntik] *adj* romantisch

roof [ru:f] *n* Dach *nt*; **thatched** ~ Strohdach *nt*

room [ru:m] *n* Raum *m*, Zimmer *nt*; Platz *m*; ~ **and board** Zimmer mit Vollpension; ~ **service** Zimmerbedienung *f*; ~ **temperature** Zimmertemperatur *f*

roomy ['ru:mi] *adj* geräumig

root [ru:t] *n* Wurzel *f*

rope [roup] *n* Seil *nt*

rosary ['rouzəri] *n* Rosenkranz *m*

rose [rouz] *n* Rose *f*; *adj* rosa

rotten ['rɔtən] *adj* verdorben

rouge [ru:ʒ] *n* Rouge *nt*

rough [rʌf] *adj* holperig

roulette [ru:'let] *n* Roulett *nt*

round [raund] *adj* rund; *prep* um ... herum, um; *n* Runde *f*; ~ **trip** *Am* Hin- und Rückfahrt

rounded ['raundid] *adj* abgerundet

route [ru:t] *n* Route *f*

routine [ru:'ti:n] *n* Routine *f*

row[1] [rou] *n* Reihe *f*; *v* rudern

row[2] [rau] *n* Krach *m*

rowdy ['raudi] *adj* streitsüchtig

rowing-boat ['rouiŋbout] *n* Ruderboot *nt*

royal ['rɔiəl] *adj* königlich

rub [rʌb] *v* *reiben

rubber ['rʌbə] *n* Gummi *m*; Radiergummi *m*; ~ **band** Gummiband *nt*

rubbish ['rʌbiʃ] *n* Abfall *m*; Quatsch *m*, Unsinn *m*; **talk** ~ quatschen

rubbish-bin ['rʌbiʃbin] *n* Abfalleimer *m*

ruby ['ru:bi] *n* Rubin *m*

rucksack ['rʌksæk] *n* Rucksack *m*

rudder ['rʌdə] *n* Steuerruder *nt*

rude [ru:d] *adj* grob

rug [rʌg] *n* Vorleger *m*

ruin ['ru:in] *v* ruinieren; *n* Untergang *m*; **ruins** Ruine *f*

ruination [,ru:i'neiʃən] *n* Zusammensturz *m*

rule [ru:l] *n* Regel *f*; Verwaltung *f*, Regierung *f*, Herrschaft *f*; *v* regieren, herrschen; **as a** ~ gewöhnlich, in der Regel

ruler ['ru:lə] *n* Monarch *m*, Herrscher *m*; Lineal *nt*

Rumania [ru:'meiniə] Rumänien

Rumanian [ru:'meiniən] *adj* rumänisch; *n* Rumäne *m*

rumour ['ru:mə] *n* Gerücht *nt*

***run** [rʌn] *v* *laufen; ~ **into** zufällig begegnen

runaway ['rʌnəwei] *n* Ausreißer *m*

rung [rʌn] *v* (pp ring)

runway ['rʌnwei] n Startbahn f
rural ['ruərəl] adj ländlich
ruse [ru:z] n List f
rush [rʌʃ] v eilen; n Binse f
rush-hour ['rʌʃauə] n Hauptverkehrszeit f
Russia ['rʌʃə] Rußland
Russian ['rʌʃən] adj russisch; n Russe m
rust [rʌst] n Rost m
rustic ['rʌstik] adj ländlich
rusty ['rʌsti] adj rostig

S

saccharin ['sækərin] n Saccharin nt
sack [sæk] n Sack m
sacred ['seikrid] adj heilig
sacrifice ['sækrifais] n Opfer nt; v aufopfern
sacrilege ['sækrilidʒ] n Entheiligung f
sad [sæd] adj traurig; niedergeschlagen, betrübt, trübsinnig
saddle ['sædəl] n Sattel m
sadness ['sædnəs] n Traurigkeit f
safe [seif] adj sicher; n Geldschrank m, Safe m
safety ['seifti] n Sicherheit f
safety-belt ['seiftibelt] n Sicherheitsgurt m
safety-pin ['seiftipin] n Sicherheitsnadel f
safety-razor ['seifti,reizə] n Rasierapparat m
sail [seil] v *befahren, *fahren; n Segel nt
sailing-boat ['seiliŋbout] n Segelboot nt
sailor ['seilə] n Matrose m
saint [seint] n Heilige m
salad ['sæləd] n Salat m
salad-oil ['sælədɔil] n Salatöl nt

salary ['sæləri] n Lohn m, Gehalt nt
sale [seil] n Verkauf m; **clearance ~** Ausverkauf m; **for ~** zu verkaufen; **sales** Schlußverkauf m; **sales tax** Verbrauchssteuer f
saleable ['seiləbəl] adj verkäuflich
salesgirl ['seilzgə:l] n Verkäuferin f
salesman ['seilzmən] n (pl -men) Verkäufer m
salmon ['sæmən] n (pl ~) Lachs m
salon ['sælɔ:] n Salon m
saloon [sə'lu:n] n Bar f
salt [sɔ:lt] n Salz nt
salt-cellar ['sɔ:lt,selə] n Salzfäßchen nt
salty ['sɔ:lti] adj salzig
salute [sə'lu:t] v grüßen
salve [sɑ:v] n Salbe f
same [seim] adj selb
sample ['sɑ:mpəl] n Muster nt
sanatorium [,sænə'tɔ:riəm] n (pl ~s, -ria) Sanatorium nt
sand [sænd] n Sand m
sandal ['sændəl] n Sandale f
sandpaper ['sænd,peipə] n Schmirgelpapier nt
sandwich ['sænwidʒ] n Sandwich nt; Butterbrot nt
sandy ['sændi] adj sandig
sanitary ['sænitəri] adj sanitär; **~ towel** Damenbinde f
sapphire ['sæfaiə] n Saphir m
sardine [sɑ:'di:n] n Sardine f
satchel ['sætʃəl] n Schultasche f
satellite ['sætəlait] n Satellit m
satin ['sætin] n Satin m
satisfaction [,sætis'fækʃən] n Befriedigung f, Genugtuung f
satisfy ['sætisfai] v zufriedenstellen, befriedigen; **satisfied** satt, zufrieden
Saturday ['sætədi] Sonnabend m
sauce [sɔ:s] n Soße f
saucepan ['sɔ:spən] n Pfanne f
saucer ['sɔ:sə] n Untertasse f

Saudi Arabia [,saudiə'reibiə] Saudi-Arabien

Saudi Arabian [,saudiə'reibiən] adj saudiarabisch

sauna ['sɔ:nə] n Sauna f

sausage ['sɔsidʒ] n Wurst f

savage ['sævidʒ] adj wild

save [seiv] v retten; sparen

savings ['seiviŋz] pl Ersparnisse fpl; ~ **bank** Sparkasse f

saviour ['seivjə] n Retter m

savoury ['seivəri] adj schmackhaft; pikant

saw[1] [sɔ:] v (p see)

saw[2] [sɔ:] n Säge f

sawdust ['sɔ:dʌst] n Sägemehl nt

saw-mill ['sɔ:mil] n Sägemühle f

***say** [sei] v sagen

scaffolding ['skæfəldiŋ] n Gerüst nt

scale [skeil] n Maßstab m; Tonleiter f; Schuppe f; **scales** pl Waage f

scandal ['skændəl] n Skandal m

Scandinavia [,skændi'neiviə] Skandinavien

Scandinavian [,skændi'neiviən] adj skandinavisch; n Skandinavier m

scapegoat ['skeipgout] n Sündenbock m

scar [skɑ:] n Narbe f

scarce [skeəs] adj knapp

scarcely ['skeəsli] adv kaum

scarcity ['skeəsəti] n Mangel m

scare [skeə] v *erschrecken; n Schreck m

scarf [skɑ:f] n (pl ~s, scarves) Schal m

scarlet ['skɑ:lət] adj scharlachrot

scary ['skeəri] adj unheimlich

scatter ['skætə] v verstreuen

scene [si:n] n Szene f

scenery ['si:nəri] n Landschaft f

scenic ['si:nik] adj malerisch

scent [sent] n Parfüm nt

schedule ['ʃedju:l] n Fahrplan m, Plan m

scheme [ski:m] n Schema nt; Plan m

scholar ['skɔlə] n Gelehrte m; Schüler m

scholarship ['skɔləʃip] n Stipendium nt

school [sku:l] n Schule f

schoolboy ['sku:lbɔi] n Schüler m

schoolgirl ['sku:lgə:l] n Schülerin f

schoolmaster ['sku:l,mɑ:stə] n Lehrer m, Volksschullehrer m

schoolteacher ['sku:l,ti:tʃə] n Lehrer m

science ['saiəns] n Wissenschaft f

scientific [,saiən'tifik] adj wissenschaftlich

scientist ['saiəntist] n Wissenschaftler m

scissors ['sizəz] pl Schere f

scold [skould] v schimpfen

scooter ['sku:tə] n Motorroller m; Roller m

score [skɔ:] n Spielstand m; v *anschreiben

scorn [skɔ:n] n Hohn m, Verachtung f; v verachten

Scot [skɔt] n Schotte m

Scotch [skɔtʃ] adj schottisch; **scotch tape** Selbstklebeband nt

Scotland ['skɔtlənd] Schottland

Scottish ['skɔtiʃ] adj schottisch

scout [skaut] n Pfadfinder m

scrap [skræp] n Stückchen nt

scrap-book ['skræpbuk] n Klebealbum nt

scrape [skreip] v schaben

scrap-iron ['skræpaiən] n Alteisen nt

scratch [skrætʃ] v kratzen; n Kratzer m, Schramme f

scream [skri:m] v kreischen, *schreien; n Ruf m, Schrei m

screen [skri:n] n Schirm m; Bildschirm m, Filmleinwand f

screw [skru:] n Schraube f; v schrauben

screw-driver ['skru:,draivə] n Schraubenzieher m

scrub [skrʌb] v scheuern; n Gestrüpp nt

sculptor ['skʌlptə] n Bildhauer m

sculpture ['skʌlptʃə] n Skulptur f

sea [si:] n Meer nt

sea-bird ['si:bə:d] n Seevogel m

sea-coast ['si:koust] n Meeresküste f

seagull ['si:gʌl] n Seemöwe f

seal [si:l] n Siegel nt; Robbe f, Seehund m

seam [si:m] n Naht f

seaman ['si:mən] n (pl -men) Matrose m

seamless ['si:mləs] adj nahtlos

seaport ['si:pɔ:t] n Seehafen m

search [sə:tʃ] v suchen; visitieren, durchsuchen; n Suche f

searchlight ['sə:tʃlait] n Scheinwerfer m

sea-shell ['si:ʃel] n Muschel f

seashore ['si:ʃɔ:] n Meeresküste f

seasick ['si:sik] adj seekrank

seasickness ['si:,siknəs] n Seekrankheit f

seaside ['si:said] n Küste f; ~ resort Seebad nt

season ['si:zən] n Jahreszeit f, Saison f; high ~ Hochsaison f; low ~ Nachsaison f; off ~ außer Saison

season-ticket ['si:zən,tikit] n Dauerkarte f

seat [si:t] n Sitz m; Platz m

seat-belt ['si:tbelt] n Sicherheitsgurt m

sea-urchin ['si:,ə:tʃin] n Seeigel m

sea-water ['si:,wɔ:tə] n Meerwasser nt

second ['sekənd] num zweite; n Sekunde f; Augenblick m

secondary ['sekəndəri] adj untergeordnet; ~ school höhere Schule

second-hand [,sekənd'hænd] adj gebraucht

secret ['si:krət] n Geheimnis nt; adj geheim

secretary ['sekrətri] n Sekretärin f; Sekretär m

section ['sekʃən] n Abschnitt m; Fach nt, Abteilung f

secure [si'kjuə] adj sicher; v sich bemächtigen

security [si'kjuərəti] n Sicherheit f; Pfand nt

sedate [si'deit] adj gesetzt

sedative ['sedətiv] n Beruhigungsmittel nt

seduce [si'dju:s] v verführen

*see [si:] v *sehen; *begreifen, *einsehen; ~ to sorgen für

seed [si:d] n Samen m

*seek [si:k] v suchen

seem [si:m] v *erscheinen, *scheinen

seen [si:n] v (pp see)

seesaw ['si:sɔ:] n Wippe f

seize [si:z] v *ergreifen

seldom ['seldəm] adv selten

select [si'lekt] v *auslesen, auswählen; adj auserlesen, erlesen

selection [si'lekʃən] n Wahl f, Auswahl f

self-centred [,self'sentəd] adj ichbezogen

self-employed [,selfim'plɔid] adj selbständig

self-evident [,sel'fevidənt] adj selbstverständlich

self-government [,self'gʌvəmənt] n Selbstverwaltung f

selfish ['selfiʃ] adj selbstsüchtig

selfishness ['selfiʃnəs] n Selbstsucht f

self-service [,self'sə:vis] n Selbstbedienung f; ~ restaurant Selbstbedienungsrestaurant nt

*sell [sel] v verkaufen

semblance ['sembləns] n Anschein m

semi- ['semi] Halb-

semicircle ['semi,sə:kəl] n Halbkreis m

semi-colon [,semi'koulən] n Strich-

punkt *m*
senate ['senət] *n* Senat *m*
senator ['senətə] *n* Senator *m*
*send [send] *v* schicken, *senden; ~
back zurückschicken, *zurücksenden; ~ for kommen *lassen; ~ off
*absenden
senile ['si:nail] *adj* senil
sensation [sen'seiʃən] *n* Sensation *f*;
Eindruck *m*, Empfindung *f*
sensational [sen'seiʃənəl] *adj* aufsehenerregend, sensationell
sense [sens] *n* Sinn *m*; Verstand *m*,
Vernunft *f*; Bedeutung *f*; *v* spüren;
~ of honour Ehrgefühl *nt*
senseless ['sensləs] *adj* unsinnig
sensible ['sensəbəl] *adj* verständig
sensitive ['sensitiv] *adj* empfindlich
sentence ['sentəns] *n* Satz *m*; Urteil
nt; *v* verurteilen
sentimental [,senti'mentəl] *adj* sentimental
separate¹ ['sepəreit] *v* trennen
separate² ['sepərət] *adj* besonder, getrennt
separately ['sepərətli] *adv* apart
September [sep'tembə] September
septic ['septik] *adj* septisch; *become
~ entzünden
sequel ['si:kwəl] *n* Folge *f*
sequence ['si:kwəns] *n* Reihenfolge *f*;
Folge *f*
serene [sə'ri:n] *adj* ruhig; klar
serial ['siəriəl] *n* Feuilleton *nt*
series ['siəri:z] *n* (pl ~) Folge *f*, Serie *f*
serious ['siəriəs] *adj* seriös, ernst
seriousness ['siəriəsnəs] *n* Ernst *m*
sermon ['sə:mən] *n* Predigt *f*
serum ['siərəm] *n* Serum *nt*
servant ['sə:vənt] *n* Diener *m*
serve [sə:v] *v* bedienen
service ['sə:vis] *n* Dienst *m*; Bedienung *f*; ~ charge Bedienung *f*; ~
station Tankstelle *f*

serviette [,sə:vi'et] *n* Serviette *f*
session ['seʃən] *n* Sitzung *f*
set [set] *n* Satz *m*, Gruppe *f*
*set [set] *v* stellen; ~ menu festes
Menü; ~ out abreisen
setting ['setiŋ] *n* Umgebung *f*; ~ lotion Haarfixativ *nt*
settle ['setəl] *v* erledigen, regeln; ~
down sich *niederlassen
settlement ['setəlmənt] *n* Regelung *f*,
Vergleich *m*, Übereinkunft *f*
seven ['sevən] *num* sieben
seventeen [,sevən'ti:n] *num* siebzehn
seventeenth [,sevən'ti:nθ] *num* siebzehnte
seventh ['sevənθ] *num* siebente
seventy ['sevənti] *num* siebzig
several ['sevərəl] *adj* etliche, mehrere
severe [si'viə] *adj* heftig, streng, ernst
sew [sou] *v* nähen; ~ up nähen
sewer ['su:ə] *n* Abwasserkanal *m*
sewing-machine ['souiŋməˌʃi:n] *n*
Nähmaschine *f*
sex [seks] *n* Geschlecht *nt*; Sex *m*
sexton ['sekstən] *n* Küster *m*
sexual ['sekʃuəl] *adj* sexuell
sexuality [,sekʃu'æləti] *n* Sexualität *f*
shade [ʃeid] *n* Schatten *m*; Farbton
m
shadow ['ʃædou] *n* Schatten *m*
shady ['ʃeidi] *adj* schattig
*shake [ʃeik] *v* schütteln
shaky ['ʃeiki] *adj* wacklig
*shall [ʃæl] *v* *werden; sollen
shallow ['ʃælou] *adj* seicht
shame [ʃeim] *n* Schande *f*; shame!
pfui!
shampoo [ʃæm'pu:] *n* Shampoo *nt*
shamrock ['ʃæmrɔk] *n* Kleeblatt *nt*
shape [ʃeip] *n* Form *f*; *v* bilden
share [ʃeə] *v* teilen; *n* Teil *m*; Aktie *f*
shark [ʃɑ:k] *n* Hai *m*
sharp [ʃɑ:p] *adj* scharf
sharpen ['ʃɑ:pən] *v* *schleifen, schär-

fen

shave [ʃeiv] v sich rasieren

shaver ['ʃeivə] n Rasierapparat m

shaving-brush ['ʃeiviŋbrʌʃ] n Rasierpinsel m

shaving-cream ['ʃeiviŋkri:m] n Rasierkrem f

shaving-soap ['ʃeiviŋsoup] n Rasierseife f

shawl [ʃɔ:l] n Umschlagtuch nt, Schal m

she [ʃi:] pron sie

shed [ʃed] n Schuppen m

* **shed** [ʃed] v *vergießen; verbreiten

sheep [ʃi:p] n (pl ~) Schaf nt

sheer [ʃiə] adj absolut, rein; dünn, durchscheinend

sheet [ʃi:t] n Laken nt; Blatt nt; Platte f

shelf [ʃelf] n (pl shelves) Regal nt

shell [ʃel] n Muschel f; Schale f

shellfish ['ʃelfiʃ] n Schalentier nt

shelter ['ʃeltə] n Schutz m; v schützen

shepherd ['ʃepəd] n Hirt m

shift [ʃift] n Schicht f

* **shine** [ʃain] v strahlen; leuchten, glänzen

ship [ʃip] n Schiff nt; v *versenden; **shipping line** Schiffahrtslinie f

shipowner ['ʃi,pounə] n Reeder m

shipyard ['ʃipjɑ:d] n Schiffswerft f

shirt [ʃə:t] n Hemd nt

shiver ['ʃivə] v zittern, frösteln; n Frösteln nt

shivery ['ʃivəri] adj fröstelnd

shock [ʃɔk] n Schock m; v schockieren; ~ **absorber** Stoßdämpfer m

shocking ['ʃɔkiŋ] adj empörend

shoe [ʃu:] n Schuh m; **gym shoes** Turnschuhe mpl; ~ **polish** Schuhkrem f

shoe-lace ['ʃu:leis] n Schnürsenkel m

shoemaker ['ʃu:,meikə] n Schuhmacher m

shoe-shop ['ʃu:ʃɔp] n Schuhgeschäft nt

shook [ʃuk] v (p shake)

* **shoot** [ʃu:t] v *schießen

shop [ʃɔp] n Geschäft nt; v einkaufen; ~ **assistant** Verkäufer m; **shopping bag** Einkaufstasche f; **shopping centre** Einkaufszentrum nt

shopkeeper ['ʃɔp,ki:pə] n Ladeninhaber m

shop-window [,ʃɔp'windou] n Schaufenster nt

shore [ʃɔ:] n Ufer nt, Küste f

short [ʃɔ:t] adj kurz; klein; ~ **circuit** Kurzschluß m

shortage ['ʃɔ:tidʒ] n Mangel m, Knappheit f

shortcoming ['ʃɔ:t,kʌmiŋ] n Unzulänglichkeit f

shorten ['ʃɔ:tən] v verkürzen

shorthand ['ʃɔ:thænd] n Stenographie f

shortly ['ʃɔ:tli] adv in kurzem, bald

shorts [ʃɔ:ts] pl kurze Hose; plAm Unterhose f

short-sighted [,ʃɔ:t'saitid] adj kurzsichtig

shot [ʃɔt] n Schuß m; Spritze f; Aufnahme f

* **should** [ʃud] v *müssen

shoulder ['ʃouldə] n Schulter f

shout [ʃaut] v *schreien, *rufen; n Schrei m

shovel ['ʃʌvəl] n Schaufel f

show [ʃou] n Aufführung f, Vorstellung f; Ausstellung f

* **show** [ʃou] v zeigen; sehen *lassen, ausstellen; *beweisen

show-case ['ʃoukeis] n Vitrine f

shower [ʃauə] n Dusche f; Schauer m, Regenschauer m

showroom ['ʃouru:m] n Ausstellungsraum m

shriek [ʃriːk] v kreischen; n Gekreisch nt

shrimp [ʃrimp] n Garnele f

shrine [ʃrain] n Heiligtum nt, Schrein m

*shrink [ʃriŋk] v schrumpfen

shrinkproof ['ʃriŋkpruːf] adj nicht einlaufend

shrub [ʃrʌb] n Strauch m

shudder ['ʃʌdə] n Schauder m

shuffle ['ʃʌfəl] v mischen

*shut [ʃʌt] v *abschließen, *schließen; shut zu, geschlossen; ~ in *einschließen

shutter ['ʃʌtə] n Jalousie f, Fensterladen m

shy [ʃai] adj scheu, schüchtern

shyness ['ʃainəs] n Schüchternheit f

Siam [sai'æm] Siam

Siamese [,saiə'miːz] adj siamesisch; n Siamese m

sick [sik] adj krank; übel

sickness ['siknəs] n Krankheit f; Übelkeit f

side [said] n Seite f; Partei f; one-sided adj einseitig

sideburns ['saidbəːnz] pl Koteletten

sidelight ['saidlait] n Seitenlicht nt

side-street ['saidstriːt] n Seitenstraße f

sidewalk ['saidwɔːk] nAm Gehweg m, Bürgersteig m

sideways ['saidweiz] adv seitwärts

siege [siːdʒ] n Belagerung f

sieve [siv] n Sieb nt; v sieben

sift [sift] v sieben

sight [sait] n Aussicht f; Sicht f, Anblick m; Sehenswürdigkeit f

sign [sain] n Zeichen nt; Gebärde f, Wink m; v unterzeichnen, *unterschreiben

signal ['signəl] n Signal nt; Zeichen nt; v signalisieren

signature ['signətʃə] n Unterschrift f

significant [sig'nifikənt] adj bedeutungsvoll

signpost ['sainpoust] n Wegweiser m

silence ['sailəns] n Stille f; v zum Schweigen *bringen

silencer ['sailənsə] n Auspufftopf m

silent ['sailənt] adj schweigend, still; *be ~ *schweigen

silk [silk] n Seide f

silken ['silkən] adj seiden

silly ['sili] adj töricht, albern

silver ['silvə] n Silber nt; silbern

silversmith ['silvəsmiθ] n Silberschmied m

silverware ['silvəwɛə] n Silber nt

similar ['similə] adj derartig, ähnlich

similarity [,simi'lærəti] n Ähnlichkeit f

simple ['simpəl] adj schlicht, einfach; üblich

simply ['simpli] adv einfach

simulate ['simjuleit] v heucheln

simultaneous [,siml'teiniəs] adj gleichzeitig

sin [sin] n Sünde f

since [sins] prep seit; adv seither; conj seitdem; da

sincere [sin'siə] adj aufrichtig

sinew ['sinjuː] n Sehne f

*sing [siŋ] v *singen

singer ['siŋə] n Sänger m; Sängerin f

single ['siŋgəl] adj einzig; ledig

singular ['siŋgjulə] n Einzahl f; adj merkwürdig

sinister ['sinistə] adj unheilvoll

sink [siŋk] n Ausguß m

*sink [siŋk] v *sinken

sip [sip] n Schlückchen nt

siphon ['saifən] n Siphon m

sir [səː] mein Herr

siren ['saiərən] n Sirene f

sister ['sistə] n Schwester f

sister-in-law ['sistərinlɔː] n (pl sisters-) Schwägerin f

*sit [sit] v *sitzen; ~ down sich setzen

site [sait] *n* Gelände *nt*; Lage *f*

sitting-room ['sitiŋru:m] *n* Wohnzimmer *nt*

situated ['sitʃueitid] *adj* gelegen

situation [,sitʃu'eiʃən] *n* Lage *f*

six [siks] *num* sechs

sixteen [,siks'ti:n] *num* sechzehn

sixteenth [,siks'ti:nθ] *num* sechzehnte

sixth [siksθ] *num* sechste

sixty ['siksti] *num* sechzig

size [saiz] *n* Größe *f*, Nummer *f*; Ausmaß *nt*; Format *nt*

skate [skeit] *v* *eislaufen; *n* Schlittschuh *m*

skating-rink ['skeitiŋriŋk] *n* Schlittschuhbahn *f*, Eisbahn *f*

skeleton ['skelitən] *n* Gerippe *nt*, Skelett *nt*

sketch [sketʃ] *n* Zeichnung *f*, Skizze *f*; *v* zeichnen, skizzieren

sketch-book ['sketʃbuk] *n* Skizzenbuch *nt*

ski¹ [ski:] *v* Schi *laufen

ski² [ski:] *n* (pl ~, ~s) Schi *m*; ~ **boots** Schischuhe *mpl*; ~ **pants** Schihose *f*; ~ **poles** *Am* Schistöcke *mpl*; ~ **sticks** Schistöcke *mpl*

skid [skid] *v* schleudern

skier ['ski:ə] *n* Schiläufer *m*

skiing ['ski:iŋ] *n* Schilauf *m*

ski-jump ['ski:dʒʌmp] *n* Schisprung *m*

skilful ['skilfəl] *adj* geschickt, behende, gewandt

ski-lift ['ski:lift] *n* Schilift *m*

skill [skil] *n* Fertigkeit *f*

skilled [skild] *adj* geübt, geschickt; erfahren

skin [skin] *n* Fell *nt*, Haut *f*; Schale *f*; ~ **cream** Hautkrem *f*

skip [skip] *v* hüpfen; *übergehen

skirt [skə:t] *n* Rock *m*

skull [skʌl] *n* Schädel *m*

sky [skai] *n* Himmel *m*; Luft *f*

skyscraper ['skai,skreipə] *n* Wolkenkratzer *m*

slack [slæk] *adj* träge

slacks [slæks] *pl* Hose *f*

slam [slæm] *v* *zuschlagen

slander ['sla:ndə] *n* Verleumdung *f*

slant [slɑ:nt] *v* sich neigen

slanting ['sla:ntiŋ] *adj* schief, abschüssig, schräg

slap [slæp] *v* *schlagen; *n* Schlag *m*

slate [sleit] *n* Schiefer *m*

slave [sleiv] *n* Sklave *m*

sledge [sledʒ] *n* Schlitten *m*

sleep [sli:p] *n* Schlaf *m*

*sleep [sli:p] *v* *schlafen

sleeping-bag ['sli:piŋbæg] *n* Schlafsack *m*

sleeping-car ['sli:piŋka:] *n* Schlafwagen *m*

sleeping-pill ['sli:piŋpil] *n* Schlafmittel *nt*

sleepless ['sli:pləs] *adj* schlaflos

sleepy ['sli:pi] *adj* schläfrig

sleeve [sli:v] *n* Ärmel *m*; Hülle *f*

sleigh [slei] *n* Schlitten *m*

slender ['slendə] *adj* schlank

slice [slais] *n* Schnitte *f*

slide [slaid] *n* Rutschbahn *f*; Dia *nt*

*slide [slaid] *v* *gleiten

slight [slait] *adj* leicht; geringfügig

slim [slim] *adj* schlank; *v* *abnehmen

slip [slip] *v* *ausgleiten *f*, ausrutschen; entwischen; *n* Fehltritt *m*; Unterrock *m*

slipper ['slipə] *n* Hausschuh *m*, Pantoffel *m*

slippery ['slipəri] *adj* glitschig, schlüpfrig

slogan ['slougən] *n* Wahlspruch *m*, Schlagwort *nt*

slope [sloup] *n* Abhang *m*; *v* *abfallen

sloping ['sloupiŋ] *adj* abschüssig

sloppy ['slɔpi] *adj* schlampig

slot [slɔt] *n* Schlitz *m*

slot-machine ['slɔt,məʃi:n] *n* Automat *m*

slovenly ['slʌvənli] *adj* unordentlich

slow [slou] *adj* schwerfällig, langsam; ~ **down** verzögern, verlangsamen; abbremsen

sluice [slu:s] *n* Schleuse *f*

slum [slʌm] *n* Elendsviertel *nt*

slump [slʌmp] *n* Preissenkung *f*

slush [slʌʃ] *n* Matsch *m*

sly [slai] *adj* listig

smack [smæk] *v* *schlagen; *n* Klaps *m*

small [smɔ:l] *adj* klein; gering

smallpox ['smɔ:lpɔks] *n* Pocken *fpl*

smart [sma:t] *adj* elegant; gewandt, gescheit

smell [smel] *n* Geruch *m*

***smell** [smel] *v* *riechen; *stinken

smelly ['smeli] *adj* übelriechend

smile [smail] *v* lächeln; *n* Lächeln *nt*

smith [smiθ] *n* Schmied *m*

smoke [smouk] *v* rauchen; *n* Rauch *m*; **no smoking** Rauchen verboten

smoker ['smoukə] *n* Raucher *m*; Raucherabteil *nt*

smoking-compartment ['smoukiŋkəm,pa:tmənt] *n* Raucherabteil *nt*

smoking-room ['smoukiŋru:m] *n* Rauchzimmer *nt*

smooth [smu:ð] *adj* eben, flach, glatt; geschmeidig

smuggle ['smʌgəl] *v* schmuggeln

snack [snæk] *n* Imbiß *m*

snack-bar ['snækba:] *n* Snackbar *f*

snail [sneil] *n* Schnecke *f*

snake [sneik] *n* Schlange *f*

snapshot ['snæpʃɔt] *n* Schnappschuß *m*

sneakers ['sni:kəz] *plAm* Turnschuhe *mpl*

sneeze [sni:z] *v* niesen

sniper ['snaipə] *n* Heckenschütze *m*

snooty ['snu:ti] *adj* hochnäsig

snore [snɔ:] *v* schnarchen

snorkel ['snɔ:kəl] *n* Schnorchel *m*

snout [snaut] *n* Schnauze *f*

snow [snou] *n* Schnee *m*; *v* schneien

snowstorm ['snoustɔ:m] *n* Schneesturm *m*

snowy ['snoui] *adj* schneebedeckt

so [sou] *conj* also; *adv* so; dermaßen; **and ~ on** und so weiter; ~ **far** bisher; ~ **that** so daß, damit

soak [souk] *v* einweichen, weichen, durchnässen

soap [soup] *n* Seife *f*; ~ **powder** Seifenpulver *nt*

sober ['soubə] *adj* nüchtern; besonnen

so-called [,sou'kɔ:ld] *adj* sogenannt

soccer ['sɔkə] *n* Fußball *m*; ~ **team** Elf *f*

social ['souʃəl] *adj* Gesellschafts-, sozial

socialism ['souʃəlizəm] *n* Sozialismus *m*

socialist ['souʃəlist] *adj* sozialistisch; *n* Sozialist *m*

society [sə'saiəti] *n* Gesellschaft *f*; Verein *m*

sock [sɔk] *n* Socke *f*

socket ['sɔkit] *n* Fassung *f*

soda-water ['soudə,wɔ:tə] *n* Selterswasser *nt*, Sodawasser *nt*

sofa ['soufə] *n* Sofa *nt*

soft [sɔft] *adj* weich; ~ **drink** alkoholfreies Getränk

soften ['sɔfən] *v* mildern

soil [sɔil] *n* Erde *f*; Erdboden *m*, Boden *m*

soiled [sɔild] *adj* beschmutzt

sold [sould] *v* (p, pp sell); ~ **out** ausverkauft

solder ['sɔldə] *v* löten

soldering-iron ['sɔldəriŋaiən] *n* Lötkolben *m*

soldier ['souldʒə] *n* Soldat *m*

sole¹ [soul] adj einzig

sole² [soul] n Sohle f; Seezunge f

solely ['soulli] adv ausschließlich

solemn ['sɔləm] adj feierlich

solicitor [sə'lisitə] n Anwalt m

solid ['sɔlid] adj stark, fest; massiv; n Festkörper m

soluble ['sɔljubəl] adj löslich

solution [sə'lu:ʃən] n Lösung f

solve [sɔlv] v lösen

sombre ['sɔmbə] adj düster

some [sʌm] adj einige; pron manche; was; ~ day eines Tages; ~ more etwas mehr; ~ time einmal

somebody ['sʌmbədi] pron jemand

somehow ['sʌmhau] adv irgendwie

someone ['sʌmwʌn] pron jemand

something ['sʌmθiŋ] pron etwas

sometimes ['sʌmtaimz] adv manchmal

somewhat ['sʌmwɔt] adv ziemlich

somewhere ['sʌmwɛə] adv irgendwo

son [sʌn] n Sohn m

song [sɔŋ] n Lied nt

son-in-law ['sʌninlɔ:] n (pl sons-) Schwiegersohn m

soon [su:n] adv in Kürze, bald, alsbald; as ~ as sobald als

sooner ['su:nə] adv lieber

sore [sɔ:] adj schmerzhaft, wund; n wunde Stelle; Geschwür nt; ~ throat Halsschmerzen mpl

sorrow ['sɔrou] n Betrübnis f, Leid nt, Kummer m

sorry ['sɔri] adj bekümmert; sorry! Verzeihung!, Entschuldigung!

sort [sɔ:t] v sortieren, ordnen; n Art f, Sorte f; all sorts of allerlei

soul [soul] n Seele f; Geist m

sound [saund] n Klang m, Schall m; v *klingen, erschallen; adj zuverlässig

soundproof ['saundpru:f] adj schalldicht

soup [su:p] n Suppe f

soup-plate ['su:ppleit] n Suppenteller m

soup-spoon ['su:pspu:n] n Suppenlöffel m

sour [sauə] adj sauer

source [sɔ:s] n Quelle f

south [sauθ] n Süden m; South Pole Südpol m

South Africa [sauθ 'æfrikə] Südafrika

south-east [,sauθ'i:st] n Südosten m

southerly ['sʌðəli] adj südlich

southern ['sʌðən] adj südlich

south-west [,sauθ'west] n Südwesten m

souvenir ['su:vəniə] n Andenken nt

sovereign ['sɔvrin] n Herrscher m

Soviet ['souviət] adj sowjetisch

Soviet Union ['souviət 'ju:njən] Sowjetunion f

*sow [sou] v säen

spa [spa:] n Heilbad nt

space [speis] n Raum m; Abstand m, Zwischenraum m; v in Abständen anordnen

spacious ['speiʃəs] adj geräumig

spade [speid] n Schaufel f, Spaten m

Spain [spein] Spanien

Spaniard ['spænjəd] n Spanier m

Spanish ['spæniʃ] adj spanisch

spanking ['spæŋkiŋ] n Prügel pl

spanner ['spænə] n Schraubenschlüssel m

spare [spɛə] adj Reserve-, überschüssig; v entbehren; ~ part Ersatzteil nt; ~ room Gästezimmer nt; ~ time Freizeit f; ~ tyre Ersatzreifen m; ~ wheel Reserverad nt

spark [spa:k] n Funken m

sparking-plug ['spa:kiŋplʌg] n Zündkerze f

sparkling ['spa:kliŋ] adj funkelnd; perlend

sparrow ['spærou] n Sperling m

*speak [spi:k] v *sprechen

spear [spiə] n Speer m

special ['speʃəl] adj besonder, speziell; ~ delivery Eilpost

specialist ['speʃəlist] n Spezialist m

speciality [ˌspeʃi'æləti] n Spezialität f

specialize ['speʃəlaiz] v sich spezialisieren

specially ['speʃəli] adv im einzelnen

species ['spi:ʃi:z] n (pl ~) Art f

specific [spə'sifik] adj spezifisch

specimen ['spesimən] n Exemplar nt

speck [spek] n Fleck m

spectacle ['spektəkəl] n Schauspiel nt; spectacles Brille f

spectator [spek'teitə] n Zuschauer m

speculate ['spekjuleit] v spekulieren

speech [spi:tʃ] n Sprache f; Ansprache f, Rede f

speechless ['spi:tʃləs] adj sprachlos

speed [spi:d] n Geschwindigkeit f; Schnelligkeit f, Eile f; cruising ~ Reisegeschwindigkeit f; ~ limit Höchstgeschwindigkeit f, Geschwindigkeitsbegrenzung f

* speed [spi:d] v rasen; zu schnell *fahren

speeding ['spi:diŋ] n Geschwindigkeitsübertretung f

speedometer [spi:'dɔmitə] n Geschwindigkeitsmesser m

spell [spel] n Zauber m

* spell [spel] v buchstabieren

spelling ['speliŋ] n Rechtschreibung f

* spend [spend] v verausgaben, *ausgeben; *verbringen

sphere [sfiə] n Kugel f; Kreis m

spice [spais] n Gewürz nt

spiced [spaist] adj gewürzt

spicy ['spaisi] adj pikant

spider ['spaidə] n Spinne f; spider's web Spinnwebe f

* spill [spil] v verschütten

* spin [spin] v *spinnen; wirbeln

spinach ['spinidʒ] n Spinat m

spine [spain] n Rückgrat nt

spinster ['spinstə] n alte Jungfer

spire [spaiə] n Spitze f

spirit ['spirit] n Geist m; Laune f; spirits alkoholische Getränke, Spirituosen pl; Stimmung f; ~ stove Spirituskocher m

spiritual ['spiritʃuəl] adj geistig

spit [spit] n Speichel m, Spucke f; Bratspieß m

* spit [spit] v spucken

in spite of [in spait ɔv] ungeachtet, trotz

spiteful ['spaitfəl] adj gehässig

splash [splæʃ] v bespritzen

splendid ['splendid] adj prächtig, herrlich

splendour ['splendə] n Pracht f

splint [splint] n Schiene f

splinter ['splintə] n Splitter m

* split [split] v spalten

* spoil [spɔil] v *verderben; verwöhnen

spoke¹ [spouk] v (p speak)

spoke² [spouk] n Speiche f

sponge [spʌndʒ] n Schwamm m

spook [spu:k] n Gespenst nt, Geist m

spool [spu:l] n Spule f

spoon [spu:n] n Löffel m

spoonful ['spu:nful] n Löffel voll

sport [spɔ:t] n Sport m

sports-car ['spɔ:tska:] n Sportwagen m

sports-jacket ['spɔ:ts,dʒækit] n Sportjacke f

sportsman ['spɔ:tsmən] n (pl -men) Sportler m

sportswear ['spɔ:tsweə] n Sportkleidung f

spot [spɔt] n Klecks m, Fleck m; Stelle f, Platz m

spotless ['spɔtləs] adj fleckenlos

spotlight ['spɔtlait] n Scheinwerfer m

spotted ['spɔtid] adj gesprenkelt

spout [spaut] n Strahl m

sprain [sprein] v verstauchen; n Verstauchung f

* **spread** [spred] v ausbreiten

spring [spriŋ] n Lenz m, Frühling m; Feder f; Quelle f

springtime ['spriŋtaim] n Frühling m

sprouts [sprauts] pl Rosenkohl m

spy [spai] n Spion m

squadron ['skwɔdrən] n Geschwader nt

square [skwɛə] adj quadratisch; n Quadrat nt; Platz m

squash [skwɔʃ] n Fruchtsaft m

squirrel ['skwirəl] n Eichhörnchen nt

squirt [skwə:t] n Strahl m

stable ['steibəl] adj stabil; n Stall m

stack [stæk] n Stapel m

stadium ['steidiəm] n Stadion nt

staff [stɑ:f] n Personal nt

stage [steidʒ] n Bühne f; Phase f, Stadium nt; Etappe f

stain [stein] v beflecken; n Klecks m, Fleck m; **stained glass** buntes Glas; ~ **remover** Fleckenreinigungsmittel nt

stainless ['steinləs] adj fleckenlos; ~ **steel** nichtrostender Stahl

staircase ['stɛəkeis] n Treppe f

stairs [stɛəz] pl Treppe f

stale [steil] adj altbacken

stall [stɔ:l] n Stand m; Sperrsitz m

stamina ['stæminə] n Widerstandsfähigkeit f

stamp [stæmp] n Briefmarke f; Stempel m; v frankieren; stampfen; ~ **machine** Markenautomat m

stand [stænd] n Stand m; Tribüne f

* **stand** [stænd] v *stehen

standard ['stændəd] n Norm f, Maßstab m; Standard-; ~ **of living** Lebensstandard m

stanza ['stænzə] n Strophe f

staple ['steipəl] n Heftklammer f

star [stɑ:] n Stern m

starboard ['stɑ:bəd] n Steuerbord nt

starch [stɑ:tʃ] n Stärke f; v stärken

stare [stɛə] v starren

starling ['stɑ:liŋ] n Star m

start [stɑ:t] v *anfangen; n Anfang m; **starter motor** Anlasser m

starting-point ['stɑ:tiŋpɔint] n Ausgangspunkt m

state [steit] n Staat m; Zustand m; v darlegen

the States Vereinigte Staaten

statement ['steitmənt] n Erklärung f

statesman ['steitsmən] n (pl -men) Staatsmann m

station ['steiʃən] n Bahnhof m; Stelle f

stationary ['steiʃənəri] adj stillstehend

stationer's ['steiʃənəz] n Schreibwarenhandlung f

stationery ['steiʃənəri] n Schreibwaren fpl

station-master ['steiʃən,mɑ:stə] n Stationsvorsteher m

statistics [stə'tistiks] pl Statistik f

statue ['stætʃu:] n Standbild nt

stay [stei] v *bleiben; verweilen, sich *aufhalten; n Aufenthalt m

steadfast ['stedfɑ:st] adj standhaft

steady ['stedi] adj beständig

steak [steik] n Steak nt

* **steal** [sti:l] v *stehlen

steam [sti:m] n Dampf m

steamer ['sti:mə] n Dampfer m

steel [sti:l] n Stahl m

steep [sti:p] adj schroff, steil

steeple ['sti:pəl] n Kirchturm m

steering-column ['stiəriŋ,kɔləm] n Lenksäule f

steering-wheel ['stiəriŋwi:l] n Steuerrad nt

steersman ['stiəzmən] n (pl -men) Steuermann m

stem [stem] n Stiel m

stenographer [ste'nɔgrəfə] n Stenograph *m*

step [step] *n* Schritt *m*, Tritt *m*; Stufe *f*; *v* *treten

stepchild ['steptʃaild] *n* (pl -children) Stiefkind *nt*

stepfather ['step,fa:ðə] *n* Stiefvater *m*

stepmother ['step,mʌðə] *n* Stiefmutter *f*

sterile ['sterail] *adj* steril

sterilize ['sterilaiz] *v* sterilisieren

steward ['stju:əd] *n* Steward *m*

stewardess ['stju:ədes] *n* Stewardeß *f*

stick [stik] *n* Stock *m*

*** stick** [stik] *v* kleben, ankleben

sticky ['stiki] *adj* klebrig

stiff [stif] *adj* steif

still [stil] *adv* noch; dennoch; *adj* still

stillness ['stilnəs] *n* Stille *f*

stimulant ['stimjulənt] *n* Reizmittel *nt*

stimulate ['stimjuleit] *v* anspornen

sting [stiŋ] *n* Stich *m*

*** sting** [stiŋ] *v* *stechen

stingy ['stindʒi] *adj* kleinlich

*** stink** [stiŋk] *v* *stinken

stipulate ['stipjuleit] *v* abmachen, festsetzen

stipulation [,stipju'leifən] *n* Klausel *f*

stir [stə:] *v* bewegen; rühren

stirrup ['stirəp] *n* Steigbügel *m*

stitch [stitʃ] *n* Stich *m*, Stechen *nt*

stock [stɔk] *n* Vorrat *m*; *v* vorrätig *haben; ~ exchange Effektenbörse *f*, Börse *f*; ~ market Börse *f*; stocks and shares Aktien

stocking ['stɔkiŋ] *n* Strumpf *m*

stole¹ [stoul] *v* (p steal)

stole² [stoul] *n* Stola *f*

stomach ['stʌmək] *n* Magen *m*

stomach-ache ['stʌməkeik] *n* Bauchschmerzen *mpl*, Magenschmerzen *mpl*

stone [stoun] *n* Stein *m*; Edelstein *m*; Kern *m*; steinern; **pumice ~** Bimsstein *m*

stood [stud] *v* (p, pp stand)

stop [stɔp] *v* aufhören; aufhören mit, einstellen; *n* Haltestelle *f*; **stop!** halt!

stopper ['stɔpə] *n* Stöpsel *m*

storage ['stɔ:ridʒ] *n* Lagerung *f*

store [stɔ:] *n* Vorrat *m*; Laden *m*; *v* lagern

store-house ['stɔ:haus] *n* Lagerhaus *nt*

storey ['stɔ:ri] *n* Etage *f*, Stockwerk *nt*

stork [stɔ:k] *n* Storch *m*

storm [stɔ:m] *n* Sturm *m*

stormy ['stɔ:mi] *adj* stürmisch

story ['stɔ:ri] *n* Geschichte *f*

stout [staut] *adj* dick, stämmig, korpulent

stove [stouv] *n* Ofen *m*; Herd *m*

straight [streit] *adj* gerade; ehrlich; *adv* geradewegs; ~ **ahead** geradeaus; ~ **away** sofort; ~ **on** geradeaus

strain [strein] *n* Anstrengung *f*; Anspannung *f*; *v* forcieren; sieben

strainer ['streinə] *n* Durchschlag *m*

strange [streindʒ] *adj* fremd; komisch

stranger ['streindʒə] *n* Fremde *m*; Unbekannte *m*

strangle ['stræŋgəl] *v* erwürgen

strap [stræp] *n* Riemen *m*

straw [strɔ:] *n* Stroh *nt*

strawberry ['strɔ:bəri] *n* Erdbeere *f*

stream [stri:m] *n* Bach *m*; Wasserlauf *m*; *v* strömen

street [stri:t] *n* Straße *f*

streetcar ['stri:tka:] *nAm* Straßenbahn *f*

street-organ ['stri:,tɔ:gən] *n* Leierkasten *m*

strength [streŋθ] *n* Stärke *f*, Kraft *f*

stress [stres] *n* Spannung *f*; Betonung *f*; *v* betonen

stretch [stretʃ] *v* dehnen; *n* Strecke *f*

strict [strikt] *adj* streng

strife [straif] *n* Streit *m*

strike [straik] n Streik m

*strike [straik] v *schlagen; *zuschlagen; *auffallen; streiken; *streichen

striking ['straikiŋ] adj treffend, erstaunlich, auffallend

string [striŋ] n Schnur f; Saite f

strip [strip] n Streifen m

stripe [straip] n Streifen m

striped [straipt] adj gestreift

stroke [strouk] n Schlaganfall m

stroll [stroul] v bummeln; n Bummel m

strong [strɔŋ] adj stark; kräftig

stronghold ['strɔŋhould] n Burg f

structure ['strʌktʃə] n Struktur f

struggle ['strʌgəl] n Kampf m, Ringen nt; v *ringen, kämpfen

stub [stʌb] n Kontrollabschnitt m

stubborn ['stʌbən] adj hartnäckig

student ['stju:dənt] n Student m; Studentin f

study ['stʌdi] v studieren; n Studium nt; Arbeitszimmer nt

stuff [stʌf] n Stoff m; Zeug nt

stuffed [stʌft] adj gefüllt

stuffing ['stʌfiŋ] n Füllung f

stuffy ['stʌfi] adj stickig

stumble ['stʌmbəl] v stolpern

stung [stʌŋ] v (p, pp sting)

stupid ['stju:pid] adj dumm

style [stail] n Stil m

subject[1] ['sʌbdʒikt] n Subjekt nt; Staatsangehörige m; ~ to ausgesetzt

subject[2] [səb'dʒekt] v *unterwerfen

submit [səb'mit] v sich *unterwerfen

subordinate [sə'bɔ:dinət] adj Unter-; untergeordnet

subscriber [səb'skraibə] n Abonnent m

subscription [səb'skripʃən] n Abonnement nt

subsequent ['sʌbsikwənt] adj folgend

subsidy ['sʌbsidi] n Subvention f

substance ['sʌbstəns] n Substanz f

substantial [səb'stænʃəl] adj sachlich; wirklich; bedeutend

substitute ['sʌbstitju:t] v ersetzen; n Ersatz m; Stellvertreter m

subtitle ['sʌb,taitəl] n Untertitel m

subtle ['sʌtəl] adj subtil

subtract [səb'trækt] v subtrahieren

suburb ['sʌbə:b] n Vorort m, Vorstadt f

suburban [sə'bə:bən] adj vorstädtisch

subway ['sʌbwei] nAm Untergrundbahn f

succeed [sək'si:d] v *gelingen; nachfolgen

success [sək'ses] n Erfolg m

successful [sək'sesfəl] adj erfolgreich

succumb [sə'kʌm] v *erliegen

such [sʌtʃ] adj solch; adv so; ~ as wie

suck [sʌk] v lutschen

sudden ['sʌdən] adj plötzlich

suddenly ['sʌdənli] adv plötzlich

suede [sweid] n Wildleder nt

suffer ['sʌfə] v *leiden; *erleiden

suffering ['sʌfəriŋ] n Leiden nt

suffice [sə'fais] v reichen

sufficient [sə'fiʃənt] adj hinreichend, genügend

suffrage ['sʌfridʒ] n Wahlrecht nt

sugar ['ʃugə] n Zucker m

suggest [sə'dʒest] v *vorschlagen

suggestion [sə'dʒestʃən] n Vorschlag m

suicide ['su:isaid] n Selbstmord m

suit [su:t] v passen; anpassen an; kleiden; n Anzug m

suitable ['su:təbəl] adj angemessen, geeignet

suitcase ['su:tkeis] n Handkoffer m

suite [swi:t] n Zimmerflucht f

sum [sʌm] n Summe f

summary ['sʌməri] n Zusammenfassung f

summer ['sʌmə] n Sommer m; ~ **time** Sommerzeit f

summit ['sʌmit] n Gipfel m

summons ['sʌmənz] n (pl ~es) Vorladung f

sun [sʌn] n Sonne f

sunbathe ['sʌnbeið] v sich sonnen

sunburn ['sʌnbə:n] n Sonnenbrand m

Sunday ['sʌndi] Sonntag m

sun-glasses ['sʌn,glɑ:siz] pl Sonnenbrille f

sunlight ['sʌnlait] n Sonnenlicht nt

sunny ['sʌni] adj sonnig

sunrise ['sʌnraiz] n Sonnenaufgang m

sunset ['sʌnset] n Sonnenuntergang m

sunshade ['sʌnʃeid] n Sonnenschirm m

sunshine ['sʌnʃain] n Sonnenschein m

sunstroke ['sʌnstrouk] n Sonnenstich m

suntan oil ['sʌntænɔil] Sonnenöl nt

superb [su'pə:b] adj großartig, prächtig

superficial [,su:pə'fiʃəl] adj oberflächlich

superfluous [su'pə:fluəs] adj überflüssig

superior [su'piəriə] adj überlegen, besser, überragend, ober

superlative [su'pə:lətiv] adj überragend; n Superlativ m

supermarket ['su:pə,ma:kit] n Supermarkt m

superstition [,su:pə'stiʃən] n Aberglaube m

supervise ['su:pəvaiz] v beaufsichtigen

supervision [,su:pə'viʒən] n Kontrolle f, Aufsicht f

supervisor ['su:pəvaizə] n Aufseher m

supper ['sʌpə] n Abendessen nt

supple ['sʌpəl] adj biegsam, geschmeidig, gelenkig

supplement ['sʌplimənt] n Beilage f

supply [sə'plai] n Zufuhr f, Lieferung f; Vorrat m; Angebot nt; v liefern

support [sə'pɔ:t] v unterstützen, stützen; n Unterstützung f; ~ **hose** elastische Strümpfe

supporter [sə'pɔ:tə] n Anhänger m

suppose [sə'pouz] v vermuten, *annehmen; **supposing that** angenommen daß

suppository [sə'pɔzitəri] n Zäpfchen nt

suppress [sə'pres] v unterdrücken

surcharge ['sə:tʃa:dʒ] n Zuschlag m

sure [ʃuə] adj sicher

surely ['ʃuəli] adv sicherlich

surface ['sə:fis] n Oberfläche f

surf-board ['sə:fbɔ:d] n Wellenreiterbrett nt

surgeon ['sə:dʒən] n Chirurg m; **veterinary** ~ Tierarzt m

surgery ['sə:dʒəri] n Operation f; Sprechzimmer nt

surname ['sə:neim] n Familienname m

surplus ['sə:pləs] n Überschuß m

surprise [sə'praiz] n Überraschung f; v überraschen; erstaunen

surrender [sə'rendə] v sich *ergeben; n Übergabe f

surround [sə'raund] v umringen, *umgeben

surrounding [sə'raundiŋ] adj umliegend

surroundings [sə'raundiŋz] pl Umgebung f

survey ['sə:vei] n Übersicht f

survival [sə'vaivəl] n Überleben nt

survive [sə'vaiv] v überleben

suspect[1] [sə'spekt] v verdächtigen; vermuten

suspect[2] ['sʌspekt] n Verdächtige m

suspend [sə'spend] v suspendieren

suspenders [sə'spendəz] plAm Hosenträger mpl; **suspender belt** Hüfthalter m

suspension [sə'spenʃən] n Federung f,

Aufhängung *f*; ~ **bridge** Hängebrücke *f*

suspicion [sə'spiʃən] *n* Verdacht *m*;
Argwohn *m*, Mißtrauen *nt*

suspicious [sə'spiʃəs] *adj* verdächtig;
argwöhnisch, mißtrauisch

sustain [sə'stein] *v* *aushalten

Swahili [swɑ'hi:li] *n* Suaheli *nt*

swallow ['swɔlou] *v* *verschlingen,
schlucken; *n* Schwalbe *f*

swam [swæm] *v* (p swim)

swamp [swɔmp] *n* Morast *m*

swan [swɔn] *n* Schwan *m*

swap [swɔp] *v* tauschen

*** swear** [sweə] *v* *schwören; fluchen

sweat [swet] *n* Schweiß *m*; *v* schwitzen

sweater ['swetə] *n* Sweater *m*

Swede [swi:d] *n* Schwede *m*

Sweden ['swi:dən] Schweden

Swedish ['swi:diʃ] *adj* schwedisch

*** sweep** [swi:p] *v* fegen

sweet [swi:t] *adj* süß; lieb; *n* Bonbon
m; Nachtisch *m*; **sweets** Süßigkeiten *fpl*

sweeten ['swi:tən] *v* süßen

sweetheart ['swi:thɑ:t] *n* Schatz *m*,
Liebling *m*

sweetshop ['swi:tʃɔp] *n* Süßwarengeschäft *nt*

swell [swel] *adj* wunderbar

*** swell** [swel] *v* *schwellen

swelling ['sweliŋ] *n* Geschwulst *f*

swift [swift] *adj* geschwind

*** swim** [swim] *v* *schwimmen

swimmer ['swimə] *n* Schwimmer *m*

swimming ['swimiŋ] *n* Schwimmsport
m; ~ **pool** Schwimmbad *nt*

swimming-trunks ['swimiŋtrʌŋks] *n*
Badehose *f*

swim-suit ['swimsu:t] *n* Badeanzug *m*

swindle ['swindəl] *v* *betrügen; *n* Betrug *m*

swindler ['swindlə] *n* Betrüger *m*

swing [swiŋ] *n* Schaukel *f*

*** swing** [swiŋ] *v* schaukeln

Swiss [swis] *adj* schweizerisch; *n*
Schweizer *m*

switch [switʃ] *n* Schalter *m*; *v* wechseln; ~ **off** ausschalten; ~ **on** einschalten

switchboard ['switʃbɔ:d] *n* Schaltbrett
nt

Switzerland ['switsələnd] Schweiz *f*

sword [sɔ:d] *n* Schwert *nt*

swum [swʌm] *v* (pp swim)

syllable ['siləbəl] *n* Silbe *f*

symbol ['simbəl] *n* Symbol *nt*

sympathetic [,simpə'θetik] *adj* sympathisch, mitfühlend

sympathy ['simpəθi] *n* Sympathie *f*;
Mitgefühl *nt*

symphony ['simfəni] *n* Symphonie *f*

symptom ['simtəm] *n* Symptom *nt*

synagogue ['sinəgɔg] *n* Synagoge *f*

synonym ['sinənim] *n* Synonym *nt*

synthetic [sin'θetik] *adj* synthetisch

syphon ['saifən] *n* Siphon *m*

Syria ['siriə] Syrien

Syrian ['siriən] *adj* syrisch; *n* Syrer *m*

syringe [si'rindʒ] *n* Spritze *f*

syrup ['sirəp] *n* Sirup *m*

system ['sistəm] *n* System *nt*; Ordnung *f*; **decimal** ~ Dezimalsystem
nt

systematic [,sistə'mætik] *adj* systematisch

T

table ['teibəl] *n* Tisch *m*; Tabelle *f*; ~
of contents Inhaltsverzeichnis *nt*;
~ **tennis** Tischtennis *n*

table-cloth ['teibəlklɔθ] *n* Tischtuch *nt*

tablespoon ['teibəlspu:n] *n* Eßlöffel *m*

tablet ['tæblit] *n* Tablette *f*

taboo [tə'buː] n Tabu nt
tactics ['tæktiks] pl Taktik f
tag [tæg] n Etikett nt
tail [teil] n Schwanz m
tail-light ['teillait] n Rücklicht nt
tailor ['teilə] n Schneider m
tailor-made ['teiləmeid] adj nach Maß
*take [teik] v *nehmen; *greifen;
*bringen; *verstehen, kapieren; ~
away entfernen; *abnehmen, *wegnehmen; ~ off starten; ~ out *herausnehmen; ~ over *übernehmen;
~ place *stattfinden; ~ up *einnehmen
take-off ['teikɔf] n Start m
tale [teil] n Geschichte f, Erzählung f
talent ['tælənt] n Begabung f, Talent
nt
talented ['tæləntid] adj begabt
talk [tɔːk] v reden, *sprechen; n Gespräch nt
talkative ['tɔːkətiv] adj gesprächig
tall [tɔːl] adj hoch; lang, groß
tame [teim] adj zahm; v zähmen
tampon ['tæmpən] n Tampon m
tangerine [,tændʒə'riːn] n Mandarine f
tangible ['tændʒibəl] adj greifbar
tank [tæŋk] n Tank m
tanker ['tæŋkə] n Tankschiff nt
tanned [tænd] adj braun
tap [tæp] n Hahn m; Klopfen nt; v
pochen
tape [teip] n Band nt; Kordel f; adhesive ~ Klebestreifen m; Heftpflaster nt
tape-measure ['teip,meʒə] n Bandmaß
nt
tape-recorder ['teipri,kɔːdə] n Tonbandgerät nt
tapestry ['tæpistri] n Wandteppich m,
Gobelin m
tar [taː] n Teer m
target ['taːgit] n Ziel nt, Zielscheibe f
tariff ['tærif] n Tarif m

tarpaulin [taː'pɔːlin] n Plane f
task [taːsk] n Aufgabe f
taste [teist] n Geschmack m; v
schmecken; kosten
tasteless ['teistləs] adj geschmacklos
tasty ['teisti] adj lecker, schmackhaft
taught [tɔːt] v (p, pp teach)
tavern ['tævən] n Schenke f
tax [tæks] n Steuer f; v besteuern
taxation [tæk'seiʃən] n Besteuerung f
tax-free ['tæksfriː] adj steuerfrei
taxi ['tæksi] n Taxi nt; ~ rank Taxistand m; ~ stand Am Taxistand m
taxi-driver ['tæksi,draivə] n Taxichauffeur m
taxi-meter ['tæksi,miːtə] n Taxameter
m
tea [tiː] n Tee m; Teestunde f
*teach [tiːtʃ] v lehren, unterrichten
teacher ['tiːtʃə] n Lehrer m; Lehrerin
f; Volksschullehrer m, Schullehrer
m
teachings ['tiːtʃiŋz] pl Lehre f
tea-cloth ['tiːklɔθ] n Geschirrtuch nt
teacup ['tiːkʌp] n Teetasse f
team [tiːm] n Team nt, Mannschaft f
teapot ['tiːpɔt] n Teekanne f
tear¹ [tiə] n Träne f
tear² [tɛə] n Riß m; *tear v *reißen
tear-jerker ['tiə,dʒəːkə] n Schmalz m
tease [tiːz] v necken
tea-set ['tiːset] n Teeservice nt
tea-shop ['tiːʃɔp] n Teestube f
teaspoon ['tiːspuːn] n Teelöffel m
teaspoonful ['tiːspuːn,ful] n Teelöffel
voll m
technical ['teknikəl] adj technisch
technician [tek'niʃən] n Techniker m
technique [tek'niːk] n Technik f
technology [tek'nɔlədʒi] n Technologie
f
teenager ['tiː,neidʒə] n Teenager m
teetotaller [tiː'toutələ] n Abstinenzler
m

telegram ['teligræm] n Telegramm nt

telegraph ['teligra:f] v telegraphieren

telepathy [ti'lepəθi] n Telepathie f

telephone ['telifoun] n Telephon nt; ~ book Am Fernsprechverzeichnis nt, Telephonbuch nt; ~ booth Fernsprechzelle f; ~ call Anruf m, Telephonanruf m; ~ directory Telephonbuch nt; ~ exchange Telephonzentrale f; ~ operator Telephonistin f

telephonist [ti'lefənist] n Telephonistin f

television ['telivi3ən] n Fernsehen nt; ~ set Fernsehgerät nt

telex ['teleks] n Telex nt

*tell [tel] v sagen; erzählen

temper ['tempə] n Wut f

temperature ['temprətʃə] n Temperatur f

tempest ['tempist] n Unwetter nt

temple ['tempəl] n Tempel m; Schläfe f

temporary ['tempərəri] adj vorläufig, zeitweilig

tempt [tempt] v versuchen

temptation [temp'teiʃən] n Versuchung f

ten [ten] num zehn

tenant ['tenənt] n Mieter m

tend [tend] v neigen; pflegen; ~ to neigen zu

tendency ['tendənsi] n Neigung f, Tendenz f

tender ['tendə] adj zärtlich, zart

tendon ['tendən] n Sehne f

tennis ['tenis] n Tennis nt; ~ shoes Tennisschuhe mpl

tennis-court ['teniskɔ:t] n Tennisplatz m

tense [tens] adj gespannt

tension ['tenʃən] n Spannung f

tent [tent] n Zelt nt

tenth [tenθ] num zehnte

tepid ['tepid] adj lauwarm

term [tə:m] n Ausdruck m; Termin m, Frist f; Bedingung f

terminal ['tə:minəl] n Endstation f

terrace ['terəs] n Terrasse f

terrain [te'rein] n Gelände nt

terrible ['teribəl] adj abscheulich, furchtbar, schrecklich

terrific [tə'rifik] adj großartig

terrify ['terifai] v *erschrecken; terrifying furchterregend

territory ['teritəri] n Gebiet nt

terror ['terə] n Furcht f

terrorism ['terərizəm] n Terrorismus m, Terror m

terrorist ['terərist] n Terrorist m

terylene ['terəli:n] n Terylene nt

test [test] n Probe f, Test m; v testen, prüfen

testify ['testifai] v bezeugen

text [tekst] n Text m

textbook ['teksbuk] n Lehrbuch nt

textile ['tekstail] n Textilien pl

texture ['tekstʃə] n Struktur f

Thai [tai] adj thailändisch; n Thailänder m

Thailand ['tailænd] Thailand

than [ðæn] conj als

thank [θæŋk] v danken; ~ you danke schön

thankful ['θæŋkfəl] adj dankbar

that [ðæt] adj jener; pron das; der; conj daß

thaw [θɔ:] v tauen, auftauen; n Tauwetter nt

the [ðə,ði] art der art; the ... the je ...je

theatre ['θiətə] n Schauspielhaus nt, Theater nt

theft [θeft] n Diebstahl m

their [ðeə] adj ihr

them [ðem] pron sie; ihnen

theme [θi:m] n Thema nt, Stoff m

themselves [ðəm'selvz] pron sich;

selbst

then [ðen] *adv* damals; darauf, dann

theology [θiˈɔlədʒi] *n* Theologie *f*

theoretical [θiəˈretikəl] *adj* theoretisch

theory [ˈθiəri] *n* Theorie *f*

therapy [ˈθerəpi] *n* Therapie *f*

there [ðeə] *adv* dort; dorthin

therefore [ˈðeəfɔː] *conj* darum

thermometer [θəˈmɔmitə] *n* Thermometer *nt*

thermostat [ˈθəːmɔstæt] *n* Thermostat *m*

these [ðiːz] *adj* diese

thesis [ˈθiːsis] *n* (pl theses) These *f*

they [ðei] *pron* sie

thick [θik] *adj* dick; dicht

thicken [ˈθikən] *v* verdicken

thickness [ˈθiknəs] *n* Dicke *f*

thief [θiːf] *n* (pl thieves) Dieb *m*

thigh [θai] *n* Oberschenkel *m*

thimble [ˈθimbəl] *n* Fingerhut *m*

thin [θin] *adj* dünn; mager

thing [θiŋ] *n* Ding *nt*

***think** [θiŋk] *v* *denken; *nachdenken; ~ **of** *denken an; ~ **over** überlegen

thinker [ˈθiŋkə] *n* Denker *m*

third [θəːd] *num* dritte

thirst [θəːst] *n* Durst *m*

thirsty [ˈθəːsti] *adj* durstig

thirteen [ˌθəːˈtiːn] *num* dreizehn

thirteenth [ˌθəːˈtiːnθ] *num* dreizehnte

thirtieth [ˈθəːtiəθ] *num* dreißigste

thirty [ˈθəːti] *num* dreißig

this [ðis] *adj* dieser; *pron* dies

thistle [ˈθisəl] *n* Distel *f*

thorn [θɔːn] *n* Dorn *m*

thorough [ˈθʌrə] *adj* gründlich, sorgfältig

thoroughbred [ˈθʌrəbred] *adj* vollblütig

thoroughfare [ˈθʌrəfeə] *n* Durchgangsstraße *f*, Hauptverkehrsstraße *f*

those [ðouz] *adj* jene

though [ðou] *conj* obwohl, wenn auch, obgleich; *adv* jedoch

thought¹ [θɔːt] *v* (p, pp think)

thought² [θɔːt] *n* Gedanke *m*

thoughtful [ˈθɔːtfəl] *adj* nachdenklich; zuvorkommend

thousand [ˈθauzənd] *num* tausend

thread [θred] *n* Faden *m*; Zwirn *m*; *v* aufreihen

threadbare [ˈθredbeə] *adj* verschlissen

threat [θret] *n* Drohung *f*, Bedrohung *f*

threaten [ˈθretən] *v* drohen, bedrohen; **threatening** bedrohlich

three [θriː] *num* drei

three-quarter [ˌθriːˈkwɔːtə] *adj* dreiviertel

threshold [ˈθreʃould] *n* Schwelle *f*

threw [θruː] *v* (p throw)

thrifty [ˈθrifti] *adj* sparsam

throat [θrout] *n* Kehle *f*; Hals *m*

throne [θroun] *n* Thron *m*

through [θruː] *prep* durch

throughout [θruːˈaut] *adv* überall

throw [θrou] *n* Wurf *m*

***throw** [θrou] *v* schleudern, *werfen

thrush [θrʌʃ] *n* Drossel *f*

thumb [θʌm] *n* Daumen *m*

thumbtack [ˈθʌmtæk] *nAm* Reißnagel *m*

thump [θʌmp] *v* *schlagen

thunder [ˈθʌndə] *n* Donner *m*; *v* donnern

thunderstorm [ˈθʌndəstɔːm] *n* Gewitter *nt*

thundery [ˈθʌndəri] *adj* gewitterschwül

Thursday [ˈθəːzdi] Donnerstag *m*

thus [ðʌs] *adv* so

thyme [taim] *n* Thymian *m*

tick [tik] *n* Vermerkhäkchen *nt*; ~ **off** anhaken

ticket [ˈtikit] *n* Karte *f*; Anzeige *f*; ~ **collector** Schaffner *m*; ~ **machine**

Fahrkartenautomat *m*

tickle ['tikəl] *v* kitzeln

tide [taid] *n* Tide *f*; **high ~** Flut *f*; **low ~** Ebbe *f*

tidings ['taidiŋz] *pl* Nachrichten

tidy ['taidi] *adj* ordentlich; **~ up** aufräumen

tie [tai] *v* knoten, *binden; *n* Krawatte *f*

tiger ['taigə] *n* Tiger *m*

tight [tait] *adj* stramm; eng, knapp; *adv* fest

tighten ['taitən] *v* *zusammenziehen, straffen, spannen; enger machen; enger *werden

tights [taits] *pl* Trikot *nt*

tile [tail] *n* Kachel *f*; Dachziegel *m*

till [til] *prep* bis zu, bis; *conj* bis

timber ['timbə] *n* Bauholz *nt*

time [taim] *n* Zeit *f*; Mal *nt*; **all the ~** immerzu; **in ~** rechtzeitig; **~ of arrival** Ankunftszeit *f*; **~ of departure** Abfahrtszeit *f*

time-saving ['taim,seiviŋ] *adj* zeitsparend

timetable ['taim,teibəl] *n* Fahrplan *m*

timid ['timid] *adj* schüchtern

timidity [ti'midəti] *n* Schüchternheit *f*

tin [tin] *n* Zinn *nt*; Büchse *f*; **tinned food** Konserven *fpl*

tinfoil ['tinfɔil] *n* Stanniol *nt*

tin-opener ['ti,noupənə] *n* Dosenöffner *m*

tiny ['taini] *adj* winzig

tip [tip] *n* Spitze *f*; Trinkgeld *nt*

tire[1] [taiə] *n* Reifen *m*

tire[2] [taiə] *v* ermüden

tired [taiəd] *adj* erschöpft, müde; **~ of** überdrüssig

tiring ['taiəriŋ] *adj* ermüdend

tissue ['tiʃuː] *n* Gewebe *nt*; Papiertaschentuch *nt*

title ['taitəl] *n* Titel *m*

to [tuː] *prep* bis; zu, vor, nach; um zu

toad [toud] *n* Kröte *f*

toadstool ['toudstuːl] *n* Pilz *m*

toast [toust] *n* Toast *m*; Trinkspruch *m*

tobacco [tə'bækou] *n* (pl ~s) Tabak *m*; **~ pouch** Tabaksbeutel *m*

tobacconist [tə'bækənist] *n* Tabakhändler *m*; **tobacconist's** Tabakladen *m*

today [tə'dei] *adv* heute

toddler ['tɔdlə] *n* Kleinkind *nt*

toe [tou] *n* Zehe *f*

toffee ['tɔfi] *n* Sahnebonbon *nt*

together [tə'geðə] *adv* zusammen

toilet ['tɔilət] *n* Toilette *f*; **~ case** Toilettennecessaire *nt*

toilet-paper ['tɔilət,peipə] *n* Toilettenpapier *nt*

toiletry ['tɔilətri] *n* Toilettenartikel *mpl*

token ['toukən] *n* Zeichen *nt*; Beweis *m*; Münze *f*

told [tould] *v* (p, pp tell)

tolerable ['tɔlərəbəl] *adj* erträglich

toll [toul] *n* Wegegeld *nt*

tomato [tə'maːtou] *n* (pl ~es) Tomate *f*

tomb [tuːm] *n* Grab *nt*

tombstone ['tuːmstoun] *n* Grabstein *m*

tomorrow [tə'mɔrou] *adv* morgen

ton [tʌn] *n* Tonne *f*

tone [toun] *n* Ton *m*; Klang *m*

tongs [tɔŋz] *pl* Zange *f*

tongue [tʌŋ] *n* Zunge *f*

tonic ['tɔnik] *n* Stärkungsmittel *nt*

tonight [tə'nait] *adv* heute nacht, heute abend

tonsilitis [,tɔnsə'laitis] *n* Mandelentzündung *f*

tonsils ['tɔnsəlz] *pl* Mandeln

too [tuː] *adv* zu; auch

took [tuk] *v* (p take)

tool [tuːl] *n* Gerät *nt*, Werkzeug *nt*;

~ **kit** Werkzeugtasche f
toot [tu:t] vAm hupen
tooth [tu:θ] n (pl teeth) Zahn m
toothache ['tu:θeik] n Zahnweh nt
toothbrush ['tu:θbrʌʃ] n Zahnbürste f
toothpaste ['tu:θpeist] n Zahnpaste f
toothpick ['tu:θpik] n Zahnstocher m
toothpowder ['tu:θ,paudə] n Zahnpulver nt
top [tɔp] n Gipfel m; Spitze f; Deckel m; oberst; **on ~ of** oben auf; ~ **side** Oberseite f
topcoat ['tɔpkout] n Überrock m
topic ['tɔpik] n Thema nt
topical ['tɔpikəl] adj aktuell
torch [tɔ:tʃ] n Fackel f; Taschenlampe f
torment[1] [tɔ:'ment] v quälen
torment[2] ['tɔ:ment] n Qual f
torture ['tɔ:tʃə] n Marter f; v martern
toss [tɔs] v *werfen
tot [tɔt] n kleines Kind
total ['toutəl] adj total; ganz, gänzlich; n Gesamtsumme f
totalitarian [,toutæli'teəriən] adj totalitär
totalizator ['toutəlaizeitə] n Totalisator m
touch [tʌtʃ] v berühren, anrühren; *betreffen; n Kontakt m, Berührung f; Tastsinn m
touching ['tʌtʃiŋ] adj rührend
tough [tʌf] adj zäh
tour [tuə] n Rundreise f
tourism ['tuərizəm] n Fremdenverkehr m
tourist ['tuərist] n Tourist m; ~ **class** Touristenklasse f; ~ **office** Verkehrsverein m
tournament ['tuənəmənt] n Turnier nt
tow [tou] v schleppen
towards [tə'wɔ:dz] prep nach; zu
towel [tauəl] n Handtuch nt
towelling ['tauəliŋ] n Frottierstoff m

tower [tauə] n Turm m
town [taun] n Stadt f; ~ **centre** Stadtzentrum nt; ~ **hall** Rathaus nt
townspeople ['taunz,pi:pəl] pl Städter mpl
toxic ['tɔksik] adj toxisch
toy [tɔi] n Spielzeug nt
toyshop ['tɔiʃɔp] n Spielwarenladen m
trace [treis] n Spur f; v nachspüren
track [træk] n Gleis nt; Bahn f
tractor ['træktə] n Traktor m
trade [treid] n Gewerbe nt, Handel m; Fach nt, Beruf m; v handeln
trademark ['treidma:k] n Schutzmarke f
trader ['treidə] n Händler m
tradesman ['treidzmən] n (pl -men) Geschäftsmann m
trade-union [,treid'ju:njən] n Gewerkschaft f
tradition [trə'diʃən] n Tradition f
traditional [trə'diʃənəl] adj traditionell
traffic ['træfik] n Verkehr m; ~ **jam** Verkehrsstauung f; ~ **light** Verkehrsampel f
trafficator ['træfikeitə] n Winker m
tragedy ['trædʒədi] n Tragödie f
tragic ['trædʒik] adj tragisch
trail [treil] n Fährte f, Pfad m
trailer ['treilə] n Anhänger m; nAm Wohnwagen m
train [trein] n Zug m; v dressieren, ausbilden; **stopping ~** Bummelzug m; **through ~** durchgehender Zug; ~ **ferry** Eisenbahnfähre f
training ['treiniŋ] n Ausbildung f
trait [treit] n Zug m
traitor ['treitə] n Verräter m
tram [træm] n Straßenbahn f
tramp [træmp] n Landstreicher m, Vagabund m; v wandern
tranquil ['træŋkwil] adj ruhig
tranquillizer ['træŋkwilaizə] n Beruhi-

gungsmittel *nt*

transaction [træn'zækʃən] *n* Transaktion *f*

transatlantic [,trænzət'læntik] *adj* transatlantisch

transfer [træns'fɔ:] *v* *übertragen

transform [træns'fɔ:m] *v* verwandeln

transformer [træns'fɔ:mə] *n* Transformator *m*

transition [træn'siʃən] *n* Übergang *m*

translate [træns'leit] *v* übersetzen

translation [træns'leiʃən] *n* Übersetzung *f*

translator [træns'leitə] *n* Übersetzer *m*

transmission [trænz'miʃən] *n* Sendung *f*

transmit [trænz'mit] *v* *senden

transmitter [trænz'mitə] *n* Sender *m*

transparent [træn'speərənt] *adj* durchsichtig

transport¹ ['trænspɔ:t] *n* Beförderung *f*

transport² [træn'spɔ:t] *v* transportieren

transportation [,trænspɔ:'teiʃən] *n* Transport *m*

trap [træp] *n* Falle *f*

trash [træʃ] *n* Müll *m*; ~ **can** *Am* Abfalleimer *m*

travel ['trævəl] *v* reisen; ~ **agency** Reisebüro *nt*; ~ **insurance** Reiseversicherung *f*; **travelling expenses** Reisespesen *pl*

traveller ['trævələ] *n* Reisende *m*; **traveller's cheque** Reisescheck *m*

tray [trei] *n* Tablett *nt*

treason ['tri:zən] *n* Verrat *m*

treasure ['treʒə] *n* Schatz *m*

treasurer ['treʒərə] *n* Zahlmeister *m*

treasury ['treʒəri] *n* Schatzamt *nt*

treat [tri:t] *v* behandeln

treatment ['tri:tmənt] *n* Behandlung *f*

treaty ['tri:ti] *n* Vertrag *m*

tree [tri:] *n* Baum *m*

tremble ['trembəl] *v* zittern; beben

tremendous [tri'mendəs] *adj* ungeheuer

trespass ['trespəs] *v* *eindringen

trespasser ['trespəsə] *n* Eindringling *m*

trial [traiəl] *n* Gerichtsverfahren *nt*; Versuch *m*

triangle ['traiæŋgəl] *n* Dreieck *nt*

triangular [trai'æŋgjulə] *adj* dreieckig

tribe [traib] *n* Stamm *m*

tributary ['tribjutəri] *n* Nebenfluß *m*

tribute ['tribju:t] *n* Huldigung *f*

trick [trik] *n* Kniff *m*; Trick *m*

trigger ['trigə] *n* Abzug *m*

trim [trim] *v* stutzen

trip [trip] *n* Ausflug *m*, Reise *f*

triumph ['traiəmf] *n* Triumph *m*; *v* triumphieren

triumphant [trai'ʌmfənt] *adj* triumphierend

trolley-bus ['trɔlibʌs] *n* Obus *m*

troops [tru:ps] *pl* Truppen *fpl*

tropical ['trɔpikəl] *adj* tropisch

tropics ['trɔpiks] *pl* Tropen *pl*

trouble ['trʌbəl] *n* Sorge *f*, Mühe *f*, Last *f*; *v* bemühen

troublesome ['trʌbəlsəm] *adj* lästig

trousers ['trauzəz] *pl* Hose *f*

trout [traut] *n* (pl ~) Forelle *f*

truck [trʌk] *nAm* Lastwagen *m*

true [tru:] *adj* wahr; wirklich, echt; treu, aufrichtig

trumpet ['trʌmpit] *n* Trompete *f*

trunk [trʌŋk] *n* Koffer *m*; Stamm *m*; *nAm* Kofferraum *m*; **trunks** *pl* Turnhose *f*

trunk-call ['trʌŋkkɔ:l] *n* Ferngespräch *nt*

trust [trʌst] *v* vertrauen; *n* Vertrauen *nt*

trustworthy ['trʌst,wə:ði] *adj* zuverlässig

truth [tru:θ] *n* Wahrheit *f*

truthful ['tru:θfəl] *adj* wahrhaft

try [trai] *v* versuchen; probieren, sich bemühen; *n* Versuch *m*; ~ **on** anprobieren

tube [tju:b] *n* Röhre *f*, Rohr *nt*; Tube *f*

tuberculosis [tju:,bə:kju'lousis] *n* Tuberkulose *f*

Tuesday ['tju:zdi] Dienstag *m*

tug [tʌg] *v* schleppen; *n* Schlepper *m*; Ruck *m*

tuition [tju:'iʃən] *n* Unterricht *m*

tulip ['tju:lip] *n* Tulpe *f*

tumbler ['tʌmblə] *n* Becher *m*

tumour ['tju:mə] *n* Geschwulst *f*, Tumor *m*

tuna ['tju:nə] *n* (pl ~, ~s) Thunfisch *m*

tune [tju:n] *n* Lied *nt*, Melodie *f*; ~ **in** einstellen

tuneful ['tju:nfəl] *adj* melodisch

tunic ['tju:nik] *n* Tunika *f*

Tunisia [tju:'niziə] Tunesien

Tunisian [tju:'niziən] *adj* tunesisch; *n* Tunesier *m*

tunnel ['tʌnəl] *n* Tunnel *m*

turbine ['tə:bain] *n* Turbine *f*

turbojet [,tə:bou'dʒet] *n* Strahlturbine *f*

Turk [tə:k] *n* Türke *m*

Turkey ['tə:ki] Türkei

turkey ['tə:ki] *n* Truthahn *m*

Turkish ['tə:kiʃ] *adj* türkisch; ~ **bath** Schwitzbad *nt*

turn [tə:n] *v* *wenden; kehren, umdrehen; *n* Wendung *f*, Drehung *f*; Biegung *f*; Reihe *f*; ~ **back** umkehren; ~ **down** *verwerfen; ~ **into** sich verwandeln in; ~ **off** abdrehen; ~ **on** einschalten; andrehen; ~ **over** *umwenden; ~ **round** umkehren; sich umdrehen

turning ['tə:niŋ] *n* Kurve *f*

turning-point ['tə:niŋpɔint] *n* Wendepunkt *m*

turnover ['tə:,nouvə] *n* Umsatz *m*; ~ **tax** Umsatzsteuer *f*

turnpike ['tə:npaik] *nAm* gebührenpflichtige Verkehrsstraße

turpentine ['tə:pəntain] *n* Terpentin *nt*

turtle ['tə:təl] *n* Schildkröte *f*

tutor ['tju:tə] *n* Hauslehrer *m*; Vormund *m*

tuxedo [tʌk'si:dou] *nAm* (pl ~s, ~es) Smoking *m*

tweed [twi:d] *n* Tweed *m*

tweezers ['twi:zəz] *pl* Pinzette *f*

twelfth [twelfθ] *num* zwölfte

twelve [twelv] *num* zwölf

twentieth ['twentiəθ] *num* zwanzigste

twenty ['twenti] *num* zwanzig

twice [twais] *adv* zweimal

twig [twig] *n* Zweig *m*

twilight ['twailait] *n* Zwielicht *nt*

twine [twain] *n* Schnur *f*

twins [twinz] *pl* Zwillinge *mpl*; **twin beds** Doppelbett *nt*

twist [twist] *v* *winden; drehen; *n* Drehung *f*

two [tu:] *num* zwei

two-piece [,tu:'pi:s] *adj* zweiteilig

type [taip] *v* tippen, Maschine *schreiben; *n* Typ *m*

typewriter ['taipraitə] *n* Schreibmaschine *f*

typewritten ['taipritən] maschinengeschrieben

typhoid ['taifɔid] *n* Typhus *m*

typical ['tipikəl] *adj* bezeichnend, typisch

typist ['taipist] *n* Stenotypistin *f*

tyrant ['taiərənt] *n* Tyrann *m*

tyre [taiə] *n* Reifen *m*; ~ **pressure** Reifendruck *m*

U

ugly ['ʌgli] *adj* häßlich
ulcer ['ʌlsə] *n* Geschwür *nt*
ultimate ['ʌltimət] *adj* letzt
ultraviolet [ˌʌltrə'vaiələt] *adj* ultraviolett
umbrella [ʌm'brelə] *n* Regenschirm *m*
umpire ['ʌmpaiə] *n* Schiedsrichter *m*
unable [ʌ'neibəl] *adj* unfähig
unacceptable [ˌʌnək'septəbəl] *adj* unannehmbar
unaccountable [ˌʌnə'kauntəbəl] *adj* unerklärlich
unaccustomed [ˌʌnə'kʌstəmd] *adj* ungewohnt
unanimous [juː'næniməs] *adj* einstimmig
unanswered [ʌ'nɑːnsəd] *adj* unbeantwortet
unauthorized [ʌ'nɔːθəraizd] *adj* unbefugt
unavoidable [ˌʌnə'vɔidəbəl] *adj* unvermeidlich
unaware [ˌʌnə'weə] *adj* unbewußt
unbearable [ʌn'beərəbəl] *adj* unerträglich
unbreakable [ˌʌn'breikəbəl] *adj* unzerbrechlich
unbroken [ˌʌn'broukən] *adj* unversehrt
unbutton [ˌʌn'bʌtən] *v* aufknöpfen
uncertain [ʌn'səːtən] *adj* unsicher
uncle ['ʌŋkəl] *n* Onkel *m*
unclean [ʌn'kliːn] *adj* unrein
uncomfortable [ʌn'kʌmfətəbəl] *adj* ungemütlich
uncommon [ʌn'kɔmən] *adj* ungewöhnlich, selten
unconditional [ˌʌnkən'diʃənəl] *adj* bedingungslos
unconscious [ʌn'kɔnʃəs] *adj* bewußtlos
uncork [ˌʌn'kɔːk] *v* entkorken

uncover [ʌn'kʌvə] *v* aufdecken
uncultivated [ˌʌn'kʌltiveitid] *adj* unkultiviert
under ['ʌndə] *prep* unterhalb, unter
undercurrent ['ʌndəˌkʌrənt] *n* Unterströmung *f*
underestimate [ˌʌndə'restimeit] *v* unterschätzen
underground ['ʌndəgraund] *adj* unterirdisch; *n* U-Bahn *f*
underline [ˌʌndə'lain] *v* *unterstreichen
underneath [ˌʌndə'niːθ] *adv* unten
underpants ['ʌndəpænts] *plAm* Unterhose *f*
undershirt ['ʌndəʃəːt] *n* Unterhemd *nt*
undersigned ['ʌndəsaind] *n* Unterzeichnete *m*
***understand** [ˌʌndə'stænd] *v* *begreifen, *verstehen
understanding [ˌʌndə'stændiŋ] *n* Verständigung *f*
***undertake** [ˌʌndə'teik] *v* *unternehmen
undertaking [ˌʌndə'teikiŋ] *n* Unternehmung *f*
underwater ['ʌndəˌwɔːtə] *adj* Unterwasser-
underwear ['ʌndəweə] *n* Unterwäsche *fpl*
undesirable [ˌʌndi'zaiərəbəl] *adj* unerwünscht
***undo** [ˌʌn'duː] *v* aufmachen
undoubtedly [ʌn'dautidli] *adv* zweifellos
undress [ˌʌn'dres] *v* sich entkleiden
undulating ['ʌndjuleitiŋ] *adj* wellig
unearned [ʌ'nəːnd] *adj* unverdient
uneasy [ʌ'niːzi] *adj* unruhig
uneducated [ˌʌ'nedjukeitid] *adj* ungebildet
unemployed [ˌʌnim'plɔid] *adj* arbeitslos
unemployment [ˌʌnim'plɔimənt] *n* Ar-

beitslosigkeit f
unequal [,ʌ'ni:kwəl] adj ungleich
uneven [,ʌ'ni:vən] adj ungleich, uneben
unexpected [,ʌnik'spektid] adj unvorhergesehen, unerwartet
unfair [,ʌn'feə] adj unbillig, ungerecht
unfaithful [,ʌn'feiθfəl] adj untreu
unfamiliar [,ʌnfə'miljə] adj unbekannt
unfasten [,ʌn'fɑ:sən] v aufmachen
unfavourable [,ʌn'feivərəbəl] adj ungünstig
unfit [,ʌn'fit] adj untauglich
unfold [ʌn'fould] v entfalten
unfortunate [ʌn'fɔ:tʃənət] adj unglücklich
unfortunately [ʌn'fɔ:tʃənətli] adv unglücklicherweise, leider
unfriendly [,ʌn'frendli] adj unfreundlich
unfurnished [,ʌn'fə:niʃt] adj unmöbliert
ungrateful [ʌn'greitfəl] adj undankbar
unhappy [ʌn'hæpi] adj unglücklich
unhealthy [ʌn'helθi] adj ungesund
unhurt [,ʌn'hə:t] adj unverletzt
uniform ['ju:nifɔ:m] n Uniform f; adj
gleichförmig
unimportant [,ʌnim'pɔ:tənt] adj unwichtig
uninhabitable [,ʌnin'hæbitəbəl] adj unbewohnbar
uninhabited [,ʌnin'hæbitid] adj unbewohnt
unintentional [,ʌnin'tenʃənəl] adj
unabsichtlich
union ['ju:njən] n Vereinigung f;
Union f
unique [ju:'ni:k] adj einzigartig
unit ['ju:nit] n Einheit f
unite [ju:'nait] v vereinigen
United States [ju:'naitid steits] Vereinigte Staaten
unity ['ju:nəti] n Einheit f

universal [,ju:ni'və:səl] adj allgemein,
universal
universe ['ju:nivə:s] n Weltall nt
university [,ju:ni'və:səti] n Universität
f
unjust [,ʌn'dʒʌst] adj ungerecht
unkind [ʌn'kaind] adj unliebenswürdig, unfreundlich
unknown [,ʌn'noun] adj unbekannt
unlawful [,ʌn'lɔ:fəl] adj rechtswidrig
unlearn [,ʌn'lə:n] v verlernen
unless [ən'les] conj außer wenn
unlike [,ʌn'laik] adj unähnlich
unlikely [ʌn'laikli] adj unwahrscheinlich
unlimited [ʌn'limitid] adj unbegrenzt,
unbeschränkt
unload [,ʌn'loud] v *ausladen, *abladen
unlock [,ʌn'lɔk] v *aufschließen
unlucky [ʌn'lʌki] adj unglücklich
unnecessary [ʌn'nesəsəri] adj unnötig
unoccupied [,ʌ'nɔkjupaid] adj unbesetzt
unofficial [,ʌnə'fiʃəl] adj offiziös
unpack [,ʌn'pæk] v auspacken
unpleasant [ʌn'plezənt] adj langweilig,
unangenehm; unerfreulich, unsympathisch
unpopular [,ʌn'pɔpjulə] adj unpopulär,
unbeliebt
unprotected [,ʌnprə'tektid] adj ungeschützt
unqualified [,ʌn'kwɔlifaid] adj unqualifiziert
unreal [,ʌn'riəl] adj irreal
unreasonable [ʌn'ri:zənəbəl] adj unvernünftig
unreliable [,ʌnri'laiəbəl] adj unzuverlässig
unrest [,ʌn'rest] n Unruhe f; Ruhelosigkeit f
unsafe [,ʌn'seif] adj unsicher
unsatisfactory [,ʌnsætis'fæktəri] adj

unbefriedigend

unscrew [ˌʌn'skru:] v abschrauben

unselfish [ˌʌn'selfiʃ] adj selbstlos

unskilled [ˌʌn'skild] adj ungelernt

unsound [ˌʌn'saund] adj ungesund

unstable [ˌʌn'steibəl] adj labil

unsteady [ˌʌn'stedi] adj wacklig, unstet; wankelmütig

unsuccessful [ˌʌnsək'sesfəl] adj erfolglos

unsuitable [ˌʌn'su:təbəl] adj ungeeignet

unsurpassed [ˌʌnsə'pɑ:st] adj unübertroffen

untidy [ʌn'taidi] adj unordentlich

untie [ˌʌn'tai] v aufknoten

until [ən'til] prep bis

untrue [ˌʌn'tru:] adj unwahr

untrustworthy [ˌʌn'trʌst,wə:ði] adj unzuverlässig

unusual [ʌn'ju:ʒuəl] adj ungebräuchlich, ungewöhnlich

unwell [ˌʌn'wel] adj unwohl

unwilling [ˌʌn'wiliŋ] adj unwillig

unwise [ˌʌn'waiz] adj unüberlegt

unwrap [ˌʌn'ræp] v auspacken

up [ʌp] adv nach oben, empor, hinauf

upholster [ʌp'houlstə] v polstern, *überziehen

upkeep ['ʌpki:p] n Unterhalt m

uplands ['ʌpləndz] pl Hochland nt

upon [ə'pɔn] prep auf

upper ['ʌpə] adj höher, ober

upright ['ʌprait] adj aufrecht; adv aufrecht

upset [ʌp'set] v stören; adj bestürzt

upside-down [ˌʌpsaid'daun] adv umgekehrt

upstairs [ˌʌp'steəz] adv oben; nach oben

upstream [ˌʌp'stri:m] adv stromaufwärts

upwards ['ʌpwədz] adv aufwärts

urban ['ə:bən] adj städtisch

urge [ə:dʒ] v drängen; n Impuls m

urgency ['ə:dʒənsi] n Dringlichkeit f

urgent ['ə:dʒənt] adj dringend

urine ['juərin] n Urin m

Uruguay ['juərəgwai] Uruguay

Uruguayan [ˌjuərə'gwaiən] adj uruguayisch

us [ʌs] pron uns

usable ['ju:zəbəl] adj brauchbar

usage ['ju:zidʒ] n Brauch m

use¹ [ju:z] v benutzen, gebrauchen; *be used to gewohnt *sein; ~ up verbrauchen

use² [ju:s] n Gebrauch m; Nutzen m; *be of ~ nützen

useful ['ju:sfəl] adj brauchbar, nützlich

useless ['ju:sləs] adj nutzlos

user ['ju:zə] n Benutzer m

usher ['ʌʃə] n Platzanweiser m

usherette [ˌʌʃə'ret] n Platzanweiserin f

usual ['ju:ʒuəl] adj gewöhnlich

usually ['ju:ʒuəli] adv gewöhnlich

utensil [ju:'tensəl] n Werkzeug nt, Gerät nt; Gebrauchsgegenstand m

utility [ju:'tiləti] n Nutzen m

utilize ['ju:tilaiz] v benutzen

utmost ['ʌtmoust] adj äußerst

utter ['ʌtə] adj völlig, gänzlich; v äußern

V

vacancy ['veikənsi] n Vakanz f

vacant ['veikənt] adj frei

vacate [və'keit] v räumen

vacation [və'keiʃən] n Ferien pl

vaccinate ['væksineit] v impfen

vaccination [ˌvæksi'neiʃən] n Impfung f

vacuum ['vækjuəm] n Vakuum nt;

vAm staubsaugen; ~ **cleaner** Staubsauger *m*; ~ **flask** Thermosflasche *f*

vagrancy ['veigrənsi] *n* Landstreicherei *f*

vague [veig] *adj* undeutlich

vain [vein] *adj* eitel; unnütz; **in** ~ vergebens, umsonst

valet ['vælit] *n* Diener *m*

valid ['vælid] *adj* gültig

valley ['væli] *n* Tal *nt*

valuable ['væljubəl] *adj* wertvoll, kostbar; **valuables** *pl* Wertsachen *fpl*

value ['vælju:] *n* Wert *m*; *v* schätzen

valve [vælv] *n* Ventil *nt*

van [væn] *n* Lieferauto *nt*

vanilla [və'nilə] *n* Vanille *f*

vanish ['væniʃ] *v* *verschwinden

vapour ['veipə] *n* Dunst *m*

variable ['vɛəriəbəl] *adj* veränderlich

variation [,vɛəri'eiʃən] *n* Abwechslung *f*; Veränderung *f*

varied ['vɛərid] *adj* verschieden

variety [və'raiəti] *n* Auswahl *f*; ~ **show** Varietévorstellung *f*; ~ **theatre** Varietétheater *nt*

various ['vɛəriəs] *adj* allerlei, verschiedene

varnish ['va:niʃ] *n* Lack *m*, Firnis *m*; *v* lackieren

vary ['vɛəri] *v* variieren, wechseln; verändern; verschieden *sein

vase [va:z] *n* Vase *f*

vaseline ['væsəli:n] *n* Vaseline *f*

vast [va:st] *adj* unermeßlich, weit

vault [vɔ:lt] *n* Gewölbe *nt*; Stahlkammer *f*

veal [vi:l] *n* Kalbfleisch *nt*

vegetable ['vedʒətəbəl] *n* Gemüse *nt*; ~ **merchant** Gemüsehändler *m*

vegetarian [,vedʒi'tɛəriən] *n* Vegetarier *m*

vegetation [,vedʒi'teiʃən] *n* Vegetation *f*

vehicle ['vi:əkəl] *n* Fahrzeug *nt*

veil [veil] *n* Schleier *m*

vein [vein] *n* Ader *f*; **varicose** ~ Krampfader *f*

velvet ['velvit] *n* Samt *m*

velveteen [,velvi'ti:n] *n* Baumwollsamt *m*

venerable ['venərəbəl] *adj* ehrwürdig

venereal disease [vi'niəriəl di'zi:z] Geschlechtskrankheit *f*

Venezuela [,veni'zweilə] Venezuela

Venezuelan [,veni'zweilən] *adj* venezolanisch; *n* Venezolaner *m*

ventilate ['ventileit] *v* ventilieren; lüften

ventilation [,venti'leiʃən] *n* Ventilation *f*; Lüftung *f*

ventilator ['ventileitə] *n* Ventilator *m*

venture ['ventʃə] *v* wagen

veranda [və'rændə] *n* Veranda *f*

verb [və:b] *n* Zeitwort *nt*

verbal ['və:bəl] *adj* mündlich

verdict ['və:dikt] *n* Urteil *nt*, Urteilsspruch *m*

verge [və:dʒ] *n* Rand *m*

verify ['verifai] *v* nachprüfen

verse [və:s] *n* Vers *m*

version ['və:ʃən] *n* Darstellung *f*; Übersetzung *f*

versus ['və:səs] *prep* gegen

vertical ['və:tikəl] *adj* senkrecht

vertigo ['və:tigou] *n* Schwindelanfall *m*

very ['veri] *adv* sehr; *adj* wahr, wirklich, exakt; äußerst

vessel ['vesəl] *n* Schiff *nt*; Gefäß *nt*

vest [vest] *n* Hemd *nt*; *nAm* Weste *f*

veterinary surgeon ['vetrinəri 'sə:dʒən] Tierarzt *m*

via [vaiə] *prep* über

viaduct ['vaiədʌkt] *n* Viadukt *m*

vibrate [vai'breit] *v* vibrieren

vibration [vai'breiʃən] *n* Schwingung *f*

vicar ['vikə] *n* Vikar *m*

vicarage ['vikəridʒ] n Pfarrhaus nt

vice-president [,vais'prezidənt] n Vizepräsident m

vicinity [vi'sinəti] n Nähe f, Nachbarschaft f

vicious ['viʃəs] adj bösartig

victim ['viktim] n Opfer nt; Geschädigte m

victory ['viktəri] n Sieg m

view [vju:] n Aussicht f; Meinung f, Ansicht f; v besichtigen

view-finder ['vju:,faində] n Sucher m

vigilant ['vidʒilənt] adj wachsam

villa ['vilə] n Villa f

village ['vilidʒ] n Dorf nt

villain ['vilən] n Schuft m

vine [vain] n Weinrebe f

vinegar ['vinigə] n Essig m

vineyard ['vinjəd] n Weinberg m

vintage ['vintidʒ] n Weinlese f

violation [vaiə'leiʃən] n Verletzung f

violence ['vaiələns] n Gewalt f

violent ['vaiələnt] adj gewaltsam; heftig

violet ['vaiələt] n Veilchen nt; adj violett

violin [vaiə'lin] n Geige f

virgin ['və:dʒin] n Jungfrau f

virtue ['və:tʃu:] n Tugend f

visa ['vi:zə] n Visum nt

visibility [,vizə'biləti] n Sichtweite f

visible ['vizəbəl] adj sichtbar

vision ['viʒən] n Einsicht f

visit ['vizit] v besuchen; n Besuch m; **visiting hours** Besuchsstunden fpl

visiting-card ['vizitiŋka:d] n Visitenkarte f

visitor ['vizitə] n Gast m

vital ['vaitəl] adj wesentlich

vitamin ['vitəmin] n Vitamin nt

vivid ['vivid] adj lebhaft

vocabulary [və'kæbjuləri] n Vokabular nt, Wortschatz m; Wörterverzeichnis nt

vocal ['voukəl] adj vokal

vocalist ['voukəlist] n Sänger m

voice [vɔis] n Stimme f

void [vɔid] adj nichtig

volcano [vɔl'keinou] n (pl ~es, ~s) Vulkan m

volt [voult] n Volt nt

voltage ['voultidʒ] n Spannung f

volume ['vɔljum] n Volumen nt; Teil m, Band m

voluntary ['vɔləntəri] adj freiwillig

volunteer [,vɔlən'tiə] n Freiwillige m

vomit ['vɔmit] v sich *übergeben, *erbrechen

vote [vout] v stimmen; n Stimme f; Abstimmung f

voucher ['vautʃə] n Beleg m, Gutschein m

vow [vau] n Gelübde nt, Eid m; v *schwören

vowel [vauəl] n Selbstlaut m

voyage ['vɔiidʒ] n Reise f

vulgar ['vʌlgə] adj gemein; Volks-, ordinär

vulnerable ['vʌlnərəbəl] adj verletzbar

vulture ['vʌltʃə] n Geier m

W

wade [weid] v waten

wafer ['weifə] n Oblate f

waffle ['wɔfəl] n Waffel f

wages ['weidʒiz] pl Lohn m

waggon ['wægən] n Waggon m

waist [weist] n Taille f

waistcoat ['weiskout] n Weste f

wait [weit] v warten; ~ **on** bedienen

waiter ['weitə] n Ober m, Kellner m

waiting n das Warten

waiting-list ['weitiŋlist] n Warteliste f

waiting-room ['weitiŋru:m] n Wartezimmer nt

waitress ['weitris] n Kellnerin f

*** wake** [weik] v wecken; ~ **up** aufwachen, wach *werden

walk [wɔ:k] v *gehen; spazieren; n Spaziergang m; Gang m; **walking** zu Fuß

walker ['wɔ:kə] n Spaziergänger m

walking-stick ['wɔ:kiŋstik] n Spazierstock m

wall [wɔ:l] n Mauer f; Wand f

wallet ['wɔlit] n Brieftasche f

wallpaper ['wɔ:l,peipə] n Tapete f

walnut ['wɔ:lnʌt] n Walnuß f

waltz [wɔ:ls] n Walzer m

wander ['wɔndə] v umherschweifen, umherwandern

want [wɔnt] v *wollen; wünschen; n Bedarf m; Mangel m, Fehlen nt

war [wɔ:] n Krieg m

warden ['wɔ:dən] n Wächter m, Aufseher m

wardrobe ['wɔ:droub] n Kleiderschrank m, Garderobe f

warehouse ['wɛəhaus] n Lager nt, Depot nt

wares [wɛəz] pl Waren

warm [wɔ:m] adj heiß, warm; v wärmen

warmth [wɔ:mθ] n Wärme f

warn [wɔ:n] v warnen

warning ['wɔ:niŋ] n Warnung f

wary ['wɛəri] adj bedächtig

was [wɔz] v (p be)

wash [wɔʃ] v *waschen; ~ **and wear** bügelfrei; ~ **up** *abwaschen

washable ['wɔʃəbəl] adj waschbar

wash-basin ['wɔʃ,beisən] n Waschbecken nt

washing ['wɔʃiŋ] n Waschen nt; Wäsche f

washing-machine ['wɔʃiŋməˌʃi:n] n Waschmaschine f

washing-powder ['wɔʃiŋ,paudə] n Waschpulver nt

washroom ['wɔʃru:m] nAm Toilette f

wash-stand ['wɔʃstænd] n Waschtisch m

wasp [wɔsp] n Wespe f

waste [weist] v vergeuden; n Verschwendung f; adj brach

wasteful ['weistfəl] adj verschwenderisch

wastepaper-basket [weist'peipə,bɑ:-skit] n Papierkorb m

watch [wɔtʃ] v *achtgeben auf, beobachten; überwachen; n Uhr f; ~ **for** auflauern; ~ **out** aufpassen

watch-maker ['wɔtʃ,meikə] n Uhrmacher m

watch-strap ['wɔtʃstræp] n Uhrband nt

water ['wɔ:tə] n Wasser nt; **iced** ~ Eiswasser nt; **running** ~ fließendes Wasser; ~ **pump** Wasserpumpe f; ~ **ski** Wasserschi m

water-colour ['wɔ:tə,kʌlə] n Wasserfarbe f; Aquarell nt

watercress ['wɔ:təkres] n Brunnenkresse f

waterfall ['wɔ:təfɔ:l] n Wasserfall m

watermelon ['wɔ:tə,melən] n Wassermelone f

waterproof ['wɔ:təpru:f] adj wasserdicht

water-softener [,wɔ:tə,sɔfnə] n Enthärtungsmittel nt

waterway ['wɔ:təwei] n Wasserstraße f

watt [wɔt] n Watt nt

wave [weiv] n Welle f; v winken

wave-length ['weivleŋθ] n Wellenlänge f

wavy ['weivi] adj wellig

wax [wæks] n Wachs nt

waxworks ['wækswə:ks] pl Wachsfigurenkabinett nt

way [wei] n Art f, Weise f; Weg m; Seite f, Richtung f; Entfernung f; **any** ~ wie auch immer; **by the** ~

übrigens; **one-way traffic** Einbahnverkehr *m*; **out of the** ~ entlegen; **the other** ~ **round** andersherum; ~ **back** Rückweg *m*; ~ **in** Eingang *m*; ~ **out** Ausgang *m*

wayside ['weisaid] *n* Wegrand *m*

we [wi:] *pron* wir

weak [wi:k] *adj* schwach; dünn

weakness ['wi:knəs] *n* Schwäche *f*

wealth [welθ] *n* Reichtum *m*

wealthy ['welθi] *adj* reich

weapon ['wepən] *n* Waffe *f*

*****wear** [weə] *v* *anhaben, *tragen; ~ **out** *abtragen

weary ['wiəri] *adj* überdrüssig, müde

weather ['weðə] *n* Wetter *nt*; ~ **forecast** Wetterbericht *m*

*****weave** [wi:v] *v* weben

weaver ['wi:və] *n* Weber *m*

wedding ['wediŋ] *n* Heirat *f*, Hochzeit *f*

wedding-ring ['wediŋriŋ] *n* Ehering *m*

wedge [wedʒ] *n* Keil *m*

Wednesday ['wenzdi] Mittwoch *m*

weed [wi:d] *n* Unkraut *nt*

week [wi:k] *n* Woche *f*

weekday ['wi:kdei] *n* Wochentag *m*

weekend ['wi:kend] *n* Wochenende *nt*

weekly ['wi:kli] *adj* wöchentlich

*****weep** [wi:p] *v* weinen

weigh [wei] *v* *wiegen

weighing-machine ['weiiŋməʃi:n] *n* Waage *f*

weight [weit] *n* Gewicht *nt*

welcome ['welkəm] *adj* willkommen; *n* Willkommen *nt*; *v* bewillkommnen

weld [weld] *v* schweißen

welfare ['welfeə] *n* Wohlbefinden *nt*

well[1] [wel] *adv* gut; *adj* gesund; **as** ~ auch, ebenfalls; **as** ~ **as** ebenso wie; **well!** gut!

well[2] [wel] *n* Quelle *f*, Brunnen *m*

well-founded [,wel'faundid] *adj* wohlbegründet

well-known ['welnoun] *adj* bekannt

well-to-do [,weltə'du:] *adj* wohlhabend

went [went] *v* (p go)

were [wə:] *v* (p be)

west [west] *n* Westen *m*

westerly ['westəli] *adj* westlich

western ['westən] *adj* westlich

wet [wet] *adj* naß; feucht

whale [weil] *n* Wal *m*

wharf [wɔ:f] *n* (pl ~s, wharves) Kai *m*

what [wɔt] *pron* was; ~ **for** wozu

whatever [wɔ'tevə] *pron* was auch immer

wheat [wi:t] *n* Weizen *m*

wheel [wi:l] *n* Rad *nt*

wheelbarrow ['wi:l,bærou] *n* Schubkarren *m*

wheelchair ['wi:ltʃeə] *n* Rollstuhl *m*

when [wen] *adv* wann; *conj* als, wenn

whenever [we'nevə] *conj* wann immer

where [weə] *adv* wo; *conj* wo

wherever [weə'revə] *conj* wo immer

whether ['weðə] *conj* ob; **whether ... or** ob ... oder

which [witʃ] *pron* welcher; der

whichever [wi'tʃevə] *adj* welcher auch immer

while [wail] *conj* während; *n* Weile *f*

whilst [wailst] *conj* indem

whim [wim] *n* Grille *f*, Laune *f*

whip [wip] *n* Peitsche *f*; *v* *schlagen

whiskers ['wiskəz] *pl* Backenbart *m*

whisper ['wispə] *v* flüstern; *n* Geflüster *nt*

whistle ['wisəl] *v* *pfeifen; *n* Pfeife *f*

white [wait] *adj* weiß

whitebait ['waitbeit] *n* Breitling *m*

whiting ['waitiŋ] *n* (pl ~) Weißfisch *m*

Whitsun ['witsən] Pfingsten

who [hu:] *pron* wer; welcher

whoever [hu:'evə] *pron* wer auch immer

whole [houl] *adj* vollständig, ganz;

unbeschädigt; n Ganze nt
wholesale ['houlseil] n Großhandel m; ~ **dealer** Großhändler m
wholesome ['houlsəm] adj bekömmlich
wholly ['houli] adv gänzlich
whom [hu:m] pron wem
whore [hɔ:] n Hure f
whose [hu:z] pron dessen; wessen
why [wai] adv warum
wicked ['wikid] adj böse
wide [waid] adj weit, breit
widen ['waidən] v erweitern
widow ['widou] n Witwe f
widower ['widouə] n Witwer m
width [widθ] n Breite f
wife [waif] n (pl wives) Gattin f, Frau f
wig [wig] n Perücke f
wild [waild] adj wild; wüst
will [wil] n Wille m; Testament nt
*__will__ [wil] v *wollen; *werden
willing ['wiliŋ] adj willig
willingly ['wiliŋli] adv gern
will-power ['wilpauə] n Willenskraft f
*__win__ [win] v *gewinnen
wind [wind] n Wind m
*__wind__ [waind] v sich *winden; *aufziehen, *winden
winding ['waindiŋ] adj gewunden
windmill ['windmil] n Windmühle f
window ['windou] n Fenster nt
window-sill ['windousil] n Fensterbrett nt
windscreen ['windskri:n] n Windschutzscheibe f; ~ **wiper** Scheibenwischer m
windshield ['windʃi:ld] nAm Windschutzscheibe f; ~ **wiper** Am Scheibenwischer m
windy ['windi] adj windig
wine [wain] n Wein m
wine-cellar ['wain,selə] n Weinkeller m

wine-list ['wainlist] n Weinkarte f
wine-merchant ['wain,mə:tʃənt] n Weinhändler m
wine-waiter ['wain,weitə] n Kellermeister m
wing [wiŋ] n Flügel m
winkle ['wiŋkəl] n Uferschnecke f
winner ['winə] n Sieger m
winning ['winiŋ] adj gewinnend; **winnings** pl Gewinn m
winter ['wintə] n Winter m; ~ **sports** Wintersport m
wipe [waip] v abwischen; auswischen
wire [waiə] n Draht m
wireless ['waiələs] n Rundfunk m
wisdom ['wizdəm] n Weisheit f
wise [waiz] adj weise
wish [wiʃ] v begehren, wünschen; n Begehren nt, Wunsch m
witch [witʃ] n Hexe f
with [wið] prep mit; bei; von
*__withdraw__ [wið'drɔ:] v *zurückziehen
within [wi'ðin] prep innerhalb; adv im Innern
without [wi'ðaut] prep ohne
witness ['witnəs] n Zeuge m
wits [wits] pl Verstand m
witty ['witi] adj geistreich
wolf [wulf] n (pl wolves) Wolf m
woman ['wumən] n (pl women) Frau f
womb [wu:m] n Gebärmutter f
won [wʌn] v (p, pp win)
wonder ['wʌndə] n Wunder nt; Verwunderung f; v sich fragen
wonderful ['wʌndəfəl] adj prächtig, wunderbar; herrlich
wood [wud] n Holz nt; Wald m
wood-carving ['wud,kɑ:viŋ] n Holzschnitzerei f
wooded ['wudid] adj bewaldet
wooden ['wudən] adj hölzern; ~ **shoe** Holzschuh m
woodland ['wudlənd] n Waldung f
wool [wul] n Wolle f; **darning** ~

Stopfgarn *nt*
woollen ['wulən] *adj* wollen
word [wəːd] *n* Wort *nt*
wore [wɔː] *v* (p wear)
work [wəːk] *n* Arbeit *f*; Tätigkeit *f*; *v* arbeiten; funktionieren; **working day** Werktag *m*; **~ of art** Kunstwerk *nt*; **~ permit** Arbeitsbewilligung *f*
worker ['wəːkə] *n* Arbeiter *m*
working ['wəːkiŋ] *n* Betrieb *m*
workman ['wəːkmən] *n* (pl -men) Arbeiter *m*
works [wəːks] *pl* Fabrik *f*
workshop ['wəːkʃɔp] *n* Werkstatt *f*
world [wəːld] *n* Welt *f*; **~ war** Weltkrieg *m*
world-famous [,wəːld'feiməs] *adj* weltberühmt
world-wide ['wəːldwaid] *adj* weltweit
worm [wəːm] *n* Wurm *m*
worn [wɔːn] *adj* (pp wear) abgetragen
worn-out [,wɔːn'aut] *adj* abgenutzt
worried ['wʌrid] *adj* beunruhigt
worry ['wʌri] *v* sich beunruhigen; *n* Sorge *f*, Besorgtheit *f*
worse [wəːs] *adj* schlechter; *adv* schlechter
worship ['wəːʃip] *v* verehren; *n* Gottesdienst *m*
worst [wəːst] *adj* schlechtest; *adv* am schlechtesten
worsted ['wustid] *n* Kammgarn *nt*
worth [wəːθ] *n* Wert *m*; ***be ~** wert *sein; ***be worth-while** sich lohnen
worthless ['wəːθləs] *adj* wertlos
worthy of ['wəːði əv] würdig
would [wud] *v* (p will) pflegen
wound¹ [wuːnd] *n* Wunde *f*; *v* verletzen, verwunden
wound² [waund] *v* (p, pp wind)
wrap [ræp] *v* einwickeln
wreck [rek] *n* Wrack *nt*; *v* vernichten
wrench [rentʃ] *n* Schraubenschlüssel

m; Ruck *m*; *v* verdrehen
wrinkle ['riŋkəl] *n* Falte *f*
wrist [rist] *n* Handgelenk *nt*
wrist-watch ['ristwɔtʃ] *n* Armbanduhr *f*
*write [rait] *v* *schreiben; **in writing** schriftlich; **~ down** *aufschreiben
writer ['raitə] *n* Schriftsteller *m*
writing-pad ['raitiŋpæd] *n* Notizblock *m*, Schreibblock *m*
writing-paper ['raitiŋ,peipə] *n* Schreibpapier *nt*
written ['ritən] *adj* (pp write) schriftlich
wrong [rɔŋ] *adj* unrecht, falsch; *n* Unrecht *nt*; *v* Unrecht *tun; ***be ~** unrecht *haben
wrote [rout] *v* (p write)

X

Xmas ['krisməs] Weihnachten
X-ray ['eksrei] *n* Röntgenbild *nt*; *v* röntgen

Y

yacht [jɔt] *n* Jacht *f*
yacht-club ['jɔtklʌb] *n* Segelklub *m*
yachting ['jɔtiŋ] *n* Segelsport *m*
yard [jɑːd] *n* Hof *m*
yarn [jɑːn] *n* Garn *nt*
yawn [jɔːn] *v* gähnen
year [jiə] *n* Jahr *nt*
yearly ['jiəli] *adj* jährlich
yeast [jiːst] *n* Hefe *f*
yell [jel] *v* *schreien; *n* Schrei *m*
yellow ['jelou] *adj* gelb
yes [jes] ja
yesterday ['jestədi] *adv* gestern

yet [jet] *adv* noch; *conj* dennoch, jedoch, doch
yield [ji:ld] *v* *einbringen; *nachgeben
yoke [jouk] *n* Joch *nt*
yolk [jouk] *n* Dotter *nt*
you [ju:] *pron* du; dir; Sie; Ihnen; ihr; euch
young [jʌŋ] *adj* jung
your [jɔ:] *adj* Ihr; dein; euer
yourself [jɔ:'self] *pron* dich; selbst
yourselves [jɔ:'selvz] *pron* euch; selbst
youth [ju:θ] *n* Jugend *f*; ~ **hostel** Jugendherberge *f*
Yugoslav [ˌju:gə'sla:v] *n* Jugoslawe *m*
Yugoslavia [ˌju:gə'sla:viə] Jugoslawien

Z

zeal [zi:l] *n* Eifer *m*
zealous ['zeləs] *adj* eifrig
zebra ['zi:brə] *n* Zebra *nt*
zenith ['zeniθ] *n* Zenit *m*; Hohepunkt *m*
zero ['ziərou] *n* (pl ~s) Null *f*
zest [zest] *n* Lust *f*
zinc [ziŋk] *n* Zink *nt*
zip [zip] *n* Reißverschluß *m*; ~ **code** *Am* Postleitzahl *f*
zipper ['zipə] *n* Reißverschluß *m*
zodiac ['zoudiæk] *n* Tierkreis *m*
zone [zoun] *n* Zone *f*; Gebiet *nt*
zoo [zu:] *n* (pl ~s) Zoo *m*
zoology [zou'ɔlədʒi] *n* Zoologie *f*

Aus der Speisekarte

Speisen

almond Mandel
anchovy Sardelle
angel food cake Kuchen aus Eiweißschnee
angels on horseback auf Toast servierte, in Speck eingerollte und gegrillte Austern
appetizer Appetithäppchen
apple Apfel
  ~ **dumpling** Apfel im Schlafrock
  ~ **sauce** Apfelmus
apricot Aprikose
Arbroath smoky geräucherter Schellfisch
artichoke Artischocke
asparagus Spargel
  ~ **tip** Spargelspitze
aspic Aspik, Gelee, Sülze
assorted gemischt
avocado (pear) Avocado(birne)
bacon Speck
  ~ **and eggs** Spiegeleier und Speck
bagel Brötchen in Kranzform
baked im Ofen gebacken
  ~ **Alaska** norwegisches Omelett
  ~ **beans** gebackene weiße Bohnen mit Tomatensoße

  ~ **potato** gebackene Pellkartoffel
Bakewell tart Kuchen aus gemahlenen Mandeln und Marmelade
baloney eine Art Mortadella
banana Banane
  ~ **split** halbierte Banane, verschiedene Eiskremsorten, Nüsse und Sirup oder Schokolade
barbecue 1) Rindfleischgehacktes, mit pikanter Tomatensoße in einem Brötchen serviert 2) Grillparty
  ~ **sauce** pikante Tomatensoße
barbecued über offenem Holzfeuer gegrillt
basil Basilikum
bass Barsch
bean Bohne
beef Rindfleisch
  ~ **olive** Rinderroulade
beefburger gehacktes Beefsteak, gegrillt und in einem Brötchen serviert
beet, beetroot rote Rübe
bilberry Heidel-, Blaubeere
bill Rechnung
  ~ **of fare** Speisekarte
biscuit 1) Kleingebäck, Keks (GB) 2) kleines Brötchen (US)

blackberry Brombeere

blackcurrant schwarze Johannisbeere

black pudding Blutwurst

bloater Bückling

blood sausage Blutwurst

blueberry Heidel-, Blaubeere

boiled gekocht, gesotten

Bologna (sausage) eine Art Mortadella

bone Knochen

boned ausgebeint

Boston baked beans weiße Bohnen, Speckwürfel und Melasse im Ofen gebacken

Boston cream pie mehrschichtige Torte mit Kremfüllung und Schokoladenglasur

brains Hirn

braised gedämpft, geschmort

bramble pudding Brombeerpudding, oft mit Apfelscheiben

braunschweiger Leberwurst

bread Brot

breaded paniert

breakfast Frühstück

bream Brasse

breast Brust, Brüstchen

brisket Bruststück

broad bean Saubohne

broth Fleischbrühe, Bouillon

brown Betty eine Art Charlotte aus Äpfeln und Gewürzen, mit Paniermehl bestreut

brunch spätes, reichhaltiges Frühstück, das zugleich das Mittagessen ersetzt; Gabelfrühstück

brussels sprout Rosenkohl

bubble and squeak eine Art Pfannkuchen aus Kartoffeln und Weißkohl

bun 1) süßes Milchbrötchen mit Rosinen oder anderen getrockneten Früchten (GB) 2) Hefebrötchen (US)

buttered gebuttert

cabbage Weißkohl

Caesar salad Salat mit Brotwürfeln, Sardellen, Knoblauch und geriebenem Käse

cake Kuchen

cakes Kekse

calf Kalb

Canadian bacon geräucherter Lendenspeck

canapé Appetitschnittchen, belegtes Brötchen

cantaloupe Melone

caper Kaper

capercaillie, capercailzie Auerhahn

carp Karpfen

carrot Mohrrübe, Karotte

cashew Cashewnuß, Elefantenlaus

casserole in der Kasserolle serviertes Gericht

catfish 1) Steinbeißer, Seewolf 2) Katzenwels

catsup Ketchup

cauliflower Blumenkohl

celery Sellerie

cereal Getreideflocken
hot ~ Haferbrei

check Rechnung

Cheddar (cheese) fetter, orangegelber Hartkäse

cheese Käse
~ **board** Käseplatte
~ **cake** Käsekuchen

cheeseburger eine Art deutsches Beefsteak, mit geschmolzenem Käse in einem Brötchen serviert

chef's salad Salat mit Schinken, Rindfleisch, Hühnerfleisch, Eiern, Tomaten und Käse

cherry Kirsche

chestnut Eßkastanie, Marone

chicken Huhn, Hühnchen

chicory 1) Brüsseler Endivie, Chicorée (GB) 2) Endivie (US)

chili con carne dicker Eintopf aus Rindfleisch mit roten Bohnen, Zwiebeln und Chilipfeffer

chili pepper Chilipfeffer

chips 1) Pommes frites (GB) 2) Kartoffelchips (US)

chitt(er)lings Schweinskaldaunen, -kutteln

chive Schnittlauch

chocolate Schokolade

choice Auswahl

chop Kotelett
~ **suey** Gericht aus fein geschnittenem Hühner- oder Schweinefleisch, Gemüse und Reis

chopped gehackt, feingeschnitten

chowder dicke Suppe mit Meeresfrüchten

Christmas pudding englischer Weihnachtspudding aus getrockneten Früchten, Paniermehl, Gewürzen; manchmal flambiert

chutney scharfgewürzte indische Tafelsoße

cinnamon Zimt

clam Sandmuschel

club sandwich doppeltes Sandwich mit gebratenem Frühstücksspeck, Hühnerfleisch, Tomaten, Salat und Mayonnaise

cobbler eine Art gedeckter Obstkuchen

cock-a-leekie soup Hühnerbrühe mit Porree

coconut Kokosnuß

cod Kabeljau, Dorsch

Colchester oyster die beste englische Auster

cold cuts/meat Aufschnitt

coleslaw Weißkohlsalat

compote Kompott

condiment Gewürz

consommé Fleischbrühe, Bouillon

cooked gekocht

cookie Keks

corn 1) Korn, Weizen (GB) 2) Mais (US)
~ **on the cob** Maiskolben

cornflakes geröstete Maisflocken

corned beef gepökeltes Rindfleisch

cottage cheese Bauernkäse aus Quark

cottage pie Auflauf aus Hackfleisch, Zwiebeln und Kartoffelpüree

course Gericht, Gang

cover charge Gedeck extra

crab Krabbe

cracker kleines knuspriges Salzgebäck

cranberry Kranbeere, nordamerikanische Preiselbeere
~ **sauce** Kranbeersoße

crawfish, crayfish 1) Krebs 2) Languste (GB) 3) Kaisergranat (US)

cream 1) Sahne 2) Krem 3) Kremsuppe
~ **cheese** Rahmkäse
~ **puff** Windbeutel

creamed potatoes Sahnekartoffeln

creole Kreolenart; meistens mit Tomaten, Paprikaschoten und Zwiebeln gewürzt, mit Reis serviert

cress Kresse

crisps Kartoffelchips

crumpet rundes, mit Butter bestrichenes Hefebrötchen, wird warm gegessen

cucumber Gurke

Cumberland ham bekannter englischer Räucherschinken

Cumberland sauce pikante Tafelsoße aus rotem Johannisbeergelee, Orangensaft und Wein

cupcake kleiner, runder Kuchen

cured geräuchert, gebeizt, gepökelt

currant 1) Korinthe 2) Johannisbeere

curried mit Curry

custard 1) englische Krem 2) Puddingtörtchen

cutlet Schnitzel, Kotelett

dab Kliesche, rauhe Scholle

Danish pastry Plundergebäck

date Dattel

Derby cheese blaßgelber Schnittkäse von mildem bis würzigem Geschmack

devilled sehr stark gewürzt

devil's food cake Schokoladentorte

devils on horseback in Rotwein gekochte Backpflaumen, mit Mandeln und Sardellen gefüllt, in Speck eingerollt und gegrillt

Devonshire cream dicke Sahne

diced gewürfelt

diet food Diätkost

dinner (großes) Abendessen

dish Gericht, Gang

donut, doughnut süßer Krapfen, Berliner Pfannkuchen in Ringform

double cream Doppelrahm

Dover sole Dover-Seezunge, gilt als die beste Englands

dressing 1) Salatsoße 2) Füllung für Geflügel (US)

Dublin Bay prawn Kaisergranat

duck Ente

duckling junge Ente

dumpling Teigkloß, Knödel

Dutch apple pie Apfeltorte mit

Streusel aus Rohzucker, Zimt und Butter

éclair Blitzkuchen, gefüllte Brandteigstange

eel Aal

egg Ei

  boiled ~ gekocht

  fried ~ Spiegelei

  hard-boiled ~ hartgekocht

  poached ~ pochiert, verloren

  scrambled ~ Rührei

  soft-boiled ~ weichgekocht

eggplant Aubergine

endive 1) Endivie (GB) 2) Brüsseler Endivie, Chicorée (US)

entrée 1) Vorspeise (GB) 2) Hauptgericht (US)

escalope Schnitzel

fennel Fenchel

fig Feige

fillet Fleisch- oder Fischfilet

finnan haddock geräucherter Schellfisch

fish Fisch

  ~ **and chips** fritierter Fisch und Pommes frites

  ~ **cake** Frikadelle aus Fisch und Kartoffelpüree

flan Obst-, Käsekuchen

flapjack kleiner, dicker Pfannkuchen

flounder Flunder

forcemeat gehacktes Füllfleisch

fowl Geflügel

French bean grüne Bohne

French bread Pariser Brot

French dressing 1) würzige kalte Kräutersoße (GB) 2) sahnige Salatsoße mit Ketchup (US)

french fries Pommes frites

French toast armer Ritter, Goldschnitte

fresh frisch

fried gebraten oder in Öl gebacken

fritter Krapfen
frogs' legs Froschschenkel
frosting Zuckerguß, Glasur
fruit Obst
fry Fritüre
galantine Rollpastete
game Wild
gammon Räucherschinken
garfish Hornhecht
garlic Knoblauch
garnish Garnierung, Beilage
gherkin Essig-, Gewürzgurke
giblets Geflügelklein
ginger Ingwer
goose Gans
  ~ **berry** Stachelbeere
grape Weintraube
  ~ **fruit** Pampelmuse
grated gerieben
gravy Bratensaft, -soße
grayling Äsche
green bean grüne Bohne
green pepper grüne Paprikaschote
green salad grüner Salat, Gartensalat
greens grünes Gemüse
grilled gegrillt
grilse junger Lachs
grouse schottisches Moorhuhn
gumbo 1) Gombo (unreife Frucht einer mittelamerikanischen Eibischart) 2) kreolisches Fleisch- oder Fischgericht mit *okra*
haddock Schellfisch
haggis Hammelmagen mit einer Füllung aus gehackten Innereien und Haferflocken
hake Seehecht
half Hälfte, halb
halibut Heilbutt
ham Schinken
  ~ **and eggs** Spiegeleier mit Schinken

hare Hase
haricot bean weiße Bohne
hash 1) gehacktes oder feinge-schnittenes Fleisch 2) Gericht aus feingeschnittenem Fleisch, Kartoffeln und Gemüse
hazelnut Haselnuß
heart Herz
herb Gewürzkraut
herring Hering
home-made hausgemacht
hominy grits Maisbrei
honey Honig
  ~ **dew melon** Honigmelone, sehr süß, mit gelbgrünem Fruchtfleisch
hors-d'œuvre Vorspeise
horse-radish Meerrettich
hot 1) warm, heiß 2) scharf
  ~ **cross bun** Rosinenbrötchen mit kreuzförmiger Verzierung (zur Fastenzeit)
  ~ **dog** heißes Würstchen in einem aufgeschnittenen Brötchen
huckleberry Heidel-, Blaubeere
hush puppy Krapfen aus Maismehl
ice-cream Speiseeis
iced eisgekühlt
icing Zuckerguß, Glasur
Idaho baked potato im Ofen gebackene Pellkartoffel
Irish stew Eintopfgericht mit Hammelfleisch, Kartoffeln und Zwiebeln
Italian dressing würzige kalte Kräutersoße
jam Marmelade
jellied in Gelee
Jell-O Geleenachspeise, Götterspeise
jelly Gelee, Sülze
Jerusalem artichoke Erdartischocke, Topinambur

John Dory Heringskönig, Peters-fisch
jugged hare Hasenpfeffer
juice Saft
juniper berry Wacholderbeere
junket gezuckerte Dickmilch
kale Kraus-, Grünkohl
kedgeree stark gewürztes Früh-stücksgericht aus feingeschnit-tenem Fisch mit Reis, Eiern und Butter
kidney Niere
kipper geräucherter Hering
lamb Lamm
Lancashire hot pot Eintopf aus Lammkoteletts und -nieren, Kartoffeln und Zwiebeln
larded gespickt
lean mager
leek Porree, Lauch
leg Keule, Schlegel
lemon Zitrone
~ **sole** Rotzunge
lentil Linse
lettuce Kopfsalat, Lattich
lima bean Limabohne
lime Limetta, Zitrusfrucht mit grüner Schale
liver Leber
loaf Brotlaib
lobster Hummer
loin Filet, Lendenstück
Long Island duck Long-Island-Ente, besonders wohlschmek-kend
low-calorie kalorienarm
lox Räucherlachs
lunch Mittagessen
macaroon Makrone
mackerel Makrele
maize Mais
mandarin Mandarine
maple syrup Ahornsirup
marinated mariniert, eingelegt

marjoram Majoran
marmalade Marmelade aus Zi-trusfrüchten (besonders Apfel-sinen)
marrow Mark
~ **bone** Markknochen
marshmallow eine Art türkischer Honig
mashed potatoes Kartoffelpüree
meal Mahlzeit
meat Fleisch
~ **ball** Fleischkloß
~ **loaf** Hackbraten
medium (done) halb durchgebra-ten, halbgar
melon Melone
melted geschmolzen
Melton Mowbray pie eine eng-lische Fleischpastete, wird kalt gegessen
menu Speisekarte
meringue Baiser, Meringe
milk Milch
mince Gehacktes, Hackfleisch
~ **meat** Hackfleisch
~ **pie** Kuchen oder Pastete mit Füllung aus Äpfeln, Rosinen, feingehacktes Orangeat und Zi-tronat, Gewürze; mit oder ohne Fleisch
minced gehackt
mint Minze
mixed gemischt
~ **grill** verschiedene Fleisch-stücke mit Bratwürstchen, Speckscheibchen, Tomaten, Pil-zen und Zwiebeln; gegrillt
molasses Melasse
morel Morchel
mousse eine Art Kremeis
mulberry Maulbeere
mullet Meerbarbe
mulligatawny soup stark gewürzte indische Hühnersuppe

mushroom Pilz
muskmelon Melone
mussel Miesmuschel
mustard Senf
mutton Hammelfleisch
noodle Nudel
nut Nuß
oatmeal (porridge) Haferbrei
oil Öl
okra schlanke Gomboschote
omelet Omelett
onion Zwiebel
orange Apfelsine
ox tongue Ochsenzunge
oxtail Ochsenschwanz
oyster Auster
pancake Eierkuchen
parsley Petersilie
parsnip Pastinake, Hirschmöhre
partridge Rebhuhn
pastry feines Backwerk
pasty Pastetchen, Fleischpastete
pea Erbse
peach Pfirsich
peanut Erdnuß
pear Birne
pearl barley Perlgraupen
pepper Pfeffer
  ~ **mint** Pfefferminze
perch Barsch
persimmon Dattel-, Kakipflaume
pheasant Fasan
pickerel junger Hecht
pickle 1) mit Kräutern und Gewürzen in Essig eingelegte Gemüse und Frucht 2) kleine Gewürzgurke (US)
pickled in Essig eingelegt, gepökelt
pie englische Pastete (mit würziger oder süßer Füllung und meistens mit Teigdeckel)
pig Schwein
pigeon Taube

pike Hecht
pineapple Ananas
plaice Scholle
plain einfach, naturell
plate Teller, Platte, Gang
plum Pflaume
  ~ **pudding** englischer Weihnachtspudding aus getrockneten Früchten, Paniermehl, Gewürzen; manchmal flambiert
poached pochiert
popcorn Puffmais
popover kleines, stark aufgegangenes Brötchen
pork Schweinefleisch
porridge Haferbrei
porterhouse steak doppeltes Lendensteak (vom Rind)
pot roast Schmorbraten mit Gemüsebeilage
potato Kartoffel
  ~ **chips** 1) Pommes frites (GB) 2) Kartoffelchips (US)
  ~ **in its jacket** Pellkartoffel
potted shrimps in Butter eingemachte Garnelen
poultry Geflügel
prawn Steingarnele
prune Backpflaume
ptarmigan Schneehuhn
pudding meist eine weiche oder feste Mehlspeise, entweder mit Fleisch, Fisch, Gemüse oder Früchten, gebacken oder gedämpft
pumpkin Kürbis
quail Wachtel
quince Quitte
rabbit Kaninchen
radish Rettich, Radieschen
rainbow trout Regenbogenforelle
raisins Rosinen
rare halbgar
raspberry Himbeere

raw roh
red mullet Rotbarbe
red (sweet) pepper rote Paprikaschote
redcurrant rote Johannisbeere
relish Würzsoße
rhubarb Rhabarber
rib (of beef) Rippenstück (vom
Rind)
rice Reis
rissole Fleisch- oder Fischfrika-
delle
river trout Bachforelle
roast Braten
roasted gebraten
Rock Cornish hen Masthühnchen
roe Rogen, Fischeier
roll Brötchen, Semmel
rollmop herring Rollmops
round steak Steak aus der Rinderkeule
Rubens sandwich gepökeltes
Rindfleisch auf Toast mit
Sauerkraut, Käse und Salatsoße; heiß serviert
rump steak Steak aus der Rinder-
hüfte
rusk Zwieback
rye bread Roggenbrot
saddle Rücken
saffron Safran
sage Salbei
salad Salat
  ~ **bar** Auswahl an Salaten
  ~ **cream** leicht gezuckerte sahnige Salatsoße
  ~ **dressing** Salatsoße
salmon Lachs
  ~ **trout** Lachsforelle
salt Salz
salted gesalzen
sauce Soße
sausage Wurst
sauté(ed) schnell gebraten, ge-
schwenkt

scallop 1) Jakobsmuschel 2)
Kalbsschnitzel
scone weicher Gersten- oder Wei-
zenmehlkuchen
Scotch broth Lammfleischbrühe
mit Gemüse
Scotch woodcock Toast mit fein
gehackten Eiern, Gewürzen
und Sardellenpaste
sea bass Wolfs-, Seebarsch
sea kale Meer-, Strandkohl
seafood Fisch und Meeres-
früchte
(in) season (je nach) Jahreszeit
seasoning Gewürz, Würze
service charge Bedienungszu-
schlag
service (not) included Bedienung
(nicht) inbegriffen
set menu Gedeck, Menü
shad Alse, Maifisch
shallot Schalotte
shellfish Krusten- und Schalen-
tiere
sherbet Sorbet, Schnee-Eis, Scher-
bett
shoulder Schulter
shredded wheat Weizenschrot
(zum Frühstück)
shrimp Garnele, Krevette
silverside (of beef) bester Teil der
Rinderkeule
sirloin steak Lendensteak (vom
Rind)
skewer Bratspießchen
slice Scheibe
sliced aufgeschnitten
sloppy Joe gehacktes Rindfleisch
mit Chilisoße, in einem Brötchen serviert
smelt Stint, Spierling (ein Lachs-
fisch)
smoked geräuchert

snack Imbiß

sole Seezunge

soup Suppe

sour sauer

soused herring in Essig und Gewürzen eingelegter Hering

spare rib Schweinerippchen

spice Gewürz

spinach Spinat

spiny lobster Languste

(on a) spit (am) Spieß

sponge cake leichter Hefekuchen

sprat Sprotte

squash Kürbis

starter Vorspeise

steak and kidney pie englische Rindfleisch- und Nierenpastete

steamed gedämpft

stew Ragout, Eintopf

Stilton (cheese) englischer Edelpilzkäse, weiß und mild oder blaugeädert und scharf

strawberry Erdbeere

string bean grüne Bohne

stuffed gefüllt

stuffing Füllung

suck(l)ing pig Spanferkel

sugar Zucker

sugarless ungezuckert

sundae Eisbecher mit Früchten, Nüssen, Schlagsahne und manchmal Sirup

supper Abendbrot

swede gelbe Kohlrübe

sweet 1) süß 2) Nachspeise

~ **corn** Zuckermais

~ **potato** Süßkartoffel

sweetbread Kalbsbries, -milch

Swiss cheese Schweizer Käse, Emmentaler

Swiss roll Biskuitrolle

Swiss steak mit Gemüse und Gewürzen geschmorte Rindfleischscheibe

T-bone steak Lendensteak (vom Rind)

table d'hôte Gedeck, Menü

tangerine Mandarinenart

tarragon Estragon

tart Törtchen, Torte, Obstkuchen

tenderloin Lendenstück (vom Rind oder Schwein)

Thousand Island dressing würzige Salatsoße aus Mayonnaise und feingehackten Paprikaschoten

thyme Thymian

toad-in-the-hole Fleischstücke oder Würste, in Teig eingehüllt und gebacken

toasted geröstet

~ **cheese** Toast mit geschmolzenem Käse

tomato Tomate

tongue Zunge

treacle Melasse

trifle mit Sherry oder Branntwein getränkte leichte Biskuitmasse, mit Mandeln, Marmelade, Schlagsahne und englischer Krem

tripe Kaldaunen, Kutteln

trout Forelle

truffle Trüffel

tuna, tunny Thunfisch

turbot Steinbutt

turkey Truthahn

turnip Kohlrübe

turnover gefülltes Törtchen, Tasche

turtle Schildkröte

underdone halbgar

vanilla Vanille

veal Kalbfleisch

~ **bird** Kalbsroulade

vegetable Gemüse

~ **marrow** Kürbischen, Zucchini

venison Wildbret

vichyssoise kalte Suppe mit Porree, Kartoffeln und Sahne

vinegar Essig

Virginia baked ham im Ofen gebackener Schinken, mit Gewürznelken gespickt, mit Ananasscheiben und Kirschen dekoriert und mit dem Saft dieser Früchte glasiert

wafer Oblate, Waffel

waffle heiße Waffel, mit Melasse oder Ahornsirup serviert

walnut Walnuß

water ice Fruchteis

watercress Brunnenkresse

watermelon Wassermelone

well-done durchgebraten, gar

Welsh rabbit/rarebit eine Art warme Käseschnitte

whelk Wellhorn(schnecke)

whipped cream Schlagsahne

whitebait Weißfischchen

wine list Weinkarte

woodcock Waldschnepfe

Worcestershire sauce aromatische Würzsoße

York ham bekannter englischer Räucherschinken

Yorkshire pudding eine Art Eierkuchen, im Ofen gebacken und als Beilage zu Roastbeef serviert

Getränke

ale obergäriges, kohlensäurearmes Bier, nicht zu kühl ausgeschenkt

bitter ~ goldgelbes, stark gehopftes Faßbier

brown ~ dunkles, süßliches Flaschenbier

light ~ helles Flaschenbier

mild ~ dunkles, süßliches Faßbier

pale ~ helles Flaschenbier

applejack amerikanischer Apfelbranntwein

Athol Brose schottisches Getränk aus Whisky, Honig und manchmal Hafermehl

Bacardi cocktail Mischgetränk aus Rum, Zucker, Granatapfelsirup und Limettensaft

barley water ein Getränk aus Gerste mit Zitronengeschmack

barley wine starkes Bier

beer Bier

bottled ~ Flaschenbier

draft, draught ~ Faßbier

bitters aus Bitterextrakten hergestellte Aperitifs, Magenliköre usw.

black velvet Mischgetränk aus Champagner und *stout* (wird oft zu Austern serviert)

bloody Mary Wodka, Tomatensaft und Gewürze

bourbon amerikanischer Whisky, hauptsächlich aus Mais gebrannt

brandy 1) Branntwein 2) Weinbrand, Kognak

~ **Alexander** Weinbrand, Kakaolikör und Sahne

British wines Weine, die aus importierten Trauben oder Traubensäften in Großbritannien hergestellt werden

cherry brandy Kirschlikör

chocolate Schokolade

cider Apfelwein

~ **cup** Mischgetränk aus Apfelwein, Gewürzen, Zucker und Eis

claret roter Bordeauxwein

cobbler ein *long drink* aus Fruchtsaft mit Wein oder Likör und Eis

cocktail alkoholisches Mischgetränk, vor den Mahlzeiten serviert

coffee Kaffee

~ **with cream** Kaffee mit Sahne

black ~ schwarzer Kaffee

cafeine-free ~ koffeinfreier Kaffee

white ~ Milchkaffee

cordial magen- oder herzstärkender Likör

cream 1) Krem 2) Sahne

cup Erfrischungsgetränk aus eisgekühltem Wein, Sodawasser und einem Likör oder Alkohol, mit einer Apfelsinen- oder Zitronenscheibe garniert

daiquiri Mischgetränk aus Rum, Limetten- und Ananassaft

double doppeltes Maß

Drambuie Likör aus Whisky und Honig

dry martini 1) trockener Wermut (GB) 2) Gin mit trockenem Wermut (US)

egg-nog warmes Mischgetränk aus Rum oder Branntwein, geschlagenem Eigelb und Zucker

gin and it Gin mit italienischem Wermut

gin-fizz Gin mit Zitronensaft, Zucker und Sodawasser

ginger ale alkoholfreies Getränk mit Ingwergeschmack

ginger beer leicht alkoholisches Getränk aus Ingwer und Zucker

grasshopper Mischgetränk aus Pfefferminz- und Kakaolikör mit Sahne

Guinness (stout) sehr dunkles, stark gehopftes Malzbier

half pint ungefähr 3 Deziliter

highball Whisky oder Branntwein mit Sodawasser oder *ginger ale* verdünnt

iced eisgekühlt

Irish coffee Kaffee mit Zucker, irischem Whisky und Schlagsahne

Irish Mist irischer Likör aus Whisky und Honig

Irish whiskey irischer Whisky; er enthält außer Gerste auch Roggen, Hafer und Weizen und ist etwas milder im Geschmack als der schottische Whisky

juice Saft

lager helles Lagerbier, kühl ausgeschenkt

lemon squash Zitronensaft mit Sodawasser

lemonade Limonade

lime juice Limettensaft

liqueur Likör

liquor Spirituosen

long drink alle alkoholischen Bargetränke, mit Wasser oder Sprudel verdünnt; mit Eiswürfeln

Manhattan amerikanischer Whisky, Wermut und Angostura-

bitter
milk Milch
mineral water Mineralwasser
mulled wine Glühwein
neat unverdünnt, pur
old-fashioned Cocktail aus Whisky, Zucker, Angosturabitter und Maraschinokirschen
on the rocks mit Eiswürfeln
Ovaltine Ovomaltine
Pimm's cup(s) eine Art Likör, wird mit Fruchtsaft oder Sodawasser gemischt
~ **No. 1** mit Gin
~ **No. 2** mit Whisky
~ **No. 3** mit Rum
~ **No. 4** mit Weinbrand
pink champagne Rosé-Sekt
pink lady Cocktail aus Eiweiß, Apfelbranntwein, Zitronensaft, Granatapfelsirup und Gin
pint ungefähr 6 Deziliter
port (wine) Portwein
porter starkes, dunkles Bier mit süßlichem Geschmack
quart 1,14 Liter (US 0,95 Liter)
root beer aus verschiedenen Wurzeln und Kräutern bereitete Brauselimonade
rye (whiskey) Roggenwhisky, eher schwerer und kräftiger als *bourbon*
scotch (whisky) schottischer Whisky, meist aus Gerstenmalz- und Getreidewhisky »geblendet« (gemischt)

screwdriver Wodka und Orangensaft
shandy *bitter ale* mit Limonade oder *ginger beer*
short drink unverdünntes alkoholisches Getränk
shot ein Schuß Whisky, Kognak oder Branntwein
sloe gin-fizz Schlehenlikör mit Zitronensaft und Sodawasser
soda water Soda-, Sprudelwasser
soft drink alkoholfreies Erfrischungsgetränk
spirits Branntweine
stinger Kognak mit Pfefferminzlikör
stout sehr dunkles, stark gehopftes Malzbier
straight unverdünnt, pur
tea Tee
toddy eine Art Grog
Tom Collins Gin, Zitronensaft, Zucker und Sodawasser
tonic (water) Tonic(wasser); Sprudel, meist mit Chiningeschmack
vodka Wodka
water Wasser
whisky sour Whisky, Zitronensaft, Zucker und Maraschinokirschen
wine Wein
　　dry ~ trockener Wein
　　red ~ Rotwein
　　sparkling ~ Schaumwein, Sekt
　　sweet ~ Süßwein, Dessertwein
　　white ~ Weißwein

Englische unregelmäßige Verben

Wir führen nachstehend die englischen unregelmäßigen Verben auf. Die Zusammensetzung und die Präfixverben werden ebenso konjugiert wie das zugrundeliegende Verb. Beispiel: *withdraw* konjugiert man wie *draw* und *mistake* wie *take*.

Infinitiv	Präteritum	Partizip Perfekt	
arise	arose	arisen	*sich erheben*
awake	awoke	awoken	*erwecken*
be	was	been	*sein*
bear	bore	borne	*(er)tragen*
beat	beat	beaten	*schlagen*
become	became	become	*werden*
begin	began	begun	*beginnen*
bend	bent	bent	*biegen*
bet	bet	bet	*wetten*
bid	bade/bid	bidden/bid	*gebieten*
bind	bound	bound	*binden*
bite	bit	bitten	*beißen*
bleed	bled	bled	*bluten*
blow	blew	blown	*blasen*
break	broke	broken	*brechen*
breed	bred	bred	*züchten*
bring	brought	brought	*bringen*
build	built	built	*bauen*
burn	burnt/burned	burnt/burned	*(ver)brennen*
burst	burst	burst	*platzen*
buy	bought	bought	*kaufen*
can*	could	—	*können*
cast	cast	cast	*werfen*
catch	caught	caught	*fangen*
choose	chose	chosen	*wählen*
cling	clung	clung	*sich klammern*
clothe	clothed/clad	clothed/clad	*kleiden*
come	came	come	*kommen*
cost	cost	cost	*kosten*
creep	crept	crept	*kriechen*
cut	cut	cut	*schneiden*
deal	dealt	dealt	*Handel treiben*
dig	dug	dug	*graben*
do (he does)	did	done	*tun*
draw	drew	drawn	*ziehen*
dream	dreamt/dreamed	dreamt/dreamed	*träumen*
drink	drank	drunk	*trinken*
drive	drove	driven	*fahren*
dwell	dwelt	dwelt	*wohnen*
eat	ate	eaten	*essen*
fall	fell	fallen	*fallen*

* Indikativ Präsens

feed	fed	fed	*füttern*
feel	felt	felt	*fühlen*
fight	fought	fought	*kämpfen*
find	found	found	*finden*
flee	fled	fled	*fliehen*
fling	flung	flung	*schleudern*
fly	flew	flown	*fliegen*
forsake	forsook	forsaken	*verlassen*
freeze	froze	frozen	*gefrieren*
get	got	got	*bekommen*
give	gave	given	*geben*
go	went	gone	*gehen*
grind	ground	ground	*mahlen*
grow	grew	grown	*wachsen*
hang	hung	hung	*hängen*
have	had	had	*haben*
hear	heard	heard	*hören*
hew	hewed	hewed/hewn	*hacken*
hide	hid	hidden	*verbergen*
hit	hit	hit	*schlagen*
hold	held	held	*halten*
hurt	hurt	hurt	*verletzen*
keep	kept	kept	*behalten*
kneel	knelt	knelt	*knien*
knit	knitted/knit	knitted/knit	*stricken*
know	knew	known	*kennen*
lay	laid	laid	*legen*
lead	led	led	*führen*
lean	leant/leaned	leant/leaned	*lehnen*
leap	leapt/leaped	leapt/leaped	*springen*
learn	learnt/learned	learnt/learned	*lernen*
leave	left	left	*verlassen*
lend	lent	lent	*leihen*
let	let	let	*lassen*
lie	lay	lain	*liegen*
light	lit/lighted	lit/lighted	*anzünden*
lose	lost	lost	*verlieren*
make	made	made	*machen*
may*	might	—	*dürfen*
mean	meant	meant	*bedeuten*
meet	met	met	*begegnen*
mow	mowed	mowed/mown	*mähen*
must*	—	—	*müssen*
ought (to)*	—	—	*sollen*
pay	paid	paid	*zahlen*
put	put	put	*legen*
read	read	read	*lesen*
rid	rid	rid	*sich entledigen*
ride	rode	ridden	*reiten*

* Indikativ Präsens

ring	rang	rung	*läuten*
rise	rose	risen	*aufstehen*
run	ran	run	*rennen*
saw	sawed	sawn	*sägen*
say	said	said	*sagen*
see	saw	seen	*sehen*
seek	sought	sought	*suchen*
sell	sold	sold	*verkaufen*
send	sent	sent	*senden*
set	set	set	*setzen*
sew	sewed	sewed/sewn	*nähen*
shake	shook	shaken	*schütteln*
shall*	should	—	*sollen*
shed	shed	shed	*vergießen*
shine	shone	shone	*leuchten*
shoot	shot	shot	*schießen*
show	showed	shown	*zeigen*
shrink	shrank	shrunk	*schrumpfen*
shut	shut	shut	*schließen*
sing	sang	sung	*singen*
sink	sank	sunk	*sinken, versenken*
sit	sat	sat	*sitzen*
sleep	slept	slept	*schlafen*
slide	slid	slid	*gleiten*
sling	slung	slung	*schleudern*
slink	slunk	slunk	*schleichen*
slit	slit	slit	*schlitzen*
smell	smelled/smelt	smelled/smelt	*riechen*
sow	sowed	sown/sowed	*säen*
speak	spoke	spoken	*sprechen*
speed	sped/speeded	sped/speeded	*eilen*
spell	spelt/spelled	spelt/spelled	*buchstabieren*
spend	spent	spent	*ausgeben, verbringen*
spill	spilt/spilled	spilt/spilled	*verschütten*
spin	spun	spun	*spinnen*
spit	spat	spat	*spucken*
split	split	split	*spalten*
spoil	spoilt/spoiled	spoilt/spoiled	*verderben*
spread	spread	spread	*ausbreiten*
spring	sprang	sprung	*springen*
stand	stood	stood	*stehen*
steal	stole	stolen	*stehlen*
stick	stuck	stuck	*kleben*
sting	stung	stung	*stechen*
stink	stank/stunk	stunk	*stinken*
strew	strewed	strewed/strewn	*streuen*
stride	strode	stridden	*schreiten*
strike	struck	struck/stricken	*schlagen*
string	strung	strung	*aufreihen*

* Indikativ Präsens

strive	strove	striven	*streben*
swear	swore	sworn	*schwören*
sweep	swept	swept	*fegen*
swell	swelled	swollen	*schwellen*
swim	swam	swum	*schwimmen*
swing	swung	swung	*schwingen*
take	took	taken	*nehmen*
teach	taught	taught	*lehren*
tear	tore	torn	*zerreißen*
tell	told	told	*erzählen*
think	thought	thought	*denken*
throw	threw	thrown	*werfen*
thrust	thrust	thrust	*stoßen*
tread	trod	trodden	*treten*
wake	woke/waked	woken/waked	*(auf)wachen*
wear	wore	worn	*tragen (Kleider)*
weave	wove	woven	*weben*
weep	wept	wept	*weinen*
will*	would	—	*wollen*
win	won	won	*gewinnen*
wind	wound	wound	*winden*
wring	wrung	wrung	*(w)ringen*
write	wrote	written	*schreiben*

---

* Indikativ Präsens

Englische Abkürzungen

AA	*Automobile Association*	britischer Automobilklub
AAA	*American Automobile Association*	Amerikanischer Automobilklub
ABC	*American Broadcasting Company*	amerikanische Rundfunkgesellschaft
A.D.	*anno Domini*	nach Christus
Am.	*America; American*	Amerika; amerikanisch
a.m.	*ante meridiem (before noon)*	vormittags (genauer: von 00.01 bis 11.59 Uhr)
Amtrak	*American railroad corporation*	amerikanisches Eisenbahnkonsortium
AT & T	*American Telephone and Telegraph Company*	Amerikanische Telefon- und Telegrafengesellschaft
Ave.	*avenue*	Allee (Prachtstraße)
BBC	*British Broadcasting Corporation*	Britische Rundfunkgesellschaft
B.C.	*before Christ*	vor Christus
bldg.	*building*	Gebäude
Blvd.	*boulevard*	Boulevard (Ringstraße)
B.R.	*British Rail*	Britische Staatsbahnen
Brit.	*Britain; British*	Großbritannien; britisch
Bros.	*brothers*	Gebrüder
¢	*cent*	Cent, 1/100 vom Dollar
Can.	*Canada; Canadian*	Kanada; kanadisch
CBS	*Columbia Broadcasting System*	amerikanische Rundfunkgesellschaft
CID	*Criminal Investigation Department*	britische Kriminalpolizei
CNR	*Canadian National Railway*	Kanadische Bundesbahnen
c/o	*(in) care of*	bei, per Adresse
Co.	*company*	Handelsgesellschaft
Corp.	*corporation*	Handelsgesellschaft
CPR	*Canadian Pacific Railways*	kanadische Eisenbahngesellschaft
D.C.	*District of Columbia*	Bundesdistrikt der USA
DDS	*Doctor of Dental Science*	Doktor der Zahnheilkunde
dept.	*department*	Abteilung
EEC	*European Economic Community*	Europäische Wirtschaftsgemeinschaft (EWG)
e.g.	*for instance*	zum Beispiel

Eng.	*England; English*	England; englisch
excl.	*excluding; exclusive*	ausschließlich, nicht inbegriffen
ft.	*foot/feet*	Fuß (30,5 cm)
GB	*Great Britain*	Großbritannien
H.E.	*His/Her Excellency; His Eminence*	Seine/Ihre Exzellenz; Seine Eminenz
H.H.	*His Holiness*	Seine Heiligkeit
H.M.	*His/Her Majesty*	Seine/Ihre Majestät
H.M.S.	*Her Majesty's ship*	wörtlich: Schiff Ihrer Majestät (Kriegsmarine)
hp	*horsepower*	Pferdestärke
Hwy	*highway*	Schnellstraße
i.e.	*that is to say*	das heißt
in.	*inch*	Zoll (2,54 cm)
Inc.	*incorporated*	amerikanische Aktiengesellschaft
incl.	*including, inclusive*	einschließlich, inbegriffen
£	*pound sterling*	Pfund Sterling
L.A.	*Los Angeles*	Los Angeles
Ltd.	*limited*	Aktiengesellschaft
M.D.	*Doctor of Medicine*	Arzt
M.P.	*Member of Parliament*	Mitglied des Parlaments
mph	*miles per hour*	Meilen pro Stunde
Mr.	*Mister*	Herr
Mrs.	*Missis*	Frau
Ms.	*Missis/Miss*	Frau/Fräulein
nat.	*national*	staatlich
NBC	*National Broadcasting Company*	amerikanische Rundfunkgesellschaft
No.	*number*	Nummer
N.Y.C.	*New York City*	Stadt New York
O.B.E.	*Officer (of the Order) of the British Empire*	Offizier (des Ordens) des Britischen Weltreiches
p.	*page; penny/pence*	Seite; Penny, 1/100 vom Pfund Sterling
p.a.	*per annum*	pro Jahr
Ph.D.	*Doctor of Philosophy*	Doktor der Philosophie
p.m.	*post meridiem (after noon)*	nachmittags (genauer: von 12.01 bis 23.59 Uhr)
PO	*Post Office*	Postamt
POO	*post office order*	Postanweisung
pop.	*population*	Einwohner(zahl)
P.T.O.	*please turn over*	bitte wenden

RAC	*Royal Automobile Club*	Königlicher Automobilklub (von England)
RCMP	*Royal Canadian Mounted Police*	Königliche berittene Polizei von Kanada
Rd.	*road*	Straße, Weg
ref.	*reference*	vergleiche, siehe
Rev.	*reverend*	Pfarrer
RFD	*rural free delivery*	Briefzustellung per Postfach in ländlichen Gegenden
RR	*railroad*	Eisenbahn
RSVP	*please reply*	Antwort erbeten
$	*dollar*	Dollar
Soc.	*society*	Gesellschaft
St.	*saint; street*	Sankt; Straße
STD	*Subscriber Trunk Dialling*	Selbstwählferndienst
UN	*United Nations*	Vereinte Nationen
UPS	*United Parcel Service*	privater Paketbeförderungsdienst
US	*United States*	Vereinigte Staaten von Amerika
USS	*United States Ship*	wörtlich: Schiff der Vereinigten Staaten (Kriegsmarine)
VAT	*value added tax*	Mehrwertsteuer
VIP	*very important person*	bevorzugt behandelte Persönlichkeit (im Reiseverkehr usw.)
Xmas	*Christmas*	Weihnachten
yd.	*yard*	Yard
YMCA	*Young Men's Christian Association*	Christlicher Verein Junger Männer
YWCA	*Young Women's Christian Association*	Christlicher Verein Junger Mädchen
ZIP	*ZIP code*	Postleitzahl

Zahlwörter

Grundzahlen		Ordnungszahlen	
0	zero	1st	first
1	one	2nd	second
2	two	3rd	third
3	three	4th	fourth
4	four	5th	fifth
5	five	6th	sixth
6	six	7th	seventh
7	seven	8th	eighth
8	eight	9th	ninth
9	nine	10th	tenth
10	ten	11th	eleventh
11	eleven	12th	twelfth
12	twelve	13th	thirteenth
13	thirteen	14th	fourteenth
14	fourteen	15th	fifteenth
15	fifteen	16th	sixteenth
16	sixteen	17th	seventeenth
17	seventeen	18th	eighteenth
18	eighteen	19th	nineteenth
19	nineteen	20th	twentieth
20	twenty	21st	twenty-first
21	twenty-one	22nd	twenty-second
22	twenty-two	23rd	twenty-third
23	twenty-three	24th	twenty-fourth
24	twenty-four	25th	twenty-fifth
25	twenty-five	26th	twenty-sixth
30	thirty	27th	twenty-seventh
40	forty	28th	twenty-eighth
50	fifty	29th	twenty-ninth
60	sixty	30th	thirtieth
70	seventy	40th	fortieth
80	eighty	50th	fiftieth
90	ninety	60th	sixtieth
100	a/one hundred	70th	seventieth
230	two hundred and thirty	80th	eightieth
		90th	ninetieth
1,000	a/one thousand	100th	hundredth
10,000	ten thousand	230th	two hundred and thirtieth
100,000	a/one hundred thousand		
1,000,000	a/one million	1,000th	thousandth

Uhrzeit

Engländer und Amerikaner verwenden allgemein das Zwölfstunden-
system. Dabei bezeichnet die Abkürzung *a.m. (ante meridiem)* die
Stunden der ersten Tageshälfte, *p.m. (post meridiem)* die der zweiten.
In Großbritannien allerdings geht man mehr und mehr zum Vierund-
zwanzigstundensystem über.

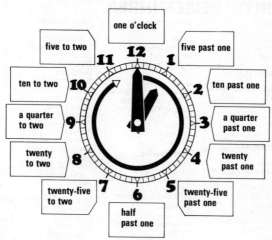

I'll come at seven a.m.   Ich werde um 7 Uhr morgens
                                     kommen.
I'll come at two p.m.   Ich werde um 2 Uhr nachmittags
                                     kommen.
I'll come at eight p.m.   Ich werde um 8 Uhr abends
                                     kommen.

Wochentage

Sunday	Sonntag	*Thursday*	Donnerstag
Monday	Montag	*Friday*	Freitag
Tuesday	Dienstag	*Saturday*	Samstag,
Wednesday	Mittwoch		Sonnabend

BERLITZ REISEFÜHRER